D1193629

CHAIM WEIZMANN

Chaim Weizmann in 1918

CHAIM WEIZMANN

The Making of a Zionist Leader

JEHUDA REINHARZ

New York • Oxford
OXFORD UNIVERSITY PRESS
1985

Oxford University Press

Oxford   London   New York   Toronto
Delhi   Bombay   Calcutta   Madras   Karachi
Kuala Lumpur   Singapore   Hong Kong   Tokyo
Nairobi   Dar es Salaam   Cape Town
Melbourne   Auckland

and associated companies in
Beirut   Berlin   Ibadan   Mexico City   Nicosia

Library of Congress Cataloging in Publication Data

Reinharz, Jehuda.
Chaim Weizmann : The making of a Zionist leader.

Bibliography: p.
Includes index.
1. Weizmann, Chaim, 1874–1952—Political career
before 1914.   2. Israel—Presidents—Biography.
3. Zionists—Great Britain—Biography.   I. Title.
DS125.3.W45R45   1985   956.94′05′0924 [B]   84-7898
ISBN 0-19-503446-5

All photos courtesy Weizmann Archives, Rehovot, Israel.

Printing (last digit):   9 8 7 6 5 4 3 2 1

Printed in the United States of America

For Shula, Yali and Naomi

Preface

Almost three decades ago Sir Isaiah Berlin wrote that he envied the future biographer of Weizmann.[1] Though to date no one has written a scholarly biography of Weizmann, he continues to arouse interest among historians. Although many of the controversies about Weizmann's work and achievements are well known, they have not been settled, which makes their exploration all the more worthwhile.

One could, of course, begin with the controversy about whether Weizmann was a true historic "hero" or not.[2] Since I feel this is not a relevant issue when considering his early life, one should focus instead on leadership.[3] How Weizmann came to possess the qualities of leadership necessary to propel him to prominence at the right moment is an appropriate subject for debate in the period prior to World War I and is thus one of the major themes in this book. In attempting to explain his complex personality, I have focused on the two driving forces which shaped Weizmann's life before World War I: Zionism and chemistry. I have tried to explain the interplay and conflict between these forces and how they were eventually harmonized on the eve of the war.

It is not my intention in this book to review the history of Zionism or Jewish history but rather to provide the reader with a background sufficient to explain the milieu in which Weizmann functioned. Clearly, no one is shaped as a leader in isolation, and it is the biographer's duty to study that leader within the proper historical context. As will be seen, the story of Weizmann as an individual and the history of his time do not necessarily mesh, but they do intersect in a way that makes it important to keep both in mind.

The writing of this book was made much easier by the publication of the twenty-three volumes of *The Letters and Papers of Chaim Weizmann*, which began to appear in 1968. My own interest in writing a biography of Chaim Weizmann was awakened when I began editing one of the volumes of letters. I completed that task on the eve of the hundredth anniversary of the birth of Chaim Weizmann. Apart from conferences and public discussions[4] on the life and times of Chaim Weizmann, that anniversary date—November 1974—produced a spate of newspaper articles and editorials on Weizmann's Zionist ideology and its meaning in our time.[5] One common theme underlies these articles: Weizmann has been neglected. One writer went so far as to state that there had been a deliberate attempt in Israel to relegate Weizmann to the far recesses of Zionist and Israeli historiography.[6]

Indeed, it is true that the State of Israel has been dominated for many years by the personality and achievements of David Ben Gurion and, more recently, by the previously neglected Vladimir Jabotinsky. Weizmann never cultivated a group of disciples, either in the Diaspora or among the pioneering elements of the Jewish community in Palestine. His power was not based on political parties or institutions within the Zionist movement. Rather, he placed his trust in a number of intellectuals and confidants. Since Weizmann's influence often depended on forces outside the Zionist movement, when these were weakened or severed he did not have the internal bureaucratic machinery to back him or perpetuate his memory. Perhaps another factor which has deterred historians from writing Weizmann's biography is the existence of his own well-written and engaging autobiography *Trial and Error.*[7] Weizmann dictated this autobiography to Maurice Samuel in old age, without consulting records or documents; thus it is not surprising that these memoirs are replete with errors.[8] For this reason I have tried to present a reliable account of Weizmann's life until the outbreak of World War I.

Historians have been interested in Weizmann's Zionist career since the war, while ignoring the earlier period. Yet it was then that his personality, Zionist weltanschauung, and scientific direction were forged. By the age of forty Weizmann had already achieved his highest academic post and had laid the foundation for his most important discoveries in chemistry. His Zionist Weltanschauung had been shaped in the aftermath of Herzl's death and his personal life was stable. He seems to have arrived at an emotional and psychic equilibrium.

The documentation for this early period is unfortunately spotty until Weizmann is made a Doctor of Chemistry in Geneva in 1899, at the age of twenty-five. Thus, the first third of his life lacks adequate records save for some memoirs of Weizmann's mother and sister.[9] The exception to this are letters written by Weizmann to his first fiancée, Sophia Getzova, between 1897 and 1902. These letters are in the hands of a Los Angeles woman who, for reasons of her own, refuses to make them available. These letters could presumably shed light on Weizmann's youth.

Apart from this disappointment, I was very fortunate to have the co-operation of various archivists, librarians, and their staff in England, Israel, and the United States. The archives and libraries used are listed in the bibliography, but I would like to single out Mrs. Leonard Stein, who graciously gave me permission to peruse her husband's papers, housed in the Bodleian Library.

Likewise, my friends and colleagues have provided me with encouragement, guidance, and help throughout the various phases of the manuscript. In 1977 Professor Walter Z. Laqueur—then the official biographer of Chaim Weizmann (appointed by Yad Chaim Weizmann) invited me to coauthor the biography with him. In this capacity I was able to consult notes and other materials prepared by the late Right Honorable Richard H. S. Crossman, who, until his untimely death in 1974, had preceded Laqueur as the official Weizmann biographer. I greatly benefited from Mr. Crossman's insights and formulations. When it became unfeasible for Professor Laqueur to continue working on the biography, he encouraged me to do it on my own and supported me throughout the six years it took to complete this manuscript. Professor Bill Williams was the perfect host during my stay at his house in Manchester and guided me through the archives of the city. Dr. David Patterson, president of the Oxford Centre for Postgraduate Hebrew Studies, graciously accommodated me in Yarnton Manor and his staff was most cooperative while I perused the Kressel Collection. Dr. Michael Heymann, director of the Central Zionist Archives, was as helpful on this project as he had been in the past. Ms. Nehama A. Chalom, the curator of the Weizmann Archives, spared no effort to provide me with documents during and after my sojourn in Israel. She also commented on the penultimate draft of the biography. Likewise, all those with whom I came in contact at Yad Chaim Weizmann supported me graciously in the preparation of this volume. Professors Chimen Abramsky, Stuart A. Cohen, Shmuel Ettinger, Lloyd P. Gartner, Ezra Mendelsohn, David Vital, and Mr. Shabtai Teveth made helpful comments on various drafts of the manuscript and saved me from many embarrassments. Mr. Peter Shaw made suggestions on the first two chapters of the book. Mr. Benjamin Ben-Baruch followed some leads for me in Manchester and helped secure additional documents. The late Professor Philip E. Elving of the University of Michigan read and commented on the chapter dealing with chemistry, as did Professor Saul G. Cohen of Brandeis University. I was particularly fortunate during the last phase of writing to discuss my book on many occasions with my teacher and friend, Professor Ben Halpern. My severest and most patient critic was my wife, Shulamit, who made many constructive suggestions. Needless to say, none of the above-mentioned individuals bear any responsibility for the final version of the book.

Financial support for the project was provided by a number of foundations. The National Endowment for the Humanities granted me a Fellowship for Independent Study and Research in 1979–80. Other funds were granted during various periods by the American Philosophical Society, the American Council of Learned Societies, the Memorial Foundation for Jewish Culture, and the Horace H. Rackham School of Graduate Studies of the University of Michigan. My thanks to all of them.

I would like to thank Mimi Fricks for typing and retyping the final drafts of the manuscript and Gregory J. Shesko of Brandeis University for providing the necessary resources. David Schoenbach, Harvey J. Sukenic, Sarah J. Geffen, and Paul F. Salstrom helped in various technical aspects of this book's production. Henry Krawitz of Oxford University Press painstakingly copyedited my manuscript and Ms. Cecile Golan prepared the index. The advice and friendship of my editor, Nancy Lane, were a constant source of strength.

The unselfish aid I have received fortifies me to tackle a subsequent volume which will treat Weizmann's career at its zenith.

Waltham, Mass.   J.R.
June 1984

Notes

1. Isaiah Berlin, *Chaim Weizmann* (New York, 1958), p. 60.
2. See the introduction by Israel Kolatt to his book *Avot u-Meyasdim* (Jerusalem, 1975), pp. 7–29. Kolatt relates some general theories on the relationship of the hero to Zionist history.
3. For some interesting comments on the role of leaders and the function of leadership, see Dankwart A. Rustow, introduction to "Philosophers and Kings: Studies in Leadership," *Daedalus* (special issue) (Summer 1968): 683–84.
4. The proceedings of one such conference were published in Yosef Gorni and Gedalia Yogev, eds., *Medinai be-Itot Mashber* (Tel Aviv, 1977).
5. See, e.g., *Maariv*, November 8, 1974; *Haaretz*, November 1, 1974; *Dvar ha-Shavua*, November 8, 1974.
6. Moshe Shamir, "Mi Mashkiah et Weizmann?" *Maariv*, November 8, 1974.
7. On this see Naurice Samuel, *Little Did I Know* (New York, 1963), pp. 194–201. See also Robert Weltsch, "A Tragedy of Leadership," *Jewish Social Studies* 13, no. 3 (July 1951): 211–12.
8. See Oskar K. Rabinowicz, *Fifty Years of Zionism: A Historical Analysis of Dr. Weizmann's 'Trial and Error'* (London, 1951).
9. On the documentation available on Weizmann see Meyer W. Weisgal, general foreword, *The Letters and Papers of Chaim Weizmann* (series A), vol. 1 (London, 1968).

Contents

    I. Origins, 3

    II. Pinsk, 15

    III. Berlin, 27

    IV. Herzl, 45

    V. The Democratic Faction, 65

    VI. Public Ventures and Private Affairs, 92

    VII. Conflicts and Disappointments, 121

    VIII. From Kishinev to Uganda, 145

    IX. The Uganda Controversy, 167

    X. New Beginnings, 211

    XI. An Alien in Manchester, 233

    XII. Wary Adjustment, 261

    XIII. The Theory and Practice of Synthetic Zionism, 289

    XIV. The End of the Wolffsohn Era, 318

    XV. Society, Science, and the Professorship, 349

    XVI. A Hebrew University in Jerusalem, 375

    XVII. Conclusion, 402

    Notes, 409

    Bibliography, 529

    Index, 557

CHAIM WEIZMANN

I

Origins

A legend told by Jews and non-Jews has it that during the Swedish invasion of Poland in the mid-seventeenth century, a Swedish general was murdered by a Polish woman, who then stole from him important military documents. To avenge his death the Swedish army surrounded the home village of the woman and burnt it to the ground, killing all its inhabitants. Only one Jew escaped the fire—Mordechai the Undertaker, known as "Motol"—by hiding in the cemetery. After the retreat of the Swedish army he built himself a house, which in time became an inn and a way station for merchants who traveled between Pinsk and Minsk. This tavern was particularly appealing to the peasants of neighboring villages, who used to spur each other on by saying, "Poidom do Motoleh" ("Let's go to Motol").

In time other Jews and non-Jews began to build their houses near Motol's and the village gradually assumed an important role among its neighboring villages. However, in the nineteenth century no one remembered the origin of the now official name of the town—"Motol."[1]

Another version attributed to the same period claims that at the time of the Cossack revolt against Polish oppression, led by Bohdan Chmielnicki,[2] there were many Jews living in this village, which then had another name. When the Cossacks came upon it, they killed all the Jews except one named Motol. When they left, he built a tavern. The rest of this version is similar to the first.[3]

It seems, then, that in the collective memory of its inhabitants the Jews had been resident in Motol for a very long time. Their numbers grew to 222 in 1847 and fifty years later they constituted 1,354 souls within a total Motol population of 4,297.[4]

Motol was a small townlet within the Pale of Settlement in the district of Kobrin, in the department of Grodno, in Western Russia, on the border of the kingdom of Poland. It was located on the Yasolda River, which joined the Pina River, a tributary of the Pripet, which was itself a tributary of the Dnieper, which ran into the Black Sea many hundreds of miles away.[5] Motol was located in a region called Polesie or Polesia, a geographic entity extending along the Pripet River in a wedge bounded roughly by Brest, Gomel, and Kiev. The Pripet has a number of tributaries which form an excellent communications network for the region. Nevertheless, throughout its history Polesie had been one of the most economically and culturally backward areas in the Slavic world.

The inhabitants of Polesie were divided into two basic cultural-linguistic groups, those in the north, who spoke Byelorussian dialects, and those in the south, who spoke Ukrainian dialects. In each group one could further distinguish subgroups characterized by dialectical variations and differences in religion, dress, custom, and architecture. Polesie was inhabited by a small Polish population, largely landowners in the villages and intellectuals and tradesmen in the towns. More numerous than the Poles was the Jewish population of Polesie.[6]

Polesie can be generally characterized as a region of marshland and forest—in fact, the most extensive marshland in Europe. Only a small amount of the total land area was cultivated. Forests played a dominant role in the economy of Polesie, and the region was a center of the timber industry. In most of Polesie cultivation centered on rye, oats, barley, buckwheat, and potatoes. The level of agriculture was primitive. Livestock raising was more highly developed thanks to the availability of pastureland. By the end of the nineteenth century the average peasant household in southwestern Polesie kept five to fifteen head of cattle and several pigs and sheep. Fishing, based on the abundant waterways and lakes, was the major supplement of the Polesian economy, followed by beekeeping and horticulture.[7]

With communication between villages only possible by wagon and small boat, the economy of Polesie was at a near-subsistence level. Almost every village produced virtually all the necessary products, from bast shoes to furniture and houses. Most village men had some skill in carpentry and construction. Up until the end of the nineteenth century most homes had open fires. They were constructed exclusively of wood; roofs were generally covered with straw thatch. Barns were built by the richer peasants. Poorer peasants stored straw and hay in ricks near the house. The peasants of Polesie were also artisans in leather working, weaving, basketry, pottery, wheel making, cooperage, and other household crafts.

For the people of Polesie the only contact with urban life was through the town marketplaces. The most important of these was the city of Pinsk on the Pripet, where large fairs were held annually.[8] Other important market centers were located in Kobryn, Stolin, Lunynets, and Mozyr in southern Polesie, and in Kamien, Kosirski, Sarny, and Ovruc in the north. Polesian villagers also traveled south to Volhynia to such cities as Kovel and north to Baranowicze and Gomel.

Some twenty miles away from Pinsk lay the village of Motol, a typical Polesie settlement without railway or paved road, and with no post office or any other regular means of communication with the outside world. The road to Pinsk was flooded with mud in the spring and autumn and rutted with ice in winter. Motol was divided into three sections along its one major street. The oldest, "Der Mark" (marketplace), was inhabited by the more respected and well-to-do citizens in town—White Russians as well as Poles and some Jews. Here were located the institutions of the local government, the schools, pharmacies, the "Old Synagogue," the *mikveh* (ritual bath), and the church. The middle section of this main street was called by the Jews the "Street of the Goyim." It was the quarter of the well-to-do Belorussian artisans. Beyond the bridge lay the "Street of the Jews," or the "Neistadt." This section, which also housed the "New Synagogue," constituted the center of Motol's Jewish life and activities. Here were located all the Jewish shops and workshops, whose inhabitants constituted the poorer element in town.[9] For the Jews of Motol the "world" was contained within the geographic confines of the village, in the large family circle, and in the company of one's neighbors and friends. The family, the *heder* (literally "room"; a privately run elementary school specializing in Judaic subjects), the synagogue, the Sabbath, and holidays constituted the most important elements in the life of every individual. Like Jews in hundreds of other forlorn villages throughout the Pale of Settlement, Motol's Jews were very well acquainted with the geography of *Eretz Israel*. On every Sabbath and holiday the village turned into a miniature Jewish state and every house became a castle of the Jewish spirit. The Sabbath was a day of holiness and pleasure. The sand was removed, the children washed and donned Sabbath clothes, and peace and quiet descended on the village. Jewish custom and tradition reigned supreme for generations until the turn of the twentieth century.[10]

By the 1870s most of West European Jewry had been legally emancipated. For the majority of Europe's Jewish population which lived within the frontiers of Imperial Russia, however, the pendulum continued to swing toward reaction and oppression.[11] This repression was compounded by conditions in the Pale of Settlement:[12] rapid growth of the Jewish population,[13] unemployment,[14] and abject poverty.[15] By all accounts it was a dismal and unhappy world for a Jewish child to enter.

The Weizmann family did not belong to this destitute and starving mass of Russian Jewry; Ozer Weizmann, Chaim's father, belonged to what might be termed—though strictly in the context of his environment—the middle class. He was a scion of a very distinguished family. One of his ancestors, five generations back, was Rabbi Abraham-Abba-Josef of Soroka, one of the disciples of Rabbi Dov-Ber of Mezeritch ("The Great Maggid"). His son was Rabbi Shemaryah Weingarten, who founded the great hasidic dynasty of Libeshei, a small town near Pinsk. He had hasidic followers in Pinsk and its environs, including Motol.[16] Rabbi Weingarten married the granddaughter of Yehiel Michel of Zlotchov, a disciple of the Baal Shem Tov, the founder of hasidism. Their son was the well-known Dayan Yehiel Michel Weingarten from Libeshei,[17] whose grandson was Chaim Azriel Fialkov of Serniki. Though he was a merchant, Azriel Fialkov was noted for his scholarship. He married Gittl-Rivka Chemerinski of Motol. Five of their sons changed their names, in-

Chaim's mother, Rachel Leah Weizmann

Chaim's father, Ozer Weizmann

cluding Ozer, Chaim Weizmann's father.[18] The change in name was, no doubt, a means of escaping service in the Russian army; they were "adopted" as only sons by other families.

Educational possibilities were limited in the village of Serniki, so it was decided to send the thirteen-year-old Ozer to Motol, to his uncle Shmuel-Itche and aunt Hannah Chemerinski. It is here that he met the eleven-year-old Rachel Leah Chemerinski (no relationship to Ozer's family), the youngest of twelve children,[19] who was born in the village of Poretchye and moved with her parents to Motol when she was seven or eight years old. Rachel Leah's father, Yehiel-Michel Chemerinski, a Stolin hasid, had worked for the estate of Count Skirmunt,[20] and in the context of Motol's economic stratification was considered a prosperous man. He had planned to make a good match for his daughter and did not consider Ozer—who was a poor free boarder next door—to be a suitable groom. Rachel Leah related in her eighties that

> at the time [she was thirteen years old] they began to talk of marrying me off. And as I was afraid of losing Ozer, I told my father to send all the matchmakers away, as I have already chosen my man. My father looked at me in astonishment. Yes, I said, Ozer is my fiancé and if you don't want me to remain an old maid you better go to Shmuel-Itche [Ozer's uncle] and arrange for the marriage. My father said: If it is Ozer you want, let it be Ozer. Good luck! That was all I wanted to hear. The marriage was arranged.[21]

They were married in 1867. Rachel Leah was not quite fourteen years old and Ozer was nearly sixteen. In 1871 their first child, Miriam, was born—the first of fifteen children to be born within a span of twenty-five years. Three of the children died in infancy. Chaim Weizmann was born in Motol on November 27, 1874.[22] The large Weizmann family was part of the Jewish population explosion of the nineteenth century.

For the first few years of their marriage the couple stayed with Reb Michel, who cared for all their needs. Ozer pursued his talmudic studies and Rachel Leah continued to play with her girlfriends.[23] It was only when their fourth child, Chaim, was born[24] that the couple moved to their own house. The Weizmann house—which was probably acquired by Reb Michel—stood in the center of Motol, opposite the priest's house. Considering Motol's architecture and the town's prevailing impoverished material condition, it was an unusually large house, containing six or seven rooms.[25] The house also had large windows and was surrounded by a sizable flower and tree garden, unusual features in Jewish homes in Motol. They indicate an appreciation on the part of Ozer and Leah for a grander lifestyle, imitating the well-to-do bourgeoisie. Reb Michel had in the meantime become old and weak and Ozer had to give up his studies. He became a tree feller and subcontractor of lumber—a *transportierer* who floated rafts of logs along the streams and rivers to Danzig, where they were sawed and then exported.[26] Chaim and his younger sister Hayah have described in vivid colors their father's exhausting occupation, constantly exposed and dependent on the elements. He employed, on a

The Weizmann house in Motol

seasonal basis, sixty men with whom he spent the better part of the year, from the festival of Sukkot (Tabernacles) in October to Passover in the spring, choosing the trees to be felled and supervising the hauling and roping of wood. After Passover he supervised the floating of the rafts on the Pina River to Pinsk and thence along the Vistula to Danzig. Ozer tried to come home for the Sabbath and holidays whenever he could, but quite often he stayed with his men weeks at a time. He managed to earn about 6,000 roubles a year (250 to 300 dollars), a not inconsiderable sum in those days. Nevertheless, and despite the fact that the Weizmanns owned a large house, some acres of land, chickens, two cows, a vegetable garden, and a few fruit trees, Ozer's income was insufficient to provide for his rapidly growing family.[27]

Despite his strictly traditional upbringing, Ozer was touched by the Jewish national trend of the *haskalah* (Enlightenment within Jewish society).[28] He was a Hebraist who read the current press and saw to it that his children received a general education in addition to their Jewish education. Ten of his twelve sons and daughters eventually earned academic degrees.[29] Ozer's erudition and personal virtues made him a respected figure in Motol. He was a scholarly type, silent and aristocratic in bearing. Despite his frequent absences from Motol, he was chosen to be the *starosta* (the elder or "head man") of Motol—the first and only Jew ever chosen to such a post. It was a mark of affection and respect for him by gentiles and Jews alike. He was a highly regarded member of the Jewish community.[30]

Ozer was a *maskil* (an "Enlightened Jew") who knew some Russian, had traveled, and had been exposed to gentile customs and folkways. His children, boys and girls, went to *heder*. The government school of Motol, where the educational sysem was extremely primitive, was attended primarily by the children of the peasants, and since there was no compulsory education, their attendance was irregular and haphazard. There was a cultural abyss between Jews and gentiles in Motol. The majority of Jews in Motol, as elsewhere in the Pale, did not know Slavic or Western languages; thus the cultures and literatures of these languages, as well as their sciences and political ideologies, were remote and alien. Though the exposure of the Jews of Motol to gentile folkways was greater than that of the Jews living in the city ghettos of the Pale, their resistance was more conscious and more effective.

The internal cohesion of these Jews was based on the firm belief that the Jews were in *golus* (exile), that they must wait for the Messiah to deliver them of their current miserable condition and return them to Zion. In the meantime the Jews in Eastern Europe developed their own unique civilization, and they did so without inhibitions and without apologies. Theirs was a self-contained yet all-pervasive world, a vast network of religious, social, and even political institutions. Here blossomed a way of life where spiritual values and ideals blended into a folk culture, where kabbalistic mysticism and talmudic rationality were inextricably interwoven. Many of the male inhabitants of the *shtetlakh* (Jewish rural communities) were Talmudic scholars. The synagogues and houses of study thus reverberated to the chants of Talmudic *pilpul* (casuistry). Almost every male Jew gave of his time to learning either in private study or by joining one of the societies established for the purpose of studying the Talmud or some other branch of rabbinic literature. The book, the Torah, was their essence.[31]

Judaism in the Pale of Settlement was all-embracing in both its doctrine and its demands for daily observance. This total Jewish milieu also protected the Jews, to a certain extent, from their hostile environment. Religious life centered around the synagogue and the school as well as their main officials, the rabbis and the teachers.[32] The Jewish community saw to it that no male child should be deprived of the opportunity to acquire at least a good elementary education. Most girls were taught how to recite prayers and read Yiddish translations of the Bible at home. The curriculum was, of course, limited to Bible and Mishnah, Talmud, and rabbinics. Elementary education was often taught in inadequate quarters, consisting of a room in a ramshackle building with few sanitary provisions, accommodating pupils of various ages and stages of preparedness. Most male children attended these *hadarim*. Sometimes the teachers themselves were unqualified, but as a rule this institution achieved its goal of providing basic education in Jewish subjects and preparing a substantial minority for more advanced studies after the age of thirteen.[33]

Chaim Weizmann's lifelong and deep sense of Jewishness, his attachment to Jewish folkways, was cradled and formed in this intense Jewish environment of the Pale. The content and texture of Jewish life in Motol was not significantly changed by the secular ideologies that had made inroads in Western Europe some hundred years earlier. Thus, until he moved to Pinsk at the age of eleven Chaim's life was more or less a replica of the traditional Jewish patterns of Eastern European Jewry. In later years, when he had occasion to speak to diplomats and power brokers about the tragedies and triumphs of Jewish history, about Jewish hopelessness and aspirations, he did not need to recall these events from textbooks; the history of his people was, as it were, ingrained in his very being.

It was only natural that Chaim began to attend *heder* at the age of four.[34] Seven decades later he looked back at that first experience with distaste: "Like nearly all *heders*, mine was a squalid one-room school, which also constituted the sole quarters of the teacher's family. If my *heder* differed from others, it was perhaps in the possession of a family goat which took shelter with us in cold weather. And if my first Rabbi or teacher differed from others, it was in the degree of his pedagogic incompetence . . ."[35]

His parents picked as his first teacher the *dardakei melamed* (teacher of the youngest children), Rabbi Tunehleh. But Chaim—asserting early in life his strong will—declared that he would study only with the rabbi of his older sister Miriam, Rabbi Zvi Bloch-Blumenfeld—nicknamed "Berele der Weissinker" probably because of his white hair or pale complexion—a traditional *melamed* who was apparently brought from Pinsk to teach the Weizmann children.[36] There are no references in Weizmann's memoirs to Rabbi Bloch-Blumenfeld, but it is clear that he liked Rabbi Motolianski, with whom he began to study at the age of six. Rabbi Abraham Isaac Motolianski—called "Avrom-Yizhok der Schwarze" because of his dark hair and complexion—was an unusual person, considering the time and place he lived in: a deeply religious man who opposed any sign of fanaticism, a man who respected and sought enlightenment. Weizmann referred to him in his memoirs—though not by name—as a humane and kindly teacher who imparted to his students a love for the Bible and Hebrew literature.[37]

Motolianski taught his young charges not only the Prophets but also grammar and Hebrew composition. He interested them in social and political issues of the day, taught them how to read a newspaper, and introduced them to the writings of Mapu, Smolenskin, Judah Leib Gordon, and Adam Hacohen Levensohn. He also introduced them to the rudiments of science. It is perhaps here that Chaim first heard about the writings of Jewish nationalists, such as Smolenskin's "Et Lataat."[38] It is perhaps here that the atmosphere of Hebrew and Jewish culture was blended with a national motif tied to the ancient homeland, daily referred to in his prayers and his studies of the Prophets. Motolianski adored Chaim, and when the latter would come home for visits after he had moved to Pinsk, it was a holiday for the rabbi. Weizmann's sister Hayah related that when he was in Pinsk Chaim privately learned French and

Weizmann at age eight, 1882

German and began to read Schiller. On one of his visits to Motol, Chaim sat on the porch one Sabbath afternoon with Ozer Weizmann and Rabbi Motolianski, drinking tea and reciting Schiller's famous poem "Die Glocke." The rabbi did not understand a single word in German, yet when Chaim explained the meaning of certain passages the rabbi was beside himself with awe and delight, begging Chaim time and again to repeat the passages.[39] Until his death Motolianski remained attached to Chaim. At the age of nine Weizmann began to learn Russian from Shlomo Tsvi Sokolovsky in preparation for his secondary education.[40] By the time he was ready to move on to Pinsk, he knew the entire Bible, a few tractates of the Talmud, Hebrew grammar, some basic Hebrew, and a smattering of Hebrew literature.[41] He had acquired the reputation of being a very diligent and pious student.[42]

It is clear that the *melamed* and rabbi had made a deep impression on Chaim, especially since Ozer Weizmann was away a great deal. They functioned *in loco parentis*, as it were. Another early influence on Chaim and the whole Weizmann family was his maternal grandfather—whose house stood adjacent to the Weizmanns'. At the age of two[43] Chaim went to live with his grandparents Yehiel-Michel and Frouma Chemerinski, who doted over the child and fulfilled his every wish. His grandfather would travel all the way to Pinsk to buy him a special toy.[44] In winter he would pile up heaps of snow so that Chaim could enjoy sliding down. He would regale Chaim with stories of the great rabbis and heroes in Israel, including the contemporary heroes Moses Montefiore and the Rothschilds. Outwardly Chaim looked like the other children: thin, pale-faced, and sharp-eyed. On the other hand, he was more demanding than the others. For instance, he preferred silk shirts, which his grandmother would struggle to sew for him. It was clear that he was being spoiled, and he behaved like an only child, rarely helping with household chores.[45] When Chaim was four his grandmother died, and Yehiel-Michel and Chaim came to live with the Weizmanns.

Yehiel-Michel had his own room at the Weizmanns' house. For the last three years of his life he was partially paralyzed, and on Sabbaths and holidays a *minyan* (quorum of ten) would be called so he could pray at home. By the time he died, in 1887, the Weizmanns already had nine children. Even with a maid and the manservant Yakim[46] it must have been a formidable task to manage the household. Moreover, Ozer's two younger sisters and brother, who were orphaned at an early age, also came to live with the Weizmanns.[47] In 1888, when Miriam, Chaim's oldest sister, married Chaim Lubzhinsky—who for the previous two years had been associated with Ozer in the timber transport—the latter also joined the household.[48]

It was a very hospitable and busy home, in which Chaim's mother was the central figure. Until she was in her forties she continued having babies; she was already a grandmother when Chaim's youngest brother, Chilik, was born in 1892. At this point Miriam, his oldest sister, already had two children, who rejoiced at the birth of an uncle.[49] Rachel Leah spent a lot of her time with babies and in the kitchen, mending, sewing, tending the garden, and even handling the business when necessary. Yet she had time to read Yiddish literature and was appalled by any form of cultural or physical stagnation. After they moved to Pinsk and her children were enrolled in the *Gymnasium,* she secretly studied Russian and read Tolstoi with great interest.[50] She was a kind and patient woman.

In Pinsk the Weizmann house became something of a public institution, and during school vacations it was pandemonium, with friends of the children coming and going, arguing interminably the ideologies of the day. Though she was pious, she was tolerant toward alien views. Most of all she was always cheerful and optimistic. She would say, "Whatever happens, I shall be well off. If Shmuel [born in 1882, the revolutionary in the family] is right, we shall be happy in Russia; and if Chaim is right, then I shall go to live in Palestine."[51]

Chaim's parents—at least according to their son's memoirs in old age—were nonauthoritarian. At the same time, they did not seem to give much direction and guidance to their offspring. The dozen or so children who occupied the house at any one point seem to have given one another support and were assisted by one of the adults in the extended family,[52] by close relatives in Motol and Pinsk, and by the teachers and rabbis with whom they studied. In Chaim's case, he seems to have established an especially close relationship with his grandfather, his favorite *rebbe*, and a childless uncle who eventually adopted him—no doubt in order to help him avoid conscription. The rest of the children must have found other surrogate parents to substitute for the often absent Ozer and for the overworked Rachel Leah. It is perhaps not surprising that in his memoirs Weizmann displays not only love for his parents but also pity. There is even a slight trace of condescension in his discussion of his mother. Clearly he missed having parents who played a central role in the household, singling out the maid for having maintained discipline among the Weizmann brood. Nevertheless, if he felt neglected as a young child, Weizmann did not harbor feelings of resentment. Throughout his adult life he maintained the warmest and most respectful relations with his parents. At the same time he himself acted as a surrogate father for his younger siblings and other relatives as well.

That Chaim's interest in the Hibbat Zion (Love of Zion) movement was early implanted in him by his parents as well as his milieu is well known. At the age of eleven, just prior to his departure for Pinsk, where he was about to move to attend the Pinsk Secondary School, he wrote a letter to his teacher Shlomo Tsvi Sokolovsky. This, the earliest extant letter, was written a few months after the Kattowitz Conference of November 1884, the first conference of the Hibbat Zion movement. Much has been made of this letter to demonstrate the boy's vision of England's future role in Jewish history. What the letter does reveal are the kinds of ideas then prevailing in the Pale of Settlement,[53] or perhaps, more accurately, in the Weizmann household. Possibly the young boy was also influenced by stories he had heard about Moses Montefiore, the most famous Anglo-Jew of the nineteenth century, who had just passed away.

> . . . I shall observe your command not to throw away behind me our sacred tongue and the teachings of our sages of blessed memory because I am bound to study the Hebrew language. And please, my dear teacher, do not imagine that when I attend the Gymnasium I shall throw off the garb of Judaism. No! On no account. I have determined in my heart to observe Judaism and I shall oppose the opinion of those who say that one becomes a doctor because he casts off his faith . . .
>
> I am sending you one of my ideas for you to see, *and that concerns Hevrat Hovevei Zion* [The Society of Lovers of Zion] *and Jerusalem which is in our land.* How lofty and elevated the idea which inspired our brethren the sons of Israel to establish the Hovevei Zion Society. Because by this we can rescue our exiled, oppressed brethren who are scattered in all corners of the world.
> . . . In conclusion, we must support this society which understands what lies before it and sees the evil threatening us, therefore the obligation rests upon us to establish a place to which we can flee for help . . . Let us carry our banner to Zion and return to our first mother upon whose knee we were

born. —For why should we look to the Kings of Europe for compassion that they should take pity upon us and give us a resting place? In vain! All have decided: *The Jew must die*, but England will nevertheless have mercy upon us.[54] In conclusion, to Zion!—Jews—to Zion! let us go.[55]

It was in Pinsk, to which the family moved in the summer of 1885, that Weizmann would begin his first activities on behalf of the Hibbat Zion movement.[56]

II

Pinsk

In his memoirs Weizmann noted that

> except during the Christmas and Easter festivals, when they were roused to
> a high pitch of religious excitement by their priests, they [the peasants of
> Motol] were quite friendly toward us. At worst they never got wholly out
> of hand, and there were never any pogroms in Motol or the neighboring
> villages. It is a melancholy reflection on human relationships when the ab-
> sence of murder must be noted as a special circumstance which calls for
> gratitude.[1]

In fact, the Jews of Motol were spared from pogroms at a time when
many Jewish communities were exposed to the murderous waves that
swept Russia in 1881–84. By the time Weizmann entered the Pinsk *Gymnasium* in 1885, the worst of the pogroms were over, but the air in the
Pale was heavy with disaster and insecurity.

Chaim Weizmann was only seven years old when the pogroms began.
In his autobiography he mentions them briefly, though it is highly unlikely that these events were not a major topic of conversation in the
Weizmann household.[2] Perhaps the Weizmanns' escape from the physical horrors of the pogroms, as well as the family's relatively more comfortable economic condition, may explain the fact that not one of their
members joined the great migration to America.[3]

For those who had experienced these horrors,[4] the pogroms became
an important ingredient in their formative experience, and they carried
in their mind's eye pictures of these gruesome scenes until old age.[5]
Psychologically the impact of the pogroms was even greater than the
physical and material damage. Eastern Europe had not been the scene
of such massacres since the Cossack rebellion in 1648–50—with the exception of the pogroms in 1744 and 1768. There was a widespread feeling of insecurity which pervaded the entire community.[6] To most Jews
it now became clear that the government was trying to make the Jewish
position in the empire untenable. Moreover, many believed that Jewish
emancipation would never be consummated in Russia.[7] Indeed, the shock
of the pogroms, the feeling of many Jews that the generally light pun-

ishments of offenders were evidence of the government's collusion and coordination of the disturbances, coupled with the otherwise miserable economic and social position of the Jews, plunged many into despair.[8]

Desperate and frightened, Jews sought immediate remedies to their intolerable condition. The pogroms and lack of Jewish rights in Russia combined to shake the Jewish masses out of their passivity and prompted one of the greatest mass migrations in modern times; most of them chose America for remedying, first and foremost, their economic misery.[9] Not since their expulsion from the Iberian Peninsula had Jews undergone such a tremendous dislocation. In the thirty years between the assassination of Alexander II and the outbreak of World War I, approximately one third of the East European Jews left their homeland.[10] There had already been a trickle of Jewish immigration to America of some 7,500 Russian and Polish Jews between 1820 and 1870 and somewhat more than 40,000 in the 1870s.[11] These figures now increased by a quantum leap.[12] The United States received about 70 percent of all Jewish expatriates,[13] but there was a simultaneous migration from Russia to Canada, with an annual peak of 11,252 arrivals in 1914. That year England harbored some 120,000 Jewish immigrants. There was also a panic-driven and unorganized immigration to Palestine, for which there are no reliable statistics; but it seems that hundreds of immigrants from Russia and other parts of Eastern Europe began to arrive in Palestine as early as October 1881.[14] Altogether nearly two million Jews left Russia between 1880 and 1914.[15]

The year 1881 in many ways represents a turning point in modern Jewish history. The travail of Russian Jewry had an impact on the Jews of the West since it coincided with the rise of political anti-Semitism in Germany, France, and Austria-Hungary.[16] The disasters of Russian Jewry and the realization that even in the West the gains of emancipation were still precarious led to a reexamination of Jewish history since the French Revolution. For the Jews of the United States this wave of immigration was crucial since it radically altered American Jewish institutions and gave them the character which they retained for many decades. In the East the dream of Jewish emancipation under the Tsar was now, at the very least, badly shaken. The Russian *haskalah* as an ideology was weakened, and there was now room for two other ideologies (in addition to assimilation): Zionism and Russian-Jewish socialism. Between 1789 and 1880 most of the important ideological currents and movements in Jewry came from the West; the new ideological movements after 1880 came from the East, which now became the center for several varieties of Jewish nationalism.

The beginning of the Hibbat Zion movement can be traced to the secularized generation of Jewish *maskilim* who had experienced the pogroms of the 1880s and their condonation by the Russian radicals.[17] Those who had held hope for emancipation in Russia now turned vehemently against their erstwhile ideals and ideas. They now held that anti-Semitism was a perennial feature of the Jewish situation in the *Galut* (Diaspora), which was rooted in the Jews' homelessness and minority status. Jews now needed to free themselves—to "auto-emancipate" themselves through collective action. The Jews also needed to regain their culture, not by imitating the Western Enlightenment but by cultivating their own historic heritage. Moshe Leib Lilienblum, one of the foremost Hovevei Zion (Lovers of Zion) of the period, at this time came to formulate his ideas about the Jewish problem. Jewish alienation, he believed, was the fundamental cause of anti-Semitism, which therefore was inevitable in the Diaspora. The only remedy was resettlement in the historic Jewish homeland.[18]

Lilienblum was soon joined by Perez Smolenskin, Lev Levanda, and others who had shared similar emotional and intellectual experiences. They all now felt themselves identified with a distinct party and ideological movement in Jewry. The members of this group had undergone various degrees of Russification and acculturation in the 1860s and 1870s; in fact, acculturation was almost a precondition for their Jewish nationalism since it had helped break the spell of the traditional quietist messianic idea. It is therefore not surprising that some of the first progenitors of Jewish nationalism were formerly removed from things Jewish. Now all of them shared a group identity which served them as a common rallying point, no matter what particular program each individual advocated for the emerging Jewish national movement. The journals *Hashahar*, *Hamaggid*, *Hamelitz*, and *Razsvet* disseminated the ideas of Hibbat Zion. Some of the Hovevei Zion societies wanted immediate immigration to Palestine, others emphasized preparation and propagation of national ideas, but all of them agreed that Palestine needed to be settled by a new class of Jewish farmers and workers.

In fact, the crisis of the 1880s produced the consolidation of a variety of attitudes. What was important for the nationalists was identification with the group; their common goals and strategies would arise as a collective process. Thus, in the immediate period after the pogroms there was a great deal of adjustment of opinions and suggestions, leading, in many cases, to a rapid shifting of lines.[19] There were those among the Russian-trained intellectuals converted to Jewish loyalty by the pogroms who advocated America as a land of immigration, albeit within a national framework.[20] However, the most prevalent point of view among the nationalist *maskilim* was the settlement of Palestine, and this became, of course, the ruling opinion among them as among the proto-Zionist traditionalists.[21] Ultimately Russian-trained Jewish intellectuals, the Hebrew *maskilim*, and the enlightened orthodox laymen and rabbis were involved in the project to settle Zion, and they emerged as a major ideological component of the Jewish community.

Leo Pinsker's pamphlet *Auto-Emancipation, Mahnruf an seine Stammesgenossen von einem russischen Juden* (1882) provided the movement with a systematic ideological basis. As the title of his pamphlet indicates, Pinsker called on the Jewish nation to aid itself and return to national consciousness and a life of territorial independence. Anti-Semitism was a universal peril and would not be solved by mere migration to minority status in another country. Under the influence of Lilienblum, Hermann Schapira, and others, he joined the Hibbat Zion and helped shape the organization of the movement. On November 6, 1884, on the hundredth birthday of Moses Montefiore, the first conference of Hovevei Zion took place in Kattowitz, in Upper Silesia, where Pinsker was elected president of the movement's presidium.[22] The main value of the Kattowitz Conference was its consolidation of the movement. There were almost a hundred societies in attendance, with a membership of approximately fourteen thousand, which collected about thirty thousand rubles a year from donations and another twenty thousand rubles from various enterprises.[23]

Even before Pinsker's *Auto-Emancipation* and the Kattowitz Conference, a group of Jewish students founded on February 6, 1882, the Bilu, whose Hebrew initials were an acronym for "House of Jacob, come ye and let us go."[24] Its program was ambitious—immigration to and settlement in *Eretz Israel*.[25] The first group of Biluim arrived in Palestine on July 6, 1882. Eventually, after many disappointments, including lack of support by the Russian Hovevei Zion, the Biluim did manage to found their own settlement, Gederah, in December 1884.[26]

Chaim Weizmann's letter to Shlomo Tsvi Sokolovsky was written one year after the Kattowitz Conference, in the summer of 1885 in Motol, shortly before he moved to Pinsk. It indicates that the eleven-year-old boy was already familiar, at least superficially, with the Hibbat Zion leadership and ideology.[27] The Hibbat Zion movement had taken deep root in Pinsk, and it is here that Weizmann's early notions and sympathies were beginning to crystallize into an ideology. Compared to Motol, Pinsk was a bustling, large city; a completely new world opened up to young Chaim. As he himself put it succinctly, "From Motol to Pinsk was a matter of six Russian miles, or twenty-five English miles; but in terms of intellectual displacement the distance was astronomical. For Pinsk was a real provincial metropolis. . . . It could not pretend to the cultural standing of great centers like Warsaw, Vilna, Odessa and Moscow; but neither was it a nameless village."[28]

The Pinsk Jewish community began in 1506, when seventy-five Jews coming from the West established themselves en bloc in a "Judengasse" close by the prince's castle and received permission to build a synagogue. In 1886 there were 19,017 Jews in Pinsk out of a total population of 22,967, comprising 82.8 percent.[29] Thus, by the time Weizmann arrived Pinsk was the second Russian city, after Berdichev, with such a high percentage of Jews. It was, as it were, a Jewish city with the non-Jews living in the outskirts. Its Jewish character was especially pronounced during the Sabbath and holidays. Many of the Jewish-owned factories had their own synagogues, and time was set aside for morning and evening prayers. On the eve of Sabbath and various festivals the workers in the shops and factories would lay down their tools an hour before the time for lighting the candles. Two long blasts on the siren from the Lurie factory would usher in the Sabbath—the first announcing the time for closing the shops, and the second, about half an hour later, the time for lighting the candles. The workshops of Pinsk were closed on Sabbaths and festivals and some of them stopped work on Tishah b'Av— the traditional day of mourning for disasters that have befallen the Jewish people.[30] In 1751 a Jewish community was established in Karlin, to the east of Pinsk. The number of Jews in Karlin increased steadily and Karlin itself grew in size until it eventually reached the boundaries of Pinsk. At the end of the eighteenth century two separate Jewish communities existed within the city of Pinsk, namely, the Pinsk community and the Karlin community.[31]

Even after the official abolition in Russia of the institution of the *kehillah* (the official Jewish community), those of Karlin and Pinsk continued to function, and like other Lithuanian *kehillot* they retained their social, juridical, and cultural autonomy. The affairs of the *kehillot* were administered by the president *(Av Bet-Din)* and members of the religious courts in cooperation with leading public figures and the officially appointed rabbi. A very important factor in the preservation and extension of this autonomy in Pinsk was the local rich philanthropists, who established and maintained educational and charitable institutions and were influential with the secular authorities. These benefactors were the Levin, Lurie, Halpern, and Eliasberg families, whose devoted service earned them the title of "the Rothschilds of Pinsk and Karlin."[32]

The Jewish community of Pinsk became economically independent of the gentile population in the nineteenth century. It was then that Jews turned increasingly to wholesale and retail business, gaining more and more control over the city's commerce. The development of Pinsk's economy was favored by the change for the better in the city's geopolitical position after the abolition of the Russo-Polish border (1795), and by the improvement of its transport facilities at the end of the eighteenth and during the nineteenth centuries, involving the construction of new canals and the laying of railway lines westward to Zhabinka-Brest-Litovsk (1844) and eastward to Luninets (1887). Jews set the pace for the city's economy, based first on commerce and then on industry. In the nineteenth century the Jews set up large business concerns which developed the city into an inland harbor capable of handling goods coming from distant places. Pinsk thus became an important transit station on the great commercial arteries running along the inland network of rivers. A link with the outside world was thus firmly established.[33] By 1898 Pinsk increasingly became an industrial town, with most of its twenty-seven factories in Jewish hands. The number of Jewish workers—men and women—greatly increased. By 1902 there were fifty-four shops in Pinsk in which at least 2,500 to 3,000 Jews worked, many of them heads of households. Thus an industrial and clerical proletariat came into being, with 50 percent of the city's Jewish population making its living by manual labor. There was also an increase in the number of Jewish artisans, such as construction workers, furniture makers, tailors, and furriers. Since economic ties with gentiles were minimal, Jews also provided the labor force for all their needs, including carters, porters, fishermen, and clerks.[34]

Pinsk was also a lively and important cultural center. Here, as elsewhere, every generation had its own scholars and sages who molded the spiritual character of Pinsk and Karlin. In the early 1760s Karlin became a hasidic center under the guidance of Reb Aharon the Great and his disciples.[35] The rise of Karlin hasidim was one of the reasons for the rabbinic ban promulgated against hasidim in Lithuania and split both the Pinsk and Karlin communities into two bitter factions.[36] Gradually the tensions eased. Karlin eventually became the "right side of the tracks." The intelligentsia, wealthy industrialists, and other worthies made their home there. The main street of Pinsk, which ran down to the docks, was called the Kievver Gasse. Beyond Kievver Gasse, in the low marshy area near the lake, lived a large population of Jewish dock workers and traders. All in all, the hasidim in Pinsk and Karlin had six prayer houses (*shulkhen*) out of the forty-two synagogues in the city.[37] About the middle of the nineteenth century the first signs of the *haskalah* movement began to appear in Pinsk and Karlin, gaining greater momentum over the next generation.

Until the mid-nineteenth century the system of traditional education of *hadarim* and *yeshivot* was the only educational option for Pinsk's Jews. The first secular (Crown) elementary school for Jews was founded in Pinsk in 1853 but did not manage to attract many students. In 1873 a private school which taught secular studies in Russian but emphasized Jewish studies was more successful. In the 1860s Jews began to send their children to the Russian high school (*Gymnasium*), whose principal was interested in attracting Jewish students. By the end of the 1870s the *Real-Gymnasium*—the public high school emphasizing the sciences—was heavily attended by Jewish pupils: Thirty-nine percent of the seventy pupils were Jews.[38] It is this school which Weizmann attended after he proved his proficiency in Russian. Two years later, when the *numerus clausus* of 1887 decreed that no more than 10 percent of the students admitted to high schools within the Pale could be Jews,[39] it would have been extremely difficult for him to gain entrance regardless of his qualifications.

Chaim's brother Feivel was two years older.[40] He was past his *bar mitzvah* and did not have a great desire for learning; Rabbi Motolianski almost lost hope for him. Ozer, however, had a different outlook on education and made a decision that was unusual for a man of his generation and upbringing. The boy's intelligence and dexterity, in addition to his love and talent for crafts, were apparent to everyone, and Ozer was not inclined to force him to continue his studies; he was happy to let him become an artisan rather than a middleman. Perhaps one consideration in sending the two boys to Pinsk was that it would ease somewhat the overcrowding in the family's home in Motol. There is no clue anywhere as to how Rachel and Ozer Weizmann felt about sending two boys out of the house at such a tender age. In any case, the decision was reached to send both Feivel and Chaim to Pinsk, Feivel to learn lithography from an expert (Aaron Solz)[41] and Chaim to attend the *Real-Gymnasium*. Interestingly, it was under pressure from Reb Michel, Chaim's grandfather, that Chaim was sent to a *Real-Gymnasium* rather than a *yeshivah*. "He is a prodigy," said the old man, "and he must continue learning."[42] This was an unusual statement from a devout and pious Jew, but it also reflected the hopes and expectations that the entire Weizmann family placed in Chaim. Though Feivel was the oldest son, it was Chaim whom everyone expected to succeed. He would also be pointed out as an example to his younger siblings. This placed a special burden on the young boy, but it also provided him with all the moral support usually reserved for a firstborn. It was a challenge he needed and wanted to meet. In fact, the first challenge came even before he entered the *Gymnasium*, when he had to master sufficient Russian to pass his entrance examinations. Later, in Germany, he would often have to study hard to catch up with his peers. Weizmann's educational path was followed by his siblings, none of whom attended a *yeshivah*. They all—no doubt with the approval of their parents—opted for a secular higher education. This would seem to indicate that Reb Michel really did not have to lobby very hard to send Chaim to a *Gymnasium*, since the atmosphere at home was, in any case, conducive to such an educational course.

For the first period the boys boarded with a family called Pollack; a while later Ozer's widowed sister Bracha moved to Pinsk to take care of the boys' needs.[43] Chaim passed his entrance examination to the *Real-Gymnasium* and began his studies. At the same time he continued his Hebrew studies with Reb Shmuel Vilkominer. His bar mitzvah was celebrated in Pinsk. Chaim delivered his address in Yiddish, but afterward, relates his mother, "Chaim engaged in conversations in Russian and Hebrew and I began to feel that he is no longer one of us, from Motol. But when he spoke to me he was still the same 'Chaim-niu' I knew. . . ."[44]

It is unlikely that Chaim actually spoke Hebrew, though he may have spent time studying the language. In fact, though he now wore a blue school uniform with shiny buttons and spoke Russian well, Chaim continued his Jewish studies and for many years kept a promise he had made to his grandfather to refrain from writing in school on the Sabbath.[45] Though later in life he described his Pinsk years as grim,[46] at the time he did not consider himself unhappy. The *Real-Gymnasium* was nothing to boast about academically; it was a typical Russian school, where the teachers were appointed less on the basis of their scholarly qualification than their contacts in the Russian bureaucracy. The teachers' main concern was advancement, which could be attained only by strict adherence to the myriad rules and regulations handed down from above, designed to impede any independent thinking. Students and teachers were hemmed in by an inflexible and oppressive system. It was hardly an intellectual challenge to Chaim and the other Jewish boys, who often outsmarted their instructors, and it was not surprising that Chaim received top marks, though he does not seem to have been a bookworm. There was only one exception to the mediocrity of the school—Chaim's chemistry teacher Kornienko, an intelligent and humane person, knowledgeable in his field and willing to share his knowledge with students—indeed, an anomaly in the system. It is understandable why he attracted the brighter students, Chaim being among them. Later in life Weizmann credited Kornienko with having given him the first push toward chemistry, though his statement "I owe [him] whatever I have been able to achieve in the way of science"[47] seems more like an expression of gratitude for the uniqueness and warmth of the man than a statement of fact. Indeed, when Weizmann entered a German university he had a great deal of chemistry to make up in order to reach the level of his German peers.

In 1888, three years after their arrival in Pinsk, Feivel was forced to interrupt his apprenticeship and return to Motol. Though relatively well off, Ozer Weizmann was more inclined toward Jewish studies than business, and the Weizmann family was not financially secure until much later, when Chaim Lubshinsky and Feivel took over the business. Moreover, this was a particularly bad time for the timber trade, and the older boy had to help out in the family's shaky business. Chaim was now fourteen years old and quite aware of his father's inability to pay the hundred rubles (fifty dollars) a year needed to keep him in Pinsk. There is some evidence that even earlier Chaim had tried unsuccessfully to support himself.[48] What is clear is that when Feivel and Aunt Bracha returned to Motol, Chaim began to supervise the homework of Saul Lurie, who was just starting at the *Gymnasium.* The Lurie family had vast interests in the timber trade, and it is possible that they even had some business connections with Ozer Weizmann. Saul's father, Idel (Samuel) Lurie, was a member of the very rich Lurie clan. Together with his brother Grigory he owned banks in Homel and in the small towns of Klintsi, Pochep, and Zhlobin.[49] He hired Chaim to supervise his son's homework in exchange for board, a little room, and fifty rubles (twenty-five dollars) a year, which paid for Chaim's tuition fees, books, and other minor expenses. Thus, at the age of fourteen Chaim was no longer dependent on his father. He lived with the Luries in their Karlin home until the end of his Pinsk days in 1892. It was probably not easy for so young an adolescent as Chaim to shoulder the responsibility of caring for his own material needs, but the experience in Pinsk is an early illustration of his strong will to persevere no matter what the obstacles. He also developed early on the confidence that he could master all difficulties.

None of Chaim's letters to his family from Pinsk have survived, but the few extant letters written to Saul's brother Ovsey (Hosea) Lurie, who was a student in Courland, indicate his seriousness and interest in his studies. He advised the latter to read Gogol, Turgenev, Grigorovich, Dostoevsky, Pisemsky, and others.[50] Indeed, it is clear that Chaim found delight and took pride in Russian literature. There are likewise references to Homer, Virgil, Dante, Shakespeare, Aristotle, Galileo, and other illustrious thinkers.[51] He tried to save his kopeks, took private lessons in German and French, and was overjoyed when Ozer would bring him from Danzig the works of Schiller and other German classics.[52] Chaim's letters to Ovsey are filled with discussions of his own and Ovsey's studies and grades. Early on his attitude toward academic study crystallized: He advocated study not only as an end in itself but as a means to extricate oneself from poverty and achieve economic security. Writing to Ovsey at the age of sixteen, he tried to impart to him the habits and norms he himself had acquired:

> Of course, if you will continue to study in the same way, if you read a lot and generally strive to improve yourself, you will soon fill the gap which still remains. Your diligence will then help you to overcome any obstacle which may appear in your path, and you will firmly march toward your goal and certainly reach it. Laziness, on the other hand, is the basest of human failings; it brings in its wake a complete confusion in the human being; both in the moral and the physical sense, a complete demoralization. May the Almighty be praised for having delivered you from this state, for having woken you out of the somnolent inertia into which you let yourself sink for some years. You have come to your senses now, you have come to understand all that is all-important to any respectable man, and especially to us, the sons of Jacob, poor wanderers, martyrs for our sacred and pure faith. We need incessant toil, constant labor; we need quick intellectual development; we must learn everything that is noble and useful and as yet unknown to us. If you engage in this worthy task you will be happy all your life.[53]

This would be a recurring theme in Weizmann's life and a cause for much anxiety for himself and anger at those he considered *batlanim*, eternal students, without a responsible and practical sense of their present situation and future prospects.[54] Despite his early tendency to serious study and thinking, Weizmann also reveals in these letters a propensity for clowning and humor:

> I am a simple fellow; when I have no time, I don't write, and when I do, I go and spin a long yarn—and if there is no sense in such a letter, that is not my business: take a deep breath and read it if you want to, and if you don't—throw it under the bench or use it for another purpose . . . if the paper is soft and doesn't hurt. Well, you ought to know our sort; we are plain chaps, we don't think a lot, just get down to it and patch up a letter. Here you are, here is a blot on the paper; pity, but on the other hand, doesn't it add to the effect? Wait, let me add another blot for good measure. Look how elegant: two most respectable blots hand in hand against a white background . . .[55]

Thus wrote Chaim at the age of eighteen. In later years he was careful not to reveal his more mischievous traits. He would confine his humor to sarcastic remarks and an occasional joke.

While in Pinsk, Chaim was able to enjoy his leisure time, such as the summer vacations spent journeying on his uncle's rafts up the canal to

Brest-Litovsk and down the Bug to Warsaw. There were, of course, also the visits home, which in themselves were daylong adventures. But even during the school session there was room for other activities. School lasted from nine to two-thirty in the afternoon. Schoolwork, Hebrew studies, supervision of his pupil, and his own private reading and study did not consume all of his time. Chaim did not have gentile friends. In his autobiography Weizmann often remarks that in his early years he knew little of gentiles; they were to him the symbols of menacing forces against which he had to protect himself, and in Pinsk, as in Motol, he had no social contact with them.[56] We have no information on Jewish friends with whom he might have spent his spare time. We do know that his intellectual and emotional interests lay outside the Christian world, and it was in Pinsk that his attraction, from his fifteenth year on, to the nascent Zionist movement increased.

The Hibbat Zion movement played an important part in the history of Pinsk. In studying Russian Jewish history it is particularly important to keep in mind the regional factors operating in each instance. It is of great significance that Chaim Weizmann's roots were in Lithuanian-Belorussian Jewry. The idea of settlement in Palestine, which had been developing steadily since the 1860s, was adopted by Rabbi David Friedman—also known as Reb Dovidel Karliner—the *Av Bet-Din* of Karlin, and Rabbi Elazar Moshe Hurwitz, the *Av Bet-Din* of Pinsk. In the middle of the 1870s, when word spread of the possibility of settlement in Palestine, with the aid of Laurence Oliphant many of the city's Jews prepared for the journey.[57] Rabbi Friedman, who was renowned for his two-volume *Piskei Halakhot*, an exposition and summary of matrimonial law, participated actively in the Hibbat Zion. As early as 1863 he published articles in the *Levanon* which reflected his favorable attitude toward settlement in Palestine, thus influencing many observant Jews to join in. He even had the idea to establish a bank that would purchase land in Palestine.[58] Friedman participated in the Kattowitz Conference[59] and remained active in the Hibbat Zion movement for the next two decades. Another important propagator of the Hibbat Zion was the popular Yiddish orator and preacher *(maggid)* Zvi Hirsch Masliansky, who became active shortly after the 1881 pogroms.[60] In 1884–85 the number of Hovevei Zion in Pinsk reached 250 and somewhat later even attained 400. Some two hundred Jews emigrated from Pinsk to Palestine between 1882 and 1891.[61] A special society, *Agudat ha-Elef*, was founded to raise funds, and its emissaries went to Palestine to buy land. Upon the organization of Bnei Moshe in 1889, under the leadership of Ahad Ha'Am, a branch was organized in Pinsk under the name *Lishkat Zerubavel*. When, in 1890, the "Company for support of Jewish farmers in Syria and Palestine" was organized under the leadership of the Odessa Committee, there was a relatively large number of members registered in Pinsk.[62] Thus, it is not surprising that when Herzl convened the First Zionist Congress in Basle in 1897, its membership contained three delegates from Pinsk.[63]

It also came as no surprise that one of the three Pinsk delegates to the

1897 Congress was Saul Lurie, Chaim Weizmann's pupil from 1888 to 1892.[64] It was during these years that Chaim was inspired by the Zionist idea. Perhaps it was Rabbi Friedman who first anchored Chaim's emotional attachments to Zion and helped harness them in the cause of Zionism.[65] It was in Rabbi Friedman's little synagogue that Chaim attended services. Reb Dovidel's brother-in-law was Yehiel Michel Pines, who had settled in Palestine as early as 1878. He was closely involved with the Hovevei Zion, and helped purchase the Gederah lands for the Bilu. No doubt his brother-in-law's extensive activities in Palestine deepened Rabbi Friedman's attachment to Zion. Chaim, who admired Friedman's saintliness and scholarship,[66] became imbued with his rabbi's attitudes. In addition, the departures to Palestine of many Pinsk Jews (e.g., the Eisenbergs and Shertoks), the inspiring orations of Masliansky, and the involvement of so many of Pinsk's families, including members of the Lurie family, in the Hibbat Zion could not have failed to leave a deep impression on young Chaim. The Weizmann home had already predisposed him to a love of Zion. Given this home environment, it is not surprising that nine of the surviving twelve children of Ozer and Rachel Weizmann eventually settled permanently in Palestine. It is, of course, quite possible that Chaim Weizmann may have contemplated the value of ideologies other than Zionism. If he did, there is no trace of this in the available documentation. All evidence points to the fact that the combined influences of his home in Motol and his milieu in Pinsk directed the adolescent, almost inevitably, into the nascent Zionist groups.

The organizational methods of the Hovevei Zion in Pinsk were poor and its financial resources poorer still; one dealt in kopecks, not rubles. Chaim was too young at the time to be included in the more impressive Zionist activities, such as meetings, writing of circulars, and speech making. What he excelled in was door-to-door money collection during the Purim fund-raising. It is here, tramping in Pinsk's March thaw, that he gained his first Zionist apprenticeship.[67] Getting involved in this way was perhaps natural for a boy whose father refused to correspond with him in any language but Hebrew, the symbol of the Zionist revival.[68]

Members of the Hibbat Zion were among the first to preach the revival of Hebrew as a spoken language and to press for a modernization of the *heder*. In 1890, only one year after the establishment of the *Safah Berurah* society for the revival of spoken Hebrew, first in Jerusalem and then in Odessa, some of the young Jews in Pinsk set up a society with the same name and purpose in Pinsk.[69] They encountered great difficulties from the orthodox elements in town, especially when they founded in Pinsk, in 1895, a *heder metukan*—progressive *heder*.[70] The *Safah Berurah* society and the *heder metukan* played an important part in the revival of Hebrew as a spoken language and in the reform of Jewish education. Weizmann's actual impact on Zionist life in Pinsk was rather minimal,[71] but the city's Zionist leaders and activities shaped his weltanschauung.[72]

At the same time, he did not remain indifferent to Russian civilization and culture. By the time he left Pinsk in 1892, he spoke fluent Russian and was acquainted with Russian culture. Moreover, his interest in science had matured into a firm desire to study chemistry. Thus, Pinsk set the double pattern of his life: an interest in science, on the one hand, and an involvement in Zionist affairs, on the other. Moreover, he now had definite ideas about the importance of education, and for the time being his most important goal would be to attain the best academic qualifications he could. A *batlan* was degenerate morally and physically. A Jew needed to further his intellectual development if he wanted to survive in the hostile world of the gentiles.[73] Chaim's strong bonds with his East European roots never weakened, but at the same time he also knew that he needed to transcend and outgrow the intellectual and physical boundaries of the Pale of Settlement.

III

Berlin

Chaim Weizmann graduated from the *Real-Gymnasium* with the highest marks in every subject except drawing. It would have been natural for him to enter a Russian university, but he had had enough of Russia. The *numerus clausus* for universities had been permanently set at 10 percent of the student body within the Pale, 5 percent outside it, and 3 percent in St. Petersburg and Moscow. Although this *numerus clausus* was not always rigidly observed,[1] it would have required endless chicanery, deception and humiliation to enter a university within the quota.[2] As a result of the restrictions in Russia, many East European Jews turned to the West to seek higher education. Chaim Weizmann was among them.

The choice of a specific university was accidental. A friend of the family, Reb Yitzhak Pulik, had two sons attending a Jewish boarding school in the village of Pfungstadt, near Darmstadt, in Germany. He recommended Chaim for a position as a junior Hebrew and Russian teacher for his sons and other Russian children. Weizmann was offered the position. The attraction of the job was that Weizmann could attend the university in Darmstadt, some thirty minutes away by train, and with a little assistance from home he could get by with the three hundred marks (seventy-five dollars) the school paid him, plus room and board. In order to avoid paying for an expensive foreign passport, in the fall of 1892 Weizmann posed as a worker on a raft which headed toward Danzig.[3] At Thorn, the first stop in German territory, he took his possessions and skipped, traveling the rest of the distance to Pfungstadt by fourth-class train via Frankfurt am Main.[4]

Pfungstadt was a well-to-do community—known all over Germany for its brewery—which had served since the Middle Ages as a central administrative and economic seat for the smaller villages nearby. The first Jews settled there as early as 1616. Weizmann arrived when the Jewish population in the village was at its peak.[5] Of great significance for the Jewish community, and for Pfungstadt in general, was the founding in 1857 of a high school/boarding school which accepted Jewish students from all over Germany and abroad, as well as Christian children from Pfungstadt. The school, which was located at Mainstrasse 6, was founded by Dr. D. E. Joel. Until 1886 it was called "Dr. Joelsches Lehr-und Erzieh-ungsinstitut." In 1880 it had about one hundred students who were in-structed by eight teachers and junior teachers, of whom five were Jew-ish. Dr. Joel, the school's founder, was director until Dr. D. Barnass took over toward the end of the 1880s. By 1890, two years before Weizmann's arrival, the number of students had already declined to eighty, and after the founding of a local secular high school the number declined further. The school finally closed its gates in 1907. During Weizmann's eight months in the school (1892–93) it was still famous all over Germany for its extensive curriculum in Judaic studies, as well as its instruction in Latin, German, English, French, Russian, mathematics, and the natural sci-ences. News about the school's accomplishments often appeared in the press.[6]

Weizmann's first experiences in Germany were unhappy. In Pfung-stadt, as in many other so-called *Landesgemeinden* (rural communities) of Hessen and elsewhere, there was greater social control in the Jewish community than in the big cities, where it was easy to maintain one's anonymity. Religion was a given, not an object of individual choice.[7] Dr. Barnass was extremely pious, but in a rigid and formal way. The school was kosher, there were no classes on the Sabbath, and prayers were re-cited at the appointed times each morning, afternoon, and evening. But it was not the kind of folk piety Chaim had known at home; it lacked warmth and intimacy and was rigid and stuffy. In addition, Dr. Barnass was a German patriot of the first order. The years before Chaim's arrival in Germany were a period of heightened anti-Semitism.[8] It was there-fore natural for Dr. Barnass to be preoccupied with the question of anti-Semitism. But it was his obsequious and spineless response to the phe-nomenon which grated on Weizmann's nerves. Dr. Barnass preached in and out of season about the sterling qualities of German Jewry and about the need for spreading this message among Germans predisposed to-ward hatred of Jews.

Unfortunately, Dr. Barnass's sermons on this and similar subjects often served as substitutes for a solid meal. This institution of learning was also a private business, and students and teachers often suffered from lack of food, heat, and light; a lung hemorrhage suffered by Weizmann many years later was traced by his doctor to the privations of his first eight months in Germany.[9] In a letter to his family written toward the end of his sojourn in Pfungstadt, Chaim described with a great deal of humor the meal served on the eve of the holiday of Shavuot (Pentecost): Instead of soup was served some strange liquid; the meat dish was re-placed by Dr. Barnass's speech, which was as far from Torah wisdom as is the distance between pork and kosher meat; and instead of dessert and sweets there were some sweet remarks by the director.[10] Weiz-mann's discomfort with the school's brand of orthodoxy was due, in no small degree, to the fact that the Weizmann family was observing reli-gious rules more loosely. Weizmann, for example, had brought to Motol from Pfungstadt the game of croquet, which the children in the family,

Weizmann as a student at the Darmstadt Polytechnic, 1892

as well as some of the adults, played throughout the summer of 1893, including the Sabbath, without a reprimand from Ozer.[11]

Weizmann registered first as a *Hospitant* (auditor) and then as an *ausserordentlicher Studierender*—a student taking a full course, but not qualified by a high school certificate for admission as an *ordentlicher Studierender*—at the Grossherzoglich Hessischen Technischen Hochschule in Darmstadt for the academic year 1892–93. The train ride from Pfungstadt to Darmstadt took thirty minutes,[12] but he had to rise every day at five in order to make the train, which arrived at six-thirty, and would walk around until the university opened at seven-thirty. He returned to Pfungstadt in the late afternoon, taught his Russian and Hebrew lessons, ate his supper, and worked late into the night. The Technische Hochschule in Darmstadt was a well-respected university specializing in engineering, architecture, chemistry, and pharmacy.[13] Weizmann's high school education in Pinsk was not comparable to his German peers,' and he had to work hard to catch up.[14] Though Darmstadt was a pleasant town, he hardly had time to enjoy it. He was constantly on the run, overworked, undernourished, and lonely. His distaste for German Jews and for Pfungstadt was colored by the fact that it was his first time away from home. Pinsk, after all, was a larger version of Motol, an overgrown Jewish village teeming with familiar Jews, friends, and sometimes relatives. Pfungstadt, on the other hand, was an alien environment where he had no support group or even a person to confide in. He was cheerless and desperately homesick. Finally he broke down and decided to interrupt his studies. At the end of the academic year he went back to Pinsk, leaving Pfungstadt without regrets.[15]

Weizmann returned to Pinsk in the spring of 1893. The unfortunate experience he had had in Pfungstadt did not deter him from a strong desire to continue his university education or from studying in Germany. In the fall of 1893 he went to study at the Charlottenburg Polytechnik in Berlin. The West, and Western culture in particular, had now taken hold of him. It was an accident that Chaim's first encounter with German culture was in Pfungstadt. It was hardly an accident that his next choice of university was again on German soil in the heart of Prussia. The decision to study in Germany was common among Russian intellectual youth in the period before World War I. To young Russian Jews Germany held out the prospect of freedom and achievement. Wilhelminian Germany was at its zenith: It represented political stability, scientific achievement, and cultural ascendance or perhaps even superiority. Weizmann himself put it thusly:

> For the Jews and the intellectuals generally of Russia, the West ended at the Rhine, and beyond that boundary there was only an unknown world. They knew Germany, they spoke German, and they were vastly impressed by German achievement, German discipline and German power. They knew, as I did, that Russia was rotten through and through, eaten up by graft, incompetence and indolence . . . Germany, it is true, was also anti-Semitic, but German anti-Semitism did not show as much on the surface. It bore a milder aspect.[16]

Those who had a Jewish national bent did not reject their attachment to the strong Jewish values of Eastern Europe, but in many ways they internalized and adopted the standards of West European culture.[17] It was not surprising that many Zionist intellectuals and students made their home in Germany in the pre–World War I era and that Berlin became a center of such East European Hebraists as David Frischmann, Saul Tschernichowski, Michah Berdichesvski, and later also Shmuel Agnon.[18] Though they were frequently humiliated and resented the attitude of the gentile and Jewish Germans toward them and their culture, the young East European Jews who came to Berlin could not fail to be impressed by this city of massive stone, gigantic statues, and monuments celebrating the Hohenzollern. The Spree, the Tiergarten, the Lustgarten, and the Brandenburg Gate awed and inspired them. The opera, the theater, the literary idols of this period—all fascinated the young men and women who arrived from the East. In an atmosphere of almost complete freedom they could sit in the cafés all night, arguing the questions of the day. It is little wonder that in June 1895, after having been in Berlin for two years, Weizmann wrote to Leo Motzkin about "the God-forsaken town of Pinsk . . ."[19]

The Russian and Russian-Jewish intellectuals were, of course, part of the immigration to the West. From 1890 to 1915, 3,348,000 people left

Russia. More than half were Jews, who settled mostly in the United States. With the aid of the Alliance Israélite Universelle and the German Central Committee for Russian-Jewish Refugees, hundreds of thousands of Jews bound for the United States or other places overseas went through German ports in the 1880s and 1890s.[20] However, many also settled in Germany after 1881. Russians made up more than half the number of foreign students at most universities, and often a majority of these were Jewish.[21]

Most of the East European Jews settled in large cities.[22] Thus, by 1910 East European Jews constituted 15 percent of the total Jewish population of Greater Berlin.[23] Toward the end of the nineteenth century Berlin was already the center of the national German-Jewish organizations. Most of the important German-Jewish periodicals and newspapers were published in Berlin as well. As Berlin continued to grow in importance as a commercial and industrial center, Jews played an increasingly important role in the city's economic life.[24]

By the time Weizmann arrived in Berlin, in the autumn of 1893, there was a sizable Jewish student population there. In Prussian universities the number of foreign Jewish students increased steadily: In 1886–87 there were 129 East European Jews enrolled at the ten Prussian universities—75 percent of them studied in Berlin—out of a total of 13,658 Jewish and non-Jewish students, thus comprising less than 1 percent of the total student population. The percentage of East European Jewish students among the total Jewish student population was much higher. In 1886–87 the 129 East European Jews comprised 9.8 percent of the Jewish student body of 1,313, and by 1905–6 the 483 East European students comprised 25.3 percent of 1,904 Jewish students.[25] Thus, Weizmann could have immediate access to a large group of people who shared a common background, language, and aspirations. From the start it was clear to him that life in Berlin would be better than in Pfungstadt—if not materially, then certainly socially and culturally.

The difference was not only that Pfungstadt was a small rural settlement and Berlin a large city, nor even that the Charlottenburg Polytechnik was one of the best scientific institutes in the West. What was important to Weizmann was the large Russian-Jewish student colony in Berlin. Weizmann always needed people around him; he needed social interaction, an audience, approval, and support for his ideas. All these elements were missing in Pfungstadt. He found ample gratification for these needs in a small organization called the Russischer juedischer wissenschaftlicher Verein (Russian-Jewish Scientific Society). The Verein, as it was popularly known, was founded by twelve Russian-Jewish students[26] in December 1888, some two years before the term "Zionism" had become current. The Russischer juedischer wissenschaftlicher Verein was the first student organization in Germany to advocate Jewish nationalism, though only gradually. The statutes of the Verein, dated January 1890, declared that its aim was to "afford the young Russian Jews in Berlin the opportunity to acquaint themselves with the interests and needs of the Jewish nation."[27] It was only in 1898 that the Verein, which now changed its name to Russischer juedischer wissenschaftlicher Verein—Kadimah, stated: "The purpose of the Verein is to cultivate among the Russian-Jewish academic youth a Zionist conviction, Jewish knowledge, and Jewish life."[28] The Verein often served as a public catalyst in the 1890s to arouse interest in Jewish national questions among German-Jewish academics.

The founder and undisputed leader of the Verein was Leo Motzkin, who was born in the Ukraine but had been living in Berlin since the age of fifteen. His background was similar to Weizmann's. His father was an observant Jew open to new ideas who made a living in the timber business. By the time Weizmann came to Berlin, Motzkin was a twenty-six-year-old student of mathematics at Berlin University. Motzkin led the Verein by virtue of his knowledge of German culture and German Jewry and his organizational abilities. The membership itself consisted of a number of forceful personalities who were to play an important role in Zionist affairs in later years, such as Shmarya Levin, Nachman Syrkin, and Victor Jacobson.[29] They were all nonconformists. They did not accept authority easily and loved nothing more than to engage in heated ideological debates for hours on end.[30] Most of them were poor and underfed; Weizmann said that he himself did not eat a solid meal during his entire sojourn in Berlin, except as someone's guest.[31] This was, no doubt, an exaggeration since he did receive a regular subvention from home and there is no record to indicate that he had to work to support himself. Nevertheless, it is probably true that he had no money to spare. The students of the Verein constantly borrowed money from one another and some must have frequently felt the pangs of starvation. When Shmarya Levin arrived in Berlin, he walked the three miles to his friend Nachman Syrkin's lodging to save money, while a dog tied to a small cart pulled his luggage. For a while Syrkin and Levin shared a room on the fifth floor of a typical workers' tenement, for which they each paid twelve and a half marks ($3.12) a month, including breakfast. Their breakfast consisted of a cup of coffee and two slices of black bread thinly smeared with butter. By way of variety they could order two white rolls *without* butter. During the week Syrkin, who was among the poorest of the lot, contented himself with the black bread; on the Sabbath he sacrificed his butter in order to "luxuriate" in white rolls—a faint reminder of the Sabbath white bread of his faraway home.[32] The students, Weizmann among them, were constantly pawning what they could in order to make ends meet until the last day of the month.[33]

The Verein was a self-contained group. Its members were marginal men in Berlin society, isolated from both the other Russian students as well as the German-Jewish community. This isolation sharpened and clarified the foreign students' identity—Weizmann's included—as *Russian*-Jewish intellectuals living as émigrés in their own cultural milieu. Ironically, all East European students—Galicians, Rumanians, Poles, Hungarians, Russians—were seen as an undifferentiated group by the Germans and the German-Jewish community, though they were often divided among themselves.[34] In the eyes of the Germans and German Jews all East Europeans were alien. For their part, East European Zionist, socialist, and revolutionary circles formed separate groups which did not interact with one another except to debate.[35] Upon arrival in Berlin it was typical for every East European Jew and non-Jew to seek the circle closest to his or her own ideas and background. Thus, Weizmann joined the Verein at once and remained an active member until his departure from Berlin in 1897. The Verein now became an important instrument in shaping his Zionist ideology and the new junior member at first stood in awe of Motzkin, Syrkin, Jacobson, and the other older members, who seemed to have already formed very definite ideas as to the direction the Jewish national revival ought to take. Motzkin, in particular, briefly became Weizmann's mentor and instructor in all Zionist matters. When Motzkin, who was then switching from mathematics to economics, asked Weizmann to teach him, for a modest fee, the elementary principles of science, the latter was delighted to be of service and was eager to please. After the lonely year he had spent in Pfungstadt, Weizmann was happy to be accepted by members of the Verein, with whose ideas he fully identified. Motzkin and the others became models that he tried to emulate in his personal as well as Zionist commitments.

Weizmann consistently studied six to seven hours a day, attending lectures and working in the laboratory. His conscientious attitude toward his studies stemmed from his conviction, already shaped in Pinsk, that education was his only path to financial independence and security. The well-known Professor Carl Theodor Liebermann, who had conducted, with Professor Carl Graebe, experiments in the synthesis of the dyestuff base alizarin, was director of the Charlottenburg Polytechnik and assigned Weizmann to the care of Dr. Karl Anton Augustin Bistrzycki and Professor Georg Karl von Knorre.[36] "Exploration of coal tar, from which alizarin had been released, was providing clues to the molecular structure of an almost limitless range of products for which industry hungered."[37] In the laboratories of the Polytechnic Weizmann's imagination and creativity began to be challenged; he was now acquiring his lifelong taste for research. Karl Anton Augustin Bistrzycki, a Polish-born scientist, was engaged in an investigation of the reaction of o-aldehydic acids with phenols and encouraged Weizmann to participate in his investigations. In Berlin Weizmann met a fellow student, Christian Deichler, with whom he was to collaborate in his early research in synthetic dyes for textiles under the guidance of Bistrzycki. After three years of collaboration, Weizmann and Deichler were successful in the preparation of naphtha derivatives.[38] Chemistry, then, was an exciting venture even if Weizmann occasionally felt inferior to his friends, who studied more lofty subjects such as philosophy, economics, and law.

Weizmann's evenings and weekends among the Verein members were as exciting as his days in the laboratory. In fact, he was oblivious to the German-Jewish community and, like the other members of the Verein,

quickly affirmed his identity as a Russian-Jewish intellectual. He had more
than his share in the all-consuming social and intellectual life of the Verein; in 1895 he served for a while as one of its joint secretaries.[39] The
Verein held its meetings on Saturday, mostly at a café attached to a Jewish hotel, the Hotel Zentrum, on the Alexanderplatz, because there its
members could get beer and sausages on credit during lean periods.
Weizmann described these meetings in his autobiography:

> I think with something like a shudder of the amount of talking we did. We
> never dispersed before the small hours of [the] morning. We talked of
> everything, of history, wars, revolutions, the rebuilding of society. But chiefly
> we talked of the Jewish problem and of Palestine. We sang, we celebrated
> such Jewish festivals as we did not go home for, we debated with the assim-
> ilationists, and we made vast plans for the redemption of our people. It was
> all very youthful and naive and jolly and exciting; but it was not without a
> deeper meaning.[40]

The members of the Verein spent a great deal of time clarifying issues of
the day. In so doing they hoped both to attract to their ranks the Russian-Jewish youth and to differentiate themselves from such philanthropic associations as the Verein Esra. Saturday nights were devoted
either to lectures or to debates with opponents. From time to time there
were guest lectures by scholars, such as Moritz Steinschneider, who were
willing to read a paper before the Verein. Many of the lectures and discussions dealt with Jewish history and literature.[41] The basic aim of all
these discussions and debates was to deepen the national Jewish consciousness and understanding of its members and to revitalize their
commitment to the Jewish nation.[42]

A major effort was expended by the Verein in its competition with the
socialists for the "souls" of new students who arrived from the East. Every
morning the train would bring these new and unsuspecting students,
who had not formed any opinion yet about Jewish nationalism or socialism. Their first contacts in Berlin would therefore be crucial; thus, the
competition for these "green newcomers" was fierce and Jewish nationalists and socialists would be standing in the train station waiting to
"ambush" them.[43] Having aroused the interest or curiosity of newcomers, the Verein would invite them to attend its Saturday-night meetings,
where the socialists and nationalists would often clash in heated and
prolonged debates before groups of up to 150 students.[44] The socialists
and antinationalists would attend the Verein's meetings in order to
sharpen their own arguments. They were usually at an advantage because they would bring to their assistance well-known figures from the
socialist world who would try to "crush" the members of the Verein with
their authority if they could not do so through argument. One of the
deadliest debaters on the socialist side was Parvus, who also belonged
to a Russian-Jewish organization named Wissenschaft und Leben, whose
members were all social democrats and "cosmopolitans."[45] Parvus was
born Israel Lazarevich Helphand, in the northern part of the Pale of Set-

tlement, and had turned to revolutionary activities by the age of eighteen. He resided in Berlin between 1891 and 1893, where he was an important contributor to *Vorwaerts,* the main daily organ of the German Social Democratic Party. He was, then, a dangerous and formidable opponent of the Verein.[46]

These were heady times for Weizmann. A new world was opening up to him: new concepts; a sense of and appreciation for intellectual freedom; and the formation of his first adult friendships, especially with Motzkin, whom he initially regarded as his intellectual superior. He was also making the most of Berlin as a center of music and theater. On Sundays there were special theater rates for students, and this was the favorite day for Chaim and his friends, who sometimes saw as many as three performances a day, eating their sandwiches between performances and returning home at night sated with Shakespeare, Goethe, and Ibsen. The musical hero in the Berlin of those days was Felix Weingartner—Edler von Muenzberg—a conductor and composer of music of international fame.[47] Weizmann and his friends from the Verein often attended his concerts, sitting in the cheapest seats under the roof and applauding riotously. At the end of a Beethoven performance the conductor went to see who had been making all that noise. Having been assured of their great admiration and told that his concert coincided with the festival of Purim, he took them to a Bierhalle for Wuerstchen and beer.[48] There is no indication that Weizmann sustained his interest in music and the theater after he left Berlin.

Early in 1895 the Weizmann family moved from Motol to Pinsk for practical and financial considerations. The Weizmanns were always a close-knit family and since Pinsk offered much better educational opportunities for the children, it did not make sense to remain in Motol. Four of the children had already left home: Chaim was in Berlin; his younger brother Moshe had already been in Pinsk since 1892, studying in the same *Real-Gymnasium* from which Chaim graduated and also hoping to be a chemist; Feivel was managing the rafts on the rivers; and Miriam was married to Chaim Lubzhinsky and resided in Pinsk.[49] In addition, Ozer's business was once more doing poorly and he decided to merge his business with that of Chaim Lubzhinsky, with whom he had been associated professionally since 1886. Ozer could conduct his business in Pinsk as well as he had done in Motol, and since all his rafts had to pass through Pinsk anyhow, it meant that he could be at home more often. Rachel Leah was then in her early forties and did not bear any more children,[50] but it was still a large family to support. Chaim was needed at home for a while; Ozer could not send him his monthly allowance just then, and the young student could help the family in their period of adjustment and perhaps help launch the other children in their careers; the Weizmann children always shared financial responsibility with their parents when it came to education.

It was not easy for the Weizmanns to leave Motol.[51] It was just as difficult for Weizmann to leave the sparkling and gay life of Berlin and return to provincial Pinsk at the end of the spring semester 1895, after having completed his third semester at the Charlottenburg Polytechnik. He was to remain in Pinsk until early summer 1896, when he returned to Berlin to resume his studies in the fall. He spent the year in Pinsk giving science lessons to children who were preparing to study abroad, as well as Russian and Hebrew lessons.[52] During the mornings he worked in the small chemical factory of Grygory Lurie, the brother of Samuel, his former employer in Pinsk.[53]

Soon after he arrived in Pinsk, Weizmann began to complain about his lot in letter after letter to Leo Motzkin.

> . . . after Berlin, Pinsk has made such a vile, repulsive impression on me that I find it unpleasant, even distasteful, to share it, dear friend, with you. There is nothing here and no one: instead of a town—just an enormous rubbish-heap; instead of people, one comes across creatures devoid of all personality, with no interests, no desires, no demands . . . Hundreds of Jews push on and hurry about the streets of our town, with anxious faces marked by great suffering, but they seem to do it unconsciously; as if they were in a daze. As in any other well-organized society, there is a so-called intelligentsia here too . . . In point of fact, the male "intellectuals" are busy paying court to intellectual damsels, while the married men and women spend their time playing cards . . . All this is quite natural and understandable if one bears in mind . . . how few higher or even average interests they have. From all this you will understand that I am incredibly bored here. I have, of course, a host of acquaintances who would gladly spend their time with me— a student from Berlin . . . but I don't go anywhere and have not taken up at all with the jeunesse dorée of Pinsk. . . .[54]

The young student from Berlin who had only recently complained about the assimilationist Jews of Pfungstadt had quickly emancipated himself from the values and lifestyle of the Pale. He clearly saw himself as a Russian-Jewish intellectual who had internalized some of the West's attitudes toward the East and the common Russian Jews. He was now looking with contempt and derision at the society around him through the eyes of a Westernizing Jew:

> I am pretty fed up with all this by now, and I am only waiting for the happy day that will free me *fun de goyishe hend* [i.e., Pinsk's Jews], and take me to Berlin . . . There is a depressed, dull state of mind everywhere . . . The monotony is only broken occasionally when one indulges in *indignation* at the emptiness and nastiness of our leading Jews, their slavishness and servility. It seems to me that on no one did the Golus [i.e., exile] have such a noxious influence as on the Jews of Pinsk . . .[55]

These harsh remarks were probably fueled by Weizmann's resentment at having been forced to interrupt his studies in Berlin, but they may also reflect more general debates of the time as to whether Russia ought to adopt Western traditions or move along central Russian lines. Weizmann was obviously influenced in his ideas by those Russian radicals who sought change along Western lines. Thus, he felt that he was physically "in the hands of the goyim," while his intellectual interests were in the West. Incessantly he inquired after the members of the Verein, their activities and accomplishments: "It is in your power to pull me out of this slough, at least for a time, and give me the chance to transport myself—at least in thought—into your circle and live your life."[56] Motzkin became his link to Berlin, and Weizmann was so grateful for the few replies from the latter that he could not thank him enough.[57] But Weizmann was not quite as inactive and bored as he pretended. Together with Judah Leib Berger, Mordechai Strick, and Hirsch (Tzvi) Hiller—all prominent Zionists in Pinsk—Weizmann formed a literary circle which was national in character and which included "the best people in Pinsk." On one occasion Weizmann spoke about the wide dissemination of the works of the Hebrew and Yiddish writer J. L. Peretz,[58] but his talk was not well received. "The reason is simple: The masses do not read anything and have no spiritual interests."[59] Together with the founders of the circle, he was also involved in lobbying for and establishing in 1895 a progressive *heder*, or *heder metukan*, where the traditional curriculum and pedagogic methods were modernized. It was among the first of its kind in the entire Pale of Settlement.[60] By the summer of 1896 there were approximately forty pupils in this *heder*.[61] The orthodox Jews in town were incensed at this innovation, and from time to time there were acts of violence. On one occasion they broke the windows in Berger's apartment and then began to stone the Weizmann house. Ozer walked onto the small porch and informed the demonstrators that he supported Chaim and his friends and would not be frightened by violence. His dignified and authoritative demeanor tipped the balance and the crowd dispersed.[62] Thus, Weizmann first clashed directly with the orthodox Jews of Eastern Europe. He would have many occasions to unleash his anger against both Zionist and non-Zionist rabbinical groups in both the East and the West. It is not easy to pinpoint the sources of Weizmann's hostility to orthodox circles, since he himself came from an orthodox home. Weizmann seems to have adopted his father's enlightened brand of orthodoxy, which was tolerant toward other forms of Judaism, and abhorred any kind of rigid and inflexible ideology. This explains Weizmann's discomfort in Pfungstadt and his violent opposition to any attempt by the orthodox to impose their values on the Zionist movement.

Zionist and educational activities occupied Weizmann's free time, but they could not take his mind off a problem that hung like an albatross around his neck: his obligation to serve in the tsarist army. Full-time students were usually exempt from military service, but only if they studied in Russia. Moreover, only Feivel could claim exemption as a firstborn and provider for the family. When Chaim was younger, his uncle Yankel, who had no children, "adopted" him as his only child in the hope that this would save Chaim from service. Yet Chaim received an order to report to the military authorities during his autumn vacation in Pinsk in 1894.[63] The situation was precarious: Many young Jews were emigrating and the Jews did not fill their quotas. It seemed to Chaim and his worried family that he might well end up as a soldier in the service of the Romanov dynasty.

The manager of the Jewish office, Reb Israel Chemerinsky of Motol, who kept the residence records, suggested adding a few years to Chaim's age, for he seemed slim and tall. Ozer agreed to this strategy, hoping that with the combination of his status as an only son Chaim might get off. It was also decided that Chaim would not register with others in his category but would submit an affidavit stating that he was sick: Chaim lay in bed while his family tried to entertain him. He went to bed a healthy man, but after a few days he really became ill. The whole charade affected him psychologically, and the fact that his family needed to pay large bribes troubled him as well. He suffered from pangs of conscience, and his face and features looked like those of a seriously ill patient. After two weeks a committee consisting of a military doctor and two clerks appeared in the Weizmann house. The doctor examined the candidate for soldiering, pronouncing him seriously ill, and wrote a certificate to this effect. The certificate was sent to Kobrin, the provincial capital. Weizmann was called before a special committee, which gave him a one-year deferment.[64]

The deferment lapsed soon after Chaim returned to Pinsk during the spring of 1895. Weizmann decided not to play the game a second time and embarked on his first "diplomatic" mission. A few days before he was due to appear before the committee for military affairs—sometime in October 1895—he left the Weizmann home in Pinsk under the pretext that he was traveling on important Zionist affairs. He journeyed to Kobrin, the residence of the supervisor of army affairs in the province. Chaim went to the latter's estate and explained that during his whole life he had not engaged in physical exercise, that he was not particularly strong, that he was deeply committed to his scientific studies, and that if he were compelled to waste time in the army he would be forced to flee and immigrate to America, where he could continue his studies. The Gentile looked at this audacious young Jew for a while and replied, "Yes, you are correct, Mr. Weizmann! Indeed, you don't give the impression of a soldier and we have more than enough cannon fodder. Go in peace and report before the committee. I am certain they will also understand that you were not created to hold a rifle." A few days later Weizmann reported to the committee, was released, and received the coveted "White Certificate" exempting him from active service as well as reserve duty.[65]

In an uncharacteristic understatement Weizmann summed up the whole episode in two sentences in his letter to Motzkin.[66] Given Weizmann's general tendency to try to impress others, especially his older friend Motzkin, his reticence in this case seems strange and raises the possibility that there were good reasons—perhaps the payment of a bribe—not to reveal the entire story in a letter. In any case, having successfully overcome this ordeal, he was again fully engrossed in the affairs of the Verein and Jewish nationalism. He was becoming increasingly annoyed at the way Motzkin ignored his letters and thereby effectively cut him off from affairs in Berlin. At first he was astonished that his faithful reporting to the Verein's leader on the doings at Pinsk remained unanswered: "Dear Motzkin, I am surprised at your silence. . . ."[67] Some time later: "To my regret, I have still had no reply from you! . . . Why don't you write?"[68] A month later he wrote in an insulted and hurt manner: ". . . I feel deeply offended at being ignored like this, all the more because it is you who are doing it . . . In spite of my frequent appeals and requests, you do not give a single sign of life . . . It follows [from a letter by David Makhlin] that you simply did not want to write. This would drive anybody wild."[69] Finally Weizmann resorted to an imploring and obsequious manner full of self-doubt:

 I have to write for the sixth time, and beg you for the reply I need so much. I can imagine very vividly how fed up with my letters you must be by now . . . In all probability you have your own weighty reasons, which entirely elude me. Believe me, your behavior has made me reflect more than once, but save for the purest comradely feelings, I do not feel guilty of anything . . . All I need is information! Any other details I do not dare to hope for even in my dreams . . .[70]

Weizmann felt humiliated by his older colleague. He always had a thin skin and was easily insulted. However, since Motzkin was the recognized authority in his intellectual and social circle, Weizmann could not afford to write in sharp tones. Until September 1899 he always used the respectful and formal "you" in his letters to Motzkin, but the year in Pinsk marked the beginning of erosion in their friendship. The early letters to Motzkin also reveal a number of characteristic traits in Weizmann that will later become apparent, especially in the period before the Balfour Declaration: his tendency to complain about others, his frequent bouts of self-doubt, and his need to aggrandize his own accomplishments, sometimes sliding into untruths.

Nevertheless, it was Motzkin who helped initiate Weizmann into the Berlin circle of Ahad Ha'Am (Asher Ginsberg), the most profound thinker in the Hibbat Zion movement. Of all the people who influenced Weizmann up to the end of World War I, Ahad Ha'Am's legacy was the most significant. It is thus imperative to consider very briefly the essence of Ahad Ha'Am's thought as it relates to Weizmann's own Zionist development.

Following his first essay "Lo Zeh ha-Derekh" ("This Is Not the Way"), in 1889—the very time that the Verein began its activities in Berlin—Ahad Ha'Am soon emerged as the most important member of the Hibbat Zion, though he was not its leader. He often stood in opposition to it and mercilessly attacked the movement, particularly on the issue of the colonization of Palestine.[71] He demanded that no more immigrants be settled in the colonies until a secure legal basis had been obtained, and he condemned the settlements that were dependent on donations from abroad.

Throughout his writings Ahad Ha'Am asserted that without a restored Palestine European Jewry, despite its unique languages and dense population, would not be able to withstand the influence of foreign cultures.[72] The only way to avoid this process was to create a *merkaz ruhani* (spiritual center) in Palestine[73] to infuse new life in both the East and the West.[74] Thus Ahad Ha'Am did not believe that Zionism would solve the "Problem of the Jews," namely, the economic, social, and political problems of the Jewish masses. Instead, it could solve the "Problem of Judaism" by creating a new type of Jew. This process would take place primarily in the Diaspora.

For Ahad Ha'Am Jewishness meant the ideas of absolute justice and impartial objectivity, a concept that determined his attitude toward the question of Arab-Jewish relations. Thus, he wished to create in Palestine a "spiritual center"—based on a sound economic base—which could radiate these ideas and values in the Diaspora. Ahad Ha'Am's purpose was not to define the essence of Judaism in general but to seek those values with which the Jewish intellectual could identify.[75] In sum, Ahad Ha'Am's main concern was for the internal, personal revival of Jewish education and tradition, a *tehiyat halevavot*, and of cultural and ethical values. Jews would come to Palestine not because of poverty and anti-Semitism but because they were attracted by the possibility of a spiritual rebirth. This process should begin, according to Ahad Ha'Am, in the Diaspora and later become the foundation for Jewish colonization.

More or less simultaneously with the 1889 appearance of his essay "Lo Zeh ha-Derekh" in Alexander Tzederbaum's *Hamelitz*, there was founded around Ahad Ha'Am in Odessa a semisecret order of members of the Hibbat Zion called Bnei Moshe.[76] It was an elitist society which never comprised more than two hundred members. However, the caliber of its membership was such that until its dissolution in 1897 it was able to influence the general direction of the Hibbat Zion movement toward a more radical nationalism. Though conceived in Ahad Ha'Am's image of what the Hibbat Zion movement ought to be like, it was often more impatient and radical than its progenitor.[77]

The members of Bnei Moshe carried out their ideas in many practical ventures, especially in the field of education. They established in Jaffa the first elementary school in which Hebrew was the main language of instruction. They founded the colony of Rehovot, where Hebrew was spoken and where Jews could find work. In the Diaspora they founded the publishing houses of Ahiasaf and Tushiyah and published a number of books, pamphlets, and journals which gave momentum to the revival of the Hebrew language and nationalist ideas. These cultural activities made the Bnei Moshe into the most vital force within the Hibbat Zion; indeed, in a sense the society was a counterweight to the Hibbat Zion. It also maintained, at best, an unfriendly attitude toward Orthodox Judaism, a position which made the society the center of some of the most heated Zionist debates in the 1890s.[78]

Weizmann's closest collaborators in Pinsk, Judah Leib Berger and Mordechai Strick, were active members of Bnei Moshe,[79] as were a number of members of the Verein. In October 1895 Weizmann met Leo

Motzkin in Brest-Litovsk,[80] and at the latter's suggestion he applied for and was admitted to membership in the Bnei Moshe. The Pinsk branch of the Bnei Moshe was one of the more successful branches. It was careful in admitting new members and its existence was a well-kept secret. A short while after he was admitted as a member, Weizmann was suspected by the heads of the Bnei Moshe in Pinsk of not being true to the values of the society. In a letter to the central office the Pinsk leaders warned their colleague not to trust him with too much information, since he may be "more of a Social Democrat than a 'Bnei Moshe' member . . ." They revealed that Weizmann had been considered for membership in the society for some time and that it was only Motzkin's recommendation which forced the issue. They believed that Weizmann had suggested himself for membership not because of his affinity with the Society's values but because he was influenced by his Berlin comrades to do so. "In any case," they concluded, "one has to be wary of him in the beginning. You, dear friend, please gather some information about him from our brethren in Berlin." The information from Berlin was apparently reassuring.[81] At that point Ahad Ha'Am had not been the official leader of the society for a number of years and had, in a sense, retired to pursue his various publication ventures. Sometime in 1896 Ahad Ha'Am arrived in Berlin in connection with the publication of the new Hebrew monthly *Hashiloah*—it was not possible to receive a publication license in Russia—and remained in the city for a period of nine months, during which he became the center of a group of young Hebraists, including Berdichevsky, Malter, Neimark, Ehrenpreis, Thon, and members of the Verein.[82]

In the spring of 1896 Ozer Weizmann's business had sufficiently improved—thanks to his more enterprising and ambitious son-in-law—so that the two of them now decided to finance the rest of Chaim's education. They sent him back to Berlin in the early summer of 1896 with the promise of a monthly allowance of a hundred marks ($30–$35), a not inconsiderable sum of money when compared to the lot of the other members of the Verein.[83] This regular income enabled Weizmann to devote all his time to his studies; he was also in a position to lend money or his coat (for pawning) to his less fortunate fellow students. He himself was not careful with his own money, but he never wavered from the principle he had already established as a student in the *Real-Gymnasium* in Pinsk. At all costs he was determined to attain a profession and a regular income. As much as he admired the bohemian lifestyle of Zvi Aberson or the dedication to public causes of Motzkin, he also saw them as "unproductive," needlessly wasting their talents and opportunities. His harsh and repeated criticisms of such men seem to reflect his own fear that if he relaxed his self-imposed restraints he might emulate their example.

Soon after Chaim returned to Berlin from Pinsk he went to pay his respects to Ahad Ha'Am in the company of two other members of the Verein, Isidore Eliashev and Nahum Mirkin. His first impression of Ahad

Ha'Am was less than enthusiastic: "The three of us visited Ahad Ha'Am today. The conversation turned on various rather unimportant questions. We did not touch upon anything fundamental as this first visit was of an official character . . ." Summing up the visit, Weizmann wrote in somewhat condescending tones: "On the whole Ahad H[a'Am] makes a very pleasant impression as a European. He spoke about the Palestine cause with restraint, not too much, without heat and, or perhaps it only seemed so to me, with a little pinch of skepticism."[84]

Weizmann, like other young nationalists in Berlin and elsewhere, was impatient for action: relief for the hordes of refugees from Russia, improvement of Jewish conditions in Russia itself, and for other social and economic measures that would ease the plight of the masses. These would remain his lifelong concerns. He had an affinity for Ahad Ha'Am and defended him against the attacks of the orthodox, but he was not yet in complete agreement with Ahad Ha'Am and did not support him fully. Unlike the restrained and skeptical Ahad Ha'Am, who was counseling a slow, deliberate pace and long-range policies concentrating on the "Problem of Judaism" rather than the "Problem of the Jews," Weizmann was unwilling, at this point, to defer militant action. Yet for the time being his militancy did not express itself in any concrete activities. This would come only at the beginning of the next century.

There was indeed plenty of room for action in which those senior members in the Hibbat Zion engaged. In June 1887 the second conference of the Hovevei Zion took place in Druskieniki in order to deal with the many problems facing the movement. A power struggle ensued at the conference between the orthodox, led by Rabbi Shmuel Mohilewer, and those supporting Pinsker and Lilienblum. Pinsker was finally re-elected to lead the movement together with six advisers, three of whom were rabbis.[85] In 1890—at a time when the Russian government was contemplating new designs against the Jews—Alexander Tzederbaum, editor of *Hamelitz*, succeeded in obtaining government sanction for the Society for the Support of Jewish Farmers and Artisans in Syria and Palestine, which became known as the Odessa Committee. However, the Zionists were denied the right to organize emigration or even maintain a country-wide organization.[86] They sought in vain the aid of Baron Maurice de Hirsch, who founded the Jewish Colonization Society in 1891 and had received permission to establish a central committee in St. Petersburg to resettle the bulk of Russian Jewry. The Zionists were successful only in 1894, when a center of the Hovevei Zion was established in Paris.[87] Pinsker's death in December 1891, the obstacles created by the Russian government, coupled with the cruel expulsion of twenty thousand Jews from Moscow, and the ban on immigration and settlement in Palestine imposed by the Turkish authorities after the land speculations of 1891, were blows that the fledgling movement found hard to absorb. There were, of course, successes in the Holy Land: the establishment of Rehovot and Hadera and the consolidation of Mishmar ha-Yarden. In the Diaspora there were increasing financial contributions. Writers and poets espoused the national cause. And there was, of course, ever-widening publishing activity, including newspapers and periodicals in Hebrew, Russian, and Yiddish.[88] But, all in all, the movement lacked élan and leadership.[89]

Weizmann was soon to confront directly Zionist conditions in the hinterland of the Pale. In midsummer 1897, as all eyes in the Zionist world were turned westward to Basel, where the First Zionist Congress was to take place in the last days of August, Weizmann was preparing to go east, back to Russia. In the winter term, after long and strenuous experiments during which he even forgot to write home, Weizmann discovered a formula for improving the methods of dye-processing chemistry. His teacher, Professor von Knorre, thought the formula could be sold and recommended Chaim to a friend of his, one Ilyniski, the manager of a dyeing plant in Moscow. Prior to his trip to Moscow, Weizmann went to Pinsk and threw himself wholeheartedly into the preparations for the congress, winning a mandate from Pinsk as a delegate and, for the time being, putting off until the end of the summer his invitation to go to Moscow.[90]

All spring long Weizmann traveled by cart, wagon, and boat to remote communities in the Pale lying along the swampy streams of the Pripet marshes. Weizmann returned to Berlin in June in order to settle his affairs and collect his belongings, since he was about to move to Switzerland. One matter that needed to be settled was a debt of more than thirty marks owed him by Motzkin, possibly for lessons he had not paid for or in repayment of an outright loan. Writing to the latter one formal letter after another, Weizmann first tried reason, then pleaded his own hardship and illness, and finally threatened Motzkin: "Have been waiting for your reply till now. Nothing has come. You have thus driven me to extremes—a thing I really did not expect. I expect the money tomorrow morning at eight. If you do not let me have it by then, I shall be forced to seek another solution, which may result in serious unpleasantness. To avoid this, I am warning you for the fourth or fifth time."[91] The lack of response—and payment—was not the only thing that bothered Weizmann; for unknown reasons Motzkin had now started a campaign against him among the students.[92] His erstwhile hero and guide for the past four years had turned against him, though there are no clues as to why this was the case. In any event, it was a painful realization for Weizmann, who always needed friends and company. Their friendship, which had begun to sour while Weizmann was in Pinsk, had now suffered more damage, not to be fully repaired even when they later collaborated in various causes. It would always remain, at best, a cool relationship. For the time being it left a bitter aftertaste to four happy and productive years in Berlin.

Weizmann left Berlin during the first days of August 1897—without the money. He needed funds desperately and finally traveled to Moscow during the last week of August to try to sell his invention. It was a humiliating experience, since he had no permit to travel outside the Pale and his two-day stay in Moscow was illegal. He was unable to sell the formula and—to add to his disappointment—was also late by one day for the congress. His father, who met him in Brest-Litovsk, brought along his foreign passport and ten rubles—all he could scrape together—for the journey to Basel. But having missed the opening day of the congress, Weizmann was despondent and unwilling to use Ozer's last funds.[93] The whole episode in Russia seems a bit obscure. It is not quite clear why Weizmann planned his trip to Moscow so close to the First Zionist Congress. But it will not be the last time that private affairs and Zionist commitments would clash. Whatever the reasons, Weizmann always regretted having missed the historic moment when 238 delegates from 24 countries[94] met formally to launch the World Zionist Organization.

IV

Herzl

Writing to Leo Motzkin from Pinsk in January 1896, Weizmann exclaimed, "Hardly anything happens over here. Our Jewish society is marking time. There is something in the air, and people are expecting great changes for the better . . ."[1]

Less than a month later, on February 15, Theodor Herzl, who was soon to found the World Zionist Organization, noted in his diary that the Viennese bookseller M. Breitenstein was displaying his pamphlet *The Jews' State: An Attempt at a Modern Solution of the Jewish Question.*[2]

Herzl arrived on the Zionist horizon in the nick of time; the Hibbat Zion movement in the East and West was floundering and rudderless. News from the colonies in Palestine was only marginally more encouraging than the situation in the Diaspora. The official obstacles to Zionist activity in Palestine were great. From the outset the Ottoman government was vigorously opposed to modern Jewish settlement in Palestine. In 1882 the government had placed restrictions on Jews entering Palestine which were designed to prevent Jewish settlement in the country. One decade later it also imposed restrictions on Jewish land purchase in Palestine. Ottoman opposition to Jewish settlement intensified in 1897 as a result of the official founding of the Zionist movement, and in 1901 the restrictions against Jewish entry and land purchase in Palestine were revised and the regulations consolidated.[3]

What all these rules and regulations meant was uncertain in view of the obscure method and issuance of the regulations, the laxity in administrative matters on the part of most Ottoman officials, and the customary *baksheesh* (bribe). Everything had its price, and as the Ottoman officials put it, "If it's a question of your interests and the Empire's—yours come first."[4] What eased the burden of this maze of contradictory and irregular Ottomon decrees was the fact that the European powers refused almost uniformly to acquiesce in the restrictions on the grounds that they ran counter to the privileges they and their subjects enjoyed under the capitulations. Lastly, Ottoman policy was never airtight because of the great difficulties in putting it into practice.[5]

The net result was both promising and disheartening for the Hibbat

Zion and later for the Zionist movement. On the positive side, from the Zionists' point of view, immigration to Palestine increased and for the first time a portion of the settlers established agricultural colonies. Reliable statistics on immigration for that period are unavailable, but the following figures give a general idea: In 1882 the total Jewish population of Palestine was about 24,000,[6] representing roughly 5 percent of the total; due mainly to immigration in 1881–84 and 1890–91, the number of Jews nearly doubled to 47,000 in 1890 and reached approximately 50,000 by 1897, more than half of whom resided in Jersusalem.[7]

The most important material achievement of the Hibbat Zion movement was the establishment in the eighties and nineties of the first farming settlements *(moshavot)* in Palestine. There were earlier attempts at colonization by the so-called Old Yishuv—notably in Petah Tikvah in 1878—but this and other attempts failed. Thus, the new arrivals from Russia and Rumania found an urban Jewish population of only 24,000[8] and a rural Jewish population of some 480 people, as well as the agricultural school Mikveh Israel, founded in 1870 by Charles Netter on behalf of the Alliance Israélite Universelle. In 1882–83 settlers from Russia, Rumania, and Poland founded five settlements. In 1884 Gederah was established by the Biluim south of Jaffa and Nes Ziona was founded in Judaea.[9] In the 1890s immigrants to Palestine founded twelve more communities. By 1900 there were twenty-two Jewish rural settlements widely dispersed throughout Palestine on 76,000 acres,[10] with a total Jewish rural population of 5,210 managing 705 farms.[11]

Despite their enthusiasm, the immigrants were unprepared for the task at hand, possessing insufficient material resources, physical stamina, and adequate agricultural knowledge to make the colonies economically viable. In addition, they were exposed to malaria, Bedouin raids, a harsh climate, and the constant difficulties imposed by the Ottoman regime. It is not surprising that of the estimated twenty-five thousand new immigrants, the overwhelming majority were absorbed in the urban communities. Nevertheless, the historic innovation of the First *Aliyah* (immigration to Palestine/Israel) (1882–1904), small as it was in total numbers, was the creation of agricultural colonies. These were modest but important gains. When the First Zionist Congress convened in Basel in 1897, fifteen years had elapsed since the start of modern Jewish settlement in Palestine.

Ironically, the precarious settlements were saved only by the financial generosity of Baron Edmond James de Rothschild, widely called "the Well-Known Benefactor" *(ha-Nadiv ha-Yadua)*, the fourth and youngest son of James Jacob Rothschild, the first head of the Paris branch of the family. It is estimated that the total amount invested by the baron in Jewish settlements in Palestine was 5.6 million British pounds, of which 1.6 million was invested between 1883 and 1889.[12] But Baron Edmond de Rothschild's largesse had strings attached to it. He imposed conditions that radically altered the colonies' structure, and all lands had to be registered in his name. He appointed "directors" who not only doled out

his money but also administered all affairs in the colonies. His "garden-
ers" supervised the farms. Sometimes his administrators insisted, as a
measure of control, that the villagers sign agreements stating that they
were day laborers on the baron's estates, subject to dismissal or expulsion at a moment's notice. Moreover, the concentration of the villages'
economy—at the insistence of the baron's administration—on the cultivation of grapes for wine extended the colonists' period of dependence.
Since vineyards only mature after six years, the settlers were required to
live off monthly stipends. During that time they were at the mercy of
the village directors *(Pekidut ha-Baron)*, who often exercised their authority in a petty and tyrannical fashion, prompting some colonies to "rebel"
temporarily. Elie Scheid, around whom the baron's administration revolved during its first two decades, is probably the best example of what
was wrong with the baron's administration, as Scheid himself took care
to describe in his memoirs:

> From time to time [at Zikhron Yaakov] there were discussions and argu-
> ments among [the settlers] during the day, and in the evening, after dinner,
> seated on my bed, I dispensed justice. I am pleased to be able to state that
> no one could ever say I judged badly. It is true that if I was very severe with
> misdemeanors which had been committed, then I was also excessively just.
> For my part the colonists had to be, and in reality were, all my children and
> I treated them like a father who loves his family. It made me sick at heart
> when I was obliged to punish one of them.[13]

It is hardly surprising that after his visits to Palestine in 1891 and 1893
Ahad Ha'Am blasted, among others, Baron Edmond and his administration for having created in Palestine an indolent and servile class of colonists who were dependent on the baron's handouts and the labor of
Arab workers.[14] In fact, the resettlement of Palestine after 1882 produced
results which were disappointing to many Zionists. The paternalistic
Rothschild administration made a mockery of the slogan of auto-emancipation, but at the same time it also realized dreams that seemed unat-
tainable only a generation earlier.[15] By comparison with the small-scale
activities of the daily Hovevei Zion routine—fund collections; celebra-
tions of Sir Moses Montefiore's centenary anniversary; agitational ad-
dresses in synagogues; savings societies for land purchase; future plans
for immigration—the colonies in Palestine were at least a tangible and
concrete achievement in the present and a foundation for the future. The
founding of the World Zionist Organization would initially have little
impact on the land of Israel. Symptomatic of the inability and weakness
of the World Zionist Organization in its early years was the fact that in
1896 the Jewish Colonization Association began to interest itself in the
colonies in Palestine, and in 1900, in conformity with the baron's wishes,
took them under its wing.[16]

Against this background Theodor Herzl appeared. Given the state of
the Zionist movement, it is easy to understand the wave of enthusiasm
that greeted him in the Diaspora. Much has been written about the life

and achievements of Herzl.[17] However, it seems that almost all of Herzl's biographers agree that he was a man of vision and determination who lifted Zionism out of cold storage. His impact on the Jewish intelligentsia and the masses throughout the Diaspora was enormous.[18] At the same time, Herzl's personal crisis of disillusionment led him to redirect his energies from his own career to work carried on as part of a mission. He began to dissociate himself from his former journalist and litterateur selves as part of the process of fashioning an identity which would devote itself to a new idea. He hoped to divorce himself from the life of the written word and embark instead on a new life of action. Herzl's basic tenet was that Palestine should be secured for the Jews by means of an internationally guaranteed charter.[19] Consequently he opposed any colonization projects ("infiltration") prior to the acquisition by the Jewish people of the legal right to settle in Palestine. Herzl and the Zionists who supported this idea made no long-range cultural or political plans for national Jewish life in the Diaspora and strongly believed that as a people the Jews had no future in that direction. Only in Palestine would they be able to develop their cultural and national character. He believed that the "removal of the Jews to Palestine was imminent," and he therefore strongly opposed Zionist participation and involvement in the political, economic, and cultural affairs of their host countries and even of their Jewish communities.[20]

Herzl's tasks were manifold: He had to communicate with, persuade, and unify Jews from every country, every class, and every religious sect or ideological school of thought. He had to convince them to effect a radical change in order to redirect Jewish history, namely, to take their destiny in their own hands. At the same time, he had to persuade or bargain with the international powers to support his efforts to secure land for the resettlement of the Jews. In other words, Herzl's two goals—organization of the Jewish national movement and acquisition of a political homeland for Jews—required two different sets of skills, the skills of the revolutionary leader and those of a genteel diplomat.

Herzl was a charismatic leader.[21] The charismatic leader, by definition, is set apart from the kind of leader who achieves his position by virtue of a slow and steady climb within a bureaucratic organization and who derives his authority by virtue of his possession of an institutional position. The charismatic leader does not assume a position that has inherent power; rather, he is himself the source of power. Herzl was considered by many of his followers, especially in the early years of his leadership, to be the only person capable of leading the Zionist movement by virtue of his special personal qualities. He did not earn authority, he demanded and inspired it. The group of loyal followers that surrounded him, plus the masses that were loyal to him as a result of the legends that grew up around him, were devoted to Herzl not because of the rules and regulations of the World Zionist Organization but out of a sense of dedication. Herzl's powers were only slightly curtailed by the creation of the bureaucratic organization which he founded. He was, as it were, beyond the reach of its rules.

No less a critic of Herzl than Ahad Ha'Am—the Hebrew essayist and spiritual leader of the Hibbat Zion—who had been a consistent and uncompromising opponent, wrote the following in 1904, the year of Herzl's death:

> . . . Herzl gave us the Congress, the Organization, the Bank, the National Fund. Whether these are to be reckoned great achievements we cannot yet know. All depends on whether they endure and in what form they continue to exist. But one thing Herzl gave us involuntarily which is perhaps greater than all that he did of set purpose. He gave us *himself*, to be the theme of our Hymn of Revival, a theme which imagination can take and adorn with all the attributes needed to make of him a Hebrew national hero, embodying our national aspirations *in their true form*.[22]

Ahad Ha'Am's priorities were of a different nature than those of Herzl. He advocated the revival and activation of the Jewish national consensus by patiently cultivating a free, creative Hebrew culture. This implied severely restricting other activities, especially the colonization of Palestine as it had developed under the guidance and supervision of the Rothschild administration. After his retirement from active leadership of the Bnei Moshe in the post-1891 period and the assumption of his new role as editor of *Hashiloah*, Ahad Ha'Am had ceased to be the young critic of the establishment, the leader of a rebellious cultural nationalism opposed to the practical, philanthropic Zionism of the Odessa Committee and the orthodoxy of the ultra-traditionalists. Now *he* was the conservative editor against whom younger men rebelled.[23] The essential mood of the Zionist elite was one of militancy that demanded action: Some young writers criticized Ahad Ha'Am's informative and analytic style, while others turned impatiently against his Zionist policies. In a letter to Leo Motzkin dated 1896, Joseph Lurie summed up the feelings of many of the young Zionists toward Ahad Ha'Am: "I found him to be a man of wide-ranging knowledge in philosophy, psychology and general and Hebrew literature. His moral stature is beyond question. He has a quick intellect, sober, but practical, probably too practical. His 'opportunism' expresses itself solely in caution and fear toward everything that is initiated, in lack of daring and initiative. . . ."[24]

What was most urgent to the young Zionists were the immediate material sufferings of the Jews. These were times of economic and political oppression, and the generation which matured in these turbulent years could not be told to work patiently toward a remote future when action would be possible. They responded with élan to any immediate challenges, but prior to Herzl they had not been able to coordinate their diverse efforts and ideas and crystallize them into a unified force. Herzl changed all of that. As reorganized by Theodor Herzl, all the old Zionist views, together with the new political Zionist ideology, were brought within the framework of a disciplined body committed to action. Thus, Herzl's personality, his organizational abilities, and his activist political ideology combined to tap the enormous emotional and intellectual reservoir of Jews, in both the East and the West, which was waiting to be channeled in the cause of the movement. At a time when it seemed that the goal of auto-emancipation would not be achieved in the near future, Herzl provided new sustenance for that idea.

Herzl did not create a nationalist movement; the popular movement which already existed—and particularly the younger, more discontented elements within it—sought him out and made him their leader. However, Herzl recognized at once the enormity of the task at hand—to create not merely a new national consensus, as Ahad Ha'Am wished to do, but a new national organization fit for decisive action. He gave the Zionist movement a sense of sovereignty by establishing the congress in Basel in 1897.[25] The major accomplishments of that congress were threefold: the creation of the congress as a permanent institution of the Zionist movement, which would eventually shift from a mere sense of sovereignty to actual sovereignty; the creation of the World Zionist Organization as a permanent organizational structure;[26] and the creation of the Basel program, which stated in its first sentence—parts of which were later incorporated into the Balfour Declaration—that "Zionism strives to create for the Jewish people a home in Palestine secured by public law."[27]

The organizational and programmatic innovations by Herzl were a big leap forward from the cautious and philanthropic activities of the Hibbat Zion. The members of the Russischer juedischer wissenschaftlicher Verein did not need to be convinced of Herzl's basic assumptions and conclusions; as early as 1895 they themselves had attempted to organize a general Zionist congress which was to convene in Berlin in August 1896.[28] Weizmann was in Pinsk while Joseph Lurie, Eliyahu Davidson, Shmarya Levin, and Leo Motzkin were formulating the program of the congress early in 1896, but he must have been aware of and in sympathy with their plans.[29] It was hardly surprising, then, that members of the Verein, spearheaded by Motzkin and including Weizmann, saw themselves at first as Herzlian Zionists. Ahad Ha'Am, who had attended the First Zionist Congress and immediately adopted a critical stance toward Herzl's plans,[30] was for the time being ignored by the students, who represented a large contingent at the congress. When Joshua Heshel Bukhmil came to Pinsk, at Herzl's bidding, the summer preceding the First Zionist Congress, he already found an enthusiastic and devoted supporter of Herzl in Chaim Weizmann.[31] Henceforth Chaim was to be part of the movement, affected in every turn of his life by the fortunes of Zionism.

In the autumn of 1897[32] Weizmann followed his favorite instructor from the Polytechnik, Karl Anton Augustin Bistrzycki, to the University of Fribourg, Switzerland, where the latter had been appointed professor. Since it was Bistrzycki who had guided his early research in Berlin, it was natural for Weizmann to write his dissertation under the guidance of a man whose interests in chemistry were akin to his own. Fribourg, a

Catholic university founded in 1889, was situated in a medieval town on the Saane River. It had very few Jewish students,[33] but it was only three quarters of an hour away from Bern, which had a large Russian-Jewish student colony. It was natural for Weizmann to spend much time in Bern, where in late 1897 or early 1898 he met Sophia Getzova, who came from a small town near Minsk and was studying medicine. They became engaged. Sophia was an active Zionist in the Bern circles and was a good friend of Leo Motzkin and his fiancée, Paula Rosenblum.[34] Their engagement resulted in a temporary improvement of relations between Weizmann and Motzkin.

Sophia Getzova and other Russian students studied at Swiss universities, particularly at Bern and Geneva, because of the liberal admission policies of these institutions. From the middle of the nineteenth century, Russians and Poles flocked to Switzerland for education or simply for refuge.[35] Herzen, Bakunin, Lavrov, Nechaev, and Kropotkin had all left their mark on Switzerland, and such leading revolutionaries as Paul Axelrod, Vera Figner, and G. V. Plekhanov still lived there in the first years of the twentieth century.[36] Both Lenin and Trotsky spent some time in Switzerland during the first decade of this century. They all found Switzerland a hospitable haven, so much so that according to the 1910 census, 147 of every 1,000 residents of Switzerland were citizens of another country.[37] Of the Russians in Switzerland, one fourth to one third were students at Swiss universities at any given time. In the winter semester of 1887–88, Swiss medical schools had enrolled only a total of 95 Russian citizens, 65 of them women. By 1900 the number of Russians in medical schools had risen to 365, and the actual number of Russian students at the seven universities of Switzerland totaled 805. The closing of three of the four women's medical schools in Russia in 1900 sent a flood of female students abroad, and a great many of them sought entry into the Swiss medical schools.[38]

In general, the Russians in Switzerland, like those in Germany, kept to themselves. Their alien ways aroused antagonism on the part of the Swiss.[39] Among themselves the Russians were, of course, grouped around conflicting ideologies. Due to his membership in the Verein, Weizmann was already a veteran of such ideological debates, especially with the Jewish socialists and assimilationists and the various Marxist revolutionary groups.[40] Many of them viewed with contempt Jews who felt deep allegiance to their own people and tradition. In 1897, the very year when Herzl founded the World Zionist Organization, the Bund, or General Jewish Workers' Union in Lithuania, Poland, and Russia,[41] a Jewish social democratic general labor organization, was founded. In the period before World War I, the Bund was a much stronger and larger movement than Zionism, attracting many young Jews to its ranks. The ideology of the Bund was closely tied to the social conditions of the Jews in the Pale of Settlement and was, at the same time, influenced by the Russian socialist movement. At its fourth convention in 1901, under internal and external pressures, the Bund went as far as demanding equal polit-

ical and civic rights—as well as national rights—for Jews, legitimizing this
move with the Marxist example of the Austrian Social Democratic Party.[42]
On the other hand, the Bund did not consider Jews a worldwide national entity and was concerned solely with Russian Jewry. It rejected
collaboration with other Jewish parties and defined Zionism as reactionary and bourgeois, as having sold out to the tsarist regime.[43] This point
was made explicitly:

> The Zionists kowtow and lick the hand of the slaughterer of the whole Jew-
> ish people, the tsarist autocracy, the atrocious, thieving tsarist autocracy that
> made paupers, beggers, sick, weak, and feeble wretches out of the Jews . . .
> You tell us to hide in a corner so that, God forbid, no one should notice and
> trample on us; keep our heads bowed as low as possible, so we should not
> catch anyone's eye; speak quietly, like a beggar at the door; beg for mercy
> and kindness . . . That's how the Zionists talk, the same Zionists who al-
> ways yell about national and personal self-respect, national pride and self-
> consciousness and other such jabber, and keep attacking "slavery within
> freedom!" . . . If the West European Jewish bourgeoisie is sunk in "slavery
> within freedom," then you, the Zionist Russian bourgeoisie, are sunk in a
> still bigger pile of muck—in "slavery within slavery."[44]

The battle lines between Zionists and their socialist-Marxist opponents
of all shades were drawn, of course, not only in Russia but wherever
substantial numbers of Russian Jews congregated. Ideological debates were
inevitable. Weizmann became acquainted with these debates through his
frequent visits to Sophia. For the time being, however, he did not get
involved in political or agitational activity of any kind. His first priority
was to complete his dissertation. There was one exception. From August
28 to 31, 1898, the Second Zionist Congress was held in Basel, some fifty
miles away from Fribourg. Having missed the first congress, Weizmann
was determined to participate in this one as a delegate from Pinsk.[45] Sophia Getzova also participated in this congress as a delegate in her own
right. Weizmann first attended a preliminary conference in Warsaw, a
caucus of the Russian delegates, in which they discussed issues that would
come up at the congress.[46] He then traveled westward with the large
Russian *Landsmannschaft*.[47]

The congress, which took place at the Stadtkasino, was again an impressive affair, at least from an aesthetic point of view. There were more
than four hundred delegates in attendance. Herzl lent the congress his
customary dignity and air of authority, sounding, in his opening address, the slogan "conquest of the communities" in the Diaspora and
the challenge to the assimilationists' self-appointed role as spokesmen of
the Jewish people. Nordau repeated, with some revisions, his survey of
the Jewish condition in the Diaspora. But there were also some heated
debates, and Herzl had to intervene time and again to reconcile the many
diverse opinions. Leo Motzkin had become a prominent figure among
the delegates. Impressed by Motzkin at the First Zionist Congress, Herzl
had asked him to undertake an investigative trip to Palestine. Now, after
nine weeks of travel and observation, Motzkin presented to the Second

Zionist Congress a frank, critical evaluation of the achievements of colonization in Palestine. Using statistical data, he demonstrated the colonists' economic progress but also described the moral failure of the colonists' dependence on the corrupt administration of Baron Edmond de Rothschild. Motzkin concluded that, given the present conditions, immigration ("infiltration") to Palestine must cease until the appropriate legal requirements (viz. a charter) had been obtained. Those Jews already in Palestine should be aided through agricultural and industrial projects administered by the Jewish Colonial Trust.[48]

Herzl was certainly pleased to hear his own views echoed, but now the difficult task of founding the Jewish Colonial Trust (Juedische Colonialbank) lay ahead of him. This was the other major issue at the Second Zionist Congress. Wolffsohn, the head of the bank commission, reported that four million francs had already been subscribed in small sums.[49] The bank as such met with no opposition, but there was some argument as to the formulation of its field of activity. The twenty-four-year-old chemist who had sat quietly until the third day of the congress, and had followed the proceedings with "profound respect,"[50] now entered the debate.

The beginning of his speech was in Russian and was not recorded, but when he continued in German he raised an organizational issue, namely, that of democratic control of the movement's funds. He feared that the money raised for the bank could, at some point, be used for purposes not directly connected with Zionist aims or could even be used for purposes opposed to those aims. Referring to the issue raised by Menahem Ussishkin—who objected to the draft proposal whereby the "Orient" alone was named as the bank's field of activity and demanded the substitution of the words "Syria and Palestine"—Weizmann suggested the compromise formula "that the bank develop its activity only in those countries that have direct trade relationships with Syria and Palestine and only in proportion to those relationships." He ended his speech with his major demand:

> The most important point, however, which we absolutely must know before we leave for home, is what the relationship is going to be between the Actions Committee and the Zionist organization and the administration of the bank. It is not enough to say that the Zionist congress will exercise its influence over the bank. It should also be stated how this will be done, or at least some indication should be given of what ways and means the bank conference has proposed to this end . . . As long as we are not given this guarantee, or at least some indication in this direction, we cannot tell our electors, "There you have an institution we founded for you and not just for capitalists" (lively applause).[51]

This was the extent of Weizmann's participation in the debate, but he was also elected to the twenty-man Congress Steering Committee, a position he would occupy time and again in future congresses. Throughout the proceedings Weizmann felt at home, welcome, and needed. He was profoundly impressed by the experience of sitting among Jewish representatives who came from the Caucasus dressed in their traditional attire, the London and Paris gentlemen, the hasidim from Poland and the *mitnagdim* from Lithuania. He was also thrilled by the impact the Jewish "parliament" had made on the gentile public.[52] He left the congress, inspired to continue the work, with Herzl's final speech at Basel ringing in his ears: "Zionism is not just a sad necessity, as is commonly claimed; it is also a glorious ideal."[53]

Weizmann traveled with the Russian delegates as far as Warsaw. There he booked third-class passage to Pinsk, where he was to spend the high holidays. Sophia (Sonechka) arrived in Pinsk a little later, where she met and was approved of by the Weizmann clan. The match was apparently also approved of by Leo Motzkin and Paula, his fiancée, and the unpleasant exchanges between Chaim and Leo in the summer of 1897 were now forgotten. It was a time for some rest but also for Zionist propaganda, as usual a difficult task in Russia without a legally functioning Russian Zionist federation. Instead of such an organization, the Russian members of the Grosses Aktions-Comité (Greater Actions Committee) (GAC) tried to function as the Landes-Comité (National Committee) and established, in 1898, a "Financial Office" at Kiev and a so-called "Correspondence Office" at Kishinev under the direction of Jacob Bernstein-Kohan, whose function was to receive reports from regional leaders and to disseminate information and directives.[54] Since it was under constant surveillance by the Russian police, the system's effectiveness was limited. It was up to enterprising individuals like Weizmann to take the initiative. "During *Hol Hamoed* Sukkot I shall tour the neighborhood and shall inform [you] afterwards what effect the Congress has had on these *Gottverlassene* [Godforsaken] towns."[55]

There are no further letters or other information on Weizmann's Fribourg period. In January 1899 he submitted two short dissertations—dedicated to his parents—on the action of electrolysis for the reduction of nitroanthraquinones in order to produce the amino-anthraquinones from which dyestuffs are made.[56] For this work he earned his doctorate *magna cum laude.* He spent a few months with Sophia in Bern, in March he moved to Clarens-Baugy (on Lake Geneva), and in April he moved to Geneva, following an invitation by Professor Carl Graebe to join the organic chemistry department at the University of Geneva. He became assistant to Professor Graebe and a *Privat-Dozent* (lecturer paid by student fees).[57] It was by all accounts a remarkable achievement due to Weizmann's single-mindedness and persistence, which were already evident in Pinsk. Only seven years earlier, with a poor background in chemistry and an even poorer knowledge of German, he had made his first acquaintance with the universities of the West. Now he had climbed the first rung of a coveted academic career at a first-rate university. To complete his education he was now quickly gaining a mastery of French in addition to his native Yiddish and Hebrew and his acquired Russian and German.

Weizmann often spoke of the tug-of-war in his life between Zionism and chemistry. In Pinsk and Berlin the division between these two interests had been clear-cut. His major energies were centered on his scientific studies and Zionist work was relegated to his free evenings and weekends. In Geneva we have the first evidence of tension and conflict; as Weizmann increasingly assumed the role of an opposition leader, it was no longer possible to neatly compartmentalize his obligations to science and Zionism. Until his move to Manchester in 1904, it seems clear that Zionism often had the upper hand. His active involvement in Zionist affairs, especially student activities, in Switzerland had already begun in the spring of 1898. While visiting Sophia in Bern he decided to challenge the Marxist and Bundist circles and founded a Zionist student society there with Chaim Khissin, Abraham Lichtenstein,[58] Saul Stupnitzky, Sophia and Rebbeca Getzova, Solomon Rapaport (also known under the name of Ansky), and Nachman Syrkin.[59] They held their first meeting in the back room of the Russian Colony's library while standing on their feet because their ideological opponents had gotten wind of the meeting and had removed the furniture. Thus, they founded the first Zionist society in Switzerland, called the Bern Academic Zionist Society.[60] The mere proclamation of this first society created a scandal among the students, and debates raged between the "Zionist reactionaries" and the revolutionary forces. It was a courageous step given the overwhelmingly hostile majority, which included such figures as Professor Naum Reichesberg and occasional visitors to the Russian colony such as V. I. Lenin, Anatole Lunarcharsky, Vera Figner, Georgi Plekhanov, and Paul Axelrod. A debate between Weizmann and Plekhanov took place in November 1901, probably in Geneva. Plekhanov invited those Jews assembled to break out of the ghetto, to abandon Zion, and to join the forces of progress as outlined by Marx and Lasalle. Weizmann replied that Marx was a traitor to his people and could not possibly be put up as a shining example to be emulated.[61] Thus, in Bern Weizmann was engaged in some of his earliest public debates.[62]

Later Weizmann would often have occasion to lock horns with the revolutionary circles and the Bundists, both in Switzerland and on his visits to Russia. On one of his trips home in 1903, he engaged in a famous debate with Kolya Tepper, who arrived in Pinsk in the spring of 1903. Tepper had previously been a Zionist and one of Ahad Ha'Am's followers. After joining the Bund he became one of their most gifted propagandists. An illegal public debate was held in a forest near Pinsk on Friday and Saturday nights one weekend in April 1903 between Tepper, Weizmann, and A. Rubenchik, who was a spokesman for Poalei Zion (Zionist Workers),[63] which adhered to Zionist ideology while basing itself on the condition of the Jewish proletariat. Unlike Nachman Syrkin's brand of socialist Zionism, this became a more popular and larger movement, which Weizmann always treated with respect and a measure of envy. In 1903, however, the Poalei Zion societies in Russia were still independent of one another and not yet a major force. Thus, Weizmann's attack was mainly directed at Tepper. During this same trip to Russia, in the Passover period of 1903, Weizmann spoke illegally in Minsk in a carpentry shop. The Bundists in town informed the authorities, who surrounded the building. Weizmann was hidden under some planks in the attic and was thus saved.[64]

During his years in Geneva Weizmann often debated with the Bundists in the hope that he might convince them that they had no future with the Russian social democrats.[65] The most extensive of these debates took place in Bern from February 22 to 25, 1903. The Zionists in Bern constituted a separate colony among the Russians.[66] Yet there were contacts between them and members of the Bund. Vladimir Medem relates in his memoirs that he knew Shmuel Rosenfeld, one of the Zionist leaders; that Sophia Getzova was a personal friend, and that he had amicable relations with Weizmann and other Zionists as well.[67]

One can, of course, not generalize from the case of Vladimir Medem and apply one's assumptions to all other Bundists. For most of the students the ideological debates were conducted in dead earnest, each side marshaling its best and most powerful advocates. The debate of 1903, which took place in a *Bierhalle,* rocked the entire Bern colony and was attended each evening by some four hundred persons.[68] Weizmann described it in his memoirs as a revolution. The Zionists of Bern invited Weizmann, the foremost leader of the Democratic Faction, Berthold Feiwel, and Zvi Aberson to be their representatives.[69] "The meeting," wrote Weizmann, "expanded into a sort of a congress . . . It was before the dawn of the third day, at four o'clock, that the resolution was put to a vote, and we scored a tremendous triumph. A hundred and eighty students enrolled in the Zionist Society—a striking revelation of the true inclinations and convictions of a large part of the Jewish student body."[70]

Vladimir Medem, who was present at this debate as one of the representatives of the Bund, presents a different account which throws an interesting light on Weizmann's role:

> Shortly after the anniversary [the fifth anniversary of the establishment of the Bund, founded October 7–9 in Vilna], we had a big debate in Berne with the Zionists. It was an event that shook the whole colony. There had been smaller debates on previous occasions, but this time the Zionists wished to mount a general assault. An announcement was made concerning a lecture to be delivered by Chaim Weizmann. And two other Zionist speakers arrived together with him: Dr. Berthold Feiwel, a German Jew, a poet and a writer . . . and an individual named Tsvi Aberson, who regarded himself as the theoretician of the "Democratic faction."[71]
>
> As for us, we were compelled to settle for our modest local talent . . . Thus we mobilized our rather limited resources and entered the fray. It lasted three whole evenings.[72]
>
> It opened with a lecture by Weizmann . . . On that occasion, at least, he did not excel with any particular oratorical gift. He spoke in a slow, even fashion somewhat drily; indeed he was a bit dull. Weizmann was apparently seeking to essay the role of "diplomat." He weighed and measured his words, and he kept himself under studied control. As to the lecture itself, it

was a tremendous disappointment.[73] The colony had been accustomed to lectures that were impressive and penetrating—lectures of solid content. But Weizmann spoke for about half an hour, and, just when everyone thought that he had concluded his introduction and was now warming to the essence of his presentation, he stopped to acknowledge that he had said all that he wanted to say. It seemed almost like a mockery, and the audience was terribly indignant. We asserted that the lecture was no lecture at all; that there was nothing to which to respond; and that there would be no discussion. But the next Zionist speaker, Aberson, stepped forward and "saved the situation." He proceeded to sermonize. His speech, full of the most incredible and fantastic things, did have some content nevertheless, and offered substance for discussion.

The debate was joined. We went at each other for three evenings in a row. It was extremely turbulent. Weizmann's partisans, in the main young *galitsianer*—future rabbis—behaved in the most disorderly manner. Unable to prevail amid the raging crowd, one chairman after another was compelled to relinquish his conduct of the meeting. I believe that the last chairman, the one who held on to his position to the end, was Ansky.[74] The discussion's high point was reached on the third evening, when three general spokesmen were selected for each side. Of all the Zionist speakers, the German, Feiwel, had the greatest impact. He was a poet and found recourse to poetic allusions. Pale, with shining dark eyes, he concluded his address and collapsed in a faint. It left some of the girls deeply shaken. As usual, however, both sides won; each side carried the day with its own people. The majority of the colony, of course, was on our side.

I vividly recall the words with which Weizmann concluded his final speech.[75] For the present, he said, we are engaged in a struggle with each other here, in Switzerland, far from our actual arena, from the Jewish masses. But the time will come and we will meet there, in distant Russia; and then we shall truly engage each other in a struggle, in head-on confrontation. And history will render its verdict upon us.[76]

When Weizmann arrived in Geneva in the spring of 1899, his social and intellectual contacts—as had been the case in Berlin—continued to be almost exclusively with the East European Jewish circles. The major difference was that he was no longer the young, inexperienced student looking with awe at the older members; he was a veteran party member and soon became a leader of a small segment of the movement. Moreover, he was a respected lecturer *(Privat-Dozent)* and a delegate to Zionist congresses. It is indicative of the need for leadership among the Zionist circles in Geneva that almost immediately upon his arrival in the city Weizmann was elected president of the Geneva Zionist Society on April 23, 1899.[77] It is not an exaggeration to say that during his Geneva years Weizmann crystallized his political views and consequently the views of his Zionist circle. He would, in the course of time, coin the phrases and arguments against the socialists, political Zionists, and the religious circles. For the most part, he interpreted ideas and tendencies that were already prevalent in the Swiss circles of Geneva, Zurich, Bern, Lausanne, Basel, and in the movement at large. One must, however, credit him with the ability to arrive first at conclusions and decisions that were compatible with the attitudes of his comrades. His abilities as a leader enabled him to explain ideological quandaries to the rank and file.[78] He became, as it were, head of the Zionist organization in Geneva, aided by such peers as Zvi Aberson and a number of young women.

Weizmann's appointment at Geneva also afforded him the opportunity to continue his collaboration with Christian Deichler, whose hometown was Nieder-Ingelheim-am-Rhein. Their collaboration in a number of projects in the field of dyestuffs chemistry resulted in three joint publications and four joint patents all taken out in the latter half of 1900.[79] At that time most organic chemists were engaged in the synthesis of cyclic molecules for organic dyestuffs. Weizmann and Deichler started with the customary procedures but very soon developed a new synthesis of their own, which proved of great value for the preparation of such polycyclic substances as carcinogens and other important pharmaceuticals.[80] For one of their discoveries Deichler and Weizmann received a contract in January 1901 from the Bayer Works, Elberfeld, later incorporated in I. G. Farbenindustrie.[81] This success provided Weizmann at once with a regular income of approximately three hundred marks a month—a considerable sum at that time. Moreover, it meant that he would be financially independent for the next four years, when the income ceased.[82] A little later Weizmann was able to sell to a Paris firm a discovery he had made while still a student in the Berlin Polytechnic.[83]

Paradoxically, Weizmann's very success in chemistry militated against intensive efforts in doing further research. His financial independence afforded him the leisure for Zionist activity. Science obviously meant a great deal to him, but he was attracted and intrigued by the chance afforded him, among the Swiss Zionists, to play an important leadership role. Throughout these Geneva years he was conscious of the fact that his scientific work was suffering and that this, among other things, was also jeopardizing his financial security in the long run: "I must regulate my activities in such a way that one thing (Zionism) does not interfere with the other (chemistry); I shall then be healthier and more creative. I shall work and there will be no more financial difficulties . . ."[84] By 1902 he was unable to bear the intellectual and physical demands imposed by these two disparate worlds and even contemplated giving up chemistry, at least for the moment.[85] It was his fiancée who deterred him from this rash step.[86] The balance between chemistry and Zionism would be duly restored only after his move to Manchester. For the time being he was busy arguing and debating at the Zionist *Stammtisch* (regular table) at the Café Landolt, the Geneva counterpart to Berlin's Café Zentrum, where expatriate students of many nationalities were advocating their various causes. Weizmann was attracted to this bohemian lifestyle and the interesting personalities which moved in its circle.

He had hardly settled in Geneva, in an apartment near his laboratory,[87] when it was time to commence preparations for the Third Zionist Congress. During the period between the second and third Zionist congresses, the conflicts that existed beneath the surface—between the "po-

litical" and "practical" Zionists; between those advocating and those opposing cultural work; between those advocating opposing forms of control
and uses of the Jewish Colonial Trust; as well as the tensions between
the Russian members of the Greater Actions Committee and the members of the Smaller Actions Committee, the effective executive which directed day-to-day affairs—were now becoming more pronounced. Weizmann was expressing the general anxiety felt in the movement when he
wrote the following to Paula Rosenblum: "We are all living under a terrible nervous strain. What will our Third Assembly bring us? As you
know, much in Zionism depends on it . . . There are so many enemies
on all sides, so many attacks, and all this has to be fought off in a
straightforward, open struggle. Will our delegates have enough energy
and courage to rise to the height of the task they have been called to
fulfill? . . . I am going to Basle now with Schweren Herzens [with a heavy
heart]."[88]

The year between the second and third Zionist congresses began on a
promising note but ended with many disappointments. Shortly after the
Second Zionist Congress, with the help of the Grand Duke of Baden,
Herzl succeeded in gaining the sympathy of Kaiser Wilhelm II for the
Zionist idea. At the end of September 1898 the German ambassador to
Vienna, Count Philip zu Eulenburg, informed Herzl that on the occasion
of his forthcoming journey to Palestine the kaiser would grant Herzl an
audience in Jerusalem. Armed with this encouraging news, Herzl made
an unwise speech in the East End of London on October 3, 1898, which
moved the masses to an almost messianic fervor.[89] On October 18, 1898,
on his way to Palestine, Herzl met the kaiser in Constantinople and received his promise to recommend the Zionist movement to the Sublime
Porte. In Palestine he met the kaiser twice: at the entrance to Mikveh
Israel and in Jerusalem on November 2. Here it became clear that, due
to the influence of his foreign minister, Bernhard von Buelow,[90] the kaiser had, in the interim, lost interest in the Zionist movement. In the
meantime, Herzl's efforts with the sultan remained fruitless, and the bank,
which had been incorporated in London in March 1899, was unable to
raise the hoped for capital of two million pounds.[91]

Leaving Nieder-Ingelheim in the first days of August 1899, Weizmann
made stops in Darmstadt and Heidelberg and arrived in Basel on August
6 or 7, where he again attended the preliminary conference of the Russian Zionists. The Third Zionist Congress, which began on August 15,
was relatively peaceful, but it did voice more criticisms than ever before
against Herzl personally and against the Inner Actions Committee (SAC).[92]
Motzkin, who at the Second Zionist Congress had pleased Herzl with
his report and conclusions on Palestine, now strongly criticized the leader
for his London speech of October 1898. Another criticism against Herzl
related to the statutes of the bank. Motzkin claimed that despite the resolutions of the Second Zionist Congress, the bank had not formally restricted its activities "to the Orient, and particularly to Palestine and Syria."
Herzl, however, was able to prove that the restriction had, in fact, been

reinforced in the statutes.[93] There were also criticisms against the manner in which the founders' shares had been distributed. The opposition, again led by Motzkin, insisted that the method by which founders' shares were controlled was undemocratic. Motzkin did not hesitate to imply that SAC, composed of Herzl's Viennese inner circle, was behaving in a dictatorial manner toward the members of the Greater Actions Committee (GAC), which was composed mainly of Russian Zionists.[94] Motzkin's speech was in part a sharper and more elaborate critique of points made earlier in the same congress session by Weizmann, who had concentrated on the relationship between SAC and GAC.[95]

Weizmann also touched on a matter that would soon come to occupy much of his time and require a great expenditure of his energies, namely, the place of culture in the Zionist movement. His reference to the issue seems, in retrospect, curiously flat: "With regard to the cultural question, which is treated like a stepchild, . . . not only does the [Inner] Actions Committee not make any move to stimulate cultural initiatives, but when a stimulus comes from the other side [Russian Zionists], the [Inner] Actions Committee does not even think it necessary to enlighten the foreign members on the subject."[96]

Herzl, of course, did not remain silent. In a detailed and frequently mocking retort to his critics, he singled out Weizmann and Yehiel Tschlenow, but he reserved his greatest sarcasm for Motzkin.[97] In accordance with a resolution of the Second Zionist Congress, the General Hebrew-Speaking Society was founded. At the Third Zionist Congress, as in the second, Herzl tried as much as possible to avoid the controversy surrounding the question of culture in order to forestall a conflict with the rabbis, who viewed the issue as a threat to Jewish religious values. This time the Russian Zionists held their ground and mounted a more concerted attack.[98] The congress did not adopt any resolutions on cultural activities, only a general resolution on the need for the dissemination of the Hebrew language and an agreement to support annually the printing of textbooks for schools in Palestine. A fifteen-man cultural commission, to remain in power until the Fourth Zionist Congress, included Rabbi Moses Gaster, Ahad Ha'Am (who had not attended the congress), Nahum Sokolow, Rabbi Reines, David Yellin, and Rabbi Isaac Ruelf.[99]

The Russian Zionists, Weizmann among them, were not opposed in principle to Herzl's political moves. They well realized that under the impossible conditions they had to endure in tsarist Russia, little meaningful international action could be undertaken. Their growing insistence on cultural activities stemmed from a conviction that they were at least as important as Herzl's diplomatic activities and his insistence, clearly expressed at the Third Zionist Congress, that the Zionists ought to seek a "charter" for their settlement in Palestine. To prove that their opposition was not personal, they organized a festive luncheon for Herzl immediately after the congress. Five hours after the close of the Third Zionist Congress, Weizmann and two of his friends addressed a postcard to Herzl with the latter's picture on it. The message, in Weizmann's handwriting, read: "This is the picture which is ever in our mind's eye and which we always carry and shall carry in our hearts. Hoch!"[100]

Though not without criticism of Herzl, Weizmann was generally satisfied with the outcome of the Third Zionist Congress. Immediately after its termination he left for Pinsk, where Sophia had been staying with the Weizmann family, who had taken a great liking to her.[101] As usual, Weizmann used his time in Pinsk to make propaganda speeches in Homel[102] and Mozyr, in Southern Polesie, where he probably arrived on September 12, 1899, on the eve of Yom Kippur. Weizmann arrived first in the village of Kalinkovichi, which served as a railroad station for Mozyr. There he was received by a *maskil*—Joseph-Bein Doroshko—who was known for his saintliness.[103] Weizmann has described in his memoirs what followed: "In the predawn twilight some twenty Jews were assembled in the tiny wooden synagogue. The *maskil* [not a rabbi, as Weizmann writes] had been carried to the meeting in his bed. [He was paralyzed.] He had heard of me, and before I addressed the meeting he blessed me and my work . . . Later I got into conversation with an old Jew . . . I said: 'Reb Nissan, did you understand what I was talking about?' He looked at me out of his old eyes under their bushy brows, and answered humbly: 'No, I didn't. I am an old man, and my hearing isn't very good. But this much I know: if what you spoke about wouldn't be, you wouldn't have come here.' "[104] From Kalinkovichi Weizmann went to Mozyr, the first fair-sized town to which he was invited by its first and most active Zionist. The rabbi in town, Raphael Kugel, was also sympathetic to Zionism. Weizmann was put up in a Jewish inn and remained in town four days; he spoke at the main synagogue.[105] After Yom Kippur he continued his tour to Slonim.

Summarizing his activities that summer in an optimistic mood, he wrote to Motzkin:

> Satisfaction with the outcome of the [Third] Congress will now be reflected in [increasing] activity. The distrustful, nervous attitude to political Zionism may be expected to disappear and a true understanding of its aims and tasks to take root . . . It's a pity, however, that we have not enough active workers to keep that flame alight. The need for an organization dealing exclusively with accurate, serious propaganda is all the more pressing now. This propaganda must not play on the passions and emotions of the masses; unfortunately many propagandists often consider it incumbent upon them to copy Herzl's London speech. The opposition at the Congress evokes great sympathy among the people; they appreciate it and are beginning to see it in its true light.[106]

In fact, there was no *organized* opposition to Herzl at the Third Zionist Congress. In the first years of the World Zionist Organization the student Zionist circles—even when they supported the Russian leaders of the Hibbat Zion against Herzl on specific issues—were anxious to bridge the gap between Herzl and his critics. Herzl was viewed by them as the undisputed leader. Nevertheless Weizmann realized that the conflicts that

were swept under the rug in 1899 would flare up sooner or later. He left
Pinsk for Geneva on October 14, stopping over for a day in Berlin. Until
the spring of 1900 he worked hard at his chemistry, reading a great deal
and delivering papers on his findings. Most of his time, however, was
devoted to student circles in Geneva and other Swiss cities. It was clear
to Weizmann that the students had to be won over to Zionism if the
movement was to have any future at all. But the propaganda work was
strenuous and not always fruitful. "Such an expenditure of strength and
energy would have made it possible to move mountains among our
masses in Russia, but here among the Swiss students, quasi-socialist,
poorly assimilated as regards Judaism, degenerate, rotten, lacking in
moralischer Halt [moral conviction], the atmosphere spread by Plekhanov, the General of the Russian revolution and *tutti quanti* has a pernicious effect upon them."[107] In Weizmann's view the socialism professed by the students was a result of their own insignificance and
weakness; they needed the crowd to hide behind it. They were driven
to socialism out of negative motives. They were rootless and without direction. "This is why they cannot be Zionists. They are lackeys, and
lackeys in socialism cannot understand the boldness and the great cultural and ethical significance of the idea of the liberation of Jewry."[108]
Weizmann did make a later distinction between those Jews who were
social democrats and those who were members of the Bund: "The Bund
[members] have no programme. They drift with the Russian *Fahrwasser*
[current]. This is not what they want, at least some of them. In our attitude toward them we must be more sensitive and look deeper . . . They
can become a productive, creative element in the Jewish sense, but they
need some fresh blood . . ."[109] Yet it was not all for naught. Though
the work was exceedingly difficult, the Zionists had managed to become
a force among the students and were treated with respect. Weizmann
was exhausted and longed for a vacation in Pinsk. On June 26, 1900, he
left for home, but not before touring Bern and Lausanne. On July 22 he
was once again elected delegate from Pinsk to the Fourth Zionist Congress, which was held in London from August 13 to 16, 1900.

"What, in general, may be expected of the Fourth Congress?" wrote
Weizmann to Motzkin in June 1900. "Oh, I am afraid of it."[110] Herzl's
main purpose in holding the Fourth Zionist Congress in London (at
Queens Hall, near Oxford Circus) was to bring the Zionist movement
greater publicity in the heart of the world's political arena.[111] In fact, the
temporary setback of Herzl's diplomatic maneuvers required a shifting
of gears. The sultan could not be reached for an interview; an attempt
to reach this goal via Tsar Nicholas II also failed. Though organizationally there were successes elsewhere in Russia and new adherents to
Zionism were added, there were new persecutions against the Jews in
Rumania, which resulted in a wave of frenzied emigration. The fate of
the Jewish colonies under the new administration of the Jewish Colonization Association was far from rosy, the immediate consequence being
a few hundred unemployed workers. On the whole, despite the attend-

ance of over four hundred delegates, the congress lacked enthusiasm and seemed to many to be forced and artificial, complete with a garden party in Regent's Park. In his opening speech to the delegates, Herzl clearly addressed the power brokers of the empire: "England the great, England the free, England, with her eyes fixed on the seven seas, will understand us. From this place the Zionist movement will take a higher and higher flight, of this we may be sure."[112] But though Herzl was able to meet some important politicians, and though the newspapers did take note of the Jewish assembly, England was not too interested for the time being. There were more significant events taking place just then in South Africa and China, and Zionism would have to wait its turn for attention in a calmer international and domestic climate.

The one practical achievement of the congress was the reaffirmation of a proposal to establish the Jewish National Fund, which had originally been suggested by Professor Zvi Hermann Schapira at the First Zionist Congress in 1897. The object of this fund was the acquisition, by means of voluntary contributions, of land in Palestine as an inalienable property of the Jewish people.[113]

Weizmann arrived in London on August 8 to take part in the Russian preparatory conference *(Vorkonferenz)*, where he was elected, on August 12, to the Steering Committee chaired by Motzkin. The cultural question arose over the circulars Bernstein-Kohan was sending as director of the Correspondence Center in Kishinev, which expressed his antireligious sentiments.[114] The question of cultural work cropped up time and again throughout the congress. The rabbis, headed by Reines, claimed that religious Jews were abstaining from the movement because of this issue. On the other hand, Sokolow advocated cultural work as the duty of every Zionist. The *Haham* Rabbi Moses Gaster, religious leader of the Spanish and Portuguese congregation of London, also spoke in favor of cultural work in his customary flowery language.[115] Weizmann, no longer able to control his hostility against the orthodox rabbis' adamant refusal to even put the question to a vote, gave the last major address:

. . . It has been suggested that the cultural—the so-called cultural—or educational question should be dropped from the Zionist congresses. I believe when we assemble again in a Zionist congress in five or six years' time we will feel ashamed to have heard such things at a Jewish congress, which is after all supposed to represent the synthesis of all combined Jewish forces. Why should the Congress drop the cultural question? Yesterday we heard from a whole series of rabbis, who claim to be the teachers of the people, that the Jewish masses are frightened of culture. I assert from this tribune that this claim rests on self-deception . . . The masses are afraid of culture! Has anyone considered what this would mean? Who has in fact demonstrated this fear of culture? Was it not these rabbinical gentlemen, those who for years confused the souls of the Jewish people? Before we had spoken of culture at all [at the Second Zionist Congress], they had already opened their crusade against Zionism. Where were the rabbis to warn us then? Why do they come now full of mistrust against the representatives of the Jewish spirit?

We have already told them four times [at Zionist congresses] and this time our esteemed leader [Herzl] has said it clearly: We do not interfere in religious matters. But this is not enough for them . . .

. . . The [Jewish] communities are falling to pieces. Now the Zionists are doing something and the rabbis say . . . they are the leaders of the people. Therefore I say: No compromises! . . . If the rabbis come as representatives of the people, we welcome them. But if they come as representatives of the synagogue, then this is anti-Jewish, for there is no synagogue in Judaism!

The cultural question must and will be the vital nerve and sinew . . . No matter how much you try to frighten us off, you will not be able to exclude such matters from our congress . . . I therefore request . . . the initiation of regular cultural activity. If we do this in the name of the Congress, it will have enormous value . . .[116]

Herzl was impressed neither by Weizmann's passionate speech nor by the arguments of other proponents. He successfully sidetracked the issue to avoid a conflict with the rabbis. By a small majority vote the discussion was suspended.[117] Weizmann left the congress "exhausted and weary, broken morally and physically."[118] It had left a deep negative impression which he recorded many decades later in his memoirs.[119] Even Herzl, in evaluating the congress, could only point to the fact, on the positive side, that it had been a "fine demonstration." For the rest, "it was a lot of noise, sweat, and drum beating."[120]

V

The Democratic Faction

A few weeks after his return to Geneva from the congress held on October 31, 1900, Weizmann met a beautiful nineteen-year-old medical student at the Jewish Club.[1] On that occasion they merely exchanged greetings. They were soon to meet again, when Weizmann volunteered to coach a group of Russian students, among them Vera Khatzman, in French and chemistry. Vera, one of seven children, was born to Issay and Theodosia Khatzman[2] on November 27, 1881, in Rostov-on-Don, in the heart of Cossack territory. Her father had been conscripted into the tsarist army of Nicholas I, where he served for twenty-five years and saw action in the Crimean War. His military service earned him the right to reside outside the Pale of Settlement in Rostov-on-Don, where he became a well-to-do wholesale clothes dealer. Vera's mother came from Voronezh, in central Russia, and knew little about her family's past. At the age of fifteen she married a man twenty-five years her senior.[3]

Given their background, it is surprising that the Khatzmans managed to preserve some sort of Jewish identity. Local conditions did not exactly encourage communal Jewish life. In 1874 Jews began to come to Rostov in large numbers, turning to trade, especially coal. They were seen as a dangerous element and officials challenged their right to be there. When the Ministry of the Interior declared, in January 1875, that the Jews had such a right, the local administration claimed that the Jews were competing unfairly with the Cossacks' efforts to develop commercially and industrially. Special laws were therefore adopted in 1880 stating that Jews could stay in Rostov only temporarily. Jews were forbidden to maintain permanent residence in the Don military district or to be economically active, with the exception of doctors of medicine, graduates of universities, and those who were sent on government service. Jews could not hold leases in the area.[4]

Despite these discriminatory laws, the census for 1897 shows that in the metropolitan area of Rostov-on-Don Jews comprised 13,002 out of a general population of 370,000. In the city of Rostov itself, which had a total population of 119,000, there were 11,838 Jews. By 1910 there were three Jewish schools for children *(Talmudei Torah)*, a Jewish women's

Vera Khatzman, Rostov, May 1900

general school, and another school attached to one of the synagogues.
For the most part Jews were allowed to carry on their affairs. The first
pogrom in Rostov is recorded relatively late, following the October Manifesto of 1905.[5] Vera's father headed one of the two local synagogues in
Rostov and the family celebrated Jewish holidays, but the five girls received no religious instruction and were completely ignorant of Hebrew,
not to speak of Yiddish. Vera's knowledge of Palestine and Zionism was
limited to the recognition of Ussishkin's name and a lithographic portrait
of Moses Montefiore.[6]

Vera's background, childhood memories, and puritanical upbringing[7]
were as remote from Weizmann's development in the Pale of Settlement
as could be imagined. In addition, she was by temperament distant and
reserved, rarely given to those emotional outbursts so characteristic of
Weizmann, who was warm, outgoing, and affectionate. Perhaps it was
this very reserve and dignity of bearing, coupled with her striking appearance, which so attracted Weizmann. In his autobiography he gives
us a clue to his preference for Vera over Sophia. As he saw it, the group
of young women to which Vera belonged differed from the other Jewish
students in the Swiss universities at the time:

> Their looks, their deportment, their outlook on life, set them apart. They
> were far more attractive than their contemporaries from the Pale of Settle-
> ment. They were less absorbed in Russian revolutionary politics . . . they
> paid more attention to their studies and less to the public meetings and end-

less discussions which took up so much of the time of the average Russian student abroad.

Weizmann referred to Vera's origin outside the Pale of Settlement and her privileged circumstances, concluding:

> All this had its effect on the bearing and manners of the group to which my future wife belonged, so that its members stood out in contrast from the majority of the Russian-Jewish students in Geneva, who for the most part seemed underfed, stunted, nervous and sometimes bitter—an easy prey to revolutionary propagandists.[8]

One can only assume that Vera's un-Jewish looks and bearing were more appealing to Weizmann than the more Jewish and active party comrade Sophia Getzova. It is also an indication of Weizmann's ever-growing ties to Central and West European culture; thus, Weizmann's break with Sophia Getzova symbolizes a certain break with his own East European background. Though in his very person he had bridged East European culture with that of the West, he always leaned toward the latter. To compliment someone was to be called European, as he did when he first met Ahad Ha'Am in Berlin. Vera was obviously closer to this ideal than Sophia, who hailed from a small town near Minsk.

But perhaps this was only part of the truth. Weizmann was a man of passion and impulse and was always, then as later, attracted to beautiful and interesting women. Though he was at the time engaged to Sophia, who had spent part of the previous summer vacation with his family in Pinsk, Vera was not the first woman to attract him while he was engaged. Just weeks before their love affair began to blossom, he had been courting another beautiful woman from Rostov, a friend of Vera's, who had disappointed him by pursuing her own flirtations.[9] The twenty-six-year-old lecturer was obviously occupied with other matters in addition to chemistry and Zionist affairs.

Weizmann's first notes to Vera address her in the formal second-person-plural "you." The first extant note, written on a card in early 1901, simply notified her that he would come back to visit.[10] The second note already revealed his uncontrolled passion for his new acquaintance, but it also indicated his trepidation at being found out. After all, the Russian-Jewish colony was not that large, and though Sophia was safely tucked away in Bern, she had good friends in Geneva who perhaps kept an eye on her financé: "You are bored, and I have a frantic desire to settle down with you in some corner and tell you a lot of things, but there are unwanted eyes. I am not afraid of them, but they profane both of us, or rather—the relationship between us. This gets me down, I am insulted, but I feel better when I look at you, so calm and pure and a 'human being.' Your friend. P.S. Nietzsche's only characterization of Goethe was: Goethe was a human being."[11]

For the next few months Weizmann and Vera did their best to hide their affair from "unwanted eyes," though they did meet in the Café Landolt, talking for hours over a glass of weak Russian tea.[12] It was only somewhat later that Weizmann could no longer bear his agonies of conscience and, perhaps, the pressure exerted by Vera to tell Sophia Getzova the whole truth.[13] In the meantime he restrained himself from completely revealing the depth of his growing affection and love for Vera. His letters to her are written in a light and humorous vein, trying to be witty and entertaining. The language of the letters does not indicate any intimate relations at the time, remaining confined to such expressions as "Verusya, my little girl," or "My dear girl, what respect I feel for you! If you only knew how much I think of you. Such good, straightforward people are truly rare . . ."[14] Or, to cite another example, "Were it not for you, my radiant, pure girl! How bright is the image of you that appears before me, my darling Verochka! I am not going to put into words what is now so very close to me. To put it on paper would be to profane it."[15] Weizmann's letters to Vera often end with "love" and "many many kisses"; in the course of the first few months of 1901 he openly declared his love for her, but it seems that this is as far as he dared go. Perhaps it was Vera who made it clear that before formally dissolving his relations with Sophia nothing more could be expected.

Vera was in Rostov on summer vacation in July 1901 when she received the following letter from Weizmann: "Leaving everything else aside for the moment, let me say briefly that I have told my fiancée the whole truth. You can imagine, my dear heart, that this was not an easy thing to do, but it had to happen and it did happen. The days preceding this and the time that followed were one long torment, torture, anxiety, and upset of all kinds for me. *C'est un fait accompli*, and the chapter is closed. I know that now comes the time for self-analysis, self-reproach." At the same time his longing for Vera became boundless and painful: "I feel an irresistible need to see you, to hold you . . . Such ardent, such long, such endless kisses, my Verusya . . ."[16] Having made the break with Sophia, Weizmann now felt free to openly express his desire for Vera.

Weizmann's letters do not reveal anything about the sensation his affair with Vera had triggered among their friends and acquaintances. How could a man of honor leave a respected and loyal party comrade for an assimilated woman who had just been graduated from the *Gymnasium*? Weizmann seems to have been severely upbraided by all who knew of the affair.[17] But matters apparently did not end there. According to one source, a "Court of Honor" was formed by six of Weizmann's friends, Shmarya Levin among them, headed by Leo Motzkin. Its task was to rule on Weizmann's love life. The members decreed that Weizmann must marry Sophia to do her justice; then, if he wished, he could immediately divorce her and marry Vera. It is not surprising that Weizmann refused, much to the disgust of Motzkin and his friends. Motzkin, in particular, never forgave Weizmann for his behavior.[18]

The thinking behind this bizarre suggestion was that Sophia Getzova deserved at least a token marriage after four years of betrothal. It is possible, as some claim, that during the final stage of Weizmann's studies in Fribourg Sophia partially supported her fiancé. But the matter was probably more serious than that. Judging by Weizmann's relations with Vera, it seems reasonable to assume that Weizmann and Sophia Getzova lived as man and wife soon after they became engaged. Weizmann often stayed with Sophia in Bern for long periods of time and she, in turn, spent vacations with him in Pinsk. In the eyes of their friends they were, for all practical purposes, married. By leaving Sophia so smoothly and abruptly, Weizmann had dishonored and shamed her. But he had also dishonored himself. Their friends—and there are indications that his family too—saw this as an act of betrayal which revealed his true character. If he could dispose of a woman like Sophia Getzova, how could he be trusted by any of them? The fact that none of this turmoil is reflected in Weizmann's letters would seem to indicate that he himself was aware of the gravity of his actions and was deeply ashamed of them, so much so that for a long time he did not dare tell the truth to his parents. Nevertheless, Vera had captivated him and there was no turning back.

Sophia Getzova, on the other hand, never fully recovered from the affair. According to one source, Weizmann arrived at the Fifth Zionist Congress (December 1901) with Vera on his arm. At this sight Sophia fainted and a great tumult ensued.[19] She earned her medical degree in Bern and moved to Palestine in 1925, where two years later she was appointed as professor of pathological anatomy at the Hebrew University. But her successful career did not seem to heal the wounds inflicted by the breakup of her engagement and she never married. On the other hand, she and Weizmann continued to maintain a cordial relationship.

Throughout the summer of 1901 Weizmann's letters to Vera continued to flow. He already saw in her a trusted friend whom he tried to initiate in Zionist affairs. His love letters were, at the same time, filled with news about his Zionist activities and a fervent wish that Vera become involved in the national enterprise, as his New Year's greetings of September 1901 indicate: "I wish that you may become a true and inspired worker in your native land; I wish that you may become a representative of the new generation . . . May your pure bright soul be filled with love for your people . . ."[20] The letters naturally ceased when Weizmann and Vera resumed their residence in Geneva—in separate apartments, of course. Yet separation from Vera became intolerable even for short periods of time. Writing Vera from every stop along a two-week trip in Germany, signing his letters with an occasional "Your Chaimchik," and deeply longing for her, Weizmann finally implored her to let him spend the night with her upon his return to Geneva: "I'll spend the whole night with you and tell you everything . . . How I am going to cuddle up to you, you will caress me, warm me and I shall relax at your home . . ."[21] Two days later he was more explicit and left no doubt as to the kind of relationship that had evolved between them: ". . . I cannot bear to pass Geneva without calling on you for at least a day. You must give me an evening, and then I want to be *only* with you, close to you, in you. I want to relax in your arms; Verochka, you will not deny me this. If this is very difficult for you, write to me at Ingelheim [Germany] . . ."[22] It is clear that a few days later Vera, who may not have permitted Weizmann to spend a night with her previously, had finally agreed.[23] Weizmann and Vera spent every possible minute with each other, enjoying walks by the Rhone River, with Mont Blanc in the background, and Vera probably listened to many Zionist debates at the Café Landolt. In 1902 they began seriously to discuss marriage,[24] but before they were finally married, in 1906, there were to be many painful and long separations.

From the very beginning of their relationship, Vera knew that Weizmann was completely engrossed in Zionist work, which often took precedence over spending time with her. She came to know Weizmann at a time when his stature in the movement was on the rise; when he was about to embark on his major Zionist endeavor, the Zionist Youth Conference, which soon developed into the Democratic Faction. Though she knew very little of the issues involved, she was no doubt impressed by Weizmann's authority within the Russian student groups. In his many letters, and in person, Weizmann tried to explain to Vera the reasons for the creation of an opposition movement to Herzl.

Herzl's policies had aroused resistance especially among a certain group of young students, mostly Russian, since the Second Zionist Congress. These very same students had been among the most enthusiastic participants in the First Zionist Congress. Since 1891 they had discussed the idea of a congress and had taken part in efforts, in 1893 and 1895–96, to convene such an assembly.[25] These younger Zionists felt strongly about their senior status within the Zionist movement and believed that their knowledge of the movement was more intimate than Herzl's. They were soon disappointed by Herzl's methods. They felt uneasy about his autocratic and adventurous tactics, the implied suspension of colonization in Palestine until permission could be obtained from Turkey and the European powers; but most of all they were angry at Herzl's shallow disregard for cultural Zionism.[26] Thus Herzl's most enthusiastic supporters soon became the first to create a factional opposition within the Zionist movement.

Given Herzl's road to Zionism, combined with his powerful personality, a clash with the assertive and independent Russian-born leadership was probably unavoidable.[27] Herzl considered that skillful diplomacy and financial resources would be the key factors in the attainment of Palestine. These factors did not require a parliamentary body elected by the masses; it was only when he had been turned down by the rich Jews that he turned to the popular movement. As a consequence, he often regarded the World Zionist Organization as the springboard for his diplomacy and the bank as the financial instrument which might solve Turkey's public debt. The World Zionist Organization could perform the tasks for which Herzl destined it only if it were united and decisive. With such a view of the congress, Herzl could not permit it to become a forum for unrestricted debate, let alone organizational factions.

Herzl was aware of the importance of the congress as a parliamentary body which united under its umbrella the various Zionist ideologies.[28]

He was ready to respect each one and give it recognition as long as its members adhered to the Zionist consensus. This also explains his attitude toward orthodoxy, or "clericalism," as it was called by those who made the analogy with the Christian state. There was no question of the orthodox coercing anyone into a traditional form of Judaism, or interfering with one's private affairs, but by the same token traditional Judaism deserved to be respected and even cultivated as a bulwark of loyalty to the national cause among the East European masses.[29] At all times he maintained a respectful, even appreciative attitude toward the orthodox rabbis in the congresses, even when he had his disagreements with them. At times Herzl even formed alliances with the rabbis when the issue at hand suited his overarching political objectives.

By the same token, at the Second Zionist Congress (1898) Herzl did not hesitate to oppose demands by the orthodox which he considered harmful to the movement, that is, of a divisive nature.[30] Under the circumstances, the orthodox Zionists were content with a Zionist movement which would seek both an economic solution for East European Jewish immigrants and the political conditions for such a solution in Palestine. On the other hand, they vigorously rejected the cultural Zionism of Ahad Ha'Am and his followers. These differences came to the fore as early as the Russian Zionist *Vorkonferenz* to the Second Zionist Congress, which took place in Warsaw from August 19 to 22, 1898.[31]

The majority of the Russian delegates in Warsaw, under the influence of Ahad Ha'Am's comprehensive lecture, wanted to present a resolution to the Second Zionist Congress which would commit the World Zionist Organization to practical and cultural Zionism. They hoped to realize the following objectives, vaguely outlined in subparagraphs of the First Zionist Congress's Basel Program as a means of obtaining the primary aim of a national home for the Jews in Palestine: (1) the promotion on appropriate lines of the colonization of Palestine by Jewish agricultural and industrial workers . . . (2) the strengthening and fostering of Jewish national sentiment and consciousness.[32]

The second point aroused a strong objection from the rabbis present, most of whom were from Lithuania. None of them had been present at the First Zionist Congress, but they now came in response to Herzl's direct appeal. They could support political Zionism as represented by Herzl but would not tolerate the introduction of the cultural question into the Zionist movement. Thus they made a counterproposal reminiscent of their strong hold over the affairs of the Hovevei Zion, when under Rabbi Shmuel Mohilewer a council of eminent rabbis oversaw the affairs of the movement.[33] Their proposal stated:

> We feel the obligation to make the proposal, in the name of the great Jewish masses which we represent, that Zionism be founded on the basis of the Torah, because this alone is the natural source and origin of our national consciousness, as our teacher Rabbi Samuel Mohiliwer of blessed memory has demonstrated in his letters. Only then will the foundation of Zionism be secure . . . and under the banner of Zionism will unite all those who

have recognized this principle long ago but have shied away because of religious considerations.

For this purpose it is necessary to convene a committee composed of devout rabbis from our country, as well as from abroad, who have the complete confidence of the people. The task of this committee of rabbis will be to represent the interests of Zionism and religion; of course, in matters *concerning economic and social issues the Actions Committee should have a free hand;* matters which affect *religion,* [however], should be turned over to the *Committee of Rabbis.*

The sphere of activity of the rabbis includes as well the overseeing of *the religious education of the children,* as well as the appointment of those propagating [the Zionist idea] . . .[34]

This view and other more moderate views on the part of the orthodox were decisively rejected at Warsaw. It was decided to present the congress with a resolution strongly supporting cultural Zionist activities.[35] The rabbis did not give up, and at the Second Zionist Congress they again tried to press their demands for control over Zionist educational and propaganda work—to no avail. The most Herzl would promise was that the Zionist movement would never do anything that would be offensive to religion.[36] The rabbis who stayed within the World Zionist Organization had no choice but to accept this formula, yet they were far from happy with it. For their part they pressured Herzl not to permit any discussion of the "cultural question" at the congresses, a demand he complied with in order to avoid unnecessary tensions in public.

Yet the "cultural question" came up time and again at Zionist congresses, on each occasion producing sharp exchanges between the orthodox and cultural Zionists. Despite occasional lip service concerning the importance of cultural work, and despite the appointment of cultural commissions, nothing was done by the World Zionist Organization and the proponents of cultural programs became increasingly frustrated. The last straw for many of them was the proceedings of the Fourth Zionist Congress in London. Herzl was especially anxious, in this instance, to suppress any squabbles and to give as much as possible the appearance of unity. Thus, all action on the cultural question was tabled by a slim margin.[37]

It was clear that the protagonists of cultural Zionism would not accept their defeat calmly. They left the congress dissatisfied with the surrender of the majority to the orthodox minority, but they were also aware of the fact that there was substantial support for their cause. In the winter of 1900–1901 discussions centering on the need for a special faction began within a small circle of young Zionist students in the West. These students included Leo Motzkin, Aaron Gourland, Abraham Kasteliansky, Nachman Syrkin, and others.[38] They were supported in Russia by Zionist youth societies, study circles which had been established even before the Second Zionist Congress, and incipient labor groups—in short, by the "progressive" or "democratic" elements in Zionism that wished to attract youth, labor, and the intellectual avant garde. They shared a distaste for Herzl's personal manner, his conservative alliances with reactionary regimes and the "clericals," and the constant friction between Herzl and Jacob Bernstein-Kohan, the leader of radical Zionist youth in Russia. They wished to change the content and direction of the Zionist movement.[39] Weizmann and many others had for a long time had an affinity for Ahad Ha'Am and his ideas; now common opposition to Herzl produced an alliance and consensus between the critics who stood outside the daily affairs of the World Zionist Organization and the students who rebelled from within.

Though many of the ideas which culminated in the creation of the Democratic Faction had originally been aired in the circles of the Verein,[40] the call to organize did not come from Berlin or even Geneva but rather from Munich. During the month of December 1900 two students, Gregory Abramovich and Alexander Nemser, wrote letters in the name of the Munich Zionist student society and of student groups in Paris, Montpellier, Geneva, and Karlsruhe, suggesting a meeting of Zionist youth[41] to discuss important questions which were not being considered by the congresses. On December 18, 1900, they also wrote to Weizmann.[42] The Munich group did not receive replies from most of those contacted, including Motzkin.[43] Weizmann, on the other hand, immediately realized the importance of such a meeting. At the third and fourth congresses he had already expressed his dissatisfaction with the direction the movement was taking. Moreover, he now exhibited, perhaps for the first time, his desire for political leadership, combined with an ambition to secure a role for himself in the movement. It would become a common characteristic for him to seize an interesting idea proposed elsewhere and carry it out to its logical conclusion. These qualities led him to launch an energetic campaign which would finally crystallize in the organization of the "young guard" of intellectuals into a faction. With time he was identified as the man who had founded the Democratic Faction.[44]

The first extant letter from Weizmann in connection with the Youth Conference is dated February 3, 1901.[45] It is not surprising that it was addressed to Leo Motzkin, who was still the undisputed leader of the important Russischer juedischer wissenschaftlicher Verein—Kadimah and a force to be reckoned with in all the previous Zionist congresses. Weizmann still viewed Motzkin as his superior in Zionist affairs, as the man who would map the strategies that others would carry out. Motzkin was needed to give the new venture support and credibility; he could not be ignored. But, as was often his custom when dealing with Weizmann, he did not cooperate. Finally, he cited "personal reasons" and doubted whether much could be accomplished by so heterogeneous a group. Motzkin was now married and engrossed in his studies for a doctorate in economics. He was also shocked and angered by rumors, during this very period, of Weizmann's desertion of Sophia Getzova.

Weizmann, though, could not be deterred by Motzkin. Together with the Munich group he went ahead with plans to convene a preparatory conference in Munich for April 1–2, 1901, just before Passover. Ironically, Motzkin's abstention thus helped propel Weizmann to a more prominent role among the Zionist students. However, in the early months of his activities for the realization of a youth conference Weizmann still felt insecure without the imprimatur and consent of Motzkin and the Berlin Verein. In letters reminiscent of his one-way correspondence with Motzkin from Pinsk in 1895–96, he pleaded: "I am waiting for a letter from you as for manna from heaven."[46] "Am impatiently awaiting your letter and communications about *Kadimah's* decisions concerning the conference."[47] "Dear Leo, Why don't you write? I am simply in despair at not having heard from you; your reply would have encouraged and heartened me. You know that perfectly well yourself, so why don't you do it? My God, how difficult it is to do anything! One comes up either against silence or against meaningless phrases . . ."[48] Motzkin continued to be silent; he had no intention of attending the Munich conference.[49]

Weizmann continued to drum up support for the idea among student groups in Leipzig, Bern, Geneva, Dresden, Karlsruhe, and other cities. After one more appeal for a reply from Motzkin on March 11,[50] he published a circular on March 15, co-signed by Abramovich and Nemser, which officially announced the preliminary conference in Munich in preparation for the Youth Conference to coincide with the Fifth Zionist Congress. The circular, written in Russian, read in part:

> . . . It now falls to the young to do work of the utmost importance—to awaken the masses of the Jewish people, to bring a ray of light into the dim, oppressive atmosphere of the ghetto, to fight against the prejudices and the dark forces which obscure our pure ideal. It falls to the intelligentsia to take the lead in spreading correct and conscious propaganda for our idea, to shoulder the task of information activity on a large and fruitful scale. The duty is laid upon us to draw all the creative classes in the Jewish people to the Zionist flag.
>
> The routine activity of Zionist groups—an activity that is called "practical work"—is not calculated to satisfy us—No! The Jewish people can and should demand of us a clear answer to all the questions life presents. Let us be frank and say, Zionism as displayed at the Fourth Congress is incapable of embracing wide circles of the intelligentsia. It is not by making eternal compromises nor by cloudy dreams that a solution will be found to an eternal problem. What is needed is tremendous moral force, what is needed is readiness for sacrifice. For the Jewish Question to be solved, it must be tackled with all the weapons of European science—an unfamiliar idea to many Zionists.
>
> The aim of the Zionist Youth Conference must be to establish a democratic organization of good and faithful workers in the field of Zionism.[51]

The *Vorkonferenz* to discuss arrangements for the proposed Youth Conference convened in Munich on April 1–2, 1901, at the Engelsburg Bierhalle. It was attended by nine delegates from student organizations in Germany and Switzerland, as well as by members of the Munich Zionist Association.[52] Not aware of the fact that Motzkin was at this point on his way to Russia, Weizmann kept on hoping until the last minute that he would at least send a delegate to represent the Berlin Verein. As late as March 30 Weizmann sent a desperate telegram to Motzkin: "Cannot do without you. Telegraph arrival."[53] As it turned out, things went reasonably well without Motzkin's blessing.[54] Moreover, the widening rift with Motzkin accelerated Weizmann's decision to chart his own independent course. The preparatory conference began a process which would end within a few months with Weizmann as the uncrowned leader of the Democratic Faction.

Had Motzkin attended the Munich conference, it is almost certain that he would have dominated the proceedings; he was, in Weizmann's words, a "power" in the movement and "the best brain among our young people."[55] His absence created a leadership vacuum and Weizmann stepped in quickly to fill it. For the next three years he would be the prime mover, organizer, and guiding spirit behind all the activities of the Youth Conference and the Democratic Faction.[56] After a short introduction by Nemser, who welcomed the conference on behalf of the Munich Zionist group, Weizmann was unanimously elected to preside over the proceedings and his proposal for the conference agenda was accepted. His opening address became the focus for all the discussions that ensued.[57]

In his speech Weizmann stated that the role of the Youth Organization[58] would be to serve as a vitalizing force *within* the general Zionist movement. Its main concerns ought to be cultural work and propaganda, the investigation of conditions in Palestine, the organization of Jewish economic life—by which Weizmann meant the promotion of productive forces among the Jewish masses[59]—and the creation of a Zionist press.[60] The discussions that ensued for many hours were on a high level, with Weizmann in the chair throughout. The resolutions and proposals as stated by Weizmann were carried with little alteration, and he was content.[61]

The preparatory conference resolved that the time had come for the founding of a Zionist youth organization in which the younger members of the Zionist intelligentsia, including students and others, would have an opportunity to make their distinctive contribution to the realization of Zionist goals. It was also resolved that while adhering to the Basel Program, the new organization would place its emphasis on the following tasks: the exploration of the ideological foundations of Zionism and the relationship of the Zionist movement to other social trends—presumably socialism; the improvement of the cultural and economic conditions of the Jewish masses; the attraction of the Jewish intelligentsia to Zionism through an inspired Jewish nationalist ideal; and the exploration of Palestine and the investigation of conditions under which Jews could settle there. The preparatory conference also agreed on the agenda for the Youth Conference and resolved to set up a Zionist Youth Conference Bureau—later referred to as the Organization Bureau—under Weizmann's direction in Geneva, and a Correspondence Bureau under the direction of Alexander Nemser and Gregory Abramovich in Munich. Jacob Bernstein-Kohan, Leo Motzkin, and Daniel Pasmanik were elected members of the Conference Bureau.[62]

Weizmann continued to maintain a respectful, often obsequious, posture toward Motzkin, Ahad Ha'Am, and others in the movement, but as a public figure he was also beginning to develop his own conception of what the Youth Organization would try to accomplish. In a letter to *Voskhod* titled "On Zionist Congresses" these conceptions were crystallized for the first time. After a long summary of the failure of previous congresses, having in mind mostly the Fourth Zionist Congress, Weizmann derided them as purely "demonstrative," "poor in content," filled with "useless people" *(Sommerreise-Zionisten)*.[63] Defending the Kishinev Correspondence Bureau, under the direction of Bernstein-Kohan, as well as the Russian *Vorkonferenzen,* Weizmann stated his view of such discussions within the World Zionist Organization:

> . . . We are too much afraid of supposedly academic controversies, the clarification of which is in fact of the utmost necessity; they would put an end to many misunderstandings and would have enormous educational value for every Zionist. It is true that clarification of all these issues would lead to a division of the Zionists into different camps, but this is precisely what we ought to be demanding. If Zionists with different points of view exist—and they do—they should be grouped according to these points of view; this would make work easier and many issues involving Zionists' opinions that today seem blurred and vague would gain by exact definition and delimitation. Zionists cannot form a party, but only an alliance to be composed of "factions" united by a common program.
>
> Grouping Zionists according to their place of origin makes sense merely for the discussion of purely technical and organizational problems, but it is completely absurd when crystallizing matters of principle. These [principles] have been given very little attention until now, but they must inevitably be brought to the fore if we want Zionism to gain in depth and not merely spread out and vanish on the surface like ripples on water! . . .[64]

This is the first public explanation of the function of a Zionist faction. Weizmann clearly stated that the *Landsmannschaften* (delegations according to country of origin) could play only a limited role. What was needed were homogeneous ideological factions which would have a unifying program. At the same time, there is in his letter to *Voskhod* an implicit underlying principle that the factions would be functioning *within* the Zionist organization as loyal and constructive opposition groups, not as separate entities. Thus, in all its evolutions the program Weizmann and his collaborators outlined demanded constructive goals within the World Zionist Organization which were undertaken because they had been neglected by the official leadership. It would consequently require all the tact and diplomatic ability Weizmann possessed in order to steer a course of both opposition to and cooperation with the official Zionist leadership.

The first test of Weizmann's strength of conviction regarding the purpose and task of the Youth Organization came from Ahad Ha'Am, whom Weizmann met in Paris on May 11. Ahad Ha'Am had come to Paris with an impressive delegation, organized by Hovevei Zion in Odessa, which included Bernstein-Kohan, Yehiel Tschlenow, Menahem Ussishkin, and a number of Palestinian settlers. Their purpose was to prevail upon Baron Edmond de Rothschild to revise the harsh policy of the Jewish Colonization Association (ICA), which had taken over from him the administration of the colonies; there were some four hundred unemployed Jewish workers in Palestine whom the ICA considered expendable and proposed to transfer abroad.[65] The delegates' mission was a miserable failure; instead of a sympathetic hearing they were forced to stand before the baron, cap in hand, as he heaped upon them a tirade of reprimands and criticisms.[66] Ahad Ha'Am was particularly shocked and hurt by the encounter.[67] His frustration was compounded by the lack of support from the official leadership of the World Zionist Organization. It was under the impact of this meeting in Paris that Ahad Ha'Am, who supported the idea of a youth conference, gave Weizmann two pieces of advice: to remove the Youth Conference from the official circles of the Zionist movement by convening it in a locale other than Basel,[68] and to do without the active participation of the "elders" of the Zionist movement, who were incapable of vital work.[69] Both suggestions were not accepted by Weizmann, who sought to win over influential "elders" (including Ahad Ha'Am himself), especially from the Russian circles, such as Ussishkin and Tschlenow, and was steadfast in his resolve to oppose the official leadership from within and not via a separatist organization. Though he was anxious to assure Ahad Ha'Am that the new organization would be largely independent of the World Zionist Organization, Weizmann knew well that even if he wished to, he could not openly revolt against Herzl.

Ahad Ha'Am was, of course, one of the elder statesmen whose views Weizmann respected, even if he did not always follow his advice. But it was Herzl, the movement's leader and potentially the most dangerous antagonist, that Weizmann had to take into account. The first challenge came in the summer of 1901. Herzl had just returned from Constantinople, where he was received by the sultan in a two-hour audience on May 17, 1901. Herzl had made a good impression. To be sure, the immediate tangible results of his sojourn were the receipt of the Grand Cordon of the Order of the Medjidje, a tiepin with yellow stones,[70] and enhanced personal as well as public prestige for the World Zionist Organization. But with the aid of one and a half million pounds—which he imagined he could somehow raise—to help wipe out the Turkish public debt, Herzl hoped that real progress could be made in negotiations with the sultan, to whom he had submitted the Zionist requests for the first time. It was clearly a sensitive and delicate moment in the movement's history, and Herzl was anxious lest any radical youngsters destroy his achievements.

An article in Die Welt by Daniel Pasmanik, a supporter of the Youth Conference (later turned opponent), did little to assuage Herzl's fears.[71]

From the latter's point of view it must have seemed particularly inopportune to speak of the exploration and colonization of Palestine in light of the delicate stage his conversations had reached with the sultan.[72] Less than a week later Herzl turned directly to Weizmann with a polite yet firm request to cancel the Youth Conference. Asking Weizmann to keep the content of this letter confidential, Herzl cited as reasons for cancellation his secret talks with the sultan and the principle that international Zionist meetings not take place before their agenda was approved by the World Zionist Congress.[73]

Weizmann realized at once Herzl's intention to make him personally responsible by forbidding him to show the letter to others. His first move was therefore to cable Herzl for permission to show the letter to members of the Organization Bureau. He received Herzl's consent on July 6.[74] But having succeeded in this first "diplomatic exchange of telegrams and letters" did not make things easier, and ultimately the decision rested with Weizmann. The two weeks until he formulated his reply were agonizing. Almost simultaneously with Herzl's first letter one arrived from Ahad Ha'Am, who announced his resignation from public Zionist activities to "concentrate on his inner world" in the wake of the Paris debacle.[75] Ahad Ha'Am's letter strengthened Weizmann's determination to press on for reforms within the movement: ". . . tears came to my eyes when I was reading his words and saw how the vulgarity of contemporary Zionism and the nonentities who are in it have managed to break the spirit of such a man . . ."[76] Weizmann could appreciate Ahad Ha'Am's principled behavior, since they shared the same background and values, yet he was too much the pragmatist and political animal to give up in the face of momentary setbacks.

How frightened and lonely he really felt Weizmann was willing to disclose only to Vera:

> . . . To convene the Conference means to declare war on Herzlism as a whole, and not to hold it is quite impossible. You can only wage war successfully if you know who supports you; can we say confidently that such-and-such forces are backing us? No, certainly not . . . Where are the youthfulness, the freshness that are needed now? Though I was bright and cheerful until now, I too am beginning to weaken, to feel that my deep faith in the forces of Jewry is disappearing, and I am in despair . . . and I am ready to weep now, my heart is so heavy. The captain weeps. The man setting out to war weeps. We are nervy, unstrung, flabby, and we are unfit for *the Jewish cause*. All our lives we have been serving many gods, and now we cannot concentrate on the ideal of freedom, of our own freedom. How will it all end? I can see before me the faces of our best people. They are all helpless now, yet they are giants in comparison with me . . .[77]

The letter typifies Weizmann's condition at times of stress and overwork. On the one hand, he displayed leadership qualities, resourcefulness, and intellectual maturity; on the other, he revealed his emotional instability. In speaking, in his letter to Vera, of sensitivity, vacillation, and nerviness, he was unconsciously describing his own varying moods.

His uneven disposition made for very frantic, sometimes hysterical outbursts. The smallest of incidents could cheer him, but it could also plunge him into depths of despair. It was during these moods of blackest depression that he longed for Vera more than ever.[78] "Verunya, Verunya, my lovely darling. I want you dreadfully, and I am already burning with longing to read your letters."[79]

Weizmann was always quick to respond to letters he received and, conversely, was greatly irritated when he had to wait for replies. It was therefore uncharacteristic of him to wait over two weeks before replying to Herzl, a further indication of his anxiety and sense of personal responsibility. When he finally did respond, his letter was a model of astute diplomacy.[80] It reflected none of the despair and uncertainty of the previous days and was written in the confident and resolute tone of a man who knows his own importance.

Weizmann began with a counterattack against the Smaller Actions Committee, which had only now, three months after the well-publicized Munich Conference, seen fit to focus attention on the forthcoming Youth Conference. Next, he assured Herzl that the Youth Conference would be concerned solely with internal Zionist questions, not diplomatic or political moves; these were, in any case, matters of lesser concern to Herzl. Lastly, Weizmann refrained from a direct attack against Herzl and explained that the aim of the Youth Conference was to halt the decline in the Zionist ranks and to counter the lack of initiative on the part of the majority of Russian Zionist intellectuals. Brushing aside the issue of party discipline, which Herzl had tried to invoke, Weizmann cited instead the democratic principles of the Zionist movement, which must be adhered to if one did not want to destroy the success that had been achieved in rallying young forces to the movement. One needed to be careful not to alienate the Jewish intelligentsia, the most vital force in Zionism.[81]

Although the Youth Conference clearly represented a challenge to his leadership, Herzl in fact disarmed Weizmann and his collaborators from the outset in a series of shrewd tactical moves. In his reply to Weizmann he apologized for the delay in the reaction of the Actions Committee to the proposed Youth Conference, appreciated Weizmann's promise that the conference would remain apolitical, and welcomed his intention to renew among the youth a sense of dedication to the movement.[82] His show of confidence assumed a mature political approach and once more placed responsibility on Weizmann's shoulders for proper behavior, lest he and his colleagues ruin Herzl's diplomatic achievements.[83]

Herzl had his own reasons for co-opting rather than further alienating the young Zionist intelligentsia. He considered the source of his troubles within the World Zionist Organization to be the vested interests and veteran leadership of the local organizations. Thus, any new leadership that arose might be preferable, and perhaps also more responsive, to his own influence.[84] Some of Herzl's colleagues demanded that Herzl publicly denounce the Youth Conference.[85] At the Greater Actions Committee meeting, which took place from October 9 to 12, 1901, there were sharp denunciations against the organizers of the conference.[86] Yet the following day, on October 13, Weizmann met Herzl[87] and was able to persuade him to adopt an officially favorable view toward the Youth Conference and even to assist in technical matters.[88] It was agreed that the Youth Conference would take place in Basel—instead of Geneva, as had originally been planned—a few days before the Fifth Zionist Congress was scheduled to begin.[89] As much as the results of the meeting attest to Weizmann's powers of persuasion, they also indicate Herzl's ability to defuse a potentially dangerous opposition before it got out of hand.[90] Both showed themselves to be seasoned politicians who understood the advantages of eliminating unnecessary direct confrontation. They left their lines of communication open pending further developments. Future events would attest to the wisdom of their decision.

The negotiations with Herzl reveal important characteristics in Weizmann. The young *Privat-Dozent,* whose experience in the movement hitherto was mainly as a propagandist, now showed that he was a first-rate tactician. Weizmann was essentially a pragmatic empiricist, not an opportunist, who believed in attaining the possible. He revealed an ability to maintain a flexible posture toward both the content of the ideas he represented as well as their method of implementation. He did not seek a final, decisive, and irrevocable break with the established leadership since he knew his own position and power base to be quite weak. Though he stood by his principles, at the same time he retained a skeptical attitude toward rigid ideological positions.

Emotionally draining as the negotiations with Herzl were for Weizmann—until their satisfactory conclusion two months before the Youth Conference—they represented a mere fraction of the enormous efforts he invested in this venture for some nine months, from April to December 1901. During this period there are very few references to his academic work, and it is clear that he was neglecting his research in chemistry.[91] His lodgings in Geneva became the headquarters of the Organization Bureau. He had help from four women: Anne Koenigsberg, Esther Shneerson, Rosa Grinblatt, and Catherine Dorfman.[92] Theoretically he was entitled to believe that others elected to the Conference Bureau—such as Jacob Bernstein-Kohan, Leo Motzkin, and Daniel Pasmanik—would pitch in. But Bernstein-Kohan was in a weak position, being on the payroll of the World Zionist Organization and constantly under attack by members of SAC; Motzkin could not be moved to do a thing, and Pasmanik soon switched sides. It was, in truth, the work of one man, a condition that essentially suited Weizmann's personal inclinations and style of work but was nevertheless wearying.

Although after the Munich Conference Weizmann clearly occupied the leading role in the preparation of the Youth Conference, he was still unsure of himself. He felt he needed Motzkin's support, or at least his tacit nod of approval.[93] In June Weizmann pleaded with Motzkin to present a paper at the Youth Conference. His posture toward Motzkin remained that of a student toward his teacher.[94] Upon hearing that Motzkin might not come to the Youth Conference, Weizmann practically fell on his knees before him in a gesture of self-negation: ". . . We cannot manage without our best comrades. You must realize that I am neither paying you compliments nor trying to be modest. I may be a good *Registriermaschine* [recording machine], I even have my own views on things, but you, my dear friend, you are the brains . . ."[95]

The "dear friend" finally consented to come and even take part in the debate, but throughout the long months of hard work and preparation he was as unhelpful as possible. Motzkin came up with one excuse after another. The real reasons for Motzkin's obstructiveness may have been Weizmann's break with Sophia Getzova,[96] though Weizmann continued to maintain friendly relations with her through correspondence and visits to her residence in Bern.[97] All in all, Motzkin did little to bring about the Youth Conference,[98] refused to prepare a paper for it,[99] and most of the time did not even bother to reply to Weizmann. Throughout it all Weizmann exercised infinite patience; on only one occasion did he reprimand Motzkin in "an official tone," but he hastened to apologize for this by explaining that he was angry.[100] Weizmann met with disappointment elsewhere as well. Bernard Lazare accorded Weizmann an initially friendly reception during the latter's visit to Paris in May and promised to deliver a paper at the Youth Conference on the economic condition of the Jewish people.[101] A month later Weizmann received a letter from Lazare, who declared that he did not accept the Basel Program and could not take part in the Youth Conference.[102] Ahad Ha'Am, who expressed his sympathy for the cause, also declined to participate since he was retiring from all public activities.[103]

There were problems from unexpected quarters. Together with a few colleagues, Nachman Syrkin—whose socialist views were already fully developed in 1898 in his essay "The Socialist Jewish State," which was modeled after Herzl's brochure—founded in Berlin an association named Hessiana in memory of Moses Hess.[104] On June 7, 1901, the association held its first public meeting. Syrkin's lecture was then published under the title "A Call to Jewish Youth."[105] Syrkin proposed two organizations: One would be a social democratic organization, supported by local workers, for economic and political rights in the countries where Jews lived, while the other would be a socialist Zionist group, supported by the bourgeoisie, which would work for immigration to Palestine. This two-pronged proposal was probably an attempt to appease the Bund, the Zionists' most serious opponent. He also called on socialist Zionism to fight orthodox obscurantism and attacked bourgeois Zionism for alienating progressive Jewish youth and discrediting the idea of a Jewish national renaissance. He called for class consciousness among the Jewish proletariat which could supplant the reactionary character of bourgeois Zionism.[106] Weizmann called these ideas "sheer madness." "It makes me indignant that people think it possible to feed 'youth' on such things,"[107] he told Leo Motzkin, and in a letter to Vera he wrote with condescension: ". . . A red cap with a blue and white ribbon, a national group hailing internationalism with childish yells, dancing around great names; self-worship and Jewish impudence. What an outrageous mixture of meaningless phrases and sheer stupidity!"[108] Shortly afterward it became apparent that Syrkin desired to convene a socialist Zionist conference similar to the Youth Conference, which would take place at the same time and in the same city. The Hessiana members also wished to participate in the Youth Conference as a group. There was opposition from Bernstein-Kohan to this, and Motzkin opposed the admission to the conference of Syrkin himself. In the end, the Hessiana was not represented, though Syrkin attended as a guest.

Syrkin's appeal was directed mainly toward the Russian-Jewish intellectuals. Weizmann was fully aware that he needed to drum up support among them as well if they were not to fall prey to Syrkin, the Bund, or the social democrats. On July 23, 1901, he left Geneva for Russia, passing through Bern and Berlin and arriving in Pinsk at the end of July, in time for his sister Hayah's wedding to his friend Abraham Lichtenstein. He had promised to visit Vera in Rostov but canceled his plans at the last minute with an unconvincing reason, pleading lack of time. Instead of a visit he treated her to a passionate sermon on Zionism. The cancellation may have been due to the fact that neither his nor Vera's parents knew the nature of their relationship.[109] Weizmann admitted that he failed to see in Russia much that would give him comfort. "The existing Zionist organizations suffer from a lack of people with profound understanding of their task and capable of filling positions in which circumstances have placed them; as a result, a terrible lack of vitality is evident in all groups . . . The results of all this are obvious: the body begins to weaken and disintegrate . . ."[110] His harshest criticism was reserved for Odessa, once the center of Zionist activities in Russia: ". . . Zionism there has degenerated into a paper kingdom of circulars, shekel receipts, and not fully paid-up shares of the J[ewish] C[olonial] T[rust] . . . It is my profound conviction that Odessa Zionism is a shameful blot on the entire cause . . . Not for nothing do the Litvaks say that hell burns for seven miles round Odessa . . ."[111]

Weizmann did not include in his summary report to Motzkin an incident that took place two months earlier, on August 29, 1901, in Nikolayev. While he was lecturing on Zionism in the synagogue, the building was surrounded by Cossacks, who had been tipped off by informers. Weizmann was arrested and interrogated by the chief of police, who proved not unsympathetic to the idea of Zionism if it meant getting rid of all the Jews.[112] Presenting a slightly different version of the incident, Weizmann wrote in his memoirs that the chief of police warned him as he was about to leave: "Look here! I see you're not a bad young man, really. Take my advice and have nothing more to do with those damn Jews. For if they ever get to this kingdom of theirs, the first man they'll string up to a lamppost will be you!"[113] As his report on Odessa indicates, there were indeed instances during the trip when Weizmann must have wished to have nothing more to do with those "damn Jews."

In his letter to Motzkin of October 27, 1901, Weizmann euphemistically called his summer months in Russia "vacations." In fact, he had only a few weeks of rest with his family in Pinsk immediately prior to and during the High Holidays. On October 10 he left for his meeting with Herzl and reached Geneva by the middle of the month. His new lodgings at 4, rue Lombard became the nerve center for the Organization Bureau. Given this hectic and unrelenting workload, it is not surprising that Weizmann buckled under from time to time. From the start he was beset by worries and anxiety over the attitude of Herzl and the Smaller Actions Committee, the necessity to get the right speakers on the Youth Conference agenda, and the lack of support from his peers and seniors both in the West and in Russia.[114] Weizmann described himself as a "beast of burden which after a short time gets reconciled to the load placed on its back."[115] But by the summer months this philosophical attitude often gave way to feelings of loneliness. The plans, the duties, and the worries began to weigh him down. In a letter to Vera he wrote that "if plots and intrigues are being hatched in secret I have absolutely no strength to fight them . . . I am powerless against underhanded tactics."[116] A few weeks later he wrote about the "terrible evil people" around him, for "whom nothing is sacred, who think only of profit and material gain and want to make capital out of public affairs," and even contemplated not attending the congress: "I shall simply not have the strength . . . and anyhow, what do they need me for?"[117] By the end of September his health began to deteriorate, his eyes started hurting, his nerves were shattered, and he was too weak to travel or take part in debates.[118] Three weeks before the Youth Conference he complained that "all this work is too much for me and if somebody doesn't help me I'll collapse before the Conference and shall not be able to take part . . ."[119]

At the same time Weizmann's activities were slowly propelling him to a leadership position, albeit only among a certain segment of the movement. Men like Ahad Ha'Am and Bernstein-Kohan took him seriously. Herzl had to negotiate with him. In this role he became more intimately acquainted with the movement and began to formulate its ideological implications for himself. Remarkably, Weizmann displayed a disdain for and frustration with the masses and their leaders, especially in Eastern Europe, while at the same time maintaining a commitment to Zionism as an ideology. His was an elitist approach to the solution of the Jewish Problem, a notion that only the intellectually superior could formulate Zionist ideology and lead the masses. This was a conception not unlike that of the philanthropic variety of Zionism in the West, with the qualification that throughout his life Weizmann continued to be attuned to the needs of the Jewish masses of Eastern Europe.

Weizmann was first and foremost a man of action, with very little patience for *batlanim*, for those who sat idly on the fence waiting for others to accomplish the necessary tasks. Weizmann had long since established sound working habits and expected much from himself. But he was haunted by the fear of becoming a *Luftmensch,* which made him turn with passion against what he considered unnecessary theoretical discussions and empty rhetoric. Among the East European students in his circle, he knew many he considered idlers. Since his days in Berlin, Weizmann looked at his Russian brethren with a mixture of contempt, pity, and an urgent desire to improve their lot. "Dr. Herzl," he wrote to Catherine Dorfman, "has no idea of Russian Zionism and of Russian Zionists . . . ,"[120] but Weizmann himself often described these Russian Zionists in the most derogatory language:

> . . . I often look around and see nothing but ruins, and instead of human heads—just cattle . . . They contribute nothing, absolutely nothing; they will not even sacrifice their peace of mind for the cause. We don't need such people; they're just a nuisance and only fit for cannon fodder. How much longer shall we have to wait for the right people? A very, very long time, until the day Israel gets stronger and we have assembled a group of united, honest fighters. Look around, look closely at the Jews of Russia, at their ser-vile faces, at those insipid, indolent idlers, and you can see what has be-come of this once highly cultured nation with such rich potentialities. I have no faith in the present Zionist masses. They are lifeless people who have had their day . . .[121]

The problem, as Weizmann saw it, was that Russian Zionists were smug, that phrasemaking had eaten too deep into the national fabric.

Weizmann's disappointment with the state of Zionism, in Russia and in the West, did not seem to affect his vision of what it meant to be a Zionist. Far from rejecting political Zionism out of hand, he was never-theless distressed by the neglect of what he called "the prophetic aspect of Zionism."[122] It was the duty of each individual to sacrifice everything for the cause. Weizmann mocked the *Shabes*-Zionists.[123] It was clear to him that "it is *imperative* that private life should not interfere with the fulfillment of public duty . . ."[124] His fate was to work even if he would not see the fruit of his labors.

> . . . here lies the whole horror of the Jewish problem—one has to work in such terrible conditions, where one doesn't know who is friend or foe, when the stench of decay hits one at every step. And years will pass, and many will still fall victim to these terrible conditions before creative, constructive work starts. Are we going to see all that? No. I doubt it. Our fate, the fate of people who live in a time of transition, is to be given activities of a purely negative character. To understand and ponder over old Jewish values, to understand only to discard them perhaps, or to reappraise them at a later stage . . .[125]

Weizmann's evaluation of Zionist progress was bound up with his own daily failures and successes. Despite his disappointment with the state of the movement in Russia, he felt that on the whole Zionism did have some good, honest supporters who would eventually triumph.

He completely identified with the cause of Zionism and was therefore willing to sacrifice a great deal for it. What he was not willing to do was to create a separate organization apart from the World Zionist Organization, as had been suggested by Ahad Ha'Am. In fact, he insisted that delegates to the Youth Conference be members of the World Zionist Organization.[126] His views on the Youth Conference were that it must be a democratic nucleus of young workers who would agree on a positive attitude toward the World Zionist Organization in the sense of taking part in it and working on behalf of its institutions, while maintaining a critical attitude toward the "clericals" and the Zionist bourgeoisie *(baalei-batim)*. In short, the young Zionists' role in the general World Zionist Organization must be twofold: to work and to criticize. Echoing the decisions in Munich, Weizmann singled out the following as the tasks of the Youth Conference: educational activities; the study of Jewish economic life; the theoretical study of Palestine, with the aid of the bank (here Weizmann volunteered to join a delegation for the study of Palestine); propaganda among the intelligentsia; and the establishment of mutual aid funds.[127] Weizmann made it clear that for him practical work was more important than theoretical formulations, that the debates were more significant than the major papers to be read at the conference.[128] But in a letter to the editor of *Voskhod* he emphasized that the principles guiding practical work must be based on well-thought-out theories and empirical data.[129]

Weizmann could justifiably see the covening of the Zionist Youth Conference, which met in Basel from December 18 to 23, 1901, as a personal triumph. Some forty delegates, mostly students, came from universities in Germany, Switzerland, France, Vienna, Prague, and Russia.[130] Among the delegates was Sophia Getzova, who came, it would seem, at Weizmann's suggestion.[131] Weizmann, Motzkin, and Bernstein-Kohan were elected co-chairmen of the conference. According to the incomplete minutes, Weizmann delivered the inaugural address, which called for an autonomous faction within the World Zionist Organization and repeated the reasons for the necessity of establishing such an organization.[132]

Though Motzkin had lost his temper before the conference at having been included as a speaker on the agenda without his permission, he proceeded to deliver a speech. He demanded an independent democratic faction that would also participate in diplomatic activities, the beginning of settlement work in Palestine, and the removal of all fanatic religious ideologies from Zionist activity. He also suggested that the faction undertake cultural work independently of the World Zionist Organization, and that Zionists take a hand in the organization of Jewish workers along trade union lines, yet at the same time dissociating socialism from Zionist activity in Eastern Europe.[133] There were other lectures that followed Motzkin's: Joshua Bukhmil spoke about the theoretical foundations of Zionism; Zvi Aberson scored a great success with his usual attack against the Bund and the assimilationists;[134] Israel Belkind gave a lecture on Palestine; Ferdinand Kobler discussed cultural work; and Isidore Eliashev lectured on Jewish newspapers.[135]

In the general discussion that ensued after each of the major papers,

Weizmann took issue with Motzkin. Weizmann was often cruel in debate. What is surprising is that he also used very strong language against— of all people—Motzkin, whom he still saw as his "teacher and guide." Weizmann stated that Motzkin was wrong in his view that the Faction undertake cultural work independently of the World Zionist Organization; rather, its aim should be to press for a congress resolution in favor of cultural activity; he also objected to Motzkin's Marxist-tinged notions about Jewish workers since they would involve the Faction in the domestic politics of the countries concerned. Weizmann's tone toward Motzkin was sharp and stinging throughout; it no doubt reflected the personal antagonism between the two men over the Getzova affair. Perhaps unconsciously, Weizmann sought to repay Motzkin publicly for the humiliation the latter had inflicted on him during the past few months:

> . . . Mr. Motzkin's program consists of a lot of negative points. It is not a program but a piece of polemic . . . when Mr. Motzkin does bring forward positive points, he is not consistent. One of these points is in the field of economic activity. Mr. Motzkin says that in this sphere a special investigation should be carried out into the condition of the Jewish working class, since its members suffer both as workers and as Jews . . . Mr. Motzkin puts the question in an opportunist and damaging way . . . I don't understand [Mr. Motzkin's] point about rendering assistance to the working class. Platonic participation is out of the question, and if we speak of active participation, I do not see any difference between Mr. Motzkin and the Zionists-Socialists.
>
> Mr. Motzkin speaks of the need to free ourselves from chauvinism, religion, romanticism, etc. This is altogether a question of tact . . . Whenever Mr. Motzkin spoke concerning actual Zionist work he was very lame. As regards the founders' shares of the bank that he spoke about, we are of course in complete agreement with him, but I am not satisfied with his superficial approach, that is to say, his calling for publication of the notarial document which will oblige the members of the *Aufsichtsrat* to hand over the shares to the control of Congress if they are not reelected . . .
>
> I now turn to the question of culture. Mr. Motzkin says that we must take the initiative in culture. I find this inconsistent, because we should not make any compromises. Cultural activity must be sanctioned by Congress . . .[136]

Motzkin did not forgive Weizmann for this scathing criticism, which was delivered in an ironic and derogatory tone.[137] The personal rift between the two dominant personalities in the Youth Conference was bound to create severe problems in the organization that was now to be created.

The Youth Conference, which ended on the evening of December 23, 1901, did not result, as Weizmann had originally assumed, in the establishment of a Zionist youth organization. It was finally agreed to form a *Fraktion,* a "Democratic Faction" within the World Zionist Organization which would unite all the "progressive elements" in the movement and would be free to express its views, especially concerning reforms and the structure of the World Zionist Organization and, when necessary, to oppose the leadership on any question, including political issues. The thirty-seven delegates who constituted the Democratic Faction decided to create an Information Bureau to be directed by Weizmann in Geneva. Its program was to be worked out by a committee, to be guided by a "Protocol" which stated that the structure of the World Zionist Organization must be reformed in conformity with democratic principles and could not revolve around a particular personality. In addition, the Democratic Faction must undertake cultural work independent of such activities by other bodies, and it must investigate the physical, political, and social conditions of Palestine. Lastly, the Democratic Faction asserted that any group of Zionists having distinct views in common ought to unite as a faction since such groupings were essential to the healthy development of the Zionist movement.[138]

The Democratic Faction represented the first attempt at organized opposition to the established Zionist leadership, in this case to Herzl himself. It was, if not in name, the first embryonic party in the movement's history. It was thus natural that it would meet with opposition from that very same leadership, but the first attacks against it came from the Zionist leadership in Russia, which no doubt was incensed by the new challenge to its own authority in Eastern Europe. It attacked the Democratic Faction in its *Vorkonferenz*, which began deliberation on December 23. Headed by Menahem Ussishkin, the thirty-five Russian opponents organized into a "United Faction" with the aim of opposing any move to destroy the unity of the World Zionist Organization, to encourage all segments of Jewry to join the latter, and to define as the most urgent need the creation of a Jewish center in Palestine.[139] In the end, the *Vorkonferenz* elected a committee to handle its affairs at the Fifth Zionist Congress; it was composed of twelve people, six of them members of the Democratic Faction. This ratio effectively illustrated its strength in the congress since the Russian delegates numbered eight members, whereas the Democratic Faction, which, of course, also included a minority of non-Russians, numbered thirty-seven.

It was clear to all concerned that the Fifth Zionist Congress, held from December 26 to 30, 1901, would be a stormy affair. Herzl was not in this situation for the first time and realized that he had to tread with greatest care so as not to offend either Constantinople or the various groupings within the movement: "I have written my Congress speech," he wrote on December 19, 1901, "—more of an egg dance than ever before."[140] He was referring to the need to balance and direct the proceedings at the congress as delicately as possible, a rare feat which had no spectator other than the one performing it.[141] There was good reason for his trepidation. Herzl had nothing to add to his earlier reports to the Actions Committee and to *Die Welt* regarding his relations with the sultan. In addition, many delegates still remembered with·distaste the Fourth Zionist Congress in London and were determined that this one should proceed differently and result in tangible achievements. In this context, the 37 delegates who formed the Democratic Faction represented a substantial power within the 287 delegates to the congress; as the only group with a definite program it was often able to dominate the congress proceedings.

The cultural question provoked a severe clash between Herzl and the Democratic Faction. During the second day of the Congress it became clear that matters would come to a head when Max Nordau, Herzl's confidant and staunch supporter, spoke about "questions concerning the physical, intellectual and economic amelioration of the Jews." Toward the end of this lecture he belittled the empty discussions concerning the issue of intellectual improvement of the Jews.[142] Martin Buber, who lectured the following day on Jewish art, took strong exception to Nordau's derogatory attitude toward cultural questions.[143] There were other matters on which members of the Democratic Faction disagreed with the regnant opinions and procedures at the congress. From the first day many of the delegates raised questions concerning the bank, activities of the Smaller Actions Committee, and organizational problems. On this last question the Fifth Zionist Congress—with Herzl's blessings—instituted changes in the structural principles of the movement and made it easier for new groups, including ideological factions, to organize outside the framework of the existing Zionist territorial organizations and come in direct contact with the central governing bodies of the World Zionist Organization.[144] Thus, Weizmann's and the Democratic Faction's conception of homogeneous factions within the World Zionist Organization was accepted and represented a major change in the movement's organization, with far-reaching implications for the future.

The various demonstrations and criticisms of and by members of the Democratic Faction were a prelude to the evening session of the last day of the congress, which lasted until four-thirty in the morning. On the first day of the congress a cultural commission was elected; it included five members of the Democratic Faction, among them Weizmann and Buber.[145] At the last session Buber presented the congress with its proposals, the main one being the following: "The Congress declares the cultural improvement, that is, the education of the Jewish people in the national spirit, to be one of the essential elements of the Zionist program and requires all its adherents to participate in it." Buber also presented resolutions which called for support for the Jewish national library in Jerusalem; for the Actions Committee to demand of the Stockholm-based Nobel Prize institute to accord modern Hebrew and Jewish literature their place in the library of the institute; for the establishment of a cultural commission in every territorial organization; for the collection of statistical materials on Jewry; for an examination of the feasibility of a Jewish institution of higher learning; and support for a Jewish publishing house and the distribution of its prospectus.[146]

Weizmann, who had earlier in the congress raised some questions about the democratic nature of the Jewish Colonial Trust, now rose to explain the need for preparatory work for the establishment of a Jewish *Hochschule*—a term which covered a technical institution and vocational school

The Democratic Faction, with Herzl (seated in center of second row), at Fifth Zionist Congress, 1901

as well as a regular academic university program and was thus often referred to as the Jewish University project. The idea was not new. It had been put forward at the First Zionist Congress by Professor Hermann Schapira, but no practical suggestions for the founding of a university had been made at the time or since. Weizmann had given the idea some thought during the previous year,[147] though it was not yet clear to him what shape such a university would take or where it would be located. What was clear was the fact that, due to the new restrictions against Jewish students in Russia and attempts to restrict their numbers in the West, the project needed urgent consideration. Weizmann's speech at the congress was couched in general terms. His main demand was that "we Zionists must intervene here, too, and though we are conscious of the fact that we are not yet in a position to accomplish anything concrete in this matter, we must nevertheless begin with the collection of information, and if we do this in the name of the congress we may hope that a propaganda campaign, conducted in the name of Zionism, will bear fruit. What we are asking for is the preparatory work, the preliminary research . . . Such new perspectives open up [the possibility] for a Jewish professional institute [*Fachschule*] which would also become a citadel of Jewish studies [juedische Wissenschaft] . . ."[148]

There were reactions to the demands of the cultural commission from the two orthodox rabbis present at the congress, Rabinovich and Reines, with the latter declaring outright: "The cultural question is a disaster for us. Culture will destroy everything. Our region is completely orthodox. With culture it will be lost. Cultural questions must not be part of the Basel Program . . ."[149] With some sixty delegates registered for the debate, Herzl tried to defer the discussion and decision on the resolutions submitted by the Democratic Faction until after the election of the Actions Committee, that is, until the closing hours of the congress. Motzkin, Buber, and the artist Ephraim Lilien protested and appealed this decision. Herzl forced his viewpoint after a harsh discussion on procedure. This so embittered the members of the Democratic Faction that without prior agreement they got up and left the hall for an hour as a sign of protest.[150] The exit of the Democratic Faction made a deep and, for the most part, negative impression on the congress, this being the first such instance in the movement's history and thus constituting a dangerous precedent—as became evident in the Sixth Zionist Congress. Alexander Marmorek, who immediately understood these implications, turned to Herzl with a request to stop this spontaneous exit. Herzl replied, "Don't get upset. These are not the worst people among us."[151] Later Berthold Feiwel presented Herzl with an official protest on behalf of the Democratic Faction and informed him that he and Weizmann had resigned from the congress secretariat.[152]

Having asserted his authority, Herzl opened the floor to debate on the cultural question as soon as the elections had taken place. The Faction had, in the meantime, returned to the congress hall—without Weizmann. When they began to inquire after him, they were told that Herzl's attitude toward the Democratic Faction so affected him that he took ill. Thus, Weizmann missed the final session of the congress.[153] Most of the resolutions of the cultural commission were accepted, including the major resolution which declared the cultural question an essential element of the Zionist program. A large cultural commission was set up, composed of, among others, Nahum Sokolow, Ahad Ha'Am, Bernstein-Kohan, Martin Buber, Israel Zangwill, Rabbi Moses Gaster, and Chaim Weizmann. On the other hand, no funds were set aside for subvention of the publishing house Juedischer Verlag. Concerning the university, Herzl declared that the Actions Committee was very interested in this issue and would continue to investigate it. It was clear that Herzl wanted the adoption of the resolutions, for which he voted demonstratively.[154] All in all, the members of the Faction had good reason to be satisfied with their achievements at the congress.[155]

In his concluding speech, in which he enumerated the achievements of the congress—the opening of the bank for business, the final creation of the Jewish National Fund, and the revision of the statutes of the World Zionist Organization—Herzl also expressed his pleasure at the presence at the congress of "a youthful group, which is faithful, sometimes in a rather lively way . . ."[156] Herzl was not far off the mark. The day after the close of the congress, Weizmann appeared at the head of the Democratic Faction, which he presented to Herzl with the following quip: "Before you stands His Majesty's most loyal opposition."[157] Weizmann spoke in a humorous vein, but his words accurately reflected his concept of the role and obligations of the Democratic Faction.

VI

Public Ventures and Private Affairs

Within less than a month Weizmann had a chance to prove that the Democratic Faction was, in fact, a loyal opposition which stood within the World Zionist Organization and defended not only the principles of the Basel Program but also the leader chosen to implement this program. On the eve of the Fifth Zionist Congress Herzl had sent a cable to Sultan Abdul Hamid in which he declared, in the name of those assembled at Basel, the "acknowledgment of deep devotion and of . . . gratitude which all Jews feel for the benevolence always shown them by H. I. M. the Sultan . . ."[1] This telegram was acknowledged by the Sublime Porte, a fact which Herzl made known to the congress during the evening session of December 28.[2] The participants at the congress received the news with a standing ovation. Not so the Bulgarian, Greek, Polish, Georgian, Russian, Armenian, and some anti-Zionist Jewish students of Geneva who read about it in the press. On December 30 they passed a resolution protesting indignantly Herzl's gesture toward "the arch-assassin Abdul Hamid" and expressing contempt for the Zionist congress. This was communicated to Herzl by cable.[3]

Upon returning from Basel to Geneva, Weizmann and his friends organized three meetings to defend Herzl.[4] One important outcome of these meetings was that those supporting Herzl's telegram to the sultan split away from the other Jewish students and, at the end of January 1902, formed a Zionist student society called Hashahar (The Dawn), headed by Weizmann.[5] Vera also joined. So did Zvi Aberson, whose brilliant talk at the Youth Conference gained him a special stature among the students. He was commissioned by the Faction to turn it into a pamphlet, visited some of the important European libraries for this purpose, and finally returned to Geneva empty-handed. Although Weizmann considered Aberson a *batlan* par excellence, he also admired and cherished him.[6] It is not quite clear why a group such as Hashahar was necessary since the Geneva Zionist Society, of which Weizmann was president, had been in existence since April 1899.[7] Perhaps Weizmann felt the need to regroup his followers in a revitalized organization in light of the creation of the Democratic Faction, whose members were dispersed throughout

Western and Eastern Europe. Possibly he saw this as an opportunity to found a group of loyal followers who would form a counterpoint to the Motzkin-dominated Kadimah in Berlin.

In light of the events at the Fifth Zionist Congress, it is not surprising that a telegram to Ahad Ha'Am was sent in the name of Hashahar which stated: "The Geneva Hashahar group extends its greetings to the dear and only Ahad Ha'Am, and wishes him long and glorious service to the national cause."[8] Yet a telegram of respectful greetings also went from Hashahar to Herzl.[9] Both telegrams were sent at Weizmann's initiative. They were not sent to these two personalities, who stood at opposite ends of the Zionist ideological spectrum, merely out of diplomatic considerations. That Ahad Ha'Am was seen as a spiritual mentor of the Democratic Faction is clear; one could even make the case that the Faction was the spiritual successor of the now defunct Bnei Moshe. And yet, for all his criticisms of Herzl, Weizmann continued to admire the man and have faith in the possibilities of a diplomatic triumph by him. Herzl had traveled to Constantinople in mid-February 1902 at the invitation of the Porte.[10] Writing to Vera, Weizmann commented that "great things are happening in Zionism now. Our dear, untiring leader is in Constantinople, and yesterday I received a telegram from Buber in Vienna: 'Wide concessions expected.' Keep this secret, my little girl!"[11] In the event, there was not much to keep secret. Though Herzl was able, for the first time, to actually negotiate with the sultan's subordinates, he did not come away with any tangible results.[12]

Weizmann was too much of a pragmatist to dismiss Herzl's diplomatic efforts. He realized the propagandistic value Herzl's negotiations had had on the movement itself and in the eyes of outside observers; he himself was later to employ the Herzl technique: negotiations with powerful individuals and governments as if backed by a strong, united, and well-endowed organization. As future developments were to bear out, Weizmann went one step further. He later acted in the name of the Democratic Faction after it had all but ceased to exist.

In the period after the Fifth Zionist Congress, the Democratic Faction seemed to be well launched. Its members had reason to expect an even more decisive success in the future. It also appeared to outsiders that Weizmann had emerged from the Youth Conference and the Fifth Zionist Congress as the Faction's strong man. True, Martin Buber and Leo Motzkin shone more than Weizmann at the congress, but it was clear even to casual observers that without Weizmann's persistence and organizing ability the Democratic Faction would never have been established. Yet the Faction's initial success was not left unchallenged. The important paper *Hamelitz*, which was close to orthodox circles, called the members of the Faction "the heroes of claptrap."[13] Menahem Ussishkin, the powerful leader of the Russian Zionists, who represented the United Faction, continued to view the Democratic Faction as an ineffective and artificial instrument.[14] He had little regard for the Russian-Jewish colonies in the West, calling them "the hot-air factories."[15] The annual meeting *(Delegiertentag)* of the German Zionist Federation (ZVfD), which took place in May in Mannheim, also objected to the formation of the Faction,[16] and there were other attacks in both Eastern and Western Europe.[17] There were, of course, also defenders of the Faction, notably Klausner, who went on record in *Hashiloah*'s January 1902 issue,[18] but these seem to have been fewer in number.

Had it continued to react as a cohesive group, as it showed itself capable of doing at the congress, the Democratic Faction would have been able to weather these minor skirmishes. Yet from the outset the Faction was faced with enormous organizational and interpersonal problems: The students from whom it derived its strength were preoccupied by a myriad of problems of their own, mostly the need to finish their training and earn a living. Once the congress was over, their enthusiasm subsided in the face of daily struggles. Few were in Weizmann's enviable position of having an academic appointment and some funds, and fewer still could contribute to the cause either with their time or materially. The Russians—including Bernstein-Kohan, Shmarya Levin, Isidore Eliashev, Victor Jacobson, David Farbstein, and others—who were senior to Weizmann in age and service to the movement, and whose stature was necessary to bolster the prestige of the Faction, were somewhat intimidated by Ussishkin's opposition. In any case they could not, for economic and political reasons inherent to life in Russia, help much and on an ongoing basis. But the crucial factor in the eventual demise of the Faction was the fact that the Youth Conference had not endowed any one person with the leadership role. The division of power and tasks between Berlin and Geneva bore the seeds of destruction. Such a division would have been problematic under the best of circumstances. Given the antagonism and power struggle between Motzkin and Weizmann, who respectively headed the Faction members in Berlin and Geneva, failure to carry any meaningful work to a reasonable conclusion was all but assured.

The first salvo to strike at the unity of the Faction came from none other than Motzkin. In addition to his grievance against Weizmann for the Getzova affair, he now had an added reason to be angry, namely, Weizmann's harsh criticism of his speech at the Youth Conference. Motzkin sought an opportune moment to repay him in kind and to humiliate Weizmann publicly. The opportunity presented itself immediately after the congress in the wake of an error of judgment made by Weizmann. In 1901 Nachman Syrkin had founded an organization called Herut (Freedom), which held its official founding congress in 1902.[19] The function of Herut was to wage war on the major Jewish philanthropic organizations in the West, particularly the Jewish Colonization Association (ICA). The plan was to lead the Jewish masses from Whitechapel in London in demonstrations against the ICA in order to force the organization to provide financial support for Zionist activities.[20] It was not new. ICA had often been the target of Zionist ire. Weizmann himself had mentioned a similar idea in November 1902 in a letter to Motzkin.[21] Moreover, Weizmann must have clearly remembered the humiliation inflicted upon Ahad Ha'Am and other Zionists by Baron Edmond Rothschild, which was directly linked to ICA procedures in Palestine. At the Fourth Zionist Congress there had been an unsuccessful attempt by Syrkin to extract money from the ICA for the Zionist movement by means of an organized protest demonstration.[22] Even such dignified Western representatives as Max Nordau and Israel Zangwill had used strong language in connection with the ICA at the fourth and fifth Zionist congresses.[23] When the program of the Democratic Faction was finally articulated in June 1902, it contained a resolution that called on all Zionists to "commence the battle against [the ICA] with the greatest energy . . ."[24] It was natural enough for Weizmann to accept an invitation extended by Syrkin at the Fifth Zionist Congress to a few members of the Democratic Faction to discuss the idea of a demonstration in London against the ICA.[25] Though these talks had not been authorized by the newly founded Democratic Faction as a whole, they would not have aroused controversy had the initiative not come from Syrkin. Weizmann himself had some qualms on this account, since Syrkin had been something of an outcast in respectable Zionist circles.[26] Clearly Weizmann, who had prevented Syrkin's Hessiana group from attending the Youth Conference,[27] was well aware of Syrkin's place in the movement; he had accepted the latter's invitation since the issue at stake was widely known and of immediate concern. Perhaps he thought Herzl might be attracted to the idea.[28]

Nevertheless, Weizmann made a mistake by not consulting the Democratic Faction as an organization before agreeing to a meeting with Syrkin, and Motzkin was determined to make him pay for it. The matter could certainly have been handled quietly, but Motzkin wanted a public humiliation which, at the same time, would assert the preeminence of the Faction's Berlin branch and his own personal leadership. Seven members[29] of the Democratic Faction in Berlin met on January 9, 1902, and unanimously resolved to request the Geneva Information Bureau to notify immediately all members of the Faction about the breach of discipline committed by Weizmann, Menahem Sheinkin, and Joshua Bukhmil.[30] The written protest that was sent from Berlin to Geneva stated that the Berlin members viewed the organization of activities against the ICA with great misgiving since it was taken without the knowledge of the entire membership, which had been present at the congress when this transgression took place. Other reasons were that the demonstration against the ICA was planned in concert with a person who stood outside the Faction (Syrkin), and that those involved had turned to Herzl, who may have been misled to believe that they spoke in the name of the entire Democratic Faction membership:

> All the aforesaid forces us to regard the actions of our members as going against the Faction's discipline and tactics and good common sense. Moreover, this rude breach of discipline at the beginning of the Faction's existence discredits the Faction in the eyes of other persons and demoralizes it in the eyes of the members themselves, bringing to naught its moral au-

thority and granting unlimited liberty of action to each of its members, which is inadmissible in any organization, and especially in our Democratic Faction.

We, seven of the members of the Faction, consider it our moral duty to protest against such a breach of discipline as an act which disrupts our corporate solidarity and thus adversely affects our work . . .[31]

Weizmann had the full backing of the Geneva Information Bureau in this matter, but he did not want a split in the Democratic Faction and tried at first to settle matters amicably. His first letter to Motzkin began with a Hebrew passage from the New Year liturgy: "I tremble when I open my mouth to utter my words."[32] He immediately touched, though in the form of questions, on Motzkin's real motivations for sending the official protest: ". . . is this protest the result of a carefully considered strategy? . . . I think that your action is fraught with disastrous consequences for our common cause. If you did not mean to 'protest' against us, but to point out, for the sake of the cause, the error we have made—was an 'official' protest really necessary? Could not a simple, friendly exchange of views have preceded this drastic, irrevocable step? Could you not have found some way of having it out with me otherwise than through the Information Bureau? Is it possible that you have acted on the spur of the moment?"[33]

Then came the explanations and excuses which, at the same time, did not amount to an admission of guilt: Those who took part in the deliberations had promised not to divulge anything; the initiative for the meeting did not come from Weizmann; the idea of combating the ICA was in conformity with prevailing notions within the Zionist movement and, in any case, the meetings were on a consultative basis; there could be no talk of public action since they were still debating the issue; Weizmann had the right to discuss matters in private which conformed with his own beliefs; discussions with Herzl were not on behalf of the Democratic Faction; all who took part in the meetings did so as individuals and therefore did not breach party discipline; and, finally, the Democratic Faction itself had not yet decided in principle whether one of its members could take part in an honorable matter without asking permission of the entire group. Weizmann ended his letter with an appeal to Motzkin's conscience and feelings: ". . . I have proved by my work that I am able to do anything that seems to me expedient and necessary for the cause. Is it really necessary, just like this, to reproach a man for his willingness to do some work, where *die ganze Person* [his whole being] is at stake? . . . you must not and cannot condemn your already exhausted friend."[34]

Motzkin was unmoved, alternating between periods of rude silence, in which he ignored Weizmann's appeals, and insulting demands that Weizmann appear in person in Berlin to give account of himself.[35] The Berlin members continued to insist on publication of their protest in one of the Faction's circulars. Weizmann tried to reason with Motzkin again: "We have known each other and worked together for nine years. Is one instant sufficient to destroy everything? . . . I declare that your protest will have lamentable results: it will blow up the Faction and throw to the winds everything that has started to take shape. You are throwing a bombshell without taking into consideration that it will wreck the entire venture . . . Good-bye . . . I should like to express my fervent wish to put an end to all this. It hurts."[36] Weizmann's pleas were buttressed by the more official tone of the Geneva Information Bureau, which asked Berlin on February 2 to reconsider its demand for publication. The Berliners would not reconsider and their protest was finally published as a confidential appendix to the Information Bureau's third newsletter on March 18, 1902. A rejoinder was made by Weizmann and Zvi Aberson on April 20 in the fourth newsletter, which was also the last to be published by the Information Bureau.[37]

The matter did not rest there. In mid-March Motzkin urged Weizmann to come to Berlin in order to reestablish normal relations between the Berlin group and the Information Bureau in Geneva. But this time it was Weizmann who was not in a hurry. Chemistry and his own research would take priority. Already in January he had reported that his laboratory work was going very well.[38] By mid-March he had completed an important piece of research in collaboration with Deichler which would reduce the cost of alazarin—a basic material in the manufacture of dye-stuffs—by 30 to 35 percent. He was eager to demonstrate the discovery to the Bayer Works at Elberfeld, as was required by his contract.[39] He was quite confident of the results and in a moment of ecstasy wrote: "If it proves technically sound, for from the scientific point of view there is no doubt, I shall drop chemistry for two or three years and travel to America to do propagandistic work, and throughout Russia also, all of which can easily happen . . ."[40]

It took almost two weeks for Weizmann to arrive in Berlin. On the way he visited Sophia Getzova and her dying sister in Bern, spent the Purim holiday with his friends in Heidelberg, and stayed three days with Deichler in Nieder-Ingelheim. A few hours after his arrival in Berlin, on March 28, he met with Motzkin. That night he wrote to Vera in a mood of great depression and loneliness: ". . . Motzkin, of course, is offended, and, generally, exasperates me by his false enthusiasm and his utter worthlessness. Some compromise will surely be reached, but the wound will not heal, since we can no longer have the same attitude to each other as we used to have . . . I would sacrifice everything for the cause not to suffer [because of internal bickering]."[41] Over the next two days there were a series of meetings between Weizmann and the Berlin group. A compromise was indeed reached; it is not quite clear what was decided, but it seems that Motzkin's attempt to assert his and Berlin's prime authority over the Geneva Information Bureau had failed.

The tactics Weizmann employed are unknown, but it is clear that he was at least partially successful in dividing the opposition. Among the "lively elements" in Berlin were Berthold Feiwel, whom he had already met at Basel, and Felix Pinkus, two "Western" Zionist students. "Feiwel is a joy," he wrote to Vera. "In his company one can relax."[42] And a day later: "I am spending the whole time at Feiwel's . . . He is a wonderful man and is most gifted . . . It's quite possible that he will come to me for a rest because he is physically worn out."[43] Within a couple of days after his arrival in Berlin, Feiwel had replaced Motzkin as Weizmann's most trusted friend. Weizmann left Berlin for Switzerland with Pinkus after having persuaded Feiwel to come to Switzerland for rest and joint work in Zionist affairs.[44]

Weizmann departed from Berlin in a triumphant mood. It was almost a year to the day since the preparatory conference had convened in Munich, and in this short period of time he had witnessed the creation of the Democratic Faction and weathered a serious challenge to its unity. The breach had now been patched, but the alliance between Berlin and Geneva was precarious at best. By the time he left Berlin, Motzkin was no longer the unchallenged leader of the "progressive" and "radical" forces of Russian Zionists in the West. At best he was now recognized by Weizmann as an equal. With time Weizmann's contempt for Motzkin's inertia deepened and his respect for his erstwhile teacher evaporated. Weizmann's self-esteem, which had often been bruised by Motzkin, was now restored, but, at the same time, he was unable to move the Berliners to active participation in the Faction's affairs. What made matters particularly difficult was the fact that the Youth Conference had elected a committee to draft the program of the Democratic Faction, in which Motzkin was the central figure.[45] But Motzkin, as usual, was not in a hurry to take the initiative in convening this committee. "Everybody is looking forward to the results of the program committee's work," wrote Weizmann to Motzkin. "As far as I know, nothing has yet been done by the other members—I don't know how things are with you. It's March already, and the program must be published by the end of the month."[46] Seven weeks later he inquired again: "What's happening in the program committee? Have you had a reply from the other members of the committee? Do I have to write to them? . . ."[47]

The delay in the work of the program committee was not due solely to Motzkin's inertia. Most of its members were either too poor to pay for the fare to the West or too busy with their studies. Finally five members of the committee met in Heidelberg for six days (June 16–22).[48] Most of the preparatory work and early drafts for the program were done by Motzkin, and most of his suggestions were accepted without alterations. The result was a rather cumbersome and wordy twenty-four-page document divided into six sections, including a general section on Zionist principles, one detailing the reasons for the need for factions in Zionism, one on the history of the Faction, one on its special program, a temporary statute, and a section on tactics.[49] The most detailed and informative chapter dealt with the Faction's special program, which foreshadowed many activities later undertaken by the World Zionist Organization. The program reiterated the Faction's adherence to the Basel Program, to principles of democracy in the Zionist movement, and its commitment to cultural work and social justice for all Jews, declaring that Zionism is not a reaction to anti-Semitism but stems from the will of the Jewish nation to maintain and develop its unique and individual characteristics.[50]

As to its practical program, the Faction declared war against opportunism in Zionism, against the use by nonreligious Jews of religion as a basis for Zionism, against philanthropic Zionism, and against hero worship *(Personenkultus)*, the last item being a reference to Herzl. All Zionist institutions must be run democratically, including the bank, the Jewish National Fund, and *Die Welt*, the official organ of the movement. In Palestine all land must be owned by the state and cooperative ventures are to be encouraged. The Zionist movement needs to prepare the ground for work in Palestine through research, purchase of as much land as possible, and the establishment of a special office in Palestine. The Faction will strive for the promotion of extensive cultural enterprises, such as the study of the Hebrew language and Judaica in general, Jewish languages, Jewish art, a Jewish university in Palestine, museums, and so forth. It would also promote sport, productive agricultural work, and cooperatives. As to ICA and the Alliance Israélite Universelle, it was decided to try to transfer the first into the hands of the Jewish nation (i.e., the Zionist movement) and to combat assimilation in the latter. Finally, the Faction called for immigration to Palestine.[51]

This program presented a challenge to the Zionist movement as a whole and to its leadership in particular. Many of the program points had been paid lip service previously in various Zionist forums; now the Democratic Faction demanded their activation. At the same time, the program committee, and Motzkin in particular, also presented a last personal challenge to Weizmann, since it was decided that until the Faction's full membership meeting in October, the program committee would administer its affairs.[52] There is no evidence that Weizmann even responded to the challenge. It was devoid of meaning from the start, since the members of the committee were dispersed throughout Western Europe. A month later Weizmann commented, with a mixture of anger and irony, "Motzkin has at last sent a program . . . As to convening a Faction Conference, he says (very characteristically) that he is ready to take the leadership on himself if Geneva agrees to carry out a considerable portion of the work, but Geneva doesn't want Mr. M[otzkin]'s leadership. This would mean doing all the work so that M[otzkin] could then write protests. *Tant mieux* . . ."[53] Weizmann was by now involved with the university project, which had priority in his eyes, and he waited to see how Motzkin would fare in handling the affairs of the Faction. In July he wrote to Motzkin with considerable satisfaction, referring to the committee's decision to publish news bulletins, draft a program of action, enroll new members, and arrange for the Faction's first conference: "The program has not yet arrived . . . Not a single decision has been implemented as yet . . ."[54] After countless reminders to Motzkin, who was revising and rewriting it, the Faction's program was finally printed in August 1902 in German; a Russian edition appeared in January 1903.[55]

In the midst of the controversy with Motzkin over the ICA issue, Weizmann complained, "For the present, I must report that a blissful state of inactivity reigns in the Faction. Nobody has done a thing, nobody has carried out the work he undertook, nobody has fulfilled even such passive duties as sending subscriptions . . . I can't give any reply to anyone. First, because I am just a letter-box and can't do a thing, and secondly because I have no idea what has been done by the others and in what way . . ."[56]

As so often occurred when he was trying to impress his correspondent with the urgency of his case, Weizmann was exaggerating. True, from a purely organizational point of view the Faction was in disarray almost from the start, due to lack of leadership and internecine warfare. Apart from Weizmann himself, who continued to propagate the Faction's cause actively—for example, in Munich, where he successfully debated the Bundists for three straight days[57]—there were a few other activists, such as Yitzhak Berger in Minsk.[58] Others inquired about the Faction, and there were new members.[59] On the whole, however, there was little significant progress. Yet quite a number of individual members of the Faction made important contributions in the area that had always occupied a central place in the Faction's platform, namely, cultural projects.

The Faction had not formulated in detail its approach to the question of culture, nor did it define exactly what Jewish culture meant. It was thus left to individual members to formulate their own projects and ideas in this area. The first and, eventually, the longest-lasting and most successful idea to be carried out was the founding of the Juedischer Verlag publishing house, the first Zionist publishing house in Western Europe. The idea of a Zionist publishing house was broached to members of the Fifth Zionist Congress in December 1901,[60] and in his list of resolutions in the name of the Cultural Commission Martin Buber asked for financial support of the enterprise,[61] a request which was not approved by the congress.[62] The Juedischer Verlag was launched in Berlin in January 1902, and its leading members included Martin Buber, Berthold Feiwel, Ephraim M. Lilien, and Alfred Nossig—all members of the Democratic Faction.[63] In line with the aims of the Faction, the publishing house tried to serve as an expression of the Jewish renaissance by publishing the spiritual, cultural, literary, and artistic treasures of the Jewish people as a foundation for the spiritual-cultural rebirth of the Jewish people. In September 1902 the Verlag was able to publish its first book, the *Juedischer Almanach*.[64] Edited by Feiwel and Lilien, the *Almanach* included works by authors from both East and West, some translated from the Yiddish and Hebrew. By the time it was transferred to the Zionist Organization in 1907, the Verlag had become a great cultural and literary resource of the Zionist movement.[65]

Another successful enterprise, though not immediately,[66] was the creation of the Jewish Statistical Bureau (Bureau fuer Statistik des juedischen Volkes), which was set up in Berlin in March 1902. It was organized by a committee whose membership was drawn mainly from the

Democratic Faction and included Martin Buber, Berthold Feiwel, Bernstein-Kohan, Leo Motzkin, and Chaim Weizmann.[67] Later that year the bureau was replaced by a new body called the Jewish Statistical Association (Verein fuer Juedische Statistik). The immediate aims of the Verein fuer Juedische Statistik included: collecting statistical information about Jews already available through government and other agencies; undertaking a scientific analysis of such materials and its publication; making independent inquiries on the social and economic conditions of the Jewish people; and collecting funds which would make this work possible.[68] The first publication of the Verein, *Juedische Statistik*, was published by the Juedischer Verlag in 1903.[69]

In one form or another Weizmann was active in the work of the Juedischer Verlag and the Verein fuer Juedische Statistik through fund-raising, administration, advising on content or form, and actual participation in some of the projects. Yet his heart and mind were set on a project which he increasingly came to view as his own personal goal and the most important task facing the Democratic Faction: the Jewish university project. As it became clearer that the Democratic Faction had failed from an organizational point of view, Weizmann devoted ever-increasing energies to this project. In any case, it was the kind of work that suited his temperament and inclinations best. He could not easily work with a large team, nor within an institution with a mandate from and responsibility to the masses, where he would be bound by decisions taken democratically and consuming much time. He did not have much faith in the judgment of the masses in Eastern Europe, as he often pointed out. He was essentially an elitist who was attuned to the voices of the masses and the currents of his movement but, at the same time, preferred to carry out its ideas by his own methods and at his own pace. For a junior lecturer who did not have the support and backing of many followers, it was a tremendously courageous—some of his friends called it foolhardy[70]—step to attempt to establish a Jewish university under the conditions prevailing in 1901, without funds and with the mere backing of a statement by the Fifth Zionist Congress that "the Congress requests of the Actions Committee to carefully study the question of the establishment of a Jewish institution of higher learning [*Juedische Hochschule*]."[71]

In a letter to Ahad Ha'Am, Weizmann referred to the congress resolution concerning a Jewish institution of higher learning: "I must admit that I only joined the Cultural Commission [as the representative from Switzerland] to tackle this task—its theoretical aspect first."[72] Ahad Ha'Am's cool, if not totally negative, reply[73] did not deter Weizmann, and it became clear that most of his time would be devoted to this project. Weizmann remained vague as to what kind of a university this would be and where it would be established, but that it was becoming more and more a practical necessity to have such a Jewish university he had no doubt. At the Munich preparatory conference in April 1901 Weizmann reasoned that there were signs that those Jewish students who were increasingly barred from the Russian universities[74] would soon find difficulty in gaining entrance to the German and Swiss universities as well.[75] It was a theme to which he returned in his speech at the Fifth Zionist Congress[76] and on many other occasions as well.

Weizmann was able to watch these developments at the Western universities at close range. By 1900 Swiss authorities had begun to worry over the flood of Russian students flocking to their universities and started to tighten entrance requirements. At the same time, the shutting down of three of the four women's medical schools in Russia in 1900 sent large groups of female students abroad. The universities of both Bern and Geneva experienced a great spurt in applications beginning in the winter semester 1900–1901—among them that of Vera Khatzman—which increased the unease among the administrators of Swiss universities even more.[77] There were similar developments at the German universities. In the first-known letter by Weizmann on the subject of the university, he referred directly to these new restrictions in Russia and the West and spoke about the idea of a Jewish university as if it were already a well-known subject that did not need further introduction. His first practical solution was to begin with plans for the establishment of two or three technical colleges in the Pale of Settlement—Warsaw, Vilna, and Odessa— "and afterwards we should develop the Jewish University project."[78] Weizmann's ideas concerning an institute or institution of higher learning were somewhat altered after the Fifth Zionist Congress: "I think there must be two institutions from the start: one in Palestine, devoted especially to Jewish learning, another in Europe—a general University with a technical faculty and, of course, a chair of Jewish studies . . . What an important European-Jewish intellectual centre could be created at a Jewish university; it would be a synthesis of Yavneh and Europe!"[79]

Despite the urgency for the creation of a Jewish university, Weizmann deliberately took his time in the preparation of a proposal, taking care to first assemble the necessary data. He collaborated closely with Berthold Feiwel, his new ally and like-minded friend. In turn, they were assisted by the Bureau fuer Statistik des juedischen Volkes, which had appointed a subcommittee—composed of Motzkin, Kasteliansky, and Feiwel—to collect statistical data about Jewish students.[80] Weizmann himself prepared a questionnaire which was distributed among them later that year.[81] In the meantime they turned for assistance to Herzl,[82] who thought it possible to persuade the sultan to agree to the establishment of a Jewish university in Palestine since such a project would not have immediate political consequences. On May 3, 1902, Herzl wrote a letter to the sultan's secretary, Izzet Pasha, in which he broached the idea of a Jewish university in Jerusalem.[83] On May 18, 1902, he also suggested to Izzet Pasha that "the project of a University in Jerusalem could serve as a screen for other matters . . ."[84] In any case, as Herzl pointed out to the sultan's secretary, this matter could best be treated face to face. In anticipation of another meeting in Constantinople, Herzl pressed both Weizmann and Feiwel to provide him with an estimated budget for the proposed university, as well as a syllabus of lectures.[85] The demand for quick action aroused Weizmann's—and his friends'—suspicion that Herzl might not be completely serious about the idea: "I am in no hurry. I am not at all willing to let the matter pass out of my hands and hand it over to Vienna, where it will be turned into light literature. I have every intention of going deeply into the problem . . ."[86] Weizmann had good reason to suspect lack of sincerity on the part of Herzl since on May 9—in the midst of Herzl's applications to the Sublime Porte on the matter of the university—SAC had rejected a request by Feiwel for a grant-in-aid for the preparatory work in connection with this very project.[87] To Motzkin Weizmann wrote, "He [Herzl] hurried me so much that I sat up for two nights preparing the report for him. What kind of a game is that? To all appearances he seems *not* to have wanted me to finish the work on time . . ."[88]

At the same time, he was not going to leave untried any possibility for furthering his idea. Within two weeks he crystallized the available data into a coherent "Plan for a Jewish University." The plan suggested a combination of a university providing higher education on an academic level with a wider array of subjects emphasizing Jewish studies *and* a polytechnic. If possible, this institution would be in Palestine. If this should prove impossible, the only real alternative would be Switzerland. The estimated capital cost for the university was 5,437,000 marks, and its annual budget was figured at 735,000 marks. The plan also described in broad outlines the organization of the university and contained as well a list of proposed departments and related schools, such as a teacher's training college, school of applied chemistry, and others.[89] Weizmann followed this plan with a few letters to Herzl amending and supplementing his suggestions. At the same time he used the opportunity to serve notice that at the present time he and Feiwel were engaging merely in preparatory work and did not intend to present the project until it had fully matured. Just as important, he was anxious lest Herzl take over the project altogether.[90] On this score he did not have to worry. As was pointed out, Herzl was interested in the university plan primarily for tactical reasons. Once the sultan had turned it down, he was happy to let the young "radicals" devote their time to this project.

Weizmann, for one, was so occupied with the university project, chemical experiments, propaganda forays on behalf of the Democratic Faction and against the Bund, organization of the Information Bureau, and an enormous correspondence, that he hardly had time to rest. In a letter to Herzl, Feiwel expressed his admiration for Weizmann's ability to undertake so many tasks with less than perfect health.[91] Since the Munich preparatory meeting of April 1901 he had been hard at work, with only one brief vacation in Pinsk in September 1901. Throughout the academic year 1901–2 he complained about his health. In January 1902 his condition was diagnosed as neurasthenia and weakness of the respiratory organs. He was advised to take a vacation, which he failed to do.[92] Toward the end of the academic year he complained, "The state of my health has deteriorated to such an extent that with the best of good will I could not attend to affairs as I should have liked. I do not know what is in store for me: I am going to the doctor today. My general state of mind is foul too."[93] To make things worse, Vera had left for Rostov-on-Don for a summer vacation on June 25 and for the next few days he was terribly depressed. "My head feels empty, my heart is empty and I am in a terribly dull mood . . ."[94] He now had to face a long separation from Vera and he felt dreadful, bereft of energy. His consolation consisted of his daily letters to Vera, which provide us with a detailed description of his quickly changing moods, his plans, and aspirations. Above all, this three-month separation from Vera affords us a view into their relationship.[95]

Berthold Feiwel arrived in Geneva just in time to make Vera's acquaintance before her departure for Russia. One of the remarkable things about Weizmann and many of his peers is that these relatively young men and women were often in poor health due to unusual deprivations, hard work, and especially poor economic conditions while studying at the universities. Moreover, Weizmann and his colleagues were often in a state of great agitation; they were constantly speaking of their "frayed nerves," emotional and physical exhaustion probably due no less to their fiery and restless temperaments than to objective aggravating conditions. Feiwel, too, was ailing, suffering from heart trouble originating from overstrain while in military service in the Austro-Hungarian army in the late 1890s.[96] Weizmann and Feiwel—or Toldy, as he was nicknamed— were good friends and allies by now. They both needed rest badly and planned to spend summer vacation in the mountains. Four days after Vera's departure, on June 29, the two friends went exploring and found a "marvelous place"[97] in Leysin, a small health resort near Montreux. They rented two rooms in the Pension de la Fôret, "near the sanatorium, with a splendid pine-grove (1,450 metres) . . ."[98] A postcard of Leysin shows the little house they lived in: "It's beautiful here, it's wonderfully sunny during the day and rather cool at night. The weather is excellent now. Half a minute away from us there is a lovely pine-forest and the mountains. The mountains are infinitely beautiful. There is a small village here (about 500 metres above us), and we live at a height of 1,500 m. From it we can see the whole of Lake Geneva, the river Rhône as it falls into it, Montreux, and in very clear weather even as far as Lausanne . . ."[99]

It was by all accounts an idyllic place to rest and recuperate. Yet while Toldy settled in the pension to begin his *Milchkur* (milk diet), Weizmann was forced to return to Geneva for a week. For one thing, despite his monthly retainer from the Bayer Works, he had run out of money. He had always been a bit careless in handling his financial affairs and, at the same time, was perhaps too generous with some of his friends— such as Aberson—who lived at his expense. No sooner had Vera left than he wrote that his dreams and plans for the summer were being wrecked by very formidable financial obstacles. He needed two hundred francs immediately; at one point he even threatened halfheartedly to stay in Geneva for the summer, though this seems to have been intended more to impress Vera with the urgency of his need rather than serve as an actual alternative.[100] What made things worse was that the discovery he had made with Deichler toward the end of 1901 had received an initially negative evaluation from the Bayer Works in Elberfeld. He returned to Leysin on July 7, where he learned of the factory's evaluation from Deichler. He therefore returned once more to Geneva on July 9, worked around the clock, checked his experiments, and got the same results he had previously obtained. He even suspected that the Bayer Works were cheating him.[101] It is not clear what the final verdict from Elberfeld was, but in the end Weizmann's financial woes sorted themselves out. He got rid of the "loafer" Aberson, "who is sitting on my back."[102] Deichler had sent two hundred francs that were due Weizmann from the factory,[103] and Vera had sent an additional sum which she had borrowed on his behalf in Rostov.[104]

Vera learned early that in certain matters, especially financial and health matters, she could have her way, and she did not hesitate to scold Weizmann, albeit in a language couched in endearments to soften the impact:

. . . Of course Chaimchik, I could not help noticing that of late your affairs were in a terrible mess. At the same time you did tell me that during the last few months you gave up taking the 100 fr. from Deichler to avoid finding yourself in the same equivocal position as last year. I was absolutely certain, therefore, that you'd have no trouble about your trip [to Leysin]. I am at a complete loss to understand what happened, darling . . . Besides, to live in Geneva also costs you money. I simply cannot understand, my dearest child. What can I say? How can I insist on your going when you say that it is impossible? On the other hand, Chaimchik, when will you ever again have such a free summer? I so hoped that this summer you would recuperate, restore your shattered health and next winter not be so weak and nervous. You will not get better in Geneva. It is very hot there, and also you will be alone and therefore depressed and moody. Chaimchik, my child, you know that you can't go on with this kind of disorderly (in material terms only, of course) existence. You cannot and do not want to. Do try to understand, my joy, that you must take full advantage of this summer and that the state of your health doesn't permit you to wait until next summer. I don't dare insist, but please do all you can to leave. Do it for yourself, and for me . . . I am so glad, my child, that you came to the conclusion at last that you can't go on any longer with this kind of irregular life. I hesitated to talk to you about it, but often thought with horror how irrationally you spend your money. For instance helping A. [Aberson] all the time . . .[105]

By July 12 he had returned to Leysin, where he was to spend the next five weeks. But vacationing was almost as hard for Weizmann as working full time in Geneva. He was not relaxed, he was not used to freedom from discipline, and he could not fully enjoy the beauty and serenity of Leysin without Vera. To ease his anxiety he communicated with her daily by mail. But the post, if it reached its destination, took almost one week to ten days in each direction, and the lack of daily letters from Vera—he hated postcards—sorely tested his nerves. It was just as difficult for Vera, who, after the sophisticated life of Geneva, was housebound in provincial Rostov.[106] Her major diversion during the entire summer was a ten-day vacation in the Caucasus.[107] She had pinned her hopes on the summer vacation, wishing that they could spend it together somehow,[108] but since Weizmann was determined to continue to keep their relationship secret, there was no choice but to go to Rostov. It was a frustrating and painful separation, punctuated by momentary explosions of anger or exasperation.

Writing from Munich en route to Rostov, Vera recalled:

> Dearest Chaimchik . . . I liked Munich very much, but all evening I felt terribly heavy at heart. I kept thinking of the last evening we spent together in Geneva . . . Do you know, Chaimchik, yesterday, as we strolled through the streets of Munich, every tall passerby looked like you. I am ashamed to confess to you, my child, that I, who adore my family, would rather go back to Geneva right now. It seems so terribly long since I saw you, and there are still three long, long months stretching ahead of us. It is awful . . .[109]

Their separation and the need to see each other became the major theme of their correspondence: "It is really impossible for me to imagine this vacation without you, utterly impossible. I keep imagining that the door is about to open and you will appear and I shall embrace you and cover you with kisses for all I'm worth,"[110] wrote Weizmann. Vera was bored: "At home everything was, as usual, rather dull." She longed for Weizmann but was realistic about a speedy reunion: "And so, my love, when shall we see each other again? It is a little too early, kitten, to talk about it, isn't it?" She could not leave Rostov in midsummer; the most she could manage was to come to Geneva three weeks before the beginning of the semester.[111]

By now she should have known her lover, who was much less sensible. It was certainly not too early *for him* to start talking about her return. Five days after her departure he mentioned, as if in passing, "Yesterday, during the journey, we were talking about how lovely it would be if you were to come here in August. We would rent a chalet and would all live together. It is much better than in Montreux. Well, my darling, is it feasible? Perhaps it is. We could be together for a month . . ."[112] From then on he virtually bombarded her with his letters, daily alternating his expressions of longing with demands for her return. It was a veritable campaign, in which he employed every possible incentive to woo her back. A day later he wrote, ". . . I even feel like writing 'Do come here quickly.' For hours on end I feel a gnawing pain that completely enslaves me, and all my efforts to drive my thoughts away and to forget remain futile . . . I feel like shouting out loud, so loud that you can hear me, Verochka darling: I love you so very very much."[113] As the month of July progressed, his demands became more explicit:

The greatest happiness for me would be to know that you were soon coming back and that you would not leave me for a long, long time . . . Everything in my room that reminds me of you, of those evenings we spent together, during which we became so attached to each other—all this arouses in me an acute burning pain. My heart aches all the time, gripped as if in a vise . . . I never thought myself so soft or capable of such an attachment. I am happy and unhappy, all at the same time. But then my happiness is eternal . . . because I shall be seeing you, and even soon perhaps. You will spend a little time at home and then you will come to me. I shall cover you with kisses, embrace you, clasp you in my arms, and I shall be so happy with you . . . Oh, how I love you! I love you, I love you, I love you. Chaimchik.[114]

In his last letter to Vera, before her first postcard arrived from Rostov, he wrote from Leysin, "All the time I sit and dream how good everything would be if you were with us . . . Verochka, stay home for another two weeks or so, and then come. You will be able to study and rest here very well. Should you come, I shall, of course, stay on here, and later shall go home [to Pinsk] for three weeks for the Holy Days only . . ."[115]

Vera, who must have had a hard time explaining to her parents the flood of letters and postcards by a man whose name they had never heard before, was irritated by this tirade of requests and by his selfish demands. Two weeks after her arrival in Rostov she chided him:

Chaimchik, I can't come, do try to understand; it is not that I don't want to come, I cannot. You know, Chaim, how boundlessly I love you, how I suffered in Geneva when I could not see you for twenty days, how hard it was for me to leave you. Surely you know it all. So if I don't come it is because I cannot. It might have been better if I had remained in Geneva. But to spend only one month at home and then leave is something I cannot do. I talked to you about it, my dearest. If you remember, Chaim, I offered to stay with you in Geneva. True, I was hesitant at first. Of course, to have done that, we'd have had to tell my parents about our relationship. They would have understood then that I belonged not only to them and would no longer have insisted on my going home then, and by the end of the summer we might both have gone to Russia together. But then you regarded my suggestion as too big a sacrifice on my part, so I dropped it. But, Chaim, what can I say at home now? I cannot even hint of wanting to return to Geneva so soon. My parents have no idea of how we feel about each other. Only my sisters may suspect. Everybody will consider it terribly selfish of me and a complete lack of consideration on my part, and they will be right . . . Yet my youthful egotism and infinite love for you might have blinded me were it not for another major obstacle—the financial one. Chaimchik, I cannot come home for just one month when the trip alone (there and back) costs 120 roubles. You know, Chaimchik, my dear, my nice, my good, my beloved, that it is my brother and not my parents who sends me money . . . ever since his marriage it really weighs on me. Now you see, my joy, my baby, that I can't come to you even if I long with all my soul to be with you, and to belong to you alone, my beloved friend . . .[116]

Weizmann annoyed her on yet another score. Throughout the summer he repeatedly swore her to secrecy about their relationship, eventually suggesting that she tell only her sisters. On the other hand, as the occasion moved him, he discussed their love with those he deemed worthy of sharing it with him. Finally Vera exploded in anger:

> Chajmchik, I find it very disagreeable that in quite a few of your letters you keep on reminding me *to be sure* to tell *only* my sisters about everything but absolutely no one else. I repeat, Chaimchik, I find it terribly unpleasant. You know that I have never said a word to anybody about our relationship, not even a hint, even though often I was disgusted by the need to pretend to behave toward you as formally as though you were a stranger. Especially I hated performing in front of people for whom I had no respect. It went against my grain but I never breathed a word to anyone; even *Told* you were the first to tell. As for my sisters, I can assure you that I said nothing to them about our relationship. But they are not so naive as to notice nothing. Reya could easily learn everything from your postcards to me, which she considers herself entitled to read. As to strangers' gossip—I can't be held responsible. Particularly since every new arrival from the Congress talked about us freely without first ascertaining whether or not it was to our liking. I find it very strange, Chaimchik, that you should think these warnings necessary. Forgive me, dear Chaimchik, for mentioning this. I may be upsetting you. But even in your first letter this sentence startled me, but I restrained myself. Now I find it incomprehensible and I feel offended . . .[117]

Vera could reason with Weizmann as long as she wanted; the impact on the ardent lover was short-lived. To her letter of July 14 he replied, "I hate myself for causing you distress and poisoning your stay at home. Forgive me, my darling, I realize only too clearly that it is difficult for you to come and I shall adapt myself to these circumstances and impatiently await that happy day when we find ourselves together again in the good old way . . ."[118] But four days later he forgot all about the distress he was causing her and came up yet with another of his many plans to bring her back to Switzerland before October:

> O yes, listen my darling. I thought a lot last night about how to arrange things, and most likely I shall not go home at all, especially if father manages to come to me. And then, my joy, you can come by the end of August. This you must do for me, and we shall stay about three weeks in the mountains, and then on to Geneva, where I want to attend the scientists' meeting in September and work in the library. If you *can* come by the end of August, new style, then it will be perfect. You see, Verochka, for this I shall even give up taking part in the All-Russian Zionist Conference [in Minsk]. This will be the first time I shall have forsaken a publ[ic] duty because of my private life.[119]

Toward the end of Weizmann's stay at Leysin, Vera became totally bewildered by his ever-changing plans:

> About our meeting, you confuse me completely now, my darling. First you wrote me that you definitely decided not to go to Russia, and I began to

dream of our living together somewhere in Switzerland. Then came the gloomiest letter in which you inform me that in five days you leave for Geneva and two, three weeks later you will go to Pinsk, and I began to dream of your coming here . . . Then you can't be sure of just what you will do, and in today's letter you hesitate . . .[120]

Vera was worried about Weizmann's health, which did not seem to improve much. It was difficult for her to know, however, if the gloomy tone of his letters was due to his frequent bouts of depression or to actual physical ailments.[121] At one point she advised him to go home to Pinsk even if it meant that he would not come to Rostov:

No, Chaim, you must promise me not to go on any propaganda tours, even if they demand it of you. It is enough, Chaim, you have been working without a break, constantly, and you've earned the right to have a rest. And so, Chaimchik, by the beginning of August you will be home. I am so glad. Chaimchik, darling, why shouldn't you come to us then? I am not going to insist because I know that it will be hard for you to undertake the journey, but I know that if there is the least possibility for you to do so you will come to your Verochka. Think about it and if you think it at all feasible, let me know at once . . .[122]

But a day later she changed her mind. She was not going to let him remain in Russia and avoid Rostov at the last moment with some lame excuses, the way he did the previous summer:

Chaimchik, you must permit me to take back what I said [yesterday]. I beg and implore you, I insist, etc., etc., etc., that you come to Rostov. If you think it possible for me to go to Geneva now, then why shouldn't you find a way to come here: Unless you come here, it will be so long before we meet. You will again not meet my family . . . And I am so anxious for you to meet. Think, my love, you will be in Russia and not come to me . . .[123]

Three days later she repeated: "Naturally, my dear child, I shall not ask you not to go home, but if you do go home I insist that you visit us . . ."[124]

It is strange that Vera would have needed to convince Weizmann to come to Rostov after such a long separation. His hesitancy was due solely to his constant need to keep their relations secret from both families.[125] At the same time, hardly a day passed without a letter or two from him to Vera. Her first postcard from Rostov only arrived in Leysin on July 9. By then he had written Vera eleven letters and three postcards. He felt he deserved the same treatment: "Look, darling, I write every day. Not a single day has passed without my having the most urgent need to share the day's events with you. My darling, you could at least have scribbled a few lines during the journey. After all, trains stop long enough at stations in Russia to let you give some sign of life . . ."[126] From then on he complained throughout the summer of either lack of mail or inadequate mail (postcards) from Vera. "But Verochka did not keep her word and did not write a detailed letter. Why? Why? Why?"[127] By mid-July, after he had received two letters from Vera, he assured her: "I shan't trouble you, Verochka, with requests to write to me more often. In all I have had two letters from you (I don't want postcards), while by now you must have had fifteen from me. If you would only think a little about my state of mind, you would always find an opportunity to write to me. But I am not going to say another word about this."[128] He kept his word for about two weeks: "Dear Verochka, my darling, what has happened? This is already the third day that I haven't had a letter from you, and I am very worried. Is everything all right? You should never do this, my darling, knowing how much your silence torments me . . . As for me, I don't miss a single day . . . But I have said this a hundred times already in my letters and you probably do not 'believe' me . . . I do not fail to share the slightest stirring of my soul with you and yet—I repeat—you do not respond to it. Why, I really don't know, and it torments me."[129] When Vera's next letter arrived, his mood had changed completely. Vera must have been vexed and often irritated by this constant stream of complaints and changes of mood. In a moment of reflection Weizmann himself once wrote her, "Such an enormous distance separates us that an exchange of letters proves almost impossible, especially with a person like me, whose mood is more changeable than the weather."[130] Vera had indeed been slow to write at first,[131] but she was gradually acquiring the habit. All she could do was to calm her nervous, anxious, and worrying lover periodically: "Kitten, my sweet, my dear one, am I to blame if letters get lost? I swear to you that not one day passes without my writing to you. I write every day, right after dinner, and by 5 o'clock I am quite incapable of doing anything, I am so overcome by the desire to be with you and talk! And *every day, every day* I write to you—not postcards as in the beginning, but letters . . . And so, I dismiss, Chaimchik, your rebuke that I write seldom . . ."[132]

It is highly doubtful that even daily letters from Vera would have satisfied Weizmann's tremendous longing for her. Parallel with his expressions of loneliness and frequent bouts of depression caused by their separation, his letters to her also reveal his strong sexual desires. The picture that emerges from these letters is of a lover who was often unable to contain his bursts of uncontrolled passion. Concomitant with tender and gentle expressions of love we also find outbursts such as these: "Verusya, my sweet. If you don't write about everything in the greatest possible detail, I shall kiss you so much when you come that you will start screaming."[133] A week later he wrote in a similar vein, "Verusya . . . Oh, would I kiss you . . . Oh, what a long time I would have to kiss you, Verusik, till you were black and blue all over, Veronka."[134] As the summer progressed he became more explicit: "Yes, Verochka, of course next year we shall be together every day, we shall work together, but how can we quickly reach the time when we shall be beside each other, with one another, in one another?"[135] Dreaming of the day they would meet in Russia, he wrote, "Verochka, Verochka, my joy, my beloved, beware of me: I shan't leave you alive after I get at you. My head is swimming at the mere thought of it."[136] As that day of reunion approached, he reminded her again of his uncontained passion: "We shall soon see each other . . . If only the hour would come more quickly when I shall see you, embrace you. Am I going to cover you with my kisses? Well, I am afraid nothing will be left of you, absolutely nothing, my child. I'll smother you, pinch you, bite you. But God, beware, my darling, for I am a savage!"[137] Vera, being generally a less passionate and impulsive person, was also less expressive about her own sexual needs and desires. She was thinking ahead, though, to their living arrangements for the coming year. Even in the more permissive atmosphere of student life in Geneva, they had to be circumspect if they wanted to live together. Thus, Vera already began to plan in midsummer: "I wrote to Mme. Vishni——[probably a landlady in Geneva] asking whether she would rent us an apartment. I would terribly like to live there. We shall never find such conveniences anywhere else. The main advantage is that there will be no landlady. If she refuses, I will try to find a room in your vicinity, my darling, and have dinner in your pension. That will be lovely, don't you think?"[138]

Weizmann's love and passion for Vera were not always matched by respect for her intellectual capacities or even her evaluation of daily experiences. On the train from Vienna to Volochisk she had a startling brush with anti-Semitism:

> There was an old Jew in the car with us. Our travelling companions didn't stop making fun of him, of his Jewish accent, his gestures, called him "sheeny." You can imagine my indignation. I went over to the Jew and asked him to sit next to me. Irritated by my interference, they began to pull his hair. I then gave him my place and sat in his. They decided, of course, that only a Jewess could behave like that and one of them pulled my arm and called me "sheeny" . . . Isn't it terrible, Chaimchik?[139]

Weizmann dismissed this experience in three words: "How dreadful, Verochka."[140] When she wrote to him of an article that was arousing interest in Russia,[141] he replied, "The article may arouse some interest among such *goyim* as the Jews of Rostov," thereby also showing disrespect for her own interest in the subject.[142] There are only few occasions when he seriously engaged her intellectually. Though he did occasionally seek her advice in Zionist affairs, their relations in this realm were those of a teacher and his disciple. Both Vera and Weizmann accepted this situation as completely natural.

Weizmann was a relentless taskmaster. To him it was clear that Vera needed to spend the summer vacation brushing up on a number of subjects that he deemed important for her Zionist and general education. One week after her departure from Geneva, he asked, "Have you started to study Hebrew, and is it going well? You must read the Bible with the teacher without fail. I should very much like you to become acquainted at least to some extent with the spirit of the Book of Books . . ."[143] Another subject that could stand improvement in her education, in his opinion, was German. For one thing, it would permit her to read *Die*

Welt and be informed of Zionist affairs. She could then help him with
the Jewish university project. By the end of July he commented, "Judging from your letters to Toldy, you are making very good progress, which
pleases me infinitely. When you can read German, I'll get a *wonderful*
edition of Nietzsche's [*Also Sprach*] *Zarathustra*."[144] A week later he did
reward Vera with such an edition.[145] It was important to him that she
study and admire Nietzsche as he did.[146] His frequent references to
Nietzsche are interesting in themselves, since he rarely read books that
did not deal either with Zionism or chemistry. He had a taste for the
theater and for classical music, but certainly not for philosophy or literature. There is no explanation of his admiration for Nietzsche except that
at the time the philosopher was modish in Weizmann's circle. Moreover,
one can also surmise that Weizmann juxtaposed, perhaps unconsciously, the philosopher's description of super humans to the "slavishness and servility" of Jews in the Pale,[147] and his desire to see Jews become emotionally and physically free of the *Galut*.[148]

From the start, Vera proved to be a very obedient student; she was
doing her best to acquire a taste for Hebrew, Zionist affairs, and other
subjects her taskmaster came up with. The first paragraph of her first
extant letter refers to Chaim as her teacher.[149] Beginning with her first
letter from Munich, en route to Rostov, Vera wrote, "And I, my kitten,
shall try my best to work hard at Hebrew so that I should be able to
write to you in Hebrew."[150] Many subsequent letters speak of her determination to learn Hebrew,[151] though it is doubtful that she made much
progress in this field, the only real evidence being the word "Sabbath"
written in Hebrew.[152] Despite the oppressive summer weather in Rostov, she involved herself in Zionist work, attending Zionist meetings,
raising money for the Jewish university project,[153] enlisting subscribers
for the Juedischer Verlag, and converting members of her family and close
acquaintances to the Zionist cause.[154] She was also making some efforts
to master German and read *Die Welt*, as Weizmann had demanded.[155]
Ultimately, as with Hebrew, her German did not improve that summer
beyond an elementary stage, and the Nietzsche edition probably collected dust on her bookshelf in Rostov.[156] When she finally received the
pamphlet *Eine Juedische Hochschule*, written in much simpler German than
Nietzsche's work, she could not understand it and preferred waiting for
a Russian translation.[157] Regardless of her ultimate success in all these
matters, it is clear that she was trying to follow Weizmann's advice and
instructions as closely as possible.

Two exchanges between Vera and Weizmann during the summer best
reveal their intellectual relationship in general and Vera's sense of inferiority in Jewish and Zionist affairs in particular. Three weeks after her
departure Vera wrote, "You are the first who made me think seriously
about Jewish problems, the Jewish Question; you were my first teacher,
and it is *for this* that I love you so profoundly."[158] Not surprisingly,
Weizmann "read and re-read this letter."[159] A few days later he replied
at length in a paternalistic, rather self-satisfied manner:

I analyze all these developments with delight and believe ever more in a harmony which grows slowly, little by little, but takes deep root, rather than the passionate, impulsive love which rushes like a tornado over the infatuated lovers' heads but leaves nothing behind it but memories—pleasant ones perhaps, but nevertheless only memories. With us, I dare hope, it will be different. Not only will it be, but it is. Moreover, Verochka, since you became one with me in the *cause* too, since you told me that you are a Zionist, since then, Verochka, our spiritual union has grown stronger, and what in other cases springs from passion in our case, to my mind, has grown from a spiritual affinity . . . One more thing, my beloved. I always wanted to love the disciple in you too, so dear and so pure, with a pure simple soul unstained by anything; to cleanse you, my joy, of all assimilation, to lead you into the Movement. I never spoke to you about it *directly*, yet I followed with a watchful eye every stirring of your soul, without ever, ever—do you remember, Verochka?—wishing to penetrate it, without ever wishing to bring any pressure to bear. I believe in the victorious force of the Idea, in the cogency of my arguments and of my Zionist life which you have had an opportunity to observe . . .[160]

Vera's reply to this letter indicates that—for good reasons—she had not always been so sure of Weizmann's respect for her mind but, at the same time, acknowledged the transformation he had wrought in her entire weltanschauung:

Chaimchik, in character, temperament and even in our mental make-up we are very different and this always frightened and worried me . . . Chaimchik, baby, I profoundly value your never attempting to lead me in a certain direction or to win me over to your way of thinking. Although, I confess, Chaimchik, that there were times when I found it painful that you seemed not to care or be interested in what goes on inside me . . . I need not tell you how this frightened me . . . By introducing me to Zionism and giving me an insight into Jewish and Zionist problems you turned me from a *goya* into a Jewess . . . essentially [though], my Zionism is of a very platonic type. Chaimchik, my friend, my teacher, this summer you must give me the kind of work to do that will help me to become involved rather than detached . . .[161]

Weizmann could only nod in approval: "Verochka, my sweet, if you only knew how dear your convictions are to me, if you only knew how I fostered this. I see this as a flower which yields good fruit . . . You have understood me—and this is the most intimate thing I can tell you, my beloved, the most sacred thought which I allow myself only in such hours of spiritual communion with you."[162]

It was clear that Vera could lecture Chaim with some effect on questions if money, and especially on his health, a subject she did not tire of bringing up in almost every one of her letters. From the start, however, there was little chance that she would be treated as an intellectual equal or that she could seriously change Weizmann's mind on general political or Zionist issues. He asked her advice periodically, but by the time she replied he had either forgotten what it was she was responding to or had already made up his mind. For the most part, Vera was treated by Weizmann delicately and gently, as a person who needed his protection and advice with every step she made. For her part, this seemed acceptable—at least we have almost no evidence to the contrary. There is only one fleeting moment during the long separation in 1902 that Weizmann seems to have seriously sought Vera's advice. In one of her letters to Weizmann, Vera related how she had described him to her relatives: "All I told them was that they never met such Zionists and that you have no life outside of Zionism, everything [else] is just extra. This is true, Chaim, isn't it?"[163] The truth was a bit more complicated than that at this stage of his dual development as a chemist and a neophyte in Zionist public life. There had been a number of occasions that summer when he sought to reconcile the conflict between his work in chemistry and his Zionist activities, and in each instance he had come to the conclusion that "I have firmly decided to lead a more concentrated life from now on, to think more of myself—I mean of us—I want to start building the future we are to have in common."[164] A day later he was more explicit: "I must regulate my activities in such a way that one thing [Zionism] does not interfere with the other [chemistry]; I shall then be healthier and more creative. I shall work and there will be no more financial difficulties."[165] Vera was pleased with these pronouncements and supported them wholeheartedly, but as the university project began to take shape, he wavered in his resolve to keep his two main interests in balance. Toldy and he were discussing the Jewish university project one day and how to propagate the idea on a large scale. Who could direct such a campaign? Weizmann, of course. It would require many months of campaigning in Russia, England, and America. He was excited by the idea and its potential and sat down to write Vera:

> I have to choose: either-or. If the Univer[sity] venture goes well, then it is unthinkable for me to work on my chemistry at the same time. I don't have to tell you this in so many words: you yourself know very well what chemistry means to me, the laboratory with all its joys and sorrows, but at the same time you know, my lovely one, that the idea of the University is no less dear to me, if not more. Chemistry is my private affair, an activity in which I rest from my public duties. Let me put all material considerations aside and ask you the question from a purely moral point of view. The choice is difficult, deadly difficult, and I don't want to conceal the problem from you and am putting it to you in its plain, unadorned form, as it stands before my own eyes. Having linked your life with mine, you must have your say, my darling, you must declare your attitude, and I am waiting for it.[166]

Vera answered by return mail in the most unambiguous and forceful manner, realizing that she was responding to one of Weizmann's perennial existential problems:

> Yes, Chaimchik, we face a difficult decision . . . What can I say now? . . . On the one hand, I have no right to take you away from the cause—on the other hand, I have no right to contribute to the deterioration of your health. Chaim, I can only implore you to think most carefully about yourself, your physical condition and then only a little, a very little, about me.

And now about something else, my dear friend. I cannot understand you: how you can so separate the moral aspect of the thing from the material one. I find it incomprehensible. Actually, when you give up chemistry—you will be left penniless. In other words without any means at all. Is it possible that you are considering living off Jewish money? Chaimchik, but you will never be able to reconcile yourself to this. And once you leave chemistry, you'll find it very hard to get back. This whole thing is very unclear to me, Chaimchik, so I had better not talk about it. I want only to advise you not to sever yourself from chemistry. Kohan-Bernstein went through a lot during the period when he was employed by the Jews. "He gives his time, does good work," people said. "Yes, but he gets paid for it," was the answer.[167] Chaimchik, it seems to me that all this somehow can be arranged quite differently. Toldy and a few other more or less active, able people could remain in the Geneva office. Then the work would be distributed between a number of people and not fall exclusively on you, and it would no longer be necessary for you to give up chemistry.[168]

Weizmann quite agreed:

Don't be afraid, my darling, that I shall give up to no purpose the chemistry which is so dear to me. All your arguments are quite correct, and I am bearing all this in mind . . . Vera, Vera, the whole aim of my letter was to tell you everything. I did not want to make any decisions without the boss . . . As for the financ[ial] side, I shall never get into Koh[an]-Bernstein's position: Zionism is developing differently, and I shall not be dependent on Jews.[169]

Far from giving up chemistry, Weizmann spent many hours each day preparing his lectures for the coming academic year and filling gaps in his own background.[170] While Feiwel was preparing the *Almanach* for publication by the Juedischer Verlag, as well as an edition of Morris Rosenfeld's *Lieder des Ghetto*, he wrote his chemistry lectures partly in French and partly in German and by the end of July he reported that he had been very successful and had prepared almost all his lectures, "some 150 typewritten p[ages], from various sources. I am going to G[eneva] one of these days to look up periodicals. All this gives me great satisfaction and relief."[171]

The greatest source of satisfaction for Weizmann that summer was no doubt the development and maturation of his friendship with Berthold Feiwel. In retrospect it seems clear that Toldy—unlike Motzkin—was the first real friend with whom he could relax and enjoy himself as an equal from the moment they met. Feiwel was a year younger than Weizmann. He was born in Porlice, near Bruenn, in Moravia. Unlike Weizmann, he had come from an assimilated background, but, inspired by Herzl and Zionist ideology, he gave up his studies in philosophy and devoted himself to the cause. He was one of the very few Central or West European Jews who at the turn of the century went to Russia and Poland, and had mastered Russian, Polish, Hebrew, and Yiddish. He was a dashing young man who had great success with women. Moreover, he was a first-rate German stylist who seemed to find the right expression for each occa-

Weizmann in Leysin with Berthold Feiwel and Esther Schneerson, July 1902

sion.[172] From all accounts he seems to have been a gentle and kind man, of even disposition and general good humor. By mid-1902 he was attached to Esther Shneerson, who had worked for and with Weizmann in Geneva during the first few months of 1902. Her own background was similar to Weizmann's. She was born in 1876 in Lyadi (Belorussia) and was raised in the house of her grandfather, Rabbi Menahem Mendel Shneerson of Lyadi, the leader of Habad hasidim and the grandson of Rabbi Shneur Zalman of Lyadi. By 1898 she had forsaken her hasidic background and had turned to Zionism. She admired Weizmann and was in love with Toldy.[173] It was thus quite natural that by mid-July she had joined both of them in Leysin.[174] For brief periods they were also joined by Felix Pinkus, Weizmann's protégé from Berlin.[175]

In many respects Feiwel was the antithesis of Weizmann, and yet they seemed to complement each other perfectly. They had an intuitive understanding and compassion for each other's needs and failings. Toldy seemed to radiate love and understanding from the very first meeting. Even Vera, who did not easily establish warm relations with others, felt this keenly. For almost a year and a half she had to endure a more or less hostile attitude from Weizmann's colleagues and friends, who saw her as an interloper, an assimilated beauty who had displaced the good party comrade Sophia Getzova, and she had been unable to penetrate their social circle. Though she met Toldy only briefly before her departure for Rostov, she felt instantly that he had accepted her without reservations. Vera's notes to Feiwel and her constant inquiries after his health illustrate how pleased and grateful she was for his friendly attitude toward her. For their part, Toldy and Esther Shneerson expressed their friendship to Vera by joining Weizmann in sending her flowers they had picked on the mountains.[176] Weizmann wrote with obvious relief, "I am so glad you've got to know T[oldy] and that you liked him. For he is the first of my comrades whom you've got to know like this. The others, like Kohan-B[ernstein], adopted a different attitude."[177] Weizmann and Toldy grew increasingly fond of each other over the summer. Toldy was a wonderful companion. In the absence of Vera, he was the only person in whom Weizmann could confide, and he told Vera so: "This is all I have; you and Toldy, the good, fine, really infinitely good Toldy. The better I know him the more I realize what a wonderful person he is, with a soul pure as crystal."[178] He was as concerned with Feiwel's health as he was with his own, sharing the details of Feiwel's progress or lack thereof with Vera.[179] On days when Feiwel was sick, Weizmann was miserable and could not function well. "He is feeling ill, and this affects my state of mind too."[180]

There was a perfect meeting of minds between the two, and on days when Toldy felt well enough they could work together on the Jewish university project. This close collaboration with a serious and dedicated Zionist was all the more welcome to Weizmann because of his constant frustrations with other members of the Democratic Faction: "Motzkin is outrageously lazy. I am not writing to him anymore and, generally, shall cease to take any further interest in the fate of the Faction. I am fed up with playing the rôle of an *enfant terrible* who, by the way, is paying out more than anyone else."[181] Some four weeks later he exclaimed again, "The affairs of the Faction . . . everything is in just the same state, and no force can make this bunch of good-for-nothings move. We shall have to drop them and start a new life. Apparently this generation is not yet fit; evidently it was not born to 'act,' to build, to create. Men of the Diaspora, assimilationists—a prey to phrases, to forms of words, to stereotypes. Small people, with small brains and small ambitions. There is no boldness, no daring urge to assume responsibility for the honor of the cause."[182] In the same letter, though, Weizmann revealed his noblesse oblige attitude to Zionism, his conviction that a small elite group of committed Zionists would carry on the work: "We have to work more, to work for the good-for-nothings as well. There is an old Jewish tradition . . . all Jews are responsible for one another, and you and I . . . have to pay with our nerves for the sins of others . . ."[183] He returned to this theme again two days later: "I know full well that the path, the path of Jews—Zionist Jews—is not strewn with roses, but I leave roses to rosy simpletons—roses exist only in novels . . . Please, my friend, keep in mind these words of mine: 'The whole aim of my life will be to serve our common cause together with you.' We shall make this the basic theme of our life . . .''[184]

He saw himself and Feiwel as members of the Zionist aristocracy who served on behalf of their people. Since they viewed themselves as an elite group, it was thus natural that the kinds of projects they turned their attention to were not geared to the masses but were meant to serve a much smaller group of intellectuals. The Jewish university project was a perfect example. Weizmann saw this project as particularly suited to his own interests and inclinations; from the start he displayed a keen sense of possessiveness over it, fearing that Herzl or the Actions Committee might take it over.[185] Weizmann's approach to the Jewish university project was cautious, practical, and systematic. As he indicated at the Fifth Zionist Congress, he wished to begin by collecting information: facts and figures on Jewish students all over Europe and material on the European universities—their structure, syllabi, finances. All that material would have to be collected and analyzed. It was, as it were, a scientific attack on a problem, an approach that was far from commonplace among the students in his circle. In a letter to Herzl written just prior to his departure for Leysin, he outlined the nature of the preparatory work that needed to be investigated: the position of Jewish university students in Eastern and Western universities; a study of the students' living conditions; the relationship of the university project to Zionism; the plan for the university budget; and a study of the best propaganda methods. "We believe," wrote Weizmann, "that only when the preliminary questions have been studied with sufficient care . . . will the project be ripe enough to be put before an official Zionist forum . . . we consider that harm would be done even by a premature announcement of the project or by its being [in the] meantime made a topic for public discussion . . .''[186]

During intervals between Weizmann's preparation of chemistry lectures and Feiwel's work for the Juedischer Verlag, the two friends worked hard on writing a pamphlet on the university project. They collaborated well as a team and by mid-July the pamphlet was ready for the printers.[187] Weizmann described the pamphlet as "my plan with Told's commentary, in which we substantiate everything."[188] Buber, Feiwel, and Weizmann were named as the authors of the plan, although Buber had nothing to do with writing it.[189] The pamphlet was divided into two parts. The first and larger part was Feiwel's creation.[190] It described the difficulties encountered by Jewish students in Eastern Europe in obtaining access to institutions of higher learning, as well as the increasing obstacles placed in their way by such institutions in Western Europe. It then described the moral, psychological, and economic impact of these discriminatory practices on the young Jewish intelligentsia. A solution to these difficulties would be the creation of a Jewish university (_Hochschule_), if possible in Palestine, but if this should prove impractical—since this was an emergency—then for the time being in some other country, such as England or Switzerland, with the explicit understanding that it would be transferred to Palestine at the first opportunity.[191] The second part of the pamphlet contained a slightly amended version of Weizmann's "Preliminary Plan for a Jewish University," submitted to Herzl in May 1902. The only major difference, in line with the first part of the pamphlet, was that England was added to Switzerland as an alternative temporary residence for the Jewish university, but apparently with a bias for England, since it appears in second place after Palestine.[192]

They now needed funds to publish the pamphlet—first in German. Toward the end of July Weizmann traveled to Diablerets, the Swiss vacation spot of Samuel Shriro, a Lithuanian Jew who had been at the Youth Conference in Basel, where he had an opportunity to be impressed by Weizmann's leadership. Shriro had made a fortune in the Baku oil fields. He had a tender spot for the young Zionists and gave Weizmann a hundred rubles, enough to print the pamphlet.[193] To his friend Catherine Dorfman Weizmann described it crudely: "I got hold of a 'Maecenas' here in the mountains and stripped him of everything I could."[194] In fact, Shriro eventually contributed another thousand rubles. Moreover, he promised that if Weizmann would tour the Baku region he could guarantee a few thousand rubles more toward the university project.[195] It was Weizmann's first experience in fund-raising.

For a number of reasons Weizmann was anxious to have ready for circulation before the end of the summer both the university pamphlet and the program of the Democratic Faction. Ozer Kokesch and Oskar Marmorek had informed him in early July, on behalf of SAC, that the university project would be discussed at the annual conference, which would meet in lieu of the full Zionist congress in October.[196] Since he had failed to convince Herzl to postpone public debate on the university,[197] Weizmann was determined to have in hand a well-reasoned and carefully formulated plan. He was also preparing to go on a propaganda tour in Russia on behalf of the Democratic Faction and was also planning to attend the All-Russian Zionist Conference in Minsk in early September. It was clear to him that he could not show up at that conference without the pamphlet and program. By midsummer he asked Victor Jacobson for an itinerary acceptable to the regional leaders in Russia.[198] He was aware of the importance his trip would have for the success or failure of the Democratic Faction and for the university project. He was also well aware of the opposition that he would encounter in Russia: "The [DF] program is not ready yet. But it soon will be. It must be ready before my arrival in Russia, otherwise I won't go. This is a *conditio sine qua non*. I'd be ashamed to show myself without a program, as, more than anyone else, I shall prove to be the scapegoat and the target for all attacks . . ." And he added meaningfully, "The area I have to tour is Ussishkin's—you realize what that means."[199]

Thus, he continued to badger Motzkin for the program.[200] "You see," he wrote to Catherine Dorfman, "once it is in my hands, I shall not be so worried."[201] Motzkin kept him on tenterhooks until the last moment and sent him the revised program just before Weizmann left Leysin, on August 14, 1902. There was a tearful departure from Feiwel, Esther Shneerson, and Pinkus, all of them trying to hide their emotions.[202] The following day he was on his way to Berlin, where he met his father, with whom he traveled to Pinsk. Characteristically, he was all "afire" and "terribly tense" before his departure for Russia.[203] In his mind's eye he was already in Russia, and he warned Vera that his time with her would be strictly limited: ". . . you must understand that I cannot shirk my responsibilities. People are waiting for me everywhere . . ."[204] For her part, Vera worried about something else. She knew full well that she was not his first lover and was aware of his roving eye. Thus, her last letter to Geneva contained a reminder for the road: "But, Chaimchik, don't let your weak character get the better of you, don't linger anywhere. Always remember that your Verochka is waiting impatiently for you."[205]

VII

Conflicts and Disappointments

Objectively, Weizmann had good reason to be satisfied with his summer vacation. His health had improved somewhat and his chemistry lesson plans for the coming academic year had been prepared. He set out confidently for his trip with the finished university pamphlet and Democratic Faction's program. Moreover, every day since he left Geneva brought him closer to Vera, for whom he had pined all summer long. Yet, within less than a week after his departure he already reported that "my nerves have gone utterly to pieces thanks to Berlin."[1] Indeed, before World War I Weizmann was a continuously high-strung, irritable, and impatient man who could be rejoicing one moment and become morose, with little apparent cause, the next. His description of himself in Leysin aptly characterizes him during those years: ". . . the smallest thing makes me terribly irritable and upsets my equilibrium, and I see everything larger than life."[2]

His first major stop in Russia was to be Pinsk, but he made the almost ritualistic stops in Bern, Nieder-Ingelheim, and Berlin. None of these were enjoyable. In Bern he once more met Sophia Getzova to discuss their relationship; more than a year after he had broken the engagement it was still painful for both of them,[3] yet his guilty conscience impelled him to see her repeatedly. The following day he visited Deichler in Nieder-Ingelheim, where he tried to make peace between Deichler and his parents, probably in a matter related to his colleague's relations with his own fiancée. Berlin, his erstwhile favorite city, now bore associations of intrigue and unhappiness connected with Motzkin and the Kadimah group. In general, he found the change from Leysin to Berlin unpleasant. "Altogether, I like Berlin less now and the Germans as well. They are coarser, even though more cultured, than the Swiss."[4] Yet he managed to interest some professors in Berlin in the university project.[5] He had an interesting discussion with the German revisionist socialist leader Eduard Bernstein.[6] While sitting in the Café Monopol with Davis Trietsch, Ephraim Lilien, and others, he received the latest news on the affairs of the Juedischer Verlag and other enterprises with which members of the Democratic Faction were involved. On August 22 and 23 he and his father

visited Weizmann's oldest sister, Miriam, and her husband, Chaim Lubzhinsky, in Warsaw, where Weizmann used his brief stay to arouse interest in the university.[7] The following day (August 24) they arrived in
Pinsk.

Since his student years Weizmann had always reserved some of his
most derogatory descriptions of the Pale of Settlement and its Jews for
Pinsk. As a high school student he had referred to it merely as "our dirty
Pinsk."[8] His contempt for the town and its people intensified after he
had spent three semesters at the Charlottenburg Polytechnik.[9] With time
Pinsk came to symbolize all the rottenness and misery associated with
the condition of Russian Jewry,[10] though he did not spare other localities
from his sharp tongue (e.g., Odessa) when the spirit and the occasion
moved him. True, Pinsk was not a pretty town; it was muddy during
the rainy season and it was terribly crowded. Conditions worsened there
in the spring of 1901 as a result of a widespread fire, which left 750 Jewish families homeless and many Jewish workers jobless. These conditions, however, were not unlike those of other towns and cities in the
Pale. Weizmann simply knew Pinsk more intimately and spent much more
time there on his yearly visits to Russia. His pronouncements tell us as
much about him as they do about the city and its inhabitants. The par-
adox that emerged during those years at the turn of the century—and
would intensify even more later—is that as he became more engrossed
on an intellectual and practical level in solving the plight of East European Jewry, he became correspondingly detached from its people, especially those not belonging to the Jewish intelligentsia. While he understood that Pinsk, or the Pale in general, "is our real life,"[11] he had also
arrived at the conclusion that "everything here [in Pinsk] is alien to me,
terribly alien, and during this one year I have moved further away from
this life than in five years. Another two or three years abroad, and I'll
be *sans patrie* in the full meaning of the word."[12] There was, of course,
also a positive attachment on Weizmann's part which rested, to a large
degree, on his strong ties to friends and kin, as well as certain aspects
of East European culture and folklore. This ambivalence between his
emotional ties to East European Jewry and his admiration for Western
culture would play an important role throughout his adult life. It was a
double allegiance to two cultures. He felt at home in both, but at times
they could not be reconciled. Politically he was able to use this dual allegiance and familiarity to good advantage.

In contrast to the shabby physical surroundings of Pinsk, for once all
was well in the family. The family business, which Chaim Lubzhinsky
had placed on firm foundations, was now run by Ozer's eldest son, Feivel, who two years earlier had married Lubzhinsky's sister, Fanya.
Weizmann was not especially fond of either.[13] "He is not much of a success," he once wrote of Feivel,[14] probably referring to his brother's lack
of education. On that score he was quite pleased with his younger
brothers. Moshe, who was five years younger than Weizmann, was attending the Kiev Polytechnic as a student of agriculture. Shmuel, who

had just finished the *Gymnasium*, was sitting for his entrance examinations at the same institution, where he wanted to study engineering. Michael (Chilik), only ten years old in 1902, was developing into a Talmud scholar; he was fluent in Hebrew and Yiddish but had no interest in the Russian language. The previous year Hayah had married Abraham Lichtenstein, who was now a teacher and bookseller in Pinsk. Fruma was already studying in Kiev to be a dental surgeon and Gita was studying music in Warsaw.[15] The three youngest sisters—Anna, Masha, and Minna—were still living at home and working hard at their studies. Most important of all, Weizmann's parents, Ozer and Rachel Leah, were feeling well and could enjoy, in relative prosperity, the development and success of their children.[16]

He used the week in Pinsk to prepare for the Minsk Conference and for a battle against a new opponent of the Democratic Faction, the Mizrahi, which was vigorously campaigning in the Pale. He expected the worst; to Vera he wrote: "The Conference promises to be a terrible *golus* product. The Rabbinical party is organizing itself in Jesuit fashion."[17] He had reason to worry about the strength of the new organization, which was created, in no small degree, in reaction to the founding of the Democratic Faction.[18] The demonstration of strength of the Democratic Faction at the Fifth Zionist Congress had an ominous look to the orthodox as well as other political Zionists in Russia. At the suggestion of the latter, Rabbi Isaac Jacob Reines of Lida convoked a meeting in February 1902 in Vilna.[19] The seventy-two participants were, for the most part, opposed to cultural activity by the World Zionist Organization and were committed to "pure" or political Zionism.[20] The participants founded the Mizrahi (coined from the term *merkaz ruhani*, spiritual center) as a religious faction within the World Zionist Organization. The platform, which was accepted by the majority of the participants, adhered to the Basel program. It stated, *inter alia*, that all activities concerned with settlement in Palestine were within the faction's purview; at the same time it declared that all matters not directly related to Zionism ought to be dropped from the Zionist program; furthermore, the Mizrahi groups could not operate in a manner contrary to orthodoxy and could not accept into their ranks social democrats.[21] Organizationally the Mizrahi conceived of itself as a spiritual center for Zionism, like that of Rabbi Shmuel Mohilewer, which would be integrally related to the territorial organization of Russian Zionists.[22] The appeal of the Mizrahi was enormous. Within a year after its founding it could boast 210 societies in Eastern Europe, with a membership of 5,000.[23]

Weizmann knew, of course, that a clash between the Democratic Faction and the Mizrahi was inevitable at the All-Russian Zionist Conference, which was to open in Minsk on September 4. Officially this was to be the first Russian Zionist Conference, since the Warsaw Conference of 1898 had been illegal.[24] Since von Plehve, the Minister of the Interior, had given his permission,[25] there was no hesitation on the part of Jews to attend—though they were well aware of the presence of Russian secret police during the deliberations. Some 526 persons from all over Russia came as delegates; it was to be the largest assembly of Russian Zionists prior to 1917, more impressive in size than any previous congress.[26] Of those assembled, 160 belonged to the Mizrahi and 60 to the Democratic Faction.[27] The fact that the Democratic Faction had wasted its time in internecine warfare and had failed to build up a strong organization and a large membership harmed it in Minsk. Within a short period of time the Mizrahi was able to mobilize almost three times as many delegates as the Democratic Faction. Prior to the Minsk Conference Weizmann already had revealed his fears and prejudices concerning the opposition. "So many 'Mizrahi' people will be assembling, there will be so much ignorance, that in such a concentration the putrefying bacilli of reason and culture will not be able to survive . . . I am . . . in a state of *allgemeine Depression* [general depression]."[28] What made matters worse was that he had no confidence in, or respect for, most of the Russian regional leaders. Having read their circulars in Pinsk, he exclaimed, "God, what trash, what poverty of thought, what stupidity, pettiness and lack of everything! If the leaders write like that, what can the [local Zionist] groups be like?"[29] Consequently he did everything he could to mobilize the Democratic Faction members and to persuade them to come as delegates. He himself received five mandates,[30] and he took with him to Minsk his brothers Moshe and Shmuel, while Ozer Weizmann joined them later.[31]

The cultural question was the most hotly debated topic at the conference.[32] As in Warsaw, here too Ahad Ha'Am's invited lecture served as a focal point for the debate.[33] Speaking for two hours in Russian, Ahad Ha'Am demonstrated the inseparable ties between the Jewish renaissance movement and cultural work. He pointed out that during the Hibbat Zion period there was no doubt in anyone's mind as to the necessity for cultural work; only the new, political trend in the movement had begun to cast doubt on this aspect of Zionism.[34] Ahad Ha'Am made two proposals. The first proposal, similar to the one he had made at the Warsaw Conference in 1898,[35] was that a worldwide nationalist cultural organization be set up, which would be independent of the World Zionist Organization but would cooperate with it. His second suggestion was that the World Zionist Organization establish separate commissions for progressive and orthodox educational and cultural activities.[36] Nahum Sokolow followed this with a suggestion that Hebrew be adopted as the official language of the World Zionist Organization,[37] and Rabbi Reines, who was given equal time, passionately and emotionally repeated his plea to avoid the cultural issue, which would alienate the orthodox from Zionism.[38]

Over 120 delegates registered for the debate on the cultural question, underscoring the sensitivity and emotional involvement of the Russian Zionists over this key issue. Weizmann and Leo Motzkin spoke on September 9 on behalf of the Democratic Faction during the general debate on cultural work. Weizmann stated that the very necessity of defending cultural work was absurd, since the question had already been resolved in the affirmative in Basel. What was important was a guarantee that cultural work would not remain an empty phrase. He accused the Mizrahi of desiring to collect funds for Zionist diplomatic work while neglecting cultural issues. In this context he paraphrased Herzl's words: "In the beginning was the idea, not money."[39] Weizmann, who had rejected a similar proposal by Ahad Ha'Am during the preparations for the Youth Conference, again rejected, on behalf of the Democratic Faction, the suggestion for an independent body for the advancement of cultural work. He did support Ahad Ha'Am's alternative suggestion that the conference set up two cultural commissions which would represent, respectively, the secularists and the orthodox. He rejected, as did Motzkin, the charge that the Democratic Faction was antireligious and insisted on friendly relations and cooperation among the various factions of Zionism.[40] In the end a compromise was struck in a private conference, which included Ahad Ha'Am and Rabbi Reines, and the proposal for two distinct trends of Zionist educational and cultural work was accepted.[41] On September 10 the Minsk Conference ended on a note of goodwill and amity among all the factions, symbolized for many delegates by Rabbi Reines's public embrace of Weizmann.[42]

The Minsk Conference also marked the last show of strength by the Democratic Faction as an organization. In objective terms, it had fallen apart before it was ever able to properly organize itself, yet the momentum of its success in Basel in December 1901 created the illusion of a living and functioning organization. The accidental presence of many of the members of the Democratic Faction at the Minsk Conference also helped perpetuate this fiction. Weizmann knew better all along, but it served his purposes to pretend that he was being backed by a significant group of followers and like-minded comrades. Thus, he also took part in Minsk in the plans to establish a center of the Democratic Faction in Moscow. The irony was that the Democratic Faction had, in large measure, given impetus to the creation of the Mizrahi, which continued to grow at a quick pace until the Uganda crisis, whereas the Faction itself was to recede into insignificance within a very brief period of time.

On the whole, Weizmann was probably relieved to leave Minsk. He had done what he could for the Democratic Faction, but now it was time to attend to the campaign on behalf of the university. He was also exhausted, suffering from a bad cold and laryngitis. He stopped over in Pinsk for a few days of rest before taking off on his propaganda tour. In Pinsk an unexpected and not entirely welcome guest awaited him: Major William Evans-Gordon, a British M.P., who was a member of the Royal Commission on Alien Immigration.

Weizmann knew a little about the background of the visit. Evans-Gordon was the founder of the British Brothers' League, which had consistently drawn attention to the mass immigration to England. As far back as 1888, and again in 1894 and 1898, such British conservatives as Evans-Gordon and Arnold White had opposed the immigration of "poor aliens," who were forced to leave their native lands due to the wretched economic and physical conditions in Russia and Rumania.[43] After the United States, Britain received the highest number of East European Jews in the last two decades of the nineteenth century.[44] According to a report submitted in 1905 to the Royal Statistical Society of London, only 105,000 of the 300,000 Jews who immigrated to Great Britain after 1891 took up permanent residence there,[45] but the perception of many Britons was that England was being overrun by foreigners. As a result of this immigration, anti-alien tendencies, which were intensified with the rise of unemployment following the Boer War, made headway early in the 1900s. Immigrants were seen as competing with British labor and were accused—with little justification—of a high percentage of criminal activity.[46] So intense was the outcry that on March 21, 1902, the government appointed a royal commission to investigate the entire problem of alien immigration. Chaired by Lord James, Chancellor of the Duchy of Lancaster, the commission met for two years. Among the commissioners were Evans-Gordon and one Jew, Nathaniel Meyer, First Lord Rothschild.[47]

Despite Rothschild's initial opposition, Leopold Greenberg, one of Herzl's most devoted followers in England, arranged for Herzl to be invited by the Royal Commission.[48] Herzl, who felt he had reached the end of the line with Turkey,[49] immediately perceived the opportunity contained in this invitation, namely, to publicize the cause of the movement in a country he had long recognized would be important for the realization of Zionist aspirations. He also understood that in order to make any headway at all he would have to win over to his side Rothschild, England's most influential Jew, who vigorously opposed Herzl and Zionism.[50] Herzl probably expected very little when he went to see Rothschild immediately upon his arrival in England on July 4. Rothschild, indeed, was frank and blunt. Herzl had been invited before the Royal Commission, he declared, so that the enemies of the Jews would be able to say that

> "Dr. Herzl is certainly the exemplary Jew, and he declares that a Jew can never become an Englishman."

Herzl replied:

> "It would be stupid arrogance on my part if I were to give this Commission a lecture on the characteristics of a real Englishman. I shall simply tell them what frightful misery exists in the East and that the people must either die or get out. We have known about the Rumanian distress since 1897 . . . In Galicia things may be even worse. There are more than 700,000 destitute people there. They, too, will start to move."

After lunch Herzl continued:

> "I want to ask the British government for a colonization charter."

> "Don't say charter. The word has a bad sound right now."

> "We can call it whatever you like. I want to found a Jewish colony in a British possession."

"Take Uganda!"

"No. I can only use this . . ." And because there were other people in the room, I wrote on a slip of paper . . . Sinai Peninsula, Egyptian Palestine, Cyprus. And I added: "Are you for it?"

He thought it over with a smile, and said: "Very much so." That was a victory![51]

Indeed. At the very least it was a step in the right direction, since without Rothschild's backing Herzl could expect no support from the British government. On July 10 Major Evans-Gordon read Herzl's statement before the commission, in which the latter discussed his view of the Jewish Question and stated his conclusion that the Jews needed a home.[52] Herzl felt he had made an unfavorable impression on the commission because he could not express himself well in English during the cross-examination.[53] He repaired this impression during a private meeting with Lord James, to whom he explained the plan he had indicated to Rothschild concerning Sinai, El Arish, and Cyprus. At another meeting with Rothschild he submitted an outline in English intended for Joseph Chamberlain, Secretary of State for the Colonies since 1895, of a plan for a colonization company, and an outline in German for Rothschild himself, detailing the financial side.

What made Herzl willing to consider, on a temporary basis, a territory other than Palestine was the realization that nothing could be gained at this point from the Turks. His only hope was that with Rothschild's backing he could gain a foothold in an area of the British Empire close enough to Palestine so that with time it would serve as a convenient springboard to the ultimate destination—the Jewish homeland.

Negotiations with the British government moved along quicker than he had anticipated. On October 22 he was able to obtain an interview with the influential colonial secretary, Joseph Chamberlain. Herzl's description of the interview is vivid and colorful:

October 23, London. Talked yesterday with the famous master of England, Joe Chamberlain. One hour. I explained everything . . . and he was a good listener . . .

He denied the existence of anti-Semitism in England. Perhaps there would be restrictive legislation if Jewish immigration were intensified—this evidently was a hint to me, the gypsy chieftain, to call off my hordes—but the race question did not enter into the matter . . .

He said he could make no statement on El Arish and Sinai. The government would want to hear the view of Lord Cromer, of whom they thought very highly. Too bad that Lord Cromer was no longer here. He had already returned to Egypt . . .

But he had no idea where El Arish was, and so we went to a big table where he pulled out an atlas from among other books, and in the atlas located Egypt. While he did so he said: "But in Egypt we would have the same difficulty with the present inhabitants."

"No," I said, "we will not go to Egypt. We have already been there."

He laughed again, this time bending deep over the book. Only now did he understand me completely, my desire to obtain a rallying point for the Jewish people in the vicinity of Palestine.

In El Arish and Sinai there is vacant land. England can give us that. In return she would reap an increase in power and the gratitude of ten million Jews. All this impressed him. I came right out with it:

"Would you agree to our founding a Jewish colony on the Sinai Peninsula?"

"Yes!" he said, "if Lord Cromer recommends it . . ."[54]

Chamberlain arranged a meeting for Herzl with Lord Lansdowne in the Foreign Office.[55] The afternoon meeting, which took place the following day, was equally successful. He, too, wanted to reassure himself of Lord Cromer's goodwill. They agreed that Leopold Greenberg, Herzl's trusted diplomat, would proceed to Egypt without delay. In the meantime Herzl would prepare an official memorandum for the Foreign Office.[56] Herzl left London on October 24, just in time for the *Jahreskonferenz.*

For the time being Herzl did not divulge any of these plans to the Zionist membership, or even to the Greater Actions Committee, which met in Vienna at the end of October. To all appearances he had been in London solely to testify before the Royal Commission. Weizmann had also heard about Herzl's journey and considered it to be yet another public stunt without substance. To Vera he wrote in a mocking tone, "Herzl is in London: he is taking part in the parliamentary enquête into the Jewish Question . . . Very interesting, isn't it? I can imagine all the comments of the half-baked synagogue politicians. They have probably decided that because of Edward VII's illness, Herzl has been invited to rule England for the time being; and why not?"[57] Weizmann's sarcasm was unjustified. As events were soon to prove, Herzl had used his trip to plant a seed in the hearts and minds of Colonial Secretary Joseph Chamberlain and Lord Lansdowne, the head of the Foreign Office. Both took him and the World Zionist Organization seriously. Just as important, and perhaps even more astounding, he now had the confidence and admiration of Lord Rothschild. This man, who had only weeks earlier referred to Herzl as a "demagogue," was to tell him in October, "You are a great man."[58] Weizmann was unaware of any of these developments when Evans-Gordon appeared in Pinsk in order to examine conditions in the Pale at first hand. Reluctantly Weizmann trudged with him by steamer and boat all over the local swamps for two days, touring the neighboring villages and towns.[59] He had evidently impressed the British M.P., and their acquaintance would serve him well sooner than he realized.

Weizmann was now off on one of his typically exhausting propaganda tours, visiting Kiev, Kharkov, Rostov, and Baku. He arrived back in Pinsk on October 17, exactly one month after his departure. The trip had been a success. Mrs. Khatzman, whom he had visited in Rostov, was not exactly thrilled at her first encounter with her balding future son-in-law, as he appeared much too old for her beautiful daughter,[60] but she soon grew fond of him. Weizmann himself wrote during his return journey, "I kept fearing beforehand that I should prove a stranger in your family, but it turned out quite differently."[61] From the point of view of Zionist propaganda and the university campaign, the results exceeded his expectations. In Baku he was promised 4,500 rubles, including 2,000 pledged by Samuel Shriro, and he was also promised 400 rubles in Rostov. In Kiev the Russian industrialist Brodsky had promised 300,000 rubles for the actual establishment of the university. He had also been successful in setting up a Jewish University Committee in Kharkov for which Jewish and non-Jewish academicians had pledged their support.[62] In short, he was proud of his achievements and eager to report them to the Zionist leadership. On October 25 he set out for Vienna to attend the annual conference of the World Zionist Organization, which met from October 29 to 30. He was to participate in the deliberations as the Swiss representative of the cultural commission which had been set up by the Fifth Zionist Congress.

The newspaper reports, especially in the official organ *Die Welt*, did not, as in the past, hail Herzl's diplomatic maneuverings with the sultan; for once they were more subdued, auguring a stalemate with Constantinople.[63] During the sessions of the Greater Actions Committee, Herzl's report on his diplomatic activities was even more gloomy about future prospects in Constantinople.[64] Herzl was slowly preparing the ground for a new departure in Zionist policy by readying public opinion for an abandonment of hope with regard to the sultan, thereby also conditioning the movement for new diplomatic strategies. In his report to the Greater Actions Committee Herzl declared that his negotiations with the sultan could be viewed as having failed. He could not foresee a change in the current situation unless Turkey were to suddenly find itself at war or were to undergo some international difficulties of great magnitude. As to his trip to England, he simply reported that he had testified before the Royal Commission and had hinted that future Zionist activity would be directed toward that country. Not alluding in the slightest to his remarkable success with Lord Rothschild, he added that the first step in England ought to be to win over its financial elite.[65] Among the resolutions passed during the sessions of the Greater Actions Committee, the official sanctioning of the Anglo-Palestine Company (APC) should be singled out. The APC could begin operations in the summer of 1903 with a bank in Jaffa under the management of S. D. Levontin.[66]

On the second day of the meetings Martin Buber reported on the activities of the Juedischer Verlag and the Jewish Statistical Bureau. Weizmann reported on the successes he had scored in Russia in terms of financial support and general interest and encouragement from academic and other quarters. Buber and Weizmann then moved a resolution in their own names, stating:

> The annual conference notes with satisfaction the information communicated to it by Mr. Buber and Mr. Weizmann on the question of a Jewish

university *[juedische Hochschule]*, declares itself in sympathy with their aspirations, [and] requests members to support the project to the best of their
ability, in collaboration with the Jewish University Bureau in Geneva. The
[Greater] Actions Committee is likewise enjoined, in collaboration with the
above-mentioned bureau, to send circulars on the subject, if and when appropriate, to societies and trusted representatives *[Vertrauensmaenner]*. The
conference enjoins the [Greater] Actions Committee to leave nothing undone to facilitate the establishment of the Jewish university in Palestine.[67]

Weizmann was, of course, aware of the emotional importance of Palestine in any such official declaration and therefore specifically mentioned it. But he was also a pragmatist. In the debates preceding this
resolution he had made it clear that sites other than Palestine would be
considered as a home for the university. On this issue he had Herzl's
support.[68] Yet those present who were bent on Palestine as the only site
for the university were dissatisfied with the resolution. They wanted to
be doubly sure. The conference thus adopted a resolution by Bernstein-
Kohan and Ussishkin—rather than the one proposed by Buber and
Weizmann—with the strong support of David Farbstein. It stated:

> The annual conference enjoins the [Greater] Actions Committee to leave
> nothing undone *[kein Mittel unversucht zu lassen]* to facilitate the establish-
> ment of the Jewish university, but only in Palestine *[nur in Palaestina zu er-
> moeglichen]*.[69]

This succinct resolution was carried by a vote of nine to seven.[70]

The decision by the Greater Actions Committee represented a clear
signal to Weizmann and his collaborators to refrain from attempts to
establish a university—even on a temporary basis—in Europe. It is also
clear that for the time being Weizmann completely ignored this admo-
nition and continued to go ahead with his own plans. A week after the
Bernstein-Kohan–Ussishkin resolution had carried, he stated unequivocally to one of his friends: "We shall have to give up the idea of establishing a University in Palestine even though this will lose us the goodwill of a number of Zionists."[71] Weizmann firmly believed that the
university project would rejuvenate the movement, yet implementation
of a university in Palestine was so utterly impractical that Weizmann was
willing to challenge, albeit secretly, the decision made by the Greater
Actions Committee.[72] A few weeks after his return to Geneva he further
articulated his convictions on the subject:

> My opinion is as follows: although it is *impossible* to establish a *Hochschule* in
> Palestine it is nevertheless necessary, for a whole [range] of reasons, some
> of them tactical, some of principle, to refrain at this stage from categorical
> declarations . . .
>   Even now Palestine is [undoubtedly] a romantic concept: as a concrete
> proposition it does not so much as come within our comprehension . . .
>   I know many people who are prepared to give up Palestine. I most cer-
> tainly do not subscribe to their views, but on the other hand I do not share
> the opinion of people who stand by the seashore in the expectancy of fair
> weather . . .[73]

Three days later Weizmann wrote another long letter to a collaborator in Rostov-on-Don. After a strong denunciation of the lack of accomplishments and imagination throughout the Zionist movement, including within the ranks of the Democratic Faction, he declared in a dramatic and somewhat exaggerated form that was always a by-product when he became excited or was carried away by his own rhetoric:

> The University is the key to our work. It must provide us with a generation that will rise on our ashes, a Jewish generation that will create a synthesis between Europe and the Jewish people. This is why I should like to have the University in England. For that country is the most important focal point for us. The University will head the Exilarchate . . .[74]

The letter is interesting not only because of its reference to England as a country on which the Zionists ought to focus their attention but also because Weizmann was expressly contemplating the establishment of the university in a country other than Palestine. One factor in this self-confidence may have been Herzl's support for Weizmann's scheme.[75] No doubt an added factor in his single-minded determination to explore a European base for the project, before its transfer to Palestine, was that he now had control over funds which he himself had raised.[76] This fact provided him with independence which he jealously guarded and strove to maintain.[77] As the momentum of the Democratic Faction was diminishing, Weizmann increasingly used the university project as a new power base within the movement. This additional factor helps explain why he was unwilling to be constrained by the World Zionist Organization's bureaucracy. Possibly Weizmann also believed that in time he could present the World Zionist Organization with a fait accompli: a well-endowed and academically sound university in Europe en route to being transferred to Palestine. It is interesting to note that on this particular point Weizmann was willing to disregard the bureaucratic legitimacy of the organization.

After his return to Geneva, during the first days of November 1902, he established the Jewish University Bureau (Bureau der juedischen Hochschule) in his own apartment at 4, rue Lombard. With the funds he had raised, of which some three thousand rubles were actually paid up by the summer of 1903, he bought a German typewriter at the end of November and henceforth almost his entire correspondence was conducted in German. He also assembled a small staff of part-time employees and collaborators.[78] In Geneva Weizmann relied mostly on the dedicated work of Catherine Dorfman and occasionally asked for Vera's help. A filing system was instituted, as well as highly efficient office procedures. Considering their meager financial and human resources, the group performed as a finely tuned organization able to deal with an overwhelming amount of work normally requiring a whole army of managers and office staff.

Throughout this period Weizmann's chief collaborators were Berthold Feiwel in Zurich, Martin Buber in Vienna, and Ephraim Lilien and Davis

Trietsch in Berlin. All of these individuals had already left their mark on German culture and were admired by Weizmann for their classical humanistic training and orientation, fields in which he considered himself deficient. There was an implicit understanding among them that Feiwel, Lilien, and Trietsch would devote most of their time to the Juedischer Verlag; Buber to the periodical which was to be founded, as well as to the setting up of a Vienna-based committee on behalf of the university; and Weizmann to the university project in all its aspects. Yet they all supported each other's activities, which naturally overlapped, and Feiwel was as involved as Weizmann in distributing a survey to East European Jewish students. Overall direction and financial responsibility for all the activities conducted by the bureau from late 1902 until 1904 seems to have rested on Weizmann's shoulders. The Juedischer Verlag seems to have been more independent of Weizmann's supervision. Ultimately all his collaborators looked to him for aid during periods of crisis. It was Weizmann who, more often than not, initiated the various projects and provided them with financial and moral support, even if his colleagues occasionally dominated and gave direction to a certain aspect of a particular project.

At the outset of his work in Geneva, Weizmann set three major tasks for the bureau. The first was to create an organization, headed by eminent academics, which would raise funds and assume responsibility for the university project. This organization would be supported by a number of regional Committees for a Jewish University—similar to the committee he had established in Kharkov in the fall of 1902—which would be located in the major European cities, but particularly in Vienna and Berlin. He also envisaged a central committee which would supervise and undertake the preparatory work of the bureau in Geneva. The bureau's second task was to conduct a number of surveys among Jewish students and professors in Western Europe and Russia. The results of these surveys were to provide basic information on the conditions of Jewish students and to serve as propaganda material in explaining the need for a Jewish university.[79] The third aim of the bureau was to launch a periodical to serve the needs of the Jewish University Bureau and act independently of the official Zionist press, which was dominated by Herzl.

As his letters written in early January 1903 indicate, Weizmann believed that cultural enterprises—the university, the periodical, and the Juedischer Verlag—would have far-reaching implications for the social and economic welfare of the Jews. The university project in particular seemed to be the solution to an immediate problem facing Jewish intellectuals. He approached this task with the caution of a scientist, but also with the urgency of a Zionist who could see that time was running out. Another motivating factor was to save the Jewish intelligentsia from "the claws" of Bundism and social democracy. The revolutionary activism and precarious existence of these two movements lent them a romantic and appealing aura. The dormant Zionist movement in Russia, which was even periodically sanctioned by the authorities, had some of this appeal.

Weizmann tried to capture the imagination of the Jewish intelligentsia with a practical project that would be existentially meaningful to them and would thus also draw them nearer to the Zionist movement. In addition, the university project was an internal political power base which would give him the strength and prestige needed to effect changes from within. These combined powerful motivations led Weizmann to dedicate himself totally to the task at hand. He was impatient, spurring on to action both himself and others, sending telegrams and express letters at the first hint of a delay in the university affair. From the end of 1902 until the summer of 1904 Weizmann wrote very little about personal affairs[80] or his work in chemistry, which was surely being neglected.[81]

During the first three months after the bureau's founding, practical steps were taken to establish a university committee in Vienna. Buber had agreed to undertake this task, and at times it seemed that he would be successful, but his efforts were always frustrated by last-minute withdrawals of potential members. In mid-December Buber was still hopeful that all would go well in Vienna.[82] He also sounded optimistic about the possibility that Herzl himself would join the project. Weizmann was, of course, delighted by these developments and in full accord with Buber's proposal.[83] Yet the news that followed in the next two months was less pleasing. An inaugural meeting of the Committee for a Jewish University in Vienna that had been set for January 17, 1903, had to be postponed to the twenty-fifth.[84] Despite the fact that Herzl himself, as well as some distinguished professors, had consented to join, the attempt to set up a committee in Vienna failed.[85]

The attempt to set up a committee in Berlin was only marginally more successful. Under Weizmann's constant prodding, Davis Trietsch had laid the groundwork for such a committee.[86] On his way to Russia Weizmann visited Berlin in mid-March for consultations with Buber, Trietsch, Lilien, and Feiwel; two days later he announced that a university committee had been established.[87]

Weizmann was at least partially successful with the survey of Jewish students from Eastern Europe. In this task he had the full and dedicated participation of his trusted friend Berthold Feiwel. The Jewish University Bureau in Geneva planned a number of surveys. A survey among individual foreign students in West European universities was conducted.[88] Weizmann and Feiwel prepared the questionnaires for East European students at Western universities and at the end of December 1902 and in January 1903 some twenty-five hundred questionnaires were distributed in thirty-eight university towns in Germany, France, Switzerland, Belgium, Austria, and Galicia. Approximately twelve hundred were filled out anonymously and returned.[89] The questionnaire contained thirty-eight questions covering personal data as well as general information on conditions in the students' local universities and possible recommendations for the future. It also elicited student reactions to the plan for a Jewish university.[90] The replies were partially processed and some tentative conclusions were published by Feiwel in 1903.[91]

In addition to the university project, much of Weizmann's time was devoted to the plan for publishing a new periodical. His first thoughts, at the end of December 1902, indicate the purpose of such an organ: "Clearly, we shall continue working in isolated units so long as no rallying point is created to unite all constructive elements, and this can only be achieved by a free, independent, well-edited publication."[92] A few weeks later he had a more ambitious aim for the periodical:

> The periodical I have in mind has to be directed towards the Jewish elite, towards the authentic Jewish intelligentsia of Western and Eastern Europe. Not to the masses, not to the family, but to the isolated circles that are lost to us because of their dispersal. The essential pre-condition for such a journal is absolute sincerity, avoidance of and rebellion against the commonplace, faultless makeup throughout. It must be a truly distinguished newspaper of the kind that people want to read.
>
> We are in the happy situation of being able to bring together writers of the highest European reputation for such a paper. The "Juedischer Verlag," by which it would be published, already commands such status that people who would never write for other Jewish papers (*Die Welt* or whatever) could happily come to us.
>
> If we had a paper that Jewish intellectuals would read, this would provide us with a good medium for propaganda among those circles at present difficult of access.[93]

Two weeks later he concluded that "our [Democratic Faction's] aims lie more in the achievement of a synthesis between East and West, bringing the ghetto to Europe and Europe to the ghetto . . . Hence the character of the paper we contemplate, a golden bridge, as it were, on which the intellectuals of Europe will meet with our Jews . . . it must be an Elite-Organ . . ."[94]

In fact, there already existed a very fine, albeit nonpartisan, periodical for intellectuals whose aim it was to find a synthesis between Eastern and Western Jewry. Called, appropriately enough, *Ost und West*, it was founded in 1901 in Berlin and was edited by Leo Wintz. Davis Trietsch and Ephraim Lilien, who were actively involved in Weizmann's plans for a periodical, composed a memorandum in early 1903 in which they proposed publication by the Juedischer Verlag of a monthly called *Juda, Illustrierte Monatschrift fuer Ost und West*. They sought to smother *Ost und West*, which they viewed as a dangerous competitor. Weizmann opposed aggressive or unethical tactics and preferred to rely on the good quality of the new periodical to elevate it above all other existing publications. Moreover, he pointed out to Trietsch and Lilien that their proposed table of contents for the first number—which included, among other topics, "Introduction to Jewish Culture" by Buber, a review of Herzl's novel *Altneuland* by Feiwel, and an extract from Gorky's *The Jew*—did not even mention the university project.[95]

Given his ideas and conception of the periodical, Weizmann decided that Trietsch could not be involved in an editorial capacity. Therefore, there could be only one choice. "I told you in Berne," he wrote to Feiwel, "that you are the only person who could edit such a paper. I would work for it solely under this condition."[96] But in a letter which arrived a week later Buber[97] clearly hinted that he would like to be co-editor with Feiwel and would even be willing to transfer to Berlin for that purpose. Weizmann changed his mind on the matter of editorship in order to placate both Buber and Feiwel: "As for the editorship, I must at once point out that it never occurred to me to have Toldy appointed sole editor. If you are going to Berlin, as you state in your letter, then it is obvious both of you will take charge of affairs."[98] Thus it was decided that the new journal was to be under the joint editorship of Buber and Feiwel, with Weizmann functioning as co-editor and publisher. In mid-March the three of them met in Berlin and decided to establish the journal *Der Jude, Revue der Juedischen Moderne*, to be published by the Juedischer Verlag.[99] The prospectus mentioned seven aims of the journal:

- the propagation of the Jewish national idea in its most radical form among Jews and the general public
- the scientific grounding of the Zionist program, with an emphasis on its historical roots
- a thorough and all-embracing investigation of all methods for the acquisition of Palestine for the Jews
- impartial and historically oriented positions aimed at practical solutions of contemporary social and cultural affairs of Jewry
- the spread of positive knowledge concerning important aspects in the history and contemporary life of our nation, combined with a present-day description of the Jewish nation in all aspects of life and in all lands
- objective criticism of all harmful aspects of Jewish life within and without the national movement, with the exception of *ad hominem* criticism
- a free exchange of all opinions, whose explication would contribute to further the national tasks[100]

The first issue of the periodical was scheduled to appear in May 1903, with funding from individual donors and the Democratic Faction. News in April 1903 of the vicious pogroms in Russia, however, diverted these funds for rescue work and publication was postponed until January 1904.[101]

Each of the projects briefly discussed here—the university, the survey, and the journal—was a major undertaking in its own right. Yet they were launched and achieved at least initial successes within a mere five months—from November 1902 to March 1903—when Weizmann went on his annual spring propaganda tour of Russia. Equally astonishing is the fact that Weizmann was the prime mover and major propelling force of all of them; his only source of aid was a small part-time staff. It is remarkable that Weizmann was able to concentrate on his work in the laboratory, to conduct coherent and well-planned lectures—even with the preparations he had made in Leysin—and to devote time to Vera and other private affairs. Throughout this period he did not miss a beat in his debates with the Bundists and assimilationists, including a three-night marathon in Bern in February 1903.[102] He continued his propaganda tours to other Swiss cities, took part in the Swiss Zionist Conference at the end of December 1902, and despite his deep reservation about its future, he continued to be the major spokesman for the Democratic Faction.

Little wonder, then, that throughout this period Weizmann was extremely tense and short-tempered—literally "a bundle of nerves," as he often referred to himself. Personality traits that had manifested themselves earlier in his life (e.g., impatience, self-pity and continuous shifts of mood) were heightened at this period. But we also encounter for the first time a proficient administrator, a man with executive capacity and practical initiative and, above all, a man who was absolutely sure of what it was he wanted to achieve. What is striking is that for the first time in his life he undertook a major project without constant reference to a more authoritative figure. For example, dependent as he had been on Motzkin in founding the Democratic Faction, he was now the supreme master of the university project. There are almost no references to Motzkin throughout this period except in a condescending and disparaging vein.[103] Despite the fact that he referred to himself as a bundle of nerves, he was able to devote his energies to the university project because he basically felt secure both in his love for Vera and in his career. He was a man with a vision, a concept of what direction the movement ought to take at this juncture in its history. The crown jewel in this conception was the idea that the Jewish university would rejuvenate the ailing Zionist movement both in the West and in the East. At the start of his work in November he declared that "this University business is most important, and is becoming even more so with the background of the Zionist situation being what it is today. This is my profound conviction. So far, it is the only concrete and large-scale undertaking to help rouse and uplift Jewry as a whole."[104]

For a man sincerely possessed of such a notion there was no time to be wasted. One gets the impression, after November 1902, that with the aid of a secretary and a typewriter there were times when Weizmann—always a prolific letter writer—sent an avalanche of communications out of 4, rue Lombard. He was a Zionist organization in miniature, doing everything from ordering and supervising the printing of new stationery to formulating policy questions regarding the university, *Der Jude*, and so on. The sheer number of letters he wrote seems incredible. Within nine months (from November 1902 until August 1903) he wrote nearly five hundred letters.[105] Writing in Russian, German, Yiddish, Hebrew, and French, he tried to motivate his colleagues throughout Eastern and Western Europe to do their share of the work.

On this score his colleagues repeatedly disappointed him, just as they had done in 1901, when he tried to enlist their help for the Democratic Faction. Now as then, many of his letters from the university-organizing period contain complaints, reminders to respond to unanswered letters, and messages of exasperation mixed with self-pity. No doubt his correspondents were amazed and annoyed by his constant pestering for immediate action on the myriad tasks Weizmann assigned them. To some extent Weizmann's disappointments were inevitable, given his unreasonable demands and impatience.[106]

Weizmann pleaded with his friends to reply to his letters, mixing reason with threats, self-pity with anger. On December 10, 1902, he wrote several letters to his friends. The first was addressed to Feiwel and read:

> . . . Today I again have to start my letter with a complaint. You must have noticed from the copies how I implored Buber and Glikin for information on matters touched on in my various letters. I am sitting here without a reply . . . If Martin [Buber] is now involved in other affairs to the extent that he hasn't the time to take care of small things, then there is no prospect of his being useful to the cause in any way later, when the tasks will become greater and more complicated. It makes matters all the worse when, having relied upon someone in the belief that he can be useful, one is sorely disappointed afterwards . . . Each morning brings me new frustrations . . . Please write forcefully to Buber. I shall do the same . . .[107]

Moments later he must have dictated the following letter to Buber:

> . . . You know that I am a kind and patient man, but now my patience seems to be at an end . . . If you believe that I can do anything for our cause when I am treated by my closest and dearest friends in this fashion you are definitely mistaken . . . We have great responsibilities to the cause and to public opinion. Absolute strangers have placed their confidence in us and pinned their hopes on our ability and capacity for work . . . This is the last time I shall ask you to reply in detail to all the questions put in my previous [four] letters . . .[108]

Buber replied two days later. He explained that he had been ailing and gave detailed answers to Weizmann's many queries.[109] Having roused Buber to action, Weizmann was appeased—for the moment at least—and offered his apologies:

> . . . Nothing was further from my mind than to cause you unhappiness. You can imagine, however, how anxious I was getting about your activities. If I had received your letter a week earlier it would not have occurred to me to bring pressure upon you in any way. Now everything is all right, so don't take it amiss if occasionally I let a stronger expression escape me . . .[110]

Weizmann's letters to his friends reflect not only his impatient streak but also his lack of authority, either personal or institutional. On the other hand, to Moses Glikin, the employee of the bureau, Weizmann wrote in a different vein, revealing an authoritarian and condescending streak toward a man his own age with an equally distinguished record of service in the Zionist movement.[111]

Though often bitter and reproachful, Weizmann kept on reassuring others that he would not easily be disheartened by the indolence of his co-workers. The vehemence of these assurances must have functioned to bolster his own resolve, for ultimately he believed he could rely only on his own efforts. He "knew" his friends "too well" to expect much from them. His assessment of his many co-workers was often correct.

When not voicing anger at others' incompetence, he wrote with confidence and pride—a kind of Zionist noblesse oblige—that he would take on the burden others would not shoulder.

> I realize that we are alone, just a small band of workers [bearing] a gigantic task on our shoulders, waging a desperate struggle lest we get crushed by the weight of the burden. A long time will have to elapse before better, stronger creative forces rise in Judaism. Until then we are the ones who are called upon to keep watch . . .[112]

In addition to his well-founded reproaches aimed at specific colleagues, Weizmann felt generally dissatisfied with numerous segments of Jewry: the "old, serene and overfed . . . the people who rest on their cheap Zionist laurels" and the "inept" students.[113] He was as disgusted with the inactivity of the Hashahar group in Geneva, which he had been instrumental in founding,[114] as he was with the lack of initiative among the Russians.[115]

In the face of this widespread inertia, Weizmann lost interest in the affairs of the Democratic Faction. In light of the tremendous efforts he had invested in its organization, from December 1901 to the fall of 1902, his abrupt disinterest in the Democratic Faction stands out in stark relief. Less than a week after his return to Geneva he wrote to Feiwel: "Faction: a change must be effected in this. We have already become a fiction." In response to Feiwel's demand that a faction bureau be opened in Geneva, Weizmann revealed that the Democratic Faction was no longer his top priority: "I consider the University the only right and important thing now . . ."[116] This change of heart reflected his realization that the Democratic Faction could not accomplish much for the movement at this point.[117]

Weizmann lost interest in the Faction because it could not accomplish much, whereas in the university project he saw an alternative that could succeed and thus provide him and other "progressive elements" with a power base within the movement. Weizmann had come to the conclusion that the Democratic Faction would be unable to seize control of the Zionist movement through direct confrontation. At most it could exert influence through cultural enterprises with which it was intimately tied, such as the periodical, the Juedischer Verlag, and the university.

For all intents and purposes Weizmann had given up on the Democratic Faction by the end of 1902. However, when it suited his purposes to pretend that it was still a viable force in the movement, he presented himself as its spokesman. This is particularly evident in the so-called Schauer affair. It began with a meeting of the Academic Zionist Society of Bern, most of whose membership belonged to the Democratic Faction. At a special meeting the students had decided to have meals served in their cafeteria on Yom Kippur of 1902. Dr. Joseph Seliger wrote an article in the orthodox anti-Zionist paper *Der Israelit* in which he condemned the action of the students. Though he admitted that most Zionists would not have condoned such action, he claimed that it suited the program of the Democratic Faction, "which has set the elimination of religion as its goal."[118] *Der Israelit*, which was published in Mainz, turned to the local prominent Zionist Dr. Rudolf Schauer, who replied to the Seliger article in the same issue of *Der Israelit*. Schauer condemned the behavior of the Bern students but claimed that Zionists in general dissociated themselves from people like the Factionists in Bern. He described the members of the Faction as a tiny minority in the Zionist camp, Russian assimilationists tainted with nihilistic ideas. The Faction's program, wrote Schauer, showed its members to be far removed from everyday life; they lacked contact beyond their small circle and could therefore not find any converts to their immature ideas.[119]

On behalf of the Democratic Faction Feiwel wrote a very sharp declaration protesting against the article by Schauer, attacking the author personally and refuting his claims. Feiwel's declaration was signed by the members of the Moscow faction's bureau and by Aberson, Feiwel, and Weizmann for the Geneva bureau, supplemented by forty other signatories.[120] Weizmann, who since 1900 had virtually ceased all his activities in the Swiss Zionist Federation, took part in the latter's conference in Biel, in December 1902, since the Schauer affair was to be a major topic of the discussions.[121] It seems that the Democratic Faction and its sympathizers retained the upper hand in the debates that took place there, though at the last moment condemnatory resolutions were passed against both Schauer and the Academic Zionist Society. Two weeks later Weizmann wrote on behalf of the Democratic Faction to Dr. David Farbstein, a lawyer and former member of the Berlin Verein, giving Farbstein the power of attorney to set up arbitration procedures.[122]

Weizmann's two-month involvement with the Schauer affair demonstrates that despite his growing separation from the Democratic Faction, he was still concerned that it retain its reputation as a progressive vanguard in the Zionist movement, unblemished by scandal. For the time being he was willing to let the organizational work associated with the Democratic Faction lie dormant while he pursued more important cultural activities. Despite his characterization, in November 1902, of the Faction as "fiction," he still perceived it as consisting of the best—if sometimes infuriatingly inactive—forces in Jewry. Though Ahad Ha'Am was not officially a member of the Faction, he was considered its backer and ally, which explains why Weizmann and other members of the Democratic Faction jumped to the aid of Ahad Ha'Am, the champion of "spiritual" and "cultural" Zionism, in his quarrel with Max Nordau, the champion of "political" Zionism. The context for this affair was provided by Herzl's novel *Altneuland*.

Shortly after the Minsk Conference *Altneuland* was published. The book is a utopian novel describing Palestine twenty years after receipt of a charter from the sultan in 1903. Its main protagonists are an assimilated Jewish lawyer named Friedrich Loewenberg—representing Herzl during his Paris days—who is weary of life, and a rich German officer by the name of Kingscourt, who is in the same spiritual condition. Both are on

y to a lonely island in the Cook Archipelago, where they plan
ᴉ isolation. En route to the island they stop off briefly in Pales-
1923 they leave their island to take one more look at the world.
... ₋ₒ, t they learn that Palestine had undergone changes and decide to
see for themselves. They disembark in Haifa, which is now the safest
and most modern port in the Mediterranean, and discover a completely
transformed country, namely, *Altneuland* (Old-New Land). They find that
within two decades a "new society" had been created on the basis of the
charter from the Turks. Masses of Jews have come to settle the land and
have created new technologies. They have built villages and cities, schools,
a university, an academy for the arts, theaters, an opera, and so forth.
Education is free to all, from kindergarten to the university in Jerusalem.
The new society was built on the principles of cooperatives, with a view
to safeguarding the rights of the individual. Every citizen devotes two
years of his life—from the age of eighteen to twenty—to public service.
There is tolerance toward all religions and nations and equal rights,
without any discrimination on the basis of religion, race, or gender, and
Jews and Arabs live in peace and harmony.[123]

Viewed in hindsight, the novel has an uncanny prophetic flavor to it.
This is not the way Herzl's contemporaries, including some of his close
friends, saw it. They viewed the novel as being full of unrealistic expectations and too deeply riddled with the spirit of Western culture and civilization. Ahad Ha'Am was particularly incensed. He published a devastating review of the book in *Hashiloah,* in which he also insulted Herzl
personally in a sarcastic and condescending tone. Ahad Ha'Am saw
nothing positive in the book. His chief criticism was directed at the kind
of society described in *Altneuland.* He argued that the major characteristic of such a society would be to imitate other nations in order to please
the non-Jews. Why would the academy devote itself to general human
questions while ignoring Hebrew language and culture? Was it for fear
that it would be considered too chauvinistic or too Jewish?[124] Essentially, concluded Ahad Ha'Am, the society described by Herzl would be
devoid of any national spirit. It would be an apish copy of other societies, dominated by a spirit of "slavishness in the midst of freedom,"[125]
which, according to Ahad Ha'Am, was the hallmark of Western Jewish
life.

At Herzl's request Nordau replied.[126] His defense of Herzl consisted
of a vicious attack on Ahad Ha'Am. No doubt Nordau also used this
opportunity to settle old scores with the latter.[127] His attack was insulting, personal, and almost vulgar. He called Ahad Ha'Am's arguments
"partly foolish, partly limited, and malicious." Most of Nordau's article
did not deal with the substance of Ahad Ha'Am's review but rather with
the personality and character of the reviewer. He claimed that Ahad
Ha'Am wanted the Jewish people to develop its essential uniqueness
"amid Asian savagery, the enemy of culture" (*kulturfeindlichen, wilden
Asiatentum),* and accused Ahad Ha'Am of intolerance, going so far as to
say that he wanted to institute the Russian knout and the inquisition.

Nordau dismissed Ahad Ha'Am's essays as "nonsense, empty and obscure pretensions, a hodgepodge of popular verbiage gathered from various European feuilletonists, expressions improperly understood, a chaos of mixed-up terms lacking intelligent thought." He accused him of using Zionist platforms for vile and treacherous attacks on others and described him as a secular protest-rabbi and bitter anti-Zionist.[128]

Nordau's article, distributed by *Die Welt* to Jewish papers throughout Europe, created a furor within the Zionist world. Almost everyone took a stand. There were those who defended Ahad Ha'Am and others who defended Nordau. For a long time Ahad Ha'Am maintained that there were sharply drawn differences between Eastern and Western Jewry.[129] In his eyes the controversy with Nordau was symptomatic of this cleavage. Many of their contemporaries, and some who wrote about this incident later, saw it the same way. Even Weizmann, a staunch upholder of an East-West synthesis, was carried away by the passion of the debate. His first reaction to Nordau's article is contained in a letter to Vera:

> I could never have imagined Nordau descending to slanderous vilification of this type, verging on the behavior of an informer . . . The struggle between East and West within Jewry has now worsened and the editors of *Die Welt* have lightly flung the apple of discord into our camp. I trust that we shall finally succeed in letting the world know where hegemony in Jewry rightfully belongs—in the hands of the author of Degeneration [Nordau] or in those of the young, spiritually free Eastern Jews.[130]

The issue was much more complicated than simply an East-West schism. The divisions within Jewry were not only geographic but also ideological and moral.[131] Thus, Shmarya Levin, an East European and one of Ahad Ha'Am's most devoted disciples, wrote his master an open, chastising letter:

> Herzl builds and you take issue with him. Herzl writes a 342-page novel and you write a small 12-page pamphlet and destroy Herzl's entire structure . . . This in itself is not sufficient evidence of the superiority of talent of the one who destroys over the builder. We could have brought many examples from all walks of life which would demonstrate how much more difficult it is to build than to destroy . . . Herzl writes a novel in which, as is the case with all novels, is contained a mixture of fiction and truth *[Dichtung und Wahrheit]*, and you come with the accountant's dry mentality, searching for faults, which you easily find on each and every of the 342 pages.[132]

Isaac Rothstein, a collaborator of Weizmann's from Rostov-on-Don, sharply criticized Weizmann's support of Ahad Ha'Am's position. In a poignant letter he reminded Weizmann that no matter what his failings, Herzl was the one true giant in the Zionist movement.

> With all due respect to Ahad Ha'Am . . . let's not forget that he is our opponent, that he has not ceased to mock Herzl all the time and to degrade him without cause . . . If we speak of the last affair, was he fair toward Herzl? Does his article constitute a critique? . . . Let us not forget that while Ahad Ha'Am is traveling in Russia as an inspector of the Wissotzky Tea

Company and philosophizes about some mystical rejuvenation of our souls, Herzl is traveling in Europe and worries about achieving our goals. And Herzl was truly successful in rejuvenating and uniting us. Even if isolated expressions in Nordau's article arouse anger, nevertheless, to add our signatures to the protest is to weaken ourselves, and thus we are only fortifying Ahad Ha'Am's criticism of Herzl. This is an undiplomatic move! . . . How can we exchange [Zionism] with Nationalism? That's a joke. Nationalism in the spirit of Dubnov or Ahad Ha'Am has an empty ring; it would have disappeared long ago were it not for Herzlism. Ahad Ha'Am owes Herzl more than anyone else and let us not delude ourselves: "the Jewish spirit," "the spirit of Jewish culture," Ahad Ha'Am's favorite expressions, are useful only as propaganda tools and I doubt much will remain of this once we move to Palestine. And what is the meaning of this spirit? Ahad Ha'Am himself has no idea . . .[133]

On the other hand, Leo Wintz, a Ukrainian Jew who had moved to the West, defended Ahad Ha'Am,[134] as did Berthold Feiwel, a bona fide West European Jew.[135] Even a prominent political Zionist and otherwise staunch supporter of Herzl like Adolf Friedemann of Germany admitted—albeit only to his diary—that Ahad Ha'Am was correct in his controversy with Nordau.[136]

Weizmann's letter to Vera dated March 15, 1903, in which he cast the Nordau–Ahad Ha'Am clash in East-West terms, expressed momentary anger at Nordau but did not truly reflect Weizmann's views on the relationship between Eastern and Western Jewry. Weizmann continuously strove to find a synthesis between the Jewishness of the East and the culture of the West. At the Fifth Zionist Congress, for example, when Alfred Klee of Germany compared the Russian Zionist proletariat with the West European Zionist intellectuals,[137] Weizmann stated his views very clearly: "If one speaks of intellectuals, it is true that the Germans possess a higher degree of European culture than do the Russians, but the organic Jewish culture is to be found among the Russians. I don't want to state that one is superior to the other but rather that we must strive to find a synthesis between these two tendencies, to try to fuse the European and Russian elements . . ."[138] As has been pointed out previously, Weizmann greatly respected the West, especially Western culture. By the same token, he often derided the East European masses and their leaders. He saw the university and periodical projects as arenas in which a synthesis could be forged between the two cultures. Weizmann also suggested that the Democratic Faction could bridge the gap between East and West by fusing the East European Jewish "essence" with European civilization:

What we regard as Jewish culture *[Kultur]* has till lately been confused with Jewish religious worship *[Kultus]*, and when culture in the literal sense was discussed, the Zionists of West[ern] Europe thought that it referred to the improvement of educational facilities in East[ern] Europe. Perhaps it is now understood, because of the specific activities of Faction members, that the totality of Jewish national achievement is intended—particularly that literature, art, scientific research should all be synthesized with Europeanism, translated into modern creativity, and expressed in institutions bearing their own individual character.[139]

Weizmann's conception of the East-West relationship was not the only issue on which he disagreed with Ahad Ha'Am. First, he still admired Herzl, albeit grudgingly at times, both as a human being and a master politician. His attitude toward Herzl was a mixture of amazement, jealousy, and criticism on specific issues. Even with his blemishes, Herzl was still, as Weizmann called him, the "Light of the Exile."[140] In addition, unlike Ahad Ha'Am, Weizmann had not given up on political Zionism. He had only criticized its monopoly within the movement. He wrote to Kalman Marmor, who was close to the affairs of the Democratic Faction, "You know the views of my friends and myself on this [the Nordau–Ahad Ha'Am affair]:[141] we are opposed to Ahad Ha'Am because he is not a political Zionist . . ."[142] As a political realist Weizmann could not fully accept Ahad Ha'Am's purist stance on Zionist issues. While Ahad Ha'Am followed his principles to the letter, Weizmann always considered his obligations as a leader who must attain certain goals. Inevitably this led Weizmann to tactical moves which resulted in a compromising of his principles.

Nevertheless, over the years there had been a gradual, cumulative rapprochement between Weizmann and Ahad Ha'Am on a number of issues. After all, Ahad Ha'Am was the major exponent of Hebrew language and literature and Jewish cultural projects, issues which the Democratic Faction and its spiritual forebears had raised since the Second Zionist Congress.[143] Moreover, Weizmann and his friends took offense at Nordau's condescending tone toward Ahad Ha'Am and East European Jews in general.[144] As a Russian Jew of a similar background, Weizmann clearly shared with Ahad Ha'Am the same basic values. It was only natural that Weizmann and his friends would now, out of personal loyalty, come to Ahad Ha'Am's defense. Thus, Weizmann's defense of Ahad Ha'Am stemmed from an emotional tie and not necessarily from moral conviction. What made this move easier psychologically was the fact that the battle was waged against Nordau and not directly against Herzl himself. Buber, Feiwel, and Weizmann published a declaration in many Jewish newspapers, signed by sixteen other Zionist personalities,[145] which stated, *inter alia:*

Everyone who knows Ahad Ha'Am's meritorious achievements realizes that there is no need to defend the man who helped create spiritual Zionism. This fearless man of truth in thought and deed. This ethical man who is regarded by the best East European Jews with love and trust. This genuine and perfect Jew who appeared as the most radical combatant on behalf of the national movement long before the advent of political Zionism and who issued the call for the redemption of the *people*, the *language* and the *land*. All who know this will admit that it is superfluous to defend Ahad Ha'Am against the defamations and degradations contained in Nordau's article. However, we consider ourselves honor bound to protest most vigorously, in the name of many West European Jewish authors, against this pitiful deed, which does injustice both to the man and the issue at hand.[146]

All in all, it was a dignified response to Nordau, though others, like Leo Wintz, chose to defend Ahad Ha'Am by means of personal insults against Nordau.[147] In the final analysis, there were no winners in this controversy. Everyone lost, in a sense, because of the damage this ugly dispute had done to the image and dignity of the movement vis-à-vis the non-Zionist world and its contribution to an actual worsening of relations between Eastern and Western Zionists.[148] Weizmann, who realized this at the outset, did not enter the controversy lightly. He was already embroiled in disputes with the Zionist leadership which could easily escalate into an irreparable rift. He had managed to find diplomatic solutions in the past two years and was reluctant to easily rupture his relationship with Herzl. His political sense told him that "there are bound to be fierce repercussions at the Congress."[149] He had used almost identical words in 1901 when he had refused to accede to Herzl's demand that he cease preparing for the Youth Conference. In March 1903 he could not have foreseen that within a very brief period a breach with the Zionist leadership would indeed ensue on matters that were far more serious. The Nordau–Ahad Ha'Am controversy was only a symptom of the ideological battle looming at the upcoming Zionist congress.

VIII

From Kishinev to Uganda

On March 17, 1903, Weizmann set out from Berlin on his tour of Russia, full of confidence that his various projects were finally moving in the right direction. His meetings in Berlin with Feiwel and Buber convinced him that *Der Jude* was only a few weeks away from publication; the Juedischer Verlag already had a few publications to its credit, with other manuscripts of quality arriving steadily. Most important, he had finally been able to establish a university committee in Berlin composed of distinguished academicians.[1] Thus, he could point to tangible achievements on his tour and speak with authority about plans for the future. He was still savoring his success in Berlin when he arrived in Warsaw the following day. He stayed at the home of his sister Miriam and his brother-in-law Chaim Lubzhinsky. "Berlin," he wrote to his faithful Catherine Dorfman, "was successful beyond all expectations . . . I only arrived today and am sounding things out . . . Am on fire. Full of hope."[2]

Warsaw turned out to be as successful as Berlin, though he had to work much harder to make any headway. It was difficult to find a common denominator with the various groups, the "Poles of the Mosaic persuasion, hasidim, our Litvaks."[3] His brother-in-law and Nahum Sokolow, the editor of *Hatzfirah*, helped him make contacts and arranged for the larger meetings,[4] but he had to do the legwork and call on people who had long forgotten their Jewishness. "The sight of these well-fed, unfeeling folk wrung my heart," he wrote Vera.[5] Then came a dramatic meeting "in the very heart of the assimilationist circles; the entire Polish intelligentsia had been mobilized . . . The speakers who came to the meeting are noted in Warsaw as 'silver-tongued' orators . . ."[6] The meeting began at 7 P.M. Weizmann spoke for three hours, covering "the entire Zionist platform." Then came the counterattack, led by Henrik Nussbaum, an extreme assimilationist, who thundered against Weizmann and his miserable university project, which, he claimed, was about to ruin Jewry and provoke a pogrom. Weizmann sat quietly, listening to these defamations, until his turn came at midnight. This time he spoke for four straight hours, answering the charges against Zionism and his own person. Weizmann accused Nussbaum and his friends of not being

Jews and wondered why they had come at all. "This fell like a bomb-shell, and exploded with enormous effect . . . In brief, my resolution was carried by a majority of all against two. From 4 A.M. on, the Warsaw telephone was kept busy informing Jewry of the victory." In short, he had "mopped the floor" with his opponents.[7] The next day he was be-sieged by reporters from the Jewish papers who wanted to have more details about the university project. Moreover, he was able to organize a university committee and received pledges for two thousand rubles.[8]

As always after intensive intellectual or physical exertion, Weizmann was exhausted and stayed in bed for two days. Despite his weakness, on March 27 he went to Lodz for two days. Upon his return to Warsaw he reported that he looked "worse than I did after the Fifth Congress."[9] But he was exhilarated; he was able to get pledges for another five thousand rubles in Lodz.[10] He was less pleased with the kinds of Jews he met. "Not in my wildest dreams did I imagine this kind of moral prostitution . . ."[11] His encounter with Polish Jewry had led him to evaluate them as harshly as the Jews of Pinsk, Odessa, and Rostov-on-Don.

On March 31 he arrived in Pinsk, where he planned to stay for ten days until after the Passover holiday, when he would continue his campaign in Moscow. He had now made up his mind that the time had come to tell his family about Vera. His relatives must have suspected all along that something was amiss in his relationship with Sophia, who had suddenly stopped visiting them in Pinsk. His fears of telling his parents that Vera had replaced Sophia were groundless, and they immediately invited Vera to join them for Passover.[12] In the meantime he found out that his Moscow trip would have to be canceled. The tsar was just then visiting the city, and members of the Democratic Faction in Moscow feared that any meeting connected with Zionism would arouse police suspicion.[13] Instead he went to Kharkov—even before the Passover holiday began—where the previous fall he had established a university committee. It was a useful visit in which he was able to regroup the pro-university forces for purposes of publicity and propaganda in large cities of central Russia.[14] Yet the Kharkov trip was marred by information he received there from Vladimir Tyomkin, the area leader for the Elizavet-grad region. Tyomkin confirmed rumors that had been current since February 1903 concerning an imminent ban on privileged Jews, who were entitled to settle and conduct their business affairs outside the Pale of Settlement. In a typically ambivalent passage Weizmann wrote, "I can't see how the Jews can be restricted any further. And yet deep in my heart I am rather pleased that the privileged groups will now get it. Let them find out for themselves what assimilation means. I am so consumed with rage and vexation that I am afraid to meet people. I feel like shouting abuse in their faces."[15]

He was less ambivalent and, in fact, quite worried about another piece of information brought by Tyomkin. He learned for the first time about a secret memorandum on Zionism, which had been prepared in the Russian Ministry of the Interior, whose conclusions boded ill for the movement. The legal status of the World Zionist Organization in Russia was on shaky grounds. On the one hand, a country-wide organization was forbidden, but local activities were allowed and the Minsk Conference had received a special permit. At the same time, the importation into Russia of the shares and provisional certificates of the Jewish Colonial Trust was prohibited in October 1902. It was clear, then, that a secret memorandum, written by Alexei Lopukhin, the chief of police in the Ministry of the Interior, could only signal a worsening of attitude by the government toward Zionism. Indeed, this very detailed memorandum, which dealt with the history of Zionism since the appearance of Herzl's *Der Judenstaat*, contained information and allegations that were extremely damaging.[16] Among other things, the memorandum made the unfounded allegation that there was a connection between the Democratic Faction and the social democratic movement and implied that the activities of the Democratic Faction in Russia should be banned. The memorandum revealed an intimate knowledge of the activities and opinions of individuals such as Bernstein-Kohan, who was suspected of radicalism, Ussishkin, Ahad Ha'Am, and others. Its last section dealt extensively with Weizmann and his efforts to create a Jewish university. On the basis of the Minsk Conference proceedings it concluded that Zionism no longer confined itself to promoting Jewish emigration from Russia, but had become a popular movement which sought to organize Russian Jewry as a separate nationality, with its own Hebrew culture. Finally, Zionism was turning the formerly docile Jewish masses into an opposition movement against the government.[17]

Weizmann had just enough time to get back to Pinsk via Kiev for the eve of the Passover holiday. No sooner had he arrived at home than he received a telegram from Simon Rosenbaum summoning him to Minsk to discuss the memorandum. Rosenbaum was a regional leader for the Minsk area and had been one of the organizers and a vice president of the Minsk Conference of 1902. Somehow he had managed to secure a copy of the Ministry of the Interior's secret memorandum. When Weizmann arrived in Minsk, he showed Rosenbaum a memorandum he had written about the Democratic Faction, explaining its true character to the Russian authorities. Rosenbaum was to submit this explanation to the Ministry of the Interior in St. Petersburg.[18] In light of the danger to Zionists implied in the Interior Ministry's memorandum, Weizmann's use of his time in Minsk to address an illegal meeting of the city's Poalei Zion (Zionist Workers) branch was courageous. Both Yitzhak Berger, who headed the Minsk branch, and Weizmann felt there was common ground between the Poalei Zion and the Democratic Faction, primarily their mutual interest in consolidating the "democratic elements" in Zionism. The Minsk branch of the Poalei Zion was established in 1899. Other groups followed in White Russia and Lithuania. In its early stages the objectives of the movement in Minsk included the following: to voice the views of working-class Jews who had Zionist sympathies; to satisfy the Jewish masses that adherence to Zionism was in consonance with the aim of workers to improve their lot; to stem the inroads made by the Bundists; and to press for the democratization of the Zionist momvement.[19] Weizmann was sufficiently in sympathy with these aims to risk an illegal meeting with Poalei Zion in an isolated building in the woods.[20] He came away with the feeling that "in Pinsk, Homel, Bobruisk and Minsk, Poalei Zion is a very gratifying phenomenon, our only fighting force."[21] The experience with the Poalei Zion must have given him a taste of the conditions under which the Bund was operating in Russia. He had long been envious of the aura of danger and courage surrounding the Bund, factors which helped attract the youth to their ranks.

Despite Weizmann's memorandum and the efforts of others in the movement, the government eventually decided to crack down on Zionism. On July 7, 1903, Minister of the Interior Vyacheslav von Plehve and Lopukhin, the director of his police department, sent a secret circular to the Russian provincial authorities in which they again forbade the importation of Jewish Colonial Trust shares into Russia and also prohibited collections for the Jewish National Fund. Public Zionist meetings were forbidden, as was the unauthorized establishment of Zionist schools and libraries.[22] Yet these developments were still almost three months away. For the moment Weizmann must have felt lucky to have evaded the police in Minsk. As he slowly wound his way back to Geneva—stopping off again at Pinsk, Berlin, and Karlsruhe—he must have reflected on how differently his propaganda campaign had evolved from the way he had planned it in March. At the same time he was satisfied; he had adapted well to changing circumstances, had raised a respectable sum of money, and had finally formalized and legitimized with his parents his relationship with Vera. In the train he had plenty of time to reflect on this and other matters, but like most Zionists he had no knowledge whatsoever of Herzl's actual diplomatic moves. After he heard in Berlin the news of Herzl's trip to El Arish, he wrote to Vera in a matter-of-fact tone. "Herzl's journey to Egypt has apparently been very successful and has had positive results in terms of colonization."[23] About a year earlier, upon hearing of Herzl's visit to the sultan, he had written to her in a similar vein, with equal ignorance of the true situation.[24]

Soon after his return to Geneva, in the last week of April, he received an angry letter from Vera. Upon learning that Weizmann had gone to Minsk, she exploded:

> When will an end come to all your wanderings? . . . I swear to God, it is as though everybody conspired to exploit you to the utmost. You must agree, my friend, that the Zionists themselves show you no mercy whatsoever and wring every bit of strength from you. I spoke very sharply about this with [Isaac] Rothstein. Now, when you are so worn out, so utterly exhausted, he suddenly says to me: "Couldn't we send Chaim to America now?" as though Chaim were an object of some sort. What are *they* doing? Chaim, what is Toldy doing? Buber? All the work is pushed onto your shoulders. I don't mean that you should fold your hands and wait for other people to work— you'd have to wait a long time for them to begin—but you must ask yourself

how much longer you can go on with this kind of work and conserve your strength. My dear friend, under no circumstances will I let you go anywhere this summer, no matter how much you insist. You've traveled quite enough this year.[25]

Vera's letter arrived on April 30, a few days after the infamous Kishinev pogrom, which was to leave a lasting imprint in Jewish history. If Weizmann had had any desire to listen to Vera's chiding and lead a more relaxed existence, resting on his laurels in calm Geneva, it would soon evaporate into thin air. Kishinev upset and changed all those projects he had worked for so arduously during the past two years. To explain its impact a brief recapitulation of the pogrom is necessary.

Kishinev was then the capital of Bessarabia.[26] In 1903 some 50,000 Jews lived there, constituting 42 percent of a population of 120,000.[27] The pogrom was preceded by a venomous anti-Jewish campaign led by Pavel Krushevan, editor of the local newspaper *Bessarabets,* which was heavily subsidized by the government. In this hateful atmosphere the body of a Christian boy was found and a young Christian woman died in a Jewish hospital. A blood libel circulated by *Bessarabets* spread like wildfire, followed by a pogrom on April 19 and 20, 1903. According to official statistics, 49 Jews lost their lives. More than 500 people were injured; among them 100 were seriously injured and 30 were permanently crippled. Many women were raped. Some 800 houses were looted and destroyed and 600 businesses and shops were vandalized.[28] The material damage amounted to 2,332,890 rubles (about $1.2 million) and about 2,000 families were left homeless.[29] All the available evidence points to the fact that the pogrom was aided and directed by agents of the Ministry of the Interior and high Russian officials of the Bessarabian administration, possibly with the backing of von Plehve himself.[30] While the gruesome killings took place in the streets, military bands played in the Royal Gardens and People's Park, attracting large crowds of well-dressed citizens, officers of the garrison, and elegant ladies.[31]

The young poet Haim Nahman Bialik was sent to Kishinev by the Jewish Historical Commission in Odessa in order to interview survivors of the pogrom and to prepare a report on the atrocities committed at Kishinev.[32] Upon his return, he wrote his searing poem "In the City of Slaughter," denouncing neither God nor the Russian mob but the Jews themselves. Not wholly justifiably, he accused the Jews of cowardly and supine acceptance of outrages against them, a theme that was later often used by the Zionists. At the same time, the poem also vividly describes the wanton destruction and horrendous acts of defilement and murder committed by the pogromists.[33] Bialik's poem had a tremendous impact. There were widespread moves among Jews to establish defense organizations, and there were also those who sought revenge.[34]

The first reports on the pogrom in Kishinev were telegraphed from the Rumanian border by Bernstein-Kohan's emissary.[35] One such telegram probably reached Weizmann. He immediately telegraphed back, following it with a letter to Bernstein-Kohan which expressed his feelings of alarm and concern and the wish to organize a large relief committee which would send as much funds as possible.[36] In light of the immediate, far-reaching, and continuous reverberations of the pogrom, which shook the entire Jewish world, it is surprising to read Weizmann's letter to Vera written the following day. Like so many other letters to Vera, this one also begins with a complaint about her not writing often enough and an expression of his longing for her. He then proceeds to inform her of his work in the laboratory and the bureau and tells her that he is at work on a memorandum to Herzl. "All this," he concludes, "is extremely important and must be done, at once." And then, as though of lesser importance, he adds: "The Kishinev happenings have given us added work. We want to organize a collection here in town and then start to collect pledges throughout Western Europe. This morning I collected 300 francs from students."[37] A week after writing this letter to Vera, he was still mostly concerned with his memorandum to Herzl and the university project. His long letter to Catherine Dorfman dealt primarily with a report of his successful Russian tour. Toward the end of the letter, he reported that he was cheerful and in a hopeful mood. Again, as an afterthought he added, "What poisons this state of well-being is the thought of Kishinev."[38] It is difficult to understand how Weizmann, who was in close touch with and well attuned to every event in Russia, was not moved by the virtual "earthquake" created by Kishinev to drop all his other activities and devote himself to relief work on behalf of the victims.

One possible explanation for his behavior may be the fact that he was still under the powerful impressions of his own Russian tour, or perhaps he was unconsciously engaging in wishful thinking that nothing take place now to prevent him from reaping the fruits of that tour on behalf of the university. It is astonishing that in his memoirs Weizmann ascribed to Sokolow his own behavior of almost complete detachment when hearing of the Kishinev pogrom. Weizmann's memoirs contain a wholly fictitious account of his own reaction:

> It was during those Passover days that we got the news of the ghastly Kishinev pogrom. I lost my head, and was in something like a panic. Not so Sokolow. Telegrams were pouring into the office of *Hatzfirah*, with details of the butchery. In the midst of the universal horror Sokolow remained calm . . .
>
> I had intended to proceed from Warsaw to Geneva. I abandoned my classes, such as they were, and returned to the Pale. Together with friends and acquaintances I proceeded to organize self-defense groups in all the larger Jewish centers. Not long afterward, when a pogrom broke out in Homel, not far from Pinsk, the hooligans were suddenly confronted by a strongly organized Jewish self-defense corps . . . I remember distinctly a time when a pogrom came as a positive relief to us . . . At least when the attack took place we knew the worst, we could face up to our enemies and then, when the storm had passed, we might expect a period of comparative tranquility

. . . Our dreams of Palestine, our plans of a Hebrew University receded into
the background . . . Our eyes saw nothing but the blood of slaughtered men,
women and children, our ears were deaf to everything but their cries. When
at last I did return to Geneva, I found no peace in the laboratory or the lecture hall . . .[39]

Weizmann was indeed in Warsaw when the Kishinev pogrom took place,
but there is no indication that he reacted to the butchery or, indeed, that
the news even reached him in Warsaw. In any case, he did not return
to the Pale but continued his journey to Switzerland, via Berlin and
Karlsruhe, probably arriving in Geneva on April 25, where Bernstein-
Kohan's telegram reached him. It is curious how Weizmann was able,
some forty years later, to totally reconstruct his past. Possibly over time
he wished to forget his own inappropriate behavior during a time of crisis and truly began to believe that he had been present to help the Jews
of Kishinev and Homel.

Weizmann's ascription of his own behavior to Sokolow came in old
age, when his distortion of the facts could perhaps have been excused
as a lapse of memory. But what makes it abundantly clear that he wished
he had behaved differently is a letter he wrote to Dorothy de Rothschild
eleven years after the Kishinev pogrom, in which he reconstructed his
past thus: "Eleven years ago I happened to be in Russia in the cursed
town of Kishinev during a Jewish massacre. In a group of about 100 Jews
we defended the Jewish quarter with revolvers in our hands, defended
women and girls, Jewish lives and property. We 'slept' in the cemetery—the only 'safe' place, and we saw 80 Jewish corpses [sic] brought
in, mutilated dead . . ."[40] It all sounded very heroic and honorable but,
in fact, was nothing but wishful fantasy. While Kishinev's Jews were just
beginning to rebuild their shattered lives, Weizmann was closeted at 4,
rue Lombard, engrossed in plans for rebuilding the Zionist movement.[41]

Weizmann's commitment to his projects was so intense that even the
Kishinev pogrom could not distract him. His success in Russia continued to buoy him. He was confident that the Jewish intelligentisa, if not
the masses, were slowly realizing the importance of cultural work for
Zionism. After all, had he not been able to lay the foundation for an administrative and academic supervisory body for the university? Had he
not been told by Feiwel and Buber that the first issue of *Der Jude* was
ready for the printers? The Jewish Statistical Association and the Juedischer Verlag were now going concerns, and he had financial resources
which made him independent of the official leadership in Vienna, as well
as the condescending regional leaders in Russia. He was clearly concerned with power and possibly thought that the combined human and
financial resources associated with the university project and the scattered remainder of the Democratic Faction might gain him a powerful
position at the upcoming Sixth Zionist Congress. Thus, he wrote a long
letter to Herzl which was most likely edited and turned into excellent
German by Berthold Feiwel.[42] Writing in his own and Feiwel's names,
he lectured Herzl on the past and present failures of the Zionist leader-

ship during its seven-year existence. Critical of the past, he offered a
blueprint for the future. The memorandum to Herzl was not simply a *cri
de coeur* but an attempt to prepare a platform and an ideological basis for
the upcoming congress. Far from being an objective analysis of the contemporary situation in both East and West, the memorandum was marked
by selective argumentation which hardly touched on Herzl's immense
achievements.

In an astute opening maneuver, Weizmann described to Herzl the
contents of the secret memorandum that had been shown him by Rosenbaum in Minsk in order to explain how Zionism was viewed by the
Russian government. Rather than give his own assessment, he wrote that
the movement was not taken seriously by the Russian authorities; the
Actions Committee, in particular, was charged with being incapable of
carrying out the decisions of the congress. He then moved on to a description of the conditions of Zionism in Russia, squeezed as it was between the left-wing revolutionary forces, on the one hand, and the orthodox right wing, on the other:

> . . . The larger part of the contemporary younger generation is anti-Zionist,
> not from a desire to assimilate, as in Western Europe, but through revolu-
> tionary conviction. It is impossible to calculate the number of victims, or de-
> scribe their character, that are annually, indeed daily, sacrificed because of
> their identification with Jewish Social Democracy in Russia. Hundreds of
> thousands of very young boys and girls are held in Russian prisons, or are
> being spiritually and physically destroyed in Siberia . . . Almost all those
> now being victimized in the entire Social Democratic movement are Jews,
> and their number grows every day. They are not necessarily young people
> of proletarian origin; they also come from well-to-do families, and inciden-
> tally not infrequently from Zionist families. Almost all students belong to
> the revolutionary camp . . . Saddest and most lamentable is the fact that
> although this movement consumes much Jewish energy and heroism, and
> is located within the Jewish fold, the attitude it evidences toward Jewish na-
> tionalism is one of antipathy, swelling at times to fanatical hatred. Children
> are in open revolt against their parents. The elders are confined within tra-
> dition and Orthodox inflexibility, the young make their first step a search
> for freedom from everything Jewish . . . [43]

This passage recapitulates a long-standing theme with Weizmann. Ever
since he had come to the West he had fought against the Bund and social democracy as the worst enemies of Zionism. Yet he feared them precisely because he recognized the attractiveness of the revolutionary my-
thos for young people, the yearning to sacrifice everything, including their
lives, for the sake of an ideal. He had seen many of his erstwhile Zionist
comrades, tired of waiting for a legal and formal charter to be handed
down benevolently by some European power or the sultan, turn to the
more exhilarating and immediate opportunities offered by the revolutionaries. When he wrote of rifts within families he was no doubt thinking of the heated debates with his brother Shmuel on these very issues.
And yet one detects, here and elsewhere, a tone of reluctant sympathy

toward these movements, a wish, perhaps, that Zionism could offer the same opportunities for heroism and self-sacrifice. What infuriated him much more was the "enemy" from within Zionism, the Mizrahi, which in his opinion suppressed those progressive elements—such as the Democratic Faction—that could bring about a change in the direction of the movement. He now made an attempt to persuade Herzl to abandon the Mizrahi faction:

> Now visualize the location within this environment of the few young Zionists with an adequate armor of independent thinking and European education to combine with their Jewish knowledge: on the one side the revolutionaries with their powerful arguments drawn from tragic day-to-day realities, their ideal of personal heroism and the magnetism inherent in martyrdom; on the other side Zionism as it is generally conceived and represented in Russia. First, there is the great mass of "Mizrahi," with 10,000 adherents. You know very well, dear Doctor, that this group enjoys the special patronage of the A.C. We would be the last to impose difficulties upon the effort to enroll the Orthodox into Zionism, even though our activities are frequently inhibited or paralyzed by them . . . But in the last analysis something we could not express at Congresses, and have refrained from ventilating in the press, has to be said: blatant promotion of the "Mizrahi" at the Congresses, in the press and through administrative acts not only betokens a profound lack of understanding but also carries with it incalculable damage and mischief . . . The leadership, . . . seems unable to assess or determine the kind of ideological sacrifice involved for the Zionist movement as a whole in wooing the "Mizrahi"—ideological sacrifice at present, but ultimately to be of a more concrete nature.[44]

Curiously, it was Weizmann himself who, when debating the Bund on a number of occasions, had defended the Mizrahi against their attacks. In his letter to Herzl, however, he undertook to dissuade the leader from further alliance with the orthodox circles. He argued, further, that the orthodox were slowly trying to dominate the Zionist movement and were alienating the youth of Eastern Europe in the process. This, he implied, could only have the effect of driving even more young men and women into the ranks of anti-Zionist revolutionary circles. Instead of forging a true spirit of idealism, the orthodox were fostering *golus*—nationalism which led to orthodox dogmatism and passive resistance. What other models of behavior and ideology were left to the youth of Eastern Europe? Apart from complete Russification and assimilation, only a petty bourgeois Zionism "exhausting itself in the most superficial propaganda activities." Zionism in Eastern Europe had been stagnating; there were no new faces to inspire the youth. In short, "the position of young Zionists is almost tragic. Misunderstood by the leadership, confined, driven into opposition, they have to struggle bitterly, both against foes from without as well as against adherents to Zionism, to make the slightest advance."[45]

What, then, was the solution he proposed? What could save the Zionist movement from stagnation? The Democratic Faction.

The Faction forms the connecting link between the older and the younger generation. It alone is capable of assuming the struggle against the revolutionaries, which indeed it does. It alone is freedom-loving and socially enlightened. It extracts the Jewish essence from among the masses and pours it into a European mold. But what that Jewish essence is, the European Zionists refuse to comprehend . . . Perhaps it is now understood, because of the specific activities of Faction members, that the totality of Jewish national achievement is intended—particularly that literature, art, scientific research should all be synthesized with Europeanism, translated into modern creativity, and expressed in institutions bearing their own individual character. We believe that this Jewish culture, being the most vital form of the people's self-expression, is more than a mere part of the national renaissance; next to the larger Palestine ideal of Zionism it represents its only remaining attribute, and can at least offer the modern Jew dissatisfied with a Shekel contribution an approach to a loftier view of life, with scope for enthusiastic action. Perhaps it is the only reply that we can make to our opponents, since the economic and political reply must be postponed to the future . . .[46]

One wonders how Weizmann could have possibly believed in many of the sentences contained in this last passage. Did he really believe Herzl to be so ignorant of the true state of the Democratic Faction as to seriously respond to Weizmann's offer to form a link between the generations? Only weeks earlier Weizmann himself had given up the Faction as "fiction." He knew quite well that for all intents and purposes it had ceased to exist after the Minsk Conference, if not earlier. He also knew that every cultural endeavor—the university, the Juedischer Verlag, *Der Jude*—though created in the name of the Democratic Faction, was the result of efforts by a few enterprising, strong-willed, and hard-working individuals. What, then, could have impelled him to make such a suggestion, which on the face of it seems almost absurd? Possibly two factors motivated him. The first was his recent successful trip to Russia and perhaps the illusion that in the midst of a larger, more passive organization youth and enthusiasm could be mobilized and make up in spirit what they did not possess in numbers. But he was also—perhaps unconsciously—employing one of Herzl's own favorite tactics: the pretense that he was leading a large group of followers. He was, in fact, banking on his ability to do so in the future, projecting it backward into the past and present.

Moreover, Weizmann extolled the virtues of East European Jewry over the West European Zionists, "who are utterly remote from Jewish culture." He prescribed that the "Jewish essence" of Eastern Europe should be poured "into a European mold." How this would be done he did not explain, nor did he explain the method by which European culture would be injected into the Jewish masses of Eastern Europe. His own ambivalence regarding the East-West conflict came to the fore in this letter to Herzl and elsewhere. He was a man straddling the line between these two cultures. He believed that the East European Zionists were more Jewish, more authentic, but at the same time he felt that they were incapable of real action, politically—and culturally—immature. The Western Zionists, on the other hand, had only a superficial understanding of Zionism, but "Western Jewry will have to be enlisted, particularly if the investigation and exposure of the problems of our movement are to be undertaken in earnest . . . a movement such as ours must set great store upon political maturity, and this is found in greater abundance beyond the frontiers of Russia."[47]

Reviewing the condition of Zionism country by country, he came to the conclusion that not much could be expected from the Zionists in Switzerland, Austria, Germany, and England. "Regarding America, it is best to remain silent." And yet once more he returned to the theme of Eastern versus Western Zionism. Weizmann had derided Russian Zionism for years, and his thoughts in the following passage can again only be understood in light of his recent positive experiences there two weeks earlier. It must also be understood as a passage written by an East European Jew to a West European Jew from an assimilated background who had for years been accused of ignoring the needs and wishes of the Russian Zionist leadership.[48] Thus, Weizmann informed Herzl that "Russian Zionism towers over the West European variety because of the readiness for sacrifice and its undiluted Jewish consciousness, which, taken together, constitute as it were an organic Zionist force. West European Zionism is in many respects simply a passive form of nationalism and, consciously or not, continues in an acceptance of assimilation."[49] Having also dismissed the Western Zionist press—primarily *Die Welt*—as a *"quantité négligeable,"* Weizmann informed Herzl that there was a plan afoot in certain quarters to rebel against this un-Jewish form of Zionism. Since it was his—and Feiwel's—wish to prevent a split within Zionism, they wrote this letter, which could be viewed as "the final opportunity to prevent an inner struggle."[50] In fact, he seems to have been carried away by his own rhetoric and the heat of debate. As a practical man and a believer in compromise, Weizmann usually viewed these issues in more detached and reasonable terms. Himself a "synthetic" Jew who combined in his personality and education both elements, he usually advocated a synthesis between East and West.[51] Tension between the Russian Zionist leaders and the Vienna-based leadership had indeed been rife for years, but Weizmann did not hold the view that the differences were irreconcilable.

Thus, he lectured Herzl on the steps to be taken to unify and strengthen the movement. These included: the expansion of West European Zionist activity, particularly among its youth; a rapprochement between Eastern and Western Zionism by injecting West European Zionism with Jewish content; intensified efforts to win over for Zionism the Jewish intellectuals; a demonstration of real and effective cultural achievements; and a serious expansion of practical projects. These tasks were a blueprint for the future, yet, Weizmann finally implied, they could be completely understood only by men like himself, men who "have had the opportunity to observe, live among, suffer and work with many levels of our people, from the drawing rooms of Western Europe to the masses in the ghettoes." Clearly implying that Herzl had only a partial knowledge of the movement, he added, "We have, moreover, experienced contact with all circles within Zionism, including its most estimable people. Particularly, we have come to know the youth as few others have."[52] Presuming to speak in their behalf, he ended with the hope that the congress would meet the needs of the youth, but also with a thinly veiled threat that if this should not prove to be the case, they would be driven to rebel.

If Weizmann thought he could overwhelm Herzl with this tour de force, he was quite mistaken. The letter to Herzl is surely one of Weizmann's most eloquent, yet it is not mentioned in Herzl's diaries, which often contain partial or even verbatim letters or notes addressed to him. In retrospect, it is evident that Weizmann's timing in sending the memorandum was poor. For one thing, he had signed his name to the anti-Nordau protest only a short time previously and had thus indirectly placed himself in opposition to Herzl; under different circumstances Herzl might have given the memorandum more attention as an authentic plea for cooperation and understanding. Moreover, Herzl had little patience for a junior member of the Zionist movement who did not fully support his policies. Weizmann's timing was especially poor in the aftermath of Kishinev. Herzl felt keenly the need to do something for the victims; he was already seriously contemplating a trip to Russia and was still in the midst of negotiations for El Arish. Thus, Herzl's reply to Weizmann was cool, with an unmistakable air of condescension. On the whole, it did not touch directly on the issues Weizmann had raised in his letter but rather on the attitude of the Democratic Faction toward the Zionist leadership and toward himself in particular: "Your exposé," he told Weizmann in one deflating paragraph,

has really not revealed anything new. The factual reports from Russia are unfortunately very gloomy and our greatest preoccupation here can only be to dispatch aid as speedily and as generously as possible. I do not believe, however, that the divisiveness revealed in the conduct of the Faction can serve this common purpose . . . At the same time, I would like to report that the Smaller Actions Committee is not the unstable, short-sighted and narrow-minded body that is depicted in the controversies conducted, if not by the Faction itself, then by friends whom the Faction will find difficult to repudiate. You know to what instances, to what newspapers and people my comment refers. I have always regarded the Faction favorably—for which some of the best Zionists have reproached me . . . I am not oversensitive towards a reasonable opposition, neither do I want songs of praise sung to me [ich bin weder ein Streber noch ein eitler Narr] . . . I would like to tell you that the behavior of the Faction in the case of Nordau-Ahad Ha'Am has flabbergasted me . . . This does not prevent me from studying carefully those suggestions contained in your exposé which seem worthwhile. Most of the questions raised by you can be usefully discussed only at the Congress and in the days preceding it. I regard you, Dr. Weizmann, as a person who has been temporarily misled, but nevertheless a useful force [eine voruebergehende, verirrte aber nuetzliche Kraft] who will once more find his way back and proceed along the right road together with all of us. I am becoming ever more strongly convinced, however, that not all the gentlemen in your group are in this category, and I prepare myself for the time when, sooner or later, they will be lost to our movement.[53]

A few weeks later Weizmann suggested to Herzl that they meet to discuss their differences, but he received no reply.[54]

Herzl was obviously not about to hand over the reins of leadership to the Democratic Faction, or even to seek their advice as to how to run the movement. He was at an advantage, in any case, being the only one to know which diplomatic or administrative steps the Actions Committee would take next. He had taken the movement by surprise many times before and was about to do it again. If he was previously willing to cultivate and aid Weizmann and his group as a possible alternative to the Ussishkin-led Russian *Landsmanschaft*, he could just as easily cut them off from most sources of power within the movement, be it a committee membership, financial aid from SAC, or his own blessing. Thus, Weizmann's letter to Herzl ended a relationship that was potentially more useful to the former than it could possibly be to the latter. A person as sensitive to diplomatic maneuvers as Weizmann must have been aware of the consequences his letter might have; at no time in the past did he seek an irrevocable break with Herzl. Yet, as was pointed out, he had miscalculated in his timing and possibly also in the tone of the letter. To the degree that he had had any influence in the inner circles of SAC, it evaporated in the wake of the *Altneuland* controversy and his sharp criticism of the Zionist leadership.

On the very day he wrote the final version of his letter to Herzl, Weizmann fully realized that the Kishinev pogrom had undermined his own projects and that he would have to seek new sources of support. Even in the face of this major calamity, his obsession with the university project remained unabated. Every ruble he had collected in pledges in Warsaw, Lodz, and Kharkov had now been diverted to aid the victims. He knew quite well that without independent resources the entire elaborate structure of the Jewish university plan would collapse. Since it was unlikely that he would get funds from the East, he turned to—of all people—David Wolffsohn, one of Herzl's most trusted and loyal collaborators, as well as Julius Moses of Mannheim, chairman of the Mannheim University Committee, with a request for loans to tide him over until the pledges from Eastern Europe materialized.[55] Neither of them complied. What was worse, Weizmann's friends in Russia made it clear that for the time being the university project and other cultural endeavors were completely irrelevant in the face of much greater material needs.[56] There were fears of pogroms in Kiev and elsewhere.[57] Samuel Shriro, his first major contributor to the university project, put it bluntly:

I have come to the conclusion that for Jews this is not the right time for cultural projects. Everywhere people expect pogroms [in Baku, Yelizavetgrad, Odessa, Kiev]. In short, times are turbulent and one does not have peace of mind to think about anything . . . Thus, in my opinion, not only

is this not an appropriate time for cultural projects, but also not for the Jewish University [Hochschule]. I had experienced the horrors of 1881 and I can
state [authoritatively] that 1881 had not produced such fears and feelings of
uncertainty among Jews as they exist now . . .[58]

Shriro informed Weizmann that in Baku nine thousand rubles had been
collected and sent to Kishinev at the initiative not only of Jews but also
of Armenians and Tatars. How, then, he implied, could anyone think of
other, less pressing causes?[59]

In the meantime Herzl had also made it clear to Buber and his associates that in light of their attack on Nordau he could not possibly participate in or contribute to the publication of *Der Jude*.[60] Buber's attempt
to explain that the protest against Nordau was not a sign of disloyalty to
Herzl, that it merely reflected disavowal of the form and method of distribution of Nordau's article, and that there was no connection between
himself and his associates in the Democratic Faction with the articles in
Ost und West[61] fell on deaf ears. Herzl found it difficult to accept so simple an explanation.[62] To Buber's contention that he and his friends were
kept away from Zionist affairs Herzl replied indignantly that both Feiwel
and Buber had been given the opportunity to edit the major party paper
Die Welt; what more could they—or, for that matter, anyone—expect?
He also sounded a warning signal: "I don't want to conceal my opinion
that the so-called Faction, for reasons that elude me, has taken the wrong
path. My advice is—strive to find your way back to the [Zionist] movement . . ."[63] Herzl seems to have maintained a similarly hostile attitude toward the Juedischer Verlag, which was also viewed as a center of
opposition to his leadership.[64]

The plans and projects Weizmann and his friends had worked on so
diligently were falling apart in the wake of Kishinev and the internal Zionist opposition. Yet Weizmann was not easily deterred. On the contrary, one of his greatest virtues was his resilience and ability to draw
on his own intellectual and physical resources at moments that seemed
quite hopeless. In this instance, too, having fully realized the situation
in the East and what it would mean for him and other members of the
Democratic Faction, he changed his plans and tactics almost immediately. "We must now wait for two months at least until the pain sub-
sides and people can think of something besides Kishinev,"[65] he wrote
to a friend. Once more he joined the effort to collect funds for the victims of the pogrom. At the end of May he traveled to Munich, site of his
previous battles with the Bundists. This time he was able to report to
Vera that "yesterday's [May 23] meeting lasted until two in the morning
and went off more than brilliantly. There was such an exalted mood, and
the various parties, including the Bund, responded so nobly—the like of
which I never expected."[66] At the same time he urged his friends not to
lose heart. "We of all people . . . must not lose our heads just now, but
mobilize all our energies and keep striving to build upon the ruins."[67]

Having temporarily lost the momentum that was generated by the university project, he made a desperate attempt to save the Democratic Faction as an alternate source of influence and power within the movement. He was convinced that the Vienna-based leadership, with the more or less active aid of hostile Russian Zionist leadership, was determined to destroy the Faction: "They are fighting against the Faction, with the intention of killing it off politically even before the Congress . . ."[68] He repeated the charges in a letter to Nahum Sokolow, though he admitted that he might be overstating his case:

> In Vienna a spirit seems to prevail whereby whatever does not conform to the "Viennese" concept of Zionism must be cast root and branch out of the Party. Everything is judged there from the point of view of the Ahad Ha'Am–Nordau business, and woe unto him who bears the mark of Cain in opposition to Nordau. A crusade has now been launched against the Faction, and particularly against individual personalities within it, from many sides. Herzl, Ussishkin, the "Mizrahi," all have got together to become the hangmen of the young, freedom-loving elements of the movement.[69]

The fight was on and the Democratic Faction was to be the bulwark of the "young, freedom-loving elements" in the struggle against the "old, authoritarian," Herzl-dominated Viennese leadership.[70] Weizmann's solution to the threat against the Democratic Faction was twofold: to try to elect as many Faction members to the Sixth Zionist Congress as possible[71] and to hold a preliminary Democratic Faction conference just prior to the congress.[72] The aim of the pre-congress conference would be to transform the Democratic Faction from a political faction active only during congresses into a permanent "working group" able to undertake various cultural and political tasks whenever required.[73]

In order to reach as many comrades as possible within a short period of time, Weizmann sent out a circular on June 17, 1903, which dealt with the preparations for the Sixth Zionist Congress. It included a list of localities in Russia where there were good chances of electing Democratic Faction candidates. It also contained a list of over forty candidates suggested by Weizmann and Buber, information on the proposed conference, and propaganda activities. The circular also mentioned the possibility of sending a Faction member to Palestine before the start of the congress to compose a report on the educational system there which would, once and for all, settle the question of the best location for the Jewish university. The last point mentioned was the publication of *Der Jude*, for which money was needed immediately. Funds were needed for all aspects of work until the pledges made in Russia could be called in.[74]

Some of Weizmann's friends in Russia and in the West must have been surprised by his flurry of activity in the period before the Sixth Zionist Congress. For one, they were not terribly impressed by the letter he had sent Herzl, copies of which went to a number of them.[75] In addition, his remarks concerning the Democratic Faction as the only element within the Zionist movement capable of useful work must have raised quite a few eyebrows among those who had a more realistic assessment of the

Faction. If Weizmann had any illusions about the state of the Faction, about how strong it really was, his friends were determined to remind him in no uncertain terms of the real situaton and of the kind of help he could expect from them and others. Replies to Weizmann's letters and circular of June 17 were harsh and uncompromising, even from among those who had a genuine concern and interest in the welfare of the Democratic Faction.

Abraham Idelson, one of the leading members of the Democratic Faction in Russia and a member of its Russian Central Committee, wrote that the experience of the last two years had proved that the Democratic Faction could function as a useful group only during congresses; in between congresses it was a dead organism. He stated unambiguously that members of the Faction were incapable of carrying out practical tasks, everything was formulated in vague terms, and the Faction's program did not materially differ from the general Zionist platform.[76] Joseph Pokrassa of Kharkov, a member of the Democratic Faction and the Kharkov Committee for the Jewish University, supported the perpetuation of the Faction, but only on condition that it apply itself to practical work.[77] Michael Kroll, who helped direct the activities of the Democratic Faction's bureau in Moscow, was skeptical about the Faction's pre-congress conference, fearing that it would, as in the past, be devoted to theoretical formulations. He complained that Russia was full of Faction members, but without a real Faction, each doing as he pleased.[78] Even Buber, who was in close touch with Weizmann for many months, had all but given up on the Democratic Faction, using phrases similar to those which Weizmann himself had written in moments of frustration. The Faction as such, wrote Buber, had accomplished next to nothing over the preceding seventeen months; its only accomplishment was its program. In fact, the Faction did not exist, except as a figment of the imagination of a few individuals. He suggested the total transformation of the Faction, which would involve everything from a change of its name to Bnei Chorin to its method of operation and a revised program.[79]

The most devastating indictment came from Victor Jacobson of Simferopol, in the Crimea, who had known Weizmann since their days as members of the Berlin Verein. Jacobson was at the time a member of GAC, Zionist regional leader for the Simferopol area, a member of the council of the Jewish Colonial Trust, and since 1901 director of the Russian Zionist Information Center. By virtue of his formal positions, as well as his personal influence, he was a man to be reckoned with. His opinion reflected a larger consensus among the more established, senior forces within Russian Zionism. His letter recounted the past and present sins of the Democratic Faction and assessed its future prospects:

> . . . I never hid my sympathy [for the Faction] . . . At the Fifth Congress
> I also supported it . . . . If I did not formally join the Faction, this is not due
> to lack of sympathy for its principles but to the anger it aroused in me be-
> cause of the tone of its leaders—belligerent, factional and largely insulting

toward a whole row of Zionist activists who are still active within the Zionist movement to this day, who were all lumped together as a reactionary group [*eine reactionaere Masse*]. These slogans at the Youth Conference of intelligent people, the promises to forge an army of dedicated activists which were announced in the speeches by members of the Faction, were probably intended to emphasize the difference between us and yourselves. Even now I am offended by the unjustified arrogance *passez moi le mot*. If you will actually do something, I will take off my hat and bow before you, but first do something and then lecture [to others]. This is something I wanted to tell you all along. But you did not want such an objective evaluation. You wanted that we, upon hearing your eulogies about ourselves, should listen and applaud. Believe me, we had the courage to do even this, but we are not convinced that we are really so terrible, so bourgeois, so permeated with the cult of personality . . . Thus I decided that I had to wait a while . . . I did not come to your conclusion that the Faction "had died"; I think it was never born and it was difficult for me to grasp that around us there is so much work to be done, such a dearth of people and creative forces, and the youth, which so arrogantly does away with us, is so inactive. Where are the results? . . . In my district and in other districts I am unaware of a sign of life of the Faction . . . We know for a fact about the existence of "Mizrahi" and Poalei Zion, we are asked to believe that the Faction also exists . . . In other words, I congratulate you on the Faction's program and am ready to sign my name to each of its statutes, but on the basis of the experience at the Fifth Congress, the Faction's conference in Basel and the year and one half that have elapsed since, I am not sure that it has the capacity to live . . .[80]

The signals from Russia as well as the West were clearly negative then. Weizmann and the Russian members could not even agree on the site of the projected conference: Idelson suggested Russia,[81] Kroll suggested Warsaw,[82] while Weizmann preferred Basel.[83] Nor could they agree on the agenda of the conference or the shape the Democratic Faction was to take in the future. The Russian members of the Democratic Faction made it quite clear that they were not interested in wasting their time on theoretical formulations.[84] Moreover, for the time being they were not interested in cultural projects. "You have to understand," wrote Kroll, "that the Faction [in Russia] is different from the Faction abroad [in the West]. You have cultural and journalistic activities that are suitable to your living conditions and to your talents . . . You have to understand that your cultural work (*Der Jude, Juedischer Verlag*, etc.) serves mostly the students in Western Europe, and it is difficult to imagine that we will materially support such work."[85] They also accused Weizmann of elitism, of trying to woo the "high and mighty" for his university project, something that was of dubious relevance to them at that moment.[86]

Thus, in early July, five weeks after he threw himself into the work of resuscitating the Democratic Faction in time for the congress, Weizmann wrote that he had abandoned the plan to summon a conference since "the atmosphere is not universally favorable." He was particularly disgusted with the East European members of the Faction.[87] That same day he exclaimed in obvious anger that "from now on we assume no responsibility for others. From this point of view I am not concerned with what happens to the Faction."[88] He was disappointed and frustrated, but he knew that the charges against the Faction were justified. A month prior to the Sixth Zionist Congress he openly admitted that

> the present state of the Faction is unsatisfactory. Being one of . . . those who helped to build and establish the Faction, I would be the first to say that it cannot and ought not continue to exist in its present form. Why? Because to date the Faction has hardly achieved even one of the objectives it took upon itself; because it has not as yet properly defined its program; because the theoretical work which it was to have accomplished still remains but a figment of the theoreticians' imagination; because in the field of propaganda and organization it has not yet achieved a twentieth of what it could have achieved; in brief, because most of the "activists" in the Faction were asleep when they should have been in the vanguard.[89]

It was apparent that the Democratic Faction, such as it was, had failed. By the beginning of July Weizmann had finally recognized that it was fruitless to invest more time and energy in this organization. Yet, though he had again lost a major battle, he was not willing to abandon the battlefield without some victory. The least he could do was to try to salvage a part of his large cultural scheme. Due to his incredible ability to recuperate from defeat, he once again switched tactics in his efforts to try to save the university project from oblivion. "Do everything you can for the University!" he wrote to one of his friends in Warsaw. "Give the people no rest and don't let them hide behind facile talk. We can under no circumstances permit a standstill to develop now, lest an enterprise begun with so much effort be made to suffer . . . the pogrom [of Kishinev] must not be allowed to extend to the University."[90] He was still planning and urging the setting up of a department of general studies,[91] as well as a department of Judaic studies, for which he wanted the assistance of Ahad Ha'Am and the historians David Neumark and Simon Bernfeld.[92]

The sticking point and major obstacle to his plan for the Jewish university, apart from adequate funding, remained its location. Just about everyone agreed that its ultimate seat would be in Palestine. As a realist Weizmann knew that under the conditions prevailing in Palestine in 1902–3, there was no chance of establishing such an institution there for the time being.[93] Otto Warburg, who had joined the Berlin University Committee, proposed that the university be established in Cairo if it were not practicable to do so in Palestine.[94] There were even professors who agreed to join the Vienna University Committee on condition that emphasis be placed on the non-Zionist nature of the project.[95] Yet none of these schemes stood a chance against the strong opposition of some of the Russian Zionists, headed by Ussishkin, who insisted on Palestine as the only site of the university, be it on a temporary or a permanent basis. They had defeated the Buber-Weizmann resolution for a temporary seat in Europe at the Greater Actions Committee of October 1902, and with time their opposition to any alternative became even more adamant.

These facts were well known to Weizmann. Michael Kroll, who supported Weizmann's view on this issue, reported from Moscow that "[Yehiel] Tschlenow [a member of GAC and Zionist regional leader for the Moscow area] and his circle have definitely expressed themselves against a university outside Palestine. We will have to do without those idiots."[96] But this was easier said than done. The opposition to the university being situated outside Palestine was widespread among the Russian Zionist leadership and went beyond Ussishkin.[97]

Weizmann was by then an experienced politician. He had not changed his mind on the university question, but he knew when to retreat, at least temporarily. He no longer had even the passive support of the Viennese leadership. Ussishkin and his followers were a formidable opposition not to be tackled without grave risks. The Minsk Conference, which was pretty much Ussishkin's conference, had confirmed him as the leader of Russian Zionism and had proved, to any who still doubted, that the strong-willed regional leader of the Ekaterinoslav area could easily have things his way. By comparison, Weizmann, who was eleven years Ussishkin's junior, was still, at most, the leader of the Russian Zionist student colonies in the West, with little support in Russia. As much as he needed Motzkin's support during the Berlin and early Geneva years, he now needed the consent and blessing of the powerful Russian leader on any major Zionist undertaking, especially since he no longer had any independent sources of funding. In fact, in January 1903 he already had attempted to find a *modus vivendi* with Ussishkin by expressing support for the latter's idea—articulated at the Minsk Conference—to establish a Zionist avant garde which would undertake any tasks placed upon it by the World Zionist Organization. This attempt at a rapprochement had failed. Now it was all the more urgent to try to come to terms with Ussishkin.[98]

To make a complete and abrupt about-face, after he had expressed resistance to Ussishkin's uncompromising demands,[99] was unthinkable. Thus, Weizmann suggested sending an emissary to Palestine who would investigate the educational system there and submit a report.[100] It must have seemed to Weizmann that Ussishkin and his friends were not completely serious about the university if they wanted to establish it immediately in Palestine in 1903, but he had no choice but to make some changes in his strategy. To his friend Saul Lurie he explained his personal motivation and tactical considerations for such a step. "You know my personal opinion regarding Palestine. I consider a University in Palestine to be totally impossible and wrong at present . . . You are familiar, however, with the spirit now prevailing in the Zionist world and which is so formidable a consideration. If we do not so much as attempt to examine the Palestine question, we shall immediately have Zionist officialdom in a body on our necks."[101]

Sending a representative to Palestine was a clever public relations stunt that was to demonstrate Weizmann's good faith and loyalty to the Palestine-oriented university. Eventually it was not carried out, but it is ample demonstration of Weizmann's method of operation. It was to take the wind out of the opposition's sails and to provide himself with ammunition for the inevitable confrontation with the Russian *Landsmanschaft* in Basel. Weizmann also undertook another step toward a compromise with Ussishkin. This time he did so indirectly by persuading Ben-Zion Mossinson, one of Ussishkin's close friends who was then studying in Bern, to join the Jewish University Bureau. Mossinson made his participation conditional, depending on the location of the university in Palestine. They concluded their agreement in writing, yet Weizmann's letter was phrased diplomatically:

> Our desire is to establish—if at all possible—a Jewish University in Palestine. The departments of philology and pedagogy would be opened in Europe, the other departments would be established in Palestine, but if this proves impossible we shall begin by opening them elsewhere. However, we shall erect no buildings, and make no attempt to remain abroad permanently, in order to be able to transfer the institutions to Palestine at an appropriate moment.[102]

The attempt to win over Ussishkin through Mossinson failed,[103] but it provides further proof of Weizmann's flexibility and resourcefulness in time of adversity. He seemed to seriously heed the advice of his friend Joseph Pokrassa: "Don't give up and don't be too quick on the draw. One cannot swim against the current. Learn patience from Herzl and steer stubbornly toward the ultimate goal."[104]

While Weizmann was doing his utmost to salvage the Jewish university as a cornerstone of the Zionist cultural renaissance, Herzl was working on the political front to find a territorial solution for the Jewish nation. The latter had recently been informed that his plan to establish a Jewish colony in Sinai and El Arish no longer had a chance of success. From the start Herzl had been overoptimistic about what to expect from Great Britain.

In mid-May he was informed that the Egyptian government had refused to guarantee the requisite water supply from the Nile.[105] The El Arish and Sinai project was now, for all intents and purposes, a closed chapter.[106] On May 16 Herzl recorded in his diary: "I thought the Sinai plan was such a sure thing that I no longer wanted to buy a family vault in the Doebling cemetery, where my father is provisionally laid to rest. Now I consider the affair so wrecked that I have already been to the district court and am acquiring vault No. 28."[107]

Yet even before the final negative reply from the Egyptian government, another suggestion surfaced, this time from Joseph Chamberlain, who had just returned from his African journey. On April 23, 1903, Herzl was received in a very friendly fashion by Chamberlain. Like his first meeting with the powerful statesman in October 1902, which resulted in

Great Britain's first serious negotiations with the Zionist movement, this meeting was to have a momentous impact. When Herzl first met Chamberlain in 1902, the latter had probably never heard of Zionism. By the spring of 1903 he had pretty much been converted to the idea by Herzl.[108] In fact, he was the first important British statesman to take Zionism seriously. Herzl recorded the dramatic encounter:

> April 24, London. Yesterday noon with Chamberlain [I] referred him to the Commission's report which I had sent him the day before and which was in front of him. "That is not a favorable report," he said. "Well," I said, "it is a very poor country; but we will make something out of it." "During my travels I have seen a country for you," said the great Chamberlain, "and that's Uganda. It's hot on the coast, but further inland the climate becomes excellent, even for Europeans. You can raise sugar and cotton there. And I thought to myself, that would be a land for Dr. Herzl. But of course he wants to go only to Palestine or its vicinity." "Yes, I have to," I replied. "Our base must be in or near Palestine. Later on we could also settle in Uganda, for we have masses of people ready to emigrate. But we have to build on a national foundation, and that is the political attraction of El Arish . . . ."[109]

Before Herzl learned that the El Arish initiative had failed, he withstood the bait of Uganda dangled before him by the powerful statesman. But circumstances changed quickly. On his trip back to Vienna Herzl heard the news about Kishinev, which was followed by the refusal of the Egyptian government to cooperate in the Jewish settlement of El Arish. Herzl felt he needed to take action to ameliorate the fate of Russian Jewry. He was now willing to search for every avenue that would further this aim.

Under Herzl's instructions, Greenberg began work on a charter for the company which would settle Jews in East Africa. The charter was prepared by the firm of Lloyd George, Roberts and Co., because Lloyd George, as a member of parliament with knowledge of Uganda, could find out in advance what was acceptable to the Foreign Office. The name of the settlement was to be New Palestine. It was to have its own flag and to be created "for the encouragement of the Jewish national idea [and] the promotion of the welfare of the Jewish people."[110] Greenberg, acting in Herzl's name, pressed the British government for an early reply to his outline for a charter for East Africa so it could be presented to the Sixth Zionist Congress.[111] Herzl did not wait patiently in Vienna for the British reply. He was determined not to leave any stone unturned. Thus, on August 5, 1903, he left for Russia,[112] where he held discussions with von Plehve and Sergei Witte, the Minister of Finance.[113]

On August 18 Herzl arrived at Alt-Aussee, where his family was vacationing. It was during that day that Leopold Greenberg informed him by telegram that the negotiations with the British government concerning East Africa had achieved satisfactory results. Sir Clement Hill, Permanent Departmental Head, informed Greenberg that Lord Lansdowne had studied the question with the interest which His Majesty's Government must always take in any well-considered scheme for the amelioration of the position of the Jewish race . . . Lord Lansdowne understands that the Trust desire to send some gentlemen to the East Africa Protectorate, who may ascertain personally whether there are any vacant lands suitable for the purposes in question, and if this is so, he will be happy to give them every facility to enable them to discuss with His Majesty's Commissioner the possibility of meeting the view which may be expressed at the forthcoming Zionist Congress in regard to the conditions upon which a settlement might be possible.

If a site can be found which the Trust and His Majesty's Commissioner consider suitable and which commends itself to His Majesty's Government, Lord Lansdowne will be prepared to entertain favorably proposals for the establishment of a Jewish colony or settlement, on conditions which will enable the members to observe their national customs . . .[114]

The document also went on with an offer—subject to the consent of the relevant officials—of a Jewish governorship and internal autonomy.

Throughout his negotiations with the British government, Herzl operated as the sole and supreme representative of the movement, working closely with only a few trusted individuals. Though rumors were rife concerning the El Arish scheme, Herzl officially notified the members of GAC only on June 12, 1903, that it had failed.[115] It was not surprising, then, that Weizmann was ill-informed about the outcome of Herzl's diplomatic missions. On April 23—the day Chamberlain and Herzl agreed that the report of the commission to Sinai and El Arish was unfavorable—Weizmann wrote to Vera that Herzl seemed to have succeeded.[116] Only after he had heard about the failure of the project did Weizmann begin to sense that the Sixth Zionist Congress would devote a major portion of its time to the question of colonization.

Therefore, our battle cry at this Congress must above all be a demand for clarity on the territorial question and a scientific investigation of Palestine and the neighboring countries. A stop has got to be put to the game of hide-and-seek once and for all. We shall also have to take action against the terrifying opportunism which has been so shamefully manifested by the leadership in affairs of colonization.[117]

Weizmann, of course, had no inkling of Herzl's negotiations regarding the East Africa territory. Though in the months prior to the Sixth Zionist Congress he had demanded clarity on the issue of colonization and a scientific investigation of Palestine and its environs, he himself had not yet formed a clear-cut view on this most important issue on the agenda of the Zionist organization. Four weeks before the congress he wrote to Kalman Marmor that "my mind has refused to rest with wondering how to prepare for the Congress, and by what means . . ."[118] In the weeks and months which followed the congress his thinking on the subject would crystallize. Herzl's disclosure of the East Africa offer was bound to force all Zionists to take an unequivocal stand regarding the future of Zionist orientation and settlement.

IX

The Uganda Controversy

The 592 delegates, as well as the visitors and journalists, who arrived in Basel for the Sixth Zionist Congress (August 23–28) had no inkling of what awaited them. If there were some who were at odds with Herzl's latest diplomatic moves, it was on account of his recent meetings with von Plehve.[1] Some—Weizmann, no doubt, among them—may have intended to make an issue out of it at the congress and call Herzl to task over his encounter with a man many considered responsible for the massacre in Kishinev. The disclosure of the East Africa offer to the congress was therefore the occasion, not necessarily the cause, of the challenge to Herzl's leadership. Those who voted against the project were, for the most part, men who had no confidence in Herzl and those who surrounded him and had been looking for an opportunity to change the leadership structure of the World Zionist Organization.[2] These issues were uppermost in the minds and deliberations of members of the Russian delegation to the congress, who began their *Vorkonferenz* on August 19. In the absence of Ussishkin, who was then in Palestine, they elected Bernstein-Kohan as their chairman.[3]

Presenting his report to the members of GAC on Friday, August 21, Herzl included a brief discussion of the British offer in East Africa.[4] The announcement caught everyone by surprise, and the immediate reactions were confused. Though almost all the Russian members of the Greater Actions Committee distrusted Plehve's promises,[5] they were less certain about East Africa. Bernstein-Kohan declared that, given their present condition, the Russian Jews would even go to hell *(dass die russischen Juden bei den derzeitigen Verhaeltnissen selbst in die Hoelle gehen)*. Isidore Yasinovsky agreed. Tschlenow, the effective leader of the Russian delegation, disagreed. Max Bodenheimer of Germany pointed out that the consideration of the project by the congress would represent a change in the Basel Program, which confined itself to Palestine.[6] Curiously, the sharpest immediate opposition to the proposal on East Africa came from Alexander Marmorek, a personal friend of Herzl. At his insistence it was decided that a second session of the Actions Committee be held, that the members take a stand individually, and that the decision be made subsequently.[7] Confused and incoherent as the GAC session was, however, Herzl was sufficiently aware that the Sixth Zionist Congress would be a stormy affair.[8]

That same Friday night the opposition of the Russian members of GAC had already begun to crystallize, and they reported their objections to Herzl. The next day (Saturday) the discussions between Herzl and some leading members in the movement continued, with only Israel Zangwill of London advocating the unqualified acceptance of the British offer.[9] On Sunday morning, August 23, 1903, the congress opened and Herzl presented Britain's offer to the delegates.[10] The first impact of Herzl's report on the delegates was described by Shmarya Levin:

> I was sitting, when Herzl revealed the whole matter to the delegates, on the platform of the Congress, being one of its secretaries. I was therefore able to watch closely the effect produced by the announcement on the faces of the listeners. It was one of almost agonized attention. On the faces were written astonishment and admiration—but not a sign of protest. I do not believe that any of the delegates realized at the moment the significance of what had happened. The magnanimity of the British offer sufficed, during the first instants, to obscure all other considerations. And yet the astonishment and admiration were not such as might have been expected. It was only when the general session broke up, and the various groups assembled in caucus, that it was realized that a crisis had appeared in the Zionist movement.[11]

In closing his speech, Herzl suggested setting up a small special committee to deal with the British offer.[12] The Russian *Landsmanschaft* decided to elect a committee of their own which would examine the problem and report back to the Russian delegation. The committee was composed of the eleven Russian members of GAC and thirteen other persons, including Chaim Weizmann. In the discussions which ensued there were those who wished to accept the offer without reservations and others who rejected it out of hand. A few members—Weizmann among them—favored the scheme[13] but attached numerous conditions to its eventual acceptance. Weizmann himself emphasized the importance of organizing the emigration movement under Zionist auspices—a point he had also stressed in his letter to Herzl dated May 6, 1903. He also returned to the theme he had elucidated as early as the Youth Conference of December 1901, namely, the need to cooperate with other Jewish organizations. A compromise draft resolution was finally worked out by Tschlenow and was to be presented to the *Landsmanschaft*. It called for the creation of a commission to study the new project; it would decide whether or not to recommend the dispatch of an investigative body to East Africa and bring its conclusions before a special session of GAC. It also asked congress to continue to investigate the El Arish project. Finally, the committee asked for an expression of the Zionist movement's gratitude to the British nation.[14]

As was already indicated by his conduct during the proceedings of the "Russian Committee," Weizmann was at first a moderate supporter of

Herzl's East Africa move. This initial reaction was fully in concert with his passionate concern for the problem of the Jews. Like Herzl, he recognized the urgent need to provide a place of refuge for the emigrating Jews of Eastern Europe. His opposition to Herzl in the past was only due to Herzl's exclusive political Zionism, but this did not mean that Weizmann, in turn, was a single-minded cultural Zionist. Moreover, all his projects hitherto were permeated by the need for immediate, practical, and effective action on behalf of East European Jewry. This attitude explains Weizmann's speech on August 24, the second day of the congress. Nordau, who at heart was opposed to Herzl's plan,[15] nevertheless delivered in the morning—for friendship's sake—a passionate speech supporting the leader's scheme, in which he coined the term *Nachtasyl* (night shelter) for the persecuted Jews who needed a homeland but could not yet attain Palestine. He promised that this night shelter would provide them not only with food and lodging but would also serve as a means for political training and national education.[16] The afternoon of the same day, at a session presided over by Max Bodenheimer, Weizmann again briefly touched upon the East Africa issue, publicly declaring his "positive attitude" toward the scheme.[17]

Just prior to Nordau's famous *Nachtasyl* speech during the morning session of August 24, the Russian *Landsmanschaft* assembled to hear its committee's report. In view of Tschlenow's vacillating stand on the committee's draft resolution and the heated controversy regarding its recommendations, it was decided to elect six general speakers, three of whom would argue for the draft resolution—among them Weizmann—and three against. The actual debate in the Russian *Landsmanschaft* began at nine o'clock in the evening.[18] Weizmann found himself in the unenviable position of espousing a cause that was by now—after two full days of the congress—clearly opposed by most of his Russian colleagues. Moreover, having constantly criticized Herzl, he now came dangerously close to supporting "official policy." Nevertheless, he was not yet deterred from his conviction and proposed laying the following draft resolution before the congress:

> Congress does not conceive the action in Africa as the ultimate aim of the Zionists, but deems it necessary to regulate emigration and consequently finds that the Zionists must unify all colonization societies or convene a congress in order to decide on East Africa. Zionist funds will not be expended for this purpose. The congress proposes that the AC shall not desist from action in Wadi El Arish.[19]

Weizmann further argued, in a vein similar to Ahad Ha'Am, that the gathering of Jews in East Africa would improve their position and prepare them for the ultimate return to Zion. He also called for a closer cooperation among the various Jewish bodies engaged in settlement activities. In general, he minimized the political aspect of the British offer.[20]

Weizmann's motion was not accepted by the Russian delegation; neither was the draft resolution of the "Russian Committee." Instead, the

Russian *Landsmanschaft* decided by a vote of 146 to 84 to accept the following resolution, which was later that day presented by Bernstein-
Kohan to the congress:

> The congress recognizes the great political importance of the generous offer
> by Great Britain which permits the Zionist Organization to found an auton-
> omous Jewish colony in East Africa and requests the A.C. to convey the sin-
> cere thanks of the representatives of the Jewish people to the British gov-
> ernment. As the congress remains faithful to the basic principle of Zionism
> and views the goal of the movement as the creation of a publicly recog-
> nized, legally secured home [for the Jewish people] only in Palestine, it re-
> grets having to arrive at the conclusion that the Zionist Organization cannot
> occupy itself with this project.[21]

On Wednesday, the twenty-sixth, even before the congress voted on
the East Africa issue, the Russian delegates met once again. It was at
this meeting that Weizmann reversed himself on the position he had taken
on East Africa less than forty-eight hours previously. He attributed this
change of heart to pro-Uganda speeches he had heard in the interim,
which convinced him that West European Zionists were not taking the
Basel Program seriously, and he feared that the Basel Program would be
completely altered in the course of time. Therefore, he had finally decided to vote against a commission.[22] In the meantime, at Herzl's insistence a draft resolution proposing appointment of an expedition—in addition to a commission—to explore the proposed territory in East Africa
was pushed through a meeting of GAC. The seven Russian members of
GAC were the only ones opposing Herzl's plan.[23] The single issue of
general agreement was that the Jewish National Fund, the Jewish Colonial Trust, and the Anglo-Palestine Company would not bear the cost of
the expedition. The commission itself, it was decided, would only be advising SAC.[24] Immediately following the meeting of GAC, the afternoon
congress session opened at 4:05, at which the resolution adopted by GAC
was put to a vote. The roll call showed that of the 468 delegates who
voted, 292 voted for the motion (the *Ja-Sager*) and 176 against (the *Nein-
Sager*, or Zionei Zion [Zionists for Zion]), with 143 delegates abstaining.[25] Five members of the extended Weizmann family were present as
delegates. Three voted for the resolution: Abraham Lichtenstein, Weizmann's brother-in-law, Ozer Weizmann, and Weizmann's brother
Moshe.[26] Chaim Weizmann and his future brother-in-law Selig Weitzman (or Weicman) voted against the resolution.[27] Lack of family consensus on the East Africa issue was not uncommon. Nor was it a conflict
between East and West European Jews, as Weizmann and others often
claimed. There was no consensus on the East Africa issue in either camp.[28]
This was probably best illustrated by the fact that whereas the veteran
Russian Zionists and Weizmann's friends voted against Uganda, the
Mizrahi and the socialist Zionists fully supported Herzl's stance.

By voting against Uganda, Weizmann had come full circle and returned to the fold of the Russian *Landsmanschaft*, dutifully toeing its ide-

ological line. The fact that he wavered on this most crucial question surely did not win him more admirers among the Russian Zionist leadership. After all, he was not held in high regard by the group around Ussishkin to begin with. His position, then, was further weakened by the fact that he neither had any backing from the Western Zionist leadership, nor was the Democratic Faction any longer a force to be reckoned with.[29] The question then arises as to why Weizmann had chosen to formulate a compromise resolution which by Monday evening (August 24) was clearly in defiance of the sentiment of the Russian Zionist leadership. Moreover, one of his fellow travelers during the debate was a Mizrahi leader, Rabbi Shmuel Yaakov Rabinowitz of Sopotzkin,[30] and among those he was forced to debate against were none other than his much esteemed friends Victor Jacobson and Shmarya Levin. Weizmann was clearly at a disadvantage and on the losing side. Why, then, did a person with so keen a sense of the possible in politics find himself in such an awkward position?

The question ought to be placed in perspective. Weizmann was not alone in his indecision on the East Africa question. Tschlenow himself, the leader of the Russian *Landsmanschaft* at the congress, had given the cue for this equivocation by striking a compromise stance toward the East Africa scheme,[31] and it was only his own reversal at the last moment, on the question of the commission, which decided the outcome of the vote within the Russian delegation on Tuesday, August 25. Even that decision, which stated that the World Zionist Organization could not occupy itself with the East Africa project, was not carried by an overwhelming majority. Of course, the Mizrahi delegates stood solidly behind Herzl,[32] as did those Zionists inclined toward socialist ideas.[33] This was also the position of one of Herzl's most consistent critics, Nachman Syrkin.[34] Other outstanding figures of East European Zionism, whose credentials were beyond reproach, either supported Herzl outright, as in the case of Max Mandelstamm[35] and Isidore Yasinovsky,[36] or wobbled and vacillated, as in the case of Leo Motzkin[37] and Nahum Sokolow.[38] The list of those East Europeans who either voted for Herzl or equivocated is very long indeed.[39]

The probable reasons for Weizmann's proposed resolution at the session of the Russian *Landsmanschaft* are fourfold. First, the resolution reflected his long-held belief that a split in the movement would be disastrous. Time and again he had talked about building bridges between Eastern and Western Zionism.[40] Here was a concrete chance to avert a collision between what most people saw as a conflict between Eastern and Western Zionism. Second, Weizmann, like Herzl, was a realist. He recognized that Herzl followed the only possible course open to him. Herzl could not have rejected the East Africa offer out of hand.[41] The proposal represented a great political achievement which could be used to further the aims of the movement in Zion itself. It amounted to a recognition by Great Britain of the World Zionist Organization as a representative institution of the Jewish people. It could also not fail to impress the sultan and possibly move him to change his attitude toward Zionism. Moreover, Herzl himself had not sought this particular territory; it was thrust upon him after Kishinev, when he felt that something needed to be done to alleviate the problems of the Jews.[42] Weizmann, who understood and empathized with Herzl's dilemma, wished to give the leader's diplomacy a chance to succeed. Third, like Herzl, Weizmann was concerned with the problem of the Jews first, and was thus less dogmatic about Palestine. Long before the East Africa issue had surfaced, he made this clear in his conception of the Jewish university project, which was to alleviate the plight of Jewish intellectuals, if necessary in Europe first. He refused to budge on this issue even after the GAC meeting vetoed the "Weizmann-Buber Plan" in October 1902. Thus, the plan to establish a university in Europe before it could be moved to Palestine was similar in idea and conception to Herzl's Uganda scheme.[43]

A fourth possible reason for devising his compromise resolution was that it seemed both attainable and a vehicle which could propel him into a place of prominence among the ranking Zionists. Weizmann was not a naive man. Had Ussishkin been present at the congress, it is clear that he would have imposed his anti-Uganda sentiment more forcefully than had been done by Tschlenow. The latter, who much admired Herzl, also wished to prevent a rift in the movement. Had he stood his ground, Tschlenow might possibly have swung the Russians toward a compromise resolution. Weizmann took his cue from Tschlenow and went out on a limb, articulating further Tschlenow's own sentiments. After the latter changed his position, he left Weizmann exposed; he was thus forced to take the criticism that was largely deserved by Tschlenow.

Following his compromise resolution, Weizmann had two days to observe the mounting opposition to Uganda. One must, of course, consider the possibility that Weizmann simply changed his mind on the issue of Uganda, but given his intuitive sympathies for the project and his initial strong support, this is an unlikely possibility. Rather, it became clear to him that in proposing his resolution he had miscalculated. Despite his sympathy with Herzl's position, Weizmann preferred being in the camp of the Russian Zionist leadership since it was his only chance to survive politically. He knew well that, not having any firm alliances with the Western Zionist leaders, he had no other choice. Presumably he would have to work harder in the future to erase any traces of his erstwhile equivocation. Weizmann retreated from his compromise resolution in three stages: by stating, on August 26, within the Russian *Landsmanschaft* that the reaction of Western Zionists to Uganda convinced him that the scheme must be dropped. At the general debate he kept silent but dutifully voted with the *Nein-Sager*, and when they followed Tschlenow out of the congress hall after the results of the vote were taken,[44] he joined their ranks.[45] One wonders if, while walking out with the *Nein-Sager*, Weizmann remembered a similar demonstration by the Democratic Faction at the previous congress. To underline the seriousness of his convictions Weizmann allied himself with the most extreme camp of the *Nein-Sager*, that of Ussishkin. It may be that Weizmann attached himself to Ussishkin, the extremist—thus placing himself in sharp opposition to Tschlenow—because the latter did not come to his rescue during the Russian *Landsmanschaft*'s deliberations. All in all, it was not an edifying but a politically astute performance.

If the vote was a victory for Herzl, it was a Pyrrhic victory. With the Russian Zionei Zion assembled in a separate hall, it did not make much sense to continue the proceedings. The inevitable clash between a parliamentary body and a charismatically authoritative personality, between ideology and politics, had finally brought the Zionist movement to an impasse which had to be broken if a split was to be avoided. What made the situation even more difficult was the fact that parallel with the overt ideological debate there also existed a less public struggle for power within the movement which became manifest when the East Africa project had ceased to be a viable option. Herzl was well aware of these issues and knew he had to act immediately and decisively. He began to heal the breach by coming over to speak to the secessionists. After two attempts to gain entrance he was finally given permission to address the *Nein-Sager*. Weizmann described the dramatic encounter:

> He was received in silence. Nobody rose from his seat to greet him, nobody applauded when he ended. He admonished us for having left the hall; he understood, he said, that this was merely a spontaneous demonstration and not a secession; he invited us to return. He reassured us of his unswerving devotion to Palestine, and spoke again of the urgent need for finding an immediate refuge for large masses of homeless Jews. We listened in silence; no one attempted to reply. It was probably the only time that Herzl was thus received at any Zionist gathering . . .[46]

Persuaded by Tschlenow, the Russian *Nein-Sager* finally returned to the congress hall during the morning hours of Thursday, August 27, 1903.[47] On behalf of the opposition Shmarya Levin read a declaration which stated that their withdrawal from the hall had been a spontaneous expression of a profound spiritual shock. Herzl then accepted a resolution of the opposition that the shekel funds were not to be used to finance the expedition to East Africa and that the report of the expedition was to be submitted to GAC before a new congress could be called to make the final decision.[48] The following two days passed relatively quietly.[49] During the last session of the congress on Friday afternoon (August 28) the delegates elected various officeholders in the World Zionist Organization, including the nine members of the Advisory Commission on East Africa,[50] among them Chaim Weizmann. The appointment seemed to contradict his *Nein-Sager* status. Possibly he was appointed at the behest of the Russian *Nein-Sager* to keep watch over the affairs of the commission. In time he would use this fortuitous circumstance to advance notions and ideas that suited his own ideological perspective.

The Congress closed with Herzl quoting the words of the psalmist: "If I forget thee, O Jerusalem, may my right hand wither."[51] The *Nein-Sager*, however, were not appeased. Less than forty-eight hours after the congress closed they held a public meeting in Basel, where Yehiel Tschlenow, Chaim Weizmann, Meir Dizengoff, and Menahem Sheinkin made it clear that the fight for a Palestinian-centered Zionism had only begun. There was an uncompromising tone reflected in their speeches, which totally refused even to consider the East Africa issue.[52] Among the harshest words spoken were those of Weizmann.

> The proceedings at the congress which just took place since the African project has been debated have a devastating impact. Here comes one person and with one stroke changes our entire program, and we stand confused and search for a way out of this dilemma . . . Herzl's influence on the people is great; even the *Nein-Sager* cannot escape this influence and thus were uncertain whether or not to declare in their resolutions that this East Africa project represents a departure from the Basel Program. Herzl, who found before him the idea of Hovevei Zion, forged a temporary pact with them. But as time elapsed and the idea did not produce tangible results, he regretted this pact. He took account only of external conditions, whereas the forces upon which we rely lie in the psychology of the people and in their existential strivings. We knew that it is impossible to attain Palestine within a short period of time, and therefore we do not despair when this or that attempt fails.[53]

In fact, Weizmann was unjustifiably implying that Herzl had abandoned the Basel Program and was backing any project which might grant Jews a territory.[54] To put it mildly, Weizmann's remarks were disingenuous. Less than a week earlier he had backed the leader's stance on East Africa and had shown sympathy for his motivations. Yet he was now fully in the camp of the hard-liners. With his unerring political sense he understood that in his first public pronouncement on the subject after the congress he had to earn his right to be among them. An extreme position would help erase the memory of his erstwhile aberration. Moreover, Weizmann now found it expedient to draw a sharp distinction between Eastern and Western Zionists. This was a notion long held by circles around Ahad Ha'Am, but Weizmann always had been careful to avoid making such unequivocal statements. In the heat of the debate and emotions which followed the Sixth Zionist Congress, he deviated for a while from his more pragmatic approach to this issue. In any case, if anyone had any doubts, it soon became clear that this debate was academic: The Zionist masses in Eastern Europe certainly continued to view Herzl as their undisputed leader.

In the meantime Herzl had returned to Alt-Aussee, where he continued to pursue his relations with von Plehve. Despite the attacks on him at the congress for having met with this arch-anti-Semite, he considered his negotiations with von Plehve perfectly sensible from a diplomatic point of view. On September 5, 1903, Herzl wrote von Plehve that it had become clear that the territory offered by the British government could, at most, be suitable for only a few thousand Jewish families. The only permanent solution for the Jewish masses remained in Palestine.[55] Ten days later Herzl also tried unsuccessfully to interest the Jewish Colonization Association in participating in the costs of the expedition to East Africa.[56]

For their part, immediately after the congress the Russian *Nein-Sager* began to take new organizational and practical steps to consolidate their opposition. A group of Russian members of GAC, as well as Weizmann, Martin Buber, and Berthold Feiwel, sojourned at the Swiss resort town of Beatenberg, where they created a Russian Landes-Comité (Central Committee) whose members consisted of some of Herzl's most vociferous opponents: Victor Jacobson, Vladimir Tyomkin, and Mehahem Ussishkin, with Joseph Sapir serving as secretary. They requested Herzl to communicate henceforth with this Central Committee directly rather than with the Russian members of GAC. They also relocated the "Financial Office" of the Russian Zionists, which had been headed by Herzl's friend Max Mandelstramm, from Kiev to Vilna. Moreover, the meeting agreed to support the proposed periodical *Der Jude*, which was to serve as a mouthpiece of the opposition. The discussions also touched on the possibility of converting the Democratic Faction from a political group into a working group as part of an opposition "league" which would be under the supervision of the Central Committee.[57]

Some six weeks later Herzl was faced with another challenge, this time from Menahem Ussishkin, the most formidable *Nein-Sager* in the Russian camp. Ussishkin, who in October had returned to Russia from Palestine, where he bought land for the Geulah Company, had been involved in setting up the organization of Palestinian Jewry at Zikhron Yaakov and had participated in the preparations for the establishment of an agricultural school for children orphaned during the Kishinev pogrom.[58] Ussishkin was full of confidence in the possibilities Palestine held for the future and was enraged by the proceedings and resolutions regarding East Africa at the Sixth Zionist Congress. In mid-October he addressed an open letter "To the Delegates of the Sixth Zionist Congress," in which he declared that though he accepted his election to GAC, he regarded the resolution authorizing the sending of an expedition to East Africa as not binding for him. Moreover, he pledged to do everything in his power to prevent its execution.

> A congress majority can be decisive in regard to any particular act or enterprise, but not in regard to the principle and ideal. And even as all the majorities in the world cannot divert me from Israel's faith and Israel's Torah, so the majority of the congress cannot divert me from Eretz Israel; for only those who have been dazzled by diplomacy and political fireworks [*von der Diplomatie und dem uebertriebenen Politisieren verblendet*] have failed, in their simplicity, to observe that the resolution of the Zionist Congress to send an expedition to any other country is a renunciation of Palestine and a separation from it. You will learn shortly of my propaganda and activity in this cardinal question.[59]

Herzl's reply to Ussishkin in the same issue of *Die Welt* was similarly sharp. He suggested that "Herr Ussishkin of Ekaterinoslav" resign his

With Sokolow (right) and Ussishkin (left), 1903

seat on GAC if he was unable or unwilling to accept the movement's discipline. Herzl went on to severely criticize Ussishkin's activities in Palestine, which endangered those he wished to help. He also made light of Ussishkin's land-purchasing methods, implying that he was completely unsuitable for the task.[60] Alluding to the East Africa project, Herzl asserted that it was the best way to gain Palestine since it would arouse the interest of those who possessed it to deal with the Zionists. If Ussishkin knew a better way of acquiring the land, it was not nice of him, as a good Zionist, to keep the information concealed from the Jewish people. If he knew no such method, perhaps he ought not to disturb the peace within the movement.[61]

Thus, within a month after his return from Palestine Ussishkin had succeeded in escalating the conflict between Herzl and the *Nein-Sager*. The stage was set then for the Kharkov Conference, which was called by the newly formed Landes-Comité and took place from November 11 to 14, 1903. Attended by fifteen regional leaders, the Kharkov Conference capped a long period of frustration and mounting antagonism felt by the Russian members of GAC toward Herzl and SAC. In 1899, 1901, and 1903 they complained of being ignored by the Vienna-based leadership;[62] recent events only highlighted their disagreement with Herzl's autocratic behavior. This theme, as well as the East Africa project, formed the core of the deliberations at the conference. The meeting resolved to demand of Herzl the abandonment of the East Africa project, the restriction of all territorial negotiations concerning Palestine and Syria, the inclusion of practical work in Palestine within the program of the World Zionist Organization, the submission of Herzl and SAC to the majority rulings of GAC, and the appointment of a Russian representative to the governing body of the Jewish Colonial Trust. In addition, they demanded to be consulted before Herzl negotiated with the Russian authorities on internal Russian Zionist matters, as well as before large expenditures were made. Belkovsky, Tyomkin, and Rosenbaum were appointed as members of a deputation to deliver this ultimatum to Herzl. In the event, Rosenbaum and Belkovsky went alone.[63] Those Russian leaders who supported Herzl called their own meetings on December 6 and December 24, where they formed the League for the Defense of the [World Zionist] Organization.[64]

What those meeting in Kharkov did not know was that in the meantime the East Africa project had become shaky as early as the fall of 1903, and by December it was already a doubtful enterprise. When making his offer, Chamberlain had originally spoken of an area of about forty thousand square miles "between Nairobi and the Mau Escarpment," which was traversed by the only railway in the Protectorate.[65] Herzl's letter to Greenberg dated August 14, 1903, mentioned no specific area for settlement.[66] After the proposal was made public, a vocal and even vehement opposition was manifested, especially by the white settlers in the Protectorate. Its British commissioner, Sir Charles Eliot, communicated to Lord Lansdowne his opinion that it was better to settle Jews at a distance from the railway so as to avoid friction with the other settlers.[67] He suggested offering the Jews areas in the Kenya or Nandi districts. Lansdowne concurred with this suggestion.[68]

Herzl was aware since October that the British had been having second thoughts about their original offer. In mid-December Leopold Greenberg drafted a letter to Herzl's loyal backer in England, Sir Francis Montefiore, which renounced East Africa. Herzl refused to send the letter and preferred that the British withdraw the offer themselves or offer a substitute.[69] His attitude changed after the attempted assassination of Nordau on December 19, 1903, by an irate "anti-Africa" youth. Herzl now instructed Greenberg to publish the letter he had drafted earlier.[70] A truncated version of this letter appeared on December 25, 1903, whose crucial passage was intended to blame the opposition within the Zionist ranks for the failure of the East Africa project. It stated that "the Government informed us at the beginning of December that it was withdrawing the proposal owing to the opposition of our people."[71] Two days later Herzl sent a circular to members of GAC repeating these charges.[72] The days and weeks which followed saw protests and denunciations of

Herzl's opponents in *Die Welt, Hatzfirah,* and other organs friendly to Herzl.[73]

Clearly, the atmosphere in Vienna was less than hospitable when the two delegates of the Russian Landes-Comité arrived, early in January 1904, to deliver the ultimatum agreed on at the Kharkov Conference. In fact, their mission failed completely, with Herzl now accusing *them* of wrongdoing.[74] Belkovsky and Rosenbaum left Vienna on January 8, 1904, defeated and humiliated, and proceeded to St. Petersburg without stopping at Berlin, where Weizmann and some of his friends had convened to hear their report.[75] At St. Petersburg some of the regional leaders—mostly the extreme *Nein-Sager*—met from January 13 to 15, 1904. After hearing the report of their deputation to Herzl, they resolved to send SAC a revised version of the Kharkov resolutions with explanatory notes, and to give their decisions wide publicity.[76] All in all, it was a rather tame action considering what had just taken place in Vienna. For the next three months the controversy with Herzl lost its shrill tone. With the near-collapse of the East Africa issue there was less to quarrel about. Herzl, too, had nothing to gain by further alienating the legitimate Zionist leadership of Russia, especially since his various diplomatic maneuvers in both East and West were not faring very well. The Russian government was reluctant to intervene in Constantinople, and Herzl's visit to Italy, where he met Pope Pius X, King Victor Emmanuel III, and other Vatican and Italian officials, did not have positive results. On his return to Vienna Herzl found the final offer from England, about which he was less than enthusiastic.[77]

There was a general sense and desire among the Zionist rank and file for moderation and conciliation. This was achieved at the GAC meeting of April 11–15, 1904. Following Herzl's opening speech, two days were devoted to the rift between himself and the Russian regional leaders who opposed the East Africa project. All the arguments for and against Uganda that had been voiced since the Sixth Zionist Congress were aired once again, supplemented by accusations and counteraccusations that included the events that had occurred in the nine-month interim. Finally both sides relented and a conciliatory resolution was adopted.[78] The GAC resolution was indeed a great achievement, though it did not lead to permanent peace or unity. Yet each side arrived at a better understanding of the other. The question as to how relations between the Russian Zionists and Herzl would have evolved over time became moot, because less than three months later Herzl died. One important result was attained at the April meeting: The unity of the Zionist movement had been preserved—at least for the moment.[79]

Soon after returning to Geneva from the Sixth Zionist Congress Weizmann wrote to Sokolow:

I feel as though [I'm] emerging from a very, very serious illness . . . I can find no peace . . . I am tormented by the thought that we were all so fearfully weak and awkward and unprepared at the Congress: a feeling of deep

remorse and shame . . . Personally I am tormented and scourged. I have
lost my centre of gravity and do not know whether to concentrate on one
thing or another, whether to stay here or go there—I am a question mark
. . . University, *Jude*, Encyclopedia, colonization problems, propaganda, and
last [but] not least, chemistry . . . One feels lonely and forsaken.[80]

It is perhaps not a coincidence that Weizmann shared these personal
feelings with a moderate and urbane senior colleague in the movement
who had himself been uncertain as to what position to take toward the
East Africa project.[81] Yet his sense of loss and uncertainty was momentary. If before the Sixth Zionist Congress Weizmann's ideas about colonization schemes, and particularly settlement in Palestine, had not yet
been fully crystallized, and if he had not yet evolved a clear method of
breaking out of the vicious cycle in which the World Zionist Organization found itself, the proceedings in Basel changed all that. For Weizmann, as for many others, the Sixth Zionist Congress was a watershed
in his personal and public career. The East Africa controversy was a
traumatic experience whose effects remained long after the issue had been
resolved. For years hence people remembered who had voted in accord
with Herzl and who had been in the camp of the *Nein-Sager*. Having
thrown in his lot with the opposition, Weizmann became one of the most
implacable foes of the East Africa project. Ideologically and emotionally
he was now fully entrenched in the camp of the *Nein-Sager*. His feelings
of shame at his own initial equivocation and the realization that he had
to prove himself all the more to the Russian regional leaders led him to
throw himself wholeheartedly into the debate which continued after the
congress.

The ten months from the end of the Sixth Zionist Congress until
Weizmann's departure for England were filled with plans and activities,
some of them reviving old ideas but most centering on the opposition to
East Africa. At its final session at the congress the Democratic Faction
instructed Weizmann and the members of the Moscow bureau to prepare the next Faction conference. Weizmann had, in fact, volunteered
for the task,[82] and within a few days the Democratic Faction bureau in
Geneva published Circular No. 1, which expressed strong opposition to
the East Africa scheme. It also announced the forthcoming Faction conference, appealed to members to organize propaganda meetings in
Western Europe, and suggested publication of the *Nein-Sager* point of
view.[83] At the meeting of the regional leaders in Beatenberg it was decided to help subsidize the Faction's propaganda activities, specifically
the publication of *Der Jude*.[84] This was followed by yet another gathering
of members of the Democratic Faction to discuss specific topics for propaganda pamphlets.[85]

To initiate and carry through policies within the Democratic Faction
was one thing; to win the confidence of the Russian regional leaders was
another. Throughout his remaining period in Geneva, Weizmann tried
to find his place among the Russian Zionist leaders, to carve a role for
himself on the Continent. He no longer had any illusions as to who was

in charge. The Russian leaders would be the ones to devise and direct the major line of attack against Herzl and the *Ya-Sager.* The key to their activities would clearly be Ussishkin, who would soon stampede them into open revolt against Herzl. Weizmann had unsuccessfully sought Ussishkin's friendship and cooperation before. The latter had no use for the Democratic Faction or for young upstarts like Weizmann, who did not show sufficient respect for his senior colleagues. But now the situation had changed for both of them. The Democratic Faction, such as it was, had no funds or prospects of getting any, and for his part Ussishkin could use any help he could get in his war against Vienna. Moreover, as soon as Weizmann showed deference to the regional leader of Ekaterinoslav and his colleagues, the road was open to cooperation, if not yet friendship. Keenly aware of all of this, Weizmann sought to cultivate Ussishkin's favor; his backing was crucial for all his projects. Thus, just like Motzkin before him, Ussishkin became for Weizmann a figure of authority not only in matters of Zionism but, to some extent, in the realm of private affairs as well.

Even before Ussishkin returned to Russia, Weizmann wrote him a long letter couched in a most humble tone:

> . . . your future plans and intentions are of vital interest to me and all comrades . . . If I turn to you with such questions this is not out of mere curiosity . . . It is out of the inner conviction that you and some of our other comrades in Russia are now, more than ever, called upon to stand at the head of our cause without as yet demolishing the idols of our own making . . .

Trying to save the Faction from Ussishkin's wrath, at the outset Weizmann offered to change its mode of operation even before consulting with his colleagues:

> The Faction is not as yet something definable, complete; it cannot represent a determinable force, although its various elements have rallied . . . Indisputably it is no longer possible for the Faction to continue in the shape in which it has so far existed . . . It would be a blessing if young, intelligent elements of our movement were to form an *Arbeitsgemeinschaft* [working group] and try, particularly at this moment, to work for a pure Zionism, a national Zionism . . .[86]

It was absolutely necessary to come to the next congress with a defined program concerning Palestine, the colonization and industrialization of Palestine, purchase of Palestine and cultural work among its Jews.

Having outlined his ideas and practical suggestions, Weizmann then proceeded to make the following offer: "It is my intention to direct the entire Zionist Jewish youth, insofar as this is within my power, towards this question and on this basis alone to conduct my own activities . . . But on our own we are so weak!" The most important task was the investigation of Palestine by competent people. Clearly implying that he and his close colleagues were most suitable for this task, Weizmann offered to go to Palestine in March as well as to tour Russia. He was willing to take a leave of absence from the university for eight months in order to carry out this plan.[87] In a similarly respectful tone Weizmann also explained to Bernstein-Kohan, another detractor of the Democratic Faction, what he planned for his group.

> I shall no longer guide the Faction in its old form, but will attempt to organize it as a working group. The basis for work exists: propaganda and agitation, educational work, practical and theoretical studies of the Palestine question . . .

Lest he be accused of vying for power, he hastened to add:

> Please understand me well: in the forthcoming campaign this transformed Faction neither wishes to, is able to, nor will strike the first blow. That has to be done by the "Nay-sayers" standing outside this Faction. The seven members of the A.C. [who were at the Sixth Zionist Congress] have to speak the first word; we are at the disposal of yourself and the others as soon as you call upon us . . . Naturally the "Nay-sayers" must also give us the opportunity to conduct propaganda, etc. They have the instruments of power, they have the influence—we shall place the propagandists at their disposal and we shall conduct the campaign in accordance with a plan worked out in concert . . .[88]

This was a transformed Weizmann. He was no longer defiant and belligerent toward the regional leaders. Naturally both Ussishkin and Bernstein-Kohan expressed interest in his ideas and promised to support the publication of *Der Jude.*[89]

While waiting for the response of the Russians, Weizmann decided to try to salvage two projects: the university scheme and the publication of *Der Jude.* Both were worthwhile ventures in themselves and could also serve as propaganda vehicles for the *Nein-Sager.* In the meantime Weizmann had learned that the best way to proceed was not through committees or conferences but on the basis of a small cadre of efficient and effective groups of academicians. Martin Buber was one of the first he enlisted for this working group. Writing to Buber at the end of September, he revealed his modified university plan: "It may be described in a few words—to establish Jewish University Vacation Courses with an outstanding Jewish program and the best talents we have . . . This is something concrete, grand and relatively easy to achieve; and is simultaneously the beginning of, and preparation for, the University wherever its location, besides being a most splendid national demonstration; in short, much more than the *Nachtasyl.*"[90] This was indeed a completely new concept in Jewish education; it demonstrated once again Weizmann's academic predilections, organizational know-how, and political flexibility. Buber liked the idea and promised to help.[91] Feiwel had some reservations. Before receiving Buber's reply of October 2, Weizmann was already on his way to London via Paris, where he presented his plan to Max Nordau and Nahum Sokolow, who approved. He was also able to enlist the participation and support of Professor Joseph Halévy, Director of Oriental Languages at the Ecole des Hautes Etudes.[92]

His plan for the vacation courses was conceived on a grand scale; he tried to enlist the best talents. Writing to Buber from Paris, he explained his motivations:

> Here I have won over Sokolow, Nordau, and Professor J. Halévy. We must have some first-rate names and I am thinking of [Franz] Oppenheimer, [Hermann] Cohen from Marburg, [Ludwig] Stein from Berne, and a few more: [Leo Abraham] Errera, [Joseph] Jacobs, [Moses] Gaster, etc. and then some younger men: you, [David] Neumark, etc. I am convinced that our cause will gain a great deal from this. I consider it to be enormous propaganda material for the University, for the idea, for Zionism. We must already speak of it as a *fait accompli* and draft a good memorandum on it at once. Please, Martinchen, do this and write to me at Geneva . . . I hope to extricate our University project by this undertaking . . .[93]

Later he added, ". . . apart from the great national value of such an endeavor, which is easy to implement, it remains the sole possibility of establishing a relationship between Jewish students and Jewish professors on the basis of Jewish scholarship."[94]

Buber, who was at Lemberg completing his doctoral dissertation, agreed to write the memorandum. He liked Weizmann's list of scholars, except for Errera, whose work on Russian Jewry did not impress him. He had his own suggestions. How about enlisting George Brandes, Karl Joel, Nathan Birnbaum, Markus Braude, Marcus Ehrenpreis, Osias Thon, and Bernard Wachstein?[95] From London Weizmann reported that Moses Gaster had agreed to join the courses, as did Israel Zangwill and Hermann Gollancz.[96] It was a grand scheme indeed, involving the foremost Jewish intellectuals and scholars in Western and Eastern Europe.[97] With tongue in cheek Weizmann called the project the "East-Africa project of the University—but it lies within the bounds of the permissible." ("Es ist ein Ost-Afrika der Hochschule—es liegt aber in der Linie.")[98]

The problem was not in inducing scholars to join the committee on vacation courses or to actually teach the courses during the months of August and September. The sticking point was the financing of the entire scheme. While en route home from London, Weizmann estimated the cost at twenty thousand francs.[99] When he had more leisure time in Geneva to make the calculations, he arrived at a figure twice as large.[100] After making some modifications in the plan, apparently at Nordau's suggestion, he finally calculated a more modest budget of ten thousand to fifteen thousand francs.[101]

The plan for university vacation courses occupied Weizmann for a number of weeks. In the meantime the Kharkov Conference of mid-November had endorsed the idea of setting up a polytechnic institute in Palestine. Weizmann announced jubilantly, "We are no longer on our own."[102] He even contemplated traveling to Palestine to investigate the conditions for setting up the institute. For his part Weizmann finally succumbed to Ussishkin's long-standing demand and abandoned the plan for a temporary university in Europe.[103] Even so, the modified plan for vacation courses was in trouble by the end of December. It was attacked and mocked by some as impossible of attainment; its initiators, namely, Weizmann and his friends, were viewed as incompetent and incapable of carrying out the task.[104] More important, however, this project also suffered from a perennial problem. As Weizmann wrote Joseph Lurie, "the things that one starts suffer from lack of manpower; one has to divide oneself up and tear oneself to shreds."[105] Two months later he repeated the same complaint: "As to the *Hochschule*, all efforts must be concentrated on the Courses, but for the time being the right people are not available, for they are all dispersed. All my hopes are placed on the Russian tour . . . "[106] But the Russian tour in the spring of 1904 was unsuccessful and frustrating on many counts. With it the plan for the vacation courses, which was all but dead, was finally buried. For the time being Weizmann also abandoned the idea of the *Hochschule* upon which he had embarked with such zeal and optimism two years earlier.[107]

The university vacation courses had been intended to maintain the momentum of the idea, to serve as a *Nachtasyl*—to use Weizmann's imagery—until such time as the actual university could be established in Palestine. But they were also clearly seen as instruments of propaganda in the hands of the *Nein-Sager* and, as such, deserved the support of the regional leaders. Weizmann viewed the publication of *Der Jude* in similar terms. It was a worthwhile and important endeavor on its own merit, but it also had propaganda value as a mouthpiece for those opposing Herzl's diplomacy. This had been recognized, at least theoretically, by the regional leaders who met at Beatenberg right after the congress. They promised to help the periodical, whose first issue had been ready in the spring of 1903, by selling shares of the publication and obtaining reader subscriptions.[108] The regional leaders reiterated their support in Kharkov by agreeing to set aside twelve hundred rubles for the printed propaganda of the Democratic Faction. In return they demanded control over the publication. Weizmann did not particularly respect the profession of journalism, but he understood the power of the press. He realized that a first-rate party organ could be a dangerous weapon in the hands of the Democratic Faction and its allies. Moreover, the Faction had received a bad press since its inception; the time had come for a counterattack. Thus, he assigned this project an important place on his agenda for immediate action.[109]

The major problem, as in the past, was locating sufficient funds to secure the publication of the first few issues. Samuel Shriro, Weizmann's initial and most generous financial backer for the university and *Der Jude*, had voted with the *Ya-Sager* at the Sixth Zionist Congress, and for the time being Weizmann could not turn to him for help. Relying on the promise of the regional leaders, however, Weizmann proceeded on the assumption that all was well.[110] Soon he realized that matters would not advance smoothly. Buber was demanding money in a hurry, since he wanted the first issue of *Der Jude* to appear in January 1904.[111] For his part Weizmann wrote to Victor Jacobson, "If any money has come for

Der Jude please send some of it, because Buber makes demands, and I have none—*pauvre comme un rat d'église.*"[112] The following day he cabled, "Dispatch funds for Jude (*Judengeld*) immediately—embarrassed."[113] Yet despite the efforts of Victor Jacobson, Menahem Ussishkin, and Yehiel Tschlenow, they managed to scrape together only four hundred rubles for the publication.[114] Jacobson and Gregory Belkovsky tried to persuade Weizmann to commence publication immediately, promising that after the first issue they would be able to sell more subscriptions, but Weizmann insisted on a minimum of fifteen hundred to two thousand rubles, which would guarantee the publication of future issues for the first six months.[115] At the same time, Weizmann vented his anger against those friends who had promised help but had failed to deliver.[116]

By mid-November 1903 a prospectus appeared announcing the publication of *Der Jude* for January 1904.[117] This second announcement of the periodical, most likely written by Buber, was quite similar in content to the prospectus which appeared in the spring of 1903.[118] It contained a long list of distinguished sponsors, the most obvious omission being that of Theodor Herzl.[119] Another glaring omission was that the second prospectus listed only Buber and Weizmann as publishers, omitting any mention of Berthold Feiwel except as a sponsor.[120]

The change in editorship reflected a crisis which took place early in November 1903. It was not the first editorial crisis to shake the fledgling enterprise. From the start Weizmann had been less than candid as to who would edit the paper. In February 1903 he wrote Feiwel that "you are the only person who could edit such a paper. I would work for it solely under this condition."[121] But a few days later he wrote Buber, whose ego had been wounded, "As for the editorship, I must at once point out that it never occurred to me to have Toldy appointed sole editor. If you are going to Berlin . . . then it is obvious both of you will take charge of affairs."[122] Three weeks later he informed Catherine Dorfman, "Editors: Buber, Feiwel and myself."[123] The vagueness as to who was really in charge finally took its toll. Feiwel felt that he was being ignored by Buber and announced his intention to relinquish all responsibility for the periodical.[124] Weizmann tried to dissuade him.

> Even now I don't see why you wish to withdraw. Now that such a critical situation has set in, and the few we do have must hold together, everyone is starting to go his separate way, with the sense of cohesiveness ever diminishing . . . We shan't achieve anything, because we are all people with frayed nerves . . . I have to do everything myself, at my own risk and with my own money—which I haven't got. Obligations assumed by other Faction members have until the present never been fulfilled. They all know how to talk, to talk a great deal . . . One thing is incontestably established, and that is the existence of a field of activity; it is as large and even more rewarding now than it has been in recent years. We are short of good workers, but that does not mean that we, who do not regard ourselves as bunglers, should throw in the sponge.[125]

But Feiwel remained adamant; his decision to withdraw was final.

If Feiwel quit in a pique over protocol, Buber succumbed to the insurmountable financial pressures. Since the spring of 1903 he had turned to Weizmann for funds, relying on the latter's executive and administrative abilities.[126] As the date of publication of *Der Jude* approached, his demands became more insistent and urgent. In a moment of exasperation Buber threatened to resign unless he received funds by December 20, 1903.[127] With this ultimatum Weizmann finally exploded:

> This is the first day I am feeling well enough to write a letter myself . . . I repeat for the tenth time that I wrote to everyone about *Der Jude;* that furthermore all of them replied . . . that we hope to receive, if not the entire 2,000 roubles by the 20th, then at least a large part of it. I too received a telegram from Berlin about paper and did not know what to make of it. I was in bed and without a penny. I wish I could also present ultimatums like yours, I could also withdraw as Told is doing, give up everything, everything, everything and let the others do the work for one or two years. It might even be necessary, because I can no longer bear this condition of being crushed while my closest friends do not have a like degree of responsibility and, perhaps quite unconsciously, shift the greatest responsibility onto me. I cannot help feeling bitter about standing completely alone, as though abandoned, at critical moments: "we march together" only when everything works out well. But when there is a crisis to overcome, such as now, then impatience and irritation take over from unity and mutual responsibility. I too have made a resolve that, if only for reasons of health, *I must* fulfil: after the Faction Conference I am not going to lift a finger anymore. I shall no longer accept any office. After 10 years of work, after 5 years of grinding, all-consuming activity, I too wish to have at least one year *all to myself.* I owe it to myself. I have never spoken like this, but now that I see that after everything, one is really alone, I cannot act otherwise.[128]

Buber remained unmoved. For his part he stated that he did not have the emotional stamina necessary to edit a periodical which did not have financial security. The example of the Juedischer Verlag, which existed on an insufficient endowment, was enough to deter him. Thus, he had to stick to his decision to withdraw.[129] From later correspondence it seems that, in fact, Buber had not yet resigned.[130] Weizmann still hoped to raise the necessary funds during his spring tour of Russia,[131] but as in the case of the vacation courses, the project had already lost its momentum, and his unsuccessful Russian sojourn could not revive it. Both projects proved that Weizmann's predilection for working alone could not fully succeed without sufficient organizational backing. Under completely different circumstances, and with the aid of the World Zionist Organization, Weizmann revived the university project in 1913, whereas *Der Jude* began its regular publication under Martin Buber's editorship in 1916.

The publication of *Der Jude* and the truncated university-in-the-making were among Weizmann's priorities in the last months of 1903, but his major occupation and concern was to devise a means to destroy the East

Africa project. In the process he attempted yet again to gain for himself a more prominent place in the movement on the Continent, though he was already keeping one eye on career possibilities in England. Herzl had pointed the way to England as the seat of power and the possible arbiter of a solution for the landless Zionist movement. Weizmann was well aware of the possibilities in England for a capable, enterprising, and ambitious man. Yet he needed a legitimate excuse for going to investigate both the East Africa question and his own opportunities, expecially since the trip was to be paid for with money collected for the Democratic Faction.[132] Two weeks after returning to Geneva from the Sixth Zionist Congress he wrote to Sokolow, "I am going to England . . . on University business . . . "[133] Thus, ostensibly he went to line up important lecturers for the vacation courses. Yet his real reason seems to have been to find out at first hand what the chances of the East Africa scheme were. He was not completely overstepping his role, since he was a member of the East Africa Commission that had been appointed by the congress. On the other hand, that commission was to have possessed a purely advisory, noninvestigative brief. Weizmann simply used his minor appointment on the commission and stretched and expanded his function—more so than any other members[134]—to suit his needs.

Fortunately he had made a good impression on William Evans-Gordon during the latter's tour of Russia in September 1902. He now relied on Evans-Gordon to make the necessary contacts in London for him. Weizmann informed Herzl that while in London he planned to obtain a report sent by Sir Charles Eliot, the High Commissioner in East Africa, to the British government.[135] A day later, however, he wrote to Evans-Gordon that he wished to obtain much more: government reports, Blue Books, and perhaps maps and descriptions of the proposed territory, in addition to the Eliot memorandum. To Evans-Gordon he somewhat misrepresented the function of the East Africa Commission, stating that its purpose was to "examine" the British offer and "to equip an expedition to that country [East Africa]."[136]

Evans-Gordon replied that he would be glad to receive Weizmann in London and instructed the Parliamentary Sales Office to forward the requested material on East Africa.[137] Otto Warburg, the chairman of the East Africa Commission, had also given his blessing to the trip,[138] and Weizmann was confident that he would be able to discover everything. "London," he told one of his close collaborators, "is the most important center now . . . For the present I shall probably only manage to establish our headquarters in London."[139]

On October 3, 1903, while en route to London, Weizmann stopped over in Paris. The first person he saw was Max Nordau. There is no explanation in his correspondence or elsewhere as to why an outspoken *Nein-Sager* would have wished to see the author of the speech on *Nachtasyl*. Moreover, Weizmann had been among those most prominent in siding with Ahad Ha'Am during the latter's controversy with Nordau. Ostensibly he visited the famous author to enlist him for the vacation courses, but Weizmann emphasized the friendly fashion in which he was received. Nordau even invited him to dinner. "What a friendship!" Weizmann exclaimed in his letter to Vera.[140] Vera was outspoken in her reaction to this newfound companionship. "What I don't like is that you have started a relationship with Nordau."[141] Buber was equally surprised. "How did you manage to win over Nordau [to the idea of the vacation courses]? Have you made up with him?"[142] Perhaps both Weizmann and Nordau realized that their positions on East Africa were not so far apart; Nordau expressed his own ambivalence toward the project and possibly intimated to Weizmann that it had encountered some resistance within the British government as well.[143] Weizmann's meetings with the leaders of the Jewish Colonization Association—including Narcisse Leven and Rabbi Zadoc Kahn, chief rabbi of France, who was, in addition, honorary president of the Alliance Israélite Universelle and a member of the Jewish Colonization Association (ICA) Council—also convinced him that they were more interested in Palestine than East Africa and that only pressure from Lord Nathaniel Rothschild in London induced them to enter into negotiations with Herzl concerning the expedition to East Africa.[144] Weizmann was much less satisfied after meeting with Sokolow. Only a fortnight previously he had written to the editor of *Hatzfirah* in the most obsequious manner, seeking his advice on personal and Zionist matters. "You are my friend, after all, so give some advice, grant me the word of salvation—I believe in you and trust you very, very much and you will do me good."[145] To Vera he now wrote about Sokolow in different terms. "I have practically given up hope in Sokolow and his sympathy. He will go wherever there is success, strength, etc., but till then he will prevaricate. His behavior in the Africa affair is disgusting. He wriggles as he talks to me . . ."[146] His assessment of French Jewry was equally derogatory. Referring to the public reaction in the wake of pogroms in Homel in mid-September 1903, he exclaimed, "Here the prostitute Republic surrenders to the embraces of the Russian bear and the damned French Jews are cowardly. They are *plus français que les Français [sic]*. They are afraid to come out against Russia as she is France's ally."[147]

He reached London on October 8. His first impressions were bleak. "I arrived today in this monstrous London, and have hardly managed to do a thing . . . I have been rushing about madly, and there is slush here, foul weather, fog, din and uproar, and a language which is not exactly comprehensible to me . . . I am now in Whitechapel. Lord, what horror! Stench, foul smells, emaciated Jewish faces. A mixture of a London avenue and Jewish poverty in the suburbs of Vilna."[148] Twenty-four hours later his mood had changed completely: "In contrast to yesterday—a most unpleasant day—today all went well. The sun has smiled and all my people have responded . . . I am terribly pleased that I went to London, terribly pleased. I feel very well today. I have done some work, and have had a rest . . ."[149]

His stay in London commenced auspiciously. Indeed, during his entire week there he registered to his credit one achievement after another. His first visit was to Moses Gaster, the *Haham* (chief rabbi) of the Sephardic community in Britain and his most important contact within the Anglo-Jewish community. It was the festival of Sukkot (Feast of Tabernacles) and they lunched outside in the sukkah.[150] Gaster was born in Bucharest and had studied at the Jewish Theological Seminary of Breslau. He had taught Rumanian language and literature at the University of Bucharest, but in 1885 he had been expelled from the country because he protested against its treatment of Jews. He settled in England, where he was appointed to teach Slavonic literature at Oxford University. In 1887 he was appointed to his eminent religious post. Gaster's abilities as a scholar and orator gained him an outstanding position within the Anglo-Jewish community. He had been active in the Jewish national movement since the days of the Hibbat Zion, and later in the Zionist movement he had accompanied Laurence Oliphant on his journeys to Rumania, Constantinople and Palestine, where he had played a considerable part in the establishment of Zikhron Yaakov and Rosh Pinah, the first colonies settled by Rumanian Jews. An early supporter of Herzl, he turned violently against the East Africa scheme. A combative and stubborn person by nature, he was willing to carry his dislike of Herzl to extremes.[151]

Gaster had met Weizmann at various congresses. They shared similar attitudes, especially on the issue of East Africa, and they saw each other as political allies. Their friendship was never warm and intimate. It waxed and waned between extremes, which included annoyance, usefulness, jealousy, cooperation, and sometimes volcanic eruptions of anger. Given the tendency of both to moodiness and sulking and their extreme sensitivity to slights, it could not have been otherwise. Each recognized the usefulness of the other for his own political advancement. Yet at this early stage Weizmann was mostly on the receiving end. He recognized the fact and treated Gaster—at least in public—with extreme care, calling him "My Dear Doctor," solicitously inquiring after his health and the welfare of his family, and respectfully deferring to his superior judgment in Zionist as well as personal affairs. But Weizmann could quickly assess personalities and knew instantly that Gaster was full of intrigue and hungry for power. The *Haham* saw himself as Herzl's equal and his worthy successor. To Vera Weizmann reported that "Gaster . . . is preparing to *overthrow* Herzl . . ."[152] After a few more days of observing the rabbi in action, he concluded, "He is an absolute rogue, and he knows that I am aware of it; but he is prepared to go along with us at all cost, if only to overthrow Herzl. One has to be very careful with him."[153] Paradoxically, Weizmann admired Herzl as a leader, though by 1903 he rejected most of his ideas. Gaster's views on Zionist ideology and policy were akin to Weizmann's, but he immediately sensed that the *Haham* could in no way measure up to the human qualities of the founder of the World Zionist Organization.

Gaster had agreed to lecture for the vacation courses; and Israel Zangwill, an almost complete antipode to the *Haham*, agreed to join its committee. Zangwill, among Anglo-Jewry's best-known public figures, was highly assimilated. His *Children of the Ghetto* had gained him international fame, which was sustained by many other works. Unlike Gaster, he supported Herzl vociferously on the subject of East Africa.[154] Weizmann assessed him thus: "Mr. Zangwill is the real ideologist of East Africa. He goes much further than the leaders would wish. In a certain sense he is even opposed to Palestine . . . He is not acquainted with the evolution of Judaism as a whole. Zionism, according to him, depends on accidents . . . after a discussion lasting some hours he took it in silence when I told him: 'You may well be the photographer of the Ghetto, but you are not its psychologist' . . . Like Nordau he is completely hypnotized by Herzl."[155] It says something about Weizmann's tactical approach to the question of organization-building that despite the deep-seated differences between himself and Zangwill, he did not hesitate to approach the latter for the vacation courses. As in the case of Nordau, the good of the organization transcended his personal antipathies. The fame of both men justified his tactical means.

Weizmann's meeting with the English members of the East Africa Commission, which included Leopold Greenberg, Joseph Cowen, and Leopold Kessler, was equally satisfactory from an ideological point of view, though personally he was not very pleased by them. With the exception of Greenberg, they had all reached the conclusion that the East Africa scheme had to be abandoned.[156] This was also the attitude of Herbert Bentwich, a distinguished lawyer, prominent Zionist, and close collaborator of Moses Gaster. Between them they represented a strong nucleus of *Nein-Sager*. For all practical purposes they *were* English Zionism. Moreover, they each wined and dined him as an important personage— quite a contrast to the treatment he was getting back on the Continent from the Russian regional leaders.[157]

But his main goal was to meet important and authoritative government officials, preferably from the Foreign Office, from whom he could gather sufficient anti–East Africa material to destroy the scheme. Here Evans-Gordon proved invaluable. The major was himself interested in helping Weizmann. In his autobiography Weizmann claimed that

Sir William Evans-Gordon had no particular anti-Jewish prejudices. He acted, as he thought, according to his best lights and in the most kindly way, in the interests of his country. He had been horrified by what he had seen of the oppression of the Jews of Russia, but in his opinion it was physically impossible for England to make good the wrongs which Russia had inflicted on its Jewish population. He was sorry, but he was helpless. Also, he was sincerely ready to encourage any settlement of Jews almost anywhere in the British Empire, but he failed to see why the ghettos of London or Leeds or Whitechapel should be made into a branch of the ghettos of Warsaw and Pinsk . . . Sir William Evans-Gordon gave me some insight into the psychology of the settled citizen, and though my views on immigration naturally were in sharp conflict with his, we discussed these problems in a quite objective and even friendly way.[158]

It is difficult to accept the fact that Weizmann was so naive or unin-
formed about Evans-Gordon's background and real motivation in helping him that he believed the major "had no particular anti-Jewish prejudices." Evans-Gordon had led the East End Conservative M.P.s in their
attempt to persuade the government to set up the Royal Commission on
Alien Immigration. Indeed, he did not want the East End to be even more
crowded with poor Yiddish-speaking peddlers and hawkers. Yet it was
convenient for Weizmann to disregard all this for the moment. Like Herzl
before him with von Plehve, Weizmann did not rule out bargaining with
anti-Semites. They were a fact of life, they could not be ignored, and it
was simply necessary to deal with them.[159] In any case, Evans-Gordon
had developed a personal liking for Weizmann[160] and proved to be as
good as his word. He gave Weizmann all the official materials on East
Africa, and since Lord Percy, the parliamentary Under-Secretary of State
for Foreign Affairs, was unavailable, he introduced him to Sir Harry
Johnston, the former Special Commissioner in Uganda. Sir Johnston received Weizmann very well, and this meeting—probably conducted in
French—was a success. Weizmann was virtually exploding with triumph:

> If I were to publish the entire content of the conversation, a mortal blow
> would be dealt to the Africans. But I shall keep this as a trump card. He
> fully agrees with my arguments and considers it impossible to establish a
> fairly large colonization project even in twenty-five years' time. He de-
> scribed the *proposal of the British Government as irony in respect of the Jews.* He
> said . . . that British public opinion will be against us, that everything we
> do here can be done for Palestine alone, and that he is ready to support us.
> He promised to come and address a meeting, and he is a tremendously im-
> portant man in England . . . I have learned valuable things from him about
> El Arish.

In a final note of jubilation Weizmann added, "You see, my child, how
diplomacy is conducted. Our leaders merely spoiled things and made
fools of themselves. I am convinced that Herzl would speak of 'enormous successes' [*gigantische Erfolge*] were he to know all I know now."[161]
He took delight in comparing himself with Herzl. "We, too, can be diplomats, eh?"[162]

Of course, things were not as simple as Johnston had portrayed. It is
further proof that Herzl had effectively kept diplomatic information to
himself, that Weizmann believed Johnston's assertion that El Arish could
still be made available for Jewish colonization, that Egyptian resistance
to the idea could be broken, and that the water problem could be solved
within six months. Based on this false intelligence, Weizmann exclaimed, "They [Herzl and SAC] lied to us!"[163] What Weizmann did
sense—even before it became public knowledge, and possibly even before Herzl knew for sure—was that Great Britain was already looking for
ways to extricate herself from the East Africa offer. Indeed, men like
Weizmann and other *Nein-Sager* may have given the government an added
excuse for a shift in policy.

Weizmann had good reason to be proud of his achievements, all the more so since he was a novice in the art of diplomacy, was in a foreign country, and had a very poor command of the English language. Four days in London convinced him that he had never felt better.[164] So engrossed was he in London that he dropped his plans to go to Glasgow, Leeds,[165] and Manchester, where he was to see Charles Dreyfus of the Clayton Aniline Company. His sojourn in London also gave him an added push to pursue an idea he had thus far discussed only with Vera, namely, that a move to England would afford him new and important opportunities. Evans-Gordon and Gaster promised to help him find a job,[166] and he had also inquired about the opportunities for "women doctors." All that was required, he informed Vera, was "to pass a simple examination, and then one may set up in practice, and do well."[167] He rounded off his stay with a visit to the British Museum and shopped for some presents for Vera.[168]

Departing London on October 16, Weizmann had a chance to reflect on the hectic week he had just spent. He already spoke of his move to England as a fait accompli; he saw for himself there an "enormous field for work" unencumbered by the presence of the regional leaders or members of SAC looking over his shoulder.[169] He intuitively sensed that he had found his métier in politics. He had the ability to instantly grasp the essentials surrounding events and to handle himself with grace and authority in his encounters with politicians. These were qualities he would refine on countless occasions. For the time being he realized that he had to capitalize on his first successes by making them public. In his estimate he now had all the ammunition he needed to destroy the pro-African forces. He had accumulated one further piece of evidence on his way home: The eminent geographer Elisée Reclus told him in Brussels that mass colonization in East Africa was unfeasible.[170] Weizmann divided up the task. He asked Buber, Feiwel, and Tschlenow to draft a memorandum that could be sent to Johnston and Evans-Gordon in England for circulation within influential circles.[171] He himself sat down to write two memoranda to the regional leaders and some other friends. Though he had already begun to prepare himself psychologically for a move to England, he had not yet, in fact, made an absolute commitment. In the meantime he viewed it as his responsibility to report his findings and to give advice. Possibly he could still carve for himself a place among the Continental Zionists.

Weizmann's first report soberly summarized his travels, meetings, and impressions in Paris, London, and Brussels.[172] With very few exceptions, it was an accurate and faithful recapitulation of his activities, though his own bias is evident throughout in the adjectives he used, in his framing of questions to his interlocutors, and in his conclusions.

I brought the impression away from London that we can accomplish a great deal there. We can win over influential circles; we must manifest our desire for Palestine with deeds rather than shallow phrases. We must place our political activities— . . . I simply call it propaganda—in the hands of first-rate men who will win over the sympathies of Europe and not snatch at chance success. Every serious statesman understands full well our renunciation of Africa and reckons with our aspirations to Palestine as a power factor. A small settlement in Palestine strengthens our prestige in the eyes of the world more than the half-baked projects which unhappily preoccupy us so much at present. To my regret, I must also state that our leaders have still not understood this, with the result that a great deal of time and energy has been uselessly squandered. I promise myself only one good thing from the Africa project: Perhaps our leaders have now been taught their lesson![173]

Less than a week later Weizmann sent his second memorandum, which clearly stated his views on the course of action to be undertaken by the *Nein-Sager*. It is a powerful and personal statement, reminding the reader of his memorandum to Herzl six months earlier.

Seven years of Zionist activity have finally taught us that we have sought in vain to construct a unity out of heterogeneous elements . . . One group conceives of Zionism as a mechanism, and is ignorant of its connection with the soul of the Jewish people. Consequently it seeks to "manufacture" Zionism either through diplomatic journeys or through fund-raising appeals. Elements that are partly detached from living Judaism—the assimilated Westerners on the one side, and the Orthodox confined within their rigid formulae on the other, are incapable of a better understanding of the national cause.

The other group, however, understands Zionism to be the life-giving force, both actual and potential; the free development of the nation finding its highest expression in the idea of statehood . . .

Whereas on our side the political forms of the movement were being continually shaped into an organic force as a result of our Jewish content, for the West European Zionism remained a cliché, completely devoid of Jewish content, unstable, wavering and hollow, finding its highest expression in so-called diplomacy, and in the Jewish Statism [*Judenstaatlertum*] that smells of philanthropy.[174]

After these opening remarks, he made the following suggestions: collective and strategic colonization in Palestine by means of a slow and systematic activity; forging a strong tie between the Zionist organization in the Diaspora (*Golus*) and the Jewish organization in Palestine; decentralization of the Zionist organization and assignment of important tasks to special departments, with London as the headquarters of the Actions Committee; a Zionist press not limited by territorial boundaries; a reorganization and redefinition of the task of the Jewish Colonial Trust and the Jewish National Fund, permitting them to operate only in Palestine and neighboring countries; and the conversion of the Democratic Faction into a working group serving the *Nein-Sager*, in return for which it and its projects would be supported financially.[175]

The striking element in both reports is Weizmann's characterization of the Zionist movement as composed of two camps divided ideologically and geographically between East and West. This analysis of the state of the Zionist movement should not be understood as intentionally divisive. On the contrary, his aim was to eventually close the gap between opposing camps and bridge these ideological and geographic differences. A related feature of both reports was the fact that despite their severe criticism of the Zionist leadership in the West, they refrained from direct attack upon Herzl. On the contrary, they contained explicit warnings against any attempts to unseat Herzl from the leadership. How can this be explained in light of Weizmann's attitude to Herzl until then? Weizmann's critical stance toward Herzl had undergone four major developments. At first he was full of admiration and respect for Herzl and his momentous achievements, venturing only minor criticisms from time to time.[176] However, he adopted a sustained critical attitude toward Herzl from 1901 on, an attitude which was a composite of disagreement on substantive issues, personal envy, and a need to carve out for himself a role within the movement's front ranks. The very establishment of the Democratic Faction presented a direct challenge to Herzl and the supremacy of SAC. Herzl was quick to understand this and tried to diffuse this opposition group. This was Weizmann's first period of disillusionment with Herzl.[177]

To his friends Weizmann had complained many times about Herzl's shallow understanding of Zionist and Jewish issues. In his first confrontation with Herzl, in July 1901, his veiled language only hinted at Herzl's culpability in having contributed to "the Zionists' dilatory and meditative approach to the solution even of domestic problems, or about the stagnation which has set in among the societies . . ."[178] He was much more explicit in his letter to his confidante: "Dr. Herzl has no idea of Russian Zionism and of Russian Zionists. Dr. Herzl is being misled by various creatures, flatterers, 'friends of the cause.' "[179] Describing, a few months later, Herzl's testimony before the Royal Commission on Alien Immigration, Weizmann wrote with obvious exasperation, "This is all extremely interesting—how the English statesmen see the position of the Jews, and how shockingly Herzl defined Zionism and the Jewish nation. Some of his answers are very intelligent, some are purely journalistic and show the dilettantism of a journalist who, having such an important mission, has not prepared himself for it . . ."[180]

As Weizmann's own development and involvement in Zionist affairs matured, he became more critical of Herzl, a stance that found its most trenchant and full expression in his memorandum to Herzl dated May 6, 1903. This memorandum—which took issue with Herzl's reliance on the Mizrahi, critized his lack of understanding of the moral and intellectual plight of the Russian Jewish intelligentsia, and tried to outline for Herzl a solution to the various woes afflicting the movement in both East and West—failed to attain its goal. Not only did it not succeed in changing Herzl's attitude toward the Mizrahi, but it also failed to open a new chapter between Herzl and the Democratic Faction. In personal terms it marked the end of the relationship between Weizmann and Herzl. Henceforth he was *persona non grata* in circles close to Vienna. The word was out that he was no longer viewed with favor by Herzl. Rubuffed and ignored, Weizmann's criticism toward Herzl became more sharp and wounding, mixed with irony and condescension.

Having made the switch to the *Nein-Sager* at the Sixth Zionist Congress, Weizmann presently became angry and bitter. He was furious at what Herzl was doing to the movement and to those who opposed him. As the opposition to Herzl faltered and Weizmann's own projects fell apart, he wrote in early 1904:

> It is obvious from everything that the mood is terrible; I see no end to these ordeals. Evidently, Herzl is a clever operator and "the great leader" will be able to force all decent people out of the movement, for he has weapons at his disposal that others would not dare to consider. We have but one thing to do in order not to find ourselves overboard: unite the small group of people who still live, think and feel in a Zionist way, and who have not yet sunk in the mire of Viennese diplomacy.[181]

From 1901 on, Weizmann gradually began to compare himself to Herzl with ever-increasing frequency, first in a subtle way and later more openly. Intertwined with his opposition to Herzl on substantive Zionist and general Jewish issues were feelings of admiration and intense jealousy. Herzl possessed all the attributes Weizmann had not yet acquired: personal charisma, fame, leadership, money, and diplomatic skills. These were qualities Weizmann had to acquire slowly and painfully by laboring in the more neglected and far less glamorous corners of the Zionist movement. The personal element in the more theoretically framed and formulated antagonism was therefore not a negligible factor. Moreover, the very struggle against Herzl trained Weizmann to assume organizational and leadership positions which, with time, would become important assets in his own rise to a position of authority within the movement.

And yet from the very start of organized opposition in 1901, Weizmann had made it clear—even in the face of conflicting advice from Ahad Ha'Am—that his group was a loyal opposition. He would bring about changes from within and would under no conditions split the movement. Even after Weizmann's opposition to Herzl had become intense after the Sixth Zionist Congress, he maintained this point of view. Through the cloud of arguments and counterarguments he clearly saw that there was no alternative to Herzl as leader of the movement. Propaganda against Herzl and his schemes was one thing, but his ouster was a differenrt matter altogether.

To Menahem Ussishkin Weizmann wrote two weeks after the Sixth Zionist Congress, "You and some of our other comrades in Russia are now, more than ever, called upon to stand at the head of our cause without as yet demolishing the idols [Herzl] of our own making."[182] Weizmann was completely opposed to Gaster's intention to overthrow Herzl.[183]

What, then, were Weizmann's aims for the moment? First, he urged a broader view by the Russian leadership on the question of how to conduct the struggle against East Africa: ". . . the Russian 'Nay-sayers' must abandon their regional, *Landsmanschaft*, point of view and seek to exercise an influence upon Western Zionism. What is at issue here is to carry through the struggle for hegemony; it is only because the leadership is West European and the following mostly East European . . . that misunderstandings such as have led as far as Africa could have arisen . . ."[184] What he aimed at was for Russian Zionists to share the power within the movement and to help lead it in a meaningful way. Though he professed to have serious doubts as to Herzl's diplomatic abilities and claimed that "we"—by which he meant himself—could accomplish a great deal through reasonable diplomacy,[185] he opposed the removal of Herzl.[186] Although after the GAC meeting in April 1904 Weizmann stated, ". . . and if [the] Uganda [scheme] does not collapse a split is inevitable and that is all we can wish for," this seems to have been a fleeting thought during a moment of despair.[187] His practical suggestion for sharing power was simple; he called for evolutionary reforms rather than a revolution.

Our *Golus* organization must undergo such radical reforms as to enable *all* leaders to receive a greater share of the work, with more control and responsibility over it. Broadly, the organization ought to be shaped as follows: each sphere of Zionist activity will have its special department that will be administered by a small number of capable people who will naturally be elected by the Congress. The representatives of these departments will form the [S]AC . . . Only by dividing the work can there be any guarantee that no further surprises will come.[188]

How did the Russian regional leaders respond to Weizmann's assessments and proposals? Yehiel Tschlenow, the more moderate member of the group, accepted them. So did Victor Jacobson. More important, Menahem Ussishkin wrote to thank him for his program, and for the first time he ventured to say that he was "sure that we could unite and work together."[189] Yet in his letters to Weizmann dated October 28 and November 6, 1903, Ussishkin issued a warning which was, in fact, an ultimatum: "I want you to know that I am opposed, as heretofore, to the Faction, to the Mizrahi, and every factionist principle which kills our general movement . . ." His agreement to cooperate with Weizmann was also conditional on "your getting rid of this 'monster' called Faction and then we will establish a strong organization of Zionei Zion."[190]

For the time being Weizmann did not openly take issue with Ussishkin. He was still euphoric about his success in London and proceeded to plan the Faction conference, which had been scheduled for December 27, 1903, at the Sixth Zionist Congress.[191] He would first wait and see what the regional leaders would decide in Kharkov in mid-November before taking any new and radical steps with regard to the Faction. While they met, he agreed to give a speech to the Bern Academic Zionist Society on Sunday, November 8, about the Sixth Zionist Congress and the East Africa issue.[192] It was the only debate in which he participated during the period from the Sixth Zionist Congress until his departure for

England in July 1904. This was not a coincidence; he did not want to continue to be too closely identified as a student leader and wished to move on to the more respectable role of an established party leader and negotiator. Yet for an excellent and eager propagandist like Weizmann it was an opportunity he could not refuse. The event must have seemed to him like old times, when he used to debate the Bundists. This time, however, the meeting was open only to Zionists, who debated among themselves. The meeting lasted for the traditional three days; his address on November 8 was followed by two days of debate. Weizmann's conclusion in Bern was that all Zionist efforts must be turned to Palestine at this time. A certain number of Jews had to be settled in Palestine before political rights could be aspired to. In a word, the need was for small-scale colonization. A Jewish state could not be created in a land without Jews.[193]

The Kharkov resolutions, for the most part, accorded with Weizmann's own ideas. But what was painfully obvious was that the regional leaders did not trust him with information on the proceedings. Ussishkin had been willing to disclose only that at Kharkov twelve hundred rubles had been set aside for printed propaganda for Weizmann's working group *(Arbeitsgruppe)*.[194] Weizmann found it difficult to accept this lack of information, which he initially attributed to an oversight or an outright mistake.[195] He could not understand how it was possible to place *him* in the same camp as those from whom one needed to guard secrets. Had he not proven himself since the Sixth Zionist Congress? Had he not declared, time and again, his total submission to the decisions of the regional leaders? "I cannot understand why you write *me* nothing about the Kharkov decisions. I do have to know them, as a *Direktive* for work," he wrote Ussishkin.[196] Eventually Ussishkin informed him that the Kharkov Conference's decisions were being kept secret from everyone and that he could not make any exceptions.[197] Weizmann tried a few more times to elicit some information. "I cannot imagine," he wrote to Victor Jacobson, "our comrades deciding to keep their decisions secret from me too. *Tant pis!"*[198] Finally Michael Aleinikov, Joseph Pokrassa, and in mid-December also Victor Jacobson leaked the information to him. In any case, the Kharkov resolutions were becoming well known despite the veil of secrecy, even before the deputation reached Herzl. But the incident left a bitter taste in Weizmann's mouth. It demonstrated once again that he did not belong to the inner circle of Russian Zionism. At most he could be assigned some propaganda tasks in the West.

As usual when worried and upset, Weizmann's reaction was partly physical. Early in December he reported, "I have been rather ill for some days now. I started spitting blood . . . The doctor advised me to leave everything and go south, but I cannot for the present."[199] His major reason for staying in Geneva was to continue work for the Democratic Faction's conference, which was scheduled for late December. Though he did not admit it publicly, Weizmann had arrived at the conclusion that the Democratic Faction had come to be more of a handicap than a political asset. Its very existence, though merely on paper, drew criticism and rebuke for its leaders, namely, Weizmann himself, while failing to provide him with a power base. Thus, the conference was to be the Faction's swan song and its official conversion to Ussishkin's "working group."[200] Despite the injunctions of his doctor, Weizmann was working hard to bring this transformation about. "A Faction Conference there will be. I am making every effort to hold on to what has, with such difficulty, been put together, but God! the human material is in pieces and corroded . . . Everybody goes around with such *tzores* of his own that nothing remains of him for the cause . . . The office-holders really can laugh up their sleeves about their impotent 'opponents.' I am fed up—but what can I do?"[201] The obstacles in the way of the conference proved insurmountable. There was no agreement on the agenda or the incorporation of the Faction into the *Nein-Sager*. Moreover, Ussishkin and Bernstein-Kohan informed Weizmann that the Russian deputation to Herzl would leave for Vienna at the end of December and asked that the Faction's conference be postponed by a fortnight to enable Ussishkin and perhaps another regional leader to take part in it.[202]

Instead of a conference a consultation was scheduled for early January in Berlin—a venue chosen so that Gregory Belkovsky and Simon Rosenbaum could report on their meeting with Herzl. On January 6, 1904, Weizmann assembled eleven of his friends for this purpose, among them Buber, Feiwel, Zvi Aberson, Michael Aleinikov, and Samuel Pevsner. Some came from as far as Kharkov and Warsaw,[203] while Weizmann himself had made the long journey to Berlin for the convenience of the Kharkov deputation. To Weizmann's great shock and embarrassment, Rosenbaum and Belkovsky did not keep their word. Despite Rosenbaum's promise, the two left Vienna on January 8, 1904, humiliated by Herzl, and proceeded directly to St. Petersburg without stopping in Berlin.

Weizmann was furious at having been ignored by the Kharkov deputation. It looked to him like a deliberate insult. After receiving Rosenbaum's telegram from Vienna informing him that he would not stop over in Berlin, Weizmann wrote to the regional leaders who had assembled in St. Petersburg.

> So much effort has been spent on the journey, and one sits here fuming with anger, not knowing what to do with oneself. There is no end to my indignation . . . let us know on receipt of this letter whether someone will be coming and when. *Otherwise we shall do nothing* and, as far as I can see, we are the only group that provides you with support . . . Once again, all this behavior of yours at such a time is incomprehensible to me. If this is Russian sloppiness, it is criminal to insult people in such a way.[204]

The Russians did not even bother to reply. Recognizing their lack of authority, the Faction members present at Berlin did hold their consultations, as planned, from January 10 to 12, 1904. Their most important decision was to unite with the *Nein-Sager* in a new alliance.[205]

Upon returning to Geneva, Weizmann seems to have understood why Rosenbaum and Belkovsky did not come to Berlin. Newspaper reports had revealed their ignominious failure, which stood in marked contrast to Rosenbaum's earlier boasts that he would bring about Herzl's ouster if the latter did not accede to the Kharkov demands.[206] It would certainly not have been a pleasant task for the deputation to report their failure to the members of the Faction; it was bad enough that they had to tell their story to the regional leaders in St. Petersburg. Weizmann already began to sense that the opposition to Herzl was crumbling: "Our Russian [G.]A.C. members . . . have ruined their own case through their ineptitude and I fear they will make many more gross tactical mistakes."[207] In fact, the regional leaders had decided to do nothing until the GAC session and sent an edited version of their case to SAC in Vienna.[208] Weizmann made one more halfhearted attempt to form a "league made up of reliable individuals, to organize and struggle against the present establishment throughout the world . . . I shall press for the launching of several militant journals, in London, in Berlin and in America,"[209] but this, too, was doomed to failure for lack of support.

Weizmann was now at a dead end. The Democratic Faction finally ended its existence with the meeting in Berlin. A conference was not called and the working group did not materialize. Moreover, *Der Jude* failed to appear, the vacation courses never left the drawing board, and the propaganda material in the form of pamphlets was never published. It was useless to pretend that any of these projects could be revived without the active assistance of others. But his friends in both East and West simply could not or would not keep up with his pace; nor did they display the same dedication to the cause that he exhibited. He had no choice but to face the facts. Sometime in February 1904 he began to dismantle the Jewish University bureau as well as the Democratic Faction bureau, dismissing his secretary, Saul Stupnitzky.

The single ray of hope in this bleak situation was "Ussishkin, the only man who has not yet lost his head."[210] At the end of January 1904 Ussishkin finally replied to Weizmann's letters,[211] explaining decisions made by the regional leaders and outlining the work ahead: an information campaign; the publication of a pamphlet called *The Truth about Kharkov (Die Wahrheit ueber Charkow);* and the publication of an anthology on Palestine. Ussishkin also proposed to convene a conference of the Zionist opposition in Russia. His letter ended confidently: "Don't feel downcast, dear friend, we will soon win, I sincerely believe so. *La vérité est en marche.* One needs only to work, work and work . . ."[212] Ussishkin's letter encouraged Weizmann. It would seem that he was heartened not only by its content but by the trust Ussishkin was now placing in him in revealing his detailed plans. He had finally established the personal relationship he had sought for so long. Henceforth he became Ussishkin's firm and trusted collaborator in Western Europe.[213] Typically, Weizmann's mood changed in an instant, and he bubbled over with more plans for a conference, publications, and travel to the important centers in Russia.[214] Despite his poor health, he began immediately to outline a major propaganda tour through Western Europe and Russia: London, Munich, Berlin, Kharkov, Ekaterinoslav, Odessa, and Kiev.[215] As time passed, he dropped the Western leg of his tour.

It was more important to visit the Eastern centers, though he hated to travel in Russia. The Russo-Japanese War had just begun in February 1904, and he was hoping for a Japanese victory over hated Russia. To Catherine Dorfman he wrote, "By the way, I hope you are [pro-] Japanese, otherwise it's terrible. Imagine, I have fallen so low as to read about ten newspapers a day in various languages, thinking that this way I am helping Japan beat Russia. Our [Japanese] navy suffered a defeat today, and I am very grieved. For if 'Kvas' wins now, doomsday will follow, and the whole of Europe will become *kosakisch,* and as *ein anstaendiger Mitteleuropaeer* [a decent Central European] I am terribly afraid of this."[216]

On March 22, 1904, Weizmann left for Russia. En route he visited his friends in Bern and Berlin and his sister and brother-in-law in Warsaw. He arrived in Pinsk on March 30. Everyone was assembled there. Even his new sister-in-law, Zina, Moshe's wife, turned out to be a more amicable woman than he had been led to believe by some members of his family. The only note of worry in his letters about the family concerned his brother Shmuel, who was engaged in antigovernment activities.[217] Within the family the mood was happy and content.[218] All was well, even with his parents, who, Weizmann noticed, had aged noticeably. In Pinsk Weizmann felt secure and appreciated, being looked up to as a successful scientist and man of the world. But everywhere the "Zionist mood [was] below zero," and the "mood of the Jews in our part of the world is terrible."[219] As usual when in the Pale, his observation of life around him spoiled the happiness of being with his family. His letters from Pinsk are permeated with sadness and pessimism about the Zionist condition in Russia and the hopelessness of the Jewish fate there. Written in a spirit of utter dejection, his letters foresee doom and disaster:

I too am in low spirits, which has its cause in everything: in the oppressive atmosphere of Jewish life here, in the complete helplessness, in this state of constant alarm experienced by the Jews these days.

It is difficult to say anything definite about Zionism, which once upon a time was the bright light against the background of life in the Pale. Everything has become confused, tangled. The *interregnum* within the party has muddled young, untrained minds; and immature, unfortunate programs come into being together with organizations that are just as flimsy. These are not worth a penny, but have the negative value of leading the young generation astray . . . The new young ones occupy themselves with anything but Zionism . . . Many are agitating against Palestine—the majority of Poalei Zion . . . There is no leading thread, there are no leaders. Uganda and Kishinev, the bloody reality of the everyday life of Jews in the Pale, weigh heavily on everything, everything, everything . . .[220]

Moshe, Chaim, and Shmuel Weizmann, Pinsk, 1902

He was now convinced that pro-Uganda forces had won the day. "If a Congress were now to be convened, the ratio would be not 295:178 but probably 400:50."[221]

Kishinev was very much on everyone's mind that Passover. During the first Seder the Weizmann family recalled their friend Peter Dashevsky, who had attempted to assassinate the anti-Semitic publisher Pavel Krushevan and was now in the Yaroslav jail. "There was terrible wailing, fainting."[222] It was a sad and memory-laden holiday that year. Weizmann was just as despondent after the holiday. The abject poverty he saw in Pinsk—with a handful of rich Jews who had adopted the "arrogant attitude of West European financial wizards toward their poor brethren with the lack of culture of the Pale"[223]—depressed him. But his attitude toward the miserable and oppressed Jews of the Pale had undergone a change. No longer did he describe what he saw with the arrogant self-assurance of a young student who had just returned from his first journey to Germany. Gone was the derogatory tone blaming the Jews of the Pale for their own misfortunes. Instead one detects a more

Family group, Pinsk, April 1904

mature Weizmann who sought to understand his suffering brethren. His tone consisted of a mixture of anger at their fate, sadness, and compassion. Having returned from a walk around town, he wrote a moving letter to Vera that reflects his agitation and despair at what he had just witnessed.

There is no single animated face, not a single smile; all around there are only dead shadows. I wonder what keeps people alive! You see a small shop with three roubles' worth of merchandise, and a whole family has to live on the profits of such a "business." Moreover, they have to live in fear of their lives and to experience all the horrors of Easter and similar festivals. All conversations turn around emigration, and all classes of society talk about it. Everybody is striving, but where to go? Entry to America is made difficult, restrictive bills are being passed in England . . . Every personal joy is poisoned by the oppressive recollection of the surroundings. Even now I am not worried that I may have harder times before me—not at all, but the feeling that all the Jews are suffocating, including those near to me, gives me no peace.

Things are in a fine state when one has to be glad that a week has passed tranquilly, without any Jewish blood being shed. You can well imagine the psychology of people living permanently in such nervous tension. Of course I shall work, Verochka. I shall work wherever fate takes me, for only cruel egoists who have silenced any voice of honor and conscience in themselves can fail to work for the Jewish cause. I have met such people here as well: always satiated, always arrogantly self-satisfied, people who represent the nadir of demoralization. I do not understand what moral force has prevented the Jewish masses from attacking them. One is compelled to marvel at the great moral force that lives in the hungry Jew. In such conditions others would have turned into beasts long ago![224]

It is not clear what Weizmann meant by the brief reference to "harder times" that may await him. Perhaps he meant to contrast the financial worries that always plagued him—in this case, the impending termination of the contract with Bayer—with the incomparably more cruel fate of those he observed. But the misery he saw only propelled him to work harder for the cause of the movement.

He was raring for action, awaiting only the conclusion of the GAC meetings in Vienna in mid-April. When he heard of the compromise resolutions from newspaper reports, he was disappointed. The expedition to East Africa was to proceed in accordance with the congress resolution, internal personal polemics were to cease, and the Kharkov demands were all but forgotten. Weizmann was convinced that this spelled the final capitulation of the regional leaders. "I think our people were simply outwitted . . . Our people have surrendered . . . The cause is lost. We, who have worked until now, are left without support and will have to wait for better times."[225] These impressions were confirmed once he had gone to Minsk at Simon Rosenbaum's insistence.[226] Under the circumstances, what sense did it make to go through with the Russian tour? He was still willing to undertake it, but there were no funds available. He was disgusted and embarrassed once more at the way he had been treated by the regional leaders. "I held myself *zur Verfuegung* [at the service] of our comrades, but evidently my work will not be needed here now. I am leaving Russia with a broken heart . . ."[227] To Vera he wrote, "I intend to spare my nerves by leaving all this rumpus for a while, until better times, and really get busy with my own affairs. There is nothing for us to do in the present circumstances. One can only smash one's head against the Chinese Wall, which is what Zionism has become."[228]

He left Minsk for Geneva on April 22, reflecting on how useless his one-month sojourn in Russia had been. En route he met Ussishkin in Berlin, who once more cheered him up momentarily, so much so that Weizmann wrote to Ussishkin from Geneva about the possibility of establishing a league of committed anti-Ugandists. He also reported that Chaim Bograchov and Ben-Zion Mossinson were on their way to Palestine on behalf of Ussishkin and Weizmann, where they planned to conduct propaganda against the East Africa project and examine the possibilities of setting up a secondary school and a teachers' training college as first steps toward establishing a university.[229]

But in the meantime Weizmann had almost completed his arrangements to move to England. Ever since his trip there in October, he had been in touch with Gaster and Evans-Gordon about employment opportunities. Gaster had promised to speak to Charles Dreyfus, the managing director of the Clayton Aniline Company in Manchester.[230] Evans-Gordon consulted Sir William Ramsay, professor of chemistry at the University of London, and even looked into the possibility of Weizmann teaching at a high school.[231] Weizmann made quite clear his own preference for a university post at a level comparable to his Geneva position of *Privatdozent*. His health was too delicate, he reminded Gaster, for factory work.[232] Gaster was pessimistic about obtaining an academic post ("Eine Akademische Laufbahn ist somit ausgeschlossen"),[233] but just prior to his departure for Russia on March 22, 1904, Weizmann wrote Gaster that he had received a letter from W. H. Perkin, Jr., professor of chemistry at the University of Manchester, inviting him to work in his laboratory at Owens College. "Since Perkin is one of the foremost chemists in England, and since a great dye industry exists in Manchester, this combination strikes me as very advantageous even though I have to work at first on my own account."[234] Replying on April 15, 1904, Gaster advised Weizmann to gratefully accept the offer as the only way for him to build a future for himself in England.[235] The Russian journey had finally made up Weizmann's mind. As he was about to return to Geneva, he informed Victor Jacobson, "I shall move away from Geneva. My personal affairs have reached a stage that requires me to devote more of myself to chemistry for some time, and more intensively than before. I am going to live in Manchester, as I have been appointed assistant to Perkin . . ."[236]

It would seem that Weizmann's decision was final, and that he had written to Perkin concerning the position in Manchester. Yet suddenly he was presented with an opportunity that might have changed the entire course of his life. The Hilfsverein der deutschen Juden, a German-Jewish organization founded in 1901 to improve the social and political conditions of Jews in Eastern Europe and the Orient, and guided by pro-German political objectives, was just about to inaugurate a teachers' training college in Jerusalem.[237] The Hilfsverein was looking for a science teacher. "I would accept this post," Weizmann wrote to Ussishkin, "with great pleasure and would be ready to move to Palestine at once instead of going to England. Admittedly what they are offering is rather unsatisfactory: 2,400 frs. a year, but this is not important to me . . ." He appealed to Ussishkin to help him attain the post. "I would wish to find myself in such a position. I would feel myself the luckiest of mortals, and it seems to me that this would also be very beneficial for our cause."[238] Weizmann also turned to Otto Warburg, who was on the administrative committee of the Hilfsverein, as well as to Buber for help in pushing through his candidacy. Both the position and the salary were much beneath his stature. He would have had little opportunity for research or for any significant promotion. Yet it is noteworthy that Weizmann was quite willing to compromise stature for a chance to settle in Palestine. In the end, he did not get the job, though rumors had already spread in Palestine that he was coming.[239] Weizmann explained his rejection by the fact that "The 'Hilfsverein' had earlier engaged a young man of 'their own,' and I failed to displace him, despite all Warburg's efforts and mine."[240] That same day he wrote to Gaster, trying to cover the fact that he was rejected and completely distorting the facts. "I considered the plan on the suggestion of Prof. Warburg, but have reached the conclusion that the school is still very much in its initial stages and has no need for me."[241] In his memoirs Ephraim Cohn-Reiss, the principal of the college, wrote that Hirsch Hildesheimer and Willy Bambus, who had made the decision, refused to engage Weizmann because of "the impertinence of this young man, who was among the leaders of the factionists against Herzl."[242] The real reasons for his rejection seem to lie in the fact that he was not sufficiently orthodox; the person appointed was Joseph Karlebach, son of the rabbi of Luebeck. The most important element in his rejection, however, was the fact that Weizmann was well known as a Zionist. Hirsch Hildesheimer and Willy Bambus had early on dissociated themselves from Herzl and the Zionist movement;[243] the engagement of so prominent a Zionist as Weizmann was bound to raise the ire of the anti-Zionist and non-Zionist members of the board of the Hilfsverein.

This incident sheds light on Weizmann's priorities during this period. The fact that he was willing to forego a much better offer in England and had jumped at the opportunity to teach in Jerusalem shows that despite his talk about the "hub of the world," England was only second best, and that Weizmann's pronouncements on work in Palestine were sincere. Yet his commitment to Palestine was not absolute. Unlike those who at that very moment were building the foundations of the Second *Aliyah*, (1904–14), Weizmann's immigration to Palestine was conditional on suitable employment.

In his autobiography Weizmann explained his decision to move to England:

> My flight to England, in 1904, was a deliberate and desperate step. It was not, to be sure, real flight; it was in reality a case of *reculer pour mieux sauter*. I was in danger of being eaten up by Zionism, with no benefit either to my scientific career or to Zionism. We had reached, it seemed to me, a dead point in the movement. My struggles were destroying me; an interval was needed before the possibilities of fruitful work would be restored. Achieving nothing in my public effort, neglecting my laboratory and my books, I was in danger of degenerating into a *Luftmensch* . . . To become effective in any sense, I had to continue my education in chemistry and wait for a more propitious time in the Zionist movement.[244]

The picture that emerges from this account—of a man who firmly and deliberately chose to move to England in order to further his scientific career and work constructively for the Zionist cause—has some support in Weizmann's correspondence during this period.[245] Yet his decision to leave Geneva for England was less resolute than it appears in retrospect, and his motivations were more complicated than his twin concerns for chemistry and Zionism. Indeed, since July 1903 he considered England fertile soil for Zionist work as well as a place for permanent residence. Still, as late as mid-March 1904 he wrote Victor Jacobson, "Do you know that I have decided to leave Geneva? I want to move to a large center—probably London, but I would like to talk this over with our comrades . . ."[246] In fact, it was only after the failure of his campaign in Russia in the spring of 1904, when his Zionist comrades had let him down once more, that Weizmann seems to have made the final decision to move to England.[247] As was mentioned earlier, even at that late date Weizmann would have still preferred a lowly position under the auspices of the Hilfsverein in Palestine to a potentially more promising career in London.[248]

Writing to Caroline Schuster some eight years after his arrival in England, Weizmann explained that he was obliged to leave Geneva because his mentor, Professor Carl Graebe, had announced his retirement and all his assistants were asked to leave. As a Jew he had no chance of finding a position in Germany or France and could find work only in England.[249] In fact, Graebe only retired from the University of Geneva in 1906 at the age of sixty-five.[250] That in 1904 Weizmann had no idea of Graebe's intention to leave Geneva is demonstrated by the fact that when Graebe announced his decision in the spring of 1906, Weizmann was taken by surprise.[251] Presumably Weizmann could have retained his position in Geneva for at least two more years. This would have spared him the painful and prolonged separation from Vera, who still had to complete her medical degree. The evidence seems to suggest that Weizmann was eager to leave the Continent, preferably for Palestine, provided he could find a suitable position. Failing that, he opted for England. Though by April 1904 he had made a final decision, it was virtually forced upon him by his colleagues in both East and West. Why, in fact, was he so eager to leave?

Weizmann believed he had arrived at a "dead end" in his Zionist and professional career. All his projects had failed and he was disgusted with the state of the movement. In Western Europe he was marked as Herzl's opponent, and in the East Ussishkin did not yet admit him into Russian Zionism's inner circle. Moreover, he had been repeatedly snubbed and humiliated by his comrades on the Continent.[252] To some degree his attitude toward the Continental Zionists and the condition of the movement was affected by Ahad Ha'Am, who had retired from public Zionist activities a short while earlier, as had his friend Martin Buber.[253] To some degree he may have been influenced by the general pressures and crisis-laden atmosphere which propelled many European Jews to uproot themselves from the Continent and seek securer havens in Palestine, England, or America. England seemed the most natural option from Weizmann's vantage point, being the last no-man's-land in Europe. Its Zionist organization was ineffective, and at least some of its pillars—for example, Moses Gaster—maintained a respectful and friendly attitude toward him; in fact, Gaster saw it as being in his own best interest to have Weizmann—a strong "Nay-Sayer" like himself—settle in England and provide the *Haham* with a much-needed reinforcement for his cause. With Gaster's help he could become a prominent Zionist in England and move from the periphery to center stage of the World Zionist Organization. Finally, Weizmann made up his mind—with Vera's strong backing and urging[254]—not to depend on the movement for his livelihood;

here, too, his attitude was similar to that of Ahad Ha'Am.[255] His financial resources in Geneva were drying up—the income from the Bayer Works had ceased and his erstwhile backer, Shriro, had withdrawn a promised retainer for research in petroleum chemistry. Almost thirty years old, Weizmann was deeply worried about his ability to support himself, his intended bride, and those of his siblings who still needed his financial backing. His ambition now seems to have been to acquire an important academic position before moving to Palestine.[256] It was, in fact, easier for a Jew to ascend the academic ladder in England than on the Continent. Moreover, Weizmann was fully aware that his all-consuming Zionist activity in Geneva had adversely affected his research in chemistry. What made this awareness more painful was the fact that despite this sacrifice he had little to show for it in terms of Zionist successes. Thus, he was determined to advance his professional career and achieve financial security. In sum, Weizmann's decision to move to England was not as resolute and decisive as he later claimed. It evolved over time, in response to forces over which he had little control. Once taken, though, he recognized the professional and public opportunities that lay ahead and did not fail to exploit them to the fullest. In fact, in England he did not—as he claimed in his autobiography—give up his Zionist activities. On the contrary, the first period in England is marked by very active Zionist work through which he attempted to penetrate the inner circles of the local Zionist leadership.[257] It came to a halt only after he was snubbed and humiliated yet again by the Continental Zionists in mid-August 1904.

A few days before his departure for England Weizmann took note of a debate in the British Parliament on the East Africa question. As he understood it, the debate confirmed what he had known since October 1903, namely, that the government did not consider granting the Jews autonomy in East Africa. Weizmann's information was not fully accurate; he accepted at face value a parliamentary statement by the Under-Secretary of State for Foreign Affairs that it was not England that had made the proposal to the Jews but rather the Jewish Colonial Trust that had applied for land in East Africa.[258] This was, of course, a complete distortion of the facts.

Nevertheless, the debate that occurred in the House of Commons on June 20, 1904, is revealing and of importance to the history of Zionism prior to the Balfour Declaration.[259] The debate took place on a motion to adjourn the House made by J. C. Wason to discuss "the danger to the peace of East Africa arising out of the steps now being taken, with the sanction of His Majesty's Government, for the establishment of an alien settlement in East Africa on lands now in the occupation of native populations."[260]

In the event, the motion was defeated and the House felt an obligation to support the settlement of persecuted Jews. Yet the debate which ensued in the wake of Wason's motion illustrates the negative public sentiment toward Jewish immigration at that time. It also demonstrates the disagreements between policymakers in London and those who were entrusted with carrying out these policies—a conflict that was to haunt the entire period of the mandate. On the one hand, Chamberlain, the politician who was genuinely well disposed toward Zionism, had practically thrust East Africa into Herzl's hands. However, as soon as he was out of office (September 1903), the staff of both the Colonial and Foreign offices did all they could to retreat from these promises. In both the El Arish/Sinai offer and the East Africa offer the local British officials, Cromer and Eliot, strongly resisted the politicians' demands for accommodation to Zionist aims. In both instances they could rely on their colleagues in the Colonial and Foreign offices to come to their aid and help whittle down promises made by a powerful politician.

Chamberlain had made the offer to Herzl in good faith, if hastily and without prior or proper consultation with his own officials.[261] He could not have foreseen the havoc it would create within the Zionist movement. Though in the short term the East Africa project had plunged the Zionist movement into a crisis, it was conceived within the larger framework of long-term British interest in the Jewish people's return to the Holy Land, preferably in a manner and form that would benefit the strategic concerns of the British Empire.[262] Though the Uganda offer severely affected Herzl's stature and health, his political instincts and strategies were, to a large degree, vindicated a decade and a half later. Ironically, it was Weizmann—Herzl's erstwhile opponent—who was instrumental in this turn of events.

On July 3, 1904, Herzl died. Weizmann, like all Zionists and Jews everywhere, was saddened by the news. At a memorial meeting of the Hashahar Circle he and Zvi Aberson delivered eulogies.[263] Herzl's death filled Weizmann with a mingled sense of leadership responsibility and guilt. He spoke of Herzl's death as a personal loss. More than ever before he saw himself as personally responsible for the fate of the movement. "I have had to experience a heavy blow . . . the death of *Herzl* . . . At this moment all the differences between us have disappeared, and I only have the image of a great creative worker in front of my eyes . . . He has left us a frightening legacy . . . I feel that a heavy burden has fallen on my shoulders . . ."[264]

Some thirty to forty of Weizmann's friends saw him off at the train station as he was leaving Geneva for England. Common grief united them; they felt bereaved by the loss of Herzl. "When the train moved, cries of *oid lo awdoh* [our hope is not yet lost] rose and mixed with the weeping, and something snapped inside me. A line was drawn, a period of life came to its end . . ."[265] On his way to England Weizmann stopped off in Paris and immediately went to visit Nordau.[266] The conversation turned to Herzl's successor. Nordau explained why he would not undertake the leadership of the movement; one reason for his refusal was that the movement would not accept his gentile wife. It is more likely that he was unwilling to sacrifice his whole life to Zionism as Herzl had done. Although he gave Weizmann many compliments, he added, "But you are too young!" ("Sie sind aber zu jung!")[267]

Nordau's words cannot be taken too literally. Even had Weizmann been much older, it is unlikely that he would have been among the prime contenders for Herzl's position. Rather, Nordau's statement can be understood simply as paying tribute to Weizmann's achievements within the World Zionist Organization. No one knew better than Weizmann that he had not yet secured a place among the first-rank leaders of the movement; after all, he had been put in his place too often by the regional leaders during the past ten months. At the same time, there is no doubt that his name had become a household word among active Zionists in both East and West. The press he received was not always favorable, but his initiatives, propaganda tours, and minor accomplishments did stir various groups to action, expecially among younger Zionists. During his years in Geneva he had developed as a first-rate propagandist and was a much-sought-after debater and speaker in Zionist gatherings. In the process of debating and lecturing to others, he developed his self-confidence and crystallized his own Zionist weltanschauung, though he still deferred to those in authority—sometimes obsequiously—such as Moses Gaster, Nahum Sokolow, Victor Jacobson, and, of course, Menahem Ussishkin.[268] The possibility of Weizmann leading the movement at this stage of his career was negligible. But his visit to Nordau, Herzl's heir apparent, is significant and provides further testimony to his intense interest in power politics within the World Zionist Organization. At the same time, he was careful when reporting his conversation with Nordau to Aberson and Ussishkin, not to mention Nordau's reference to his own qualifications. He knew full well that the time was not yet ripe.[269]

The East Africa controversy molded Weizmann's Zionist thinking—at the age of thirty—into a form which did not change much later. He was now convinced, more than ever, that practical and cultural efforts were necessary in the Diaspora, but primarily in Palestine, and that diplomatic maneuveurs—which he did not reject on principle—had to be combined with a systematic settlement in Palestine under the auspices, and with the help, of the World Zionist Organization. He was also convinced that the chasm between Eastern and Western Jewry had to be bridged if Zionism was to survive. Here, too, the Uganda controversy was a watershed in his weltanschauung. He had blamed Herzl for the rift between East and West and saw himself as the healer and peacemaker, a notion of his that would finally take shape as "synthetic Zionism." In fact, in his own personality Herzl was able to bridge the differences temporarily, and it was only after his death that the internal pressures within the movement became more extreme. But regardless of the facts, Weizmann's view of the events surrounding East Africa would shape and color his actions in the future. Lastly, taking his cue from Herzl, Weizmann was among the first to recognize that the movement's headquarters had to be moved to the the world's political and financial center of power, namely, London. This would occur at a time when the English Zionist forces were still an insignificant factor in the movement as a whole.

Professionally Weizmann had come a long way. At the age of thirty he was a successful chemist with a growing list of patents and scientific papers to his credit, a man whose career was assured either in industry or at a university. In terms of personality, he did not yet seem to fully possess the self-assuredness of an adult—which explains his constant need to describe himself in terms more laudatory than the facts warranted. He was still given to enormous fluctuations of mood, most often experiencing feelings of inferiority and dejection, especially when slighted by someone whose opinion he valued. He possessed a capacity for great anger, which he sometimes found hard to control. At the same time, he was often submissive and self-effacing to those with whom he wanted to curry favor; with his subordinates he was often impatient and high-strung. Indeed, he had an "unbalanced personality." Often he displayed intellectual arrogance while at the same time showing compassion for the suffering Jews of Eastern Europe. By 1904 he was "a would-be leader very much aware of his spell-binding powers, who had recently been forced to realize that if he could attract a following, he still lacked the authority to retain it."[270]

Weizmann may have lacked authority in 1904, but he possessed other qualities that would propel him to a position of leadership within a decade. He was not a man who formulated theoretical frameworks and hypotheses, who constructed or, indeed, was even capable of constructing philosophical systems or breaking new ground in the world of ideas. Rather, he often took an idea formulated by others and developed it to its fullest potential, as in the case of the university project. Weizmann was primarily a man of action. He possessed unbridled energy and an almost incredible capacity for work on multiple projects simultaneously, supplemented by enormous willpower. Weizmann also possessed an acute ear and keen eye for changes in the movement. He had an open mind and the necessary flexibility—unlike Ussishkin, for example—which allowed him to change tack, make compromises, and, on occasion to do a complete turnabout. On the whole, he had the instincts of a born politician for judicious timing and incisive action. Within a very brief period he could identify a field of activity, map out a strategy for implementing the necessary tasks, and then plunge himself into them, carrying others along in his enthusiasm. His quick intelligence and firm grasp of human nature enabled him to find close collaborators, though more often than not he was disappointed that their zeal and devotion to the cause did not match his. His disillusionment with others was inevitable, since few had his capacity for perseverance and dedication. In addition, it was almost impossible to work with a man who preferred to work alone and do things his own way. Weizmann was simply not a team man; this personality trait often worked to his advantage, but occasionally it also backfired.

Above all, during his Geneva years Weizmann had made a firm commitment to work for the cause of Zionism and the Jewish people, to change their miserable and humiliating condition. He often spoke of this commitment as growing out of a feeling of noblesse oblige. He regarded it as cowardly, for those capable of doing the work, to shirk this responsibility. He had nothing but loathing and contempt for them. "In such moments there arises in me a terrible hatred towards 'Jews' who turn away from Jewry. I perceive them as animals, unworthy of the name *homo sapiens*."[271]

During his Geneva years Weizmann's outward style of living had not altered much, the most perceptible change being that in the last year he had virtually ceased addressing and debating student groups. Otherwise he continued his work in the university, labored to get his various projects off the ground, and spent many hours at the Café Landolt and the Café du Nord. Yet inwardly he felt that he had come to the end of a period, that he was on the threshold of new developments and opportunities. As he made the psychological adjustment to wrench himself from the hub of his dreams and activities at 4, rue Lombard and the Continent, he reviewed his four years in Geneva and could not help but feel nostalgic.[272] Despite all the disappointments and frustrations, these were also productive years in his academic and Zionist development. Among his accomplishments he could count the help he had given in sustaining Swiss Zionist societies in Bern, Lausanne, Geneva, and Zurich;[273] though most of his organizational projects had failed, they had helped raise the Zionist consciousness of dozens of young men and women. The Democratic Faction, for example, left a permanent mark in Zionist life as the first legitimate opposition party in the movement's history. In the process it also propelled a number of young Zionists into positions of prominence. These men and women injected a new vitality and élan during a critical period in the movement's history. They were the first to challenge Herzl's autocratic rule, thus affirming the tradition of democracy to which the World Zionist Organization was committed. Weizmann's propaganda tours probably touched hundreds, if not thousands, of people in both East and West. He had come a long way. Though his estimate of himself may have been a bit less positive, by 1904 he was one of the most successful propagandists in the Zionist movement; a highly controversial figure, to be sure, but a man to be reckoned with. "When he arrived in England Weizmann's character was still rough-hewn, waiting to be shaped by destiny."[274] As he left the Continent, Weizmann must have thought that England would be just another station in his life's journey. He could not have known then that in England he would encounter a culture that would forever stamp his character. For nearly all the remaining years of his life England would be his physical and intellectual anchor.

X

New Beginnings

England in 1904 was hardly the hospitable country in which "a Jew might be allowed to live and work without hindrance, and where he might be judged entirely on his own merits"[1]—especially if that Jew came from Eastern Europe. The period after 1881 witnessed a mass immigration to England from Eastern Europe, which ended with World War I. During this period the size of the community increased from 65,000 to 350,000.[2] Its social composition was completely transformed by the mass of Yiddish-speaking, predominately orthodox immigrants. Whereas the existing Anglo-Jewish population was moving into the suburbs, the new immigrants formed overcrowded ghettos in London's East End,[3] Manchester, Leeds, Liverpool, and Glasgow. While the established community sought an increased diversity in its occupations, the new immigrants tended to concentrate on very few trades, such as tailoring, show business, and cabinetmaking.[4] They also created their own network of Yiddish and Hebrew newspapers and fraternal societies (*hevrot*) as well as many small synagogues (*minyanim*).[5]

The middle-class Anglo-Jewish community sought to discourage the influx of immigrants, who were mostly Jews. This was not surprising, since it was the largest movement of aliens into the country for a century and coincided with periods of high unemployment. The gentile population was outraged.[6] Charges were made that the Jews were working for low wages, doing piecework in filthy workshops, and that they lived in dangerously overcrowded accommodations.[7] The anti-alien movement was largely led by conservative members of Parliament representing East End constituencies, but they were also backed by a number of trade unions.[8]

In 1900 Herzl had already warned that immigration into Britain would constitute a danger to the Jews already there, as well as to those who might follow. For the latter would import "in their pitiful bundles the very thing they were fleeing from, namely, anti-Semitism."[9] This warning was fully justified, in view of the anti-alien agitation which had been growing in strength for more than a decade. As early as 1888 it was strong enough to call for the creation of a Select Committee appointed by the

House, which issued its report in August 1889.[10] The committee had collected a varied group of witnesses, ranging from parsons to trade unionists, from employers to employees in bootmaking and tailoring, from
doctors to sanitary inspectors, and from prominent English Jews to a rather
picturesque group of fifty aliens selected by Arnold White for their peculiarly depraved and destitute appearance; he paid them five shillings
at a time to attend the committee meetings.[11] The committee's main conclusion was that "though the number is not sufficiently large to create
alarm, the proportion of aliens to native population has been for many
years, and is, on the increase . . . the better class of immigrants only
arrive in transit to other countries, but the poorest and worst remain here.
Though the immigrants are independent, industrious and frugal and rarely
come upon the rates, they are very dirty and uncleanly in their habits,
tend to work for long hours at low wages and crowd many Englishmen
into pauperism."[12] The committee, however, did not arrive at a firm
conclusion in favor of legislation. It warned the House that there were
grave difficulties in enforcing laws similar to those of the United States,
and they were not prepared to recommend legislation at present. What
they advised was the collection of better statistics and a careful monitor-
ing of the situation.

The report on the committee was followed in 1890 by the expulsion of
the Jews from such Russian cities as Moscow and Kiev and the ruthless
enforcement of earlier oppressive decrees, which produced a sudden influx of 7,000 immigrants in 1891. But the rate of immigration fell back
during the next decade to about 2,500 to 3,000 a year.[13] Agitation against
aliens, therefore, could not be maintained at a high level. Indeed, Israel
Zangwill's *Children of the Ghetto,* which appeared in 1892 during the last
Gladstone administration, had a positive effect in creating national sympathy for the poor Jewish immigrants. The Liberal government regarded
opposition to alien legislation as part of its free-trade policy and merely
ordered the Board of Trade to provide statistics on immigration. In July
1894, however, the Conservatives, headed by Lord Salisbury, sought to
embarrass the government by introducing a Private Member's Aliens Bill.
This was the product of a parliamentary immigration committee composed of conservative M.P.s and organized by Howard Vincent and James
Lowther. The Private Member's Aliens Bill got a second reading but died
quietly after being blocked by the Liberal whips.[14]

The years 1889–1900 brought pogroms and harsh measures against the
Jews of Rumania, and 1903 witnessed the Kishinev pogrom in Russia, to
be followed by other outrages until 1906. These brutal blows to East European Jewry now brought a heavy stream of unorganized immigration
to the British Isles, which reached its peak in the years 1905–6.[15] At this
point British unemployment figures were once more on the upswing. The
parliamentary anti-aliens now began to renew their efforts. Their numbers had been strengthened since 1900 by Conservative successes in East
London, Tower Hamlets, Mile End, and other constituencies; these were
all now represented by Conservative anti-alien members. Their spokes-

man at the top of the Conservative hierarchy was Howard Vincent, chairman of the National Union of Conservative and Unionist Association from 1895 and vice-chairman of The British Brothers' League, the brainchild of Major William Evans-Gordon, William Stanley Shaw, Murray Guthrie, and Howard Vincent. The major aim of The British Brothers' League, which was established in May 1901, was to prevent any further increase of destitute and undesirable aliens.[16] Howard Vincent, who represented Sheffield Central, was fully backed by Evans-Gordon, who sat for Stepney.[17] Those in Parliament defending immigration were headed by Sir Charles Dilke and C. P. Trevelyan, as well as two spokesmen for the Labour Party, John Burns and Keir Hardie. Winston Churchill, who had then joined the Liberal Party and had chosen northwest Manchester, also supported free immigration. In Parliament the Parliamentary Pauper Immigration Committee sent a letter signed by fifty-two M.P.s to the Prime Minister, Lord Salisbury, demanding legislation, while Evans-Gordon moved an amendment to the address in 1902 recommending the establishment of a royal commission. The government finally gave way and set up a seven-man Royal Commission on Alien Immigration in 1902 under Lord James, which sat for fourteen months and covered much the same ground as the Select Committee.[18] One of the typical arguments concerning the aliens/Jews was presented before the hard-working commission.

> The Aliens will not conform to our ideas, and, above all, they have no sort of neighborly feeling . . . A foreign Jew will take a house, and he moves in on a Sunday morning, which rather, of course, upsets all the British people there. Then his habits are different . . . He will use his yard for something. He will store rags there, perhaps—mountains of smelling rags, until the neighbors all round get into a most terrible state over it, or perhaps he will start a little factory in the yard, and carry on a hammering noise all night, and then he will throw out a lot of waste stuff . . . —it is all pitched out, and in the evening the women and girls sit out on the pavement and make a joyful noise, I have no doubt, and on the Sunday the place is very different to what the English are accustomed to. Most extraordinary sights are seen . . .[19]

The Royal Commission duly reported in August 1903 in favor of limited restriction on immigration and the establishment of prohibited areas. One of its main arguments in favor of restriction was the deterrent effect of any legislation on potential immigrants. The government was quick to act.[20] On February 2, 1904, the King's speech included a reference to a Government Aliens Bill, which, following the recommendations of the Royal Commission, provided a skeletal basis for Home Office regulation. It gave the Home Secretary power, through immigration officers, to prohibit without appeal the landing of any alien either convicted of an extraditable crime or associated with prostitution, or of bad character. He also had power to order the expulsion of any alien of a similar type. The Local Government Board was given the power to designate prohibited areas for aliens where overcrowding was proven to exist. Since it was introduced under the Ten-Minute Bill and opposed in the correspondence columns of the *Times* by the Permanent Secretary to the Home Office, the government was obviously not fully committed to this policy. This is strongly supported by the fact that two months later it proposed that the bill should be sent to a grand committee, the one place where closure could not be applied. As a result, the bill could easily be choked or abandoned.[21]

Finally the bill was referred to a Committee of the whole House, and during this stage a very large number of amendments were accepted and a considerable number of concessions were made by the government. In particular, safeguards for religious refugees were built into the bill. These concessions were the result of pressure on Conservative M.P.s by the Jewish community. Another group of concessions, dealing with transmigrants, came as a result of pressure from the big shipping lines. The committee stage was completed by July 10 and the bill was given its third reading by 193 to 103 on July 19, 1905.[22] The royal assent was obtained after an uneventful passage through the House of Lords on August 10, in time to present the bill to the public as part of the Conservatives' election manifesto in the Christmas election. On January 1, 1906, the Aliens Act went into force.

When Weizmann arrived in London in July 1904, the campaign against the immigration of aliens/Jews was at its height. He could not but be impressed by the multitude of economic, social, and political arguments against the immigrants, which were sustained by stereotypes permeating all levels of British society.[23] It may have occurred to him that the Swiss treatment of aliens was much more humanitarian than that which he encountered in Britain. Yet he was personally not touched by, nor did he comment on, this hostility toward the same group with which he was intimately linked through common geographic origin, family ties, religion, and language. He had in the meantime transcended its cultural, social, and educational barriers. Moreover, he had highly marketable skills in a field in which he had already begun to make his mark and arrived in England with excellent references. He had powerful and influential connections in England, including, ironically, Evans-Gordon, who was doing his best to bar Weizmann's brethren from entering England. He even had some money to tide him over the first difficult period of adjustment. In short, his move to England was not as risky for his career as it may have seemed at first glance. With hard work and a reasonable amount of goodwill on the part of his friends, he possessed at least the basic ingredients for success. Neither in 1904 nor later is there any evidence to suggest that Weizmann suffered from anti-Semitism, either personally or in his professional life.[24]

Weizmann arrived in London on Sunday, July 10, 1904, and boarded with the Van Gelder family at 22 Grosvenor Road.[25] He immediately attempted to make contact with some of his more important acquaintances. First among them was Moses Gaster, the *Haham*, who was to return the following day from Vienna, where he attended Herzl's funeral.[26]

For some time to come the rabbi would act as Weizmann's patron, adviser, and financial backer.[27] The clash of personalities between them would come to the fore only after Weizmann was no longer fully dependent on the rabbi's goodwill. For now he was eagerly awaiting Gaster's return. London, in Weizmann's opinion, was bound to be a major Zionist center. If he played his cards right, he could assume an important role with Gaster's aid.[28]

Gaster was highly cultured and intellectually superior to many of those contending for Zionist leadership in England. But he was also pugnacious and willful, arrogant and easily offended.[29] In some ways he was similar to Ussishkin without the latter's personal authority and institutional backing. As the leading practical and cultural Zionist in England, he was engaged in a pitched battle with Herzl's local supporters, who included Leopold Greenberg, Israel Zangwill, and Joseph Cowen.[30] In truth, it was a tempest in a teacup, since the English Zionist Federation in 1904 was a rather sorry affair, with very little popular backing even from the East European immigrants and a splintered leadership at the top.[31] It was into this organization that Weizmann would pour much of his energies over the next ten years.

The origins of the English Zionist Federation can be traced back to the Hovevei Zion societies founded in the wake of the pogroms in Russia in 1881–82. The first such groups were founded in Leeds and Manchester in 1883.[32] Two years later the short-lived Palestine Colonisation Association was founded;[33] in 1887 some younger elements founded the Kadimah Society, which boasted 150 members at the height of its activities, only to be weakened by a split in its ranks in 1888.[34] Finally, the Hovevei Zion Association of Great Britain held its first public meeting at the Jewish Working Men's Club in East London on May 31, 1890. This association had the support not only of the East European masses of the East End but also of Samuel Montagu, who was then M.P. for Whitechapel, Lord (Nathan) Rothschild, Sir Benjamin Cohen, and Sir Joseph Sebag-Montefiore, as well as Rabbis Hermann Adler and Moses Gaster and the Reverend Simeon Singer.[35] The driving force in the association was another solid West Ender, Colonel Albert Edward Goldsmid, whose administrative skills and innovations did much to win the organization attention and new members.

These seemed to be auspicious beginnings. In fact, the activities of the Hovevei Zion Association moved at a crawling pace and were confined to intermittent support of Palestinian settlements or speech making on festive occasions. Its most important practical achievements included the publication, in 1894, of a quarterly journal called *Palestina* and the purchase of twenty-four thousand acres of land in the Golan, but the aims of the association were philanthropic in nature and its membership never amounted to more than two thousand.

Another achievement was the fact that the British Hovevei Zion had established early on a tradition of contacts with their government—a departure from most other Hovevei Zion societies on the Continent. Initially Theodor Herzl received a cordial response to his ideas among the Anglo-Jewish establishment—primarily due to the efforts of Israel Zangwill—and he first outlined his ideas before the prestigious and elitist Maccabean Club on November 24, 1895.[36] Three months later, at the invitation of Asher Myers, the editor of *The Jewish Chronicle*, Herzl described his program publicly, even before the publication of *Der Judenstaat*.[37] Disappointed by the lukewarm response he received from the Anglicized Jews as well as from some of the Hovevei Zion, Herzl turned to the masses on his next visit to England, in July 1896, where he was received enthusiastically in the East End.[38] His earliest supporters included the *Haham* Moses Gaster, Israel Zangwill, Jacob De Haas, Leopold Kessler, Joseph Cowen, and Leopold Greenberg. The London Hovevei Zion, on the other hand, were much cooler to Herzl's plans.[39] There were no official delegates from England at the First Zionist Congress.

A few months after the first congress, the British Hovevei Zion decided to join forces with the World Zionist Organization. At a conference held at Clerkenwell Town Hall, in north London, delegates from twenty-seven Hovevei Zion "tents" and an assortment of close to twenty Zionist societies met on March 6, 1898, and adopted the Zionist program.[40] Failing to reach an agreement on their relationship to the World Zionist Organization, the delegates created a subcommittee. After months of controversy, the subcommittee dissolved itself, having failed to unite all Hovevei Zion groups in Great Britain. Herzl's supporters therefore established their own English Zionist Federation (EZF) on January 22, 1899,[41] with Sir Francis Abraham Montefiore as its first president. Other officers of the English Zionist Federation included Moses Gaster, Leopold Greenberg, Herbert Bentwich, Joseph Cowen, and Jacob De Haas.[42] By 1902 the Hovevei Zion Association had lost its raison d'être and gone out of existence. On the whole, the English Zionist Federation remained an ineffective body during the first years of its existence. Its West End leaders shied away from the inflammatory politics and noise of the East End masses, and it felt itself too weak to challenge the established Anglo-Jewish community for control of communal resources and institutions. It became a more effective force only after the Kishinev pogrom and the communal debate it engendered, but it never did gain much ground in its attempt to conquer the community. As late as 1902 the Zionists could claim the active support of no more than 4.5 percent of the entire Anglo-Jewish population.[43]

The English Zionist Federation, which was born out of internal strife, continued to be plagued by internecine rivalry. When Weizmann arrived in England in the summer of 1904, the English Zionist Federation was experiencing a severe crisis. The dual impact of the East Africa trauma, which divided Zionists everywhere, and the very strong clash of personalities in England, left the federation divided, listless, and ineffective.[44] The most harmful personal clash took place between Leopold Greenberg and Moses Gaster as early as 1902, when they debated the usefulness of Herzl's appearance before the Royal Commission on Alien Immigration, but it was the East Africa question which exacerbated their relationship, since Gaster was the most prominent opponent of the scheme in England. Henceforth the two continued to quarrel over personal as well as substantive Zionist issues and organized coteries of supporters around them.[45] The internal rivalry within the English Zionist Federation mirrored the conflicts within the movement in general, with Greenberg representing the "political" Zionists and Gaster the "practicals." It was in this atmosphere of conflict that Weizmann had to carve out a role for himself, with one eye on broader events within the World Zionist Organization and the other on affairs within the English Zionist Federation.

Within a fortnight after his arrival in England, Weizmann was warmly received and was even courted by all the leading Zionists of London, a fact which clearly flattered his self-esteem. Indeed, given the state of the movement in England, he would have been an important asset to either of the warring camps. Leopold Greenberg, Israel Zangwill, and Joseph Cowen, who made the overtures, surely knew that on substantive Zionist issues Weizmann did not belong in their "political" camp, but they could attempt to keep him from actively joining Moses Gaster's efforts and thus neutralize the *Haham*. This tactic had little chance of success. Both Weizmann and Gaster were allied in their opposition to the East Africa project. Thus, they had slowly built up an affinity for one another, and it was natural for Weizmann to first turn to Gaster upon arrival in England. During his first years in England Weizmann treated the *Haham* as he had previously treated Motzkin and Ussishkin, namely, with deference often bordering on self-effacement. Gaster, who was not very popular in Zionist circles, could, for his part, use Weizmann's friendship and support as well as the latter's wide contacts in Western and Eastern Europe.

On the day Gaster returned from Herzl's funeral, Weizmann went to see him at his home in the well-to-do suburb of Maida Vale.[46] Their conversation, which lasted four hours, covered the entire political constellation within the Zionist movement. More than ever, Weizmann was convinced that Gaster's primary aim was to get elected to the Grosses Aktions-Comité and then to take over the leadership of the World Zionist movement.[47] The following day, July 13, Weizmann attended the memorial service for Herzl which took place in the Great Synagogue under the aegis of the English Zionist Federation.[48] Later that day he went to see Evans-Gordon, who must have viewed Weizmann as an ally in his own campaign to keep immigrants from British shores and was thus eager to help. He promised to secure Weizmann an appointment with Earl Percy, the Parliamentary Under-Secretary of State for Foreign Affairs, and Sir Clement Hill, the Superintendent of the African Protectorates. On July 14 Weizmann summed up his first impressions of London's Zionists in a long report to Ussishkin. The West End Zionists—Cowen, Greenberg and Bentwich—were dismissed in a sentence or two. But he did not spare those resident in Whitechapel either, displaying once more his distaste for the hapless masses. "Except for a small group of clean, honest and educated leaders, there are only the *plebs,* in the worst meaning of the word . . . "[49] Among the "honest and educated leaders" he counted Dov Aberson (the brother of his Geneva friend Zvi Aberson), Kalman Marmor, and Uriah Moonitz; all three were associated with left-wing Zionist causes and had been close to the affairs of the Democratic Faction. Turning to an elitist solution for the woes of the English Zionist Federation, he now urged Ussishkin to allocate five hundred rubles for the purpose of publishing a paper, presumably to promote the cause of the *Nein-Sager* within the English movement.[50]

His keen political sense, however, cautioned him to at least keep in touch with the ideological opposition. Though he belonged to the camp of the unyielding Ussishkin, Weizmann adopted a carefully controlled political stance which afforded him maximum leverage in the warring Zionist camps. As a stranger working in the English environment, this was a prudent course which served Weizmann well. In a second letter to Ussishkin, written three days after the first, he reported on a meeting with Cowen, Greenberg, and Sir Francis Montefiore. He described Montefiore as "a puppet who can be maneuvered at will." Behind him were the real actors:

> Cowen is an honest man but very weak and, I think, completely under the influence of Greenberg, who conceals his cards and is as sly as the devil . . .
>
> *Personal tactics* . . . I have decided for the time being to hold myself in reserve. Each side is trying to drag me in, but with such a constellation one can easily commit political suicide. Moreover I am disgusted with these gentlemen, for they are not thinking of the cause, merely of power . . . I have no wish to become a member of this pack. The centre of gravity is where you are. You ought to know this. You should also be aware that I shall have great influence out here so long as you support me. All these gentlemen are conscious of this . . .[51]

Weizmann obviously enjoyed being courted by the various factions of the English Zionist Federation; he was not used to this kind of treatment on the Continent. He delighted just as much in being able to reject the various overtures with an air of superiority. Ussishkin probably chuckled while reading the reports of his junior colleague and following his tactical moves. Weizmann must have seemed less than genuine, protesting, on the one hand, that he wanted to keep out of intrigues and pretending to be neutral, while on the other, making the rounds among the factions and at heart already an enemy of Greenberg, "the Jewish Chamberlain," as he nicknamed him,[52] and waiting for the right political opportunities. For a man who wanted to serve as a "bridge" and a peacemaker, he behaved most peculiarly. His claim, later in life, that during this period he had decided to curtail his Zionist activities[53] is hardly borne out by the almost feverish Zionist activity that characterized his first fortnight in London. On the contrary, the whole tone of his first report to Ussishkin bespeaks a man who is more than ready to plunge into Zionist affairs at a moment's notice; characteristic of the report is one of its concluding paragraphs: "One feels that a terrible burden has fallen on our shoulders. Herzl left a terrible legacy, but now less than ever is there time for tears. *Einigkeit macht stark.* I repeat once again: I am entirely at your disposal."[54]

Weizmann's great opportunity seemed to materialize on July 25, when he met Earl Percy in the House of Commons and Sir Clement Hill at the Foreign Office. Then, and in later years, Weizmann made much of these meetings, claiming that they had contributed to a defeat of the Uganda proposal.[55] In his memoirs Weizmann described his meetings with Lord Percy: "He . . . expressed boundless astonishment that the Jews should even so much as have considered the Uganda proposal, which he regarded as impractical, on the one hand, and, on the other, a denial of the Jewish religion. Himself deeply religious, he was bewildered by the thought that Jews could even entertain the idea of any other country than Palestine as the center of their revival; and he was delighted to hear from me that there were so many Jews who had categorically refused . . . ."[56] It comes as no surprise that in hindsight Weizmann probably exaggerated Percy's negative views on East Africa, but it was quite true that the latter was opposed to the East Africa project.

The interviews with Lord Percy and Sir Clement Hill were most probably conducted in French. Immediately after they took place Weizmann summarized both interviews and sent them to Percy and Hill on July 26, asking that they change and amend those passages they deemed inaccurate.[57] Weizmann's memorandum (also written in French) to Percy recorded the following:

> . . . I asked His Excellency to be good enough to tell me, if possible, the limits of the territory [in East Africa], and particularly to inform me of the political conditions under which colonization could be effected . . .
>
> His Excellency replied that the principal conditions were already set out in the letter addressed by Lord Lansdowne to the congress and signed by Sir Clement Hill.
>
> I objected that since the details are not precise, people had interpreted Lord Lansdowne's letter in several different ways, and that it was only after the reply given by His Excellency in the course of recent debates in Parliament that many of the details were clarified.[58] For example, the question of autonomy is still unsettled.
>
> His Excellency then replied that there could certainly be no question of Jewish autonomy, but one of "local government" at the most. As to details and the publication of documents, it is necessary to wait for the report of the expedition [to East Africa] . . .
>
> I had the honor of declaring that all Zionists (despite differences of opinion) are profoundly grateful to the government for having supported the idea of Jewish colonization under English protection, but that in this case the majority of Zionists consider the movement as a national rebirth of the people of Israel, and one which consequently could not take place elsewhere than in the Holy Land. The rebirth will either take place in Palestine or not at all.

His Excellency wished to explain to me that the English government certainly had the best of intentions of doing something for the persecuted Jews, but considered the colonization of Africa as something incompatible with the Zionist idea and Israel's aspirations to nationhood. Taking into account also the objections of the indigenous population, as well as the energetic protests raised in England against the establishment of a Jewish colony in Africa, the government felt that the African project would only give rise to an anti-Jewish movement, which would be very regrettable.[59]

Percy recommended Weizmann to Sir Clement Hill, who explained to Weizmann the exact location of the territory in question:

. . . The territory in question . . . is entirely on the far side of the railway by which all the necessary transportation for colonization would be made at very high rates. Colonization will be extremely costly and final success is very doubtful. One must add here that the English government takes no responsibility for the protection of the colonists against the natives, who, said Sir Clement, are all against you. All these points being agreed upon by the English government and the Zionist agent [Greenberg].

In my opinion, said Sir Clement, the only result would be a Jewish colonization similar to that of Argentina. There the actual condition of the project differed profoundly from its interpretation among Zionists.

If I were a Jew, added Sir Clement, I should absolutely oppose such a project. As a Zionist one has nothing to look for in Africa.[60]

The summaries suggest that Weizmann steered the conversation in a direction that led both statesmen to express themselves negatively on East Africa. They also show that both did not need too much prodding.

It is clear, though, that Clement Hill and Earl Percy were taken aback by Weizmann's memoranda to them. Hill wrote the following in minutes that were attached to Weizmann's memorandum: "Lord Percy, I did not know I was being 'interviewed' and propose to ask Dr. W. to omit the passages I have put in brackets. Hill." Lord Percy replied, "Yes, I did not understand I was being 'interviewed' either . . ."[61] Yet it is clear that both took Weizmann seriously, and that he had made an impression on them. Moreover, both took the trouble to reply to him on August 4, 1904, suggesting some deletions in his memoranda.[62] Their amendments were, on the whole, minor and simply toned down the negative attitude of the two British officials to the East Africa scheme. Hill, for instance, requested that Weizmann delete a passage which contained the following two sentences: "If I were Jewish, added Sir Clement, I would oppose such a project absolutely. For a Zionist there is nothing to look for in Africa."[63]

It is understandable that Hill and Percy wanted on record a more moderate official version of their conversations with Weizmann, but it is just as significant that in their replies they did not actually challenge the basic content and spirit of his memoranda.[64] Both were hostile to Zionist settlement in East Africa. Their own official minutes—especially those of Lord Percy—compiled the day after their interview with Weizmann, amply confirm this fact. Lord Percy recorded:

The section of the Zionists whom Weizmann represents are opposed to the scheme, though grateful to the British government, because they think the African colony will be a fixture and not a "halfway house" to Palestine, and that money spent on it will therefore be devoted to frustrate the return movement . . .

I thought it well to point out to him that we should probably expect any colonists in Africa to be men with some capital behind them and not merely destitute aliens . . . from the point of view of British interests I did not suppose we should care to go on with the scheme if the Jews themselves were lukewarm about it, as the desire to meet their views had been one of our principal motives. He is impressed with the impolicy of risking anti-Semitic feeling in a British colony and is obviously hostile to the whole project.[65]

Lord Lansdowne, Secretary of State for Foreign Affairs, added the following sentence to Lord Percy's minutes: "We shall be fortunate if the project falls through."[66] This sentiment no doubt reflected the general feeling of the government. A few days later Lord Percy supplemented his minutes with his letter to Weizmann and reiterated his view that the British government "had no particular reason to desire the establishment of a Jewish colony if the Jews themselves no longer wished for it. It was obviously not popular with the British residents out there and we should have no difficulty in disposing of the land to other settlers if the present scheme was abandoned . . ."[67]

Though he may have projected his own negative feelings toward East Africa onto Percy and Hill, there is little doubt that Weizmann must have sensed their own desire to retreat from the scheme. Possibly nonverbal communication which he picked up at the interviews strengthened his impressions. In any case, he had some reason to be proud when remarking, in a letter to Ussishkin alluding to Herzl's style of diplomacy, "As you see, we can have our own diplomacy, without spectacular effect, but more solid . . . if only it were possible to strike roots here . . . then there is no doubt about the possibility of influencing English public opinion in our favor."[68] After all, Weizmann represented no official body in the Zionist movement. He himself admitted that he had "assumed the role of some kind of self-styled diplomat of the Russian Zionists to the British Government."[69] The interviews with Percy and Hill were, in the last analysis, of no great consequence. They may have only confirmed Percy and Hill's resolve to oppose the idea of Jewish autonomy in East Africa; they did not provide Weizmann with significant new information, though he himself evaluated them differently.[70] If he had planned to show that Greenberg had overstepped his authority in dealing with the British, this too proved to be an incorrect assumption; Greenberg had merely been Herzl's faithful messenger. Yet the interviews provide a clue to Weizmann's style and personality: They disclose his penchant for acting on his own without proper authority, while giving the impression that he is speaking in the name of a larger body,[71] as well as his desire to deal with the most authoritative figures he could reach. Like Herzl, he approached gentiles in a self-assured and unapologetic manner.[72] These were traits he would subsequently develop more fully to great advantage, when he was already a man of great scientific achievements and some standing within the Zionist movement. Indeed, it was no minor accomplishment that Weizmann, a foreigner who, in July 1904, had just stepped off the boat and hardly spoke the English language,[73] could obtain and follow through on interviews with two important members of the British government. Possibly the long-range implication of the interviews was that already during his first meetings with British politicians Weizmann sensed "that we are in a position to obtain help from the British Goverment (in a most positive way) for our Palestine aims, and I can show how."[74] Perhaps they provided him with the feeling that, given the right opportunities, he could successfully negotiate with politicians.

Three days after his first venture in "high diplomacy,"[75] Weizmann arrived in Manchester. His decision to move there had not been an easy one.[76] He was determined to make the choice on the basis of the best career opportunities available to him. Possessed of a keen eye, three days after arriving in England he remarked, ". . . first of all I have to put some order into my own affairs. Until then I will be unable to do anything. One has to have standing here."[77] Professor William Perkin had already suggested in the spring that Weizmann come to Manchester, but Weizmann also had a letter of introduction from Graebe to Sir William Ramsay, professor of chemistry at the University of London, a renowned chemist who received the Nobel Prize in 1904.[78] Weizmann was not about to let this opportunity go unexplored. The problem was that London was not as informal as Geneva; he had written to Ramsay soon after his arrival in London, formally requesting an interview. He had also written to Perkin in Manchester. Until they both responded, he was on pins and needles. Meanwhile, he reasoned that, all things being equal, he would prefer staying in London.[79]

On July 18 he finally met Ramsay, who promised to do everything possible to secure Weizmann a paying job at the University of London. Considering the fact that this was already the middle of the summer, Ramsay's interest in Weizmann is ample indication that he was impressed by the young man's credentials and Graebe's letter of recommendation. However, upon returning to his lodgings Weizmann found a letter from Perkin, who had just arrived in London.[80] After meeting Perkin the following day Weizmann was in a position to coolly weigh both offers. Possibly he informed both professors of the competing invitations he had and of the fact that they were both bidding for him. In any case, Perkin couched his offer in a much less tentative form. As Weizmann related, "Perkin . . . said that if I did some good work by Christmas I would be able to secure a *Fellowship* . . . and for a capable man there is *definitely* a future. He gave an understanding that I would have students . . . He offered me a laboratory for the vacation, a room of my own and on Thursday week I can start work . . . The laboratory in Manchester is brand new and, Perkin says, better than in London. I haven't made up my mind yet. I shall talk it over with Gaster tomorrow and then decide . . ."[81] A day later he was already leaning toward Manchester, explaining, "Ramsay promised me almost the same thing, but in a somewhat less positive way, and I prefer Manchester, the more so as the University is brand new there and very well appointed. It has an excellent laboratory and library, the climate is better [sic!], the town cheaper and one can always move to London if the opportunity arises . . ."[82] The opportunity to start work at once clearly made Manchester more attractive. The day after he met with Perkin he consulted Gaster, who concurred that Manchester was more promising;[83] moreover, the *Haham* had many contacts in the city through his involvement as honorary vice-president of the newly built Victoria Memorial Jewish Hospital. He would be only too pleased to use his contacts there to Weizmann's advantage. Until Christmas Weizmann was to work in Perkin's laboratory without pay,[84] so the problem was only how to make ends meet until then. Once again his luck held out. His brother-in-law, Chaim Lubzhinsky, promised to support him until he could draw a regular salary.[85] All in all, it was not a bad arrangement; it would give him time to settle in properly in the laboratory and improve his English before he met his first class. Almost in passing Weizmann noted, "I bought myself some English books to read, including the Bible, Macaulay and Gladstone's speeches."[86]

In 1904 it seemed to Weizmann that from a Zionist point of view Manchester had little to offer in comparison with London; his decision to move to Manchester was based on his firm resolve to improve his standing as a chemist. Weizmann's belief that "standing" was a prerequisite for useful public activity tipped the scales in favor of Manchester. Less than a week earlier he had declared, in a letter to Ussishkin, his strong desire to live in London at all costs so that he could better serve the Zionist cause.[87] He knew well that this is what Ussishkin wanted to hear, but no sooner did the offer from Perkin materialize than he began to rationalize the move to Manchester from a Zionist point of view as well: "The local [London] Zionists, with very few exceptions, are idiots. The intellectual element is entirely non-existent. In general, this is characteristic of England as a whole. In Manchester I shall probably live in a 'chemical' circle; that doesn't worry me, though of course it is a deprivation . . ."[88]

Manchester was obviously not Weizmann's first choice, but from a professional point of view Owens College and the city's other industrial and chemical resources were as good a place as he could pick.[89] The University of Manchester was the first of a group of English universities which were founded in the latter part of the nineteenth and early twentieth centuries. For six centuries Oxford and Cambridge held a monopoly on university education, but by the middle of the nineteenth century this situation began to change. The two ancient universities had catered to a certain well-defined class, but now the demand for education was more widespread. Oxford and Cambridge were universities of the Anglican church, fenced in by strict tests, but Nonconformity had greatly increased and Nonconformists wanted proper education for their sons and daughters. Also, due to the industrial revolution there had been a great population shift to the north, making Oxford and Cambridge difficult to reach and expensive to live in.

Plans for a university in Manchester were in the air as early as the 1820s and 1830s, but the first effective step was taken by a private citizen, John Owens, a Manchester merchant. Upon his death in 1846 he bequeathed a large sum of money toward the foundation of a college. It was stipulated as a fundamental principle that there were to be no religious tests in the admission of students. Owens College was opened in 1851 but did not flourish until the 1870s. The college could not confer degrees and students had to sit for examinations at the University of London. In 1875 a pamphlet was issued advocating the institution of a University of Manchester. Initially, however, there was the institution of a federal university with constituent colleges, of which Manchester was the first. It was established as Victoria University in 1880.[90] The university existed side by side with Owens College until Owens College was incorporated with the university on June 24, 1904, to form the University of Manchester.[91]

When Weizmann arrived in Manchester in 1904, the university boasted a student body of some twelve hundred[92] and an excellent faculty, especially in the sciences. Chemistry had been one of the first subjects to be taught at Owens College by Professor Edward Frankland, who established his reputation through his work on the structure of carboxylic acids, on the attempted isolation of alkyl radicals, and on the general conception of molecular structure. His successor was Henry Roscoe, who was best known for his isolation of the metal vanadium and the disentangling of its chemistry. Although Roscoe's field lay in inorganic chemistry, in 1874 he helped create England's first chair in organic chemistry, which was occupied by Carl Schorlemmer until his death in 1892.[93] Roscoe, who resigned his own chair in 1886, was succeeded by Harold Baily Dixon, a pioneer in combustion chemistry and safety in mines. Schorlemmer was succeeded by William Henry Perkin, who had made the offer to Weizmann.

Perkin was the eldest son of William Henry Perkin, whose major discovery was mauve (known also as Tyrian purple, or aniline purple), the first synthetic dyestuff; the event occurred when he was a mere eighteen (1856). This discovery gave impetus to a new coaltar dyestuffs industry.[94] It so happened that in 1868 the German chemists Graebe and Liebermann announced that they had synthesized alizarin, the natural coloring matter of madder; their process, however, was too expensive to be of more than scientific interest, and again it was Perkin who worked out new methods to manufacture alizarin with the aid of coal tar products. His son, William Henry Perkin, had studied in London, at the University of Wuerzburg, and at the University of Munich under Adolf von Bayer. He was very much influenced by von Bayer and himself became almost the archetypal German professor: cultured, fond of walking holidays in the Alps, and devoted to a rather narrow field of research. His work was concerned almost exclusively with the elucidation of the structures of natural products by degradation and synthesis.[95]

Perkin, Weizmann's new mentor at the University of Manchester, was no doubt intrigued by the fact that Weizmann, who had studied under Liebermann and Graebe, was concerned with the same field of research as his father, Sir William Henry Perkin.[96] In addition, both Perkin and Weizmann had studied in Germany, and though Weizmann had no direct contact with Adolf von Bayer, he did sell his first patent to the Bayer Works. Such biographical coincidence may have played a role in Perkin's offer to Weizmann;[97] the fact is that he received Weizmann with open arms and expressed confidence in the young man's abilities.[98] However, it was not blind faith alone that motivated him. When he arrived in Manchester Weizmann had to his credit, in addition to his excellent dissertation, three papers and five patents.[99] Perkin clearly viewed Weizmann as someone who could strengthen the rather neglected subject of organic chemistry at the University of Manchester as well as someone with whom he could collaborate on occasion.

The first sight of Manchester itself must have been quite a shock to Weizmann as he came off the train on the morning of July 28. The drabness and griminess of this northern city, with a population of close to three quarters of a million people,[100] stood in sharp contrast to the serene beauty and clean air of Geneva and the majestic and cosmopolitan nature of London. Yet Manchester—often referred to as "Cottonopolis"—was a rich industrial city which offered many opportunities for those with energy and enterprise. At the turn of the century Manchester was an urban prototype; in many respects it was the first of the new generation of huge industrial cities created in the Western world in the last two hundred years. It was also a city of great vitality, not only in its economic growth but also in its political, cultural, and intellectual life, priding itself on, among other achievements, *The Manchester Guardian*, Britain's leading provincial newspaper, the Horniman Repertory Theatre, and the excellent Hallé Orchestra. The city also paid a price for its rapid growth and was plagued by high-density population, pollution of the air and water, and inadequate and poorly built houses. Its Jewish population of some twenty-five thousand was the second largest in England.[101] Approximately two thirds of the Jews in Manchester were of East European origin,[102] mostly first-generation immigrants.[103] In 1906 only one minister of a synagogue in Manchester was English-born and only four rabbis could preach in English from the pulpit. Yiddish was the lingua franca of the community.[104]

The Jewish community of Manchester was established in the late 1780s or early 1790s, acquiring a cemetery and opening a synagogue.[105] The most distinguished early resident in the city was Nathan Meyer Rothschild, who exported cotton goods to Germany.[106] After 1815 the Jewish community slowly grew into a respected and well-to-do body of merchants, professionals, and shopkeepers. Already in the 1860s East European Jewish immigrants brought to the assimilating community a more orthodox point of view. They also moved in large numbers into tailoring, cap making, slipper making, and waterproofing.[107] The 1880s brought an increase in the rate of immigration, coupled with poverty for those forced to work in the small "sweating dens," and helped spread new ideologies, particularly Zionism and socialism. The Jewish population in Manchester at the turn of the century reflected the spectrum of class structure of British Jews, with the exception of the down-and-outs. There was virtually no unemployment among Jews. The Jewish community included a substantial industrial working class, mostly engaged in small workshop trades. On the whole, the Jewish population in Manchester can be said to have been housed and employed despite some pockets of poverty. At the other end of the class structure were the very rich Jews, such as the Behrens family, one of whose members, Charles Behrens, became Lord Mayor of Manchester shortly before World War I.[108]

Given the diversity of the Jewish population, it is not surprising that it had been divided institutionally along religious and social lines since the early nineteenth century, with occasional major controversies surrounding such issues as ritual slaughter *(shehita)*.[109] The divisions and diversity of the Jewish community were also reflected in the plethora of synagogues,[110] philanthropic organizations,[111] and educational institutions.[112] The most powerful institutions in the city were the Shehita Board, which represented fifteen congregations (except the reform synagogue), and the Visiting Committee, which looked after Jewish boys in industrial schools.[113]

The Jewish quarter in Manchester comprised the whole of Cheetham Hill Road, Elizabeth Street, Hightown, and parts of Lower Broughton, Strangeways, and Salford. It was, in certain respects, unlike the Jewish quarter in London.[114] Cheetham Hill Road was a broad, spacious thoroughfare—quite a respectable residential street, with many people owning attractive small homes. Most of the larger synagogues and other Jewish institutions were located on Cheetham Hill Road. Of course, this prosperity was deceptive since in the outlying areas of this Jewish residential quarter were some very poor neighborhoods; for example, there was the area known as Red Bank, right off Cheetham Hill Road. Red Bank was a high sandstone ridge which fell away from the area of middle-class settlement on Cheetham Hill down to the railway in the valley. The houses in Red Bank were arranged in cramped rows, along excavated shelves separated by flimsy retaining walls. Thousands of Jewish immigrants lived there in overcrowded and unsanitary conditions. This was the most decrepit area of Jewish residence in Manchester.[115] The areas around Berkeley Street or Carter Street in the Strangeways district were also crowded with poor immigrants.[116]

Weizmann had only a brief initial acquaintance with the area around lower Cheetham Hill Road and Red Bank. Upon his arrival in Manchester he was met at the train by Joseph Massel,[117] a printer by profession and a Hebrew poet, who had come to Manchester from Russia in the 1890s. Massel lived at 2 Park Place, a small street that ran off the lower end of Cheetham Hill Road, and across the street from Red Bank. Massel's home faced the old Congregation of British Jews and was a little up the block from The Central Synagogue which served the East European immigrants. This was the center of Manchester's orthodox Jewish population.[118] Massel was one of Manchester's most active and early Zionists. He had attended the First Zionist Congress[119] and had probably met Weizmann as early as the Second Zionist Congress.[120] He took Weizmann to his home and then helped him find his first lodging in the city. The following day, July 29, Weizmann rented a room in the home of Rachel Levey[121] on 10 Cecil Street in an area of Chorlton-on-Medlock. In the nineteenth century this was the center of the non-Jewish German population. By 1904, when Weizmann arrived, it was a decaying neighborhood, well known for its genteel but run-down lodging houses, where many actors and actresses lived. It was also known as a red-light district. The advantage of living there was that it was very close to the university and merely a mile and a half from the center of the city. The Leveys tried hard to forget their Jewish origins on Cheetham Hill, but they were kind and made Weizmann feel at home.[122] All in all, he was satisfied with his living arrangements, for which he paid 150 francs per month, including full board, laundry, and lighting. He was even pleased with his new city. "The town is very interesting," he wrote Vera." "The Institute is marvellous, the laboratories enormous, the libraries beautiful, both the municipal ones and at the Institute."[123]

At the university Perkin also received him well. Despite the fact that Weizmann arrived in the midst of summer vacation, it is clear that Perkin went out of his way to settle Weizmann in a laboratory in order to afford him the opportunity to begin some experiments. Later in life Weizmann was less than grateful when describing his first days in the university's laboratory:

> The beginning was not encouraging. The laboratory in which Professor Perkin had bidden me make myself at home was a dingy basement room which had evidently not been used for many months. It was dark, grimy and covered with many layers of dust and soot; the necessary accommodations were there, but a great deal of cleaning and rearranging had to be done before it could be made habitable. As far as I could see, I was alone in the building, and I had no idea where to find the paraphernalia to fit up a laboratory. The first thing I did was to set to work to scrub the tables, clean the taps and wash up the dirty apparatus which stood about in picturesque disorder. This occupied my first day. It was not exactly a scientific occupation, but it kept my thoughts busy till evening when, very tired, and suffering from housemaid's knee, I stumbled back to my lodgings.[124]

This story, written long after Weizmann's relationship with Perkin had soured, contradicts the evidence. Except for the fact that he had to pay to use the laboratory,[125] Weizmann's letters of this period indicate that he was most grateful for Perkin's helpfulness and generosity. Given the general pollution in Manchester and the fact that the laboratory that was rented to Weizmann was not in use at the time, it is more than likely that it required extensive scrubbing. His first laboratory was indeed old,[126] but it was far from dismal.[127] He immediately made friends with Perkin's assistant, Samuel Shrowder Pickles, who showed him around,[128] and was delighted with the help extended him by the chief steward of the laboratories, Edwards, and the lab boy, Tom, who was placed at his disposal.[129] Within less than a week[130] he could report to Gaster that he had now become completely immersed in chemistry. The professor and the other gentlemen were extremely obliging. "I have a key to my lab and can come and go at any time without being tied to regular hours." Just prior to his departure on August 4 for an extended vacation in the Dolomites, Perkin came to say good-bye and suggested that Weizmann do a piece of work with him. "He is working on camphor—something entirely outside my own field. I hastened, of course, to accept his proposal gratefully and am now preparing myself for this collaboration by studying the relevant literature . . . The library is excellent."[131] The following week he was already completely at home in the laboratory, noting, "it's very cosy there, and the place is well appointed. I have really got everything for my work, and it is progressing full steam. Everything is very clean, very comfortable; I do as I please in my room and, imagine, it's even much nicer than in Geneva. Perkin did me a real favor giving me the laboratory for the vacation . . ."[132]

Before he began work in the laboratory, Weizmann had checked the university's list of courses and realized that organic chemistry was a neglected subject in Manchester. With the exception of Perkin, most chemists specialized in inorganic chemistry.[133] There were obviously great opportunities here for advancement, but he had to prove himself first. He was determined at all costs to have a new piece of work ready to present to Perkin upon the latter's return from his vacation, and imposed upon himself an arduous work schedule. He got up every day at around eight, leaving for work at eight forty-five. He returned for a one-hour lunch at one-thirty and then resumed his work until seven, with a thirty-minute break for tea. After a walk he had his dinner at eight-thirty, and from nine-thirty to eleven-thirty he read up on chemistry, presumably on camphor. But he hardly noticed the days go by and reiterated that he was very pleased with his new life.[134] Everything was going very well, he reported to Vera, yet he must break off his work to go to Vienna to the meetings of the Grosses Aktions-Comité and the annual conference, which were to commence on August 16. "The journey to Vienna is a great sacrifice for me, but I know I am indispensable there."[135] He had a mission on the Continent: to destroy the East Africa scheme and to expose Leopold Greenberg as the person responsible for involving the World Zionist Organization in this affair. He viewed Greenberg as Herzl's shadow, which had to be laid to rest. So eager was he to go to Vienna that he was willing to interrupt promising laboratory experiments.

During his fortnight in London Weizmann had haughtily announced to Cowen that he did not wish to be involved in the intrigues of the English Zionist Federation,[136] but he was more than eager to take part in the intrigues of GAC and the annual conference. A week after his arrival in England, before settling any of his personal and professional affairs, he already occupied himself with plans to return to the Continent. Though not a member of GAC, he used his position on the East Africa Commission as a legitimate reason for attending the meetings and implored Ussishkin to provide him with the funds necessary for travel.[137] After his meetings with Percy and Hill, Weizmann was convinced that his presence in Vienna was of the utmost importance. His first letter from Manchester was to Ussishkin, to whom he declared:

> I contend that no one in the Zionist Organization is at present in possession of the intelligence I possess regarding the situation. Africa can be eliminated, and all those who supported it will have to to fall with it. I claim, and assume the responsibility of producing proof, that everybody was led astray, and that the case presented to the Congress was entirely distorted! I have proof in my hand such as no one has ever dreamt of.[138]

He assured Ussishkin, who was then vacationing in Bad Kissingen, that he was now fully informed about the East Africa project; he would show that the real culprit was Greenberg. "The entire business is nothing but fraud. Herzl was deceived, the Congress was deceived, and Messrs. Greenberg and Co. deserve to be lynched."[139] Ussishkin was convinced that Weizmann's presence in Vienna was indeed necessary and promised to reimburse him for his travel; in the meantime Gaster loaned Weizmann enough to tide him over.[140] The *Haham* had his own reasons for supporting this trip. Weizmann would not only help defeat the East Africa project and shame Greenberg, he would also report back on all the current intrigues and opportunities and help promote Gaster to a more eminent position within the World Zionist Organization.[141]

Weizmann departed for Vienna on August 13 in high spirits and full of confidence. He had good reason to be satisfied with himself. Within a little more than a month in England he had scored great personal and professional triumphs: He had been well received by the established members of the English Zionist Federation; two top British politicians had accorded him a respectful hearing; and two of England's most distinguished chemists had vied for his services. He had quickly adjusted to Manchester and had begun to do serious work in the laboratory. In short, it was a remarkably auspicious beginning. Now he was on his way to the Continent, armed with two impressive memoranda, to rout the proponents of the East Africa project. He craved recognition and appreciation for his Zionist work and was absolutely certain he was about to receive it—and, who knows, maybe soon he would even be elected to the

Grosses Aktions-Comité. Shortly after his arrival in Vienna on August 16 these hopes were cruelly dashed.

What he found in Vienna was the nucleus of the World Zionist Organization's leadership, which had been thrown into turmoil and confusion by Herzl's premature death. Weizmann was not permitted to take part in many of the meetings, but enough rumors seeped into the corridors for him to form a clear picture of what took place within the conference rooms. Vienna was now the scene of the first skirmish for control of the movement. The Grosses Aktions-Comité, which met from August 16 to 19, elected a committee with plenary powers to handle the affairs of the movement until the Seventh Zionist Congress. This committee was ratified by the annual conference, which co-opted additional members as well and was known as the Committee of Thirteen.[142] It was clear from the start that the Committee of Thirteen was split into various factions too unwieldy to functon in a useful and efficient manner. In general, a great deal of time was spent in Vienna on the East Africa question,[143] but no decision could be reached until the return of the survey expedition, for which there was not yet sufficient funding. In reality, the movement had come to a grinding halt, politically speaking, until the return of the expedition and the convening of the next congress.

Weizmann's letters from Vienna reflect his dejection and disappointment with the proceedings. On the day of his arrival he went to visit Herzl's grave and mourned the lack of strong guidance form the man he once accused of dictatorial rule.[144] After two days of deliberations he was already less pious when referring to Herzl: "I . . . will soon leave . . . with a very nasty feeling that we are standing amidst the ruin of the cause; and that the deceased himself contributed quite a bit to it. Herzl, *for his own sake,* died in time . . . "[145] And, by the same token, much to his surprise, Weizmann learned that Leopold Greenberg was only a tool in Herzl's hands and did not act independently. To his credit, Weizmann admitted his mistake about Greenberg in no uncertain terms in a letter to Gaster: "Mr. Greenberg acted *par ordre* and is *completely* covered by letters from Herzl; of this I am personally convinced. Accordingly, attacks on Greenberg are *only* attacks on Herzl, which one must not now make, of course."[146] Greenberg had publicly protested his innocence[147] and was now fully exonerated by the written evidence. Weizmann was persuaded by Yehiel Tschlenow—probably with Ussishkin's assent—that "publication of the conversations with Percy and Hill could *only* cause frightful harm now and strengthen Greenberg's prestige while killing off politically all those who opposed Herzl's diplomacy . . . *On no account* should publication of the conversations be allowed to *take place now.*"[148]

But clearing Greenberg of all wrongdoing also meant that Weizmann had lost another opportunity to propel himself into the Zionist limelight. Once again, those conferring in Vienna made him feel like a junior participant whose time had not yet come. Moreover, the chaos and indecision at Vienna, and the rift between the Vienna-based Engeres Aktions-Comité and the Eastern Europeans, boded ill for the future. Even

Ussishkin seemed to have mellowed and was not his fiery, uncompromising self. All agreed that the expedition to East Africa would proceed as had been planned. Tschlenow summed up the mood when he declared, at the last session of the Grosses Aktions-Comité, that they had all been suspicious of Herzl's attitude toward Palestine without good reason.[149] There was nothing left for Weizmann to do on the Continent. As he packed his belongings and collected the secret memoranda in his room at the Hotel de France, he stopped for a few moments to write a note to Vera: "I am leaving now, tired and worn out, and very much regretting having come. For Zionists of our kind there is no work now, and I can see a bad transitional period before us. It is sad, but one has to wait, wait, wait and keep one's silence . . . This is my last Zionist activity. I must withdraw from the cause for a year . . ."[150]

On his way back to Manchester from the Continent, Weizmann made a few short stops in Switzerland to meet his brother Moshe,[151] see some friends, and collect laboratory equipment for his work in Manchester. While waiting for a train in Bern he wrote Vera a long letter on the snack-bar notepaper, once again assessing conditions within the movement. The only ray of hope he could discern at the annual meeting was the report of Selig Soskin and Otto Warburg on the work of the Commission for the Investigation of Palestine, which had inaugurated the periodical *Altneuland* and had made wide-ranging plans for a scientific exploration of Palestine.[152] Everything else within the movement seemed bleak, in ruins. "It is sad, my Verochka, very sad . . . I am burning with desire to see you, talk to you, open my wounded heart to you, the heart of a tired Zionist who is witnessing the crumbling of his precious cause and is unable to fight it. My time will still come, but later, later, when there will be nothing but fragments! . . . I shall withdraw and devote myself to science. I can do so now, for I burn with the desire to find repose in science. I have no doubt I shall succeed . . ."[153]

The meetings of the Grosses Aktions-Comité and the annual conference were a watershed in his attitude toward Zionist work. He had not gone to England, as he relates in his memoirs,[154] in order to end his Zionist activity. On the contrary, all the evidence shows that he saw England as a stepping-stone for renewed work in the movement. His almost immediate political success in England strengthened this conviction. Rather, it was only after the meetings in Vienna that he decided to desist from Zionist activity temporarily. Perhaps the contrast between his almost instantaneous acceptance in Zionist and professional circles in England and the snubbing he had to endure in Vienna made the experience all the more painful; it seems to have created the negative attitude toward the movement to which he referred in his memoirs. In any event, he now felt the need for a respite from Zionist activity. Ten weeks after his unhappy journey, he was able to articulate what had happened: ". . . since the famous Vienna Conference, something within me snapped, the thread linking me to the party was severed, and I suddenly felt terribly alone . . . I am so infinitely remote from you all; and all that is close to my heart is separated from me by the sea and infinite space. Here I am completely by myself and alone in the fullest and most terrible meaning of the word."[155]

In the three-month interim, however, he was hard at work in the laboratory, "lest I find myself in the street and give 'friends' the chance of nodding their heads in my direction: 'He was a gifted fellow, yet he is a failure.' "[156] As it turned out, nothing could have been further from the truth. The next ten years of Weizmann's scientific career brought him repeated success and ultimately it was chemistry which propelled him into the Zionist limelight.

XI

An Alien in Manchester

The familiar pattern in Weizmann's dual relationship with Zionism and science was at work again. When he was full of confidence in himself, his friends, and the Zionist cause, he tended to sacrifice his scientific work for the sake of Zionism. Now that he was again humiliated and depressed, he sought to renew his self-confidence in an area where he could prove his prowess beyond doubt. His success in chemistry gave him the necessary self-esteem, provided him with energy, and served as the springboard for his return to the more hazardous and uncertain Zionist work. Thus, he could not wait to get back to his experiments. The day after his return to Manchester, on August 31, he spent almost twelve hours in the laboratory and immediately felt much better.[1] He now worked without respite, continuing the experiments he had interrupted a fortnight earlier; they went well. He and Perkin's assistant, Samuel Shrowder Pickles, were on the verge of a new discovery, and Weizmann impatiently anticipated each new day when he could go to work. Within a week after his return he could proudly announce: "I have achieved a new reaction that reopens a complete area and I am very pleased. Something new again; a Manchester product this time."[2] Pickles and Weizmann established a reaction between magnesium organic compounds and phthalic anhydrides, leading to a new class of compounds which, in turn, could be converted into derivatives of anthracene, the basis of certain important dyestuffs. The scientific value of the discovery lay in the fact that the chemical structure of the anthracene derivatives so produced was unambiguous, unlike those produced by previous methods.[3] By the end of September he could report yet another successful experiment.[4]

Both experiments were published in November 1904 in the *Proceedings of the Chemical Society*.[5] Significantly, Weizmann signed his name Charles Weizmann. There is no clue in his correspondence or his autobiography as to why he chose to sign his academic papers and patents under the name Charles.[6] Was it an indication of his desire to integrate himself more fully into English academic circles? Or perhaps it was an attempt to make it easier for his gentile colleagues to pronounce his name? Or was it the result of his recognition that one needed "standing" in English society?

Whatever the reasons, the decision to anglicize his name in his professional activities was deliberate and consistent. Until 1920 he signed his scientific papers Charles, after which the simple abbreviation "Ch" appears; his patents were signed Charles until 1943.[7] The Manchester Directory for 1908 lists his name as Charles as well.[8] His passport and other official documents also bore his anglicized forename. Thus he was "Chaim" the Zionist and "Charles" the chemist.

Perkin, who had returned from his vacation at the end of September, was duly impressed with Weizmann's accomplishments[9] and immediately assigned him two additional students. Weizmann now had four students working under him, who were joined in mid-October by Carl Voegtlin, a Swiss student who had roomed with Weizmann in Geneva at the Pension Dupuis. Like Weizmann, he became a lodger at the Leveys. Thus, within two months after his return from Vienna Weizmann had a small group of workers who could relieve him of some of the more routine experiments. Moreover, Perkin promised him a research fellowship by Christmas,[10] and Weizmann typically let his imagination run wild as to what the immediate future had in store for him. To Vera he wrote that his salary would be 150 pounds.[11] To Menahem Ussishkin he reported a month later that he had been appointed a lecturer, which "corresponds to a German Extraordinary Professor! . . . The prospects for a Chair are almost certain . . ."[12] In fact, on the recommendation of Perkin Weizmann was appointed a research fellow in January 1905, with the modest salary of 50 pounds per annum; he was assigned four research students and was allowed to use the Thorpe Laboratory free of charge.[13] According to the rules of the University of Manchester, he was allowed to engage in research under the supervision of a professor or lecturer, and with the approval of the council and senate of the university he was also permitted to deliver lectures. Yet to his friend Buber he boasted, "I . . . have very good prospects of being accepted as Professor of Chemistry before long, either here or at some other University in England. I have already been appointed Lecturer and Fellow of the University . . ."[14] His need to enhance his status in the eyes of his friends reflects his desire for respect and power. It also indicates a basic insecurity and desire for approval by others. His excellent work did entitle him to hope for the professorship he sought throughout his ten years in Manchester, but he was to learn that merit alone was insufficient for its attainment.[15]

In November 1904 he began preparing his first series of lectures in organic chemistry. The lectures were to be given once a week on Saturdays from January 21 until March 4, 1905.[16] He was extremely nervous before his first lecture,[17] though he had a great deal of experience in public speaking and classroom lecturing. The fact that he undertook to lecture in English indicates that within six months he was fluent and had mastered English speech—a remarkable achievement. No doubt he could speak with authority on a subject he knew very well, but the forty-one students who awaited him in the lecture hall were an unknown and intimidating entity. He began by disarming them: "I was a foreigner, I said, and had been in the country only a few months; I was consequently at their mercy. I would do my best, but I would certainly perpetrate many howlers. They could make all the jokes they wanted at my expense—after the lecture . . ."[18] This little introduction made an impact and the Lancashire men and women sat attentively, straining to comprehend his lecture, which was delivered in a low-pitched, guttural, slyly good-natured style. His heavy Russian accent seemed to pose no problems once they got used to him.[19] "My Saturday lecture was a great success," he wrote Vera. "At the end of the lecture the students gave me an ovation. They were delighted. I was, of course, in seventh heaven. Perkin is also very pleased."[20] He did not quite get accustomed to take the lectures in his stride and spent many hours preparing for them, but he began to feel at ease with his students, who clearly appreciated his efforts.[21] "Students keep coming to me . . . I already have more than Perkin—a proper school."[22]

Perkin could only congratulate himself on his wisdom in attracting such a talented researcher and lecturer to the university. He fully realized that within a short time Weizmann could also find a position elsewhere in England and sought to anchor him in Manchester. Quite possibly he dangled before Weizmann's eyes the prospect of attaining a professorship, though Weizmann had a tendency to count his chickens before they were hatched and therefore was often miserably disappointed. In the meantime, Perkin found more concrete means for boosting Weizmann's material and professional status. Early in December 1904 he founded the Manchester Chemical Society, with himself as president and Weizmann as secretary.[23] Within his own department there was, of course, a limit to what he could do for Weizmann, but he steadily sought to advance him up the academic ladder. In July 1905 Weizmann was appointed demonstrator—namely, assistant to the departmental head and supervisor of student work in the organic chemistry laboratory—at a new annual salary of a hundred pounds.[24] Thus, in addition to his Saturday lectures to first-year students, his task was now to demonstrate in the laboratory experiments related to Perkin's lectures. He at first demonstrated to third-year chemistry honors students in the old Schorlemmer Building, but soon he had his own laboratory in the newer extension of the organic chemistry unit.[25] One of his former students recalled Weizmann thus:

It was in October 1906 that I went into Dr. Weizmann's laboratory. He had not long left Russia then. We were rather nervous of him at first; we thought we might not be able to understand his very "foreign" English or grasp what particular chemicals he meant us to use. He would refer, for instance, to calcium chloride as chlor calc., to sodium hydroxide as hydrox sod., and so on. We soon got used to him, however, as time went on and his speech grew less guttural to our ears . . .[26]

Within a year after his arrival in Manchester, then, Weizmann had already established a reputation as a fine lecturer and skillful demonstrator, while at the same time continuing to publish papers with his collaborators in the *Proceedings of the Chemical Society*.[27] His financial situation, however, remained precarious, and he sought to supplement his modest university salary with industrial work. The first such opportunity materialized with an offer made by Samuel Shriro of Baku, the first benefactor of the university project in 1902. Shriro arrived in Manchester toward the end of September 1904 and offered Weizmann fifteen pounds a month in return for three hours of work a day developing a process for the production of odorless and colorless soap from petroleum residues. In the event that he could solve this problem, he was promised five hundred pounds and a share in the profits of manufacture.[28] This arrangement was to signal a marked improvement in Weizmann's material situation. The problem was that Shriro rarely paid, and when he did the money came late, thus disrupting any orderly budgeting on Weizmann's part; he bombarded the oil man with telegrams and pleas to pay up.[29] The university salary was sufficient to support Weizmann's very modest living arrangements, but his anxiety over finances stemmed from other sources. He wanted to earn enough so that Vera could join him in Manchester as soon as possible.[30] Moreover, when he began his research fellowship, he allocated one hundred francs each month to help support his sisters Anna and Masha, who were about to begin their university studies in Zurich.[31] Like his sisters, his brother Shmuel, also a student in Zurich at the time, turned to Weizmann for financial help.[32] A year later, when his brother Moshe switched fields and also began studying chemistry in Zurich, Weizmann supported him as well.[33] Vera was quite incensed that so much of her fiancé's earnings should go to his siblings. On one occasion, when Vera guessed that the money Weizmann requested would be forwarded to his sisters, she exclaimed:

> This [request] seems so absurd to me, so strange, so impossible to understand—when you know quite well that my means are minimal, that I live so frugally and don't permit myself anything but the absolute essentials, that I had to deny myself going to you for want of money for the fare . . . that even now I still don't know how and where I'll get the money to pay for my tuition . . . Why do you need 500 roubles? Why don't you write to me about it? Actually, I can guess: You probably want to send this money to your sisters. But, Chaimchik, that's absurd. True, you didn't ask for my advice . . . All the same, I think it won't be any great misfortune if the girls were to leave a year later [for Zurich] . . .[34]

But Weizmann was not to be dissuaded. Education, in his opinion, was not a luxury but a necessity for those who did not wish to become *batlanim*, mere *Luftmenschen*. Sending money to his family members and aiding them in their careers would continue to be one of his priorities.

Until his financial situation improved, he tried to save wherever he could. At the beginning of January 1905, he and Voegtlin decided to leave the Leveys. They disliked the food and the rent was too high.[35] On February 8 he moved into his new lodgings at 20 Parkfield Street in Rusholme; the combined cost for his food, lodging, and laundry now amounted to eight pounds per month.[36] He was pleased with the improvement in his food and rent and the comfortable rooms. Rusholme was a drab neighborhood, consisting of back-to-back houses built in the last quarter of the nineteenth century and densely occupied by a poor working-class population. Parkfield Street, located in a decaying area, consisted of lodging houses occupied by white-collar, low-income persons.[37] In the midst of Rusholme stood Victoria Park, a private, well-to-do residential area with its own toll gates. It was an irritant to the entire impoverished area encircling it. Weizmann, who had to traverse this affluent suburb every day on his way to and from the university, must have been very conscious of the fact that some of his senior colleagues resided there.[38] Looking at the well-appointed and stately mansions around him, he may have reflected on how unjust it was that he had to work so hard just to make ends meet. He did make one attempt, during this early period, to move to a better neighborhood. In late August 1905 he took rooms in the home of his research assistant, Jan Quiller Orchardson, on 43 Whitby Road in Fallowfield.[39] This was a proper suburb with lots of greenery and fresh air.[40] But it turned out to be only a six-week interlude since Orchardson was leaving Manchester for a position in Leeds.[41] Thus, he returned to his old lodgings at 20 Parkfield Street, paying fifteen shillings a week, including breakfast and heating, which was "very reasonable for the locality."[42]

Luckily he met Charles Dreyfus soon after his arrival in Manchester. Dreyfus was a chemist who in 1869 had moved from Alsace to England. In 1876, at the age of twenty-eight, he founded the Clayton Aniline Company, of which he remained managing director until his retirement in 1913. The company was founded some twenty years after William Henry Perkin had prepared the first synthetic mauve coal tar dye; it was the growing demand for aniline, used in producing many of the newly developed synthetic dyes, which led to the formation of Dreyfus's company. By the turn of the century Dreyfus was a prominent citizen of Manchester, had served as a member of its municipal council from 1897 to 1906, was a leading member of the South Manchester Synagogue, and numbered among the founders of the Victoria Memorial Jewish Hospital.[43] Since 1903 he had also been the president of the Manchester Zionist Association. It is possible that he and Weizmann had met briefly at the Fifth or Sixth Zionist Congress, where Dreyfus was a delegate. In any case, Weizmann knew of Dreyfus; as early as April 1904 he asked Gaster whether he had spoken to Dreyfus about a position for Weizmann in his company,[44] and it is most likely that Gaster had indeed recommended Weizmann for employment in Dreyfus's company. Weizmann went to see Dreyfus in Manchester during November 1904 on the pretext of finding a job for Vera at the Victoria Memorial Jewish Hospital.[45] The two men took to each other immediately. They had much in

common professionally, culturally, and ideologically. Moreover, Dreyfus, just like Perkin, realized at once how advantageous it would be to
have in his employ an experienced student of Liebermann and Graebe,
that is, a direct disciple of the foremost researchers in the field of dyestuffs. Within two weeks he offered Weizmann a job with his company.[46] He often invited him to his house in salubrious Fallowfield to
meet his friends and the rest of the family.[47] Perkin fully supported
Weizmann's desire to become a consultant to industry, provided this work
did not interfere with his duties at the university during the academic
year and that experiments conducted at Weizmann's initiative be undertaken by students in the university laboratories.[48] The three-year contract with Dreyfus stipulated that Weizmann would work in the factory
only during the university vacations and would earn 175 pounds a year,
plus 25 pounds for an assistant.[49] Weizmann was also promised five
weeks' vacation during the summer.[50] Moreover, the university gave him
a well-appointed new laboratory where he could work alone—presumably also on experiments for the factory—while his students continued
to work in his old half-basement laboratory. Little by little he was en-
larging his domain within the university.[51] In mid-March, having successfully completed his last lecture and now ensconced in his well-
equipped laboratory, he was delighted with all the arrangments, positively enjoying his work.

> Luckily, the laboratory is now a source of tremendous satisfaction to me: it
> makes me feel positively stronger. I don't overwork, thanks on the one hand
> to a brilliant student of mine who relieves me of a good half of the work,
> and on the other to my assistant (paid) [Jan Quillar Orchardson], a very nice
> fellow whose attitude is not only that of an assistant, but of a friend. Thanks
> to these two I am able to cope perfectly, and by issuing instructions to my
> co-worker am even able to leave the laboratory earlier than usual.[52]

Though far from living in comfort, he was now also financially more secure, earning a combined salary of sixteen pounds a month.[53] Not only
did he no longer need his brother-in-law's monthly support; he could
now send regular contributions toward the education of his siblings.

This rosy picture was offset by work in Dreyfus's factory. On March
20 he began a monthlong, nine-thirty-to-five daily routine at Clayton. It
did not take him long to dislike the dirty and dusty conditions at the
factory, which was saturated with the odors of aniline. It also meant an
extra-long day for him, which began with his getting up at seven and
working a full day, after which he went to the university laboratory to
check on his own ongoing experiments.[54] At the end of his first week he
wrote Vera in utter disgust:

> It was very hard, because I am unused to all that filth, noise and crackle,
> and that atmosphere saturated with aniline. Generally speaking, science
> suffers a terrible degradation when every experiment is considered from the
> financial standpoint and the finest reactions are despised if they have no
> "technical," that is "commercial," significance. I feel dreadfully uncomfort-

able and sometimes, after speaking with those in charge, thoroughly disgusted as well. Three more weeks and I shall leave these ugly, unwholesome surroundings, for which I have never developed a liking and which never attracted me. What is the difference between this and a planter using Negro labor! It is even worse here. Cultured people, educated at universities, having dreamt of science, etc. etc., are working here so that the Company might prosper. Such a pity![55]

As he commenced his second week in the factory, he began counting the days until he could return to his laboratory at the university: "This is already my second week at the factory. I hope it will slip by, and the third and fourth week too . . . I am not made for technical work; it hasn't taken me long, at close quarters, to develop an aversion to it. The Germans call it *Schinderei*, chemistry perverted into alchemy."[56]

The vehemence of Weizmann's reaction to the Clayton Aniline Company was due, no doubt, to the contrast with his working conditions at the university. On the other hand, his relationship with the Dreyfus family had become more intimate,[57] and his new friend and employer, only too anxious to make him happy, arranged to release Weizmann from all dirty work at the laboratory. "The factory gave me a youngster to wait on me. He does the filtering, cleans, runs to the post office, goes shopping, performs analyses. In short, the boy is a treasure . . . Only the purely chemical work is left to me."[58] Moreover, despite the unpleasant working conditions, he had a sense of satisfaction since he and Alexander Meyenberg, his collaborator and the factory's manager, were able to send off another patent, "our 6th factory patent," an improvement in the manufacture of anthracene and dyestuffs therefrom.[59] To compound his happiness, Harold Baily Dixon, the director of the university laboratories, promised to appoint Weizmann head of a special technological laboratory with an added salary of 150 pounds per annum.[60] In view of this pending professional advance, one can perhaps better understand his constant boasting about an imminent professorship.

Successful work in the laboratory during the day and the affairs of the Manchester Chemical Society a few evenings a month, though rewarding, still left him restless. After four months of almost total abstention, he was eager to return to Zionist activity.[61] There is no explicit clue as to the immediate catalyst which prompted him to return to Zionism. His four months in Manchester no doubt sufficed for him to observe that Manchester was not blessed with too many talented Zionist activists, and that if he chose to he could certainly quickly rise to a position of leadership in England's second-largest Jewish community.[62] Possibly it was his good friend Joseph Massel, vice president of the Manchester Zionist Association, who urged him not to stand aside. More likely he was stirred into Zionist activity by news of events in Russia. The period following the outbreak of the Russo-Japanese War on February 9, 1904, was marked by renewed pogroms against the Jews. Notwithstanding the considerable number of Jews who were conscripted into the Russian armed forces in the Far East to fight for the glory of Tsar Nicholas II in his attempt to

annex Manchuria to Siberia, their Jewish co-religionists in the Pale of
Settlement and elsewhere paid with their blood for alleged Jewish assistance to the Japanese. A bloody pogrom took place in the city of Alexandria (province of Kherson) on September 19 and 20. Within a month
more violence was perpetrated in the province of Mogilev. In the city of
Mogilev the reservists pillaged Jewish homes and shops from October 20
to 22.[63] Weizmann was pained and worried by the detailed account of
these events, which he read about in *The Jewish Chronicle*[64] and in letters
from friends in Kiev.

> The letters are full of horrifying news about pogroms and the terrible state
> of mind everybody is in. I can imagine what is going on in everybody's head
> and heart. And it is precisely at this difficult time that I am not on duty as
> a Zionist. This pains me. I ought to give myself a little shaking. I hope to
> do so in a little while . . . When one hears what goes on, one feels ashamed
> at living as peacefully as we do while all who are near and dear to you suf-
> fer terribly.[65]

Thus, on the eve of his thirtieth birthday he was introduced by Charles
Dreyfus at a synagogue where Weizmann addressed the Manchester Zionist Association on the theme of "The Political Movements of Jews in
Russia."[66] He had carefully prepared for this meeting, later reporting that
the audience stood for nearly three hours, as though under a spell, listening with rapt attention. "This public, which always seemed so repul-
sive to me, was somehow different yesterday, more noble. My words
stirred them, and at least for the duration of my lecture a bond was established between them, myself, and the whole mass of suffering
Jewry."[67] Speaking in Yiddish to a group of East European immigrants
must have once again been invigorating; this was the next best thing to
his yearly propaganda tours in Russia. The mostly solitary work in the
laboratory could sustain Weizmann for only a limited period of time; it
was by and large a lonely profession, save for the weekly contact with
students. Weizmann needed people—he needed to speak, argue, and
touch them. Zionist propaganda was thus more than an abstract ideology; it was a personal need, and one clearly senses that it came as a relief to him to speak again after four months of self-imposed silence. His
listeners were just as appreciative of this skillful speaker who warmed
their hearts with familiar images and symbols. For at least a few hours
they could feel at home in this cold and alien environment, where even
Zionist activists were for the most part Anglo-Jews, removed from the
people they attempted to lead.[68] Weizmann's lecture on November 26,
1904, marked his formal reentry into Zionist work and launched him into
the affairs of the Manchester Zionist Association, which was only too
happy to assign him a prominent place within its meager ranks. Possibly
this newcomer could inject it with some new energy and vitality. For the
next decade Weizmann would be closely tied to its affairs. Thus, a brief
sketch of its history is in order.

The first Zionist society in Manchester was a branch of Hovevei Zion which called itself the Society for the Promotion of Colonization in Palestine.[69] Despite its pledge to work toward spreading the idea that "colonization of the Holy Land is an object worthy of the consideration of the entire Jewish communicty,"[70] nothing was heard of it again. The first significant push toward a Zionist organization in Manchester came in 1890 through the efforts of Reverend Hayyim Zundel Maccoby, the "Maggid of Kamenets," who had arrived that year from Russia, where he had helped establish scores of Hovevei Zion societies. On August 2 and 3, 1890, he spoke at the New Synagogue and the Manchester Jews' School, persuading 160 persons to enroll as Hovevei Zion.[71] A few months later their numbers rose to over 400 members.[72] Beginning in 1891, the Manchester branch of Hovevei Zion (soon known as the Manchester "tent") began raising funds for Jewish colonization in Palestine.[73] In general, the early period, prior to Herzl's *Der Judenstaat*, saw in Manchester weak and splintered Hovevei Zion associations, organized by country of origin, degree of Jewish tradition, and even social class.[74] Their activities were confined to occasional lectures and annual meetings.[75] For the most part the membership was composed of poor East European workers led by a number of middle-class, usually English-born, Jews.[76]

Following the First Zionist Congress, Zionism also made inroads in Manchester. The Dorshei Zion Association, a group which emphasized the fostering of the Hebrew language, was founded a year earlier, in 1896.[77] It also sponsored lectures on Zionism and Jewish history.[78] An amalgamation of a number of groups, the Zionist Association (Vaad Hazioni), with Joseph Massel as its president, was founded[79] along with another group called Bnei Zion.[80] The combined membership of all three groups was eight hundred in January 1898.[81] Of the various Zionist groups in Manchester, the Vaad Hazioni emerged as the most active and enterprising, supporting cultural, political, and fund-raising activities.[82] It was in January 1901 that Charles Dreyfus began to be involved in Zionist affairs in Manchester,[83] and in August of that year he was elected president of the Zionist Central Committee.[84] Dreyfus was probably the only industrialist and member of Manchester's Jewish elite active in Zionist affairs, and his election to the presidency was no doubt also a means of lending Zionism a measure of respectability within the Jewish establishment.

In May 1902 Dreyfus succeeded in amalgamating the various Zionist associations[85]—except for the Menachem Zion Association—into the Manchester Zionist Association (MZA), with himself as president and Joseph Massel one of its two vice presidents.[86] A few months later the newly created MZA, with its headquarters at 97 Cheetham Hill, was able to register one hundred new members.[87] It became the center of activities for other provincial Zionist associations from Leeds, Liverpool, Birmingham, Sheffield, Cardiff, and others.[88] At the annual EZF meeting, which took place in 1903 in Liverpool, Dreyfus was elected provincial vice president.[89]

Dreyfus probably encouraged Weizmann to continue to be active in the affairs of the Manchester Zionist Association. The parallels between Weizmann's relations with his two employers—Perkin and Dreyfus—is striking. Both recognized his professional talents and skill in chemistry and found him a great asset in their respective laboratories. But, beyond this, they also sought to get him involved in their own extraprofessional and intellectual interests. Perkin, who was president of the Manchester Chemical Society, and Dreyfus, who was president of the Manchester Zionist Association, each took advantage of Weizmann's services in the evenings and on weekends as well. To be sure, Weizmann's arm did not have to be twisted to participate in either activity. For one thing, his social life was minimal. He saw the Massels once a week on Saturdays and on Jewish holidays[90] and the Dreyfus family occasionally on Sundays.[91] Consequently he had some free time at his disposal, and these activities distracted him from his frequent bouts of loneliness and depression. But perhaps more important than that, he was flattered by the attention lavished upon him in Zionist circles. One can only guess that despite his frequent complaints about overwork, he was mighty glad to once again be involved in Zionist affairs.

His reception by the rank and file and the leadership of the Manchester Zionist Association and the English Zionist Federation was enthusiastic. He was an immediate success. As had previously been the case in Geneva, his sudden rise to prominence within Zionist ranks reflected both his talents and natural abilities, as well as the dearth of an available pool of able men and women.[92] His speech in November whetted his appetite for renewed Zionist propaganda. With the fellowship at the university secured and the promise of a job from Dreyfus, he felt financially reassured and thus reported to Ussishkin that, "faithful to my word, I am ready to take up work for the cause. I am this week joining the committee of the Manchester Zionist Association . . . I shall probably myself undertake a tour of Leeds, Glasgow, Edinburgh and Liverpool . . . I have gradually acquired great influence here."[93]

On this occasion Weizmann did not exaggerate when he wrote about his growing influence. He was, in fact, deluged with invitations to speak in the English provincial towns as well as in London and Scotland.[94] The East European immigrants in Manchester and elsewhere were obviously impressed by his Yiddish and German lectures. Not since the "Maggid of Kamenets" had made the rounds in the 1890s had they had a man of stature—and one of their own kind to boot—whose concerns and aspirations were, like their own, intimately tied to East European Jewry.[95] The Anglo-Jewish leadership, on the other hand, was clearly attracted to this East-West Jew who represented for them the authoritative voice of East European Jewry yet, at the same time, was familiar with and attuned to their own cultural value system. Though on the periphery of the continental Zionist leadership, he was in the context of England an experienced veteran Zionist who had been soldiering in the ranks of the movement even before it was organized as a political vehicle. He brought with him the aura of an elder statesman in the movement as well as the

professional and academic credentials necessary in a society so conscious of rank and status.

It is not surprising, then, that between December 1904 and July 1905
Weizmann quickly rose to a position of some importance within the English Zionist Federation. Together with Dreyfus and others, he was elected
delegate of the Manchester Zionist Association to the annual conference
of the English Zionist Federation, which took place in Leeds on January
22, 1905.[96] He arrived in Leeds in good spirits the day after he had delivered his first lecture at the university. Surveying the *Menschenmaterial*,
as he condescendingly reported to Vera, he came to the conclusion that
it was rather poor but better than he had expected.[97] The executive of
the English Zionist Federation reported on its activities on behalf of Russian immigrants and against the passage of the Aliens Bill, and indicated
an acceptance of the East Africa project should the survey expedition's
report be favorable.[98] Weizmann had come to Leeds in the hope of cur-
tailing the power of "Greenberg and Co." and organizing a group opposed to their control of the English Zionist Federation.[99] Their report
gave him the opening he sought and at once he launched into an attack.
He contended that the fight against the Aliens Bill was not a Zionist task
but rather the concern of all Jews in England. Zionism was not to be
branded as a philanthropic aid society on behalf of poor East European
Jews, and it certainly should have nothing to do with East Africa.[100] His
speech was well received, and even the executive retreated from its position on the Aliens Bill and the East Africa issue. Weizmann was very
pleased with himself.

> Greenberg and Cowen are wooing me. They covered me with praise and
> nominated me for the executive committee of the party in England, and I
> was elected unanimously. In the evening there was a mammoth meeting . . .
> when the official speakers had finished, there were loud calls in the crowd
> "We want Weizmann to speak" . . . To the great delight of the public I spoke
> in Yiddish . . . I was strongly applauded; I received declarations of affec-
> tion, and invitations to all cities; in short I am *lancé*. I hope to acquire an
> influence on the progress of affairs here, but I must bide my time . . .[101]

This period was the beginning of Weizmann's reentry into the political
life of Zionism—first in England and soon on the Continent. The officers
of the English Zionist Federation consisted of: Sir Francis Montefiore,
president; Joseph Cowen and Jacob Moser of Bradford, vice presidents;
and Leopold Greenberg, treasurer.[102] These men supported political
Zionism. Loyal to Herzl during his lifetime, they were not ready to dismiss the East Africa project—which they had all advocated—after his
death. Weizmann and Dreyfus constituted the strongest anti–East Africa
opinion on the executive.[103] If a successful opposition was to be mounted
against the Greenberg-dominated English Zionist Federation, Manchester as a major provincial city was a good launching pad. In order to achieve
this goal Weizmann first had to consolidate his own position locally. Thus,
by February 1905 he willingly consented to become the vice president of

the Manchester Zionist Association.[104] Next he wished to use Dreyfus as the lance that might break the defensive shield of the London group.

Dreyfus was not only a respected local industrialist who dabbled in civic affairs. His influence extended to the general national political scene as well. Within a year he was to become the president of the East Manchester Conservative Association and chairman of Prime Minister A. J. Balfour's constituency committee during the 1906 election campaign. Weizmann was impressed when Dreyfus introduced him in January to the Prime Minister during a public meeting in Manchester, though Weizmann had only a very brief conversation with Balfour.[105] Thus, in Weizmann's view it would be advantageous to promote Dreyfus from his local position in Manchester Zionism to a national position in the English Zionist Federation. Weizmann accordingly advised Ussishkin to "contact Dreyfus and use him to establish relations with the English government. Dreyfus is in favor of Palestine . . . Dreyfus must be promoted. He wields enormous influence . . ."[106]

Not content to rely on Dreyfus to wield his influence and not quite respectful of Dreyfus's judgment in Zionist affairs, Weizmann undertook to spread the true Zionist doctrine himself. He did not lack invitations to address audiences in the provinces, and even in London,[107] but it was not easy. He maintained a grueling schedule in the laboratory from Monday through Friday. On Saturdays he gave his lecture on organic chemistry and he needed his rest on Sundays.[108] He was apologetic about his refusal to accept invitations, explaining that at this point in his life his first priority was to work hard in order to ensure a living for himself.[109] At the same time he exaggerated his Zionist activity in his rather servile reports to Ussishkin.[110]

Nevertheless, though it meant a great sacrifice in terms of his health, he did venture on occasional propaganda lectures, aided by a small sum of money sent him by Ussishkin.[111] "Yesterday I spoke most successfully in Leeds [on the state of Zionism and the forthcoming World Zionist Congress] before thousands, but I must confess I haven't the strength for propaganda. After my speech I could hardly breathe, and during the night I developed a tremendous headache . . . My speech, together with replies to the discussion, lasted three hours. The audience behaved excellently throughout, and was most respectful."[112] In general, on those few occasions when he did lecture in Leeds or Liverpool[113] he was satisfied that he did very well. Once in a while he also engaged in one of his favorite public activities—a debate with anti-Zionists.[114] His oratorical skill, honed over many years of propaganda in Russia and Western Europe, served him well. The Yiddish-speaking audiences[115] sensed at once his spiritual and intellectual authority.[116] His success among Manchester Jews, for example, was so striking that in a letter to David Wolffsohn one of his local adversaries complained that Weizmann was "a first-class fanatic whose knowledge of Yiddish enabled him to speak to the hearts of the poorer elements that were bewildered by the magic word 'Jerusalem' and were unmoved by logical analysis."[117]

His success in England notwithstanding, Weizmann knew full well that the final decisions on the course of the World Zionist Organization were to be made on the Continent. Thus, he took care to maintain deferential relations with Ussishkin, who served as his link to European Zionists and acted as a barometer of the moods within the movement as a whole. Ussishkin had not been idle. In view of the confusion reigning in the movement after Herzl's death, and the pervasive split between the Zionei Zion, who opposed consideration of East Africa or any other territory other than Palestine as the future Jewish homeland, and the Ugandists and territorialists—of the socialist and nonsocialist variety—he was determined to intervene decisively to ensure the victory of Zionei Zion. Summarizing his pro-Palestinian views, which had been voiced at the Minsk Conference of 1902, the Kharkov Conference of 1903, and elsewhere, in December 1904 Ussishkin published an article entitled "Our Program" in the Russian Jewish paper *Evreiskaia Zhizn*. Reviewing the history of Zionism since the days of the Hibbat Zion, Ussishkin arrived at the conclusion that colonization, cultural Zionism, and political Zionism should all be pursued simultaneously, that success on any single front would reinforce and strengthen achievements and endeavors on the other two. In other words, he firmly believed that a synthesis of all three approaches had to be achieved in order to effect the original purpose of Zionist diplomacy as stipulated in the Basel Program.[118] Ussishkin demanded that the World Zionist Organization apply itself forthwith to practical work in Palestine, without neglecting diplomacy and while cooperating with such other non-Zionist bodies as the Jewish Colonization Association and the Hilfsverein der deutschen Juden.[119] He also returned to a theme that had been articulated at the Minsk Conference and that was central to his thinking, namely, the prime importance of involving Jewish youth in the colonization of Palestine. He suggested the creation of a worldwide pioneering force of single young people, healthy in body and spirit, who would volunteer to work in Palestine for three years, under conditions of minimal comfort, in the service of the Jewish people. At the completion of their service they would have the option of returning to their countries of origin or settling in Palestine. There was no doubt in Ussishkin's mind that such idealistic youth were to be found among the Jews of the Diaspora. "If in the 1880's we had dozens of Biluim, I believe we could now recruit thousands like them. The young generation is alert, ready for self-sacrifice. One needs [sic] only turn to it and show it the way."[120]

Forty-seven Zionei Zion, or *Palestintsy*, as they called themselves, met under Ussishkin's leadership in Vilna from January 14 to 17, 1905. The major decisions arrived at by the delegates were in the spirit of Ussishkin's article. They rejected territorialism outright and even demanded that territorialists be disqualified from purchasing the shekel or participating in the congress; the conference also resolved to reject the East Africa project at the Seventh Zionist Congress. On a positive and constructive note, the delegates resolved to establish a secondary school in Palestine named after Herzl, to promote activities which would strengthen the national consciousness in the Diaspora, and to support the election to the Seventh Zionist Congress of only those candidates who upheld these resolutions.[121] Though he was not present at the Vilna Conference, Weizmann was elected to two subcommittees concerned, respectively, with the syllabus and teaching staff for the secondary school and with the establishment of a fund for national education in Palestine.[122] Thus, Weizmann was recognized for the first time as having a leadership role in the movement in Russia itself. He was elected to a central East European Zionist forum and thus formally gained entry into Ussishkin's inner circle, a goal he had desired for so long. Ironically it came when geographic distance prevented him from enjoying his newly won status.

Those opposing the Zionei Zion took up the gauntlet with élan, calling themselves "pure Zionists." They, too, prepared for the Seventh Zionist Congress and met in Warsaw in April 1905 under the leadership of Max Mandelstamm, who was a "Ugandist" (and, in a later transformation, a territorialist). This conference decided to demand of the Seventh Zionist Congress a change in the Basel Program that would declare that Zionism aimed to create for the Jewish people a haven in any appropriate and obtainable territory. They opposed exclusive investments in Palestine—or any other country, for that matter—without the necessary political guarantees and demanded that those members of the World Zionist Organization who had failed to promote the East Africa project be disciplined. The "pure Zionists" saw themselves as ideologically close to the Ugandists.[123] The most articulate leader of the pro-Uganda faction was, without doubt, Israel Zangwill.[124] In a series of articles in *Die Welt* he defended the East Africa project. He called for settlement in East Africa as an immediate relief measure, pointing out that Palestine was not a land without its own problems for the Jews, not the least of them being the fact that the Jews constituted a minority within the country's population.[125]

While these controversies raged within the Zionist world, Weizmann consistently toed Ussishkin's line. He echoed the Vilna Conference's resolution that "all so-called Territorialists" be declared "unconstitutional elements, even though they had the perfidy to smuggle themselves into the party by way of a Shekel."[126] Yet, unlike in his Geneva years, Weizmann was now a more cautious man, not ready to abandon everything and totally immerse himself in Zionist work. Berthold Feiwel wrote in late January that a group of Zionei Zion, mostly former members of the Democratic Faction, were planning to make Berlin the headquarters of the movement. They even visualized various departments and offered Weizmann the chance to involve himself with those of organization and propaganda. A year earlier he would have been delighted by the initiative as well as the roster of members enlisted by Feiwel. This time, however, he replied politely that department or no department, he had no interest in moving to Berlin and could be just as useful in Manchester.[127] He had been delegated by the Vilna Conference to conduct Zionei Zion propaganda in England,[128] but when it came to an open conflict between the Zionei Zion and the territorialists in England, he was a bit uneasy. It was one thing to debate Greenberg or Zangwill within the ranks of the movement as an individual yet quite another to organize a separate group to fight them. Moreover, he was not quite sure he wanted to go into battle in the company of some of the English Zionei Zion, who seemed to have dubious intellectual and Zionist motivations.

On April 24, 1905, on the initiative of J. K. Goldbloom, a preparatory meeting of the Palestinian Zionist Association (Merkaz Zionei Eretz Israel) was held in London. Moses Gaster was elected president of its executive committee and Weizmann, who attended the meeting, was a member of the larger committee.[129] The main aim of the new organization was to help elect Zionei Zion delegates to the congress. "I have . . . joined the committee, albeit with a heavy heart. Not to join meant remaining outside, in a difficult, isolated position. To join meant temporary association with people who, with very few exceptions, have little in common with me."[130] It went against his principles that differences in the movement be resolved by creating separate organizations. If successful, Gaster would create a competing organization to the EZF rather than retaining the Palestinian Zionist Association as a lobby group within it. At the same time, Weizmann could not yet afford to alienate the volatile rabbi and reluctantly agreed to take part. But London also had an invigorating influence on him after the quiet months in Manchester. He was once again at a center of Zionist activities, seeing friends and being flattered by invitations to speak in cities.[131] Even before the formation of the Palestinian Zionist Association, he had tried unsuccessfully to block Zangwill from delivering a speech in Manchester; when his resolution failed, he immediately proposed that a second meeting, following Zangwill's, take place with a Zionist speaker. This resolution was passed unanimously.[132] However, he accepted an invitation to dinner in honor of Zangwill, probably since it was given by Charles Dreyfus.[133] The English Zionists had standards of etiquette of their own, and even Zangwill's opponents appreciated that he was Anglo-Jewry's most prestigious personality. Weizmann, on the other hand, did not hesitate to lock horns with the opponents of Zionei Zion. Unabashed by Zangwill's enthusiastic reception in Manchester on April 8, Weizmann declared to the same assembly[134] that he disagreed with Zangwill's every word. "I spoke for three minutes, stating that if Moses had chanced to be in this hall he would have recognized his Egyptian slaves. Nobody protested, some even applauded. Yesterday . . . I spoke against Africa before a crowd of 600, with the same success. A crowd will always remain a crowd!"[135] A month later, at a meeting organized in Manchester by Barrow Belisha and Nathan Laski—the latter was one of the most prominent members of the community[136]—at which the speakers urged that East Africa be given serious consideration,[137] Weizmann got up and told those assembled that "their enterprises were doomed in advance, as they know neither the people nor their needs. The 'poor Jews of the East,' having waited 2,000 years for Laski and Belisha to call a meeting to render aid, will go on waiting without being unduly bothered by the resolutions adopted at the session." He was quite pleased with himself: "This struck the meeting like lightning, and covered it with ridicule."[138] This was the kind of report he knew would please Gaster, with whom he constantly tried to curry favor. Moreover, it was written in the style the *Haham* himself would probably have employed. It is quite unlikely, however, that a meeting organized by territorialists would have allowed Weizmann to "cover it with ridicule." Nevertheless, it took courage to present a different point of view before such a crowd.

Though it had clearly failed, the East Africa project was not yet dead. The Grosses Aktions-Comité meetings in Vienna from January 4 to 6, 1905, decided that an extraordinary congress, to run concurrently with the Seventh Zionist Congress, would settle the East Africa issue.[139] All factions now awaited the official report of the East Africa Survey Expedition. Money for the expedition was eventually secured by Leopold Greenberg from a gentile woman, Mrs. E. A. Gordon, who donated the necessary two thousand pounds anonymously.[140] The expedition, composed of Major A. St. Hill Gibbons, Professor Alfred Kaiser, and Nahum Wilbush, finally sailed for Mombassa on December 28, 1904.[141] After surveying the territory offered by the British government for almost two months, the official report was submitted to the Grosses Aktions-Comité on May 16, 1905. But prior to this date Wilbush and Kaiser had already informed Warburg, chairman of the East Africa Commission, that they found the area proposed to be unsuitable for settlement.[142] Gibbons, on the other hand, remained equivocal, giving conflicting assessments of the area to the press, to Leopold Greenberg, and to the Foreign Office, but his official report reflected his own doubts as to mass settlement of the area.[143] GAC convened in Vienna on May 22 to 24 to hear the report of the expedition and to make final arrangements for the Seventh Zionist Congress. It decided to recommend that the congress reject the East Africa proposal, though GAC also authorized a committee to be appointed that would confer with other Jewish bodies to determine whether they had an interest in Jewish settlement in the proposed territory.[144] Further, the Grosses Aktions-Comité decided to recommend to the congress a triumvirate to lead the organization, composed of Max Nordau, David Wolffsohn, and Otto Warburg.[145]

The Seventh Zionist Congress was to open at the end of July 1905. Though GAC had rejected East Africa, the final decision was to be made by the congress. Thus, each side redoubled its efforts to elect its delegates. The debates and discussions between the territorialists and the Zionei Zion took place wherever Zionists resided and, of course, also in England, the unofficial headquarters of the territorialists.[146] Like Ussishkin, Weizmann was also pleased by Wolffsohn's election to the triumvirate and hoped that the latter might bring peace and harmony to the movement;[147] this impression was strengthened after Wolffsohn's visit to Manchester on June 4.[148] His aim had been to cool the heated tempers in the English Zionist movement, yet it was too late. While Zangwill and Greenberg attacked the East Africa Survey Expedition and the decision of the Grosses Aktions-Comité,[149] Weizmann mounted a counter campaign, especially in the provinces.[150] He took part in the semiannual conference of the English Zionist Federation, which met in London on June 12, mostly debating the resolution of GAC, and sat on the committee which approved the resolutions, declaring that Palestine alone could be the goal of the Zionist movement.[151] Weizmann never left the hall and participated in "everything." Not the least of his accomplishments was to effect a temporary reconciliation between Gaster and Greenberg.[152] He worked hard to elect Zionei Zion to the congress; he even succeeded in having Berthold Feiwel elected over Zangwill in Leeds.[153] Weizmann and Dreyfus were elected as the delegates from Manchester.[154] Moreover, Weizmann's popularity had not waned among the Zionists in Eastern Europe even during his one-year absence. Thus, he received mandates from Kovno, Uman, Novorossiisk, Kharkov, and other places as well.[155]

He had more than enough mandates in his pocket but insufficient funds to finance the trip to the Continent. A year of hard work in Manchester still left him as poor as he had been the previous year, when he traveled to Vienna to attend the Grosses Aktions-Comité meetings; much of his modest income went for the support of four of his siblings. Yet he would not borrow money from Dreyfus or Perkin. He insisted on maintaining a strictly professional relationship with them, keeping up appearances as befitted a respected academician. Moses Gaster may have had many faults, but he was also a warm and generous man and even discreet in personal matters. As a fellow East European he could better empathize with the younger man's difficult circumstances. Once again Weizmann approached the *Haham* for a loan,[156] which the latter advanced forthwith.[157] With sufficient funds at his disposal, he could now afford to take his summer vacation from the university and participate in the pre-congress activities of the Zionei Zion and the Russian *Landsmanschaft*. The Zionei Zion had won a clear majority of the mandates, and two hundred of the delegates gathered in Freiburg-in-Breisgau from July 21 to 23 in order to prepare the resolutions they would bring to the congress. Weizmann was elected to the presidium of the conference, further solidifying the recognition accorded him by the Russian Zionists at Vilna. Ussishkin chaired the sessions. Weizmann was pessimistic about the outcome of the meeting, seeing only "great chaos. A mass of people has turned up of all shades, views and species, so it is going to be very difficult to achieve a unity of outlook . . . The meeting has a juvenile look, and so has its mentality."[158] Nevertheless, after two days it was proposed that the congress affirm the inviolability of the Basel Program, recognize the need for immediate practical work in Palestine, and resolve that the Uganda scheme be dismissed and that territorialists be removed from the World Zionist Organization. It is easy to see Ussishkin's hand in these resolutions, reminiscent of those arrived at in Vilna in January 1905. As soon as the Freiburg Conference ended its deliberations on July 23, the delegates traveled to Basel, where the Russian *Vorkonferenz* was held during two stormy meetings on July 24 and 25. The three hundred Zionei Zion and eighty territorialists who attended this *Vorkonferenz* failed to reach agreement on the composition of the presidium and dispersed within a few hours.[159] These sessions presaged the stormy Seventh Zionist Congress which took place from July 27 to August 2 and was attended by more than seven hundred delegates, the largest Zionist congress ever held.

The congress had two main issues on its agenda: the East Africa project and the election of a new leadership for the World Zionist Organization. It was presided over by Max Nordau and five vice presidents, among them Wolffsohn and Bernstein-Kohan. Ussishkin was elected as a member of the presidium and Weizmann was selected as secretary/translator for Yiddish.[160] The first day was devoted to a eulogy for Herzl, delivered by Nordau, who in the afternoon session spoke about the miserable conditions of the Jews in Russia. Alexander Marmorek presented the official report of SAC on the state of the movement, which, despite the crises afflicting Jewry, had grown to 140,000 shekel-paying members.[161] The following two and a half days were devoted to the extraordinary congress on the East Africa project, which preceded the congress proper. Following reports by Warburg and Greenberg dealing with the British offer and the expedition itself, the debate began with a speech by Israel Zangwill, who skillfully defended settlement in Uganda and rejected the report of the expedition. Uganda, he claimed, was in our hands and thus constituted the realization of half the Basel Program;[162] Zangwill tried to steer the discussion away from a choice between East Africa and Palestine, promising that with Uganda in Jewish hands it would be easier to work for a realization of Zionism.[163] One hundred and twenty delegates registered in advance in order to speak in the debate that followed, of whom eight, representing the various points of view, were allowed to do so. The socialist-territorialist point of view, emphasizing the social nature of the Jewish Question and the need for an urgent solution to the plight of the Jews in Eastern Europe, was powerfully presented by, among others, Nachman Syrkin, while the main spokesman for Zionei Zion was Yehiel Tschlenow. The answer to Uganda, said Tschlenow, is no! "The core of our program is to create for the Jewish people a home in Palestine secured by public law."[164] To those who said that Palestine was unsuitable for settlement he suggested they go to Uganda.[165]

None of the arguments advanced in the debate were new, but they needed to be reiterated once more before the congress could come to a final decision. On July 30 Alexander Marmorek proposed a resolution, in the name of the Grosses Aktions-Comité, which basically incorporated Menahem Ussishkin's resolution, as formulated at Freiburg, reiterated on the first day of the congress,[166] and amended by an expression of thanks to the British government. The basic principles of rejection of any territory outside of Palestine and the insistence that only those who adhere to the Basel Program have a place in the World Zionist

Organization[167] was a clear message to the territorialists and Ugandists, practically forcing them out of the World Zionist Organization. After this resolution was overwhelmingly accepted by the congress,[168] Zangwill made one last attempt to impugn the constitutionality of the verdict, alleging that it ran counter to the statutes of the Jewish Colonial Trust.[169] When Nordau rejected his claim, Zangwill made one final statement, his last before a Zionist congress: "Herzl told me that the Seventh [Zionist] Congress will be the last congress and I hope that it will be so."[170] Syrkin was not to be outdone by Zangwill, declaring that he and his group of Zionists-socialists were leaving the congress and urging all territorialists to follow them.[171] Zangwill and his followers were taken by surprise but had no choice but to follow suit.

The twenty-eight delegates who refused to accept the verdict of the congress, as well as others who joined them, immediately convened in a separate conference (July 30–August 1), where they decided to establish an independent Jewish Territorial Organization with Israel Zangwill as its president, and with the support of Nachman Syrkin—who was elected to the executive—and his Zionist-socialist followers. The aim of the new organization as outlined in Basel was "to secure a territory upon an autonomous basis for Jews who cannot, or will not, remain in the lands in which they live at present. To achieve this end, the Organization proposes (a) to unite all Jews who are in agreement with this object; (b) to enter into relations with governments and public and private institutions; (c) to create financial institutions, labor-bureaus and other instruments that may be found necessary."[172] For a few months the Jewish Territorial Organization coexisted peacefully with the World Zionist Organization, after which it became a definite diplomatic threat; bitter controversies ensued between them, which subsided only after the Balfour Declaration.[173] Few thoughtful Zionists were truly happy about Zangwill's secession from the Zionist movement, and Zangwill himself was not eager for the break. He had toiled faithfully in the service of Zionism since Herzl's days. His brilliant style, sharp wit, and wide-ranging contacts with politicians and every major Jewish institution made him an important asset. Now that he was in opposition, he could—and did—cause harm to the Zionist movement in England and elsewhere.

But these were troubles for the future. The immediate problems facing the regular sessions of the congress, which convened at the close of the extraordinary congress on July 30, were of an organizational nature. Before the final decision on the composition of the movement's leadership, the congress listened closely to the reports of Otto Warburg and Selig Soskin on the activities of the Committee for the Investigation of Palestine.[174] These were followed, the next day, by Ussishkin's proposal that, concurrent with diplomatic activities and as a basis for them, the World Zionist Organization devote its efforts to systematic work in Palestine through multifaceted research, promotion of agriculture and industry, cultural and economic improvement of Palestinian Jewry through the infusion of new intellectual forces, and a striving for correctives in the administrative and legal areas necessary for improving conditions in Palestine. He also called for rejection of philanthropic and planless colonization *(Kleinkolonisation)*. The resolution was carried with a few amendments.[175] After a great deal of public debate and behind-the-scenes dealings, the congress elected the Engeres Aktions-Comité, composed of Wolffsohn (chairman), Warburg, Bernstein-Kohan, Kann, Ussishkin, Greenberg, and Alexander Marmorek; the seat of the World Zionist Organization was moved from Vienna to Cologne.[176] In general, the election of the Grosses Aktions-Comité proceeded peacefully—until it came to the selection of the English candidates. Gaster was originally a candidate for this body but met with great opposition and was dropped. Weizmann, who had been elected by the English delegation to the standing committee, was now, for the first time, also elected to the Grosses Aktions-Comité, together with Francis Montefiore, Joseph Cowen (who was elected despite stiff opposition), Charles Dreyfus, and Jacob Moser.[177] Gaster did not easily forget this slight and later accused Weizmann of not having done enough to get him elected to the Grosses Aktions-Comité.

Weizmann's role in the proceedings of the Seventh Zionist Congress was minimal. The stenographic protocol records his name only as a member of the secretariat and as a candidate for office. Yet for the first time he was elected as one of fifty-two members of the Grosses Aktions-Comité, a recognition of his genuine new status in the movement and an honor he hardly expected.[178] A year earlier he had not even been of sufficient stature to be informed of decisions arrived at by the Russian Zionist leadership, and only half a year earlier he was made to cool his heels in the corridors while members of GAC met in Vienna. Now he was the Russians' most trusted man in England, with official recognition to boot. True, being a member of GAC was not the most elevated position in the movement, but Weizmann was a man of ambition and this was a beginning. Now, at least, he could demand information as his right, no longer depending on friends to throw him a few crumbs of gossip. Henceforth he could not be easily dismissed as a leader of a fringe student group.

By all accounts he should have been satisfied. His professional and Zionist careers were at last on an even keel. Any objective assessment of Weizmann's first year in England would have had to call it a great success, and yet—with the exception of his initial euphoria during July and early August 1904—he had been profoundly unhappy during these past twelve months, and for a good part of the rest of 1905 and 1906 as well. "What a difficult year it has been!" he wrote to Ussishkin in mid-June 1905. "The thought alone is frightening, and I couldn't go through it all again. You cannot imagine what it means for an intellectual to live in the English provinces and work with the local Jews. It's hellish torture! I am left without a single sound nerve."[179] The following day he wrote to Vera, "Each day seems an infinity—I can no longer do anything. Verochka, I am afraid that you will find that I have aged greatly.

I have had, and continue to have, many worries and feel that this year has left its mark on me."[180]

How can one explain these statements in view of his seeming success? What were those things which weighed on him, depressed him, and left him profoundly discontented? Perhaps the clue can be found in a letter he wrote to Vera three days after his initial arrival in Manchester. "You must understand, my dear, that every familiar sound reaching me here is three times more dear. I have to live among alien people here, among strangers, and at times one feels rather sad."[181] This basic feeling of alienation did not quite leave him throughout his years in Manchester,[182] but it was particularly strong during the first period of adjustment. The abrupt transition from Geneva to Manchester allowed Weizmann to further his scientific career but demanded of him an emotional adjustment to an alien environment. The transition from the almost bohemian lifestyle he led in Geneva among student circles, in which he occupied a certain position of leadership, to the straitlaced and rather stiff formality of England was more than superficial. It also entailed an intellectual and emotional dislocation. No longer was he able to spend his evenings and nights in coffeehouses and private rooms debating the issues of the day. It was now work and more work and no one with whom to share his innermost thoughts. In England he had to keep up appearances with his co-workers and employers, pretending to be infinitely grateful for the opportunities they afforded him. His innermost thoughts could now only be shared with Vera by mail. His anger and frustration, his disappointments, and his complaints with respect to his new environment poured forth in letter after letter. His homesickness and loneliness were now projected onto his environment, with very little room for fine distinctions; he tended to paint everything black.[183] His observations are those of an alien without much sympathy for and emotional involvement with his surroundings.

England had been a great disappointment to Weizmann. The bureaucracy in the universities and elsewhere angered him greatly. "No one hurries in England and wheels turn slowly . . . and this is why they have fallen behind. I must confess that we used to have false notions about the English and England . . ."[184] Though he often complained of poverty, he himself recognized that it was not extreme; it was the impoverishment of a young professional man.[185] Social conditions in the society around him rarely concerned him, but on one occasion, when he was overwhelmed by a scene he must have witnessed that morning, he commented to Vera on the life of the British workers, which did not add to the glory of England. "Each morning I cross the working-class district of Manchester and observe the faces of workers gathering at the factory gates, monster that it is, sapping at their vitality all day long. What infinitely deep life-drama can be read on those emaciated, pale faces! I see men going through life grinding their teeth, and I sense that they are right, incontrovertibly! How horrifying!"[186] A few months later he ex-

panded on the injustice of the class stratification in England, while at the
same time lamenting the lack of intellectual vigor in the society as a whole.
"English society as such lacks the intellectual vigor one finds in Germany or France. The English labor movement, with one and a half million adherents, has not produced even one Jaurès or Bebel. The country
is governed by an oligarchy of the ancient hereditary nobility, and
everything is made to fit the system. The main centres of education in
England, Oxford and Cambridge, with their unrivalled resources and institutions, also incorporate countless relics from the Scholastic epoch.
People like us, and myself particularly, find all this very difficult to accept . . ."[187]

Except for his first two weeks there, he never learned to like Manchester.
From the very start, of course, he disliked the smog[188] and the foul
weather that persisted through a good part of the year.[189] But his feelings toward the city ran much deeper than that. Only a year after his
arrival, when he had already achieved some standing at the university
and within the Zionist ranks, he was "frightened" of having to spend a
long time there,[190] and a year later, on the eve of his marriage, he wrote
to Vera with resignation and pathos: "I am merely 'living out' the days
I am forced to spend here, and shall leave Manchester with pleasure at
the earliest moment . . . we shan't be spending all our life among these
people. We shall never be able to accept this kind of people, and shall
always feel cut off from all that is alive in our own world. The realization
that you will be obliged to live in this unattractive, cold and grim atmosphere is of course the sole explanation for my dejection. But we shall
do our best to create our own world, a world of our own dreams and
ideals inaccessible to others."[191]

What made matters worse was the fact that he also had no use for
local Jewry, non-Zionists as well as Zionists. "I must tell you," he wrote
Menahem Ussishkin in typical exaggerated fashion, "that conditions here
are frightful, in fact beyond description. You are dealing with the dregs
of Russian Jewry, a dull, ignorant crowd that knows nothing of such issues as Zionism . . . there is no Press to speak of: the *Jewish Chronicle*
and *Jewish World* are mean little papers belonging to Rothschild and Co.,
and the plebeian Yiddish press is even worse."[192] He considered English
Jews devoid of any aesthetic and intellectual sense: "There is none of
that poetical tone perceptible in Russian Jewry, the poetry compounded
of deep, centuries-old suffering that can be detected even in everyday
life. Materialist, commercial England has succeeded in burning out
everything exalted in our Jews, so that the creation of a Jewish intelligentsia here has become an impossible task. But it is dreadful, indeed
agonizingly painful, to have to admit that all is rotten and condemned
without hope."[193] Toward the close of his first year in Manchester he
summarized his view of local Jewry: ". . . I have been disappointed by
many things, first and foremost by life in England . . . Worse, however,
I haven't yet managed to accept local Jewry. I am afraid that when I am
able to, it will mean my own deterioration. It is difficult to accept igno-

rance, rudeness and triviality, and it is difficult to fight against them."[194] He kept on pounding mercilessly at Anglo-Jewry.

> With every passing day the people here lose what little interest they once held for me. Originally I used to observe them as one does something novel, but once I had seen them as they are I realized there was no point of contact between us. The Cheethamites are a mob, a rabble of the downtrodden, and those outside who consider themselves the betters of "our poor ghetto brothers" are in fact worse. Their Zionism is empty, a mere amusement. Obliged as I am to work in such a milieu after being used to something entirely different, it is little wonder that occasionally I want to weep.[195]

Underlying Weizmann's bitter contempt and disgust for life in England was a deep-seated perception that he lacked any kind of intellectual affinity with those around him, whether in the provinces or in London. His only intellectual satisfaction came from his work at the university, but this was insufficient. He still lacked the status to associate freely with his senior colleagues. He had no real circle of cultured friends; it was particularly painful after the rich social life of Geneva. This is well illustrated in the following letter to Vera, wherein he tried to explain the reason for his despondency: ". . . I used to be concerned exclusively with scholars and students, people untouched by life. I saw the 'real world' only when I was on the road, conducting propaganda, and even then I saw it merely as a pageant. All is changed now. Everything I see around me is 'real' and so dreary as to be devoid of the faintest poetical haze . . ."[196] He was disgusted with polite, meaningless conversations and found that he was bored by those he met and with whom he worked. "The people surrounding me display so little understanding, so little sensitivity to the train of my thoughts and feelings! They disgust me. Even the period when I had no acquaintances seems preferable to this. Meeting any of them and sharing their interests for a moment or two makes me feel petty, and two hours of chitchat makes my heart ache . . ."[197]

Yet there was finally a ray of light in this intellectual and cultural wilderness. At the meeting on April 30, 1905, at which Weizmann ridiculed Nathan Laski and Barrow Belisha for their support of the East Africa project, one member of the audience clapped furiously. As soon as the meeting was over, he approached Weizmann and invited him to his home. This was none other than Samuel Alexander,[198] a Jewish professor of philosophy at the University of Manchester since 1893 and author of *Moral Order and Progress* (1889), in its day the best systematic general treatise on evolutionary ethics in the English language.[199] Weizmann jumped at the invitation of this congenial and erudite man and was not disappointed. The forty-six-year-old professor was a bachelor who lived in one of Manchester's more affluent neighborhoods. Weizmann wrote Vera that "his home is so pleasant that I immediately felt like an old friend. We talked till 1 A.M. (starting from 7 P.M.) about Zionism, about Jews, about a Jewish University. I haven't had such a conversation since I left my own milieu and came to England. He is not a Zionist, but neither is he an opponent; he inclines toward Zionism and is certainly anti-African. I am very happy that I now have a friend to whom I can unburden myself."[200]

Meeting Samuel Alexander was exciting, and with time their contacts became more frequent, slowly blooming into a rewarding friendship. For the time being these meetings could only occasionally relieve Weizmann of his sense of loneliness and isolation. On a daily basis he was supported and sustained mainly by Vera; until their marriage in August 1906, most of his letters were addressed to her; more than any other document, they reveal his innermost struggles and triumphs, his disappointments and joys, his changing moods and achievements. Their correspondence from 1904 to 1906 has some resemblance to that of 1902—there are the same kinds of reproaches for failing to reply immediately—but on the whole the later letters also show a relationship that had matured, in which the initial passion had been somewhat blunted. The long separation could not but take its toll on their relationship, and their mutual frustrations were intermittently punctuated by bursts of anger or petulance, especially on the part of Weizmann, who felt more isolated and lonely than Vera, lacking the sustenance of such friends as Berthold Feiwel and Esther Shneerson, who in the summer of 1902 helped assuage the pain of separation from Vera. On the whole, there is little joy that is expressed, especially in those letters written by Weizmann. Vera, too, had her own problems. The result is a correspondence between two people who are extremely nervous, anxious, and depressed, constantly complaining to each other of their low morale, their nerves, and their worries. The letters are permeated by a strong undercurrent of sadness and tension, which were only partially alleviated when they managed to see each other from time to time.

Early in July 1904, just prior to Weizmann's move to England, Vera traveled to Rostov-on-Don for summer vacation. En route she visited Weizmann's parents in Pinsk for the first time and was warmly received. But the atmosphere in Rostov was quite different. Her grandmother had died a short while earlier and her parents were also in poor physical and emotional health;[201] her father was at the end of his days.[202] While dealing with these problems, Vera missed a few days of writing. Though he sensed that something was wrong, Weizmann, righteously claiming that he did not miss a single day, berated Vera and her family for not writing.[203] The tension between Weizmann and Vera increased whenever they did not receive letters from one another, contributing to their loneliness, which was made even less bearable by the intellectual and social isolation prevailing in Rostov and Manchester. One of Vera's letters read:

> Chaimchik, my friend, don't be angry with me for not writing; I am punished enough each time I read a letter, charged with worry and anxiety from you. How could you think that I was putting you to a test? Is it possible that you don't trust me? How can I atone! I give you my solemn word that

this will not happen again. I know that at the start of your life there, you are bound to have a rather hard time. Alone, lonely, no one to care for you. Would I play tricks on you at a time like this? I embrace you and ask you to forget it . . . It is close to four years since we began to love each other but have had to live apart from each other for such a long time. So let's try, Chaimchik, my dearest friend, to ease the terrible time ahead of us and make it more bearable by sharing our every thought and feeling.[204]

The one cheerful note that made the separation a bit more tolerable was planning for the next time they would see each other.[205]

Both Vera and Weizmann had close ties with their own families and were anxious to find ways to bring joy into their lives. Vera wanted Weizmann to write to her family and Weizmann was insistent that she write to his parents. Moreover, whenever Vera traveled to and from Rostov, Weizmann tried to persuade her to visit his family in Pinsk, an obligation she would have rather done without. She did not feel at ease in his parents' house without Weizmann,[206] but knowing Weizmann's opinion on this matter, she tried to forestall the inevitable with solid excuses. It was not that she disliked going to Pinsk, she wrote Weizmann, but his parents would be dissatisfied with a short visit, and she preferred to spend the extra time with him; moreover, she had to make other stops on the way: at his sister's house in Warsaw, with their friends in Berlin, and on top of everything else she was traveling with a friend.[207] But ultimately Weizmann prevailed by applying strong psychological pressure.

> My mother is of course puzzled at your not being able to find a few days for them . . . My poor parents have had little enough joy during the past year . . . Perhaps you really find it unpleasant to be in their company. After all, they are my parents, and not yours. There's no need to tell you that I would have preferred you to spend a few days less with me—however precious to me every day with you is—and that you should have gone to Pinsk. But you have deprived me even of the possibility of asking this of you. I am most fearfully upset, the tears are choking me. I felt very hurt and bitter after the letter from mother, who loves you so much. But enough. If you will feel like doing so, you will travel by way of Pinsk.[208]

Of course, Vera had no choice. "Chaimchik, I will stop in Pinsk and will remain there as long as my ticket allows me to. Only don't be sad and don't suffer. You cried when you wrote this letter. I know it. I shall write to Pinsk at once and ask them to forgive me . . ."[209]

Vera also had her moments of exasperation. It was difficult enough to keep up with Weizmann's almost daily letters. In addition, she was emotionally drained by problems in her own family, including severe financial strain,[210] and the suicide, in February 1905, of her brother-in-law Maxim, husband of her elder sister. She was also anxious about her forthcoming medical examinations. Their correspondence at this stage reveals little genuine intellectual exchange; it primarily consists of reports of ongoing activities. In particular, Weizmann's letters to Vera read like memoranda for future reference. They concentrate on an intense examination of their relationship. Reflecting honestly on her feelings for Weizmann after a separation of two months, Vera exclaimed:

> . . . lately I began to feel distant toward you. I am quite serious, darling
> . . . The distance that separates us removes me from you, and I must talk
> with you repeatedly in order to avoid this feeling of aloneness. Chaimchik,
> I don't want you to think that I love you less. No, not at all. But it begins
> to seem that we are not as close, as though we don't belong to each other.
> I too, baby, want terribly to see you, and the time gets nearer and nearer
> and shrinks even more when I think of the lovely days we shall spend to-
> gether. My dear friend, I'll make you forget all your troubles. I shall em-
> brace you, caress you, and for a few moments we shall live only with one
> another. All right, kitten?[211]

Just prior to commencing the academic year in Geneva, Vera came to Manchester on October 10 and remained twelve days. During her brief visit Weizmann continued his work at the university, seeing her every evening.[212] The brief and infrequent interludes when they could be with each other eased the tension between them; such periods were usually followed by a warmer and more empathic correspondence. In the afterglow of their moments together they both remembered with pleasure the good times they had shared.[213] But there were also specific issues around which there were tense moments. Vera, for example, was quite annoyed with the carelessness with which Weizmann treated her medical studies. During her sojourn in Manchester he had promised to investigate whether she could complete her medical studies in England. Weizmann could, when he wished, pursue a task with tenacity and relentlessness until he accomplished his goal. It was obvious that he was lax about the whole matter, sending Vera information based on casual conversations and raising her hopes for a continuation of her studies in England on the basis of very little evidence.[214] Vera was incensed. "I don't want information from private sources, since I can't rely on it. This time I want to be precisely and reliably informed."[215] She persisted in letter after letter, sending him materials relating to her studies, including recommendations from her professors and other documents, but she could not move Weizmann to follow through on his promises.[216] It took Weizmann three months to find out that she would need to study two years at the University of Manchester before she could even be permitted to sit for her final examinations;[217] two additional months passed before he informed her that the regulations were even more stringent in London.[218] He ignored altogether her request to inquire at the University of Edinburgh.[219]

In general, it is curious how casual and forgetful Weizmann was about certain aspects of Vera's life. Though they were born within a day of each other,[220] he forgot to congratulate her on time—two years in a row—on the occasion of her birthday, making lame excuses for this negligence.[221] More serious, perhaps, was his total refusal to take seriously

Vera's Zionist activities in the Hashahar group in Geneva. In letter after letter Vera reported the latest gossip within the group.[222] She could reasonably assume that as a founder of the group in which he had for years been the most important member, and which gave him such a tearful farewell party on the eve of his departure for England,[223] he would display some interest. But starting in November 1904 he repeatedly expressed a total lack of concern for the group's welfare. In mid-December 1904 he went to Geneva for three weeks, stipulating in advance that he did not want to be dragged into Hashahar's affairs.[224] A few weeks later he condescendingly wrote the following letter to Vera, who was now a leading member of Hashahar: "Your information about Geneva happenings made a very bad impression on me. I feel ashamed that all these people, who in reality are engaged in nonsense, nevertheless believe they are all the while saving Israel. What has our little circle come to! Ten members divided into twenty parties, each detesting the other."[225]

For the most part Weizmann and Vera were so obsessed by their own relationship that they could not devote much time in their letters to other issues. As the time between their meetings wore on, they interpreted and misinterpreted each letter or lack thereof: "Chaimchik," wrote Vera, "there are times when I get a peculiar feeling that something has changed in our relationship . . . I can only explain it by our nervous state, which I ascribe to the abnormality of our life, the fact that we are separated for such long periods of time. I hope, Chaimchik, that you'll get rid of any such feelings."[226] This was a theme which obviously occupied Weizmann as well, one to which he constantly returned, trying to explain to himself as well as to Vera what was wrong. "Distance, and the period of separation, have somehow made you cease to understand me—I don't want to say love me—and I feel hurt, sad, ashamed and sick at heart . . . Everything seems to be slipping away from me . . . my life is monotonous and perhaps unattractive; its everyday side cannot interest you. The glitter that enriched my life in former years, the old sensations, have vanished. I am old!"[227] A few days later he returned to this theme: "When I was in Geneva my life was richer, eventful. This is what I meant by glitter. I was a 'public figure.' You 'forgave' me a great deal for the sake of those moments when I interested you as a public figure. Now it's no longer so. I have become a quiet and hardworking drudge . . . The people I dealt with, and deal with now, those with whom I live and on whom I *depend*, have nothing in common with me. I am doing all this just for the sake of our life together. Only life with you is meaningful for me, and it is only by believing in it that I can believe in my own survival . . . The moment my faith in your love is really shaken I shall consider my life as finished . . ."[228] Summing up his year in Manchester and their relationship, he wrote with obvious agitation a letter which reads like a confession, attempting to explain the reason for their estrangement:

You are mistaken, my dear, if you believe that there are times when I don't love you so much and am as a consequence writing less frequently. As happens so often these past weeks, I feel that if I set myself to it I could write you a whole volume, yet when I touch the pen I can't get a solitary word down. I have become so depressed, and feel that I look so much older, that I'm afraid of our meeting, lest it cause you pain. The year spent in England has left its mark on me . . . If you were to ask me the reason for this mood, which started last Christmas, I wouldn't know exactly how to define it . . . I find my surroundings stifling. I can't acclimatize myself to the life here, nor can I imagine that we shall live here permanently. I should like to work my way up to a professorship and then go to Palestine . . . I feel a stranger everywhere, all the time, despite my superficial adaptability.[229]

And yet, despite the occasional harsh words and disappointments, they found that their love had somehow matured. On the eve of the Jewish New Year Weizmann wrote, "I find, to my great and profound joy, that we learned to understand each other better and more deeply this year, faithfully and immediately identifying with each other in spirit."[230] Throughout their difficult and lonely separation it was clear to both that their partnership was to be a lifelong venture. Their friends—Berthold Feiwel and Esther Shneerson, Zvi Aberson and Rosa Grinblatt, Benjamin Herzfeld and Esther Weinberg—were married or about to marry. They watched enviously, but they also knew that their turn would soon come.[231]

XII

Wary Adjustment

Throughout 1905 and much of 1906 one issue overshadowed Weizmann's personal miseries as well as his daily concerns with Zionism and chemistry: the fate of the Jewish people in Eastern Europe. By 1905 a number of social groups were up in arms against tsarism[1]—not only students, professional people, workers, and peasants but also gentry and liberal-minded businessmen, as well as elements of the national minorities, who seized the occasion to rebel against the oppressive policies of the Russian state.[2] These groups were naturally joined by organized political parties, such as the Constitutional Democratic Party (Cadet), the Social Democratic Party (SD), and the Socialist Revolutionary Party (SR), to mention only the most important ones. Though each was rent by internal strife and was intensely competitive, these parties were united in their determination to overthrow or radically alter the tsarist regime.[3]

The tide of opposition finally exploded on January 9, 1905, in what came to be known as "Bloody Sunday," when the police fired at a huge demonstration of workers, led by the priest George Gapon, carrying icons and portraits of the tsar and singing hymns, marching peacefully to the Winter Palace to beg the tsar for help and redress of their political and economic condition. Scores were killed and hundreds were wounded.[4] Gapon fled, and by the end of Bloody Sunday the Gaponovschina was dead as a political movement. But the massacre led to a great outburst of indignation in the country and gave another boost to the revolutionary movement.[5]

Despite attempts by Tsar Nicholas II to quell the ferment in the country by canceling redemption payments, proclaiming religious tolerance, and, finally, by issuing on August 19, 1905, an imperial manifesto creating an elective Duma with consultative powers, the tide of revolution grew unabated. The summer of 1905 witnessed new strikes and mass peasant uprisings in many provinces, culminating in a mammoth strike in October, at which point Nicholas II and his government finally capitulated.[6] At the suggestion of Prime Minister Sergei Witte, the tsar issued the October Manifesto on October 17, which guaranteed civil liberties to the Russians, announced a Duma with the legislative function of passing or rejecting all proposed laws, and promised a further expansion of the new order in Russia.[7] The October Manifesto split the opposition. The liberals and moderates were satisfied, while the radicals, such as the social democrats, wanted a constituent assembly, not handouts from above. The government began its counterattack with the arrest of members of the St. Petersburg Soviet. In the course of the winter, punitive expeditions and summary courts-martial restored order in many troubled areas. The extreme right joined the army and the police; right-wing activist groups, known as the Black Hundreds, beat and killed Jews, Poles, Finns, Armenians, and the intelligentsia. Protofascist in nature, this newly awakened right flourished on ethnic and religious hatred and was often aided and abetted by the police as well as the Russian Ortho-dox Church.[8]

For the Jews of Russia, the events leading up to and following the rev-olution of 1905 were punctuated by pogroms and ever greater blood-baths. As soon as he read about the aborted January demonstration, Weizmann's sense of the Russian way of coping with crises alerted him to what the revolutionary activities would mean for the Jews:

> I am absolutely shattered by the news from Russia . . . As I read the news-papers tears filled my eyes—it is really terrible. *Il sonne comme l'histoire*. Blood-stained pages of Russian history; that is, not only Russian but also world history and, partly, our own Jewish history too . . . I am horror-stricken by the realization that this conflagration which broke out in Petersburg . . . will spread to the provinces, and that torrents of Jewish blood will also flow. This mixing of the two streams of blood, the Russian and the Jewish, fills me with fear. All day yesterday, and today, I felt as if I were going out of my mind and God only knows to what degree my nervous system has bro-ken down . . .[9]

What was particularly frustrating to him was the fact that he could only rely on *The Times, The Jewish Chronicle*, and other news services.[10] He was anxious for more detailed information. Throughout the year he spoke of his desire to go to Russia in order not to lose contact with Russian Jewry.[11] Even Vera, who could attend the mass meetings of the exiled Russian revolutionaries in Geneva, was somehow closer to the events occurring in Russia. Knowing how anxious Weizmann was for news, she faithfully reported on those public gatherings. One of these accounts of a meeting which took place on January 26, 1905, is worth reproducing for the light it sheds on the atmosphere on the Continent:

> There were three thousand people. All parties, nationalities, men and women. Professor Wice, head of the local Social Democratic Party, presided. He spoke beautifully and very emotionally against tsarism, Russian absolutism, etc. . . . He was followed by Professor Milhaud, who also spoke with great feel-ing and very well. He referred to the tsar as petit-père, who always speaks about peace and disarmament and who was the first to attack Japan. Talked about the regime of absolutism, oppressions, but not a word about Kishinev . . . What was rather characteristic was a speech by a Russian social dem-ocrat, Trotsky. This is how he began his speech: "Comrades, I shall not re-

peat what I have already said at our *national* meeting . . ." Then he proceeded to prove that revolution is made only by social democrats. His entire speech was devoted to showing the role played by his party in the revolutionary movement. At such a moment! It was simply disgusting! At the end he summarized his speech in German for the German workers who were present, ending with: "This is an international meeting, our language is our own—international . . ."; and just imagine, my darling, this Trotsky, I have been assured, is a Jew . . .[12]

Though he would have given a great deal to be able to participate in the Geneva meetings, Weizmann dismissed them as bogus sympathy: "I can imagine how dismayed everybody is in Geneva, but all the 'heroes' stay put at the [cafés] 'Cluse' or 'Carouge' and other such places beyond the reach of Cossack whips."[13] Instead he pinned his hopes on Tamesada Kuroki, the Japanese army commander, and Heihachiro Togo, the commander in chief of the Japanese navy, and was delighted with the Japanese victory over Alexei Korupatkin, who commanded the Russian forces in the Far East.[14] His joy over Russian defeats was open and unabated; he cheered the Japanese when they won battles in Manchuria[15] or at sea in May 1905:

Verochka, what do you think of Togo? Were I a believing Jew I would certainly see the hand of God in this terrifying defeat [in the naval battle of Tsushima Straits]. Two-thirds of the [Russian] fleet destroyed, admirals lost, sailors, captains and some of the ships captured. There hasn't been so shameful a defeat in all history. Talk about a Great Power! Now all is lost and Russia will be compelled to conclude a shameful peace.[16]

His jubilation was premature. Even while it lost battle after battle on land and sea, and even while the revolution at home proceeded apace, the tsarist regime proved to be quite resilient. Moreover, the pogroms against the Jews were only exacerbated by news of Japanese victories. Religious fervor around Easter was another factor contributing to the horrors perpetrated against them. Every year, as the spring holiday approached, Weizmann expressed fear that it would be accompanied by pogroms, thus continuing a time-honored tradition in Eastern Europe. This time around he had good reason to expect the worst. In a letter to Vera he confessed that "the thought of Easter drawing inexorably nearer makes me tremble. This time I shan't be at home but here, all alone. The prospect is frightening: my imagination will run to something terrible happening at home in my absence . . ."[17] Indeed, pogroms were being openly prepared for the Easter-Passover season. They broke out on April 17, 1905, in Vinnitza (Podolia), where the soldiers and police joined the mob in the killing and looting,[18] later spreading to Bialystok, in the province of Kovno, and Melitopol, where the killing and pillaging of Jews was to a large extent contained by the Jewish self-defense groups. In Zhitomir, on the other hand, despite the valiant efforts of the Jewish youth to defend itself, dozens of Jews were killed and hundreds were wounded. This massacre was also made possible by the active participation of the army and police, which disarmed those defending themselves, leaving them to be freely slaughtered by the mob.[19]

The repeated resistance of Jews to the pogroms in many localities showed a change of attitude and consciousness within Russian Jewry.[20] A conference of Jewish communal leaders, which met in Vilna at the end of March 1905, founded the League for the Attainment of Complete Equal Rights for the Jewish People in Russia. Aiming "to implement in full measure civil, political and national rights of the Jewish people in Russia," it represented the first attempt at a struggle for freedom as a Jewish nation.[21] The Jews reacted to the pogroms by ever greater participation in the revolutionary struggle; but this made them a convenient target for the reactionary forces. Humiliated by defeat in Manchuria during the summer of 1905, the soldiers and Cossacks attained easy victories by killing Jews in Minsk, Brest-Litovsk, Siedlez, Lodz, and Bialystok.[22] As he opened *The Times* each morning, Weizmann realized how helpless he was to prevent yet another ravaged Jewish community: "Zhitomir was followed by Brest-Litovsk. It seems that a blood-stained tragedy was enacted there . . . So many horrors still remain in the future. The period of Russian revival will be written into Russian history in Jewish blood. The Russian spring is for us a time of bloodshed. The projected reforms will exclude Jewish participation in the 'new' life . . ."[23]

The worst was yet to come. Following the October Manifesto, an orgy of blood was set in motion as if on cue. In the course of twelve days (October 18–29) pogroms were perpetrated by the Black Hundreds and other Russian "patriots" in Kiev, Kishinev, Kalarash, Simferopol, Romna, Kremenchug, Yekaterinoslav, and other cities. In all, some 660 cities, towns, and villages were affected—some repeatedly—by the pogroms. At the end of this period there were 876 Jews dead and 1,770 injured. Some 200,000 Jews sustained financial losses which amounted to sixty-three million rubles.[24] The bloodiest pogrom took place in Odessa, where hooligans rampaged for four days. The Jewish self-defense group was sufficient to repulse the mob but was powerless against the army and police, which killed 55 Jews. The final toll in Odessa amounted to 302 murdered Jews and thousands wounded. More than 40,000 Jews were totally ruined economically.[25]

Weizmann was oppressed by a sense of guilt which had gradually overcome him since the spring:

> God, I am so distraught! I firmly believe it is a crime and disgrace to be here conducting chemical experiments while slaughter takes place over there. Those in Russia fare better: if their skin is in danger, their heart and conscience are pure, whereas ours . . .[26]

Two days later he returned to the same theme:

> The pen is shaking in my hand, my brain refuses to function and everything is tinged with blood . . . Again and again, thousands slain, thousands wounded, groans, weeping and wailing. And such helplessness! And why

did fate put us in such a situation that all we can do is observe from afar! Why aren't we with them, with those who fight and those who perish![27]

Unlike his reaction during the Kishinev pogrom, Weizmann was painfully aware of the disasters befalling his brethren in Eastern Europe. It was a traumatic experience which may have also deepened his guilt feelings concerning Kishinev.

What made it even more difficult to sit in Manchester, reading newspapers and teaching chemistry to Englishmen,[28] what contributed to his sense that he was failing his duty as a Zionist and a Jew, was the constant and growing concern for his and Vera's family,[29] who were displaced throughout Russia and Poland. Fortunately no family members were killed or wounded during the pogroms,[30] though quite a few of their relatives had close brushes with the tsarist authorities. Vera's brother-in-law, Solomon Rabinovich, was a member of the Social Revolutionary Party and was about to be arrested when he left Rostov.[31] Weizmann's sister Gita was engaged to the Bundist Aaron Hiller and was wanted by the police for having corresponded with him; searches took place in the family home in Pinsk and in Warsaw, but she had escaped in time.[32] His niece, Eva Lubzhinsky, had been expelled from her high school in Warsaw because of her revolutionary activities and had to be placed in a boarding school in Switzerland,[33] and his brother Moshe and sister Fruma were imprisoned in Minsk for two months for their participation in Jewish self-defense groups. It was only due to the good offices of their friend Simon Rosenbaum—a member of the first Duma—that they were released.[34] Weizmann's brother Shmuel, who had the longest record of revolutionary proclivities in the family and was by 1905 a member of the Zionist Socialist Workers' Party (territorialists), simply disappeared for a while, keeping the family in the dark about his fate—no doubt to protect them and alleviate fear.[35] Moreover, in the midst of the October upheavals Shmuel married Bazia Rubin, a fact which brought little joy to Weizmann, who worried about their inadequate means of subsistence.[36]

Of all his relatives Weizmann was most concerned about his brother Moshe, who was still in Kiev during the fall of 1905. Even before the October revolution, disaster struck Moshe's father-in-law, Samuel Petrovich Rivlin, a well-to-do industrialist in Baku. That city had long ago acquired a reputation for strikes and demonstrations. Troubles began as early as December 1904, when a general strike affected the oil fields, refineries, shipyards, and workshops. In February 1905, when Azerbaijanis and Armenians massacred one another, there were further disruptions.[37] In September 1905 fighting broke out between Tatars and Armenians in Baku and elsewhere in the Caucasus, causing great damage to the oil installations.[38] Like many others in the oil and refinery business, Samuel Rivlin was ruined by the upheavals in Baku.[39] Thus, he could no longer help his daughter Zina and his son-in-law, Moshe, who had in the meantime a two-month-old infant to support as well.

Nor could Moshe remain at the Kiev Polytechnic, which had been shut down by student strikes. Until Weizmann could help him transfer to Geneva to continue his studies as a chemist, Moshe went with his family to Pinsk.[40] How to get the funds for Moshe? While vacationing in Weggis right after the Seventh Zionist Congress, Weizmann met Judah Leon Magnes, who was soon to become rabbi of the wealthy Temple Emanu-El in New York. Magnes promised to help Moshe with a scholarship. Alexander Marmorek of Paris made the same promise.[41] Magnes finally came through with some funds,[42] and in the spring of 1906 Moshe settled with his family in Geneva to study chemistry with Weizmann's own mentor, Carl Graebe.[43]

One way for Weizmann to alleviate his anxiety and guilt over events in Russia was to plunge himself, at least for a while, into Zionist work and the protest meetings organized in the provinces. Since his first public lecture in November 1904 he had gained a reputation as an excellent speaker; events in Russia made it all the more desirable to have someone who could better understand and communicate to the East European immigrants the implications of news items in *The Times*, *The Jewish Chronicle*, and *The Manchester Guardian*. The first organized response to the plight of Russian Jewry came from London. Early in April 1905 Weizmann received a letter from Moses Gaster informing him that pogroms were imminent in Russia. At Gaster's initiative, a meeting of the Conjoint Committee of the Anglo-Jewish Association and the Board of Deputies of British Jews had decided to publish documentation on the fate of Russian Jewry.[44] In a spurt of activity reminiscent of his days in the Democratic Faction, Weizmann wrote twenty-five letters to correspondents in all parts of Russia, including the Geneva office of *Iskra* and the Bund, requesting the necessary information.[45] Gaster's hope was that such a publication of documents would help avert the dangers threatening Russian Jewry.[46] Though Weizmann was more skeptical,[47] he was willing to try anything that might be of help. He was, in any event, embarrassed by his relative Zionist inactivity[48] and was pleased to relieve his frustrations in meaningful work.

A few months later it became clear that the publication of documents would hardly help save Russian Jewry. As news reached England of the massacres following the October revolution, protest meetings were held throughout the country, with Weizmann also addressing large crowds in Liverpool and Leeds. It was, of course, particularly unfortunate that the Aliens Act had just been passed and was about to be enforced on January 1, 1906; yet, curiously, Weizmann hardly touched on that subject. He maintained a detached view of the Aliens Act, seeing it as an internal English concern with which he, as a Zionist leader, should not get involved. On the contrary, insofar as British politicians—such as Evans-Gordon—were obsessed by the specter of an alien invasion about to contaminate their shores, they could possibly be moved to look with favor upon Zionist efforts to settle Russian refugees in Palestine.[49] Instead, Weizmann's wrath was aimed at the leaders of Anglo-Jewry and their fund-raising activities, coordinated by the Russo-Jewish Committee, which included, among others, Lord (Nathaniel Meyer) Rothschild, a strong supporter of the Jewish Territorial Organization (ITO), and Claude Montefiore, president of the Anglo-Jewish Association. That body appealed for relief funds, which would only be given under the express condition that the money collected would not be used to bring Jewish refugees to England. A few days after he heard how the Russo-Jewish Committee had ignominiously bowed to the general British mood of xenophobia, Weizmann read in *The Jewish Chronicle* that the Anglo-Jewish Association had decided against holding protest meetings in London.[50] Weizmann was outraged; he considered the actions of the Anglo-Jewish leadership "a second pogrom."[51] Gaster was of the same opinion. Weizmann immediately began a speaking tour, denouncing the actions of the London groups.[52] Inspired perhaps by the reception given to his speeches, he conceived of an extraordinary and bold plan to shake the power of the Jewish patricians in London. He called it "a revolution within Jewry itself."[53] In a letter to Ussishkin he described his plan:

. . . I can declare that I have now acquired tremendous influence over the Jews throughout the provinces. I now plan to use this influence to undermine the authority of the Rothschilds and all the gentry who have behaved in a base and cowardly fashion in this terrible hour . . .

As you know, the Lord Mayors called protest meetings throughout the country, with the sole exception of London. Earl Spencer (the future Premier) *[sic]*, together with about ten of the Cabinet and University representatives, etc., will speak at a tremendous meeting to be held in the largest hall in Manchester on December 10. The Jewish speakers will be Gaster and myself. I have submitted, and shall defend, the following resolution: "the meeting holds all classes of Russian society responsible for the continued denial of rights to the Jews, who gave the Russian people their freedom. The meeting, together with English Jewry, which it represents, expresses its indignation at the cowardly behavior of certain Jews who consider themselves to be the official representatives of the Jewish people; it summons them before the tribunal of Jewish public opinion for directly and indirectly supporting the Russian Government by providing it with money and loans" . . .

The preliminary committee concerned with convening this meeting (it consisted of representatives from all Jewish communities) termed my resolution historic, and declared that it meant war against the entire existing order in West European Jewry. Nevertheless my resolution was adopted (I spoke for two hours and had a hemorrhage in the evening, as my chest was already affected by the speaking I had done) . . . we are at an historic moment, and cannot afford to miss it. We Zionists can gain control over *all English* public opinion. After the meeting a deputation, myself included, may go to the Minister and to the King.[54]

Weizmann asked that Ussishkin help draft the wording of the resolution and send a letter of support.[55] He put the same request to Max Nordau, Nahum Sokolow, Yehiel Tschlenow, Bernstein-Kohan, Max Mandelstamm, Victor Jacobson, and Shmarya Levin.[56] It was to be an all-out assault on the Anglo-Jewish establishment. His initial success on November 25, 1905, in convincing the preparatory committee to go along with his resolution was as surprising to him as it is in retrospect, and can only be attributed to his powers of persuasion and the gravity of the situation in Russia. His boast that "everybody said that this is the beginning of a new era for English Jewry"[57] was indeed not farfetched. But he made two serious errors. His information on the willingness of English Jewish bankers to loan money to Russia was erroneous. In fact, they refused to participate in such loans as long as Russian Jewry was deprived of equal rights.[58] More important, he overestimated the willingness of leading Zionists to go along with him. Max Nordau was the only one to send a letter, which was addressed to the mass meeting and which included no reference to Weizmann's resolution; it merely called on the Russian government to pay compensation to the victims as a precondition to the granting of new loans.[59] J. I. Loewy and Nathan Laski, who were members of the preparatory committee, began to have second thoughts about allowing this Russian immigrant to attack the pillars of English Jewry in the presence of some of England's most prominent politicians. Gaster tended to agree with them and also objected to the presence of Evans-Gordon—who had played such a major role in passing the Aliens Act and was now a supporter of ITO—on the speakers' platform.[60] The latter mistake was quickly rectified, but Weizmann still tried to salvage his resolution, assuring Gaster that it had been submitted with the approval of Ussishkin and Nordau and that he had agreed to participate in the December meeting only on condition that he could move his resolution.[61] Gaster stood his ground[62] and Weizmann had no choice but to acquiesce.

Thus his frontal attack on "our rich Jews"[63] resulted in a personal debacle. For weeks he had been urging Vera to come over from Geneva to be present at his moment of great triumph.[64] She arrived just in time to see Weizmann play a much more modest role in the proceedings. Moreover, Weizmann's speech at the meeting of December 11 was not even reported in the press.[65] Weizmann's embarrassment at his failure was so great that he did not mention it in any of his subsequent letters. One can only assume that his explanations to his fiancée of what had happened were not very complimentary to Moses Gaster, nor to the "local rich Yids."[66] Clearly Weizmann had been carried away by his emotions and perhaps also by a desire to be catapulted into a major public role. But he had bitten off more than he could chew and he seems to have learned his lesson: Next time he was going to lay the proper groundwork before launching an attack. Indeed, at the beginning of 1907, when he did manage to carry out a minor revolt within the English Zionist Federation (EZF), he did so with sufficient and prearranged backing, after weeks of behind-the-scenes maneuvering. For the moment his one consolation resulting from the affair of December 1905 was that Vera was with him for three weeks.

As soon as he recovered from this personal rebuff, he turned his attention to another effort on behalf of the Jewish victims of the October pogroms. The Engeres Aktions-Comité, which met in Cologne in November 1905, decided, at the initiative of David Wolffsohn, to hold a general Jewish conference in Brussels to discuss the situation of Russian Jewry. It was clearly an initiative by the "politicals" within the Zionist movement, who may have wished to beat the Jewish territorialists at their own game. It was most enthusiastically supported by Leopold Greenberg, who felt that this "is an opportunity we ought under no circumstances to miss. It is the one thing that is now possible for us to do to show that we are working and doing something that is tangible. Even if the other people refuse to come to the conference, we shall have shown to the world that we are alive and that we are taking the lead in Juedische Weltfragen."[67] Indeed, the major Jewish organizations—the Board of Deputies of British Jews, the Alliance Israélite Universelle, and the Jewish Colonization Association—refused to participate because of the conference's alleged Zionist character.[68] The Hilfsverein der deutschen Juden participated, apparently in order to keep the resolutions in line with the sentiments of the large philanthropic organizations.[69] The response from other such groups—when they even bothered to answer—was at best cool. The Russian members of the Grosses Aktions-Comité, whose opinion was sought, agreed to the Brussels Conference but were skeptical of its outcome from the outset. Even Max Nordau and Otto Warburg objected to the conference on the grounds that its failure to achieve concrete results would be more harmful to the movement than inaction.[70]

The eighty delegates who were present at the opening of the Brussels Conference on January 29, 1906, were mostly Zionists from both East and West, with a sprinkling of delegates from the Jewish Territorial Organization, the Anglo-Jewish Association and the Hilfsverein der deutschen Juden. From the Zionists' perspective, the conference was a failure. Their proposals concerning equal rights for Jews in Russia and the creation of a representative organization for the Jewish people in which all organizations would participate were rejected. The resolutions that were passed were akin to those resolved at another, philanthropic conference in Frankfurt on January 4, 1906, to which the World Zionist Organization had not even been invited.[71] The Brussels Conference resolved: to create a preparatory committee to explore the creation of a permanent body representing Jewish organizations; to establish a commission to explore settlement prospects in various countries; and to discourage Jews without sufficient funds from emigrating before they could be assured of means of livelihood.[72] Thus, as a price for cooperation with non-Zionists, the Zionists were cornered into a most embarrassing situation, despite Greenberg's attempts to call the conference a success.[73] In the aftermath of the Seventh Zionist Congress, it seems almost incomprehensible that the Zionists agreed to the second resolution, which was clearly in the spirit of the Jewish Territorial Organization. Moreover, the third resolution complemented the decision of the English Russo-Jewish Committee, which had decided against using its funds to facilitate the emigration of victims of the pogroms into England.[74] If the Zionists deserved some credit for their burning desire to help Russian Jewry and for their vision of an international Jewish conference that would deal with this issue in political terms, they also demonstrated that they lacked the necessary leadership and instruments of power to implement their ideas.

Weizmann's initial response to the convening of the Brussels Conference was favorable, and it is clear that he was eager to take part in it. He even volunteered to use the upcoming holidays for propaganda in the provinces on behalf of the conference "once I have your instructions, which, of course, I will scrupulously follow."[75] The idea of an international Jewish assembly had recently also been suggested in Manchester and very much appealed to him, provided it would enhance the Zionist cause.[76] His enthusiasm began to wane considerably when he learned that most non-Zionist organizations had refused to take part. "This was to be expected and once more we have learned the lesson that any attempt on our part to conciliate the assimilationists can only lower our prestige; cooperation with these scoundrels is not possible."[77] Nevertheless, Weizmann would have taken part—if only to have a chance to speak with the Russian delegates—had he not been prevented from doing so by an accident in the laboratory.[78] His reaction to the resolutions was acerbic and cutting; it contradicted his initial willingness to work with non-Zionist organizations and was obviously colored by his disappointment at their rejection.

> Greenberg thinks it was a success; I venture to disagree . . . The old delusion still persists that it is possible or desirable to cooperate with partly or wholly assimilated bodies. Zionism is losing its radicalism, surrendering its own moral strength and freshness to those semi-bankrupt, semi-rotten bodies without receiving anything in return.
>
> Zionists of the brand of Greenberg, Wolffsohn, I mean the opportunists, believe they have contributed a folk basis to those bodies. The contrary is true—Zionism is becoming estranged, shallow and insensitive, descending from its democratic eminence to the baize-green table of plutocratic philanthropists, and perhaps as low as to the back-door of the elements dead to Judaism . . .
>
> Don't call me a fanatic or a narrow-minded man. Zionism exercises its Maccabean force of attraction and its greatness as a freedom movement so long as it solves the Jewish question radically, or strives to do so. The moment it chases after transient successes at the expense of Jewish distress the gates are opened wide for the politics of the ghetto.[79]

The failure of the Brussels Conference may explain why it has receded into the backwaters of Zionist historiography. But even in the closing weeks of 1905 it received little public notice, especially in England. Attention was now focused on the forthcoming general election, which was then coming to a climax. Arthur James Balfour's position as Prime Minister had become untenable in the autumn of 1905. Grievances against his administration—the Education Act, the Licensing Act, tariff reform proposals, Chinese labor, parliamentary tactics—had piled up. Balfour was losing the confidence of the country and control over the Conservative majority in the Commons. On December 4, 1905, he resigned and was succeeded two days later by the veteran Liberal Sir Henry Campbell-Bannerman, with the understanding that a general election would soon follow. It was set for January 1906.[80] Balfour's resignation was probably a tactical device designed to strengthen Conservative chances in the general election by enabling them to fight unencumbered by the embarrassments of government.

It was during the closing days of the election campaign, on January 9, 1906, that Weizmann met with Balfour, who was now fighting as leader of the opposition to retain the seat he had held in the East Division of Manchester since 1885. Weizmann's account of the meeting in his memoirs has about it all the ingredients of a good story and it is only natural that it has been widely quoted in Zionist and general historiography.[81] The meeting took place in the Queen's Hotel, Balfour's campaign headquarters. Balfour inquired as to why some Zionists were so bitterly opposed to the Uganda offer, upon which Weizmann launched into a long explanation:

> I added that if Moses had come into the Sixth Zionist Congress when it was adopting the resolution in favor of the Commission for Uganda, he would surely have broken the tablets once again . . . the Jewish people would never produce either the money or the energy required in order to build up a wasteland and make it habitable, unless that land were Palestine. Palestine has this magic and romantic appeal for the Jews; our history has been what it is because of our tenacious hold on Palestine . . .
>
> I remember that I was sweating blood and I tried to find some less ponderous way of expressing myself . . .
>
> Then suddenly I said: "Mr. Balfour, supposing I were to offer you Paris instead of London, would you take it?"
>
> He sat up, looked at me, and answered: "But, Dr. Weizmann, we have London."
>
> "That is true," I said. "But we had Jerusalem when London was a marsh."
>
> He leaned back, continued to stare at me, and said two things which I remember vividly. The first was: "Are there many Jews who think like you?"
>
> I answered: "I believe I speak the minds of millions of Jews whom you will never see and who cannot speak for themselves, but with whom I could pave the streets of the country I came from."
>
> To this he said: "If that is so, you will one day be a force."
>
> Shortly before I withdrew, Balfour said: "It is curious. The Jews I meet are quite different."
>
> I answered: "Mr. Balfour, you meet the wrong kind of Jews" . . .
>
> I was drawn again into Zionist activity . . . The conversation with Balfour . . . was like a tocsin or alarm . . .[82]

Weizmann's record of the meeting the very same day of the interview is a great deal less dramatic and, no doubt, more accurate. "I had a meeting with Balfour today and had a long and interesting talk with him about Zionism. He explained that he sees no political difficulties in the attainment of Palestine—only economic difficulties. We talked about territorialism. I explained to him why this was not possible. We undertook to send him a memorandum."[83] It was completely out of character for Weizmann to downplay an important conversation or meeting. He had made much of his conversations with the less important Percy and Hill in 1904, and chances are he would have faithfully recorded the conversation with Balfour—which he purported to remember many years later— had it been as interesting as his memoirs record. Weizmann made no public reference to his conversation with Balfour until thirteen years later— in Jerusalem.[84] By the time Weizmann wrote his memoirs in the late 1940s, Balfour's niece, Blanche Dugdale, had already recorded the main elements of the story as it had been told to her by Weizmann himself.[85] Clearly Weizmann had made an impression on Balfour,[86] yet it was not sufficiently strong to foster their relationship or help in the pursuit of the subject of their conversation. Not only was Balfour not "converted" to Zionism, as was later maintained,[87] but he did not even respond to Weizmann's letters and memoranda, written in subsequent years, and refused to grant him an interview. It was not until Weizmann had won Lloyd George's interest in Zionism that Balfour consented to see him again in 1914. Why, then, was Balfour interested in meeting Weizmann in the midst of a hectic election campaign, and why did he spend over an hour with him while "the corridors were crowded with people waiting for a word with the candidate"?[88]

Blanche Dugdale has maintained that in the midst of the campaign Balfour wanted to fathom the reasons for the Zionist attitude to the East African offer and that Charles Dreyfus, his campaign chairman in Manchester, told him "that there was at that moment in Manchester one of the younger leaders of the Zionist movement, a Russian Jew, Chaim Weizmann by name," who could provide the necessary information. Dugdale then claims that Balfour "turned . . . very characteristically, for relaxation, to a subject which interested him alike as a political philosopher, a student of history, and a statesman . . ."[89] Similarly, one of Balfour's later biographers maintained that Balfour's interest in Weizmann "had little or nothing to do with the electioneering then in progress . . . Balfour, though he made some excellent speeches as the rain pelted down through the Manchester grime, had a remarkable gift for withdrawing himself and turning his active, inquiring mind to some unconnected matter . . ."[90] It may very well be that Balfour was intrigued by the final rejection of the Uganda offer by the Seventh Zionist Congress, which had taken place in July 1905. He must have been puzzled by the phenomenon of a persecuted people refusing a *Nachtasyl*, as Nordau had put it. Possibly he thought the Zionists were thankless people. How could his government, which tried to help persecuted Jews, be condemned simultaneously for anti-Jewish sentiment simply because it wished to curb the uncontrolled influx of such refugees to England? Moreover, did not everyone know that he pushed the Aliens Act for political reasons—as Winston Churchill had pointed out in the Commons—and that there were even certain segments of Anglo-Jewry who were not exactly delighted by the specter of Russian-Jewish immigration to England? The intricacies of Jewish life and politics may have indeed occupied Balfour's "inquiring mind," but this does not sufficiently explain why Weizmann had to be called in for an explanation a few days before polling began. After all, Dreyfus himself had attended the Seventh Zionist Congress and had even given an official report on it at a large Manchester gathering in September 1905.[91] Surely he could have satisfied Balfour's curiosity on the East Africa project. It seems, then, that the timing of the interview could hardly have been coincidental and had a great deal to do with electioneering. True, there were few Jews in Balfour's own constituency, but Balfour had a responsibility toward other Conservative candidates in other constituencies.

The turn of the century marked the beginning of a Zionist vote in England. Every candidate in the 1900 and 1906 elections received a letter from the English Zionist Federation offering the help of "our friends in the constituency which you seek to represent" if the recipient would declare his Zionist sympathies. Both letters made it clear that Palestine was the goal. There were 143 positive replies to the 1900 circular and over 250 to that of 1906.[92] It is unlikely that the support of Zionists for any candidate in the period prior to 1914 had an appreciable impact on the outcome of the elections, but one must keep in mind that Balfour's situation in 1906 was desperate enough for him to try to gain support for himself and his party wherever he could. Thus, there was some reason for Balfour to meet Weizmann. Moreover, as leader of the opposition it was his duty to enhance the chances of other party condidates in whatever way possible. At the same time, Balfour must have known that the English Zionist Federation represented only a small fraction of English Jewry. Moreover, the election in any of the Manchester districts did not hinge on the Uganda issue. In the next-door constituency Winston Churchill was wooing the vote of supporters of the Jewish Territorial Organization by stating that he "believed in the idea of creating an autonomous Jewish colony in East Africa" under the British flag.[93]

Overshadowing the question of Uganda, which was by now a dead issue, was a much more immediate concern of the Jewish masses: the Aliens Act, which had become law in 1905 during Balfour's premiership. It is quite understandable that Balfour preferred to talk about Uganda rather than the Aliens Act; Weizmann's detachment from British political and social problems was such that he, too, did not raise this embarrassing issue; though harsh on those Jews who sought to keep their brethren from England's shores, he could empathize with a gentile's motivations in keeping foreigners out. Yet, as was amply documented in the press of the time, for the Jewish masses in Manchester and elsewhere the Aliens Act was a major concern in the campaign. Few of them mourned Balfour's resignation when they recalled his role in taking charge of the act's passage through the Commons. It was the Prime Minister himself who not only moved the second reading but also sat through the many hours of the committee stage, when he made the statement that however disgraceful anti-Semitism might be, and however valuable Jews might be to the community,

> it would not be to the advantage of the civilization of the country that there should be an immense body of persons who, however patriotic, able, and industrious, however much they threw themselves into the national life, still, by their own action, remained a people apart, and not merely held a religion differing from the vast majority of their fellow-countrymen but only inter-married among themselves . . . some of the undoubted evils which had fallen upon portions of the country from an alien immigration which was largely Jewish, gave . . . some reason to fear that this country might be . . . in danger of following the evil example set by some other countries, and hu-man nature being what it was, it was almost impossible to guard against so great an evil unless they took reasonable precautions to prevent what was called "the right of asylum" from being abused . . . The truth was that the only immemorial right of asylum given by this country was to allow aliens in with whom the country agreed . . .[94]

Later in the debate Balfour once again clearly referred to the Jewish im-migrants in London.

> What actually happens is that these foreign immigrants go into a small area of the East End of London and they produce the evil of overcrowding . . . It means that the foreign immigrant first drives the British workman out of Whitechapel and then the small merchant has to pay the rates in order to carry out the sanitary arrangements and the Poor Law arrangements which are to remedy the state of things of which he is the victim. How can you justify it? The truth is that the evil is not only great and pressing in these districts where it prevails, but is one which these districts are perfectly in-capable of dealing with unassisted . . . In my view we have a right to keep out everybody who does not add to the strength of the community—the in-dustrial, social and intellectual strength of the community . . .[95]

Whether Balfour could rightly be called an anti-Semite on the basis of these remarks is doubtful; his mind was too subtle and balanced for so extreme a prejudice. That he was ambivalent in his attitude to Jews seems more certain even to those biographers who are sympathetic to his po-litical career and personality.[96] But to the tens of thousands of Jews who had in the meantime found asylum on British shores, Balfour's state-ments in the Commons were not substantially different from those of any anti-Semite in Stepney and Whitechapel, or of a member of the Brit-ish Brothers League. Even those who did not follow closely the parlia-mentary debates on the Aliens Act could glean sufficient information from *The Jewish Chronicle*—which had expressed surprise and disappointment at the Prime Minister's remarks—to turn them decisively against Bal-four's government.[97] In light of the pogroms raging in Russia, Balfour's statements could only be interpreted as a harsh indictment against their hapless and persecuted brethren. From a political point of view, the Aliens Act could not have been passed at a less propitious moment. It is quite possible that Balfour's meeting with Weizmann was intended as a signal to the Jewish community, or perhaps—more modestly—as an attempt to win over a man who was regarded as having influence among a segment of that community. Perhaps Weizmann could remind his brethren that Balfour's government had shown a sincere interest in the solution of the Jewish Problem. After all, was it not his government which had offered Uganda to the Zionists?

One politician who was quick to exploit the Aliens Act to his own advantage was Winston Churchill, now a Liberal, who had just been brought into the government of Henry Campbell-Bannerman as Parliamentary Under-Secretary for the Colonies. Shortly after being approached by the North-West Manchester (Cheetham) Liberals in the spring of 1904, Churchill had assured Nathan Laski, a leading member of the Jewish community, of his opposition to the Aliens Act. His letter stands in stark contrast to Balfour's remarks in the Commons.

> What has surprised me most in studying the papers you have been good enough to forward me is how few aliens there are in Great Britain. To judge by the talk there has been, one could have imagined we were being overrun by the swarming invasion and "ousted" from our island through neglect of precautions which every foreign nation has adopted. But it now appears from the Board of Trade statistics that all the aliens in Great Britain do not amount to a one-hundred-and-fortieth part of the total population, that they are increasing only 7,000 a year on the average, and that, according to the report of the Alien Commission, Germany has twice as large and France four times as large a proportion of foreigners as we have. It does not appear, therefore, that there can be urgent or sufficient reasons, racial or social, for departing from the old tolerant and generous practice of free entry and asylum to which this country has so long adhered and from which it has so often greatly gained . . . The whole bill looks like an attempt on the part of the Government to gratify a small but noisy section of their own supporters and to purchase a little popularity in the constituencies by dealing harshly with a number of unfortunate aliens who have no votes . . .
>
> It is expected to appeal to insular prejudice against foreigners, to racial prejudice against Jews, and to labor prejudice against competition, and it will no doubt supply a variety of rhetorical phrases for the approaching election . . .[98]

Churchill was as good as his word and had played a major role in smothering the Aliens Act with amendments and forcing its abandonment by the government. Nathan Laski, Joseph Dulberg, Barrow Belisha, Samuel Finburgh, and other Jewish leaders in Manchester were naturally grateful, and Laski assured Churchill that "I have got a body of splendid workers together for you, and as far as our district is concerned—victory is assured . . . There has not been a single man able to arouse the interest that you have already done—thus I am sure of your future success."[99] A few weeks before the fall of Balfour's government, the Board of Deputies of British Jews publicly thanked Churchill for his efforts to ameliorate the measures stipulated by the Aliens Act.[100]

Churchill's opposition to the Aliens Act established his reputation as a leading champion of the rights of minorities, which served to enhance his position among Manchester's Jews. During the election campaign he appealed to Jews in his constituency to support him on account of his fight against the Aliens Act[101] and fully exploited his good connections with the Manchester branch of the Jewish Territorial Organization, in which Dulberg, Belisha, and Laski played a prominent role.[102] North-West Manchester, where Churchill stood for election, had enough Jewish votes to make a difference, and Churchill used every opportunity to address public Jewish gatherings. It was during such an occasion, on December 10, 1905, that he met Weizmann for the first time. Weizmann, who had been a member of the organizing committee of the meeting to protest the Russian pogroms, had also been one of the speakers. After eighteen months in England he could easily have addressed the crowd in English, but he deliberately chose Yiddish, knowing full well that his audience appreciated this gesture all the more in the presence of gentile participants. It elevated the language to the status of a national vehicle and reminded them that their culture was a valuable asset even in exile. Churchill also spoke,[103] as did Moses Gaster. After the meeting Nathan Laski gave a dinner party in honor of Churchill, to which Weizmann was invited.[104] Churchill must have been impressed by the impact of Weizmann's Yiddish speech on the crowd and instructed his political agent to approach Weizmann and enlist his support for the coming election. After all, many of the few hundred eligible Jewish voters did not know English well and were bound to listen to the political advice given by local leaders in their own language. Moreover, Churchill's contacts in the Jewish community had hitherto been almost exclusively with the non-Zionist leadership. It would be a coup indeed if he could also move Weizmann to campaign for him.

Weizmann, who was usually quick to grasp at political opportunities, remained cool to the suggestion that he, a stranger to England, help a descendant of the Duke of Marlborough attain a seat in parliament. He fully realized his power to sway Jewish votes in Cheetham, but he did not think it wise to enter the political fray. For one, he suspected that the Liberals would not be much better than the Tories when it came to fulfilling campaign promises.[105] Moreover, Churchill's close ties with Manchester's branch of the Jewish Territorial Organization was a serious drawback in Weizmann's eyes. Perhaps more significantly, Weizmann had little interest in British politics and British internal affairs to the degree that they did not directly impinge on Zionist aspirations. He deliberately kept himself above the furious political activity around him. Writing to Ussishkin a week before the fall of Balfour's government, he remarked that Earl Spencer would be the future Prime Minister; this, while Campbell-Bannerman was already preparing his own list of cabinet members;[106] and he was unfamiliar with the correct spelling of Churchill's first name,[107] though the latter had been active on the Manchester political scene since the spring of 1904. He held himself aloof as a Russian Jew in exile—a political émigré—who felt no sense of kinship with either the British gentiles or with English Jewry and could therefore afford to ignore the tariff reform crisis and, to a large extent, even the Aliens Act. In order to remain polite to Churchill's agent and, at the same time, cover his own flank, he decided to ask Wolffsohn for advice.[108] Wolffsohn apparently also felt that British politics were none of Weizmann's business and did not reply until January 8, 1906, informing him that he would have to get his instructions from Leopold Greenberg. Wolffsohn had written to Greenberg four days earlier asking him to use his own judgment as to how to proceed.[109] By the time this reminder of his limited power within the World Zionist Organization arrived in Manchester, Weizmann had already consented to meet with Churchill on January 12, 1906—a day before Britain went to the polls. Like the interview with Balfour, this too seemed to have passed in an uneventful fashion. Its only concrete result appeared to be a promise from Churchill that the colonial secretary, Lord Elgin, would be prepared to receive a Zionist delegation.[110]

Weizmann's willingness to meet with Churchill did not place him in a delicate position with his employer, who was managing Balfour's campaign. On the contrary, Dreyfus apparently harbored sympathies for Churchill, though the latter was a defector from the Conservative camp and a vocal opponent of Balfour.[111] Dreyfus must have been aware, though, of Churchill's overtures to Weizmann and thought it would do no harm for the latter to meet Balfour as well. After all, Weizmann could provide access to the Yiddish-speaking voting public as well as to the academic community. In the event, Weizmann showed remarkable restraint and poise during both interviews, and there is no evidence that either contestant was able to persuade him to take part in his electoral campaign.[112] There also is no evidence as to Weizmann's impressions of either politician's tactics during the interview—Churchill's open and unabashed solicitation of his support and Balfour's more genteel and diversionary, almost detached attitude. They had not left an impression strong enough to be recorded at the time, though Weizmann must have been flattered by the attention lavished upon him. One can only wonder if this second experience with prominent British politicians convinced him that in England Zionism and Zionist leaders could command some attention and influence. On the other hand, one can note with somewhat more certainty that for both Balfour and Churchill Weizmann was probably the first East European Zionist of stature they had met. Approaching almost sixty years of age in 1906, Balfour was probably not swept off his feet into accepting Zionism after his interview with Weizmann; this would have been out of character with his worldly experience and sophistication. More likely he was impressed by Weizmann's ability and energy and was convinced that Palestine was indeed the only country acceptable to the Zionists.[113] For Winston Churchill the long-term lesson might have been the insight that, apart from the patrician class of English Jews he knew, there also existed a potential power in the Jewish masses who adhered to Zionism. Indeed, it is most likely that ultimately Weizmann agreed to meet both politicians because he saw it as an opportunity to enlighten them on the merit and goals of Zionism.

In retrospect, it seems clear that Weizmann could not have significantly altered the elections either in East Manchester or in the North-West a few days before polling began. The Jewish vote was solidly behind Churchill, who won by a majority of 1,241 over his opponent, Johnson-Hicks. Of the 470 Jewish voters in the Cheetham district, no fewer than 406 had pledged to support him.[114] Balfour's Liberal opponent, Thomas Horridge, had also won a resounding victory, polling 6,403 votes to Balfour's 4,423.[115] The local and national results were even more decisive. All Lancashire constituencies, which in 1900 had returned Unionist members, with Balfour at their head, had now returned six Liberals and four Labour men;[116] and in the new House of Commons the pro-government bloc totaled 513 members, as compared with only 132 Conservatives and 25 Liberal Unionists.[117]

Weizmann spent January 13—the day polling began in every division in Manchester—traveling by train to Glasgow to attend the annual conference of the English Zionist Federation, which took place the following day. This poorly attended meeting elected him, for the first time, to the executive of the English Zionist Federation.[118] It is curious that his election did not even seem important enough to report to Vera.[119] He merely wrote that the territorialists had been routed at the conference.[120] This was not true, though, of their general position in England. The "Zangwillites," as he called them, may not have been elected to the executive of the EZF, but in 1905–6 they were certainly a threat to Zionism in England. Zangwill had managed to attract an impressive group of notables to serve on the British ITO Federation. They included Meyer A. Spielman as president, Leopold de Rothschild as treasurer, and O. E. d'Avigdor-Goldsmid as senior member. Even Lucien Wolf joined the Jewish Territorial Organization and served on its international council with Clement Salaman.[121] He also enlisted the support of Paul Nathan and James Simon of Germany, Max Mandelstamm and Isidore Yasinovsky of Russia, and Meyer Sulzberger, Oscar Straus, and Daniel Guggenheim of the United States. It was a more impressive group than Herzl had ever managed to enlist.[122] The English Zionists clearly feared that Zangwill would manage to "tap the enthusiasm" of the same elements in the community which the Zionists were attempting to win over,[123] and, even more seriously, that Zangwill would have an easier and more effective entry to Whitehall.

Closer to home, Manchester, too, had a well-organized branch of the Jewish Territorial Organization, which was established immediately after the Seventh Zionist Congress, in September 1905, and was formally inaugurated a month later.[124] By December 1905 the Manchester branch of the ITO claimed a membership of five hundred.[125] In July 1906 it even established a special sub-branch for Yiddish speakers.[126]

Though Leopold Greenberg had been given a clean bill of health at the annual conference and GAC meetings in the summer of 1904, Weizmann did not cease to distrust the latter's political and personal motivations—with good reason Greenberg developed a penchant for acting independently, especially after Herzl's strong personality had ceased to dominate the movement and hamper individual initiative. Immediately after the Seventh Zionist Congress, on August 8, 1905, and without proper authorization, Greenberg notified the British Colonial Office of the World Zionist Organization's decision on Uganda.[127] Even before receiving the reply of Charles Lucas, an Assistant Under-Secretary who was writing on behalf of the Secretary of the Colonial Office, Alfred Lyttleton,[128] Greenberg had already embarked on his next step. In a letter to *The Times* dated August 24, 1905, he wrote that a British offer to the Zionists of some territory adjoining Palestine, such as the Sinai Peninsula *or* Cyprus (!), would win the active support of the World Zionist Organization.[129] This was clearly a deviation from the decision of the Seventh Zionist Congress, which rejected all colonizing activity outside Palestine and its adjacent lands. It was only after the fact, in November 1905, that Greenberg was instructed by SAC to investigate British interest in Jewish settlement in El Arish.

Weizmann had suspected all along that Greenberg and Cowen might stray from the resolutions adopted at the Seventh Zionist Congress.[130] Greenberg was managing the affairs of the EZF behind the scenes, with Sir Francis Montefiore as its weak president and Joseph Cowen as vice president. These devotees of Herzl could easily find a *modus vivendi* with Zangwill, whose absence from their councils they regretted. In any case, Greenberg's enmity toward Zangwill was mostly on personal grounds and, to a lesser degree, on political issues. Though Weizmann did not think that Zangwill would make much headway, he kept in touch with him, probably in order to be informed of his activities. After one such visit to Zangwill in October 1905, he noted, "The point is that Zangwill, whom I had always taken for a sincere but misguided man, gave the opposite impression this time: he is fond of his own image in the role of 'leader' and paper king of the *schnorrers*. Madame [Zangwill] even had the insolence to tell me the following: 'You had three remarkable figures in your movement: Herzl, Nordau, and my husband . . .' "[131] Weizmann belittled the author of the *King of the Schnorrers*, but Zangwill's cause was given new life by the continuous pogroms in Russia (e.g., in Homel on January 26 and 27, 1906) and by Greenberg and Cowen's efforts to come to an understanding with the Jewish Territorial Organization. They also tried to pressure Wolffsohn to take a more positive stance toward this organization, resulting in SAC's decision, in November 1905, to permit them to enter into negotiations with Zangwill provided they first consulted with Wolffsohn.[132]

Weizmann was opposed, from the outset, to the activities of " 'leaders' such as Cowen and others, flirting with the territorialists for the sake of a 'peace' which no one needs and no one is interested in."[133] Though he was eager for every opportunity to leave Manchester and "be among people a little,[134] he was disgusted by what he saw happening to the movement in London:

> I cannot say that I have come back very fortified. In this London hell the condition of all the "leaders" is so revolting, and their hatred of each other is such that no organized work is possible. Gaster sulks [because of his failure to gain election to GAC], Greenberg plays politics, Cowen is a snob. I also saw Zangwill. He has been very ill, is aging, exhausted, apparently disillusioned. He interrogated me about the possibility of receiving a concession from the Russian Government for a stretch of land in Siberia—for the Jews; the most bizarre, most fantastic projects appear and vanish like mushrooms. But against the background of Whitechapel's hell, all this demoralization in Zionism has an overall dreadful effect on one. I was glad to leave London, with the intention of not returning there on Zionist business for a long time.[135]

Of course, Weizmann was a moody man, and a few days later he wrote to Vera that "my meetings in London passed off very successfully, and in the summer I shall go there more often."[136] Yet in the spring his disgust and contempt with affairs in the English Zionist Federation were so deep that he did his best to stay away from Zionist meetings.[137] In any case, there was not much that could be accomplished at the moment. Though he sided with Gaster against Greenberg and Cowen, the *Haham* was, at best, a difficult colleague: He did not attend the Glasgow Conference of the EZF and refused to be nominated to its executive or serve as its delegate to Brussels. On the whole, he preferred to operate behind the scenes and go his own way. He demanded absolute loyalty to himself and could tolerate no opposition. Gaster would have to wait for better opportunities to elect him as president of the EZF. Weizmann's visit to the Continent, from April 6 to April 23, did little to change his views or attitudes toward the EZF.

The only bright moment in his Zionist world were the visits to Manchester by Menahem Ussishkin and Nahum Sokolow. Ussishkin came to England at the end of May 1906 in order to form a syndicate to help finance economic enterprises in Palestine;[138] he co-opted Weizmann, among others, to the committee, while visiting Manchester in the company of Sokolow.[139] The latter's Warsaw daily, *Hatzfirah*, had just been banned by the tsarist authorities and he was without a livelihood. Never at a loss for ideas to launch new projects, he was now gathering material for a study on Jewish emancipation in Western Europe.[140] Weizmann had genuinely warm feelings for Sokolow,[141] whose daughter, Maria, had been close to the circle of the Democratic Faction. Thus he turned once more to Moses Gaster for financial help for his friend,[142] and he also tried to arrange for a loan from Dreyfus.[143]

It was probably from Sokolow and Ussishkin that Weizmann heard, for the first time in many months, details of events in Russia. He had not visited Russia for the past two years and was eager for firsthand news. In April 1906 there were elections to the First Imperial Duma. Weizmann was pessimistic about its ability to function in a democratic fashion in the land of the tsars.[144] He had heard, no doubt, that there were voices in Russian Jewry which counseled emigration. Others hoped that constitutional changes would take place that would lead to equal civil and perhaps even national rights for the Jews. In the event, the League for the Attainment of Complete Equal Rights for the Jewish People of Russia led the campaign, and a large segment of Russian Jewry took part—with the exception of the Bund, which boycotted it—electing twelve Jewish deputies representing the several ideological tendencies of Russian Jewry.[145] The most prominent Jewish delegate in the Duma was Maxim Vinaver, who was destined to play a role during the 1917 Russian Revolution as well.[146] Yet even while the delegates to the Duma were debating the question of civil equality for Jews,[147] the Bialystok pogrom raged on from June 14 to 16, 1906, leaving eighty Jews dead.[148] The commission empowered by the Duma to investigate the massacre, which included the Zionist leader Victor Jacobson, reported unequivocally that the pogrom had been planned by the administration. The commission recommended the dismissal of all officials implicated locally, as well as that of the Minister of the Interior and his staff.[149] But the Duma's days were now numbered, and on July 22, 1906, it was dissolved by the tsar, who alleged that it had concerned itself with matters outside its jurisdiction (Bialystok).[150] Thus, the Duma brought no practical gains for the Jews,[151] confirming the suspicions of the Jewish socialists, who had remained passive on the sidelines.

The Bialystok pogrom had reverberations in England as well. Despite their public denunciation of one another,[152] Greenberg and Zangwill found a common language in responding to events in Russia. *The Jewish Chronicle* of June 22, 1906, published an appeal on behalf of the latest pogrom victims. It was jointly signed by Sir Francis Montefiore and Leopold Greenberg, representing the EZF, and by Israel Zangwill and Clement Salaman, on behalf of the ITO. This appeal stated that the renewal of pogroms in Russia justified the contention of the Zionists and territorialists that a Jewish national home alone offered the hope of speedy relief for Russian Jews. The same issue of *The Jewish Chronicle* also published an appeal by Joseph Cowen to shareholders of the Jewish Colonial Trust to reject the resolution limiting its activities to Palestine and neighboring countries.[153] Weizmann immediately wrote to Percy Baker, a fellow member on the executive of the EZF, suggesting that they and Max Shire and Herbert Bentwich, their like-minded friends on the executive, resign.[154] He also consulted Gaster, insisting that "by their actions Greenberg and Cowen have not struck a death blow at the movement . . . My mind went blank when I read the letter . . . I am determined to announce my resignation from the Federation . . . What is your view? What must be done?"[155] Gaster counseled Weizmann and Baker to withhold their resignations for the time being[156] until the facts surrounding the joint appeal could be clarified.

Weizmann now saw an opportunity for finally removing Greenberg from the national leadership of the EZF. Yet his experience during the summer of 1904 had taught him not to attack Greenberg or accuse him publicly without investigating the facts. He believed that Greenberg must have had weighty reasons for publishing the letter with the ITO.[157] He suspected that he had coordinated his action with SAC,[158] which was indeed the case. Percy Baker was informed by Wolffsohn that the latter had agreed to the EZF-ITO move as a general charitable appeal.[159] Unlike Weizmann, Wolffsohn saw no sacrifice of Zionist principles by cooperating with non-Zionist organizations during emergencies. In fact, the ITO-EZF appeal was a logical consequence of the Brussels Conference and its resolutions. Moreover, Wolffsohn's political approach to Zionism, one might safely assume, predisposed him to a certain sympathetic personal attitude toward Zangwill even if he rejected the program of the ITO.[160]

Still, Weizmann waited patiently for the meeting of the EZF Central Committee, which was to take place on July 22, 1906. That meeting totally repudiated the actions of Greenberg and Cowen. Yet in the period prior to that meeting Weizmann was again shocked when he learned that not only had Wolffsohn approved the joint appeal, but that on July 15 he had come to London to attend a Zionist-ITO meeting called by Oscar Straus, of the ITO International Committee, to further discuss the resolutions reached at the Brussels Conference. That meeting resolved to advocate large-scale settlement and eventual local autonomy in a region unspecified. Wolffsohn's proposal that Palestine and its neighboring regions be given first consideration in any settlement plans and be objectively considered was deferred for future discussion.[161] This made Wolffsohn an active and willing culprit in Greenberg and Cowen's schemes. Weizmann now understood that he had held false hopes when he had welcomed Wolffsohn as leader of the movement, trusting in his ability and goodwill.[162] It would seem that Berthold Feiwel had, after all, correctly assessed Wolffsohn some months earlier when, writing from Cologne, he complained of differences between himself, as editor in chief of *Die Welt*, and the leader of the movement.[163] Weizmann sat down to write a carefully drafted letter, warning Wolffsohn of the Greenberg-Cowen clique and their activities in England.

> . . . I learned from the Anglo-Jewish papers last Saturday [July 21] that you were in London last week, that a conference was held there, that resolutions were published, that Territorialist circles are now making capital of these matters, etc., etc. . . .
>
> You cannot fail to realize that for us—I mean Dr. Dreyfus, Mr. Moser and myself—it was most unpleasant to learn from the newspapers alone what had happened in London. We were assailed from all sides with question after question, and stood there bewildered—I knew no more than what was written in the papers . . .
>
> . . . we are after all members of the [G]AC, your direct representatives, who are only too ready *always, always*—you have only to ask—to serve you with information, advice and action. Have we deserved to be *thus* ignored?

And how important, how exceptionally important, it would be for you, dear Mr. Wolffsohn, to have an *accurate* picture of what is going on here! . . .

. . . I am completely objective, guided by no personal motive, not resident in London and so am free of the spirit of intrigue prevailing in the Sodom that goes by the name of Zionism there . . .

How nonplussed the Zionist following must have been when Greenberg, having attacked the ITO so very sharply in the Liverpool resolution [on April 22, which upheld the Basel Program and condemned philanthropic efforts on behalf of the Jewish people], issues a joint manifesto with the ITO one month later . . . Place yourself for a moment in the psychological condition of an average Zionist who knows nothing about "higher politics." What is he to think of leaders who change front at any moment, who knowingly act contrary to the decisions of the Congress . . .

At the last meeting of the Federation, on Sunday the 22nd . . . by an overwhelming majority of votes the Liverpool resolution was declared superfluous and pointless, a resolution in favor of the amendment of the Bank statutes was carried, the joint manifesto of the Federation and the ITO was deplored . . .

. . . But what is the situation in the movement now? No positive Zionist work, no proper agitation, no shekalim, etc., etc. These things are not appreciated. Instead, pride of place is given to political hot air, publicity-mongering, large mass meetings with speeches saying first one thing and then the exact opposite. It is pathetic how demoralized the movement is in London. No recruitment, no loyalty, no faith in the leadership, confusion, bog. All the "successes" are worthless . . .

I am writing this with my heart's blood, dear Mr. Wolffsohn, as your [G]AC colleague, your friend, your admirer. How, for God's sake, could you associate yourself, even though entirely privately, with that conference and mass meeting? Why did you not enquire also of us? Why did you rely on one side only? . . .

I consider any possibility of working here out of the question: any activity is frustrated in advance. We shall be reminded over and over again of the manifesto and the conference . . . the Federation Committee is collapsing, must fall to pieces, unless the situation is clarified.[164]

Clearly Weizmann intended to prepare the ground for Greenberg and Cowen's ouster from the EZF leadership and for the annual conference, which was to meet in Cologne at the end of August. Wolffsohn replied, in the meantime, that his meeting with the ITO representatives had been blown out of proportion. Remarking that the English Zionists had to work with Greenberg, Cowen, and Montefiore until they chose other leaders, he also implied that Weizmann was being used by Gaster for the *Haham*'s purposes, clearly referring to Weizmann's strong support of Gaster at the EZF executive meeting on July 22.[165] This allegation Weizmann was anxious to dispel: "I have acted in complete independence, without allowing myself to be swayed . . . I fully realize that Gaster is embittered, but I am not moved in any way by bitterness or personal motives."[166] This was not quite true, since Gaster was carefully orchestrating the moves of the opposition members of the EZF executive, which included Dreyfus, Baker, Shire, Bentwich, and Weizmann. Gaster's own preferred scenario was to embarrass Greenberg into resigning as honorary secretary of the EZF. Failing that, he was contemplating the creation of a new Zionist federation.[167] This strategy was crowned with success within a few weeks.

Despite Weizmann's exaggerated claim that since the Seventh Zionist Congress he had participated in "over sixty meetings in various towns,"[168] he was, in fact, devoting only a small part of his time to Zionist propaganda. Though he had been elected vice president of the Manchester Zionist Association in July 1906,[169] he did not even mention this to Vera, nor the fact that he had been elected to a committee to approach the new Liberal government to modify or repeal the provisions of the Aliens Act.[170] Except for emergencies in the Jewish and Zionist world—such as the pogroms in Russia or the EZF-ITO manifesto—he was not greatly moved to be involved in public affairs.[171] The main reasons for this partial abstention was his dissatisfaction with his surroundings. He was enjoying England, and particularly Manchester, less and less, he shared no common language either with the Zionists or the English Jews he met,[172] and he still missed his lively Geneva circle and, of course, Vera. So alienated was he from his surroundings that, having nowhere to go on Yom Kippur, the most solemn day in the Jewish calendar, he went to work instead—probably for the first time in his life.[173]

He worked out his frustrations mostly in the university laboratory, where he was now a demonstrator and Perkin's assistant. Here, unlike Zionist work, success was achieved in direct relation to the effort invested. He continued to dislike the grimy surroundings at Clayton,[174] but this was now a less significant factor since he could conduct most of the experiments for the factory in his own laboratory at the university, where his relations with Perkin continued to be excellent.[175] He also enjoyed teaching large numbers of students.[176] His one disappointment at the university was the long delay in his promotion, but this was as much due to his driving ambition,[177] as it was to Perkin's constant dangling of yet another opportunity before his eyes.[178] The fact that he merely attained the degree of master of science from Victoria University in 1906[179] and did not get promoted to the position of senior lecturer until 1907 did not prevent Weizmann from continuously assuring everyone he knew that he would soon be given a professorship, as if it were in Perkin's or Dixon's power just to hand him the position.

During the winter he had been making good progress in his work for the factory on experiments which Perkin had suggested as early as August 1904. With the assistance of Perkin, who had also been engaged to work for Dreyfus, he was getting very close to producing a marketable form of synthetic camphor, when it became clear to him that Alexander Meyenberg, the manager of Clayton, was sabotaging his work.[180] Dreyfus did chastise Meyenberg,[181] but the latter continued his scheming. As the process was nearing completion, Meyenberg and other chemists at the factory demanded that Weizmann's experiments be retested at the

Clayton laboratories. This gave Weizmann the opportunity he sought to put his opponents in their place once and for all. He delivered an ultimatum to Dreyfus, declaring that if a single experiment were carried out at Clayton he would drop the entire work and not touch it again. It is a testimony to Weizmann's stature at Clayton that "Dreyfus took fright. He came tearing to my home in the morning and began to explain. I told him that he is surrounded by ignoramuses and impostors who deceive and cheat him, that I require absolute independence for myself, [my assistants] Friedl and Bentley, and that we won't release a single piece of work from the College unless we have this guarantee. Dreyfus agreed to everything and now all is well."[182] Indeed, all continued to be well. By the end of March Weizmann predicted that the actual production of synthetic camphor would soon begin.[183] In early May he was shocked to learn that a German factory had taken out a patent for camphor five days before the Clayton Aniline Factory, but fortunately it was a *Spekulations-Patent* and "completely worthless."[184]

One episode connected with the camphor experiments, however, almost resulted in a serious tragedy. In mid-January 1906 a student in the laboratory blundered by working with an impure chemical substance that subsequently exploded. The 250-degree liquid from the beaker poured over Weizmann's left hand.[185] The wound was much deeper and more serious than he had imagined at first and took six weeks to heal.[186] He was confined to his lodgings for a while, and even though from the very first day one of his lab boys came to dress him in the morning and one of his assistants put him to bed at night,[187] he complained that none of the Zionists had come to visit him.[188] But he was too quick to pass judgment. A few days later he reported to Vera:

> I was unfair to the Zionists when I said they don't come to see me; nobody knew. As soon as they found out they began coming, even a little too much. Mr. and Mme. Dreyfus visit me almost daily. Perkin came again today, but didn't find me, as I was at the College. Weinreb and Friedl are nice. They send you their kindest regards and always ask about you. The same is true of Benfey and Mme., who insist on my moving in with them. I shall go to their home on Saturday and Sunday. Even Meyenberg came yesterday.[189]

The recovery was slow and his friends continued to care for him. At the beginning of February he was again confined to his bed, where he experienced unbearable pain and suffering through endless and sleepless nights. "Opening my eyes this morning I suddenly saw Dr. Dreyfus by my bed. I find this warm sympathy very touching. Perkin came to see me today with a cab. He took me out for a while, and this was very pleasant."[190]

This incident clearly illustrates that Weizmann was not as isolated as he sometimes liked to suggest. Over a period of eighteen months he had built around him a coterie of friends, assistants, and collaborators who cared about his well-being. Apart from professional medical care, they saw to it that all his needs were met over a relatively long period of time.

With Vera on their wedding day, August 23, 1906

Family group at Weizmann's wedding, Zoppot, 1906

The accident in the laboratory also reveals something of Weizmann's relations with Vera. In the first ten letters after the accident, he tried to minimize both the wound and the pain, protecting her from the truth in the paternalistic tone which he often adopted toward her. It was only three weeks after the accident that he finally admitted to her: "It is hard to imagine how much I have suffered all this time—more than three weeks."[191] On the other hand—and this is very much in character—he tended to greatly exaggerate his injury when writing to his friends. To Judah Leon Magnes he wrote, "There was an explosion in my laboratory and I was badly injured. Both my hands were severely affected, the right less than the left, luckily. But my burns were so severe that I was in danger of losing the latter. I had to stay in bed for three weeks . . . Now the right hand is completely healed, the left still bandaged and I am out of my sickroom."[192]

Vera could hardly afford to spend too much time worrying about Weizmann's hand, though she suspected all along that he was not telling her the whole truth. She was undergoing her own purgatory of examinations, "attacks of nerves," and headaches; she was more moody and on edge than ever before and was constantly advised by her fiancé—quite thoughtlessly—to take care of herself and rest. The ordeal was finished when she finally became a doctor in May 1906. When the news reached Weizmann he took his three closest colleagues—Weinreb, Friedl, and Bentley—for a drink at the Midland Hotel.[193] During the last week of May 1906 Vera boarded a train for Rostov—not without Weizmann trying to persuade her again to visit his family in Pinsk.[194] This time he was unsuccessful. The news that came from the Khatzman house in Rostov was alarming, and Vera was in a hurry to see her family, only to learn upon her arrival that her father had passed away a day earlier.[195]

Nothing seemed to stand in the way of a marriage now. In early June Weizmann made up his mind that the wedding would take place in August,[196] and though Vera's belongings from Geneva had begun to arrive in Manchester, he was slow to inform her of his final plans.[197] On the other hand, his acquaintances in Manchester were told of his impending marriage; at the end of the semester a student delegation arrived at Weizman's lab to inquire of his wishes for a wedding gift.[198] It was not that Weizmann got cold feet at the last moment; on the contrary, he was longing for a life together with Vera, in which "everything will be different, much better."[199] The problem was to find a place where the formalities for the wedding could be easily arranged and which would be agreeable to the dispersed members of the family. Weizmann would have preferred Switzerland, but the formalities there were too complicated for nonresidents.[200] His parents ruled out Warsaw because Ozer Weizmann was no longer on good terms with his son in law Chaim Lubzhinsky, ever since Feivel Weizmann had divorced Lubzhinsky's sister, Fanya.[201] A compromise solution was suggested by Weizmann's sister Miriam: Zoppot, near Danzig.[202] By the time everyone agreed to this it was already July 30, and the final formalities had to be hurriedly arranged by Weizmann at the very last moment.[203]

On August 23, 1906, a few members of Weizmann's family gathered at the small synagogue in Zoppot. The party included: his parents, Ozer and Rachel Leah Weizmann; his elder brother Feivel; and his sister Miriam Lubzhinsky.[204] No member of Vera's family could make it to the wedding, which was performed according to the traditional Jewish rite. All in all, after nearly six years of waiting, it seems that the wedding in Zoppot passed in a rather subdued mood.[205]

Two days later they left Zoppot for Cologne, where Weizmann attended the annual conference from August 28 to 31. It was hardly a honeymoon, with Weizmann returning to the hotel room in the small hours of the morning, sheepishly bringing Vera an offering of flowers and fruit.[206] It was only after the Zionist meetings were over that they bought third-class tickets to travel up the Rhine.[207]

XIII

The Theory and Practice
of Synthetic Zionism

The forty-one men attending the annual conference at Cologne (August 28–31, 1906) could hardly have been impressed by David Wolffsohn's report on the SAC's activities during the past year. He informed them about the movement's efforts on behalf of East European Jewry, the outcome of the Brussels Conference, which he called a success,[1] and the establishment of a branch of the Anglo-Palestine Company in Beirut. Wolffsohn also emphasized the ever greater role of the bank in Zionist affairs. These achievements were viewed as quite meager by those attending the conference. In addition, the general financial situation of the movement was less than rosy due to a declining shekel income. Wolffsohn ended his report with an optimistic survey of the various Zionist federations around the world.[2] The discussion which ensued did not produce any new information, since Wolffsohn refused to elaborate in public on political activities. The only excitement during the first day came when Joseph Cowen heatedly defended his opposition to any changes in the statutes of the bank. There followed unsuccessful demands for his ouster from the directorate of the bank, while the changes were approved in conformity with the decisions of the Seventh Zionist Congress. Weizmann entered the controversy with a plea for greater involvement of the bank in Palestine at the expense of new branches in neighboring territories.[3]

The central theme of the annual conference revolved around the interpretation of the resolutions of the Seventh Zionist Congress, which had been an amended version of that made in Freiburg in July 1905. The Seventh Zionist Congress had resolved to systematically consolidate Zionist positions in Palestine in concert with political and diplomatic action. This was to be accomplished by means of the following: comprehensive research; advancement in agriculture and industry; the cultural and economic organization of Palestinian Jewry by an infusion of new intellectual forces; the introduction of administrative and legal reforms. All unsystematic and philanthropic small-scale colonization was decisively rejected.[4]

The final formulation of the resolutions at the Seventh Zionist Congress had been the joint effort of Alexander Marmorek—who had suggested the amendments on behalf of the "politicals"—and of Ussishkin.[5] At the annual conference they violently disagreed over their interpretation. The catalyst for this dispute was Ussishkin's proposals for the establishment of a fund for land purchase and the creation of an agrarian bank. Marmorek saw these proposals as a deviation from the resolutions of the Seventh Zionist Congress and a return to Hovevei Zion methods. He argued that the Commission for the Investigation of Palestine, headed by Warburg, was only empowered to engage in research, not in economic activities. He also claimed that the Jewish National Fund had not been set up to found commercial enterprises.[6]

Weizmann entered the fray in support of Warburg and Ussishkin. He moved the discussion onto a broader philosophical plane in which he examined the interplay between political activities and practical work. Taking his cue from Berthold Feiwel, Weizmann, too, suggested that passive resistance to work in Palestine pervaded SAC. This, he claimed, was a widespread feeling in the movement as well as among those present at the annual conference. A dichotomy existed between the wishes of the masses and the leadership. Referring to Marmorek's charges, he continued:

> The slightest work in Palestine is often condemned as Hovevei Zionism. I can understand if one considers certain work in Palestine as insufficient or wrong. But the politicians here present, who constantly speak of their devotion to Palestine, cannot be content with total lack of initiative in regard to work in Palestine while emphatically stressing their disapproval of the performance of the Palestine Commission. I am not one of those who disparage political work as such; on the contrary, I am completely in favor of exploiting political opportunities in order to achieve our goal.[7]

But political work was not sufficient; it had to be based on concrete and practical achievements. Borrowing Leopold Greenberg's metaphor, which likened Zionism to a tunnel which had to be dug from both ends, Weizmann firmly believed in the need to pursue political and practical Zionism at one and the same time. As the foundations of practical work were strengthened, the chances for a successful political work would be increased.[8]

The immediate impact of the debate that followed Weizmann's speech was the acceptance of Ussishkin's suggestions to explore the possibilities of founding a mortgage bank and of establishing a land-purchase fund. For Weizmann, his speech at the annual conference marked the first time in which he publicly developed the principles of what would soon come to be known as "synthetic Zionism." He would develop it further at the EZF annual meeting in Birmingham in February 1907, and at the World Zionist Congress in The Hague in August of that year. The fact that he was willing to challenge Alexander Marmorek, a member of SAC, shows that he felt confident in his abilities and was unafraid to voice an opinion not popular with the majority of the executive.[9] Weizmann's speech drew him even closer to the circle around Ussishkin and marked him as one of the outspoken proponents of "practical" Zionism. His success at the annual meeting also encouraged him to openly challenge the leadership of the EZF, a goal toward which he began working immediately upon his return to Manchester.

Weizmann's aim to oust from the leadership of the EZF those he considered purely political Zionists and to install "practicals" reflected similar trends in the movement. The most important expression of the changing orientation in the movement was expressed in the third conference of Russian Zionists, which was held from December 4 to 10, 1906, in Helsingfors (Helsinki), in the Grand Duchy of Finland, safe from the harassment of the Russian police. Some of Russia's leading Zionists, such as Ussishkin, Simon Rosenbaum, Jacob Bernstein-Kohan, and Vladimir Tyomkin, were absent from its proceedings,[10] but younger, energetic men—particularly Abraham Idelson, Yitzhak Gruenbaum, and Vladimir Jabotinsky—meticulously laid the groundwork for the seventy-two participants from fifty-six cities, thereby contributing to its success.[11] The Helsingfors Conference is best known for its emphasis on *Gegenwartsarbeit*, that is, its resolutions on political work for the Jewish masses in the Diaspora, while rejecting what the delegates called "catastrophic Zionism."[12] The delegates interpreted the Basel Program as a directive to Zionists to organize the Jewish masses in the Diaspora as a national minority and lead them in the Zionist spirit. They felt that such activity would strengthen Diaspora Jewry and provide it with new cultural, material, and political means in its struggle for the creation of a sound national life in *Eretz Israel*. They called for a liberalized, democratic Russia with wide, autonomous rights for its non-Russian peoples, including the Jewish nation, which, through a comprehensive organizational framework, would exercise its political rights and cultural, educational, and, in certain respects, even administrative autonomy both in Hebrew and Yiddish. It was the firm belief of those assembled that such a program would transform Zionism from an activity remote from the Jewish masses and confined to the diplomatic and pioneering sphere into a dynamic movement concerned with the actual needs of the Jews, particularly in Russia.[13]

This program could be implemented in Russia only after 1917—albeit for a very brief period. For the immediate future the first part of the Helsingfors Program was much more significant for the impact it had on the course of the Zionist movement. Yehiel Tschlenow, the chairman of the conference, gave the tone to the discussion in his speech on the direction and goals of political Zionism and the current tasks awaiting the movement. He emphasized the failure of political Zionism and its neglect of practical work in Palestine. He called for the immediate creation in Palestine of agricultural and commercial enterprises.[14] Those who spoke after Tschlenow (e.g., Boris Goldberg and Daniel Pasmanik) elaborated on his practical suggestions and analysis. It was also here that the lawyer Simon Weissenberg, a delegate from St. Petersburg, first used the

Leon Simon

Simon Marks (left) and Israel Sieff (right)

Harry Sacher

term "synthesis" to explain the new direction in Zionism: The Hibbat Zion represented the "thesis," Herzlian diplomacy came as the "antithesis," while "synthetic Zionism" reconciled these conflicting directions in the movement, embracing and streamlining both in the common service of the Zionist movement.[15] The resolutions at the Helsingfors Conference concerning practical work in Palestine clearly charted a new course.

> Recognizing that the manifold development of our positions in Eretz Israel and the systematic preparation of the land itself as a safe haven secured by public law for the Jewish people constitute, according to the first paragraph of the Basel Program, the principal and organic elements of Zionism's political aim;
>
> That inactivity coupled with future expectations could damage the stability and productivity of our movement;
>
> That without concrete achievements in this direction our political-diplomatic struggle for Eretz Israel will be devoid of the necessary weight and actual force—
>
> This conference has resolved to demand of our executive institutions, in

accordance with the resolutions of the Seventh Congress, to engage in continuous, energetic, and planned work in Eretz Israel, concomitant with political activity which is consonant with the political character of our movement.

A settlement which aims to create an autonomous society must be well planned in its initial phases, because only thus can the foundation be created for orderly mass immigration in the future—the conference recognizes that the aim of practical work in Eretz Israel must, on the one hand, constitute the creation of necessary conditions for a natural and progressively increasing mass Jewish immigration while, on the other hand, securing the decisive influence of the Jewish element in the cultural, economic, and public life of Eretz Israel.[16]

The conference also urged the creation of a Palestine office that would coordinate all Zionist work in Palestine and the establishment of an agency in Constantinople which would remove political obstacles for orderly Zionist work. It also called for support of Jewish self-organization in Palestine, the improvement of Jewish education and working conditions, the creation of an agrarian or mortgage bank, the founding of a Hebrew periodical in Palestine, and support for reforestation and the Bezalel School in Jerusalem.

Weizmann was clearly in full accord with the resolutions concerning Palestine. One suspects that he even had some sympathy for the *Gegenwartsarbeit* program proposed at Helsingfors, which rivaled in its theoretical and practical measures that of the Bund, directing itself to the immediate hardships of Russian Jewry. It was the kind of program he would have supported during his Geneva years. But Weizmann was not firmly aligned with Ussishkin, who showed his disapproval of *Gegenwartsarbeit* by absenting himself from Helsingfors. Weizmann, too, disapproved of involving Zionists in Russian domestic politics. Moreover, he feared that the Helsingfors Conference would split the Zionist movement in Russia.[17] Yet Ussishkin and his colleagues, while definitely not recognizing Tschlenow's leadership and pointedly absenting themselves from Helsingfors, accepted the resolutions of the conference as binding. For his part, Weizmann did not publicly voice his objections to its ideological formulations. In fact, in preparation for the EZF annual conference, he and Harry Sacher, a new recruit to Zionism who had recently joined the staff of *The Manchester Guardian*, were busily writing a programmatic pamphlet which reinforced the Palestine-centered recommendations of the Helsingfors Conference. Their circular emphasized the need for practical Zionism both as an educational force and as a protection against further schism. It called for an investigation of Palestine and the strengthening of the Jewish community there through support for its cultural, educational, and economic activities as well as through the establishment of trade unions and an agricultural bank. Weizmann and Sacher maintained that the EZF's rehabilitation required the formation of a committee for Palestinian affairs which would cooperate with similar committees elsewhere in raising funds, assisting the Bezalel School, the

Herzl Forest project, and the publication of a Hebrew newspaper in Palestine.[18]

Weizmann was by now sufficiently experienced in the politics of the movement to know that changes within it would not be effected by pamphlets and propaganda alone. Structural and administrative changes would have to take place first. His letter to Wolffsohn in July 1906 marked the first step in his attempt to unseat the current leadership at the next conference of the EZF in Birmingham. His aim was to remove Cowen and Greenberg from the federation's leadership and replace them with "practicals," notably the *Haham* Moses Gaster. The task was made easier by Greenberg's voluntary resignation as EZF honorary secretary immediately after the annual conference in Cologne. Greenberg cited as one of the reasons for his departure his appointment to the board of the Jewish National Fund.[19] This was at best a flimsy excuse since he was also a member of SAC and a member of the directorate of the Jewish Colonial Trust, neither of which were very time-consuming activities. Possibly he was just not in a mood for a fight, preferring to bow out of the EZF gracefully rather than facing the prospect of working with Gaster as the president of the federation.

Weizmann's behind-the-scenes maneuvers in preparation for the Birmingham conference of the EZF, in February 1907, provide us with an interesting insight into his diplomatic and tactical skills. On September 30, 1906, he described to Gaster a plan which he attributed to Wolffsohn, with whom he had discussed it at the annual conference in Cologne. Though Wolffsohn's natural sympathies were with Greenberg and Cowen, he must have been convinced by Weizmann that the situation within the EZF called for change. If Weizmann could similarly persuade the English rank and file, Wolffsohn was not going to stand in his way.

> I have been thinking about the matter as follows, and incidentally, what I now wish to tell you is a Sokolow-Wolffsohn proposal: a sound, broader committee should be established in London as representative of the Federation. Possibly we might have the Central Office with secretariat here in Manchester. Dreyfus, Moser and I would take charge of the latter; you, Sir Francis [Montefiore] and Bentwich the former.
>
> I believe this apparatus would function well, and would do justice to all sides, by which I mean London and the Provinces.[20]

A few weeks later he had second thoughts concerning the move of the EZF secretariat to Manchester. True, Percy Baker, the new honorary secretary of the EZF, was "too insignificant intellectually to take command of the situation," but perhaps it would be advisable to let him carry on and see how he ran things. "Here it always sounds like a revolution when you speak of transferring the Bureau to Manchester."[21] He had no wish to act the revolutionary. For the time being his aim was to influence things from a distance, not to acquire the prestige of office. Moreover, title and honor were much more important to Moses Gaster; Weizmann had no wish to appear as if he was competing with the *Haham*, the key person in the new projected leadership of the EZF. But Gaster, who feigned a lack of interest in the presidency of the EZF, had to be "convinced" first that coming to Birmingham was important. Weizmann, Percy Baker, and others began a concerted effort to persuade Gaster that his presence and active participation in Birmingham were crucial: "Insignificant though the EZF is in itself, the fact unfortunately remains that only through it can one acquire influence over the *Landsmanschaft*. Outside the EZF it would be hard to achieve anything, first of all on account of the shortage of organizational talent. I am not in the slightest concerned about the 'Sir' [Francis Montefiore], who could doubtless be accommodated as 'honorary Pres.' "[22] By the beginning of January the plan for the coup had matured: Gaster would come in as the president of the EZF, while Francis Montefiore would be promoted to the meaningless post of honorary president.[23]

Moses Gaster was not an easy man to promote. If Weizmann had momentarily forgotten his past observations about Gaster's tremendous ambition,[24] suspicious nature, and pettiness,[25] he was quickly reminded of these traits as a result of a tactical error. At the suggestion of Baker, who deemed it difficult to unseat Montefiore, Weizmann dared to intimate that Gaster enter the EZF leadership first as a vice president.

> It may surprise you to find me in favor of "evolution." However, I have had a bitter price to pay for my experience . . . You do know, dear Doctor, that— pardon the expression—I don't care a damn for the 'Sirs,' but at the moment there's nothing else to be done. In 4–5 months everything will have been refashioned in your spirit.[26]

Gaster, who a week earlier had indicated that he would reconsider his decision not to attend the EZF Conference only if he were assured an absolute majority for election as president, peaceful discussions at the conference, and a position of complete freedom and authority,[27] now turned his full wrath on Weizmann. He declared that he would not agree to any compromises. Moreover, he considered it an insult to be placed on the same level with Cowen and Greenberg. He regretted the fact that Weizmann had been influenced by Baker. He would gladly forego the honor of the presidency, which he neither sought nor needed.[28] Whatever happened, Zionism would continue to be represented by him. So-called Zionists had no claim on him, unless they showed unbounded loyalty and a better understanding for the situation and his person.[29]

As in the past, when confronted by Gaster's anger Weizmann immediately retreated.

> I am terribly sorry that you are annoyed even with me, that you suspect me of having been made to change my mind . . . I only wrote how things are . . . How can you suspect me of any sort of crooked dealing? I promise you I will leave the EZF if I cannot change the state of affairs. I have only stayed on for your sake. I hate with all my soul being involved in a scuffle with those people. Should we have to quit the field, we ought to make one last attempt to save things.

I am writing you these lines with my heart's blood. *We* are in a terrible crisis.[30]

Gaster replied with a more conciliatory letter, hinting that he might come to Birmingham after all, but still insisting that all his conditions be met.[31] In addition to his requirement that his election to president of the EZF be fixed in advance, that no opposition of any consequence take place at the conference, and that Weizmann and his friends quit the EZF if this were not to materialize, he also insisted that no ceremony honoring Greenberg take place in Birmingham.[32] Finally, four days before the conference was scheduled to meet (February 3, 1907) Gaster consented to attend.[33]

Before Weizmann could fulfill his promise to Gaster, the fifty delegates present were engaged in lively and heated debates on the merits of political and practical Zionism. The debate was generated by the programmatic brochure written by Weizmann and Sacher and the resolutions of the Manchester Zionist Association, which followed from this program and were to be presented to the Eighth Zionist Congress. The resolutions, which endorsed the Helsingfors Program, were drafted by Weizmann. They stated: (1) that the diplomatic work of the (Smaller) Actions Committee represented only one part of the required political activity and that diplomacy was only effective when based on firm economic and cultural achievements in Palestine; (2) that the next Zionist congress establish in Palestine itself a committee for the thorough investigation of the country's resources; (3) that this committee give the fullest encouragement to Jewish activity in Palestine by helping to establish clubs, societies, etc., and that special attention be devoted to the creation of Jewish schools; it should also do its utmost to improve the economic conditions of Jewish wage earners, in particular by encouraging the growth of trade unions; (4) that the Eighth Zionist Congress establish an agrarian bank in Palestine for granting loans based on security to Jewish colonists.[34]

Seconded by Harry Sacher, Weizmann delivered the main speech for the practicals' endorsement of the Manchester resolutions. Zionism, he stated, had been dominated by phraseology. What was called "political Zionism" was really "diplomatic Zionism," and English Zionists had accepted the position that a time would come when the diplomatic agents of the movement would bring to it a charter for Palestine. Hence the inaction in regard to work in Palestine. The erstwhile methods of the movement, however, were no longer adequate for a solution to the current practical problems. What was needed was slow, difficult work of a different nature, which required quiet sacrifice. The charter would merely sanction peaceful penetration into Palestine. "I believe in Herzl and his politics, but charters do not drop from heaven. The charter will not come while we sit here inactive, we will only get it as a consequence of work in the country [Palestine]. Of course there are difficulties and dangers, but what people has freed itself without dangers? Do you think you will free the Jewish people by speaking at meetings at home? No, this will be possible only as a result of work in Palestine itself . . . The task should begin now, and be undertaken quietly."[35] Weizmann concluded by stating: "I don't underestimate the value of diplomacy, but our diplomatic activity is, after all, supported and made easier through economic successes in Palestine. I do take exception to the misuse of the concept 'political' Zionism, and its confusion and identification with pure diplomatic work."[36]

Cowen retorted that although practical work in Palestine had propagandistic value, he felt that this was its only merit and therefore should not be supported. It was not permissible, he said, to squander the people's money for this purpose. It would be irresponsible to expand the work in Palestine without a firm political foundation. "We already have three branches of the Anglo-Palestine Company in Palestine," Cowen asserted. "Do you demand that we open another branch every five minutes? Hovevei Zionism is very good indeed, but it has as little to do with us as does territorialism." Cowen urged instead that Zionists focus on acquiring the right to Palestine from Constantinople. Feverish activity within Palestine at the present time could only result in conflict with the Turks.[37] Cowen also cited the unfortunate history of the Rothschild colonies, which had eaten up millions of francs and which could provide a lesson to those who believed in practical work. The total income of the movement in 1906, Cowen reminded his listeners, was not more than twenty thousand marks from shekel revenue. Not too many Jews could be settled in Palestine with that kind of money. A great deal was being done in Palestine already, and the work there had to proceed slowly and carefully. "They must first learn to walk before they can run, and because they are not moving on as fast as he, in common with Dr. Weizmann, would like, they had no right to say Zionism was dead . . ."[38]

The conflict between Cowen and Weizmann at the EZF Conference reflected similar debates that had taken place within GAC in Cologne a few months earlier. Weizmann's speech at Birmingham was a forceful further development of his belief, as publicly enunciated in Cologne in August 1906, that diplomatic and practical work were both necessary and interdependent if the movement was to succeed. The resolutions he presented at Birmingham in the name of the Manchester Zionist Association were adopted with two amendments. The first deleted the word "only" before "effective" in the first resolution, thus reading: ". . . that the diplomatic work of the Actions Committee can be effective when based . . ." The second amended the fourth resolution to read: ". . . that the Eighth Congress be requested to devise means by which Jewish colonists may be granted loans upon security."[39] These two amendments somewhat weakened the resolutions, but clearly Weizmann's conception emerged victorious from the proceedings. Perhaps just as important was the fact that he found at Birmingham new supporters for his ideas among some English Zionists. These included Herbert Bentwich, a founder of the EZF and the Grand Commander of the Order of Ancient Maccabeans, which would soon become an important vehicle in Weizmann's struggles within the Zionist movement in England. There were also some young newcomers to the movement, which included Harry Sacher, Samuel Landman, Norman Bentwich (Herbert's son), and Leon Simon, son of a Manchester rabbi, a budding Hebraist who had recently begun his civil service career in the post office. This was a new generation which did not feel encumbered by any of the ideologies current during the 1880s and 1890s. They were all English-born Jews who chose to follow their commonsense brand of Zionism and became "Gasterites" around 1905–7. Weizmann's theories made sense to them. In addition, they were captivated by the personality of this authentic East European Jew, so different from the Jewish patricians they had known all their lives. Instead of rehashing old theories he brought them new, well-reasoned Zionist ideas which stood in opposition to those espoused by the established EZF leadership. The value of their support for Weizmann was magnified by the fact that almost all of them had an easy and powerful pen and access to newspapers and other publications. Thus they were able to reach large audiences. Led by Weizmann, they would shortly constitute a distinct group known as the Manchester School of Zionism.[40] In the months just prior to World War I these men of letters were joined by two young businessmen, Simon Marks and Israel Sieff. "They learned their Zionism from Weizmann; they became not only his disciples, but his friends, counselors, and coadjutors, and at all critical moments injected a largeness of practical vision and a willingness of sacrifice. They had the courage of imagination, they could see mountains of difficulty degenerating into molehills, and they always set the target at its maximum . . . they brought to bear an uncommon sureness of judgement. The women of the group [Rebecca Sieff and Miriam Sacher] were as interested and as active as their menfolk . . ."[41] This, then, constituted Weizmann's core support group, not only during the Manchester period but throughout his career. Though he never created for himself a broad constituency within the Zionist movement as a whole, it was probably at Birmingham that this small group of loyal followers began to exert their influence in support of Weizmann's ideas.

The Birmingham Conference terminated in a state of shaky peace within the EZF, symbolized by a public reconciliation between Gaster and Cowen amid the cheers of the delegates, and by the closing speeches of Greenberg and Weizmann, who spoke in Yiddish. The amended Manchester resolutions submitted by Weizmann were accepted and constitutional changes were effected whereby Montefiore was elected honorary president, Gaster president, Cowen London vice president, and Weizmann provincial vice president.[42] But despite Weizmann's efforts, his attempt to radically alter the EZF leadership structure was only partially successful; in fact, had Greenberg chosen to put up a fight, Weizmann might not have achieved as much as he did.[43] With Cowen continuing as vice president, it was only a matter of time before the truce between him and Gaster would evaporate under the heat of mutual recriminations. Weizmann's sincere efforts to effect a long-term reconciliation between these two contentious personalities[44] were futile. Cowen and Gaster were unable and unwilling to peacefully share power.[45]

Weizmann's position, on the other hand, had been strengthened. After two and a half years in England, he had achieved a respectable place in the national and even international Zionist world. Formally he held the position of EZF vice president, vice president of the Manchester Zionist Association, and membership in the Greater Actions Committee, but these were titles others also held without necessarily rising to national or international prominence. Weizmann, on the other hand, had skillfully managed to turn Manchester, an insignificant Zionist outpost, into an important power center from which he could wield influence. Berlin and Geneva had provided him with more intellectual stimulation and better company, but Manchester had proved to be an excellent base from which to rise to leadership, both within the EZF and within the World Zionist Organization. Having built his own power base on the periphery, he would, in the course of his sojourn in Manchester, strengthen and deepen his influence there until he became the dominant Zionist force in the provinces. Given London's fragmentation into Zionist enemy camps, his consolidation of the Manchester School of Zionism was indeed impressive. At the close of the conference Weizmann could easily be counted among the five or six most important and influential Zionists in England. Only Greenberg, Cowen, Bentwich, Charles Dreyfus, and possibly Percy Baker were his peers on the national level. None of them could count on a loyal young group of devotees, as could Weizmann, and none of them had his excellent ties to continental and particularly Russian Zionists. If Greenberg, and later Cowen, were Wolffsohn's most trusted men in England, Weizmann was without doubt the *Vertrauensmann* of that segment of "practicals" in the movement which was slowly gaining ground. Thus, it is quite clear that the Birmingham Conference marked the culmination of the first period in Weizmann's Zionist activity in England. During these two and a half years in Manchester he was far from inactive in the movement, as he later portrayed himself in his memoirs.[46]

He could now rest on his laurels for a while. Gaster, his closest ally in England, was president of the EZF; Weizmann's own position was firm. Moreover, Weizmann had plenty of personal problems to worry about. Vera and he arrived in Manchester after their short honeymoon without money, having literally spent their last penny on sandwiches bought on the train from London. Harry Sacher, who met them at the station, loaned them half a crown to pay for a cab to their lodgings.[47] Weizmann's rooms at Parkfield Street were adequate for a bachelor, but Vera found them depressing. A cab station in front of the house provided a background of unceasing noise, the three sparsely furnished rooms were cold and uninviting, and the landlady, untidy and lazy, was more interested in her detective novels than housekeeping. Hampered by her inability to speak English, Vera was almost perforce housebound, waiting in these miserable surroundings for Chaim to return home from his daily work at the laboratory or from weekend trips devoted to Zionist propaganda. The monotony was only broken by an occasional tea party to which the kindly professors' wives invited her, making valiant attempts to communicate with her in French,[48] and by Vera's trip to Paris at the end of March 1907 to visit her sister Sophia, who reciprocated with a visit to Manchester in July 1907. It became clear at the outset that they had to move to some more pleasant surroundings, an almost impossible undertaking given Weizmann's modest salary. At the beginning of December 1906 he therefore undertook—in addition to his work at the university and at Clayton—a job as examiner of chemistry papers for the Royal College of Science, South Kensington, which added another fifty or sixty pounds to his yearly budget.[49] Soon he was also marking papers for Oxford and Cambridge.[50] With the added income they were able to pay for new furniture, and on March 16, 1907, they moved into their new home at 57 Birchfields Road, which they rented for the surprisingly low sum of thirty-three pounds per year.[51] This would be their residence until 1913. Birchfields Road was definitely a step up from the drab surroundings of Cecil Street and Parkfield Street. It consisted of a row of semidetached houses, opposite the large and pleasant Birchfields Park. In close proximity to Victoria Park and the university, in 1907 it was one of Manchester's main roads, thus making it easily accessible by public transportation. The houses were attractive, with small gardens; in short, this was a solid, middle-class neighborhood.[52]

Feverish Zionist activity, two jobs plus additional moonlighting, worries about finances, and a generally tense and nervous state finally took their toll on Weizmann's health, which was never very good. After Birmingham he was exhausted and badly needed a rest,[53] but it was the middle of the academic semester and the work pace had to be kept up. Though he was anxious to cement the peace concluded in Birmingham between Gaster and Cowen and was fully aware that his presence as mediator was therefore necessary at meetings of the EZF executive, he tried to limit his trips to London—at least temporarily—for financial as well as health reasons. Instead, he urged Gaster by letter to issue a peace manifesto and hold large peace meetings that would consolidate the EZF.[54] Gaster finally produced such a manifesto on March 1—co-signed by Montefiore, Cowen, Weizmann, Greenberg, and Moser—which declared that political activity would be complemented by practical work.[55] Unable to attend the executive committee meeting of the EZF on February 19, 1907, which discussed the future work of the organization, Weizmann explained his absence thusly:

My state of health is unfortunately very serious as a result of fatigue and excitement of the last two years. I am so run down that any strain causes me to spit blood. After Birmingham I was not myself for a whole week. My throat was terribly painful, spasms of coughing and blood every minute. I had the greatest difficulty in concealing it from my wife. I can hardly tell you how much this hard life has taken out of me. The struggle for life and

Zionist affairs—both things have been very, very difficult. I just happen to
be a man who is terribly affected by everything . . .[56]

Even if one takes into consideration Weizmann's general proclivity to
exaggerate in reporting his personal situation—both positively and negatively—the evidence is clearly there to suggest that he badly needed some
rest. Yet even while writing to Gaster of his miserable physical condition, he was already preparing mentally for his next Zionist venture. As
so often in the past, he could not bypass a new challenge to create and
explore opportunities for the movement and for himself, no matter what
his state of mind and body. This time the challenge came from the engineer Johann Kremenetzky. Born in Odessa, Kremenetzky had settled
in Vienna, where he had become a spectacularly successful industrialist
and owner of one of the largest lamp factories in the world. One of Herzl's
earliest admirers and closest friends, he had intermittently been a member of SAC from 1897 to 1905 and of GAC from 1905 on, and was the
first head of the Jewish National Fund.[57] Though ideologically in the
"political" camp of the movement, Kremenetzky was also a builder and
a man of action who had long been able to observe Weizmann at the
congresses and GAC meetings. To a certain extent he was probably attracted to Weizmann, whose biography was not too dissimilar from his
own. Intrigued by this *Nein-Sager* firebrand, he finally decided to challenge him publicly from the pages of *Die Welt.* "Dr. Weizmann," wrote
Kremenetzky,

is a man of deeds . . . and complains that he has nothing on which to base
effective propaganda for Palestine . . . As far as I know, Dr. Weizmann is
a capable chemist. The best speech which Dr. Weizmann could make on behalf of Zionism would be for him to go to Palestine and to build a small
chemical industry . . . I don't simply want to give Dr. Weizmann advice
which he may not need; however, I would be willing to assist him, and to
raise a part of the required funds for the erection of a plant that would be
capable of maintaining itself and would be efficiently managed.[58]

In the correspondence that ensued between Weizmann and Kremenetzky, the latter suggested that Weizmann, as an industrial chemist, investigate the prospects of establishing an industry in Palestine. In particular, he was interested in the possibility of manufacturing such essential
oils as orange and lemon oil, as well as citric acid.[59] He was also interested in the production of perfumes. This assignment suited Weizmann
well since his current attempts to work out a process for the synthetic
production of camphor stood in close relation to that part of chemistry
which deals with essential oils.

Weizmann was able to persuade Kremenetzky that a preliminary study
tour of southern France and Italy was necessary. With all expenses paid
by Kremenetzky, he set out on his trip in the company of his assistant,
William Bentley, who would be working on any experiments resulting
from their journey. They stopped in London on March 21 in order to
enable Weizmann to take part in the EZF executive meeting. The follow-

ing day they set out for the Continent in the company of Vera, who would stay in Paris for three weeks with her sisters Rachel and Sophia Khatzman. On the whole, the trip went as scheduled. Weizmann probably visited Grasse, the important perfume center, and a factory producing citric oil in Messina. But he also took advantage of the opportunity to do a little sightseeing. After spending one night in Monte Carlo, he exclaimed, "Real hell! . . . I want to get away from this gang of elated scoundrels."[60] Rome was much more impressive, but he forced himself to keep it in historical perspective: ". . . the ancient ruins made a deep impression upon me. *Tout passe;* I [feel] no regrets about awe-inspiring Rome, powerful and beautiful. Feeble Jerusalem outlasted it. Only tourists walk upon the ruins of Rome, while on the ruins of Jerusalem new life is stirring! However, I feel positively dazed."[61] From Rome he went down to Sicily and then back to Switzerland via Rome and Venice. This time he visited the Vatican and was impressed by the innumerable artistic treasures. "I saw the original of Moses . . . My head is swimming from the Madonnas, Venuses, Christs, churches, frescoes, carpets, etc. . . ."[62] Venice was no less captivating. "It's a wonderful city. I didn't imagine anything like this . . . It is all interesting and beautiful, but one needs to have a great deal of money and time to make the most of it. Moreover, my artistic sense is probably very feeble, and of course I cannot appreciate all these things."[63] After a month of investigation, Weizmann reported his assessment to Kremenetzky. "Opportunities for a factory producing citric oil, tinned fruit and perfumes in Palestine are apparently unlimited. The materials would be easy to procure; climatic conditions for these special products are more favorable than in southern France or Sicily."[64] The recess between semesters was coming to an end and he hurried back to Manchester, asking Kremenetzky to make up the loss in his monthly salary from Clayton.[65] Unmindful of the weather conditions in Palestine during the summer, he decided to undertake the second part of the trip right after the Eighth Zionist Congress in August.

On June 2, 1907, Vera gave birth to a boy—Benjamin. It is remarkable that Weizmann decided to postpone his son's circumcision by three weeks in order to ensure the attendance at the ceremony of Moses Gaster, who was in Palestine at the time.[66] In the event, Gaster was unable to attend, and Harry Sacher became Benjamin's godfather.[67] But the very gesture indicates that despite his criticisms of the *Haham*, Weizmann also felt affection for the man who had done so much to help him over the past three difficult years.[68] He was now even more conscious of the need for money to support his little family and undertook to mark nine hundred papers for the Imperial College of Science and Technology.[69] But he was in good spirits. The Clayton Aniline Company was hoping to bring off the sale of the camphor patents, or at least to come to an agreement with a French firm. The sum of one hundred thousand pounds was mentioned and Weizmann already dreamed of being a rich man.[70] At the end of July he was sent by the company to negotiate the terms of the sale.[71]

As usual when he experienced moments of success in his work, Weizmann wrote to Gaster that he was about to be appointed "Senior Reader in Organic Chemistry."[72] A few months earlier he wrote to Otto Warburg that he was already a "Senior Demonstrator, which is more or less equivalent to the German Extraordinarius."[73] In fact, during the academic year 1906–7 he was still an assistant lecturer and demonstrator, and his only formal academic achievement that year was an award of a doctorate (D.Sc.) from the university.[74] It was only during the following academic year (1907–8) that he would be appointed senior lecturer,[75] and it was only in May 1913 that he was promoted to the post of reader. Clearly, his slow promotion did not keep up with his expectations and continued to be a source of frustration. For the time being, though, these setbacks were not acute problems, since his work in the movement provided a more immediate gratification.

The elections to the Eighth Zionist Congress were held in England on June 30, 1907, and Weizmann was hard at work to ensure that "practicals" would be sent as delegates. Already in the spring he had an inkling that the congress would be stormy. On March 23 he shared a Zionist platform with Max Nordau and Alexander Marmorek in Paris. Nordau contended that conditions were not yet suitable for working in Palestine, and Alexander Marmorek described such activities as fostering the *halukkah* (charity distribution) system rather than the national spirit.[76] Moreover, the reports that reached Weizmann in Manchester seemed to indicate that "a spirit of confusion and aimlessness" had taken over in Cologne, thus making the outcome of the congress uncertain.[77] This was not quite true. After two years in office Wolffsohn had become confident in his leadership abilities, and during a visit to London on July 9, 1907, he made it quite clear that the Zionist movement remained committed to its political course of action. The Zionists had to be loyal to the Turkish regime and not infiltrate Palestine without permission. Moreover, the treasury of the movement had to be husbanded carefully and much thought had to be given before undertaking any new ventures in Palestine.[78]

The main reason for Wolffsohn's visit to London was to convince Greenberg and Cowen to drop their opposition to an amendment of the Articles of Association of the Jewish Colonial Trust (JCT). The amendment concerned deleting the phrase "or any part of the world" from the company's articles, thus restricting its activities to Palestine, Syria, and the neighboring countries. This change, which had been discussed since the Third Zionist Congress, assumed a degree of urgency with the secession of the territorialists after the Seventh Zionist Congress in 1905. Israel Zangwill, who correctly perceived the harm that would ensue to the ITO from such a change, tried to stop the process through litigation in the British courts, which in July 1907 postponed judgment pending consultation of the shareholders.[79] Weizmann foresaw a heated debate on the issue at the Eighth Zionist Congress,[80] and, in fact, the entire fourth day of the sessions (August 18) was devoted to discussion of the JCT

With Vera, holding their son Benjy, November 1908

articles. Those who opposed litigation did so because of the very high
expense involved. Those who favored continuation of the battle wished
to lay the Uganda scheme to rest once and for all.[81] The discussions around
the Jewish Colonial Trust were only one indicator that the "politicals"
within the movement were not about to give up their positions without
a fight, though Herzlian Zionism in its purer form of "charterism" was
to play out its last act in 1907. The battle between the "practicals" and
"politicals," however, had yet to be fought. It was enacted in full at the
Eighth Zionist Congress.

In accordance with Herzl's tradition of keeping the Zionist movement
in the public eye, the congress met at The Hague from August 14 to 21,
1907, while the Second International Peace Congress was taking place
there. In view of the reaction that occurred in Russia following the failure of the revolution of 1905 and the dissolution of the Duma in mid-
June 1907, the Russian Zionists had no choice but to hold their Fourth
Zionist Conference in The Hague just prior to the congress (August 9–
13, 1907). Weizmann, who, in addition to a mandate from Manchester,
also held one from Vitebsk, participated in the conference and was elected

to its presidium, together with Tschlenow, Ussishkin, Rosenbaum, and Tyomkin; he also presided over the morning session of August 12.[82] He was further recognized and honored when elected as a Russian representative on the standing committee of the congress *(Permanenzausschuss)*. Weizmann tried hard to juggle his commitments to the conference, to GAC, which also met on August 12, and the standing committee, which met the following day. The Russian conference backed the resolutions of the Helsingfors Conference,[83] but it was also marked by the usual tumult and division among its members. Weizmann strongly supported Ussishkin's position on practical work in Palestine and declared that "Zionism had developed from a Zionism of a charter to a Zionism of actions and deeds in Palestine. This is evident from the many resolutions that have been accepted . . . It is Ussishkin who challenges us to carry out these resolutions and shows us how to do it . . . What is Zionism without work in Palestine?"[84] Syrkin, who replied, belittled these ideas. "Gentlemen, you lack faith. I believe with all my heart that we will get the charter! . . . Formerly [Jews] went to Palestine to die and now you want to bury our money in the land of Israel . . . In Ussishkin's speech I find only minor proposals . . . and no trace of political activity that will lead us to our goal."[85]

The debate continued for the next few days at the congress, which formally commenced on August 14 with 435 delegates, of whom 157 came from Russia.[86] In his opening speech Wolffsohn stipulated three main conditions for successful Zionist work: political activity, education of the people, and preparation of the land.[87] It was not by accident that the last priority mentioned in his speech was work in Palestine. Though he pointed to a series of achievements of the movement in Palestine, it was clear that its financial commitments to practical work were minimal. This fact was underscored by Nahum Sokolow's report on the movement and its institutions, which indicated that out of a pitiful total budget of eighty-one thousand marks (approximately twenty thousand dollars), only twenty-five hundred had been allocated to the Palestine commission.[88] Not surprisingly, many of the delegates criticized SAC's lack of achievements in Palestine, and even personal attacks against Wolffsohn were not absent.[89] One indication of the shifting priorities in the movement was the fact that the only one to speak at length on the importance of cultural work in the Diaspora—a major topic of debate in previous congresses—was Marcus Ehrenpreis.[90] The emphasis had clearly shifted to practical work in Palestine. Thus, Otto Warburg's comprehensive lecture on practical work in Palestine, supplemented by Max Bodenheimer's lecture on the work of the Jewish National Fund and Nissan Katzenelson's lecture on the Jewish Colonial Trust, served as background for the discussions which dominated the second part of the congress.[91]

What provided the "practicals" with some of their best arguments was the report by Shmarya Levin, who had just returned from Palestine and claimed that philanthropic work was ruinous to the Jewish spirit. Delivering a paper on Jewish education in Palestine, Levin showed how children were taught in the language of whatever parent institution was sponsoring their school. More than that, the pupils were taught that their school was an outpost of the respective civilization of the parent body, whether it was the Alliance Israélite Universelle, the Hilfsverein der deutschen Juden or the English-sponsored Evelina de Rothschild school for girls. Levin also lamented the influence of the missionary schools and the lack of any systematic and centralized curriculum in Palestine. He called for the establishment of a country-wide system of education, as well as the founding of a high school and a university *(Hochschule)*.[92] The debate reached its climax during the afternoon session of August 19, when Leo Motzkin and Alexander Marmorek, among others, spoke on behalf of the "politicals" and Weizmann did so as one of the "practicals." Both Motzkin and Marmorek warned against exaggerated hopes for practical work. Both emphasized that they were not opposed to practical work in Palestine in principle, but that this was only one means to achieve Zionist goals. Motzkin, in particular, repeatedly insisted that the movement not abandon the idea of a charter, whose time would come sooner or later. Marmorek also argued against wasting the meager financial resources of the movement, which would be better spent for political work.[93]

Weizmann made his first major congress address immediately after Marmorek. He took notice of Motzkin and Marmorek's well-delivered and well-reasoned speeches.[94] He was probably aware, while speaking, of the irony in the situation, which pitted him against Motzkin, whom he once held in high esteem as his teacher in the anti-Herzlian camp. That same Motzkin was now defending Herzl's views against his erstwhile disciple. Weizmann's speech has often been cited as the one in which he defined his concept of Zionism and gave it the name "synthetic Zionism." It is therefore appropriate to examine it carefully.

> . . . Until now Zionism was exclusively diplomatic Zionism. One thought it possible to inspire the Jewish people by creating a modern version of *shtadlanus* [intercession by notables]. One thought it possible to inspire the Jewish people by telling them: This or that potentate views our aspirations with favor. That was your political Zionism and this is the source of the enthusiasm you have aroused. You succeeded in this to a certain degree, because the Jewish people really like to think that potentates were concerned with them. They soon realized, however, that the goodwill of potentates and the acknowledgment of Jewish rights by the governments were not sufficient. Though acknowledging Jewish rights, and in spite of Nordau's brilliant advocacy, the governments will not lift a finger to do us justice; they will do nothing to help us, because with justice alone one does not get help in today's Europe. We must admit that this is a pessimistic point of view, but it is true . . .
>
> There was something ironic in the fact that Jewish policy had been reduced to mere diplomacy. Those gentlemen who had a one-sided conception of political Zionism are to be blamed for this. What we want is an honest synthesis of both existing trends of Zionist thought . . .
>
> As soon as I see this honest, sound synthesis of both trends achieved in our movement, there will be no need to stress only one aspect. But I must

say that I have not yet seen the realization of this synthesis. And perhaps it was just this [one-sided approach] which has brought about the slow decline of the movement we are now witnessing. Certainly, Mr. Motzkin was right in saying that Herzl had pointed out new possibilities; but Herzl did not take into account the existing possibilities in the Jewish world, because he did not know them: Perhaps this was his good luck and has made him the great leader he was. . . .

You must realize this: The governments will listen to you only when they see that you have the ability to possess Palestine . . . The road is difficult, but we must take this road, and I wish the [World] Zionist Organization to take it. None of us would wish to reject the great idea that Zionism is a political movement . . . But do not reduce politics to supplication toward governments, asking their opinion about Zionism. This will be of no use. We have already approached all the governments. We cannot start again on this track . . .

By political Zionism I mean that the Jewish problem should be stated as an international problem. We must say: "Of course, the Jewish Question implies an international danger for the governments." We Jews claim our rights from the governments! And we Jews say: "We need your help! But we ourselves also do everything in order to gradually strengthen our position in the country which we regard as our homeland." Then the governments will understand us. Up to now no English statesman has been able to understand why the Zionist Congress rejected Uganda . . . We must, therefore, make Zionist policy so clear to the governments that they understand it as the Jews understand it.

Mr. Motzkin said: "We cannot take the risk of a failure, for it will be said not the attempts have failed but Zionism has failed . . . " But if you pursue such a policy you cannot do anything at all. Have we always taken into consideration what the others might say? No! It is difficult and unpleasant to suffer failure! But we have no guarantees whatsoever that all the precautions we could possibly take would save us from failure. And those gentlemen who are not present, who were enthusiastic about Uganda, did they think that there everything would develop smoothly and failure would be out of the question? . . .

If we consider Zionism as an historic movement, we must accept the idea that there may be momentary failures. But to make no start at all!

. . . I conceive of political Zionism as a synthesis of activities in all spheres; I consider practical activity to be the means of attaining the political aim, the charter; the charter is to be the result of practical activity. I hold that the Jewish problem should be unfolded as an international problem with the greatest vigor . . . But the work must be done on both sides.

[The relation between political and practical activity might be] compared to the digging of a tunnel, which must be started from both ends until the men meet in the middle. This, too, is dangerous. The tunnel might collapse. On the one side, I have at least seen the earnest will to start digging; the other side, however, contends that the ground is too hard or the tunnel might collapse. I should like—and this is the synthesis I strive for—the digging to start at last.

The congress should give a clear, well-defined mandate to the Actions Committee. The charter should be striven for, but only as the result of our endeavors in Palestine. If the governments give us a charter today, it will be a scrap of paper; not so, if we work in Palestine: then it will be written and insolubly cemented with sweat and blood. (Long, persistent applause and hand clapping.)[95]

As noted above, since the Eighth Zionist Congress Weizmann has been credited as having invented the term "synthetic Zionism."[96] Weizmann himself reinforced this notion by stating in his autobiography that "I coined the phrase 'synthetic Zionism,' which became a slogan among the practical Zionists."[97] However, when one reads the text in the protocols of the congress, Weizmann's speech strikes one as biting and provocative but hardly a statesmanlike, well-thought-out piece. At least on the page the speech seems to lose its sparkle. One gets the impression that, apart from the notes he took while listening to those who preceded him,[98] he had no prepared speech in front of him. For an experienced debater like Weizmann this did not present a problem, but the result is that a large part of the speech was devoted to scoring points, and there is no real attempt to define in depth the meaning and nature of synthetic Zionism. Although synthetic Zionism implied a fusion of practical and political Zionism, for rhetorical purposes Weizmann chose to contrast it with political Zionism. Indeed, the speech is a challenge to the "politicals" to accept the position of the "practicals," and in many places it is blatantly polemical.[99] As an example of a dialectic argument his speech is admirable. He never quoted opponents except in order to clarify his own arguments and often put in their mouths words they had never used in order to explain what *he* really meant. It is small wonder that Alexander Marmorek and Joseph Cowen occasionally lost their composure and interrupted him.

It seems quite clear, however, that Weizmann's speech made a tremendous impression.[100] It was not so much what Weizmann said but the authority, confidence, and oratorical skill with which he spoke. His role as the representative of the "practicals" was not to compromise with the "politicals" but rather to demolish their arguments. His skills as a polemicist had been refined for years against Jewish and non-Jewish adversaries on the Continent. As an experienced debater, Weizmann always had his hand on tthe pulse of his audience. With perfect timing he delivered a speech for which the "practicals" were waiting, indeed, one which they were expecting.

The central idea in his speech was hardly novel. The very thought that synthetic Zionism was born and was immediately accepted in one afternoon at a congress teeming with ideas, plans, and controversies of all shades and hues is unreasonable in itself. The groundwork for the speech had been laid long before the Eighth Zionist Congress—and not only by Weizmann. The basic ideas contained in Weizmann's speech had been articulated—using different words—by Menahem Ussishkin in his pamphlet *Our Program*.[101] Martin Buber also had written in 1905 about the need for a synthesis between cultural and political Zionism.[102] These ideas were also contained in the platform of the Democratic Faction itself. They were dominant at the Freiburg Conference of 1905 and at the Seventh Zionist Congress, which accepted the Freiburg resolution and passed its own resolution to this effect.[103] At the extraordinary congress which preceded this same congress, Yehiel Tschlenow insisted forcefully on the need to pursue simultaneously political and practical work. The same theme had been sounded at GAC meetings in August 1906 and at the Helsingfors Conference—which Weizmann did not attend—of December 1906, where the term "synthetic Zionism" was probably coined for the first time. Indeed, prior to his famous speech at the Eighth Zionist Congress, Weizmann himself had voiced the same opinions at GAC meetings the previous year and at the EZF Conference in Birmingham in February 1907. Lastly, the term "synthesis" was used by at least five men who spoke prior to Weizmann at the Eighth Zionist Congress.[104] During his own speech, Weizmann did not use the term "synthetic Zionism"; he only spoke of a synthesis of both practical and political work.[105] Weizmann adopted rather than invented the term "synthetic Zionism," recognizing its appeal as a slogan. His ability to identify with new trends in the movement and the fact that he was a forceful and articulate representative of the "practicals" at the most important public forum of the Zionist movement tended to give his speech added weight and prominence. Thus he was credited with coining or identifying a term which, in fact, had been in the air for a number of years.

Two elements were missing from Weizmann's speech: a discussion of Zionist work in the Diaspora and a demand for cultural work. This was not simply an oversight. Both then and later in his Zionist career Weizmann exhibited very little interest in the Zionists' involvement in the political affairs of their countries, indeed, even in Zionist proposals for autonomy. This approach probably had little to do with his absence from the Helsingfors Conference.[106] After all, at this period he was very well informed about what transpired among Russian Zionists. Rather, this may have to do with his long residence in the West, which may have contributed to his lack of appreciation for demands for autonomy. More striking is the fact that since the formal demise of the Democratic Faction and his transfer to England, Weizmann had turned his attention from Zionist cultural work and was directing his energies more toward practical work in Palestine. This may have been due to several factors: his deep disappointment in the failure of his various cultural projects on the Continent; his temporary physical removal from the influence of such men as Ahad Ha'Am, Berthold Feiwel, and Martin Buber; and the general mood in the movement, which increasingly tended toward practical work. His speech at The Hague represented the height of Weizmann's Palestine-oriented approach to Zionist problems before World War I, though the almost full eclipse of his interest in cultural work was only temporary. Cultural concerns, and especially the university project, were taken up again with vigor in the period immediately before 1914.

The "practicals" won an important tactical victory at The Hague: The congress decided to expand its practical work in Palestine and to establish the Palestine Department, which set up the Palestine Office in 1908 under the direction of Arthur Ruppin. It also decided to spend one quarter of the movement's budget on work in Palestine.[107] Yet the battle had not been completely won for the "practicals." The new SAC consisted of Wolffsohn as president, Jacobus Kann, and Otto Warburg, thus clearly giving the old "politicals" the decisive voice in the decision-making process. To no small degree this new situation was due to the infighting among the "practicals" themselves, chiefly Ussishkin and Tschlenow, who canceled each other out of SAC membership.

Weizmann did not stay around to hear the results of the elections to various offices, which again granted him a seat on GAC as an English representative.[108] He left the congress a day early for Paris, where he had a business meeting relating to his camphor experiments. He was physically spent but elated about his performance at the congress. He realized that he had reached à new height in his Zionist career.

> . . . By everyone's admission it was a great evening, great in significance, purity and beauty . . . six main speakers were elected . . . Then began a tournament without precedent in the annals of the Congress. Motzkin and Marmorek spoke extremely well, especially the former. The old Motzkin roused himself, and the Faction was revived. I was the last speaker and opposed both with unusual success and vigor, even better than in Cologne. The Congress gave me a colossal ovation—everyone without exception, including my opponents . . . Personal problems receded into the background, something sacred went through the hall and purified the atmosphere.[109]

For years he had been listening to the firsthand reports about Palestine by Motzkin, Ussishkin, Tschlenow, and Shmarya Levin. It was fortuitous that at this very moment in his Zionist reorientation he could finally see for himself what had been accomplished in Palestine. Though arranged only at the last moment, Kremenetzky did reconfirm his commitments to pay for Weizmann's trip,[110] and on August 22, 1907, Weizmann set out for Palestine from Marseilles aboard the steamship *Orénoque*. Vera went to Wales for a vacation with their ten-week-old son. This was the first of many vacations she would spend alone (or with the children), while her husband was engaged in professional or Zionist activities.

Weizmann's first encounter with Palestine[111] was during the Second *Aliyah* (1904–14). The first phase of this *Aliyah* was inaugurated by fourteen Jews who had been active in the defense of Homel and arrived in Palestine during the winter of 1903–4. Those who followed this group came for a variety of reasons: the pogroms in Kishinev and Homel, which had a traumatic impact; their association with socialist-Zionist groups; the failure of the revolution of 1905 and the rise of anti-Semitic reaction which came in its wake; and the atmosphere of despair and confusion following the Uganda crisis and Herzl's sudden death.[112] Young women and men, deeply disappointed by the lack of direction in the Zionist movement and its continued political orientation, were moved by the idealistic challenge of men like Menahem Ussishkin, whose pamphlet *Our Program* exhorted them to devote three years of their lives to building up Palestine. They were equally impressed by a circular written in March 1905 by Yosef Vitkin, a teacher in Palestine, who called on them to do pioneer work. Michael Halperin, a Palestinian Jew, traveled from town to town in Russia and called on young men and women to immigrate to Palestine to undertake agricultural work and defend the Jewish settlements.[113] Another factor contributing to the wave of immigration was the Russo-Japanese War, which began in 1904. Many young men (called "Japanese" by the Yishuv) preferred immigration to Palestine to service in the tsarist army.

It is quite unlikely that in 1907 Weizmann knew much about the Second *Aliyah* or of the general political, economic, and social transformations then taking place in Palestine. But if he needed an introduction to life in Palestine, he could not have had a better guide than Manya Wilbushevitz (later Shohat), who was also traveling aboard the *Orénoque*.[114] Manya Wilbushevitz hailed from Russia, where she had briefly been a member of the terrorist section of the Socialist Revolutionary Party.[115] After her first visit to Palestine in 1904, she began actively pursuing her plans for collective settlements in Palestine. Max Nordau informed her that she was suffering from feverish delusions and advised her to consult a psychiatrist.[116] She was not the kind of woman who could be deterred by derision, however, and went on to become the driving force behind Sejera, the setting for the first attempt at collective agricultural settlement. Also on board was David Klimker, manager of the Hermon olive oil factory in Motza, outside Jerusalem. Thus, the trip began auspiciously. The weather was excellent. Since few people were on board, Weizmann had a cabin all to himself, and though he traveled third class, the food was very good.[117] The company at his table was interesting: Klimker, Wilbushevitz, two "decent-looking Englishmen and a young Jew from Brussels." The rest were "mostly scum," he assured Vera.[118]

They arrived in Alexandria on August 27, where Manya Wilbushevitz and Weizmann reported to two local Zionist groups on the congress.[119] Three days later the boat went up the coast to Beirut, where the passengers were placed in quarantine for five days because of a cholera epidemic in Egypt—not an unusual occurrence in the area.[120] Conditions in quarantine were abominable. Weizmann wrote Vera, "We have been locked up in dreadful barracks lacking the most elemental comforts . . . It is dirty and foul—in short, Turkish style. It is even impossible to read, as all kinds of savages are milling around and are being a disturbance. The food is pretty bad; moreover, I am paying 8 frs. a day for the privilege."[121] The tedium was broken by a visit from Victor Jacobson, who a year earlier had opened the Beirut branch of the Anglo-Palestine Company, using his office to make contacts with Turkish officials in Constantinople. By the time Weizmann was released from quarantine, the boat for Jaffa had already departed, forcing him to spend two extra days in

Beirut and bringing the net loss of his travel time to ten days. He was rescued by Samuel Pevsner, Ahad Ha'Am's son-in-law, founder of the Atid Company and manager of its Haifa plant, who was then vacationing with his wife, Lea, in Burmanna, a resort town near Beirut. No doubt the two days spent with the Pevsners were a useful further introduction to life in Palestine, and it was certainly a relief to be able to spend the eve of the New Year with them rather than in quarantine.[122]

On September 10 Weizmann arrived in Jaffa, the gateway to Palestine for thousands of immigrants, tourists, and pilgrims. It was a bustling, overcrowded, and fast-growing city. Prior to the founding of neighboring Tel Aviv in 1909,[123] it served as the center of Zionist institutions and of the New Yishuv in Palestine.[124] But Weizmann spent only one day in the city. "I saw a lot of people, heard many contradictory opinions. People are dissatisfied with a lot of things and speak harshly against the work of the Congress. But one has to listen to all this in silence, without entering into discussions . . . I cannot tell you anything as yet, except that the sky and the sea are very beautiful here, and the mood entirely different from ours."[125] Jaffa, he had time enough to observe, was a place where people concerned themselves with "squabbles, gossip and homemade politics," where they "know only one thing: tearing everything apart." A two-day trip to the Jewish colonies in the Sharon plains presented an altogether different picture. Here, at last, he saw for himself practical Zionism at work; his enthusiasm for Jewish farmers and their lifestyle would remain with him throughout his life. He was impressed by Petach Tikvah, Rishon le-Zion, and Rehovot, where he stayed in the home of Aaron Eisenberg, who had emigrated from Pinsk. The latter's daughter, Yehudit, and her husband, Chaim, showed him their vineyard on a nearby hill, upon which Weizmann would one day build his home and the Daniel Sieff Institute. He reported enthusiastically to Vera:

> It's worth a lifetime to glimpse the work of Jewish hands, to see how, after twenty years of toil, former sand and swamps support flourishing orchards, to see Jewish farmers. I understood many things much better, more clearly; the potentiality of Palestine is immense . . . It is impossible not to feel well in a colony. My general conclusion is briefly the following: if everything progresses so slowly, with such difficulties, the fault lies not with the *soil of Palestine,* nor even with the political conditions in the country (indisputably difficult), but rather with *ourselves—and only ourselves.* If our Jewish capitalists, say even only the Zionist capitalists, were to invest their capital in Palestine, if only in part, there is no doubt that the lifeline of Palestine—all the coastal strip—would be in Jewish hands within 25 years. No force in the world would then be able to destroy what was built.
>
> I am not shutting my eyes to the tremendous difficulties, the obstacles, the hard life, but my conviction is strong and unwavering. Let the Jews want it, and everything will be ours![126]

He spent less than two days in Jerusalem (September 16–17), where he gave a talk on the congress. "It was extremely interesting," he wrote to Vera,[127] but clearly Jerusalem had made a negative impression on him, as he later recalled in his memoirs:

> My most unhappy experience during the . . . tour of the country . . . was Jerusalem . . . Jerusalem was the city of the *Challukah,* a city living on charity, on begging letters, on collections . . . From the Jewish point of view it was a miserable ghetto, derelict and without dignity. All the grand places belonged to others. There were innumerable churches, of every sect and nationality. We had not a decent building of our own. All the world had a foothold in Jerusalem—except the Jews. The hotel to which we were directed was a dilapidated and verminous ruin, with nondescript people pouring in and out all day long, and all of them engaged apparently in wasting their own and each other's time. It depressed me beyond words . . . I remained prejudiced against the city for many years . . .[128]

After Jerusalem, the flow of letters to Vera ceased—for good reason. He was traveling with Yehoshua Hankin by horse-drawn carriage and on horseback in isolated and extremely difficult terrain; moreover, it was dusty and quite hot in early September. Once again he was fortunate in having a man such as Hankin serving as his guide. Hankin had come to Palestine from the Ukraine in 1882 at the age of eighteen. In due course he became one of the country's foremost experts in dealing with the Arab population, as well as in the acquisition of land; his first purchase in 1890 was the acquisition of the land on which Rehovot—Weizmann's future residence—was founded.[129] Beginning their nine-day-long tour in Jaffa, which served as Weizmann's base, they headed north toward Metullah, through Zikhron Yaakov—where Weizmann lay ill with fever for three days—and on to Haifa, Nazareth, Yavniel, Sejera, and Tiberias.[130] Hankin, whose father was one of the founders of Rishon le-Zion, could enlighten Weizmann from firsthand experience about the impact of Baron Edmond de Rothschild on the First *Aliyah.* There was no question about the fact that he had single-handedly saved the colonies during a critical period.[131] But the Rothschild administration also sapped the colonists' initial zest for pioneering, first making them into virtual employees of the baron and eventually—after their land began to yield rich harvests— into estate owners who depended on hired hands, mainly Arabs. "New blood had to be brought into the country; a new spirit of enterprise had to be introduced."[132]

The last stop of the tour, on September 26, was Haifa, where he visited the Atid Factory and waited for the steamer to take him back to Europe. According to his memoirs, he met Arthur Ruppin in Samuel Pevsner's house in Haifa,[133] though none of his letters and subsequent reports mention Ruppin's name. This is not surprising, since the man who was destined to become the "father of Zionist settlement" was hardly a household name in Zionist circles in 1907. Born in Posen and raised in Magdeburg, Ruppin was a lawyer by profession and an economist and sociologist by avocation. His fame as a sociologist began to spread after the publication in 1904 of his book *Die Juden der Gegenwart.* In 1907 he was asked by David Wolffsohn and Otto Warburg to investigate settlement possibilities in Palestine;[134] his few months in the country over-lapped with Weizmann's trip. This journey led to Ruppin's appointment in 1908 as head of the Palestine Office (Palaestina Amt) and of the Palestine Land Development Company, which the World Zionist Organization set up in Jaffa.[135] From then until his death in 1943—with inter-ruptions devoted to scientific work—Ruppin was largely responsible for organizing Zionist settlement in Palestine.[136]

Ruppin's report to the World Zionist Organization in November 1907 indicates that he had quickly grasped the most important needs of the Yishuv and of the movement in Palestine.[137] One may safely assume that the combined observations and advice of Ruppin, Hankin, and Pevsner had an impact on Weizmann. Even though he had spent only sixteen days in Palestine (during three or four of which he was bedridden), Weizmann's newly found friends helped place his impressions in per-spective. Just prior to his departure from Palestine, while the sights he had witnessed and the conversations he had had were still fresh, he wrote his report to Kremenetzky concerning industrial prospects in Palestine. He advised against perfume manufacture or fruit canning; the former had been tried unsuccessfully by Baron Edmond de Rothschild[138] and the latter was not sufficiently profitable. He saw the greatest promise in an indus-try based on olive oil. He suggested that Kremenetzky join forces with the Atid enterprises by introducing more capital:

> I proposed to the gentlemen that . . . together with Atid [we] found a sin-gle company that will control the entire oil industry of the country. Atid will give us its two years' experience and knowledge of conditions; we shall con-tribute fresh capital, new chemists, etc. . . . We could have a single central administration and make the new venture easier and more economical in every respect . . . *I therefore suggest to you that we start with an oil factory, then add a small lemon-[processing] factory and distillation plant.*[139]

Nothing came of these suggestions. Kremenetzky remained cool to Weizmann's ideas, and though the latter kept on asking for a decision, the industrialist stalled. A year and a half later Kremenetzky asked for a more detailed memorandum on Weizmann's findings and a report as well as laboratory tests.[140] Probably realizing that nothing would come of this, Weizmann failed to comply. Instead he asked for reimbursement for his expenses,[141] which greatly angered Kremenetzky.[142] The latter was ob-viously not convinced by Weizmann's preliminary reports and did not rush to invest his money in the Atid Company;[143] only after World War I did he establish the Silicat brickworks in Palestine.[144]

As a hard-nosed businessman, Kremenetzky expected more informa-tion from Weizmann to justify his hundred-pound investment in the lat-ter's trip. For his part, Weizmann admitted later in life that the initial object of his journey—the establishment of a factory—"receded into the background" during his trip.[145] What, then, were his general conclu-sions on what was to be done in Palestine? Above all, Zionists had to press immediately for practical work in Palestine, which this new breed

of pioneers of the Second *Aliyah*, free of the spirit of philanthropy, would
undertake. How was this to be accomplished? To Vera he had written
that the initiative had to come from "our Jewish capitalists, [or] even only
the Zionist capitalists"; then Palestine would be in Jewish hands within
twenty-five years.[146] To Sokolow he wrote two months later, "Even the
[Zionist] organization, and not only the Zionists in their private capacity, could do a great deal."[147] In short, he did not have a clear-cut economic, political, or even social conception of *how* land was to be acquired—nor was this important in the final analysis. Rather, his was a
pragmatic approach which clearly viewed concrete achievements as having political and diplomatic weight in and of themselves. He concluded
his letter to Sokolow thus: "The whole program for Palestine could almost be summed up in one word: land. Ussishkin was not so wrong
when he said that in another 25 years it will be impossible to get Palestine unless we buy up the land now."[148]

On October 19—a cool Saturday evening, far from the dusty heat of
Palestine—Weizmann summed up his views in an impressive speech before the Manchester Zionists.[149] He told his audience that Palestine was
continually changing, improving. Zionism's mistake was to worry about
preconditions for founding colonies rather than their actual existence.
Political influence would follow in the wake of institutions already
founded, not by diplomacy alone.

> . . . The Baron had accomplished more in the country than the collective
> labors of the Zionist Organization. It was true that this work was not na-
> tional, but was built on philanthropy, and that it fostered the ghetto spirit
> of dependence on *schnorring* . . . nevertheless the work of the Baron had
> been the work of a statesman. It had shown that Palestine was colonizable
> and that the Jews were the proper people to colonize it.
>
> . . . However, the welfare of the colonies was seriously affected by the
> Arab labor question. Sixty to eighty percent of the laborers were Arabs . . .
> This involves two issues: (a) Arabs are being civilized at the expense of their
> Jewish neighbors, and (b) it places the prosperity of the Jewish colonies too
> much in the hands of the Arab population. The Arab retains his primitive
> attachment to the land, the soil-instinct is strong in him, and by being con-
> tinuously employed on it there is a danger that he might feel himself indis-
> pensable to it, with a moral right to it.
>
> The Jewish colonies could not be regarded as really Jewish so long as Ar-
> abs formed so powerful a part of the labor force. There were Jewish labor-
> ers, but they could not be expected to enter into competition with Arabs,
> whose requirements were few, and whose mode of living was uncivilized.
> The course open to Jewish labor was to contribute superior intelligence and
> civilization, which would render it more valuable to the employer. He praised
> Poalei Zion and Hapoel Hazair, especially the latter, which competed with
> Arab labor by better, more efficient work . . .
>
> The purchase of land was difficult, but much depended on how one went
> about it . . . The JNF [Jewish National Fund] was still too small for signifi-
> cant land purchase,[150] but the Zionists should open an office in Constanti-
> nople to facilitate legalities. This would stimulate private initiative. The JNF

should buy plots between the colonies to form geographically united centers belonging entirely to Jews. This strategic buying should be the basis for their practical work.[151]

In fact, Weizmann had little faith that the World Zionist Organization would undertake major efforts in Palestine: "We have no people in the country and it is all paperwork . . . our bankers are only money-changers and our diplomats only intercessors. They are not equal to the complicated conditions in the East, and their ignorance is bottomless."[152] For the time being Weizmann put his faith in the revamped EZF and Gaster's leadership: "The redemption of the land is only a phrase with us, and the Germans [the Templars] are buying land in Palestine while we make Congresses . . . I beg you, dear Doctor, to write immediately. We could win over Moser and Dreyfus as well as some other people here and in London for Palestine . . . I am waiting to be summoned."[153]

Gaster was not ready for large-scale practical work either,[154] but for Weizmann the trip to Palestine—the only one he made before the Balfour Declaration—was of decisive importance in his own personal development. He saw with his own eyes that what he had preached at the Eighth Zionist Congress concerning synthetic Zionism could actually be accomplished. It confirmed his resolve to push the cause of the "practicals." For the Zionists time was of the essence; they could not afford to squander it.

XIV

The End of the Wolffsohn Era

Upon his return from Palestine on October 10, 1907, and throughout 1908 Weizmann did not contribute much to the life of the reconstituted English Zionist Federation. The main reason for his abstention from internal politics seems to have been ill health. Throughout the winter he experienced serious weakness, loss of weight, and painful abscesses which required some surgery.[1] An indication of the seriousness of his condition is the fact that in April 1908 he went on a ten-day vacation to Old Colwyn in North Wales,[2] to which he returned during the summer to spend the month of August[3] with Vera and Benjy. Instead of working for Clayton or in the lab, he confined his academic work to a paper which he presented before the British Association for the Advancement of Science early in September.[4] Despite these rest periods, his chest pains did not subside—forcing him, on at least one occasion, to cancel a public lecture[5]—and in mid-December he went to Cannes to convalesce in a sanatorium for one month.[6]

In contrast to his frenetic pace in 1906–7, Weizmann severely curtailed—though he did not totally eliminate—his Zionist activities throughout this period. For example, at the end of December 1907 he traveled to Geneva to conclude a contract for his camphor patents with the company of Leon Givaudan,[7] which earned him a monthly check of a few hundred francs until just prior to World War I.[8] After a stopover in Vienna to visit Kremenetzky and his brother-in-law Abraham Lichtenstein, he attended GAC meetings in Berlin on January 6 and 7, 1908.[9] During these meetings Weizmann criticized the leadership for its lack of systematic planning in Palestine during the past three years: "What will you do if your political work should be crowned with success?"[10] He was clearly alluding to Wolffsohn's recent trip to Constantinople at the invitation of Effendi Bekhor, who was acting on behalf of the sultan. In exchange for twenty-six million pounds, which would help wipe out the Turkish public debt, the Sublime Porte was willing to permit the settlement of fifty thousand Jewish families in Palestine over a period of twenty-five years. It was an indication of the exaggerated Turkish notions of Zionist financial prowess. When Wolffsohn offered two million pounds in return the negotiations broke down. On the positive side, Wolffsohn was able to successfully negotiate for permission to open the Anglo-Levantine Banking Company in August 1908 as a partnership of the Jewish Colonial Trust and Mitrani Bros. The Zionist director of the bank, Victor Jacobson, was also to function as the political representative of the World Zionist Organization.[11]

Weizmann was not the only person to criticize the leadership's performance since the Eighth Zionist Congress, but Wolffsohn took personal offense at his needling remarks, which were made outside the context of the debate: "Dr. Weizmann's remarks astound me. We are presently discussing grants from the National Fund and here comes Mr. Weizmann, who, year in, year out, has demanded this work from us . . . and asks what political aims we have and according to which system we operate. When we charted a political course, it was Mr. Weizmann who demanded practical work of us; now that we have undertaken practical work, Mr. Weizmann demands political action. We were always told to undertake practical work in Palestine; now it is being asserted that all that is being done is bad."[12]

To all appearances, the annual conference of the English Zionist Federation, which met in Manchester on February 2, 1908, was much less eventful. Beneath the surface the old rivalries of Greenberg and Cowen versus Gaster continued unabated—so much so that Gaster refused to address public meetings to which Greenberg had been invited. The 1908 conference, therefore, had to be held *in camera*.[13] Gaster was again elected president, with Herbert Bentwich and Jacob Moser as vice presidents for London and the provinces, respectively. Weizmann and Harry Sacher were elected to the Provincial Council of the EZF, while Leon Simon was elected to the London Council.[14] Cowen still protested unsuccessfully against any changes in the statutes of the Jewish Colonial Trust, and perhaps because of this the "politicals" in the EZF were not elected to its executive body.[15] At a public meeting following the conference, Gaster launched into a tirade against the territorialists, declaring his adherence to the Basel Program. Probably the only event of great significance at the Manchester Conference was the public reading of a letter from Winston Churchill to Gaster in which he declared that his visit to East Africa had acquainted him "with many difficulties which seem to lie in the path in that country. And, of course, Jerusalem must be the only ultimate goal. *When* it will be achieved it is vain to prophesy. But that it *will* someday be achieved is one of the few certainties of the future. And the establishment of a strong, free Jewish State astride of the bridge between Europe and Africa, flanking the land roads to the East, would be not only an immense advantage to the British Empire, but a notable step towards the harmonious disposition of the world among its peoples."[16]

Weizmann was hardly involved in the Manchester Conference of the EZF and willingly gave up the provincial vice presidency in favor of Moser. That same weekend he was busy with Ahad Ha'Am, who was then in England for a few months exploring a suggestion by the heads of the

Wissotzky tea firm that he become manager of their recently opened London office.[17] Weizmann's concern was to keep his promise to Ahad Ha'Am, who agreed to come to Manchester for the weekend on condition that he be kept from the Zionist limelight;[18] what Ahad Ha'Am saw of the Zionist conference in Manchester depressed and disappointed him.[19] Weizmann, on the other hand, was overjoyed when Ahad Ha'Am moved to London in May 1908 as Wissotzky's agent. At last there was someone in England he respected and trusted without any reservations, to whom he could turn for personal guidance and advice and with whom he could discuss Zionist problems.[20] Though by now more integrated in England, Weizmann still had a greater affinity to his former patrons on the Continent. Ahad Ha'Am's towering intellect and moral authority would serve Weizmann as a sure compass in charting the political and intellectual problems confronting the Zionist movement, making it less imperative to await Ussishkin's directives from afar. Ahad Ha'Am's cautious approach would reflect itself in the substance and style of Weizmann's subsequent formulations and positions. For his part, Ahad Ha'Am felt lonely and estranged in England and greatly cherished the company of Weizmann and a few chosen individuals from the Old Country as well as from among the younger generation of English Zionists. Weizmann visited Ahad Ha'Am when in London, often staying the night in his home in the northwestern suburb of Belsize Park and arranging to meet there with other men from Ahad Ha'Am's circle of intimates. Within a brief period Ahad Ha'Am completely replaced Moses Gaster. It was to the Odessa philosopher that Weizmann now turned not only for moral encouragement but also for occasional financial help.[21]

A visit by Ahad Ha'Am to Manchester was a holiday for Weizmann, so much so that he hardly attended the EZF sessions of the Manchester annual conference. Well aware that his colleagues in the EZF had noted his reduced level of activity and pronounced lack of interest, soon after the Manchester Conference he offered to resign his seat on the executive—a suggestion that was rejected by both Percy Baker, the honorary secretary, and Moses Gaster.[22] Likewise, he failed to attend GAC meetings in Cologne in mid-August 1908, preferring to continue his vacation in North Wales.[23] When Otto Warburg invited him, in November 1908, to accept an honorary directorship in the newly formed Palestine Land Development Company (PLDC), Weizmann accepted with uncharacteristic reluctance. "If you can find no better director for the PLDC, if you think I could be of some use in this position, then I will accept it."[24] His one concrete achievement during this period was to help establish the Manchester University Students' Zionist Association, of which he was elected president in mid-January 1909.[25]

If Weizmann can be credited with having engineered the results of the Birmingham Conference in February 1907, he must also share some of the blame for the disastrous results of the annual conference of the EZF in Sheffield at the end of January 1909. For the past three or four years Weizmann had played a key role in corralling the provinces, and especially Manchester, into the Gasterite camp. His concerted attempts helped bring Gaster into the presidency of the EZF on his own terms. But what Weizmann should have known was that Gaster was temperamentally incapable of playing the impartial role that his office demanded. Instead, within two years he managed to throw even his followers into despair over his tactless and unimaginative handling of the affairs of the EZF. The membership had declined rapidly and the financial situation of the organization had reached a new nadir. Moreover, in the absence of Weizmann's skillful behind-the-scenes negotiations—which he had conducted so masterfully two years earlier—the "practicals" came to Sheffield disorganized, dispirited, and totally unprepared for the fight that awaited them there. Even though Greenberg was absent from Sheffield, the "politicals," headed by Joseph Cowen, staged a well-planned counterattack, catching Gaster and his followers off guard. Joseph Cowen, Jacob Goldbloom, and Israel Cohen sharply attacked Gaster for the lackluster performance of the movement. He was accused of dictatorial behavior and a demonstrative lack of respect toward the movement's veterans, namely, Greenberg and Cowen. Despite Weizmann's conciliatory speech, the executive's report, moved by Herbert Bentwich and Samuel Daiches, was passed by only a slim margin of twenty-six votes to twelve. Nevertheless, Gaster was unanimously reelected for the third year in a row as president of the EZF, and Jacob Moser was returned as provincial vice president. A problem arose over the position of the London vice president. Supported by Cowen, Greenberg barely won, with twenty-two votes to the twenty-one of Herbert Bentwich, who challenged the elections even before the results were made known.[26] When the results were announced, Gaster and Moser declared that they would not serve with Greenberg and resigned. All their followers, including Weizmann and Leon Simon, also resigned from the executive.[27] Though Greenberg continued to have the support of some influential London Zionists—among them Cowen, Israel Cohen, S. B. Rubenstein, Jacob Goldbloom, Harris Ginzburg, Samuel Goldreich, and Leopold Kessler—he was unsuccessful in his attempts to continue the work of the federation. Gaster refused to hand over the federation's office keys and papers since he did not recognize the truncated executive as having a sufficient mandate.[28] Greenberg's requests for Sir Francis Montefiore's intercession were also futile.[29] The shameful scenes that ensued made the EZF the laughingstock of the entire movement.

Naturally the various factions turned to David Wolffsohn, the president of the World Zionist Organization. Greenberg advised Wolffsohn to stay out of the fray,[30] a suggestion that suited the latter's inclinations in any case.[31] Weizmann and his supporters, however, saw the situation as an opportunity to wrest power from the "politicals" once and for all and move the federation headquarters to Manchester.[32] Though he feigned personal disinterest, Weizmann informed the president that "it is tremendously hard for me to plead this way, which in my opinion and that of many others is the only sound way out of the crisis, because it could mean at the same time that I want to grab the 'power' (nebbich!) for my-self. Until now I have been above any suspicion of personal motives, and I would now naturally lay myself open to attacks. But this is my profound conviction: London is absolutely rotten and useless. In the provinces we have less choice, but we could find people who would work and not quarrel."[33] Two years earlier Weizmann had made a similar suggestion, but not in quite so explicit a manner; the fact that he re-ceived the largest number of votes in the elections at Sheffield may have emboldened and encouraged him to be more frank.[34] Herbert Bentwich and Jacob Moser, who met Wolffsohn in Cologne, reinforced the sug-gestion for a move to Manchester with Dreyfus as president, Bentwich and Moser as vice presidents and Weizmann as honorary secretary.[35] Even Samuel Goldreich, who supported Greenberg, saw no alternative to Manchester. He summarized the situation in English Zionism thus:

> . . . I hold more firmly than ever to the opinion that the only remedy is to remove the headquarters to Manchester and let Dr. Weizmann take the chair. He is a strong man and will most likely rise to his responsibilities, and I hope he will do better than any of his predecessors; he cannot do worse. I hold that he was entirely wrong in resigning [from the executive] in Shef-field and I know of no justification for it but sheer Jesuitical cowardice.
>
> As you know, I have no respect for Dr. Gaster. He is a megalomaniac of the worst kind, and as it is coupled with an appalling incapacity for work or leadership, his removal from the chair can do no harm. Mr. Greenberg has too many enemies to be a really effective chairman . . . Cowen is the most capable Englishman in the whole group, but he is so tactless and im-pulsive that I am afraid to entrust him with the chairmanship at the present moment . . .
>
> I have thought about this for some time and feel sure that the removal of the headquarters of the federation to Manchester is best.[36]

Wolffsohn was now persuaded that Manchester was a viable alterna-tive, but he insisted that the final decision had to be made by the En-glish Zionists themselves. He even entertained the idea that a separate federation could be established in the provinces, with headquarters in Manchester, which would later unite with the London group.[37] Green-berg, who claimed he had nothing against Manchester in principle, re-sisted any attempt for change before the membership itself could decide the issue.[38] The impasse was broken when, at the suggestion of the Manchester Zionist Association, a special conference was convened in Leeds on March 28, 1909.[39] With the exception of Harry Sacher, Gaster's supporters boycotted this meeting and a supposedly neutral leadership was elected, with Charles Dreyfus as president, Leopold Greenberg as London vice president, and Jacob Moser as provincial vice president. No Manchester Zionist was elected to the executive.[40] Moser refused to serve, and the EZF, whose headquarters remained in London, limped along as an ineffective and lifeless body for the next few years. Though he was reelected at the EZF annual conference held in January 1910,[41] Dreyfus resigned from his office in July of that year, after the EZF executive's recommendation to dissolve the federation was rejected by the membership.[42] Joseph Cowen, his successor, would not stand for election, and the post was reluctantly assumed by Leopold Kessler in February 1912.[43]

Gaster's long-term prediction that another Zionist organization would be created apart from the EZF finally came true. Conveniently, such a body already existed and simply needed to be revamped by the Gasterites. The Order of Ancient Maccabeans (OAM) was founded in 1896 by Ephraim Ish-Kishor, probably at the suggestion of Theodor Herzl.[44] This was an order of friendly societies whose aim was to combine support of Zionism with mutual social benefits; thus it remained distinct from the English Zionist Federation after that body had been established. Its membership was mainly drawn from the working class and numbered about a thousand by 1909. It suited the purposes of the Gaster group perfectly, not only because it was a well-knit organization but because in 1909 its grand commander was none other than Herbert Bentwich, a loyal Gasterite, and its headquarters were in Manchester.[45] It was only natural that Bentwich now summoned the commanders of every Maccabean "beacon" to help challenge the EZF and replace it with the Order of Ancient Maccabeans as the legitimate voice of English Zionism.[46] With Gaster pulling the strings behind the scenes, it was decided to turn OAM into a *Sonderverband* directly affiliated with the World Zionist Organization. This could be done once proof was submitted of a minimum of 3,000 shekel purchasers.[47] Wolffsohn sanctioned OAM's independent distribution of shekels that year,[48] and by December 1910 he was notified that the order had sold 3,010 shekels.[49] The EZF protested,[50] but to no avail. By the time the Ninth Zionist Congress met in Hamburg in December 1909, Weizmann had helped elect Maccabeans as delegates.[51] Meetings of the EZF with OAM in May 1910 and in August 1911 did not lead to reconciliation.[52] In its meeting in early November 1911 GAC finally imposed its own solution, recognizing OAM as a *Sonderverband*, provided the OAM and the EZF formed a Joint Zionist Council that would act for both bodies.[53] In February 1912 both sides finally agreed to this solution under the neutral leadership of Samuel Hirsch.[54] Within a short period the newly created council was dominated by the Gaster group.

Throughout much of this period Weizmann was careful not to sever ties either with the EZF leadership or with Wolffsohn, writing conciliatory and even friendly letters to the latter until the Ninth Zionist Congress met in Hamburg in December 1909. Even afterward he maintained his relations with the London group, though in a letter to Gaster he wrote, "I have had a somewhat acrimonious correspondence with Sacher. Sacher believes he will be doing the right thing by making another attempt with the EZF. The younger people just do not have the experience we have so bitterly undergone, and it is only to be expected that they will soon find out the hard way that the situation is impossible."[55] Gaster was not deceived by Weizmann's words. He became increasingly suspicious of his protégé's movements and motivations.[56] Gaster had good reason to be wary of Weizmann. Unlike Gaster, Weizmann wished to effect peace

between the warring camps of English Zionism. At the annual conference of the EZF, which took place in Manchester on February 26, 1911,
Weizmann accepted the vice presidency of the EZF under the presidency of Joseph Cowen.[57] Weizmann's close associates—Norman Bentwich, Harry Sacher, and Leon Simon—also joined the executive.[58] Not
surprisingly, Weizmann and Gaster stopped corresponding until the
spring of 1913—a sharp contrast to the frequent contacts and warm relations during the previous seven years. It was clear that the more Weizmann's stature grew on the Continent, the more he felt independent of
the *Haham*, free to choose his own political path amid the intrigues of
English Zionism. Despite his disappointment with the EZF's rejection of
his proposal that Gaster be elected president of a "homogeneous" leadership, Weizmann again accepted the vice presidency of the EZF under
Cowen at the annual conference of June 1, 1913,[59] as well as at the Leeds
Conference of February 1914.[60] Throughout he remained the pragmatic
politician, knowing full well that it was easier to influence the EZF to
adopt a "practical" course from within rather than continue splintering
the Zionist forces further. Firmly entrenched in both the EZF and OAM,
he was in a singular position to achieve unity between them when the
time came. His acceptance of an official post in what Gaster considered
the enemy camp fully accorded with his long-standing principle of
avoiding, as much as possible, secession within Zionism. By February
1911 he had given up hope that Gaster would compromise with the EZF,
having decided that a break with Gaster was preferable to a split with
English Zionism. Lastly, as a member of both the EZF and OAM, he
would have a better chance in persuading their memberships to oppose
Wolffsohn at the Tenth Zionist Congress.[61]

Weizmann realized early in 1909 that as long as Wolffsohn remained
in power, Greenberg and "his gang," as Gaster referred to them,[62] would
continue to steer the movement along the old "political" path. Wolffsohn's (and Kann's) natural sympathies lay with Greenberg and Cowen,
making internal changes within the EZF difficult to effect. It was clear
that if the "practicals" were to get anywhere, Wolffsohn would have to
go. This, of course, was also the view of others in the movement, especially Ussishkin, who knew that because of Wolfssohn he had been
excluded from SAC at the 1907 congress in The Hague. Since mid-1906,
when he was elected chairman of the Society for the Support of Jewish
Farmers and Artisans in Syria and Palestine (the Odessa Committee),
Ussishkin had become the leader par excellence of "practical" Zionism.[63]
If he failed to get rid of the "politicals" at The Hague, this only made
Ussishkin all the more eager to try again at Hamburg. Even Tschlenow,
who hitherto had advocated a more moderate course, now changed his
conciliatory stance toward the Wolffsohn-led SAC. The battle would take
place in Hamburg at the Ninth Zionist Congress.

The congress had been postponed from its usual summer date to the
end of December 1909 in order to afford the World Zionist Organization

the necessary time for assessment of the new situation in the Ottoman Empire. On July 24, 1908, a bloodless revolution led by the Young Turks took place. Under pressure, Sultan Abdul Hamid II restored the constitution which he himself had granted in 1876 and had suspended two years later. Press censorship was abolished and arrangements were made to reconvene the parliament for the first time in thirty years.[64] The Young Turks, represented primarily by the Committee of Union and Progress, established themselves as the dominant force behind the new regime. In April 1909, following an abortive counterrevolution, Abdul Hamid was deposed and the committee's influence was further enhanced.[65] The Young Turks were initially welcomed with almost delirious joy by the empire's subjects. Turks, Armenians, and members of other ethnic groups embraced on the street, believing that the age of freedom and brotherhood had arrived.[66] Jews also joined the Committee of Union and Progress and soon attained considerable prominence. Zionists everywhere initially expected far-reaching changes in the Ottoman Empire's hostile attitude toward Zionism.[67] Weizmann, too, was infected by the general enthusiasm. At a public meeting of the Manchester Zionist Association he equated the new constitution to a charter. The changes in the Ottoman Empire had come as a surprise to everyone, including the political experts. He believed that three quarters of the difficulties which had previously confronted the Zionist movement had now been removed. He foresaw reform of the Palestine land laws, unrestricted immigration, and the free development of industry and the press. In his mind's eye he could already see the legally secured and publicly safeguarded home in Palestine.[68]

During the first few months after the revolution, the signs were indeed encouraging. Max Nordau, who had maintained contacts with the Young Turks in Paris in the period before the revolution, was particularly optimistic.[69] On the other hand, Victor Jacobson, who had come to Constantinople in August 1908 as the representative of the World Zionist Organization, warned from the outset that it was premature to ascribe to the new regime a positive attitude toward Zionism.[70] Wolffsohn adopted a cautious posture toward the new regime, not committing the Zionist movement to any definite policy, while striving to cultivate the favor of those now in power.[71] This infuriated many Zionists, especially in Russia, who saw in this policy a failure to seize new opportunities. A meeting of Russian Zionists, headed by the perennial rivals Tschlenow and Ussishkin, convened in Odessa in October 1908 and recommended the establishment of a Jewish press in Constantinople, pledging to raise fifty thousand rubles for this purpose. To Wolffsohn's surprise and annoyance, they succeeded in raising the money.[72] GAC, which discussed these developments in its meetings in mid-March 1909—which Weizmann did not attend—relented in the face of this fait accompli and voted to increase the subsidy for newspapers in the Turkish capital.[73] Following Wolffsohn's visit to Constantinople in June 1909, it was decided to support a number of French and Ladino newspapers which took a pro-Zionist stance and to publish a Hebrew weekly. Vladimir Jabotinsky was appointed the editor and coordinator of these enterprises.[74]

Thus, the views of the Russian Zionist opposition prevailed against Wolffsohn's objections on an important issue. Moreover, the Zionist appointees in Constantinople, Jacobson and Jabotinsky, were clearly Ussishkin's men. The Russian opposition had been marshaling its forces and coordinating its policies since the fall of 1908. At the beginning of February 1909 a general meeting of the Odessa Committee, chaired by Ussishkin and attended by some 450 delegates, turned into an impressive demonstration of opposition to the Zionist leadership. By their sheer mass the delegates constituted a quasi-congress of those dissatisfied with Wolffsohn.[75] The Russian Zionists published a circular in early October 1909 in which they demanded new means for political and practical work in Palestine in accordance with the changed political conditions. They demanded serious Zionist activity among Turkish Jewry and within the Yishuv, as well as increased work in Palestine, including the establishment of new settlements, training farms, factories, and, of course, the founding of an agrarian bank. Lastly, they also called for the election of a new president of the SAC.[76] The ten Russian members of GAC were so sure of their victory in Hamburg that they openly discussed the composition of the new SAC—Nordau, Marmorek, Sokolow, Stand, Tschlenow, Ussishkin, Warburg, and Wolffsohn—which would have its headquarters in Paris.[77] Weizmann, no doubt remembering how the opposition had faltered in The Hague two years earlier, commented skeptically, "I see that our comrades in Holy Russia have raised the banner of revolt against Wolffsohn, but [I] am afraid that in Hamburg they will agree on every point, as almost always happens. They are considering the transfer of the 'centre' to Paris. Maybe Marmorek's [anti-TB serum, which he had discovered] will have a salutary effect here."[78]

In fact, Weizmann contemplated not going to Hamburg; he had more immediate and important concerns. As a step toward the coveted professorship, he intended to secure a Fellowship in the Royal Society (F.R.S.) and was therefore anxious to publish the results of his ongoing experiments during the winter vacation so as to make his case as strong as possible.[79] However, a fortnight prior to the congress Gaster, in one of his unpredictable moves, decided not to attend "because of the personal nature of the debates."[80] Thus, maintained Gaster, Weizmann had to make the sacrifice and lead the fifteen members of the Order of Ancient Maccabeans during the congress debates and, in cooperation with the Russians, defeat Wolffsohn.[81] He gave Weizmann last-minute instructions when the latter passed through London on his way to the congress.[82] Weizmann was wary of Ussishkin's plan and much less confident than either the Russians or Gaster.[83] In the meantime he had been cornered into a situation which would force upon him the leading role in the concerted attack on Wolffsohn: The Russians elected him chairman of the standing committee (the *Permanenzausschuss*) of the congress.[84] In effect, he was in the powerful position of stage-managing all the subjects brought to the floor for debate.

The Ninth Zionist Congress, which was attended by 435 delegates, opened on December 26, 1909. Wolffsohn began the proceedings with an optimistic assessment of developments in the Ottoman Empire, emphasizing Zionism's potential contributions to the general welfare of the new regime. "There is no conflict between Ottoman interests and Zionist aspirations . . . Ottoman laws will be the blueprint for all our enterprises . . ."[85] Wolffsohn's address contained few surprises, but this was more than balanced by Max Nordau, who also spoke in the opening session. Instead of his usual oration on the state of world Jewry and Zionism, he delivered a polemical defense of Zionism and the leadership of the organization, while at the same time frankly analyzing recent events in the Ottoman Empire. With an eye on the opposition at the congress, he described the feverish excitement engendered by these events among certain Zionist circles, which demanded from Wolffsohn that he establish close ties between the World Zionist Organization and the new regime in Turkey. He complimented the leadership for remaining levelheaded under pressure. He opposed the transfer of the Zionist center to Constantinople.[86] He also opposed the abandonment of the Basel Program, though he conceded that the charter idea could be dropped and that the clause "public law" in the Basel Program had to be reinterpreted to mean "under Turkish protection"[87] rather than international or European protection.

> Our final aim is to live undisturbed in the land of our fathers as a modern, highly civilized nation . . . Certain of our opponents have claimed that we wish to appropriate a province from the Turkish Empire and, after we find ourselves in Palestine, to declare it a kingdom or a republic . . . What we want is to live as a nationality within the framework of the Ottoman state, like all other nationalities in the Empire; it is our wish to deserve the reputation as the most loyal, reliable, and useful of all Turkish nationalities . . .[88]

No sooner was the presidium of the congress elected[89] than a virtual avalanche of attacks was directed against David Wolffsohn and SAC's policies. The opening salvo was delivered by Daniel Pasmanik, Wolffsohn's erstwhile supporter, who made some very uncomplimentary comparisons between the current president of the World Zionist Organization and Herzl.[90] He was followed by a host of other critics. Wolffsohn, who even prior to the congress was well aware of the impending revolt against him, was not about to sit for five long days on the defendant's bench. He decided to take the wind out of his opponents' sails and announced his resignation from the presidency on the morning of the second day of the congress. He used the opportunity to reply to his detractors and to defend his own policies. He was particularly harsh toward the Russian Zionists, who, in his opinion, constantly criticized and demanded action but could not agree on any issue among themselves.

On the other hand, he paid generous tribute to Otto Warburg. He considered the Russians' proposal for an eight-member SAC impractical; they needed to find the right people and he could not recommend a better president than Warburg.[91] It was an aggressive, well-delivered speech, which so moved the delegates that they rose to sing "Hatikvah," the Zionist national anthem. It is not clear whether Wolffsohn really meant all he said about Warburg, nor whether he had indeed made up his mind to relinquish Zionist leadership. What is certain is that the opposition had vastly underestimated both his abilities as a politician and the widespread sentiment among the delegates—especially the German delegates—to keep him in office. Wolffsohn's resignation did not totally quell the attacks against him, though for the most part they subsequently bore a moderate tone. An exception to this was Weizmann, who probably did not quite believe Wolffsohn's public announcement that he had had enough of running the movement. Weizmann may have suspected a tactical maneuver; otherwise it is difficult to explain his bitter personal attack on Wolffsohn, whom he accused of speaking about Russian students in terms that befitted a German chancellor. He readily conceded Wolffsohn's accomplishments but reminded him that there were others who had made similar contributions: "Go to the cemetery of Hedera and see the graves of all the dead Jewish workers about whom no one speaks in the congress; yet they have to their credit as much as some [of our] great leaders . . ." True, Wolffsohn had managed well the finances of the movement, but there were other values in Zionism apart from its businesslike operation. But it was impossible for one person alone to handle all the complicated affairs of the movement. Why not experiment and transfer the offices of the movement to one of the large Jewish intellectual centers where more capable people could get involved? "I know nothing of business practices, but I assert that it is more likely to find inspiration in Berlin than in the little town on the Rhine."[92] Careful bookkeeping had obscured the single most important ideal in Zionism: the settlement of Palestine. Of course, the movement needed financiers, but it also needed a large group of intellectuals. "Mr. Wolffsohn, don't accuse Warburg of making mistakes. You and all of us make mistakes . . . And when the great undertaking of Jewish colonization will get under way, then the 3.3 million pounds [he probably meant 300,000] of the Jewish Colonial Bank will be a mere trifle. A mistake could be made which would cost us the entire capital of the movement, but does that terrify a great historical movement? Yet there you are, always holding the pen in your hand like a petty accountant. Always repeating 'We might lose everything.' " Weizmann suggested trying something new and moving out of Cologne. "Berlin has the largest concentration of Jewish intellectuals. We must win them over; in this milieu we will be able to work better. Don't hide yourself in a corner . . . a great national movement belongs in Berlin, with its large Jewish community, with its intellectual center."[93]

Two more days passed in debates, not only between Wolffsohn's supporters and detractors but also on issues concerning the work in Palestine, which concluded with a vote of confidence for Warburg's "unceasing and successful endeavors."[94] The most important decision arrived at during the debate was the adopton of Franz Oppenheimer's plan for cooperative agricultural settlement in Palestine, realized two years later by the founding of Merhavyah.[95] Late on the evening of the fifth and last day of the congress, Max Bodenheimer, a vice president, announced the standing committee's recommendations. Weizmann and his colleagues on the committee proposed the election of a twenty-one-person actions committee, from among which three to seven members would constitute the SAC, three of whom had tò live in the same city. The president of the Jewish Colonial Trust (viz. Wolffsohn) would have the right of participation in SAC as an *ex officio* member.[96] This was a transparent move to ensure that Wolffsohn would not remain the president of SAC, since he had declared in his earlier speech that he would not transfer to Berlin. The implicit tactic behind the suggestion was that Otto Warburg, Arthur Hantke, and Nahum Sokolow would become members of SAC; Ussishkin and Tschlenow could possibly also transfer to Berlin. There was immediate unrest among the delegates. Heinrich Loewe, a member of the German delegation, suggested that Wolffsohn be elected president of SAC, with the center remaining in Cologne.[97] The agitation among the delegates grew and Wolffsohn had to plead with them to give the suggestions of the *Permanenzausschuss* a hearing.[98] Yet his supporters would not relent and insisted on the right of the congress as a whole to choose its president, namely, Wolffsohn. Thus, the proposals of the standing committee were defeated by a vote of 148 to 128.[99] It was now almost midnight and Weizmann asked for an adjournment of the congress so that the standing committee could consider the situation anew before making further recommendations. Wolffsohn followed the committee to a private room. When the meetings resumed at one thirty in the morning, he asked the congress to reverse its earlier decision. The delegates reluctantly obliged.

It was under these humiliating circumstances—with the man he tried to depose in essence creating the conditions for him to attempt to do so—that Weizmann proposed the following SAC members: Warburg, Sokolow, Tschlenow, Ussishkin, Hantke, Stand, and Sandler. To add to Weizmann's embarrassment, three of those proposed—Hantke, Sandler, and Warburg—possibly acting under pressure from the German delegation, declined the honor.[100] Thus, Weizmann's plan crumbled even before the delegates had a chance to vote. The refusal of Warburg and Hantke caught him by surprise. Without Warburg Weizmann's committee had no one else of comparable stature to nominate. Again pandemonium ensued, and the congress was adjourned at 2 A.M. When the proceedings resumed at a quarter to four in the morning, it was clear that the opposition had been decisively routed. Bodenheimer declared that there was no solution but to reelect the previous triumvirate, consisting of Wolffsohn, Warburg, and Kann. The congress approved this suggestion, as well as the reelection of GAC.[101] Thus ended the most confusing and unsatisfactory congress in the movement's history. The results of the congress displeased all parties and resulted in an even sharper division in the Zionist movement. For Wolffsohn, his reelection was a Pyrrhic victory; though he had scored a few points against his Russian opponents, he knew full well that he was marked for another, more bitter attack two years hence. His opponents, humiliated and bitter, vowed to regroup and return better prepared to the Tenth Zionist Congress.

Weizmann was now decisively and personally embroiled in the struggles within the movement. He became increasingly committed to a well-defined ideological position. In retrospect, it seems that the conflicts at the Hamburg congress and the personal debates with Ussishkin that followed in 1910 pushed Weizmann more and more to adopt a position that would, after World War I, be termed "Weizmannism." After all, until the Sixth Zionist Congress Weizmann was open to political and short-term palliatives suggested by the World Zionist Organization leadership. In the wake of that congress, Weizmann was forced by Ussishkin and his circle to adopt a less compromising stance and was henceforth opposed both to cooperation with non-Zionist organizations (e.g., the Brussels Conference), to *Gegenwartsarbeit*—as defined in Helsingfors—or to any other involvement in the political affairs of countries where Jews resided. He was increasingly concerned with Jewish settlement in Palestine. Yet at the Eighth Zionist Congress, where he adopted "synthetic Zionism" as his own term, Weizmann still viewed it as a compromise formula according to which settlement policies in Palestine would complement, not exclude, political action. However, as his personal relations with Wolffsohn worsened, Weizmann and his friends became ever more insistent in arguing that practical and cultural work in Palestine were a prerequisite for political action. Zionism was to be a slow, evolutionary process, with a view toward the long-range needs of Jews.

Weizmann returned to Manchester in an angry mood, with Wolffsohn's words ("You will, all of you, come crawling to me on your bended knees") still ringing in his ears.[102] Writing to Nahum Sokolow,[103] Weizmann made it clear that he was ready for the inevitable fight with the movement's leadership: ". . . it all seems to me like a bad dream now . . . On my return journey I stopped in London, met Gaster, Bentwich, and we agreed that a beginning should be made at once by firmly organizing the Maccabeans as well as *our* scattered non-Maccabeans. I am in correspondence with [Jacob] Moser [at that time a member of GAC and Lord Mayor of Bradford] and have suggested to him that we start a fighting fund . . . I am full of courage and zeal, and we will not rest till we have turned the movement into a Zionist one."[104] He proposed to raise one thousand pounds, of which half would serve as the "fighting fund" and the other half be sent to the new center of opposition in Berlin.[105] It seems that immediately after the Ninth Zionist Congress, members of the opposition met in Hamburg to coordinate their future efforts. They included Nahum Sokolow and Berthold Feiwel; the latter had resigned his position in the World Zionist Organization's secretariat in 1909. They were to coordinate the activities in Berlin and co-opted into their circle Martin Buber and, a bit later, Julius Berger, who gave up his work at the Central Zionist Office. Weizmann was assigned the task of streamlining all activities in England. In Hamburg they agreed to publish an official letter of protest against the policies of SAC and to suggest ways for stemming further deterioration within the movement. Time was of the essence, and within four weeks after the congress Weizmann delivered his first assessment of what had transpired in Hamburg. Speaking in Yiddish, he told a meeting in Leeds that the congress had once again placed in stark relief the wide gulf between Eastern and Western Zionism. He belittled political Zionism and—with a much more cautious assessment of the new Turkish regime than he had made a few months earlier—warned his listeners not to expect much of the Turks. The charter would forever remain a dead letter unless Jews settled in Palestine. He defended the Russians' policies at the Ninth Zionist Congress as efforts to compromise with the leadership. At the same time, he denied that he was personally against Wolffsohn; the latter was their leader, though he had certainly complicated the affairs of the movement. To the accompaniment of loud applause Weizmann promised that the mistakes made in Hamburg would be rectified at the Tenth Zionist Congress.[106]

The "politicals" in the local movement were also campaigning for their point of view. In Liverpool, Edinburgh, Newcastle, Belfast, Dublin, Glasgow, and London, Zionist associations declared their loyalty to Wolffsohn and SAC.[107] Even those whose enthusiasm for the Young Turks had cooled—like Max Nordau—still maintained their opposition to the "practicals." In a speech to a French Zionist meeting in early February 1910, Nordau belittled the demand of the "practicals" to settle in Palestine while the Turkish prohibitions were still in force. Undeterred, Weizmann, Moses Gaster, Leon Simon, Harry Sacher, Herbert and Norman Bentwich, Samuel Daiches, and others continued to plan their opposition campaign against Wolffsohn's policies throughout the first few months of 1910, though with little success. The "center" in Berlin did not amount to much, and the "fighting fund" did not collect more than fifty pounds—a far cry from the thousand pounds Weizmann had hoped to raise. Even Otto Warburg, the one "practical" on the SAC, discouraged the opposition, assessing its chances of success as minimal, especially since he had of late detected a more positive attitude in Wolffsohn and Kann toward work in Palestine.[108]

The debate soon gravitated to a more personal plane. After he received a letter from Jacob Moser, in which the latter explained events at the Ninth Zionist Congress from Weizmann's perspective,[109] Wolffsohn gave his own version. In his reply Wolffsohn directly attacked Weizmann:

If Dr. Weizmann now attempts to portray events on the last night of the congress as if the fault lies with me or with the majority, then I really have no words to describe his behavior . . . Even in the last hour I urgently pleaded with the five gentlemen who had been proposed for the SAC to take over the leadership. They declined via Tschlenow. Dr. Weizmann was present at these negotiations and knows very well that the fault does not lie with me, that I had to take over the leadership. One must blame the incompetence and thoughtlessness of the gentlemen who brought strife and discord into the congress. A great deal of the blame rests with Dr. Weizmann, who, as chairman of the standing committee, threw that body into great confusion.

Wolffsohn drew Moser's attention to reports in *Die Welt* which detailed some of the unsavory methods of the opposition. If Weizmann now sought to give a different account, he was simply distorting the facts.[110] Moser showed Weizmann the correspondence. Obviously shaken by the attack, which portrayed him as a schemer and intriguer, Weizmann wrote Wolffsohn a long letter which alternated between moods of anger, self-pity, and apologetics. He then launched into an extended review of what had transpired at the congress, trying rather unsuccessfully to justify his own behavior as chairman of the standing committee, as well as that of other members of the opposition, and then returning to his appeal for justice and fairness:

> . . . Mr. Wolffsohn, it is not right to try and shift the blame onto the opposition. The cause of everything is the mistrust, the lack of respect, which has become a principle in the party and which infects and embitters everything. It is only because of this that the Congress and the entire movement have got into a blind alley.
>
> Incidentally, you said in your letter to Moser that you were glad things had turned out as they did, because there was no saying what the opposition would have done to the movement. What has the opposition done to you since the Congress? But we are pulled down, everything is dragged into the mire. We are for work in Palestine because we are after good posts . . . Russian Jew and Zionist is equated with conspirator, destructive, incompetent, etc., etc. Scholars are *hooligans*. In short—long live the ancient and proven tactic of the Black Hundreds, which, as we know, has registered such brilliant successes under Russian Tsarism . . .
>
> Well, you have won all along the line. This I also asserted in Leeds, and appealed for loyal cooperation. Your supporters—presumably in an excess of zeal for the "good cause"—see fit to adopt the tactics described to make us leave the ranks in disgust. And they will succeed. Another year of this kind of "victorious" Zionism, and we shall go, shall leave the field. Things will go on even without Russians, conspirators, Petersburg privy counsellors, academics! One thing cannot be taken away from us, and that is a place of refuge—Palestine. Even if people go on saying that we are just after posts there, we shall work for Palestine, and in that effort as well as in other serious professional work we shall find satisfaction until the storm passes.
>
> This is what an old Zionist, and not a bad one, has to tell you. *Ad memoriam!*[111]

Weizmann's emotional and pained outcry reflected his general state of stress, which seems to have also affected his relationship with Vera. En route to Paris in late March 1910, having had time to reflect on what impact Zionist affairs had had on their domestic life, Weizmann explained to Vera:

> As to our relationship, the present differences between us should not be taken as you, Verochka, take them. You know yourself how many different obligations and problems are piled on me. Ever since I arrived from Hamburg I have been unable to relax because of Zionist affairs . . . Where did you get the idea, Verochka, that I am angry? It only hurts me that you think I am angry and aloof. This is not true. I am only *préoccupé*, which is natural in my position . . . This will pass. You must understand, feel that I love you without limit, and respect you, and you must not talk of my being superior to you. This is untrue and ridiculous. I have great shortcomings, which I am trying in every possible way to overcome, and I hope I shall overcome them. Don't be sad, Verusya . . . Don't think for a moment that I am angry with you—I love you, appreciate you and respect you and I don't even want to put it into words.[112]

Since Vera's letters to Weizmann during this period are not extant, it is difficult to know what had been transpiring in their domestic life. The explanation that Zionist affairs depressed and preoccupied him is no doubt true, but one wonders if Vera did not have other complaints which gave rise to the unhappiness between them. No doubt Vera must have felt quite lonely in Manchester: She was without many friends, with a small baby in tow, constantly struggling to make ends meet while her husband was either at the university or involved in Zionist affairs. Weizmann hardly had the time to give her the attention she felt she deserved. It is not unlikely that she occasionally complained about the order of priorities in her husband's life.

If Weizmann felt under pressure, so did Wolffsohn, some of whose problems came from a quarter he least expected—Jacobus Kann, his closest ally in the movement. In 1909 Kann published his impressions of a visit to Palestine in a book entitled *Erez Israel, das Jüdische Land*,[113] in which he proposed Jewish autonomy for Palestine under Turkish suzerainty. He demanded a charter, with a concession of at least one hundred years for all lands not in private hands, to a Jewish organization representing the Jewish people (i.e., the World Zionist Organization). All authority would be placed in the hands of the Jewish administration, which would also guard the interests of the local population. A sum of twelve million English pounds would be raised, half of which would go toward alleviating the Ottoman debt, the other half to be placed at the disposal of the Jewish administration for the development and settlement of the land. The Jews would become Ottoman subjects and would not be a burden to the Turkish treasury. Kann also spoke of a Jewish governor, a Jewish army, and even a parliament.[114] It was the most far-reaching public statement on Zionist aims to date, and though Kann emphasized that he

only expressed his personal views, it was difficult to dissociate his political demands from his official position as a member of SAC. The book
aroused little interest as long as it was available only in German and
Dutch, but the distribution of a French version—the language of the
Turkish intelligentsia—a short while after the Ninth Zionist Congress
aroused fears and suspicions in circles hostile to the Zionists. The press
committee in Constantinople demanded the withdrawal of the book,
disavowal of Kann's plan, and his resignation from SAC; it even threatened to go public on its own, declaring its dissociation from Kann.
Wolffsohn, on the other hand, charged Vladimir Jabotinsky with gross
insubordination and forbade such a public disavowal.[115] The result was
that Jabotinsky, who had made excellent progress in winning the confidence of local journalists and politicians, resigned his position. The Russian Zionists, who supported him and Victor Jacobson on this issue, took
a dim view of Wolffsohn's conduct[116] and intensified their struggle to
replace SAC at the Tenth Zionist Congress.[117]

Attacks against SAC also came from other quarters. The public "Manifesto of Nineteen," which had already been discussed by the opposition
at Hamburg, was finally published in *Die Welt* on February 25, 1910.
Among its nineteen signatories were Martin Buber, Berthold Feiwel,
Richard Lichtheim, Vladimir Jabotinsky, Herbert Bentwich, and Chaim
Weizmann.[118] The authors of the manifesto declared that the Ninth Zionist Congress had failed in its assigned tasks: charting of methods and
direction of political Zionism; crystallization of Zionist forces in light of
new political developments; and presentation of a general blueprint for
future work. They called upon all opposition elements in the movement
to rally their forces at the Tenth Zionist Congress and demand that
Zionism be based on a complete integration between East and West;
that Palestine be placed at the center of all political and practical work;
that a realistic form of diplomacy be conducted in Turkey; that the center
of the movement be transferred to a large Jewish community; that GAC
have the decisive voice in determining policy, with SAC serving as its
executive arm; and that the "cult of personality" in the movement be
replaced with democratic procedures.[119] Weizmann's friends and collaborators in England—Harry Sacher, Leon Simon, and Norman Bentwich—composed a similar manifesto in English which had some additional suggestions for the future course of the movement.[120] Even among
the German Zionists there were signs of a growing opposition to Wolffsohn,[121] and Yehiel Tschlenow and Max Nordau attacked one another in
the pages of *Die Welt* concerning the "impractical and tactless Russians."[122]

Shortly before Passover Wolffsohn traveled to England. Well informed
of Weizmann's role in stoking the fires of opposition on the Continent
and in England, and aware that Weizmann was sitting in the audience,
Wolffsohn made the following derogatory reference to him in his first
speech in England, held at the Pavilion-Theatre in Mile End:

Our friends, who demand practical work, are well meaning, but they do not work themselves . . . Herr Dr. Weizmann, surely a good Zionist, one of the leaders of the opposition in Hamburg, who has worked for our cause all his life, who has given of his body and soul, has said in his great opposition speech at the last congress: "A great mistake may be made which would involve the entire share capital of the bank, the entire three hundred thousand pounds may be lost. Is a historic movement intimidated by that?" Dr. Weizmann believes that the most important thing is the idea. If it only lasts! The idea is not new, it was not invented by Dr. Herzl or anyone else, it is thousands of years old and will forever exist as long as there are still Jews on God's earth (lively applause). But when Dr. Weizmann says, "What does it matter if three hundred thousand pounds are lost!" then I must say that Dr. Weizmann is an impractical man in business matters (hear, hear!). If we did not know Dr. Weizmann, we would have to say that our worst enemy could not have given us such advice. The idea itself would not be bankrupt if we were to lose these three hundred thousand pounds, but the Zionist Organization would be! . . . We cannot lightly gamble with the heritage bequeathed us by Herzl (stormy applause).[123]

Weizmann had been preparing for Wolffsohn's tour in England, fully intending to challenge him in public. His colleagues on the Continent, particularly Nahum Sokolow, supplied him with the ideological ammunition with which Wolffsohn could be attacked.[124] Moreover, he felt a bit more confident that his ideas would be given a public hearing. If Wolffsohn had on his side such major organs as *Die Welt*, which he himself controlled, and *The Jewish Chronicle*, which was managed by the loyal Leopold Greenberg, Weizmann had the support of a brand-new Manchester-based monthly, *The Zionist Banner*, which was inaugurated by the Manchester Young Men's Zionist Society in October 1909 and commenced publication in April 1910.[125] Wolffsohn's *ad hominem* charges gave Weizmann a convenient opportunity to strike back. On April 25, 1910, at the inaugural meeting of the Manchester Young Men's Zionist Society, which also saw the adoption of a resolution in the spirit of the "Manifesto of Nineteen,"[126] Weizmann replied to Wolffsohn's charges.

. . . Herr Wolffsohn, with his monotonous demand for businessmen, confuses a leader with a secretary. Who has promulgated the axiom that the Movement must be led by a businessman? Was Herzl a businessman? Did anyone ever require that he should be one? Was Beaconsfield a businessman? Or is Asquith? And, for the moment, admitting that this is a correct view, where are the startling business capabilities of those in charge now! Is the 2½% which constitutes the dividend of the JCT an example of high business acumen? Businessmen are fine in their way, but they must be given ideas. And what we require of our leader is not the proper supervision of an office—we have many paid officials to do this; our leader must give us a program.

He must think! He must inspire us with ideas, and with energy to carry those ideas into practice . . .

Given the right plans, men and money will always be forthcoming . . .

[Practical schemes] have been established despite the inactivity of the Actions Committee. It has always been so . . .

Herr Wolffsohn quoted my words at [the Ninth Zionist] Congress. What I said was—"there may come a day when we shall have to risk as much money as there is now in the bank for experiments." And is this not a good wish, a wish that all will echo? For Palestine they are unwilling to risk [money], and for Uganda they were willing.[127]

Wolffsohn was furious. At a speech in Manchester on May 2, 1910[128]— once more in the presence of Weizmann—he responded to Weizmann's insulting remark in a similar vein: "It is not written anywhere that a leader must necessarily be a Doctor of Chemistry." But this time he also went a step further and insinuated that Weizmann was both incompetent and not fully honorable in his financial dealings, and that he mishandled the Jewish university and Kremenetzky funds placed at his disposal.[129] Weizmann did not react immediately to Wolffsohn's Manchester speech. It is quite possible that it did not sound as offensive as it seemed in print.[130] It was only after reports appeared in *Die Welt* and *Hayehudi* that Weizmann insisted Wolffsohn correct any misperceptions about Weizmann's integrity.[131] He also asked Johann Kremenetzky to clear up the record publicly in regard to Weizmann's handling of the latter's funds.[132] While willing to publish a clarification, Wolffsohn expressed surprise at the interpretation Weizmann put on his Manchester speech.[133] Yet Weizmann was not the only one to interpret the speech as casting aspersion on his character and moral conduct. At a meeting of the central committee of the Russian Zionists, a resolution was passed protesting Wolffsohn's speech and expressing the committee members' high regard for Weizmann.[134] But Weizmann was not satisfied. The public insult gnawed at him; it made him look foolish and untrustworthy.[135] Three weeks after Wolffsohn's speech he wrote him a letter demanding the complete withdrawal of all charges and announcing his resignation from all Zionist offices—GAC, the board of the Palestine Land Development Company, and the World Zionist Organization in general:

I had a long struggle with myself before arriving at this bitter and, for me, weighty decision. After fifteen years' work, fifteen of the best years of my life, in which I gave the best I had in me to the movement, I am compelled to cut the ties. So long as the struggle was serious and clean, it could be carried on. But I am too good to be torn to pieces for nothing, and I can see no use in it either for the movement or for myself as a Zionist.

I am a poor man, [and I] must work hard to maintain my position in life. All my free time, and indeed some of my time that was not free, all my energy, I gave to the propaganda work, with the result that I am abused and pelted with stones. Now, I would have suffered this joyfully had I been able to see even the slightest benefit from it to the movement. But I can see nothing but discord, weakness and disorganization. It was never my ambition to lead the movement. I never strove for that. My purpose was to give myself for Palestine. I can foresee an end to these *Galuth* activities, and in a relatively short time I shall have the possibility of going to Palestine. I want to use the time to learn, to prepare myself further for Palestine and to rest so as to arrive there a healthy man.

I willingly accept the certificate of incompetence; but—and this is meant quite sincerely—it applies not only to our party, but to all.

You will forgive this rather lengthy letter. In recollection of the old, friendly relations which now, alas, are poisoned, I considered it my duty to write to you in detail for the last time.[136]

Wolffsohn's reply came within a fortnight. He enclosed a retraction—but not an apology—subsequently published in *Die Welt*, which stated that he did not wish to cast doubt upon Weizmann's honesty and merely sought to point out that Weizmann and some of his friends who made the most vociferous demands for practical work were themselves unsuited to carry out such work.[137] In his private letter, though, Wolffsohn was far from being apologetic.

. . . You who are now complaining to me, dear doctor, should remember, first of all, that as far as personal attacks, abuse, and insinuations are concerned, you are by far a more accomplished trickster than I am.[138] Still, I have never allowed my spirits to sink [under such attacks] and have steadfastly upheld the principles entrusted to me by the movement. I am surprised that you now express the intention of leaving for Aretz [Palestine] and I can hardly believe that you have seriously weighed the problem and that your decision is irrevocable. If you are really going to stop your work altogether, I can only say that this would be a great disappointment. That I will make no official use of your resignation goes without saying.[139]

The conflict between Wolffsohn and Weizmann was further discussed at the annual conference held in June 1910, where the parties to the dispute decided to end their differences amicably.[140]

How was it possible to conclude the dispute so amicably in view of the grave charges made by Wolffsohn? One must see this unseemly controversy as an extension and final phase of the Ninth Zionist Congress. Despite his victory at the congress, Wolffsohn was apparently eager to put Weizmann in his place for his role as chairman of the standing committee. As his correspondence with Moser indicates, Wolffsohn was seething with rage. He waited four months for the opportunity to lash out at Weizmann publicly on Weizmann's own home territory so as to make certain that his public remarks would have the greatest effect. Weizmann, though deeply hurt, apparently understood the psychological need of Wolffsohn for some form of catharsis. Deep down he may have even blamed himself for not having sufficiently prepared the ground for a coup at the Ninth Zionist Congress and for letting Ussishkin manipulate him from behind the scenes. In any case, not much could be gained by Weizmann in a protracted dispute with the leader of the movement, who was bound to win any public debate. The wisest option for Weizmann was to retreat temporarily in a face-saving maneuver, biding his time until the next opportune moment.

At first reading, Weizmann's remark to Wolffsohn that he intended to go to Palestine within "a relatively short time" seems surprising. Since mid-May 1909 he had made up his mind to present his candidacy for a Fellowship of the Royal Society, an almost necessary step in the direction of the professorship. His research was going very well, and he felt that with a few more publications and the backing of his senior colleagues he could achieve this goal. This was very much in keeping with Vera's wishes; she was more interested in Weizmann's professional advancement than his Zionist aspirations. She herself was making plans to resume her medical studies and start practicing in England.[141] Weizmann intended to submit his name for election in mid-December 1910, but a snag materialized at the last moment, since he had not yet been naturalized—a necessary precondition.[142] Once again he turned to his old and trusted friend Moses Gaster, whom he asked to expedite the matter by turning to Home Secretary Winston Churchill.[143] The *Haham*, ever ready to help, turned instead to Herbert Samuel, then Postmaster General, who indeed helped smooth Weizmann's naturalization process[144] in time for the submission of his candidacy to the Royal Society. On December 12, 1910, Weizmann's name was proposed to the society by Harold Dixon and William Henry Perkin, the two senior chemists at the University of Manchester. How, then, did Weizmann's desire for academic status and honor in England square with his wish to go to Palestine in the near future? It was only to Ahad Ha'Am and to Vera that he confided his most cherished plans: the attainment of a Royal Society fellowship, a professorship, and then, at the zenith of the academic ladder, a move to Palestine. During periods of disappointment with the World Zionist Organization or his professional career, his wish to go to Palestine became more urgent. At such times Palestine became an idealized refuge. As time passed, he was less ready to actually immigrate to Palestine, but psychologically it was a comforting thought to imagine an alternative setting for himself. Under the impact of the defeat at the Ninth Zionist Congress he wrote Ahad Ha'Am, "Oh, if only to Palestine sooner! I really am waiting with great impatience. By the way . . . my candidature for the Royal Society is going to be put forward . . . But I am afraid I shall be ready sooner than the Technicum."[145]

The Technicum to which Weizmann referred was the brainchild of Paul Nathan, secretary of the Hilfsverein der deutschen Juden, in the wake of his visit to Palestine in 1907. In his report to the annual meeting of the Hilfsverein in March 1908, Nathan maintained that an important ingredient in the development of Palestine would be the founding of a Technicum. He envisaged a modern institute for the training of engineers and technicians, who would play an important role in the building of railroads, ports, roads, bridges, and so forth. Nathan also suggested that such an institute be built in Haifa, which was bound to be the linchpin for the industrialization of the country.[146] As the plans for the Technicum crystallized, it was decided by Nathan and his collaborators to combine it with a science-oriented high school.[147] The Hilfsverein could not by itself raise all the necessary funds. In January 1908 Nathan met

Shmarya Levin, who was immediately won over to the project.[148] Both then turned to David Wissotzky, whose father, Kalman (Wolf) Wissotzky, had left in his will a substantial sum of money for the creation of institutions that would bear his name. With the support of Ahad Ha'Am, one of the trustees of the fund, David Wissotzky promised financial help. Nathan then returned to Palestine in April 1908 and purchased land for the projected Technicum. He also approached the banker Jacob H. Schiff, who promised to donate one hundred thousand dollars. That summer the World Zionist Organization, through the Jewish National Fund, offered to pay for the land in Haifa upon which the Technicum would be erected, an offer which the Hilfsverein was pleased to accept.[149] On March 29, 1909, the Hilfsverein and the Wolf Wissotzky Fund established the Juedische Institut fuer technische Erziehung in Palaestina. The chairman of its first board (Kuratorium) was James Simon, president of the Hilfsverein, with Paul Nathan as his deputy and executive director. The first executive committee consisted of Ahad Ha'Am, Shmarya Levin, Paul Nathan, James Simon, and Ludwig Schiff, Jacob Schiff's brother.[150]

From the outset, Weizmann assumed that a chemistry department, under his chairmanship, would be one of the first to be established at the Technicum. As early as February 1909 he made it clear that "as my situation here gets more secure I feel like tearing out those young roots; I should like to leave England; and how happy I should be to go to the Jewish Technicum . . ."[151] Two weeks later, as the legal formalities between the Wissotzky Fund and the Hilfsverein were about to be concluded, he added, "Obviously the whole matter comes into the sphere of reality. That is good. And I expect very, very much from a Hebrew Institute of Higher Learning in Palestine [viz. the Technicum]—almost everything. But shall we have the strength to create something first rate, a temple of learning better than the *goyim's*? I hope so!"[152] Ahad Ha'Am, the ranking Zionist on the executive of the Kuratorium, strongly supported and encouraged Weizmann's aspirations,[153] at one point even nominating him as his deputy to the board. Weizmann's letters to Ahad Ha'Am reveal his dual aspirations: to build an institute which would provide Palestine with a sound scientific base in order to contribute to the development of the Yishuv, and a position for himself that would be commensurate with his academic status while affording him the opportunity for Zionist self-fulfillment.[154] But despite the seemingly solid financial backing for the enterprise, matters did not proceed as smoothly as he had hoped. From the very start Ahad Ha'Am had warned of delays in establishing departments of chemistry and agriculture, but Weizmann still remained optimistic. He became disturbed about future prospects when he himself inquired in Berlin about plans for the Technicum. The chief adviser for the Technicum, Georg Schlesinger, was a professor of industrial science who, in Weizmann's opinion, placed too much emphasis on the engineering department at the Technicum at the expense of other needs.

I'm afraid that there will be a repetition of the mistake made by the Baron, who organized things in Palestine according to the *dernier cri,* forgetting the basic fact that in such a country one ought to begin with the modest, most necessary things and allow them to develop.

I took the trouble to investigate how many concessions had been granted recently for "mining" projects in Asia Minor and Anatolia. There were about twenty. If our Technicum is supposed to satisfy Turkey's needs, then obviously there should be a mining department at least in embryonic form, i.e., chemical laboratories . . . It is of course awkward for me to talk about this, as in a sense I am personally interested, but you do know that I am only seeking the good of the cause.

I am not afraid to say that if in the future I were to be entrusted with the organization of the chemistry department I should be able . . . to find means and people for this. In two years I shall have finished my "stage" here and would readily devote half a year to such work.[155]

It seemed to Weizmann that despite inadequate planning there was still a chance that his aspirations would materialize. But already by December 1910 the first obstacles loomed large on the issues of language and religion—not to speak of financial problems and Turkish interference[156]—which placed the founding of a chemistry department at the Technicum low on the list of priorities. By the time Weizmann was truly ready to move to Palestine, in the period after the Tenth Zionist Congress, the dream of occupying the first chair in chemistry at the Technicum had evaporated.

But these were troubles for the future. In the months following the Ninth Zionist Congress Weizmann devoted a great deal of energy to mobilizing the opposition in England for the Tenth Zionist Congress. His election to the vice presidency of the EZF, coupled with his strong identification as a Maccabean, placed him in a very favorable position to propagate his ideas among all segments of English Jewry. He concentrated his attention on a hitherto neglected group: the university students of Oxford, Cambridge, and London. This increased Zionist activity often came at the expense of his family life. Frequently he spent weekends traveling by train to Glasgow, Leeds, Liverpool, and other provincial towns. Vera, who had her own professional aspirations, was resentful of Weizmann's absences, having to single-handedly care for Benjy, who was often ailing. The full-time nanny and the periodic vacation in Wales or in the French Alps only partially made up for long periods of unhappiness she experienced in Manchester. Weizmann himself often commented on the sacrifices he made on behalf of the cause; he was a doting father, devoted to Vera, and disliked being without them. He made up for his enforced absences by working even harder to attain financial independence, continuing to mark examination papers,[157] trying to sell his patents, and looking for new professional opportunities. At one point he was even intrigued by an offer of a professorship in India, which would have solved all his material problems.[158] His immediate and extended family looked to him for advice, financial help, and professional guidance. He continued to send monthly checks to his sisters in Switzerland regardless of his own financial straits. His brother Shmuel came to live with the Weizmanns sometime in 1908.[159] Eva Lubzhinsky, Weizmann's niece, studied in Manchester from 1909 to 1912. Though she did not live with the Weizmanns, she seems to have spent much time with them.[160] Weizmann's sister Anna came to Manchester for the academic year 1913–14 after she had finished her studies in chemistry at Zurich. She came at her brother's invitation, lived with the Weizmanns, and worked at the University of Manchester under her brother's supervision.[161] There were thus many family members and affairs to be taken care of. Weizmann dispatched these obligations as a matter of course, never complaining about the extra burden placed on his shoulders.

All in all, the Weizmann family members in Russia as well as in the West seemed to be making steady progress in their business as well as professional careers. One matter that deeply concerned all of them was Ozer Weizmann's health. He had been ailing for a while, and in the summer of 1910 Weizmann visited his parents in Bad Kissingen and in Freiburg-in-Breisgau, where Ozer went to recuperate.[162] But Ozer never fully recovered. The following April (1911) Weizmann traveled to his parents' home for the Passover holiday. It was to be his last visit to Pinsk. He made the mandatory stopover in Warsaw to visit his sister Miriam and his brother-in-law Chaim Lubzhinsky, who, with their children, accompanied Weizmann to Pinsk.[163] After visiting Warsaw, even Manchester seemed a civilized place. Jewish life in Warsaw filled him with disgust. He described it as a *"Totentanz, danse macabre.* Ostentatious overdressing, overflowing cafés, gaiety and amusement, while the screw turns tighter and tighter, the circle of misfortune gets narrower."[164] While 98 percent of the Jews were starving, 2 percent were feasting and overeating, dressing in the latest Parisian fashions.[165]

Pinsk had not changed since he had last been there. There was the usual contrast between the warmth and happiness in the family circle[166] and the terrible degradation of Jewish life that dominated in the Pale of Settlement.[167] It was the last Passover the family would spend together with Ozer. A few weeks later, on May 31, 1911, he died at the age of sixty-one.

At the end of his letter of April 15 to Vera, Weizmann returned to the theme of government oppression in Russia. "The circle of restrictive measures has become narrower the whole time, the noose tightens and it is impossible to prophesy what will come next . . ."[168] Weizmann was referring to the chain of restrictions instituted against the Jews since the changes in election laws to the Duma of June 1907. Peter Stolypin, Minister of the Interior, devised one cruel anti-Jewish measure after another. In the spring of 1910, for example, twelve hundred Jewish families were exiled from Kiev in a most brutal fashion. Under his administration the quotas for Jews in secondary schools and at the universities were strictly enforced. In February 1911 the Congress of the United Nobility, which represented the most reactionary elements of the landowners, demanded the retention of all existing restrictions and advocated, in addition, the elimination of Jews from the country. It reinforced its demands with the charge of ritual murder. The rightist press made even more drastic demands: "The government must recognize that the Jews are dangerous to the life of mankind in the same measure as wolves, scorpions, reptiles, poisonous spiders and similar creatures which are destroyed because they are deadly for human beings . . . The Jews must be placed under such conditions that they will gradually die out . . ."[169] Thus the groundwork for a monstrous blood libel was prepared. Just a fortnight before Weizmann's arrival in Russia, the mutilated body of a boy was discovered near Kiev, providing the government and the rightist press the opportunity of accusing Jews of killing the boy for ritual purposes.[170] In July a Jewish factory worker, Mendel Beilis, was arrested and imprisoned for two years before he was acquitted.[171] The infamous Beilis trial attracted world attention, revealing the corruption of the Russian regime and the plight of its Jewish subjects.

At the same time that the Beilis case got under way in Russia, the Zionists witnessed with dismay the increased and widespread opposition to Jewish settlement expressed by the Turkish government and various Arab spokesmen.[172] Thus, an attempt was made by David Wolffsohn at the Tenth Zionist Congress to refute the charges leveled against Zionism,[173] knowing full well that both Turks and Arabs had by now acquired the habit of carefully examining Zionist speeches and publications.

The increased hostility of Turks and Arabs to Zionism was a major item on the agenda of GAC, which met from June 27 to 29, 1910.[174] Weizmann did not attend these meetings—neither did Ussishkin or Tschlenow—which in fact predetermined the outcome of the Tenth Zionist Congress. The sessions were often stormy and there was no lack of personal attack against Wolffsohn by Shmarya Levin and Alexander Marmorek, the president's erstwhile supporter and friend.[175] Nevertheless, after both sides had vented their complaints and frustrations, the conference ended on a note of reconciliation and was henceforth dubbed the "Peace Conference."[176] Practically all the demands of the opposition, which had been rejected at the Ninth Zionist Congress in Hamburg, were now accepted through the efforts of an *Einigungskonferenz*. The following was decided: to give GAC a larger voice in the conduct of the movement; to submit to the next congress proposals to transfer the seat of the central office from Cologne to a larger Jewish center, where at least three members of SAC would be resident; and to increase SAC membership to 5 to 7 members who would elect from their midst the chairman/president of the movement.[177] Lastly, it was proposed that the president of the Council (*Aufsichtsrat*) of the Jewish Colonial Trust (namely Wolffsohn) would be a full member of SAC.[178] Weizmann was delighted by these proposals. "Now a little rest is called for, then we shall pull ourselves together and prepare the Xth Congress thoroughly. Perhaps we shall succeed in getting rid of the rabble. When Christ wanted to save the Temple, he drove out the money-changers."[179]

Weizmann's rather extreme reaction must be seen in the light of the prolonged and acrimonious debate he had only recently had with Wolffsohn. In fact, at the close of GAC meetings in June 1910 it had become clear that Wolffsohn would terminate his tenure as president of the World Zionist Organization with the next congress.[180] His supporters were deserting him and his health had severely deteriorated; he was now physically and emotionally prepared for a changing of the guard.[181] Though officially a member of the OAM delegation to the congress, Weizmann also had a Russian mandate and participated in the Sixth Conference of Russian Zionists, which opened on August 6, 1911, in Basel, three days prior to the congress. The debates in this conference were naturally focused on the worsening condition of Russian Jewry, as well as the question of political versus practical work.[182] Weizmann participated actively in the debate with his by now familiar call for organic and methodical work in Palestine—"stone by stone"—and an abandonment of "Charter-Zionism."[183]

The congress, which opened on August 9, 1911, with 429 delegates from 28 countries in attendance, was largely uneventful, the major issues having been resolved more than a year earlier. Weizmann, who was elected vice chairman of the standing committee, replaced Alexander Marmorek as acting chairman, once again giving him a key role in the congress. Wolffsohn announced his resignation during the first session of the congress.[184] It made little sense to attack the departing president for his past sins. The controversies at the Tenth Zionist Congress centered less on the work of SAC than on questions of national education, religious coercion in Palestine, the role of religion and culture, and the attitude of the movement toward these issues. Naturally the Mizrahi took an active part in these debates, with some of its members even threatening to leave the movement on the cultural question as well as on the issue of applying Jewish law to JNF properties. A compromise was finally struck by the cultural subcommittee, which proposed the organization of cultural work in Palestine by SAC, with the assurance that nothing should be done that would offend Jewish observance; it was left to the individual national federations to adopt their own resolutions on this issue.[185] Two innovations at the congress were the extensive use of the Hebrew language and the display of "moving pictures" on Palestine by Murray Rosenberg, the estate agent who had only recently returned from a tour there.

The most important issue—the organizational framework of the movement—was left for the last day of the congress, August 15. It was during this session that the standing committee suggested some changes, the most important being limiting the membership of GAC to twenty-five and the election of the chairman and his deputy from among the SAC membership. This was accepted by the congress, but a storm of protest ensued when the representatives of small federations complained about the composition of the standing committee itself. It was only through Wolffsohn's intervention that tempers cooled and the congress went on to deal with the remaining items on the agenda.[186] Weizmann did not participate in these debates and generally kept aloof from all other issues during the previous five days of the congress. His work was done far from the public eye. One reason for his silence was perhaps due to the fact that many of the important issues at the congress had been decided earlier; Wolffsohn's voluntary resignation assured the victory of the opposition and made much of the discussion a *pro forma* exercise. In fact, this turn of events made Weizmann's task as chairman of the standing committee much easier. But perhaps Weizmann also learned from the Ninth Zionist Congress that he needed to be more cautious in his public deliberation. It was safer—and more effective—to decide matters far from the limelight. It was only during the very last hours of the congress that Weizmann read to the delegates the names of those nominated for various offices in the movement.[187] The most difficult task for the standing committee was to put together an acceptable GAC membership, since its size had been sharply reduced to twenty-five and federation representation had been discontinued. In presenting the list, Weizmann emphasized that it was arrived at after many hours of debate and consultation with all parties, and after taking into account all the points of view represented at the congress. "We, members of the *Permanenzausschuss,* call this the 'List of Peace.' May this list and the work of the gentlemen . . . contribute to the peace and restoration of health of the movement."[188] The list was almost perfectly balanced, with thirteen members of the opposition, ten belonging to Wolffsohn's cause and two without a definite alignment. Symbolically, the list opened with Wolffsohn and ended with Weizmann.[189] Some names were notable by their absence (e.g., Leopold Greenberg, Joseph Cowen, Herbert Bentwich, and Moses Gaster, to mention only England's veteran Zionists). Nevertheless the new GAC's composition was accepted by the congress, as were those suggested for SAC. The new SAC included Otto Warburg, Arthur Hantke, Shmarya Levin, Nahum Sokolow, and Victor Jacobson.[190] Here, too, a balance was achieved in the successful merger of East and West European Zionists— one of Weizmann's long-standing goals. These were men after Weizmann's heart, all "practicals" and all men with whom he had good personal relations. If there was anything to mar the total sense of victory by the "practicals," it was the fact that the "politicals" managed to hold on to the purse strings of the movement, namely, the Jewish Colonial Trust and the Jewish National Fund.[191]

The congress was a personal triumph for Wolffsohn, who, at the suggestion of Joshua Thon, was acknowledged for his work.[192] During the last hour of the congress Yehiel Tschlenow also praised Wolffsohn for his accomplishments, not the least of which was to make the Tenth Zionist Congress the "Congress of Peace."[193] But it also meant political defeat for Wolffsohn and his camp. For Weizmann, on the other hand, it was both a personal and political triumph. His success compensated for the inelegant and unsophisticated manner in which he had conducted the affairs of the standing committee two years earlier in Hamburg. It also meant that he no longer belonged to the opposition camp. After years of working against the elected leadership, he was now one of the closest confidants of SAC, a firm believer in the new direction in the movement, and a beneficiary of this reorientation. From now on he could rely on powerful support for his various cultural and practical projects from the new central office in Berlin. After all, Warburg, the new chairman of SAC, was as keen as Weizmann himself to develop colonization and science in Palestine; Levin was working full time for the Technicum;[194] Sokolow would guarantee that cultural affairs would not be neglected; Hantke was sure to put order into the organizational chaos reigning in the movement;[195] and Jacobson was a diplomat who could be relied upon to consult with others before irreversibly committing the movement. Indeed, the entire concept of political work, which Weizmann had so often derided in the past, came to have new meaning and significance. Now that he was part of the "establishment," he reaffirmed even more forcefully than in the past the necessity of engaging in political and diplomatic work.[196] It was a very different Zionist movement, one with which he could fully identify, and his letters concerning its future would henceforth reflect optimism and confidence.

But identification with and support for the movement also brought new responsibilities. These new Zionist obligations often conflicted with Weizmann's personal and professional aspirations. Despite the contradictory claims of both, he made remarkable strides in each in the next few years. Only during World War I did the two unite to serve the same cause.

XV

Society, Science,
and the Professorship

Had he so wished, Weizmann could now have become directly involved
in shaping Zionist policy. The opportunities and temptations were readily available. As soon as he returned from the congress to Manchester
early in September, he was besieged by SAC with various requests for
information, advice, and participation in meetings. After spending years
in the opposition, he now found himself dispensing advice on matters
pertaining to the Jewish Colonial Trust, the means of uniting the warring factions of the OAM and EZF, and Zionist relations with the press.[1]
During the first week of November 1911 he traveled to Berlin to participate in meetings of GAC, which discussed proposals for political and
propaganda activities in Turkey and Palestine.[2] It was decided to create
a committee to deal with such matters, of which Weizmann would become a member. Weizmann was accommodating, replying to Arthur
Hantke's many queries in detail and with a new air of self-confidence.
He promised to do his best to get pro-Zionist articles into *The Manchester
Guardian* through his good friend and disciple Harry Sacher.[3] Following
the outbreak of the Turko-Italian War in September 1911, which reopened the Eastern Question and Anglo-Russian negotiations concerning their respective spheres of influence in Persia, Weizmann felt that
Britain had to be shown "how vital it can be . . . to have a friendly and
'strong' element in Palestine, in the Asian Near East in general, that we
can be the link between England and the Muslim world. England will,
after all, also have a lot to do with the Muslims . . . I believe that the
basis on which we can negotiate with the men in power here probably
lies in this direction. We want nothing from them, except that for the
time being the Government should do us no harm."[4] Weizmann was
not yet calling for the exclusive reliance of the Zionist movement on England. On the contrary, a month earlier, at the meetings of GAC in Berlin, Weizmann stated unequivocally: "We have only Palestine and Turkey as a political sphere of interest and we must take care to strengthen
and support it [i.e., the Ottoman Empire] as best we can. Everything
else is utopian. We can build our politics only on the basis of a strong
and regenerated Turkey . . ."[5] Nevertheless, after seven years in a

country whose interest in the Near East was growing, he increasingly appreciated the necessity of political work within English government circles. Recalling his conversation with Balfour in 1906, he naturally— but unsuccessfully—sought to engage him on this issue.[6] Balfour could or would not find the time to receive him. A similar attempt to gain access to Lord Haldane, the British Secretary for War, also failed.[7]

There was a limit, though, to what Weizmann was willing to do on behalf of SAC. In February 1912 Hantke inquired whether Weizmann would undertake a propaganda tour in the United States.[8] Weizmann refused, accepting only a much shorter tour during the semester break in March, to include Berlin, Vienna, Prague, and Heidelberg.[9] In explaining his reasons for declining the American tour, Weizmann revealed some of his future plans.

> As you know, I want to go to Palestine in 3–4 years. *But* I want to go to Palestine not when I have nothing to lose here, but, on the contrary, after having achieved everything here. This "everything" consists of two things: a full professorship and admission to the Royal Society. The former has been achieved except for the official announcement, which will presumably come during the summer term [*sic*]. The second is somewhat more difficult for a Russian Jew. However, the matter has got to the point where my candidature has been established. How long the candidature will "stand" depends on the scope and character of my scientific work, for in my case this is the only decisive criterion. I must therefore strain every nerve to work and publish a great deal, for admission to the Royal Society will open all doors for me here. I shall then be worth ten times as much to you . . . I have a definite aim in view, and I have worked hard for years to attain it. I have achieved a great deal here, and this is my last ambition here in the *Golus*, for it will make me independent and give me the best introduction for Palestine. I shall not conceal from you that I have yet another ambition—to become English Consul in Palestine, and if necessary I shall take the examination for it.[10]

Weizmann's frank discussion of his goals only hinted at one other ambition. By "independence" he meant, no doubt, financial independence as well as professional independence. As a child in Motol, growing up in a family dependent on the elements for its livelihood, Weizmann was plagued by a lack of financial security. Ever since he began to work—at the age of eleven—one of Weizmann's goals was to achieve the financial security he had always lacked. For years he had been patenting his chemical inventions, hoping that one of them would eventually bring him a large and steady income. Ironically, he had achieved a partial financial independence only during his Geneva years, when he and Christian Deichler sold one of their first patents in 1901 to the Bayer Works in Elberfeld.[11] By the beginning of 1912 Weizmann had seventeen patents registered in his name and those of his collaborators.[12] Yet he was able to sell only his camphor patent, which brought him three hundred francs each month until just prior to World War I.[13] This income, plus his 300-pound salary from the University of Manchester, which was supplemented by the correction of examination papers for other universities, amounted at most to 450 or 500 pounds per year.[14] Moreover, in April 1912 his appointment at the university underwent a change: He was placed in charge of a course in chemistry for medicine and a course on coloring matters—and his university salary was increased to 450 pounds per year.[15] Thus, by all accounts Weizmann's combined annual income was quite substantial. Nevertheless, it seemed inadequate to maintain the Weizmann household, as Weizmann's frequent loans from Gaster and later from Ahad Ha'Am and Julius Simon clearly prove.[16]

From the very beginning of their married life, Chaim and Vera Weizmann lived beyond their means. Vera had never earned an income. While still a student in Geneva she was supported by her parents and—when their financial situation deteriorated—by an older brother.[17] It was at her insistence that the Weizmanns moved to the house on Birchfields Road and bought new furniture. Since she did not know how to cook and never cared to learn, they employed a maid who did the cooking, washing, and cleaning.[18] As soon as Benjy was born, they also employed a nanny. From the start, the Weizmanns took vacations a few times a year, preferably in the Austrian, Italian, or French Alps, in Switzerland or the South of France, and on other occasions in Wales or on the southern coast of England. Both liked the good life.[19] According to Vera, Weizmann's tastes were expensive and he had little monetary sense.[20] Vera was more aware of the need to save money, but she also wanted to live in style. If she tried to save money, it was, according to her own autobiography, by attempting to check Weizmann's generous financial contributions toward his siblings' education and by choosing a good dressmaker in a little back street who made her three well-cut dresses a year, which she took care to preserve.[21]

Having to cut corners[22] and being aware that they did have to count their pounds before spending them sensitized the Weizmanns to the wealth of their acquaintances and friends. While on his propaganda trip to the Continent in late March 1912, Weizmann was invited to the Berlin apartment of Richard Lichtheim, a German Zionist who came from a wealthy family.[23] "They have a very elegant apartment and live in the Berlin fashion like everybody else," wrote Weizmann the following day. "We two are real proletarians compared with all that crowd."[24] At the end of his trip he stopped over in Heidelberg, where his friend Julius Simon lived in the style of the upper bourgeoisie. "They have a jewel of a villa in terrific taste, everything very expensive, but not *parvenu*," Weizmann reported.[25] He felt so comfortable in this environment that he decided to extend his stay, ostensibly in order to be able to attend the circumcision ceremony of Berthold Feiwel's son. He continued to regale Vera with details of the Simon household. "It's very pleasant in this house. Julius and his wife are very nice people and very cultured. She's a bit too loud, but very cultured and intelligent. He is pure gold. They have a gorgeous house. A lot of beautiful things, beautiful books and a great deal of real taste in everything. They certainly live better than we do . . . It isn't like Manchester, where everything is so grim and heavy."[26]

This was the kind of life Chaim and Vera aspired to. They were both elitists who felt that they rightly belonged within the higher economic and intellectual strata of society. Though Weizmann knew how to communicate with the East European immigrants, he rarely spent time with them in England, not even with their intelligentsia; it certainly never occurred to him to live in their neighborhoods.[27] The exceptions to this rule were men like Ahad Ha'Am and Sokolow, whose standing in the Zionist movement was unquestionable. The one person who was below his station, as it were, and with whom Weizmann did keep up contact in England was Joseph Massel, who had sheltered and provided for him during his first days in Manchester. Though he liked to talk to the members of Manchester's Zionist groups, he never really got close to them. "There was no intimacy of contact, no real warmth or affection. Of course there were some Zionists with whom he was delighted to talk. But once the conversation was finished, he wanted to escape to his laboratories or to his home."[28] If Weizmann remained personally aloof from the masses, he did retain an emotional bond with them. Vera, on the other hand, had no emotional ties to them at all. If Weizmann could, in a moment of anger, exclaim that he was "fed up" with his fellow Jews,[29] it was because he cared about them and wanted to refashion them into different, "better" Jews. Vera could only express impatience with the whole lot of them.[30] Her assimilationist background[31] and elitist—if not snobbish—attitudes dictated her social preferences and behavior. In Manchester, as later, she always preferred the company of high-class Jews and British gentiles.

Though she was the wife of a lowly lecturer and could hardly speak proper English, Vera's entry into Manchester's upper society was rather swift and uncomplicated. This was partly due to her striking appearance. Vera was "of medium height, graceful and well poised, dressed with distinctive taste, though not expensively. Her eyes were hazel, her hair between colors, her brow was open and serene, her mouth broad, generous, amused. She was a beautiful woman."[32] Though most of the professors' wives were twice her age, they immediately adopted her. They must have sensed that this impressive-looking woman belonged—if not by class, then by inclination—to their own elitist circle. Though puzzled by some of the habits and customs of polite society, Vera clearly took a liking to the weekly "at homes," with their innumerable cups of tea, toast, and cakes.[33] Before her arrival in Manchester, Weizmann spent his free hours mainly with the Dreyfus family—"Pa" and "Ma" Perkin, as he called them—and occasionally with Professor Samuel Alexander and some of the chemists working for the Clayton Aniline Company. In time, of course, he also gathered around him an intimate Zionist group which included Norman Bentwich, Leon Simon, Harry Sacher, and a few others. Vera, however, was not content with this circle and aimed to climb the social ladder; she was eager to be invited into Manchester's better homes. Within a short time she became a frequent visitor to the fashionable homes of the ladies Lapworth, Schuster, Behrens, Perkin, Kolp, and others. It was during one of these social occasions that Vera met Caroline Schuster. Mrs. Schuster, the wife of Professor Arthur Schuster, admired Vera's charm and abilities and took a great liking to her. In the period before World War I the Weizmanns were frequent visitors to the Schusters' home in the exclusive neighborhood of Victoria Park, a short distance from their own house on Birchfields Road.

Arthur Schuster was born in Frankfurt-am-Main. His father was a well-to-do Jewish textile merchant with business connections in Great Britain. Following the war with Austria, which saw the free city annexed by Prussia, the elder Schuster decided to emigrate, and in 1869 he joined the Manchester branch of the family's merchant-banking firm. A year later, at the age of nineteen, Arthur Schuster entered the business, but he soon decided on an academic career. He studied physics and mathematics at Owens College and Heidelberg and was soon recognized as a brilliant mathematical physicist. In 1881, at the age of thirty, he was named professor of applied mathematics, and seven years later he succeeded Balfour Stewart as professor of physics.[34] He was a Fellow of the Royal Society and was involved in the administration not only of the University of Manchester but also of those of Liverpool and Leeds.[35]

Arthur Schuster was baptized as a young boy and had little knowledge of or interest in Jewish affairs. In 1887 he married a gentile girl, the daughter of a minister from Wardington, Oxfordshire. Caroline Schuster, perhaps influenced by her father, more than made up for her husband's lack of interest in Jewish or Zionist affairs. As much as she was impressed by Vera, she was absolutely captivated by Weizmann.[36] She was struck by his personality and appearance. In his late thirties Weizmann cut an imposing figure. He was of slightly more than medium height, had a dark, small, pointed beard and a rather unusually youthful, pinkish face for a Central European Jew. His eyes were full of life, but they were somber. His mien was that of a man who knew he carried a burden, yet it was vigorous and unpretentious. He was always immaculately dressed.[37] While Arthur Schuster enjoyed spending time with a fellow scientist, Caroline Schuster was converted within a brief period into an enthusiastic Zionist, an enthusiasm she tried to impart to her children as well.[38] In turn, Weizmann was fascinated—even infatuated—with this bright, vivacious, and good-looking woman who was the first gentile woman he got to know well. He was more than willing to spend many hours instructing her in the history of the Jewish people.

The Schusters, who were very well off, kept an open house and were greatly involved in Manchester affairs. They were considered liberals—even radicals—by the standards of those days. Caroline Schuster was active in university and civic affairs, was a friend and patroness of young academicians and people of promise generally.[39] Arthur Schuster, a man of remarkable originality and ingenuity, was highly respected. At various times he was elected to office in the Royal Society, the International Research Council, and the British Association.[40] He also had a sense of humor which made his guests feel at home. The Weizmanns, for one, were charmed by the Schusters and their lifestyle. This was a different English society from the one so disparaged by Weizmann when he first arrived in Manchester. They were determined to emulate, as best they could, this home and standard of living. This, however, would take more money than Weizmann was earning. Vera decided to obtain her British qualification in medicine—a goal she had had in mind since 1907.[41] Because she had earned her medical degree in Geneva, she was required to take the last two years of the medical curriculum in Manchester. In 1910 she began her studies. Despite frequent bouts of ill health that plagued her and Benjy, she succeeded in obtaining her Bachelor of Medicine and Surgery degree on December 19, 1912.[42] After an extended vacation in Cannes during the winter of 1912–13, she took a position in May 1913 as public health officer in Manchester in charge of clinics for expectant mothers.[43] She could finally contribute a second salary to the family budget.

If Vera was resentful of Weizmann's onerous Zionist activities, she did encourage him to expand his horizons in various branches of chemistry. Though his studies were undertaken during vacations from the university—times they could have spent together in Manchester or in the mountains—they both willingly made the sacrifice, hoping that his research would finally bring them financial security. A few years after he had settled in Manchester, Weizmann became interested in biological chemistry and in bacteriology, which he regarded as a special branch of organic chemistry. No facilities for this work were available at the University of Manchester, where biochemistry did not yet form part of the curriculum, while the study of bacteriology was confined to the medical school.[44] Beginning in March 1909, therefore, Weizmann regularly gave up his spring and summer university vacations—as well as his work and income at the Clayton Aniline Company—in order to work at the Pasteur Institute's bacteriological and microbiological departments, under the direction of the well-known biochemist Auguste Fernbach, director of the fermentation laboratory at the institute.[45] In Paris Weizmann learned something more than chemistry; he became acquainted with French civilization and the French way of life. He usually stayed in the Latin Quarter with Vera's sister Rachel and her husband Joseph Blumenfeld, a chemical engineer. In Paris Weizmann met some of the most brilliant chemists and physicists of the day, including Georges Urbain, Jean Baptiste Perrin, Paul Langevin, and others. For a time he worked in Perrin's laboratory at the Sorbonne, learning something about colloidal chemistry. He did not let any opportunity for deepening his knowledge in chemistry go by. During one of the Weizmanns' vacations in Switzerland, he spent a few weeks doing research on milk bacteriology with the distinguished scientist Robert Burri. The rest of his training in biochemistry he supplemented with his own reading and work in Manchester.[46]

Weizmann's frequent sojourns in Paris brought him in contact not only with French scientists but also with many Russian émigré chemists, some of whom worked at the Pasteur Institute, including Nikolai Semeshko, later Commissar for Health in the Soviet Union, and Ilya Metchnikov. According to a memoir by one of Weizmann's confidants during his declining years, it was in Paris, in early April 1910, that Weizmann met Vladimir Ilyich Lenin.[47] Weizmann may have heard Lenin speak at public meetings in Geneva in 1904. Now he was formally introduced, possibly by Nikolai Semeshko. Lenin was in exile for the second time, after the collapse of the 1905 Revolution.[48] He had plenty of time to study and turned to the natural sciences, among other subjects. Lenin knew of the work at the Pasteur Institute. He had also heard of the discoveries of Ernest Rutherford and was interested in meeting a Mancunian who was said to be a friend of Rutherford. According to the sole evidence in our possession, the two met in Lenin's favorite Parisian café on the boulevard d'Orléans. Their discussion ran the gamut from tsarist Russia to physics and chemistry. For the most part, it seems that Weizmann explained scientific terminology to Lenin while the latter held forth on Machists, Russian Empirio-Monists, Empirio-Symbolists, and other backward groups and theories. He also did not refrain from making disparaging remarks about the Zionists, especially the Zionist-socialists of Ber Borochov's school. Lenin did not spare the Bund either.[49] Nevertheless they seem to have parted on friendly terms, because a few days later Lenin sent Weizmann his recently published book *Materialism and Empirio-Criticism*,[50] which included the following handwritten dedication: "Compliments of the Author."[51] If indeed Weizmann met Lenin, there is no evidence of this in his letters to Vera, to whom he reported almost daily on all his activities.

He did report with great excitement, that spring of 1910, about the new work he was undertaking at the Pasteur Institute. His regular visits to the institute attained a new sense of purpose. On February 8, 1910, Professor William Perkin employed Weizmann in research on the production of synthetic rubber, for which Perkin had a contract with the London-based Strange and Graham Ltd. At the beginning of the twentieth century there occurred a crisis in the supply of natural rubber from the Far East, caused both by the rapidly increasing demand for this commodity and by local difficulties of production.[52] This shortage led to speculation as to whether it would not be possible to create a synthetic substitute for natural rubber that would exhibit mechanical properties similar to those of the natural substance. At that time this was a revolutionary idea: Though synthetic substitutes for natural products had been known and were used, for example, in the pharmaceutical and dyestuff industries, this was not the case for such complex high-molecular-weight materials as rubber and natural fibers. In Germany the chemist Carl Harries had just discovered that natural rubber is a hydrocarbon which, when heated to high temperatures, releases isoprene. The conclusion was, therefore, that if one could find a good method of making isoprene, one might be able to convert it into synthetic rubber.[53]

The prospects, then, of making a fortune in producing a scarce commodity attracted the firm of Strange and Graham. Edward Halford

Strange, the company's director, engaged Professor William Perkin[54] to assist the company in technical research, offering to pay him 1,000 pounds a year plus royalties.[55] Perkin accepted this generous offer and, in turn, asked Weizmann if he would care to serve as his research assistant, for which he would pay him 250 pounds a year plus 33 percent of the profits which Perkin would receive from any royalties or patents resulting from their joint work. Eager for a larger income, Weizmann jumped at the offer.[56] Thus, when he went to the Pasteur Institute in the spring of 1910, Weizmann was no doubt more excited about the prospect of finally making a lot of money in the world of industrial chemistry than he was with the ideological controversy he had with Lenin. It occurred to Weizmann right away that it would be a good idea to draw into the research team Professor Auguste Fernbach, who knew more about alcohol fermentation processes than either Weizmann or Perkin. Fernbach was interested, and upon his return to England Weizmann broached the idea with Edward Strange, who promptly invited the French chemist to join the team.[57] Fernbach agreed to join on terms that were far less generous than those offered Perkin.[58] He brought with him one of his own assistants at the Pasteur Institute, Moses Schoen.[59] Halford Strange, who had a general background in chemistry, was also considered part of the research group. Thus, by the fall of 1910 an Anglo-French research syndicate was formed which set itself the task of simultaneously investigating the question of synthetic rubber in Manchester and in Paris.

To create synthetic rubber on a commerical scale, the research team concentrated at first on the production of amyl and butyl alcohols by fermentation processes.[60] Fernbach and Schoen worked in Paris, the others in England, with Weizmann and Strange visiting the Pasteur Institute from time to time. The attention of the group was directed chiefly toward a means of producing amyl alcohol. In January 1911 Fernbach and Weizmann found a mixture of bacteria that would ferment the starch in potatoes, yielding amyl alcohol in the process. The following month Weizmann was able to produce the same substance with other bacteria.[61] The members of the group thereupon concentrated their efforts on the amyl alcohol route to isoprene and synthetic rubber. But at the end of March 1911 it was found that during certain experiments conducted in Paris and Manchester the fermentations had produced butyl alcohol, and from that time the energies of the group were diverted toward ascertaining the means by which this material could best be obtained. The first order of business was to select or discover the particular bacillus that would yield the best results. Such a bacillus—referred to variously as BF (Bacillus Fernbach) or FB—was discovered by Fernbach in June 1911. A culture of this bacillus was isolated and that same month it was sent to Weizmann via Strange.[62] Fernbach and Weizmann now endeavored to produce butyl alcohol in bulk by fermenting starch in potatoes.[63] At that time it was already known that in the fermentation of sugar to alcohol by yeast, a minor by-product was "fusel oil," essentially a mixture of amyl alcohols, each of which contains five carbon atoms. It was assumed—erroneously, as it turned out—that these alcohols, like ethyl alcohol itself, were produced by the fermentation of sugar, and Weizmann's attention was therefore drawn to fermentation processes in general—an unusual subject for an organic chemist at that time—and to the problem of finding a microorganism which would yield five-carbon alcohols as the main product, not just a by-product, of fermentation. The Russian microbiologist Winogrodsky had already discovered the existence of a bacterium, or a group of bacteria, able to ferment carbohydrates and produce an alcohol with an odor similar to that of "fusel oil," as well as another well-known chemical substance, acetone. However, this alcohol was butyl alcohol, containing only four carbon atoms, a compound already known but at the time not used for any practical purpose. William Perkin, who of all members of the team understood least about fermentation, therefore recommended that this substance be called not "butyl" but "futile" alcohol and suggested that "the stuff be poured down the sink."[64]

Despite Perkin's pessimism, Strange decided to erect a plant at Rainham, Lincolnshire, for the production of materials developed in the intermediate stages of research. In contrast to Perkin, Weizmann was confident of the outcome of his research. To Ahad Ha'Am he boasted, "I have actually reached the end and overcome all difficulties in the synthesis of rubber and the laboratory stage is finished. This business should now be transferred to the factory. Whether my *Industrieritter* will have enough patience and ability to take advantage of what I am convinced is a really good job, or whether they will turn it into something purely for speculation, I don't know; and this problem is causing me a lot of worry, because I shouldn't like to be left with nothing but my chemical 'fame.'"[65] Characteristically, he had been impatient, rushing to inform Strange that he would soon send the isoprene he would produce in his lab. His report turned out to be inaccurate, resulting in recriminations from Strange.[66]

While Weizmann and Fernbach were struggling to make headway on the question of fermentation, with a view to converting sugar starch into higher alcohols,[67] an important discovery was made in March 1912 by one Mr. Kane, the works manager at Rainham. Using BF and some crude methods of distillation, Kane realized that in addition to other products of the fermentation of starch conducted by him, there could also be found a considerable quantity of acetone.[68] The discovery of acetone was made known, of course, to Weizmann, who did not immediately grasp its industrial implications.[69] Strange, on the other hand, realized at once that this discovery could have momentous implications for his business.[70] Acetone, largely used at the time as a solvent, was made by dry distillation of wood. One of its important uses was its ability to make gunpowder "smokeless." When treated with acetone, gunpowder burns with a minimum of smoke, a discovery which would become very important when World War I broke out, since it meant that the location of guns, especially big naval guns, could be concealed.[71]

Halford Strange had for some time labored under the difficulty of raising sufficient capital for his research syndicate.[72] With the discovery by Kane of an efficient method for the production of acetone, he decided that the moment had come to expand his company, which was to be renamed The Synthetic Rubber, Fusel Oil and Acetone Manufacturing Co., Ltd., with a capital of five hundred thousand pounds to be raised by public subscriptions for shares.[73] In order to induce the public to buy shares in the new company, Strange commissioned a certain Dr. Otto Hehner, who was in his employ, to write a scientific report on the production of acetone, amyl and butyl alcohols through fermentation of potatoes.[74] The report claimed a much higher yield than had in fact been hitherto discovered with any bacteria.[75] Strange knew quite well that he could not get away with making such a claim concerning the experiments at Rainham. What he needed was the backing of well-known chemists whose statements would not be questioned by anyone. Sir William Ramsay, professor of chemistry at the University of London and recipient of the Nobel Prize in 1904, had already expressed his interest in joining the board of the new company.[76] Strange had no problem persuading Perkin to vouch for experiments that had been made at Rainham.[77] Moreover, Perkin agreed to give a lecture on June 17, 1912, to the Society of Chemical Industry, which would promote the new company—twelve days before the prospectus was to be issued.[78]

It was more difficult to move Fernbach to write a report, based on experiments at the Pasteur Institute, that would excite both the scientific community and the public. In reply to Strange's request of May 8, 1912, Fernbach truthfully reported that he lacked sufficient evidence to write the kind of report that Strange had in mind. Yet he, too, like Ramsay and Perkin, was tempted by the prospect of making money. He therefore demanded a seat on the board of directors of the new company as a *conditio sine qua non*. He also urged that a new experiment be conducted before he wrote the report. Both conditions were accepted immediately by Strange.[79] Fernbach had been conducting an experiment with maize (rather than potatoes) as the raw material. The experiment went well for about ten days, but at the end it turned out to be a failure, yielding no more than 25 to 28 percent acetone and higher alcohols—about equal to the amount which had been obtained by Mr. Kane in Rainham.[80] Nevertheless Fernbach discarded his earlier pangs of conscience and wrote a report that was purposely misleading and could be interpreted as if he had been able to extract as much as 42 percent of the substances in question from maize, whereas, in fact, those results had been obtained by him only from potatoes.[81] Thus, Strange finally had his professors where he wanted them: Lured by money, they were in effect backing false advertisement. The distinguished galaxy of Ramsay, Perkin, and Fernbach did not fail to impress the public, and at least seventy-five thousand pounds were raised through subscriptions.[82]

Weizmann knew all along that the reports from Rainham and the Pasteur Institute were incorrect.[83] He nevertheless kept quiet because he,

too, saw a chance of finally becoming rich. He could assuage his conscience by telling himself that he neither wrote the misleading reports
nor did his name appear in the company's prospectus. Moreover, Fernbach, who realized that Weizmann was the real brain in the English team,
sought to tie Weizmann closer to the project by improving his financial
terms with the new company. In anticipation of Strange's visit to Paris
on May 18, 1912, Fernbach invited Weizmann to stipulate his own conditions.[84] Realizing that this was a once-in-a-lifetime chance, Weizmann
decided that he would personally travel to Paris (May 17, 1912) to prepare with Fernbach for their meeting with Strange.[85] By the time he
reached Paris, Weizmann had already read the first draft of Perkin's lecture, scheduled for delivery a month hence. The lecture was apparently
written for Perkin—who had little knowledge of the substance of the experiments—by Francis Edwards Matthews, a chemist employed by Strange
and Graham, in collaboration with Halford Strange. Late in April Strange
sent the draft to Weizmann, with a request "for the addition of any scientific stuff which you think ought to go in. I have arranged with Perkin
that he will give due credit to the chemists and bacteriologists who have
been engaged on the work . . ."[86] It is unclear what "scientific stuff"
Weizmann may have added to the paper, but the incident again made
him painfully aware that Perkin was getting credit for doing little or
nothing. But if Perkin was going to have all the prestige, Weizmann was
determined to improve his contract with Strange. Having worked out the
strategy with Vera in advance, Weizmann described the outcome of negotiations on May 18:

> A hard day is over. I have been up since 8 in the morning, at the Institute
> from 9. Shall let you know the results briefly. I have concluded an agree-
> ment which we shall put in writing in a few days by means of an *échange de
> lettres,* according to which I shall get 25% of what Fernbach makes as profit,
> and in addition to that Fernbach will pay me 100 pounds a year from the
> salary he receives from Strange. I consider this arrangement very satisfac-
> tory. I certainly didn't expect to succeed in getting anything in cash beyond
> the 25%.
>
> Besides, I was fully convinced that Strange would take all measures to get
> me under contract to them, as he knows that I have no obligations whatever
> to Perkin as regards keeping secrets, etc., etc. I told him I would sign a con-
> tract with them only if they gave me a guarantee to pay me a decent and
> regular salary. He understands this perfectly and it is in his interest to have
> me tied up—if I let him—and to pay for it. His affairs are apparently going
> very well . . . I hope my Verochka will be pleased. I kept in mind that you
> told me "to think of you during these business talks . . ."[87]

Strange was willing to sign a contract with Fernbach, but only after June,
presumably in order to first see the rate of public subscriptions.[88]
All he had to do now, Weizmann thought, was to sit quietly while
waiting for Strange to give a new contract to Fernbach, who would, in
turn, write Weizmann a letter confirming their verbal arrangements. Once

In his laboratory at the University of Manchester, 1912

he had this letter from Fernbach he would demand from Perkin a larger share of the latter's yearly retainer of one thousand pounds. Should Perkin refuse, he would threaten to walk out on him, free to use the knowledge he had acquired on fermentation processes as he wished.[89] To Vera, who had in the meantime taken a two-week vacation in Baslow, Derbyshire, he wrote on May 21 that Perkin was unaware of what was going on.[90] But Perkin was not deceived. Possibly he had been alerted to the new situation by Strange. Perkin fully understood that once Weizmann had made an arrangement with Fernbach, he would be beyond his control. A day later he pressed Weizmann to inform him in detail of the agreement made in Paris. When he was informed, he warned Weizmann to cancel this new deal since, according to Perkin, Weizmann had made a commitment to the University Council—prior to the change in his appointment in April—not to undertake any new outside work.[91] Weizmann refused to budge and Perkin went to London to see Strange.[92] Within less than a fortnight Perkin had changed from Weizmann's mentor into his most dangerous enemy, writing openly to Strange that he was sick of Weizmann and wished that "the affair in Jerusalem would hurry up."[93] Moreover, Perkin had Strange's full cooperation in plotting against Weizmann. Strange still held a grudge against Weizmann for having misled him on the question of isoprene and having aggressively pressed, a few months earlier, for permission to publish the results of some of the experiments undertaken on behalf of the company. Strange suspected that Weizmann wished to claim credit for work that was not his own.[94] This reservoir of suspicion and resentment now overflowed when Strange realized that Weizmann's strategy was to corner him and Fernbach, forcing them into an agreement which could then be used against Perkin, whom Strange held in high esteem as a loyal friend.[95] In consultation with Perkin, Strange undertook to turn Fernbach against Weizmann as well. With all three of them lined up in one camp, Weizmann would have to give up his exaggerated demands or be dismissed from the team. Strange returned to Paris and reported to Perkin concerning his conversation with Fernbach.

> I commenced by asking Fernbach whether Weizmann was an old friend of his, as I had been rather led to understand so from Weizmann's remarks. Fernbach told me that he may have known him three months previously and that only casually. I said: "Is he a man upon whom you have any reason to doubt his absolute reliance?" He said: "No, and I should be very shocked if we found we could not give him our full confidence." I then told him what I knew of Weizmann's history and his proved tendency to lying in ordinary and scientific matters, and of his continual campaign for slightly more cash. Fernbach told me that he had agreed to the 25 percent commission to Weizmann because he felt that he undoubtedly owed some commission to Weizmann for his valuable introduction between himself and Strange and Graham Ltd. He also felt that it was unsafe that such valuable knowledge should be in the possession of a man of Weizmann's type without his having some direct interest in it. I told him of Weizmann's threats to you, that he considered himself free to do what he liked with any information, including rubber, if he did not obtain terms from you which he considered satisfactory. I also told him of the promise not to do any outside work which he is alleged to have given, by which he has secured his new appointment [at the university]. Fernbach has agreed to give Weizmann nothing in writing until we have discussed the thing and drawn up a joint plan of campaign.
>
> I have been considering the agreement between yourself and Weizmann and I am more astonished [at] Weizmann's effrontery in making the threats he did to you and also to me in London . . . I do not wish to have any fuss about this while the flotation [of the new company's shares] is in progress, but when it is over I think the best plan will be to invite Weizmann to meet yourself, myself, Matthews, and Fernbach, produce an agreement giving him the maximum we are prepared to agree to, and if he does not sign it, we will fire him out.
>
> In my opinion it is quite a question whether we cannot get an injunction from the High Court to restrain Weizmann from uttering threats to disclose secret information in his possession . . . This is a weapon up our sleeve . . .
>
> Finally, I have come to the conclusion that attempts to work in a friendly way with Weizmann only invited aggression on his part, and in future I am afraid the policy with regard to him must be of unmitigated firmness. The fact that we are not ready to deal with the situation for a few weeks will act

in our favor, as at present he has strained himself up to a move on impudence and daring, but I think this will evaporate during the next few weeks of uncertainty . . .[96]

Weizmann had no inkling of Strange's machinations against him,[97] but he realized that Fernbach had become the linchpin of the team, and that his decision would make or break Weizmann's case. Consequently Weizmann journeyed to Paris once again on May 29 to present his arguments to Fernbach, who was then conferring with Strange as well. Fernbach may have had some reservations about Weizmann's personal style, but he had no doubt that this brilliant chemist was essential to the success of the project. After hearing both sides of the argument, he thought Perkin was trying to misuse his rank to browbeat Weizmann into submitting to his own financial demands. Fernbach therefore made a suggestion according to which Weizmann would hand over to Perkin one third of what he got from Fernbach, whereas Perkin would concede to Weizmann one third of his own profits on synthetic rubber.[98] This agreement favored Perkin in any case, since the work on butyl and amyl alcohols and on acetone at the Pasteur Institute and at Rainham seemed more promising at the time. Strange agreed to this scheme, though without too much enthusiasm, promising to take up the matter with Perkin.[99] Perkin also agreed,[100] but at the same time he proposed to reduce Weizmann's share of his own retainer, insisting once again that Weizmann's new appointment at the university had been based on his promise not to accept new work, and that Weizmann had violated this agreement by his contract with Fernbach.[101] Strange, to whom Weizmann complained, was by now convinced by Fernbach that Weizmann must be retained. Strange tried, on the one hand, to prevent Perkin from damaging Weizmann's position at the university while, at the same time, cutting Weizmann down to size. "In my opinion," wrote Strange to Perkin, "we can force your said assistant to agree to anything we consider reasonable, as Fernbach, I believe, is not willing to give him a share of profits unless he is properly tied up past, present and future."[102]

It is possible that a final arrangement could have been worked out between Weizmann and Perkin had it not been for the latter's lecture on June 17, 1912. When Weizmann, who may have contributed some "scientific stuff" to the paper, heard that Perkin had given credit in his speech only to Francis Edward Matthews and Auguste Fernbach, totally ignoring his assistant's pivotal role in the research, he lost his composure. He criticized Perkin openly and demanded to be free of the professor's control while retaining the same share of Perkin's yearly salary of one thousand pounds; otherwise he would consider himself a free agent.[103] By the time Strange's letter of July 3, in which he proposed to tie Weizmann legally to the company, was received by Perkin, it was too late. Furious at his assistant's brashness, Perkin dismissed Weizmann from the Anglo-French team on June 23.[104] Strange, who was largely to blame for having

pitted the parties against one another to begin with, had belatedly arrived at a radically different assessment of Weizmann from the one he
offered seven weeks earlier.

> I should like to add that in my opinion Weizmann is a valuable member of
> our group. He is well up in chemical literature, knowing many languages
> and having valuable connections throughout Europe. He is amazingly in-
> dustrious and has a quick brain. He is not an accurate experimenter and this,
> of course, involves repeating his experiments very carefully. On the other
> hand, I do not think he is untrustworthy . . . Lastly, I am very conscious
> of the fact that we owe Weizmann a very heavy debt for bringing us in con-
> tact with yourself.

This reassessment was combined with Strange's concession that "Perkin
has done very little actual work."[105] He now proposed, with Perkin's
consent, that Weizmann become Fernbach's assistant so he could continue to collaborate on the fermentation processes.[106] The summer and
fall of 1912 were spent in working out a new arrangement among Weizmann, Fernbach, and Strange.[107] Fernbach and Strange took the precaution, in the meantime, not to give Weizmann any information on experiments in progress. This time Weizmann, too, was more cautious than
he had been in February 1910 and consulted a lawyer before agreeing to
any new contracts.[108]

Weizmann took one other precaution and decided that the time had
come to consult his senior colleagues at the university: Arthur Schuster,
Samuel Alexander, and Ernest Rutherford. It is not clear how much he
told them about his scientific work for Strange and Graham, but he did
inform them that his personal ties with Perkin were severed. He needed
their protection and advice now that Perkin had become his implacable
enemy. His friends took his side, of course, and asked him to calm down
and maintain cordial relations with Perkin.[109] Weizmann continued his
work at the university as if nothing had happened, but the Perkins and
the Weizmanns moved in some of the same social circles, which made
life in Manchester very uncomfortable. In the close-knit society of
Manchester academics it quickly became known that the Perkins were
no longer "Ma" and "Pa" to the Weizmanns, and that it was best not to
invite them to the same teas and garden parties.[110] Once again Weizmann began to talk about his "Palestinian plans," not only to Ahad Ha'Am
but also to members of the faculty at Manchester. He was also considering applying for vacancies at Oxford, London, and Edinburgh.[111] Then,
all of a sudden, it was announced at the beginning of December 1912
that Perkin had accepted the Waynflete professorship at Oxford[112] and
planned to move there at the end of the academic year. Perkin's departure for Oxford was a sudden and unexpected move. It is quite likely
that it came in the wake of national publicity surrounding the synthetic
rubber and acetone experiments for which Perkin took all the credit.[113]
It is quite clear that Weizmann was surprised by Perkin's move; otherwise he might very well have avoided controversy with the professor at

that stage. For a moment Weizmann deluded himself into believing that he was still the natural successor to Perkin: "It is not impossible," he wrote to Ahad Ha'Am, "that I shall get either Perkin's Chair or *the Chair* of Biochemistry. I've already been asked in a roundabout way about my Palestinian plans (Schuster and Alexander). For the time being I'm saying nothing, and the question of the appointment is not yet *actuelle . . .*"[114] To be on the safe side, he informed Schuster that he would be prepared to stay at the university for at least five years.

Characteristically, he counted his chickens too early. Perkin's chance to pay Weizmann back for his insubordination came sooner than he had expected. For years he had promoted Weizmann through the university ranks, giving him every possible opportunity to advance himself. He had carefully groomed his protégé, possibly promising Weizmann that he would succeed him to the chair in organic chemistry; in the process Perkin took out a number of patents with Weizmann.[115] Even if we take into account Weizmann's tendency to exaggerate his own status, his persistent claim for nine years that he was in line for a professorship may indicate that Perkin gave him good reason to believe it. Instead of showing gratitude and deference, Weizmann had acted in a most disrespectful and insulting manner. Perkin was determined to show his assistant that he could also use his prestige and influence to ruin Weizmann's chances for promotion. He pointed out to the University Council that Weizmann was more interested in money than pure research and that, in any case, his stay at Manchester was temporary by his own admission and only served as a springboard to a position in Palestine. Why then not give the chair to an upright, native Englishman, to his brother-in-law Arthur Lapworth, for example? True, Lapworth's specialty—though he had begun his career as an organic chemist—happened to be inorganic chemistry, but, on the other hand, he was about to be elected a Fellow of the Royal Society (in 1913) and could be counted upon to serve the university loyally for many years to come.[116] Thus, the battle for the professorship was to ensue at the worst possible time for Weizmann: Vera was sitting for her exams and Benjy was sick with a severe ear infection. As soon as Vera passed her exams and Benjy felt better, Weizmann sent them off to Cannes, affording him time to devote himself to the inevitable and painful showdown ahead.

Luckily, Weizmann had at his disposal the active support and sound advice of Schuster, Rutherford, and Alexander. When he told them that he was about to sign a new contract with Strange, they were appalled. Perkin was indeed right: The University Council would view such extensive work outside academe as being in conflict with Weizmann's university duties. Strange, who had initially thought he could get along without Weizmann's services, now tried to persuade him, at all costs, to keep the agreement secret: "It is highly undesirable to ask the Council whether you may enter into the agreements. I strongly advise the course of entering into the agreements and saying nothing . . . It can easily be explained that this is simply a confirmation of the old arrangement in a slightly different form."[117] But Weizmann, who only a week earlier thought he could ride on both horses by getting the professorship and entering into a lucrative industrial consultantship, was quickly sobered on both accounts. Perkin could get away with certain improprieties, given his family's prestige and impeccable lineage. Perkin could even hypocritically and shamelessly try to deny others what he sought for himself. It was quite another thing for a Russian immigrant to step out of line. He would have to renounce all outside employment if he wanted his senior colleagues and friends to work out a compromise with the vice chancellor.

Immediately after Christmas 1912, Schuster—who was a member of the search committee—began to work out an arrangement with the vice chancellor, Alfred Hopkinson, regarding Weizmann's position. The search committee was constituted on January 8, 1913, and in its first meeting it sought the advice of Harold Dixon and William Perkin. It was not at all clear at the outset what was to be done, and the initial suggestion was to advertise the position for a professorship and to appoint both Lapworth and Weizmann as readers. Another suggestion was to appoint only two readers.[118] Weizmann and Lapworth had the same rank in 1913. Lapworth was Senior Lecturer and Assistant Director of the inorganic laboratories, while Weizmann was Senior Lecturer and Assistant Director of the organic laboratories.[119] In February 1913 the committee resolved to write to seven distinguished chemists in Britain, the United States, and Germany to ascertain their opinion on candidates for the position.[120] Yet after all but one answer—that of Professor Richards—were duly received, the committee decided to make a permanent appointment to the chair in organic chemistry and *not* to advertise the position, as was customary.[121] The vice chancellor was asked to write to the following: J. Norman Collie, W. J. Pope, James Walker, J. J. Dobbie, and G. T. Beilby—all of England—and to Theodore William Richards of Harvard University. Harold Dixon was asked to write to Professor Hermann Emil Fischer, an organic chemist in Berlin who had received the Nobel Prize in chemistry in 1902. In its full report to the senate of the university the committee stated: "No useful purpose would be served by an advertisement which necessarily would cause delay and would, in the circumstances of this case, have other very serious disadvantages."[122] On May 1 the University Senate resolved that Perkin's brother-in-law was to get the professorship in organic chemistry, while Weizmann would be appointed to a new position as reader in biochemistry, with a raise in his salary to six hundred pounds a year plus fifty pounds for an assistant;[123] this arrangement did not place Lapworth in a supervisory role to that of Weizmann.

Harold Dixon, who was senior even to Perkin in the chemistry department, was chosen by the University Council to sound out Weizmann on this arrangement before the official decision was handed down to him.[124] Though he had known for some time (through Schuster) what the university would propose,[125] Weizmann pretended to be surprised and told Dixon that if he asked whether he approved of this arrangement, his answer was categorically "no." Dixon left, requesting a firm reply by 2:15, two hours after they met. Weizmann rushed over to the Schusters and over lunch Arthur Schuster—now wearing the hat of an adviser, rather than that of a committee member—approved of Weizmann's reply, which was presumably given to Dixon at the required time: *"I cannot afford to reject or accept proposals. I shall have to obey the decision of the University. I consider your proposal as wrong in the interests of the University and as an offense to me. It will affect me in such a way that I shall try to get out of this place as soon as I can."* He did not fail to add that Perkin had cheated him materially and morally and that Dixon was condoning it.[126]

After the new arrangement was officially announced in May 1913, Weizmann tried to make the best of it—at least publicly.[127] To Vera he wrote that the whole affair smacked of anti-Semitism.[128] On the face of it, it may have indeed seemed that way. Weizmann could not be faulted on his teaching, for example. He was known as a good teacher and cared about his students, who in turn showed him great respect and even affection.[129] Moreover, by 1913 he had almost fifty publications to his credit. He was known in the department as a brilliant chemist, more promising than Lapworth,[130] who had published more than Weizmann but worked by accumulation of detail rather than by publishing seminal papers.[131] In fact, Harold Dixon and William Perkin were among those who in December 1910 sponsored Weizmann for a fellowship in the Royal Society, obviously because they held him in high esteem. Exactly two years later they had turned against him, making sure he would not receive the professorship, which in turn made it impossible for him to attain the coveted fellowship.[132] Weizmann never got over the loss of the professorship. He considered this to be the most serious setback of his life.[133] In the immediate aftermath of Dixon's official proposal he became physically ill and extremely dejected: "If you only knew," he wrote to Vera, "how tired I am of all these *'goyim,'* how much of a stranger I feel here, how isolated . . ."[134] Two days later, in a moment of desperation, he exclaimed: "Ach, Verochka, I wish we could go to Palestine soon and put an end to *Galuth* in all its forms."[135]

A careful reading of the search committee's documents, however, reveals that anti-Semitism did not play a role in Weizmann's loss of the professorship. The simple truth is that all parties involved in the messy affair—Weizmann included—were guilty of only two things: greed and vanity. Perhaps Perkin was the worst offender, because he received a large retainer from Strange and Graham, reaping financial and professional benefits without doing any of the work and using Weizmann without giving him due credit. It is possible that had Weizmann received recognition for his fermentation experiments, he would have had a better chance to attain the professorship. Moreover, Perkin was willing to go so far as to read a purposely misleading scientific paper, written by others, in other to promote a commercial enterprise. Lastly, when faced with the possibility of a challenge which would have exposed his dishonesty in scientific matters, he attributed to Weizmann those offenses of which he was most guilty. But it was only a question of degree of guilt. Fernbach had knowingly contributed his prestige to an enterprise he knew would defraud the public. Throughout Weizmann was guilty by association and by his failure to call his colleagues to task or expose them publicly. He, too, like Perkin, had worked on projects which he knew were against university rules. He was willing, as late as December 1912, to repeat this mistake, and it was only thanks to Schuster, Alexander, and Rutherford that he severed his association with Strange and Graham at the last moment. What helped undermine Weizmann's chances for the professorship, then, was not anti-Semitism. Perkin would no doubt have continued to favor him as his successor had Weizmann not challenged Perkin's reputation and financial arrangements; given Perkin's great influence at the university, he might have been able to arrange for Weizmann to attain the professorship. Weizmann's attempt to exploit his own indispensability in the Anglo-French research group by presenting the professor with an ultimatum backfired when Perkin refused to be blackmailed. In his anxiety to break out of his own financial straits, Weizmann forfeited not only the new deal with Strange and Fernbach but also his old contract with Perkin. He had lost not only a second income but his status in the department as Perkin's protégé and heir apparent. The fact of the matter is that Weizmann was guilty not only of greed and disloyalty to his benefactor but also of impatience and lack of sound political judgment. This, in the final analysis, contributed to his undoing.

Clearly, the procedures for filling Perkin's chair were highly irregular, most notably the decision not to advertise the position. In his letters to eminent chemists in Britain, Germany, and the United States, the vice chancellor listed the names of candidates other than Weizmann and Lapworth, yet it is obvious from reading the committee's and senate's minutes that these other candidates were never seriously considered as successors to the chair in organic chemistry.[136] The irregularities in this particular case are all the more striking when one examines the other appointments made that year by the University Senate. None of these appointments to professorships involved the same type of special committee that was constituted to deal with the chair of organic chemistry, and in none did the vice chancellor of the university take so active a role as in this case. None of the committees asked for and received permission to deal with departmental matters other than recommending a candidate for the chair. None asked for permission not to advertise and none ever considered not filling the professorship in question and making "special arrangements." All other committees seemed to seriously consider candidates from within and without the university.[137] In light of the reference in the report of the "Committee on Arrangements Consequent on Professor Perkin's Resignation" to "the [special] circumstances of this case," one must arrive at the conclusion that the committee's decisions were strongly influenced by political considerations.

But what of the intellectual and academic merits of the case? Did

Weizmann deserve the professorship on his own merits? Was he a better candidate for the position than Lapworth? Was perhaps neither appropriate for such a position at this stage in their careers? It is unlikely that a clear-cut and decisive answer could ever be given to all of these questions; this is a particularly difficult task seven decades after the fact. Yet the evidence seems to suggest that even without the irregularities associated with Lapworth's appointment, Weizmann would not necessarily have been awarded the professorship at this stage in his career even if Perkin had strongly backed such an appointment. The most decisive extant evidence for this statement is contained in the correspondence between the vice chancellor of the Victoria University of Manchester, Sir Alfred Hopkinson, and Professor Theodore William Richards, Erving Professor of Chemistry at Harvard and director of the Wolcott Gibbs Memorial Laboratory.[138] In view of the fact that all other replies to the committee have disappeared, this correspondence assumes special significance and is therefore extensively cited. Hopkinson's letter to Richards of February 18, 1913, reads as follows:

Dear Professor Richards,

As you are no doubt aware Professor Perkin has been appointed to the Chair of Chemistry in the University of Oxford and will shortly be leaving Manchester. We are now making enquiries with a view to the arrangements to be made here in consequence of his resignation. It is of vital importance to us, having regard to the extent of the Chemical Department, the number of students to be trained and the continuance and promotion of research in Chemistry, that we should secure the best men available to carry on the work, and I have been asked by the Committee of Senate which has the matter under consideration, to make confidential enquiries with a view to obtaining the best information.

Among the younger organic chemists of distinction the following have been mentioned as men of special ability and promise:

Dr. A. W. Crossley, F.R.S., Professor of Chemistry in the Pharmaceutical Society.

Dr. M. O. Forster, F.R.S., Assistant-Professor at the Imperial College of Science.

Dr. A. McKenzie, Birkbeck Institute.

Dr. R. H. Pickard, Technical School, Blackburn.

Dr. R. Robinson, Professor of Organic Chemistry in the University of Sydney, N.S.W.

Dr. Smiles, Assistant Professor of Organic Chemistry, University College, London.

Dr. J. Thorpe, F.R.S., Sorby Fellow, University of Sheffield.

We have also before us the names of two chemists now on our Senior Staff:—Dr. Lapworth, F.R.S., Lecturer in Physical Chemistry and Assistant Director of the Inorganic Laboratories, and Dr. Weizmann, Lecturer in Bio-Chemistry and Assistant Director of the Organic Laboratories.

I should be very grateful for any expression of opinion you would give me, which I can communicate to the Committee in confidence, on the subject of the qualifications of any of the above mentioned or of any other chemists either in England or America who may appear to you to have the desired qualifications—our object being to maintain the efficiency of the Department of Organic Chemistry as a School of learning and research . . .[139]

Professor Richards replied as follows on March 7, 1913:

My dear Sir Alfred:
  Your kind letter came two or three days ago, and I have been thinking about it ever since. It seems to me that you have named the candidates about in the order desirable. Dr. Crossley and Dr. Forster are both able men and known all over the world, and of the two I should be inclined to put Dr. Crossley first as you have. Next, I should be inclined to put Dr. Lapworth and next Dr. McKenzie. The others I know little about, for my specialty is not organic chemistry, as you know.
  . . . Among the young Americans Professor Brunel, now of Bryn Mawr, seems to be considered as perhaps the most brilliant. He has not a reputation, however, comparable to that of Dr. Crossley or Dr. Forster . . .
  . . . I find that our resident professor of organic chemistry E.[lmer] P.[eter] Kohler agrees essentially with me in the order of preference named above . . .[140]

One must keep in mind that Richards was best known for his atomic weight studies; it is therefore not surprising that he was more likely to hear of Lapworth, a physical chemist, than of Weizmann. Yet Crossley and Forster, whom he held in high esteem, were organic chemists; that is, they were outside his own specialty. Clearly Richards had no knowledge of Weizmann's work, though he had visited Manchester a few years earlier and had an honorary degree from the university. Moreover, Richards's colleague, Kohler, who *was* an organic chemist, also did not rank Weizmann among the top candidates. Weizmann had not at that stage made significant theoretical breakthroughs. He had been working in the new field of biochemistry for only two years and had not yet made any major contributions in that field. Those he did make were claimed by Perkin as his own.

Yet even assuming that Weizmann was not the undisputed candidate for the position, one must conclude that the appointment was handled in a strange way by the University Senate. It decided to give the chair in organic chemistry to a man who was clearly an inorganic chemist (in 1922 Lapworth officially assumed responsibility for inorganic chemistry and was succeeded by Robert Robinson, who had appeared on the vice chancellor's list in February 1913), while appointing Weizmann reader in biochemistry—a field in which he had not yet distinguished himself. The explanation for this may be fourfold: Setting aside the question of his personal merit, Weizmann's appointment to the professorship would have been a direct insult to Perkin, one of England's more distinguished chemists. Possibly the council was also angered by Weizmann's extensive nonuniversity chemical activities, which went against his agreement with the university. Weizmann had not yet attained a fellowship in the Royal Society. Lastly, there were political motivations underlying the appointment which are not explicit in the minutes of the committee that are extant. Obviously the university was trying to avoid embarrassment and a possible scandal, but it is not clear what factors were at play here. Whatever the reason, the committee and the senate acted in an unusual manner by failing to advertise the position, as was customary. Clearly they wished to retain Weizmann, but not at any price. From the outset he never had a good chance to succeed Perkin to the chair in organic chemistry since it had been decided as early as January 1913 that he would be appointed reader. Whether Lapworth was indeed the strongest candidate for the chair is doubtful, but it is impossible to answer this question with absolute certainty in view of the missing documentation on the other candidates and the availability of only one reply from those eminent chemists who had been approached. On the face of it, it seems that Lapworth's appointment to a chair—any chair—was premature. As for Weizmann, attaining a readership at this stage in his career was a respectable achievement marred only by his unrealistic expectations, which had been fanned for years by Perkin. Nevertheless, Lapworth's appointment to a chair seems to indicate that had Weizmann been able to obtain Perkin's backing, he, too, would have been a viable candidate for the position. He lost the professorship not only on scholarly but also on political grounds.

To add insult to injury, Weizmann was soon to suffer another rebuff. To a certain degree, this added disappointment was all the more painful and humiliating since it involved two members of the Schuster household: Caroline and her daughter Norah. If Caroline Schuster was fascinated by his Zionist idealism, Weizmann was quickly captured by her charm and beauty. It was to her that he bore his innermost aspirations and desires. If Arthur Schuster gave him sound advice on university matters, Caroline knew how to comfort and encourage him, spending many hours uplifting his spirits when he was most depressed by the Perkin affair.[141] With Vera in Cannes, it was to the Schuster house that he came, almost daily, to plan the next moves in the battle for the professorship. It was during these weeks of daily contact that Weizmann became infatuated with Caroline Schuster. The source of this infatuation may simply be that Caroline was an attractive and warm individual. After all, she was not the first woman to whom Weizmann felt attracted even after his marriage to Vera, nor was she to be the last. What may have enhanced the intensity of this particular relationship was the loneliness he felt, with Vera far away in Cannes, at a time when he needed emotional support more than ever. Possibly he was also intrigued by the fact that Caroline was the first gentile woman he got to know well; moreover, she seemed receptive to his ideas and was obviously fascinated by his personality. He may have simply misread the signals of a woman who lived in a world so different from his own and misinterpreted her intellectual interest for physical attraction. Caroline may not at first have noticed the precise moment when Weizmann had ceased to be interested in her as merely another Zionist disciple and his infatuation had taken over. But she was a sophisticated woman who must have become aware, at some point, of the erotic flavor that had crept into their long conversations. Surely it was not merely the teacher instructing the pupil when he wrote to Caroline: "It is again for me to thank you . . . for all you did for me and gave me . . . Coming from you—from a personality which I admire so highly—it should make me a better, a stronger man . . . I am frightened to continue these lines . . . It comes from the deepest source in me! . . . Let me come into your house more often . . . Send me away when you think you are busy or not disposed to talk, I shall understand."[142] But if Caroline was only vaguely aware of Weizmann's feelings toward her, she found out on January 6, 1913, how strong they really were. That afternoon Weizmann poured his heart out to her without any inhibitions. Caroline understood that this intense and fiery chemist was actually falling in love with her. Perhaps consciously Caroline changed the conversation to another subject. She had no intention of hurting Weizmann and turning him out of the Schusters' social circle. Indeed, Caroline may have even felt flattered by Weizmann's attentions. If she was not attracted to him physically, he was nevertheless for her a noble representative of the Jewish people. Thus, she suggested that Weizmann initiate her twenty-year-old daughter, Norah—a Cambridge student—into the inner world of Judaism and Zionism. After all, Norah was partly Jewish and therefore an even more logical candidate than her mother for the Zionist cause. Weizmann's letter to Caroline that evening reveals the emotional turmoil which this highly charged conversation had unleashed in him.

My dearest friend, guide, teacher, mother, everything—it is scarcely possible for me to describe how sad I feel—but it is not sadness which oppresses, on the contrary. Probably it occurs only once in one's life and I dare not go to bed for fear I shall not live through fully this beautiful moment in my life. I should think you are capable of elevating a man to any height, however low he has been before he knew you. The few words you spoke this afternoon were so momentous that each syllable burnt me like fire and I was and still am trembling . . . I think such must have been the sensation of the Jews when they stood round the Sinai and heard the voice through the fiery clouds. I am so happy, so heavenly happy, that really I should not live further for fear that happiness may go away . . . Friend, darling darling friend— I feel so weak and so strong, so sad and so joyful, every little cell is awake in me, every little nerve vibrates . . .

What do you want me to do? I shall work and toil and nothing shall be too hard for me. But you will always encourage me, won't you? I shall strain all that is best [in] me to reclaim dear Norah, to get her to feel in unison with us. I know it is a hard task, but the prize is high enough for it . . . You are a saint and my head burns when I look to you, just as if I would look on a magnificent glacier in full sunshine. Keep this letter and give it to Benny when I am dead. He should know what you were for me. Vera knows it already.[143]

It is not clear whether Norah, who returned to Cambridge the following week, knew of the substance of the discussion concerning her which had transpired between Weizmann and her mother. Yet a month after her mother's moving encounter with Weizmann, she found herself in the same awkward situation. After a short bout with influenza, during which the Schusters nursed him at their home,[144] they sent Weizmann to Westcliff, on the southern coast of England, for a few days' rest. On his return trip, he stayed for a weekend at the home of Ahad Ha'Am. Somehow he persuaded Norah to also spend the weekend at the Hampstead home. What transpired between them is not clear from the correspondence. Yet Weizmann must have made it clear to Norah that he was infatuated with her.[145] Norah, who had innocently accepted the invitation to Hampstead, must have been quite shaken by this incident. Unlike her mother, she did not have the same daily and intimate contact with Weizmann. Nor was she fascinated by the appearance or the ideas of this man who was twice her age. She must have made it quite clear that though she respected him as a valued friend of the family, she had no interest in any other ties with him. She realized that it would be unwise—or perhaps unsafe—to stay with him under one roof for another night and returned to Cambridge on Saturday morning. One can only wonder what explanation Norah and/or Weizmann gave Ahad Ha'Am and his wife for this sudden departure. Feeling foolish at what had just transpired and alarmed at the possible consequences, Weizmann wrote Norah a letter that same afternoon:

Sunny Norah,

When your train left, I felt so isolated in this cold big London and a fear overcame me, that it is the last time I see you. I pray to God that my fear may prove wrong, may prove a mere hallucination, provoked by overstrung, harassed nerves . . . I plead for your mercy, sunny Norah . . . The personal element which worried you so and created the present state of affairs is *eliminated* now and will never arise again . . . Having disposed of the personal, or so called personal, equation as a mere accidental fact, [there] remain the other higher and deeper factors. There is no doubt in my mind about the community of intellect . . . If I am not mistaken in you, there is good hope for the future and the tender plant which we were nursing may develop.

I was no doubt going too fast, I trusted too much to my mentality, and to the power of what is to me the sterling truth, the only truth worth living for. I forgot that you have been taught from a different book, that your truth is not my truth and I under-rated the force and significance of the odds against my teaching. What I named today by the term "Galilean" assumes different shapes and aspects: today it's Peggy [Norah's sister-in-law—an actress], tomorrow it's Cambridge, then it's England, British culture, freedom, greatness, strength and weakness. Who am I to fight against all those giants. I'm only a bundle of nerves, emerging from the gutter of the Ghetto, probably unable to appreciate the brightness and the height of the "Galilean." What seems normal light to you, normal conditions, normal standards and canons, all those elements which make for your happiness . . . all those elements are foreign to me, nay, hurt me, tell me in [a] thousand tongues the story, that I have no claim on them, have no right to call them my own, send me forcibly back to the ghetto . . .

It was this difference and your intrinsic value and the 50% of Jewish blood in you which attracted me with such violent force, set my whole complex mentality at work and drove my small engine at a fearful speed . . .

. . . I made no secret of how I feel towards you . . . I am not an adherent of the semi English, semi spartanic virtue of hiding your feelings at any cost . . . this has estranged you from me today . . . well I am the so-called "exotic" to you . . . But I think your mother is the same, I go further and think that you carry the same spark, I saw it in your eyes, I felt it in your letters, I felt it in you when you were in London [for] the week-end. You are trying to suppress it . . . Let me remind you once more the feeling which you ought to have is not for *my* personality. I am a *zero* as such. But I represent to you a product of 2,000 years in human suffering, of a downtrodden great race which is making a gallant and bold attempt to free itself from chains which have eaten deeply into its flesh.[146]

The following day (Sunday, February 9), Weizmann went to Cambridge to deliver a lecture, which had been arranged two months earlier, to the Cambridge University Zionist Association. When Norah came to London for the weekend, he had probably imagined that they would travel together back to Cambridge. Norah and a friend of hers were in the audience. Did he personally hand Norah the letter he had written her the previous afternoon? To Vera he simply wrote in passing that the Schuster girl had been in attendance; he did not say a word about the fact that they had both spent the night in Ahad Ha'Am's home. This was a convenient omission, but Weizmann's letters to his wife indicate that Vera knew or sensed something of the depth of his feelings for Caroline and Norah Schuster. A week after his memorable conversation with Caroline and a day after Norah left for Cambridge, he apparently needed to reassure Vera.

You should not think, child, that I shall become estranged from you. I really wouldn't be able to live without you. It always seems to you, Verochka, that I love you less than you do me. Perhaps I love you differently, but this love is indissoluble and unshakable. If, as you say, I become "infatuated," this doesn't affect that love for you which is the center of my whole consciousness and existence. And the infatuations have passed. I have suffered and got over last year's incident [sic] and forgotten it, and I hope that you no longer think about it either. Please don't blame me, Verusya![147]

But doubts kept gnawing at Vera. She had known of Weizmann's susceptibility to beautiful women ever since she first met him, and, as his letter to her indicates, there were previous occasions during their marriage when he became infatuated with other women. Vera's suspicion that something was afoot must have been deepened by her husband's constant admonitions not to return too soon to Manchester from the Riviera.[148] The day Norah left Ahad Ha'Am's house to return to Cambridge, he wrote to Vera once again. "No, Veronka, my friendship with Schuster will not estrange me from you; on the contrary, I feel it binds me to you. I find it hard to explain at present, but feel it most sincerely."[149]

On a picnic with Caroline (left) and Norah Schuster (right), 1911

After the incident in Hampstead, his visits to the Schusters became less frequent. Did Norah tell her mother what had transpired in London? Perhaps. If she did not, Caroline's own experience with Weizmann led her to suspect that something had happened. There is no evidence, however, to suggest that the Schusters had changed their attitude toward Weizmann. On the contrary, they continued to support his battle for the professorship and welcomed him whenever he chose to come to their home. Rather, it was Weizmann who had been wounded to the core: He had been humiliated once again by members of the British elite. In his own mind he could dismiss Perkin as an anti-Semite, but this could hardly be the case with Caroline and Norah. He needed time before he could face them anew as a friend and not as an intimate. Again Vera sensed that something was wrong. Weizmann could not very well tell her about his infatuation with the Schuster women and the rebuff he had suffered. But how to explain his changed attitude toward people who went out of their way to prepare borscht for him, who took him into their house when he was sick,[150] about whom he had waxed poetic in almost every letter? His explanation must have struck Vera as strange and disingenuous. He now claimed that the Schusters

are certainly charming people, nevertheless in those fundamental questions which constitute the center of our whole existence they are strangers, indifferent, and, moreover, very remote.

You see, child, when we used to meet assimilated Jews, we used to turn away from them with disdain; we didn't even regret that these people had left us, or were doing so. But here it wounds me every time to see all these fresh, balanced, cultured, nice people, for whom all our painful questions are nothing but sounds. They might become "interested," but it would go no further. This is a pity, a great pity. Sometimes, sitting in their homes, I see how deeply concerned they are by some petty topical problem, and I, having just read the Jewish papers, with the sighs and the moans of the Jewish ghetto still sounding in my ears, begin to feel doubly hurt, and say to myself: it would have been better for you not to have known or loved these people. They are not for you. This is not your feast . . . Having been born in the ghetto, one belongs in the ghetto all one's life. Life will seem artificial to us outside its walls . . .[151]

Somehow the Schusters' inability to feel really Jewish had never bothered Weizmann before the incident with Norah in Hampstead. It certainly did not impress Vera as a sound reason for severing relations with the Schusters. For her part, Vera had already wholeheartedly accepted English society. She felt comfortable among the patricians of Manchester and was about to increase her status and prestige among them with her newly won medical degree and position. She was willing to work hard to see to it that she and Chaim would achieve a position that was due them in English society. The last thing she could imagine was a breach with the Schusters, who, to a large extent, had made it possible for the Weizmanns to enter that society. She was unconvinced by Weizmann's sudden change of heart toward the Schusters and must have inquired once again as to what had happened, to which Weizmann replied:

I have already written to you, dear Verunya, why I now visit the Schusters less often. Not because I love and respect them less. Nor have they changed their attitude one iota towards me, towards us. But it hurts me so much, and there is something bad coming into my feelings, something like envy and bitterness. I don't envy them, I envy the *goyim* who calmly devour the best we have and scream that we are exploiting them.[152]

He was not disappointed with the Schusters, he assured Vera; he always knew that they were only half or quarter Jews. "But it is only here that I have seen with my own eyes how deep and cruel the Jewish *Galuth* is, even when it adopts an attractive and not just a pogromlike form."[153]

Vera did not have to worry for long that their relations with the Schusters had been impaired. Within a brief period of time Weizmann began to report again on visits to the Schusters. Presumably he resumed his discussions on Zionism with Caroline and on science and university affairs with Arthur Schuster. Nor were the ties with Norah severed. On the contrary, the two maintained a lively correspondence. As Weizmann promised her on February 8, "the personal element" had been eliminated. But he did not give up trying to convert her to Zionism,[154] albeit with little success.[155] To please him, though, Norah joined her mother in attending, as guests, the proceedings of the Eleventh Zionist Congress in Vienna that year.[156] Afterward the Weizmanns, Harry Sacher, and Norah went on a two-week mountain tour in the Austrian and Italian Alps.[157]

What did worry Vera, however, was an invitation from SAC to Weizmann, early in March 1913, to join the executive.[158] Three days earlier—while still in Manchester—he informed Norah with great excitement that he had been offered the position of Zionist representative in Constantinople, and that he was ready to "throw myself head over heels into it . . . never return from it,"[159] but by the time he arrived in Berlin he found that the even greater honor of SAC membership was to be bestowed upon him. The invitation came at a time when his self-esteem had been badly bruised by his public and private failures. He was particularly vulnerable to any gestures of respect, especially from the leadership of the Zionist movement, whose ranks he had yearned to join for more than a decade. In contrast to Manchester, he found the atmosphere in Berlin warm and friendly, and he was tempted—at least for a few days—to consider seriously the offer by SAC. The nostalgia he always felt for the Continent was aroused once again. "Here in Berlin there's a good and sound Zionist mood, and in general there really is a Jewish life—people, books, ideas, aspirations. Not as it is with us in England."[160]

But Vera put her foot down firmly. Beneath the elegant and delicate exterior there lurked a woman of iron will who knew how to manage her husband. There were areas in their married life where she was willing to give him more freedom; for example, in his occasional infatuations with women. But on certain other matters, such as money and career, she held her ground. They might have to go to Palestine one day—and she had already told Chaim that she would—but only when they were ready to do so, and not out of desperation or on an impulse. If Weizmann suffered setbacks in his career, she was going to see to it that he would not use Palestine as a personal refuge. While they were still in the Diaspora, she set clear limitations as to what she would permit Chaim to do for the Jews. To volunteer his time for Zionist causes was one thing, but she would not allow him to become a paid official of the Zionist movement. Since that issue had come up for the first time, in the summer of 1902, she had not wavered on this point.[161] Moreover, having taken her medical degree for the second time and on the verge of a career as a public health officer,[162] she was not willing to give it all up and sit for her exams for a third time in Germany.[163] Deep down she knew that Weizmann would not relinquish his university position, even if it turned out to be a readership rather than the coveted professorship. This was confirmed by Weizmann himself on many occasions. While wishing he could go to Palestine and put an end to the *Galut* in all its forms,[164] and assuring Vera that "it will soon be time for us to get out of this swamp and go to Palestine,"[165] he basically adhered to what he had written to Arthur Hantke in February 1912. Even during his deepest depression over the lost professorship, he reaffirmed his basic goal in a letter addressed to Vera: "Your readiness to go to Palestine has made me *very* happy, but, child, we shall go there as *free* people and not driven by devils like Dixon and Perkin."[166] Had the Weizmanns moved to Berlin in 1913 and remained there during World War I, it is quite possible that Zionist history would have taken a different turn.

To repeat, Weizmann would have had at least a reasonable chance to attain the professorship had he not thoughtlessly rushed into a conflict with Perkin. He never fully recovered psychologically from this affair. The insult gnawed at him for the rest of his life.[167] Whatever lessons he may have learned from the episode about human nature and academic politics, it was too late to implement them within the university context. His future actions indicate that he would implement one important lesson from the events of 1912–13: He would be more cautious before entering any business agreement.[168] Conversely, he did not become more discreet in his attitudes to and relations with other women. What made the suppression of his bitter experiences more bearable was the fact that Weizmann soon achieved the financial security, public recognition, and prestige he had sought all along. Vera was at long last able to supplement the family budget with her salary, and by the end of the summer of 1913 Weizmann had concluded a discreet arrangement with his friend Julius Simon, by which the latter financed Weizmann's continued experiments on fermentation in return for half the profits resulting from any discovery.[169] Weizmann was now free to work as he pleased in his new capacity as an independent researcher and eventually made sufficient profit from his discoveries to live in the style to which he and Vera aspired. The post of reader freed him from almost all teaching duties, giving him plenty of time for laboratory work.[170] It also enabled him to devote a great deal of his time to an old-new project which would preoccupy him until World War I: the founding of a Hebrew university in Jerusalem.

XVI

A Hebrew University in Jerusalem

Prior to the conflict with Perkin—early in May 1912—Weizmann wrote to Judah Leon Magnes, outlining a new scheme. Weizmann had just read in the press that Mr. Nathan Straus, a German-born philanthropist now residing in New York, had established in Hadera (Palestine) a health station under the direction of Dr. Wilhelm Bruenn. Since he had for some time urged the establishment of a chemistry department within the Technicum—under his own direction—Weizmann suggested the following: Why not combine the various projects into one big institute, "something like a small Pasteur Institute[?] . . . Such an institute could fulfill two functions: a teaching institute and a research institute, and could develop into the nucleus of the great Jewish research centers of the future. The Hilfsverein would be greatly interested in the establishment of this institution, since it would supply them with the chemical department of the Technicum; other circles would lend support to the colonizing, hygienic aspect." In short, such a project would consolidate all the small scientific enterprises in Palestine, eliminate overlap and waste, and ensure high-quality research and personnel.[1]

Magnes was not convinced that a central organization combining such institutions as the Agricultural Experimental Station at Atlit, which was headed by Aaron Aaronsohn, the Health Bureau, and the Technicum was feasible, but he had great faith in Weizmann's personal and scientific qualities. Replying to Isaac Straus, who also advocated centralization, Magnes wrote:

> . . . I called your attention to the fact that Mr. Aaronsohn and Dr. Lewin came in person to this country in order to secure the establishment of the institutions in which they were interested. I am mentioning this for the purpose of convincing you that in case any other institution of whatever nature is to be established in Palestine by means of American money, it will be necessary for a man of ability and energy to come here in person and to convince unwilling financiers that his mission in life is to establish the institution in which he is interested. I am sure that [if] a man with the ability, scientific achievements and pleasing personality of Prof. Weitzmann [sic] were to come here on behalf of *his* institution, and were to make it his mission to

secure the establishment of this institution, he would meet with success. . . .
Securing money for the establishment of an institution is much easier than
for the scientific work of any individual, however worthy he may be. I should
like to do everything possible to enable Prof. Weitzmann [sic] to settle in
Palestine; and the scientific results he would doubtless achieve would be an
inspiration to a large number of men and women throughout the world. . . .[2]

Magnes did not specify the institution on whose behalf Weizmann
would exert his energies, but he knew enough of the Manchester chemist to be able to say that he would succeed in his endeavors. In fact, as
early as the spring of 1912, while on his propaganda tour on the Continent, Weizmann and his close friends Julius Simon and Berthold Feiwel
had discussed the idea of reviving the Jewish university project.[3] But the
idea remained dormant until early March 1913, when it was brought up
again in Berlin at a closed meeting of SAC and a few GAC members.
The time seemed particularly propitious for advancing the idea of a Hebrew or Jewish university in Palestine.[4] Italy's seizure of Tripolitania from
the Turks in the fall of 1911, followed a year later by the First Balkan
War, did much to weaken the Ottoman Empire, which lost almost a third
of its European territory in the reshuffle which ensued. The protracted
war aggravated Turkey's perennial liquidity problems. For a while it
seemed that the Zionists would extract some concrete concessions from
the Turks, such as softening their stiff opposition to Zionist immigration
and land purchase in Palestine in return for financial help.[5] Moreover,
Baron Edmond de Rothschild was moving closer to Zionism and had expressed interest in purchasing large tracts of land in Palestine.[6] Could
this unpredictable philanthropist possibly be interested in the Jewish
university as well? Weizmann tended to believe that the baron could be
persuaded to lend his support. Weizmann had had a high regard for the
baron's achievements ever since his visit to Palestine in 1907.[7] Weizmann had reiterated his hopes of winning Edmond de Rothschild over
to the Zionist cause on a number of occasions. At GAC meetings in November 1911 he stated:

I well know that the Baron [Edmond de Rothschild] is a man imbued with
love for work in Palestine but is under the influence of courtiers. There is
no doubt that if we were to approach him without fanfare, on the basis of
solid work, we would gain his support—at least this is what I have heard
from many people. I know, e.g., that Rothschild was for a while favorably
inclined toward Zionism. True, these were sporadic exceptions, but it is up
to us to steer him in this direction.[8]

Now the baron was indeed prepared to cooperate with the Zionist
movement. Weizmann, too, was readier than ever to throw himself into
the university project. The idea could not have resurfaced at a better time.
The humiliation he had suffered over the loss of the chair at Manchester
had left him disillusioned and depressed. Though he was promoted and
received a good salary, he viewed both the university and Manchester
itself as a gilded cage.[9] He had not quite given up the idea of establish-

ing himself in Palestine as the first professor of chemistry at the Technicum, but his chances seemed to be dwindling. Yet he needed to feel that—at least intellectually—he could transcend his immediate surroundings. Thus, the reemergence of the idea of a Jewish university in Palestine had the potential of rescuing him from the dead end he had reached in his career.[10] Moreover, the project was now to receive the backing of SAC, which was composed of men who shared Weizmann's vision of a cultural renaissance in Palestine. Conditions for such a project were more favorable than in 1901–4. There now existed a Hebrew *Gymnasium,* and a new generation of Palestinian Jews was maturing and would eventually seek higher education. At its meetings in Berlin early in March 1913, GAC appointed a committee comprised of Weizmann, Berthold Feiwel, and Leo Motzkin—with the authority to co-opt others as well—and assigned it the task of gathering material and preparing a report on the feasibility of establishing a university in Jerusalem.[11] Weizmann was to make the official report to the Eleventh Zionist Congress.[12] As usual, Weizmann endowed GAC decisions with more meaning than they initially contained: "We've worked out the *Tagesordnung* for the Congress . . . the *clou* of the Congress will be the question of the creation of a Jewish University in Jerusalem and the whole Zionist machinery will be put to work for the speedy implementation of this project."[13]

Weizmann did not waste a minute. On the same day on which GAC concluded its meetings he called on Leopold Landau, a gynecologist in Berlin, who had been favorably disposed toward the university project for over a decade. Landau was a relative of Paul Ehrlich, one of Germany's most eminent scientists, credited with contributions toward the cure of diphtheria and syphilis and a Nobel Prize laureate. Since the turn of the century Ehrlich had been director of the Speyer Institute for Experimental Medicine in Frankfurt. Landau telephoned his illustrious relative and persuaded him to receive Weizmann, who hoped to enlist him as an ally in the university campaign. Fortified as well with a recommendation from his erstwhile mentor Carl Graebe, Weizmann met Ehrlich in the latter's laboratory on March 10, 1913.[14] Ehrlich took Weizmann on a quick tour of the laboratories, explaining his theories with force and excitement. Finally, Weizmann rallied his courage and explained the purpose of his visit. "But why Jerusalem?" exclaimed Ehrlich, giving Weizmann the opportunity to air the reasons for establishing a Hebrew university in Jerusalem. They had spent more than an hour together when Ehrlich suddenly pulled out his watch and said, "Do you know that out there, in the corridor, there are counts, princes and ministers who are waiting to see me and who will be happy if I give them ten minutes of my time?" Weizmann replied, "Yes, Professor Ehrlich, but the difference between me and your other visitors is that they come to receive an injection from you, but I came to give you one."[15] The encounter with Ehrlich had clearly been embellished when Weizmann wrote his memoirs,[16] but what is certain is that when he left Ehrlich's office after a conversation that lasted well over an hour, Weizmann had won over an important new ally.[17] Characteristically, Weizmann later combined his professional and Zionist goals by working in Ehrlich's laboratory.

Weizmann returned to Manchester full of energy. His friends on the Continent and in England promised their full support,[18] and he felt that his moment had come. "The movement has begun to smack of gunpowder," he wrote Vera, who was still in Cannes with Benjy. "I too now feel as one does during a heated battle. Every nerve is taut, every cell is alive and feelings are more acute. . . . I won't succumb to the Manchester mood. I feel that I don't belong to Manchester at all. Everything here is 'temporary' and alien. . . . I'm beginning to feel a great responsibility over the report that I am to prepare for the Congress. . . . To my way of thinking, this is the one slogan that can evoke a response just now—the Hebrew University. *Die Zionsuniversitaet auf dem Berge Zion!* The Third Temple!"[19] He was virtually bursting with good feelings and optimism about the future. One can practically hear and see the Weizmann of the Democratic Faction days reawakening, combative at the new challenge presented to him by the movement. As usual during such moments, he was carried away by emotions.

> The work calls . . . and the time is near when it will devolve upon us to show how deeply the yearning for freedom is embedded in us, which you and I, Verusya, will not see, but Benichka will. I don't write this with any feeling of sadness, but with pride, yes, and with gladness, in that perhaps it will fall to us to have the good fortune to sacrifice ourselves on behalf of Jewish freedom. You and I, Verusya, much like Moses from the heights of Horeb, will see the free, Jewish Palestine in the distance though we shall still be living in the Diaspora.[20]

He threw himself into his work. Once again letters began to pour out of Manchester at a furious pace, requesting advice, information, and cooperation. Unlike the Geneva period, Weizmann did not have to rely on volunteers to do the office work. He had at his disposal a part-time paid assistant and a typewriter, both provided by SAC.[21] Moreover, beginning in April 1913 SAC engaged the services of Leo Herrmann, a Prague journalist, one of whose special duties was to aid Weizmann in work connected with the Hebrew university. With Leo Motzkin and Berthold Feiwel—who had both been involved in the Jewish university project during the Geneva period—at his side once again, Weizmann felt that the old spirit of the Democratic Faction had been reborn.[22] This feeling was strengthened when Martin Buber asked to be co-opted onto the university commission.[23] Relations with old comrades like Julius Simon and Judah Magnes were strengthened through their common work. Even while embarking on the university project, Weizmann continued to hope for a position as head of the chemistry department at the Technicum, prompting Ahad Ha'Am to put his name forward at the next curatorium meeting.[24] He was even willing to accept an appointment as the administrator of the Technicum.[25] Clearly, he saw no conflict between these two institutions and preferred an immediate appointment at the Technicum[26] to a later position at an institution that existed only in his mind's eye. Yet, as he well realized, the Technicum was dependent on the largesse of people who mostly stood outside the Zionist movement and to whom he had to come hat in hand. Ever since Hermann Schapira first suggested the idea in 1882, the Jewish university had been an entirely Zionist affair. The idea was born out of Zionist impulses and would be realized by Zionists. Circumstances coalesced to give Weizmann great authority and control over how it would be planned.

By the end of March 1913 he had formulated the first draft of a plan for the university which clearly demonstrates that his suggestion, in May 1912, to establish a Pasteur-like institute had been only a fleeting idea. It arose naturally in 1912 because of his work with Fernbach, but now that he actually had to produce a plan, he had a much greater scheme in mind. Writing to Menahem Ussishkin, his old and reliable barometer for Russian Zionist attitudes toward any project, he suggested that the university begin with a medical school, faculty of philosophy which would include Orientalia and Hebraica, and faculty of law and political science.[27] He reiterated this plan more succinctly to Judah Magnes, whose cooperation he deemed crucial for the success of the project. Magnes was Weizmann's major link to the American Jewish elite and he had to be consulted every step of the way. "From both practical and political points of view, it appears to me that one should start with a Medical school and with a school for Law. Both adapted to the requirements of Turkey and the East . . ."[28] Magnes objected to the priorities outlined in Weizmann's proposal and suggested instead "that a beginning ought to be made with what might appear to be the least practical thing of the whole subject, but which, in reality, might prove to be the most practical of all . . . a Jewish school of archaeology, which should be developed . . . into a school of Geisteswissenschaften treated from the Jewish point of view . . ."[29] That he valued Magnes's opinion is evident from the subsequent reversal of priorities in Weizmann's conception of a Jewish university. On June 12, 1913, he wrote to SAC, "Of course we shall have to emphasize that the ultimate aim is a university, but that we are beginning with those institutes that are easier to realize, such as perhaps an archaeological institute, a law faculty, if possible a modest medical school . . ."[30]

Weizmann's approach in preparing the proposal for the Eleventh Zionist Congress closely resembled his preparations in writing the pamphlet *Eine Juedische Hochschule* in 1902: enlisting the support of Jewish scholars throughout the world and soliciting opinions from them on the nature and feasibility of a Jewish university;[31] obtaining permission and approval from the Turkish authorities;[32] collecting statistical information on the material and intellectual condition of Jewish students in both Eastern and Western Europe;[33] conducting propaganda tours in advance of the congress[34] and obtaining information on the financial operation and administrative regulations of other universities in the Middle East rather than Europe.[35] Above all, as in the past, he tended to feel responsible for all the work and paid scant attention to the formal division of labor assigned within the university commission.[36]

Given his tendency to take charge and his outburst of sustained energy in pursuing his goal, he was soon disappointed when he discovered—as in the past—that his co-workers could not, or would not, keep pace with him. Within two months of outlining his plan for a university to Ussishkin, he began complaining that his closest collaborators in the project, Leo Motzkin and Leo Herrmann, had done nothing to advance the idea.[37] In a passage which sounds as if it had been written during one of his periods of frustration in Geneva, Weizmann complained:

> Altogether, I have myself had to do everything I have so far undertaken, as colleagues and friends are so slow that one cannot make headway at all. I do realize that the execution of such a gigantic project is almost impossible when one finds such weak interest in the most intimate circle . . . This perpetual correspondence, which mainly consists of outgoing letters only, is repugnant to me, and personally I am going to decline any further work under such conditions. Until the Congress I shall certainly do my best conscientiously to discharge what I have undertaken, but after that I will not let myself in for this kind of work.[38]

In fact, what seemed to militate against progress in the university scheme was not only laziness and lack of interest but also opposition from within the movement. Max Nordau, who was still seen by SAC as an invaluable symbol of the movement's link with Herzl, a man whom SAC sought to persuade at all costs to come to the Eleventh Zionist Congress,[39] where he would presumably lend legitimacy to the new "nonpolitical" leadership, publicly opposed and even ridiculed the university project. He repeated the old canard, which had been one of the bones of contention when Wolffsohn came to England, that Weizmann and his colleagues had a decade earlier squandered university funds.[40] But even those who in principle supported Weizmann's ideas within the movement seemed to be having second thoughts. Ahad Ha'Am thought the idea of a university dangerous since it might "arouse the suspicions of states whose eyes are turned to Jerusalem."[41] Arthur Ruppin felt, at least initially, that a university in Palestine was not as important as agricultural settlements and that the movement could ill afford to expend money on such a project.[42] This was also the view of the Palestinian Poalei Zion.[43] Nahum Sokolow and Judah Magnes counseled Weizmann against a propaganda tour on behalf of the university.[44] Even Weizmann's faithful friend Berthold Feiwel advised against pressing forward too fast with the scheme since the time was not yet ripe for it.[45] Finally, SAC seemed to be somewhat uncertain about the scheme,[46] prompting Weizmann to exclaim in anger: "I don't want to look like someone with muddled and crack-pot schemes."[47] The strongest opponent to the university plan within GAC was Jean Fischer,[48] who warned against the creation of an intellectual proletariat in Palestine.[49]

In fact, the assignment by SAC to Weizmann, Motzkin, and Feiwel was merely to produce a report, and it is understandable that Weizmann's friends became nervous at the prospect of his committing the movement to a scheme that had not yet been approved by the congress. But those who thought they could deter him from charging ahead did not properly assesses the man. Though he agreed that there was some merit in the argument that too much publicity for the Hebrew university at this early stage might scare both the Turks and Rothschild,[50] Weizmann was driven by the thought that the movement might not take full advantage of the current political situation. His zeal to realize his cherished dream was fueled by his belief that the university would occupy a central role in the cultural and spiritual renaissance of Zionism and would form an important element in settling the land in Palestine, serving as a political statement underlining the Zionists' intentions to establish permanent roots in the land.[51] Likewise he was spurred by the hope that the university's establishment would result in a position for himself as head of the university's chemistry department. Thus, despite his fulminations against SAC and his regret at the loss of "the spirit of 4, rue Lombard,"[52] he was not about to abandon the project. GAC, which met in Berlin from June 15 to 16, 1913, decided that at the Eleventh Zionist Congress Weizmann would address the delegates on the question of the university, the need for such an institution, and the feasibility of carrying out the project. It also stated in advance that it would be premature for the congress to arrive at concrete decisions on the question and that it should only recommend the desirability of further study of the project.[53] Yet even this lukewarm and noncommittal resolution did not deter Weizmann, who was already planning his moves after the congress. The next step, he wrote to SAC, would be to form an effective committee in England. Unlike the current and ineffective commission, this new committee—composed of himself, Ahad Ha'Am, Harry Sacher, and Leon Simon—would be a working committee. "The advantage is that they are all close at hand, and the whole thing will acquire an 'English' character. Of course there will also be a German committee, but the main work should be done by these people."[54] At Ahad Ha'Am's request he changed the nature of the committee to "Anglo-American."[55] Thus, even before the congress met, he received SAC's consent to concentrate the university activities in England.[56]

This brought up once again the subject of Moses Gaster. At GAC meetings in Berlin in March 1913, the state of Zionism in England came up. The untenable stalemate between the EZF, controlled by the old Herzlians Joseph Cowen and Leopold Kessler, and the Order of Ancient Maccabeans (OAM) continued to be an embarrassment to the movement as a whole.[57] Both SAC and Weizmann were interested in enlisting the *Haham* within their camp. SAC wanted to see a strong English Zionist organization which would once again contribute meaningfully to the movement's support for the university project. In addition, both SAC and Weizmann felt that only the *Haham* could provide the strong lead-

ership necessary to pull the English movement out of the mire of intrigue in which it seemed hopelessly entangled. Thus, shortly after returning from the Continent in March 1913, Weizmann contacted Gaster—
after a break of two years in their relationship—pledging his friendship
once again. "You know," he wrote to Gaster,

> what we all want [is] to see you at the head of the movement here, so that
> your great force is available also for the general international movement . . .
> Therefore if I approach you now in the name of, and on instructions from,
> the SAC, it is done with the intention of cooperating with you most closely
> to prepare the Congress in a proper manner both here and on the Conti-
> nent, to restore the organization in England to its true importance and vi-
> tality. It will succeed, it must succeed if you and [Jacob] Moser and the whole
> circle of younger friends return . . . I beg you, dear Doctor, to let mercy
> prevail over justice and write to me soon . . .[58]

The "dear Doctor," who had been biding his time since 1911, carefully
nursing his anger and contempt for the leadership of the EZF, replied
by return mail. It was not in Gaster's character to be gracious. Treating
his erstwhile protégé as if he were a truant schoolboy, he wrote, "Though
you are a sinner, you are in a penitent mood, and I shall be pleased to
accept the penitent sinner on one condition: no relapse. If you have now
seen [the] light and have been able to convince yourself of the hopelessness of conditions . . . you may perhaps be cured of some vagaries in
which you indulged and find that 'chochmas' do not pay. I had warned
you long ago and you would not listen . . . you wanted to be too clever
by half. . . ."[59] Beyond scoring points, though, the *Haham* repeated his
long-standing demands for absolute loyalty and cooperation. More important was his *conditio sine qua non* that the EZF be dissolved and replaced by a new organization.[60] Though he was convinced that Gaster
must be drawn back into the leadership of English Zionism, Weizmann,
who was influenced in this matter by Leon Simon,[61] found this demand
difficult to swallow.[62] SAC was of two minds in the matter, alternately
negotiating with Gaster while promising funds to the Joint Zionist Council
(i.e., the EZF), which was bound to keep the organization alive.[63] It even
considered the idea of having Leon Simon and Harry Sacher take over
the leadership of the EZF.[64]

SAC finally gave in to Gaster's unbending demands to create a tabula
rasa and to form a new organization,[65] though formally it had no constitutional power to dissolve the EZF.[66] In a letter to Weizmann, Hantke
proposed that the Joint Zionist Council be dissolved and that the EZF be
replaced by a new body, the English Zionist Association, and that OAM
be given a newly defined status within it.[67] With Weizmann and Sacher's approval,[68] it was decided that Hantke, Victor Jacobson, and Otto
Warburg would attend the annual conference of the EZF scheduled for
June 1, 1913, in order to lend their support for this new arrangement.[69]

If Hantke and his colleagues thought they could intimidate the EZF
leadership into submitting to their suggestion that they resign, they were

in for a surprise. As early as April, Joseph Cowen took the battle into SAC's own camp, accusing the new leadership of an excessive pro-German orientation.[70] At the London annual conference it turned out that the delegates were determined to run their own affairs without interference from Berlin. Despite Weizmann's call for a "homogeneous executive" composed of Gaster (as president), Jacob Moser, and Herbert Bentwich, and the declaration by these gentlemen that they were willing to take over, the EZF refused to dissolve itself, as demanded by Gaster.[71] Resentful of the heavy-handed manner in which SAC handled the whole affair, the delegates defiantly returned Joseph Cowen—the "political"—as president of the EZF, with an executive composed mostly of Cowen's own men.[72] Thus, the attempt by SAC and Weizmann to bring about a reorganization of the movement in England failed miserably. Perhaps spurred by the near collapse of the organization, the EZF seemed to slowly revive under Cowen's leadership. Though he continued to support OAM as a "practical organization," Weizmann was, as always, a pragmatist; he now realized that the movement could only be changed from within. At the annual conference in Leeds in February 1914, he consented once again to be elected vice president of the EZF.[73] His election marked the beginning of the end in England concerning controversy between the "politicals" and the "practicals," which had been raging since Uganda. The strife between these two camps ended with the outbreak of World War I.

Weizmann's interest in the affairs of the EZF and OAM declined rapidly as soon as the June annual conference ended its deliberations. Though he was interested in bringing to the congress as strong an OAM delegation as possible, and even exerted some effort in that direction,[74] he concentrated almost entirely on the presentation of his university project before the congress, aware of some of the negative reactions his address might provoke. He also continued to explore other possibilities for the founding of a chemistry department in Palestine. In 1912 a Society of Jewish Physicians and Scientists for the Improvement of Sanitary Conditions in Palestine was founded in Berlin.[75] Its moving spirit, Ephraim Pinczower, asked Weizmann to form an English branch of the society. Despite Sacher's objection to cooperation with a German society which might be controlled by the German government,[76] Weizmann immediately foresaw the possibility of attaching a "chemical section" to the society which could eventually become the nucleus of the medical faculty of the Hebrew university in Jerusalem.[77] He was likewise positively inclined toward the suggestion of Aaron Sandler, a member of the society and a leading German Zionist, to attach an institute of chemistry or microbiology to the International Health Bureau in Jerusalem, which would later be incorporated into the university. Sandler's reasoning was that the university project could provoke German academic circles to compete with that institution.[78] Weizmann took the warning seriously but was not deterred by the possible competition. Nor did he, at this point, fully accept Baron Edmond de Rothschild's oft-repeated demand for a behind-the-scenes operation. He was firm on the need to discuss the project at the congress. "I cannot think how one might initiate the university propaganda unless the idea is publicly proclaimed at the congress and, moreover, with all emphasis and all earnestness . . . On mature reflection I cannot see why and how we should now start to retreat."[79]

The Eleventh Zionist Congress opened in Vienna on September 2, 1913, and was attended by 540 delegates. It included twenty Palestinian representatives who repeatedly insisted that Hebrew be the language of the congress. Zionist activity in Palestine was one of the dominant themes, and its importance was fully underscored by SAC's own pronouncements. The "politicals" found themselves on the defensive. Significantly, Otto Warburg did not mention the practical accomplishments of the "politicals" during Wolffsohn's tenure in office, attributing them to the new leadership which had been in office since 1911. He emphasized the loyalty of the Jews to Turkey and their support for its efforts at regeneration. Likewise, he expressed the wish of the Zionists for a cooperative relationship with the Arab population in Palestine. The cultural and economic improvements in Palestine would benefit both Jews and Arabs and would become the basis for such cooperation.[80] In place of Nordau, who stayed away from the congress after all,[81] it fell to Sokolow to present the traditional survey of the condition of the Jewish people, while Shmarya Levin—hinting at the controversy just then brewing in Palestine—concentrated on the accomplishments of the Yishuv in Palestine and demanded that all educational activities in the country be placed in the hands of the Zionist movement.[82]

The next five days of the congress were dominated by the struggle between the "practicals" and the "politicals" for control over the Jewish Colonial Trust. The new SAC had been planning to take over the financial institutions of the Zionist movement, correctly assuming that without such control they would continue to depend on Wolffsohn and his associates, who preached constant vigilance in incurring any expenditures. At the Eleventh Zionist Congress arguments for and against the new SAC's policy for increased expenditures for practical work were made once again; its supporters including Menahem Ussishkin and Yehiel Tschlenow, and its detractors including Nissan Katzenelson, Jean Fischer, and, of course, Wolffsohn himself. One of the last to join the debate was Weizmann, who emphasized the importance of synthetic Zionism, a term which he claimed to have coined. He also reiterated his long-standing belief that Zionist policies could not be solely directed on the basis of financial considerations. Even if a certain set of activities were to result in financial loss, it would have a positive moral and political impact. He advocated an aggressive investment, on the part of the Zionist movement, in the economic and cultural life of the Yishuv.

> There are moments in the life of peoples and also in the life of the Jewish people *when a school, too, is a political act* . . .
> The fundamental principle of our diplomacy is the following: The chief

great power with whom we are negotiating is the Jewish people. From this great power we expect everything, from the other great powers very little. . . . In a Hebrew speech made by Ussishkin, he raised some points that . . . in my opinion form the underpinning of our basic political work in the future. We must keep open the door to the East, and above all win back Ottoman Jewry and the Jewry of the East. In Palestine we must promote the *Kibbuz Hoorez* [acquiring contiguous tracts of land]. These are the two basic principles of our politics . . . We must also take care to enlighten the Arab population. The Arabs, who have a kinship with us, will show understanding for our endeavors and will become our friends. . . .

Weizmann closed with a demand that all segments of the movement unite behind SAC and give it a chance to carry out its policies successfully.[83] SAC did receive a vote of confidence, but unofficially it also decided to give up its demands for control over the financial institutions of the movement. Though a sick man, Wolffsohn proved to be stronger than had been anticipated. SAC had little choice but to temporarily give up the fight if it wanted to preserve the unity of the movement. Wolffsohn and his friends remained in control of the Jewish Colonial Trust.

One of the more impressive speeches at the congress was delivered by Arthur Ruppin, who gave a dispassionate account of the conditions, achievements, goals, and problems of Zionist work in Palestine. Ruppin demonstrated in his speech not only a thorough knowledge of Palestine and of economic issues facing the movement but also a clarity of thinking and a mind open to other solutions. Though he admitted that Zionist achievements had not been overwhelming thus far, he was confident that a solid base had been prepared for the future. He evinced his understanding for the spirit of the young in Palestine and underlined the importance of pioneer settlements, but he also stated his support for the old colonies and for urban and industrial development, emphasizing that private initiative and investments were crucial to the success of the Zionist enterprise. Like Warburg and Weizmann—who reiterated the point during his presentation of the university project—Ruppin also insisted on the need for peaceful cooperation with the Arabs in Palestine and for the greatest tact and sensitivity in the acquisition of land. No time should be lost in arriving at a peaceful understanding with the Arabs and achieving a *modus vivendi* in which Jews and Arabs could develop their cultures side by side.[84] Like Weizmann, he also reiterated that a national enterprise could not be measured only in economic terms but also in national terms, even if no immediate material gains were apparent. "We have reconciled ourselves to the fact that we must reach our goal not through the charter but through practical work."[85]

It would have been unwise for Warburg, Weizmann, or Ruppin to have said more than they did in a public forum, knowing that all the proceedings would be published. Yet there are clear indications that by 1913 Weizmann was aware that the Arabs' opposition to the Zionists was more than a mere economic matter. In a letter to Vera he wrote that

Passport photo, early 1915

there is alarming news from Syria about the Arab national movement. With the weakening of central authority in Constantinople, the periphery of Asia Minor is beginning to organize, though in a very primitive manner. They consider Palestine their own and have embarked on an intensive propaganda campaign in their semi-national, semi-Christian, and "semi-antisemitic"—an expression that can hardly apply to the Arabs—press against the selling of land to "Zionists," the enemies of Turkey and the usurpers of Palestine. We shall soon face a serious enemy, and it won't be enough to pay just money for the land. In this connection, it's most important to launch a strong propaganda drive for the transfer of Yemenite Jews to Palestine as quickly as possible. It's more important than ever to transfer sound and reliable Jewish elements to Palestine.[86]

It was during the penultimate evening of the congress (September 8) that the university scheme finally had a hearing. The subject was introduced by Menahem Ussishkin, who discussed the problems of education and culture and demanded the predominance of Hebrew in the educational system in Palestine. At the end of his speech, which was again delivered in Hebrew, he brought forth a resolution for the establishment of a Hebrew university in Jerusalem in which all subjects would be taught in Hebrew from the outset.[87] Weizmann then launched into a detailed explanation of the proposal. Since Motzkin had, despite his promises, failed to produce a draft, the speech was Weizmann's own creation, though it had been subjected to Berthold Feiwel and Judah Magnes's scrutiny (and approval) beforehand.[88] Weizmann's basic thesis for the creation of a university had remained unchanged since his Geneva years.

His train of thought and even his phrasing of arguments were at times identical with those that can be found in *Eine Juedische Hochschule* and in his long letter to Herzl dated May 6, 1903. But there are also differences that are immediately apparent. In his speech before the congress, as in 1902, he brought up the fact that anti-Semitism prevented students and scholars, especially those from Russia, from entering the universities, but he did not dwell on the subject as he had previously done. Possibly he did not wish to place the Russian delegates to the congress in a difficult position by attacking their government publicly. More important is the fact that the pamphlet of 1902 had viewed Palestine as one of several possible sites for the erection of a university, along with England and Switzerland. In Weizmann's speech before the congress no land other than Palestine was even mentioned.

Weizmann emphasized in his speech the positive impact the university would have on all Jewry. His approach to the subject was marked by moderation and an attempt to avoid antagonizing any faction at the congress. He divided his speech into two parts: the necessity of founding a university and the feasibility of founding such an institution.

It is superfluous to discuss at length before a Zionist congress the national necessity and importance of a Jewish university. We all feel the immense value of an intellectual center, where Jews could learn, teach, and do research in a sympathetic atmosphere free from hindrances, in the fellowship of Jews, free from the oppression of an alien culture, and inspired by the resolve to create new Jewish values and bring our great traditions into harmony with the modern world. Out of such a synthesis genuine Jewish education would arise, from which the Jewish nation as a whole would profit most. The influence of such a center on the Diaspora would be profound; the self-esteem of the Jewish intellectuals would be greatly enhanced. When one considers what influence the Jewish *Gymnasium* in Jaffa is already exercising on the *golus,* and what so weak and so young an organization as the Merkas Hamorim [the Union of Jewish teachers in Palestine] is already accomplishing, one must agree that the national importance of a university would be unlimited. Most of all the university would be the guardian of those values which are most precious to the future of the nation; it would cultivate the living Jewish national tongue, it would be a meeting place for all Jewish creative activity in literature, art, and science: In a word, it would be "the cultural center." What wealth of Jewish spiritual power could win freedom and live out its life in the Jewish university! Eminent Jewish scholars—who are now denied advancement because they are Jews, cannot find a sphere of action, and often are exposed to serious material and moral humiliation because they will not abandon their people—would have a place in which they could dedicate themselves wholly to science and their people. Such a concentration of Jewish scientific endeavor would be an immeasurable advantage for the scholars themselves and for science in general.

Today, so many of our young men are lost to the cause of national emancipation because of the pernicious influence of an alien environment. Trained in a Jewish university, they would be its best and stoutest champions, men who would make the Jewish national spirit live in the noblest fashion and communicate it to the whole people. The new, upright, creative Jew would become ours. The Jewish people would draw from this national enterprise much force and a new inspiration. It would see the most splendid proof that its creative power lives, and it would gain courage and confidence for the highest national achievements.

A university would have the highest significance for our position in Palestine. It would be a most useful instrument in our peaceful development of the land. It would attract new forces to the land. It would contribute to the opening up and development of the country. It would raise our prestige in the eyes of the native population. Of much importance is the fact that the university would train the teachers for our schools in Palestine and the Diaspora. Today most of our teachers are educated in non-Jewish seminaries, and to a large extent their training lacks a national basis. Very different would be the lot of Jewish education if the teachers came from a Jewish university and were in constant touch with a Jewish university . . .

I have till now discussed the necessity of a university wholly from the national Palestinian point of view, but unhappily the project for a Jewish university draws support from one of the needs of Diaspora-Jewry, which has become the most burning question of the day. Everybody knows how bitter is the denial of rights to which most of our people are subjected. Of the restrictions on Russian Jews perhaps the most severely felt is the exclusion from secondary schools and universities imposed by the state. To describe these in detail would carry us too far. I need only say that these circumstances will compel non-Zionists to hasten to help. Ten years ago the movement for the exclusion of Russo-Jewish students from the European universities began. Every year the oppression has become keener, so that today the Jewish student nearly everywhere stands before closed doors. The position of the Jewish student from Eastern Europe has become critical . . .

However great the need may be, we must not conceal the fact that it may not be materially diminished by a small university in Jerusalem. The university can only be a palliative. But it is a palliative of a very special kind. A considerable percentage, not to be belittled, of our youth would have an alma mater. Morally, the mere existence of a Jewish university would bring hope and comfort and strength to our youth. To the university project can be applied successfully and logically the argument of our entire movement. We make no claim that Zionism can supply a speedy cure for Jewish poverty. Zionism is the bread of tomorrow, and therefore it is an urgent duty to prepare it today. The university is a stone in this structure of the future, which we mean to set up for the new Jewry in Palestine. That it may become such, we must begin earnestly now.

What are the prospects before the alumni of the university? Turkey and the whole Orient are an immense field of activity. The capacity of these lands will grow as they are developed, and if the education is adapted to the needs of the Orient a market is ready. The alumni of our university will be our best pioneers materially and morally. We shall furnish Turkey with the trained men she needs. A university in which the Turkish and Arab populations are accepted would help establish good relations with our neighbors. That indicates the high political significance of the university . . .

A university's reputation, its capacity for work, and the value of its degrees will depend upon the scientific worth of its teachers. If we succeed in calling to the service of our university men of reputation, its status must rise at once and its graduates [will] have the same chances, even in Europe, as the Jewish graduates of a European university. There follows a conclusion weighty even from the practical standpoint: We must strive to attract young and promising talent and spend our money on the teaching personnel rather than on buildings and equipment. The teachers must be good researchers and free research must have full scope. This leads to the practical execution of our plan.

In Jerusalem there already exist some of the conditions necessary for the establishment of a medical faculty after a while. The activity of the Society of Jewish Physicians has laid the foundations of a bacteriological and pathological institute. Consolidate these institutions and it is not hard to conceive of them as the kernel of what will in the future become a good medical school . . . For the faculty of humanities the undertaking is much simpler . . .

It would be premature now to make definite proposals. The congress must settle the question of principle, and it will be the duty of its executive branch to work out the details.

One of the most important questions of principle, which must be discussed at once, is what the language of instruction shall be. There can be no doubt now that the science of Judaism and most humanities can be taught in Hebrew. If any doubts are raised, they are directed to the mathematical and physical sciences. True, the natural sciences are taught at the Jaffa *Gymnasium* in Hebrew, but it is still debatable whether at this point in time Hebrew possesses an adequate terminology for higher instruction and whether the scientific quality of the instruction would not suffer seriously if Hebrew were at once introduced. I do not think this an insurmountable difficulty . . . The flexibility of Hebrew makes it very amenable for the expression of scientific ideas, and if the teachers are given sufficient time to prepare, they can gradually adjust to their difficult task. Possibly in the first years there might be more than one language of instruction, but the aim should be a complete Hebraization . . . From what has been said an important practical requirement follows: the extension and development of our national library in Jerusalem. However modest our university at the beginning, for her existence and her proper development, and particularly for the creation of Hebrew textbooks, a good library will be indispensable. Our national library would be a foundation stone of the university . . .

The proposals I have to lay before congress are simple in their nature. We are all aware of the enormity of the undertaking, and we desire to avoid launching projects into the world without a material foundation or means of realization. We believe, however, that the time has come for earnest preparation . . . [89]

Following a lengthy debate, which continued until the last day of the congress (September 9), a resolution was carried, with three dissenters, charging the Actions Committee "to form a commission to undertake the preparatory work necessary for the foundation of a Hebrew university in Jerusalem."[90] The first contribution for the project of one hundred thousand marks was given, anonymously, by David Wolffsohn.[91] Having resumed his role as chairman of the steering committee, Weizmann now brought before the congress the slate of the new SAC, which, besides Warburg, Hantke, Jacobson, Levin, and Sokolow, also included

Yehiel Tschlenow, who had expressed his willingness to move to Berlin.[92] Weizmann himself was reelected to GAC.[93] Given the general tenor and theme of the congress, it was appropriate that Chaim Nachman Bialik gave the last speech in Hebrew, congratulating the congress on its decision regarding the university. It was an end of an era in the history of the Zionist congresses and the movement. Wolffsohn, who bid the delegates farewell and "Auf Wiedersehen" at the Twelfth Zionist Congress, died a year later, in September 1914.

For Weizmann the Eleventh Zionist Congress represented another milestone in his advancement within the movement. Never before was he so much a part of the "establishment" and so little involved in controversy as at this congress. More important, the first stage in the implementation of his university scheme had been completed successfully, thus overcoming its most difficult test. True, the resolution itself was vague and rather innocuous, specifying no dates and not even defining the nature of the institution to be founded. Yet this is exactly why it sailed so smoothly through the congress despite dire predictions to the contrary. It gave Weizmann the utmost flexibility in maneuvering the project past various pitfalls, affording him an opportunity to interpret the mandate from the congress in light of new circumstances as they arose. Now that he had an agreement in principle, he would, as always, interpret it in his own way, adjusting and changing it to fit new situations. He had successfully learned from past experience that in order to win agreement on any matter which could possibly be divisive it was best not to press the principles in which he believed too forcefully at the very outset. Later a consensus would be reached when the movement was faced with a fait accompli. It was therefore with an easy heart that he could spend four weeks on the Continent, the first three on a walking tour through the Tyrol and Swiss Alps with Vera, Norah Schuster, and Harry Sacher, and the last at the Bern Institute for Dairy Farming and Bacteriology, headed by Professor Robert Burri.

He returned to Manchester early in October 1913. While he was in Burri's laboratory, Vera had moved the household from 57 Birchfields Road to 30 Brunswick Road. Thus, ironically, at the very moment in his career when he had lost the professorship and a lucrative consulting job with Strange's company, he was finally able to afford a fine house in a neighborhood in which Manchester's academic and social elite chose to live. It was not quite Victoria Park, where the Schusters resided, but Professor Samuel Alexander lived at number 24 Brunswick Road and the former occupant of the new Weizmann residence was none other than F. E. Weiss, the vice chancellor of the University of Manchester.[94] Charles Dreyfus and C. P. Scott, the editor of *The Manchester Guardian,* lived within walking distance, and quite a few members of the elite South Manchester Synagogue[95] resided in Weizmann's new neighborhood. The house itself was comfortable. It contained a large drawing room, with three bedrooms on the second floor and two on the third floor. It had a semidetached garage and—most important—a very large square garden. At last Vera could have her own garden parties.[96]

Weizmann had little time to enjoy the house. Upon his return from the Continent early in October 1913, he had to take account of a major crisis which had just begun to face the Zionist organization and which potentially threatened the success of the university project. This crisis, known as the "language debate" *(Sprachenkampf)*, has been the subject of extensive scholarly treatment and need only be briefly summarized in the present context.[97] The *Sprachenkampf* was rooted in the divergence of opinion between, on the one hand, the Yishuv and the Zionists—represented by Ahad Ha'Am, Shmarya Levin, and Yehiel Tschlenow—and, on the other, the Hilfsverein—represented by Paul Nathan and James Simon—concerning the language of instruction in the Technicum and the secondary school which was to be attached to it. On June 8, 1913, Levin had suggested to the curatorium that Hebrew be the language of general instruction in the secondary school and that at least one subject at the Technicum also be taught in Hebrew.[98] At its meeting of October 26, 1913, the curatorium rejected this demand,[99] apparently under pressure from the German Foreign Office.[100] Instead, a motion by Paul Nathan—suggesting that no official language be prescribed in either institution, but that Hebrew would be emphasized except in the natural sciences and technical subjects, where the language of instruction was to be German—was carried.[101] After consultation with SAC,[102] Ahad Ha'Am, Levin, and Tschlenow resigned on the grounds that the resolution passed could not be reconciled with their national ideals.[103]

Following the decision of the curatorium on October 26, 1913, the Hilfsverein teachers and students in Palestine—with the support and encouragement of SAC—launched a campaign—which was accompanied by resignations, protest meetings, and strikes—for control of the educational system in the country, with Hebrew as the sole language of instruction. The Merkaz ha-Morim (Palestinian Teachers Association) decided to establish its own schools,[104] with SAC allocating funds for a secondary school in Haifa, a boys' school in Jaffa, and a teacher-training program in Jerusalem.[105] After months of acrimonious debate in Palestine and on the Continent between the Zionists and those who supported the Hilfsverein, the American members of the curatorium (Adler, Kraus, Mark, Marshall, Schechter, Schiff, Strauss, and Sulzberger) demanded a compromise, which both sides accepted, providing that the language of instruction in the Technicum would be left to the decision of the curatorium, with the understanding that Hebrew, as far as practicable, would be predominant, with its adoption within seven years for all courses except those lacking appropriate instructors and textbooks.[106] At its meeting of February 22, 1914, the curatorium decided to abandon its plan to establish a secondary school affiliated with the Technicum and accepted, with minor alterations, the suggestion made by the American members, further resolving to replace with other Zionists the three who

had resigned, two of whom would join the curatorium's executive committee.[107]

The Zionists viewed this outcome as a victory,[108] but the Hilfsverein
was far from happy with the decision and used various opportunities to
recoup its loss of control of the Technicum.[109] Moreover, the *Sprachenkampf* contributed to the intense struggle waged at that very time in Germany between Zionists and anti-Zionists. After more than a decade of
cooperation with the Zionistische Vereinigung fuer Deutschland, many
of the leading members of the Hilfsverein now openly joined the anti-
Zionist camp. Quite a few of its leading members signed their names to
the full-page anti-Zionist advertisement which appeared on February 5,
1914, in Germany's leading newspapers.[110] Yet the *Sprachenkampf* was
functional for both the German Zionists and the movement as a whole.
It provided, among other things, an opportunity for the World Zionist
Organization to finally gain control of the educational institutions in Palestine and to infuse its own ranks with new ideals and goals. Lastly, it
gave the movement an opportunity to refute the oft-heard charge that it
was Germano-centric not only organizationally but ideologically as well.

Though he was clearly in sympathy with the Yishuv and SAC's struggle in the language debate, Weizmann was far from happy with the way
it unfolded.[111] Weizmann was not at all eager to alienate the German Jews,
whose financial support he sought. Moreover, in line with his pragmatic
approach to the university, he was less dogmatic than Ussishkin as to
the language of instruction. Thus, even before the struggle between the
Hilfsverein and the Zionists had erupted into a major crisis,[112] Weizmann remained equivocal about the language to be used at the university in Jerusalem, pointing to the difficulties in using Hebrew for the
mathematical and physical sciences.[113] Weizmann must therefore have
understood the Hilfsverein position on the issue of the language of instruction at the Technicum since, motivations apart, his own views were
not radically divergent from its own.[114] Obviously he could not express
such sentiments openly to SAC.[115] His strategy in dealing with the language debate was threefold: to ignore it personally as much as possible,
to dissociate the university project completely from the *Sprachenkampf*,
and to use the crisis itself to the advantage of the Hebrew university in
Jerusalem.

Weizmann had been Ahad Ha'Am's deputy on the curatorium since
June 1910, but he had no intention of replacing his mentor after the latter's resignation.[116] This was not merely a question of loyalty to Ahad
Ha'Am; his own involvement would have meant that the university project
would, *ipso facto*, also be embroiled in the dispute. From the outset,
Weizmann viewed the *Sprachenkampf* in terms of how it would affect the
university project. "We must now triple our energies and establish the
Hebrew University," he wrote to Ahad Ha'Am within a week after the
curatorium's momentous decision.[117] The *Sprachenkampf* was for Weizmann an issue that did not directly concern him; while describing

to Shmarya Levin his own involvement in the university affairs, Weizmann wrote, "I know that you are very much absorbed by *your* school-dispute. . . ."[118] That is, he viewed the *Sprachenkampf* as Levin's affair; he had his own concerns. To be sure, in the early weeks of "the unfortunate affair with the Technicum," which he believed would set many Jews against the Zionist movement, he could still see a silver lining in the controversy. "I think it will make people understand that in Palestine only . . . Jewish things can be created. . . ." The affair, he wrote to Magnes, served to put the Zionists on guard against undue German influence in Palestine and against the notion that a language other than Hebrew could ultimately be the language of instruction in Jewish institutions.[119] In public Weizmann continued to maintain a posture of strong support for SAC's activities on behalf of the Merkaz ha-Morim. At the EZF conference in Leeds in February 1914, he condemned the attitude of the Hilfsverein and was largely responsible for passage of a resolution to collect money for the Zionist schools.[120] As time went on, however, and as the dispute assumed ever larger proportions, affecting Jews in Europe and America as well, Weizmann became increasingly worried. After all, Jacob Schiff and Nathan Straus were German-born and far removed from Zionist ideology, and if they were to exert their influence among the American and European philanthropists and urge them to withdraw support from Zionist enterprises, what would happen to the university project? Moreover, SAC's decision to support Jewish schools in Palestine could only result in the dissipation of funds allocated to the Hebrew university. "The Technicum affair appears to have become a very bad business and I am afraid we have got ourselves involved in a fight from which we are going to emerge with heavy losses. . . . I wonder where we shall get the necessary money for the schools [in Palestine]. The fit of protests will pass quickly and leave us standing with a heavy burden on our shoulders that will incapacitate us for further action. I well understand that the SAC was forced into the fight by the Palestinians, but it will have to stop in good time."[121]

Weizmann was particularly concerned lest Paul Ehrlich, a German patriot, be influenced by the debates raging in Germany around the topic of Zionism. Weizmann warned SAC that "a strong anti-Zionist wind is now blowing in Germany. I am afraid that Ehrlich will catch cold from it."[122] But by February 1914, when Weizmann wrote these lines, Ehrlich seemed to have been able to withstand pressure—if such was applied—to abandon the university scheme. Moreover, Weizmann's success in disengaging the university project from the publicity and notoriety which accompanied the *Sprachenkampf* and other debates in Germany made it possible for men like Paul Ehrlich, Leopold Landau, Nathan Straus, and others with German affinities to continue their ties to the project without compromising their own positions. For both tactical and psychological reasons Weizmann brought up the subject of the *Sprachenkampf* only when absolutely necessary. The project itself had, in any case, progressed to a stage where even Ehrlich could not do it mortal damage. In the few months since the Eleventh Zionist Congress, Weizmann had worked relentlessly and systematically to move the project a major step forward.

Soon after the congress Weizmann received expressions of support from many quarters. The first to write was Judah Leon Magnes, who warmly praised his moderate and carefully crafted speech at the congress.[123] Israel Abrahams and Charles Fox co-chaired a meeting of Jewish students at Cambridge which passed a resolution in support of the university project.[124] Sir Philip Magnus, at that time an M.P., a leader of Anglo-Jewry, and an anti-Zionist, expressed support for the founding of a Hebrew university.[125] In Baltimore, Maryland, a Committee for the Securing of Funds for the Jewish University was established in October 1913.[126] Even Ussishkin made it known through intermediaries that he wished to be included in the preparatory work for the university.[127] Some eighty student societies from all over Europe, representing twenty-five hundred members, sent Weizmann a joint declaration of support for the university in March 1914.[128] Weizmann's propaganda speeches in Paris and elsewhere were well received.[129] Moreover, during this very period he gained the firm friendship and loyal support of four young men: Leonard Stein, a lawyer just out of Oxford; Selig Brodetsky, a mathematician who was just beginning his career as a lecturer at Bristol University; and Israel Sieff and Simon Marks, who were already making an impact on the world of business.[130] Together with Ahad Ha'Am, Julius Simon, Harry Sacher, and Leon Simon they formed a loyal advisory group with which Weizmann discussed his ideas and strategies.

His most important challenge, of course, was gaining Baron Edmond de Rothschild's support and financial backing for the Hebrew university. Weizmann was fully aware that achieving this goal required different tactics. The baron was a very private and authoritarian person. This meant that those protecting his privacy had to first be persuaded of the importance of the project and the seriousness of its progenitor, and be willing to listen more and talk less. Weizmann understood these requirements intuitively and acted accordingly. He turned to Joseph Spanien, one of the pioneers of French Zionism, who was also closely associated with the baron. Together with Jacques Bramson, who had ties with the baron, Spanien worked to gain Weizmann access to Rothschild. On October 30, 1913, he notified Weizmann that the baron was ready to help finance the project at a later stage[131] and that a meeting could be arranged with Gaston Wormser, the baron's adviser, and probably with the baron himself.[132] Weizmann planned for these meetings carefully, urging SAC to establish a structural framework for the project.[133] SAC approved Weizmann's basic organizational plan, though it expressed some reservations about beginning the university with a medical school.[134] At the meeting of GAC which followed, that body constituted itself as the University Preparatory Committee. It also established four subcommittees and a working committee composed of SAC members plus Weizmann and Menahem Ussishkin.[135] Weizmann invited Heinrich Loewe, a German

Zionist and a professional librarian, to head the university's library department.[136] Disregarding SAC's reservations, Weizmann continued to advocate the idea of a medical school up until his first meeting with the baron.[137] He described to Ussishkin how, as the next step in pursuing the university project, "we select for these sections [subcommittees] people in agreement with the basic principles, i.e., the Hebrew language and Jerusalem, from the scientific, political world, etc., of non-Zionists. The sections draw up a plan and carry out preliminary propaganda, to begin with only *von Mann zu Mann*, touring city after city and working on interested individuals. This done, they proceed to found the 'Association for the Hebrew University.' This Association has *Vereine* throughout the world; it has a Central Committee that builds the University and is its proprietor. . . ."[138]

On January 3, 1914, dressed in coattails and a top hat, Weizmann met Baron Edmond de Rothschild for three quarters of an hour. The meeting was a success: The baron promised to contribute funds.[139] At the same time, he also destroyed Weizmann's carefully worked out plan. Rothschild made it clear that he was only interested in a research institute similar to the Pasteur Institute[140] or a Rockefeller Institute, "where about 30 or 40 good men would work at scientific research," publish it from Jerusalem and gradually attract pupils, and so in time form a University.[141] On the very day on which he met the baron, Nathan Straus cabled Weizmann that he would be willing to donate a plot of land for the university.[142] When the working committee of the university met three days later in Berlin, it decided to purchase a tract of land on the Mount of Olives in Jerusalem and to begin negotiations with the Turkish government for the purpose of obtaining a concession for the site from them.[143] Weizmann was empowered to continue negotiating with the baron and Straus.[144]

Even under normal circumstances it might not have been an easy task to bring Straus and the baron to an agreement on so complicated an issue. Given the *Sprachenkampf*, it was all the more difficult. The baron, a firm French patriot, was pleased about the difficulties the Hilfsverein was having in Palestine. His hostility toward the Hilfsverein and its control over the Technicum "was based partly on his passionate advocacy of Hebrew, rather than German, as a 'national tongue,' but partly also on his dislike of the *Kaiser Juden* and their efforts to find a place in the sun for their community."[145] If anything, the conflict may have made him more receptive toward the university project. His anti-German sentiments came through in the discussion with Weizmann. "If Ehrlich works in Frankfurt, it is of no value to us; he will be eaten up by the Germans." More importantly, he advised Weizmann to see Nathan Straus and to "dégager M. Straus des mains des allemands." Straus, however, had strong pro-German sentiments and affinities and could not easily be disengaged from them. Moreover, he had no desire to dissolve the identity of his own health institute in the baron's research institute.[146] Nevertheless, Weizmann enlisted Magnes's help in persuading Straus to cooperate with the baron rather than with the German Society for Combatting Malaria in Jerusalem, with whom Paul Ehrlich was also associated.[147] Though noncommittal for the moment on the health station, Straus merely reiterated his readiness to donate his land in Jerusalem for the university.[148] Next, the baron wished to have Paul Ehrlich's imprimatur on the research institute, which Weizmann obtained. Later, he also requested detailed estimates on the costs involved in building such an institution, and Weizmann quickly made inquiries at the Speyer Institute and elsewhere. Above all, the baron insisted on discretion and in keeping his name out of the news. As Weizmann explained it, the baron was a Jewish "nationalist with a distrust of the national movement, and of the people . . . He wanted everything to be done quietly, by order, without a national movement. He disliked the paraphernalia of the organization."[149] The baron was also worried about the political interpretation that the Turks would assign to a university project, especially if Rothschild's name was linked to it. In the final analysis such a public, splashy project could harm the university and the Zionists. When reports did leak out to the press,[150] Weizmann published denials in *Die Welt* and *Hatzfirah*, claiming that "the alleged negotiations between the baron, Professor Ehrlich and myself are fabricated . . . Furthermore, I know nothing about a donation by the baron to the university."[151]

What to do, though, about the baron's most important demand that the idea of a university be abandoned, for the time being, in favor of a research institute? How to explain the fact that Weizmann, who began work on the project with a vision of a full-fledged university—"*Die Zionsuniversitaet auf dem Berge Zion!*," as he put it—later scaling it down to a medical school, was now willing to accept a research facility akin to the Pasteur or Rockefeller institutes? Weizmann was able to change his view because of his pragmatic approach. The most important thing for the moment was to draw the baron into collaborating with the Zionists. He knew well that the baron would not abandon a project which had the Rothschild name associated with it. Thus, unlike Herzl, Weizmann was willing to listen to the baron and was not personally wounded when the latter dismissed his projects as unworkable. Of course, the baron, too, had a much more positive view of the Zionists since he had first met Herzl more than a decade and a half ago. The change of attitude and the fact that the baron was being asked to finance a particular institute—not help launch a movement—made Weizmann's task somewhat easier. Perhaps the clue to Weizmann's approach to the baron may be found in his own words. Even before he went to see the baron, Weizmann conceded that, with the exception of the Hebrew language and Jerusalem, "we are quite ready to compromise on everything else."[152]

As he began to accept the baron's idea, Weizmann quoted in its defense Sokolow's words that "if the Baron would think that one has to start with an astronomical observatory we would have to take his view."[153] These were tactical considerations, but as he was seeking justification for his own radical reorientation, his tactics were transformed into an ideological point of view. Three weeks after his meeting with the baron, Weizmann wrote, "I consider the Rothschild proposal simply magnificent. Just think of it: we succeed, let us assume, in establishing a kind of Pasteur Institute or Rockefeller Institute in miniature, 20–25 capable men work there in various fields, biology, chemistry, physics, bacteriology, serology, etc. They publish their own Journal, gradually accumulate a library, make a name for themselves . . . this is the most natural and in our circumstances the most practicable way."[154] By April 1914 he called the idea of building a teaching institute right away "a dangerous, deadly point of view." The *only* way to build a university, he now insisted, was through a research institute which, in time, would evolve into a university.[155] Though there is no direct evidence for this assertion, it is quite possible that Weizmann's enthusiasm for the baron's idea was also fueled by his own overriding interest in research rather than in teaching. Be this as it may, it is clear that the baron's wishes would have been decisive no matter what he proposed.

Judah Magnes, who only in December 1913 had insisted once again that the university in Jerusalem must begin with a school of arts and science,[156] was now won over by Weizmann to adopt the baron's notion of a research institute.[157] Ahad Ha'Am supported the idea wholeheartedly.[158] At the end of February 1914 GAC also approved the founding of a research institute in Jerusalem[159] and SAC authorized Weizmann to negotiate for its establishment as the first stage of the future university.[160] In the final analysis they all came to the conclusion that Sokolow and Weizmann were correct in their assessments. The baron's very participation in the project was an asset the Zionists could not afford to disregard. From past experience they knew that once Rothschild was involved in a project, he tended to support it until it was firmly established. In principle, a research institute with an orientation toward the natural sciences was not all that far removed from Weizmann's own plan for a medical school, though the baron eliminated from his plan any teaching faculty. What was important for the moment, Weizmann reasoned, was to collaborate with the baron, to engage him in the project; in time he could no doubt be persuaded that the research institute would form the nucleus for a future university.[161] As it turned out, it was a greater obstacle than Weizmann or GAC had anticipated.

Since the baron was on an extended tour of Palestine from January through March 1914, Weizmann had plenty of time to prepare for their next meeting. Armed with a thick folder—it included letters from Paul Ehrlich and other distinguished scientists, messages from Nathan Straus concerning the transfer of land to the university, as well as a detailed project which had previously been inspected and signed by Leopold Landau and Ehrlich[162]—Weizmann met the baron in Paris on March 27, 1914. The proposal itself was for a research institute, which was to include departments of chemistry, physics, and experimental medicine, with construction costs of 2.2 million francs and an annual budget of 600,000 francs. Following the meeting, Wormser intimated that the baron would contribute 500,000 francs for the construction of the institute and about 150,000 to 200,000 annually, but the baron refused to hear about the idea of a university.[163] Though he was concerned about the baron's refusal to accept the research institute as the embryo for the future university, Weizmann was also heartened by the baron's impressions of his recent trip, which he summed up thusly: "Without me the Zionists could not have accomplished anything, without the Zionists my project would have died."[164] Nor was he discouraged that the baron was contributing less than the Zionists had expected. "He will give later. He always starts with a little, and then becomes involved. He is a very wise old man, but a terribly *meshugener fish*. He talks enough for 20 and never lets anyone get a word in, which makes it very difficult to convince him, and one is obliged to listen to a lot of nonsense before putting a word in. All the same he's a darling and it's a pity that he is so old."[165]

In the period before their next meeting,[166] Weizmann continued to present Wormser and the baron with budgets of institutes similar to the one envisioned in Palestine, as well as an even more comprehensive memorandum on the entire project. Despite the baron's warning that he would not contribute a single sou for a university, he held his ground that the research institute be seen as the university's nucleus. The showdown came at their meeting on April 9, 1914, when the baron brought up the idea of a microbiological institute. He abandoned this notion when Weizmann pointed out that this was useless in Palestine, which did not have subsidiary sciences like physics and chemistry.[167] It was a difficult session. The baron brought up one argument after another against associating his research institute with a university: The Great Powers and Turkey would be alerted; the university scheme could harm Palestinian colonization; and so forth. Finally Weizmann told the baron that he had no right to deprive the Jewish youth, who were hoping for a university within this institution; if he did so, thousands would seek baptism out of despair. Thus, despite the danger of being misunderstood in Turkey, they must preserve the idea of the university. This apparently hit the mark, and the baron gave in. Since the latter now agreed in principle, it was decided not to work out the exact formula right away. When Weizmann told Rothschild that he hoped the university would be completed in ten years, the latter replied, "But that's much too long."[168] Moreover, the baron reiterated a wish he had harbored for some time, namely, that James, his thirty-six-year-old son, be involved in the university project. The "Old Man," as Weizmann referred to him, saw this project as a means of interesting James in his own Jewish tradition and in Palestine. That same afternoon Wormser arranged for Weizmann to meet James. Weizmann scored his second success of the day. "It's much easier to talk to this gentleman. He is 40 [sic] years of age, very sensible and simple. We discussed all the details and arrived at complete agreement."[169] James Rothschild—or Jimmy, as the Zionists called him—would become Weizmann's close collaborator for many years to come. Weizmann and SAC could now proceed to form a university committee which would include James de Rothschild, Gaston Wormser, and Paul Ehrlich as the baron's representatives.

For the past few months Weizmann had been working very hard on the university project. Since January 1914 he had been on the Continent once or twice every month to see the baron, Ehrlich, Landau, and to attend meetings of GAC. He even found time for public appearances.[170] His accomplishments in the brief period since the Eleventh Zionist Congress were impressive, and as he celebrated the Passover holiday with his family in Manchester he had good reason to feel proud and content. He could have also expected some praise from Zionist circles for having almost single-handedly persuaded Baron Edmond de Rothschild to collaborate with the World Zionist Organization. The prospects for the future were even rosier. Instead of receiving praise, he suddenly found himself defending his greatest Zionist achievement.[171] Vladimir Jabotinsky, who had also been co-opted into the university working committee, wrote a letter to that committee on April 10, 1914, in which he objected to the concept of a research institute under conditions imposed by Rothschild, whose participation was not essential, whose contribution was inadequate, and whose name could not be used because of his reservations concerning a university. Furthermore, Jabotinsky considered that research institutes were not acceptable unless they were regarded as the nucleus of a university adapted to teaching purposes and the Hebrew language. The SAC letter which accompanied Jabotinsky's own letter also expressed fears of undue Rothschild influence over the project and quoted Tschlenow's opinion that the agreement with the baron was unacceptable and that negotiations should be reopened.[172]

Weizmann was stupefied at the unexpected turn of events. Was this the thanks for months of patient and skillful negotiations? In a long letter to SAC he reminded his colleagues that he had been careful to obtain their authorization for his negotiations at every step of the way. If they had qualms about how matters were proceeding, there had been plenty of time in the past few months to call a halt to them—"the gentlemen are coming one train too late." He then directly attacked Jabotinsky and his colleagues in the sharpest terms.

They want a teaching institute straight away because an urgency exists in Russia. I stress with the greatest emphasis that this is a dangerous, deadly point of view . . . We fought against the utopia of the Charter and educated the party—to some degree at least—to view Zionism as a historic evolution. Now, in the realization of the *greatest* national project, those same fighters again want to tread the ground of beliefs in miracles, of Zionism living by the grace of anti-Semitism.

We shall certainly experience miracles. For a time we may perhaps be able to persuade some *"bourgeois,"* as Jabotinsky calls them, that we are going to have a university of our own; the glorious prospect of Jewish diplomas with the Star of David can be held before their eyes and they will pay for that;

one million, two million, three million roubles will be obtained . . . Then the professors we have "bred" and "prepared" will go *schnorring,* as they do for the [Herzliah] Gymnasium, for Bezalel . . .

If the gentlemen believe that they can conjure books, a language of instruction, professors, money, science, out of the ground, let them find bliss in their belief. *Epater le bourgeois [sic]* is easy; at the same time, however, it involves repelling the others, the perceptive ones, who are well aware of the value of bluff and a one-day housefly . . .

The principle of the research institute becomes clearer the longer one reflects on it. Precisely in the circumstances prevailing with us, with the lack of all the necessary prerequisites, the smooth preparation of professors, books, terminology is *only* possible within a research institute. For us, from the national point of view, from the point of view of the conquest of the land, that part of the university to be realized in the research institute, which is, as it were, the higher, purely scientific part, is the most important and not the teaching, i.e., applied part. As the highest intellectual center, as the assembly point of Jewish creativity, the research institute is more than a university, higher than a university . . .

Consider only one possibility which is not utopian: one of our workers gains the Nobel Prize. Or take another, simpler case: the work of our institute will be recognized, quoted, our journal displayed in all universities. . . .[173]

That same day he also poured his heart out to Shmarya Levin, a leading member of the working committee: "If the views of Jabotinsky-Tschlenow are shared by the other members of the Arbeits-Ausschuss, as is to be foreseen,[174] I consider the University cause killed from the beginning . . . Jabotinsky's letter wounded me deeply by its lack of seriousness about one of the most important questions . . . All this is so painful to me that I can't carry on."[175]

But at this point in his life his moods of depression over setbacks in the movement were becoming shorter, if not less painful. Though his disagreements with Vladimir Jabotinsky continued, he was soon back at work. In any case, the university scheme had generated its own momentum. Early in April 1914 Arthur Ruppin informed Weizmann that he had already begun to buy land on Mount Scopus in the names of David Yellin, Judah L. Magnes, and Weizmann.[176] The project was further discussed at the working committee meetings on June 6 and 10, 1914,[177] and by GAC, which sat as a preparatory committee on June 7.[178] Jabotinsky argued at the meeting against cooperation with the baron, while Weizmann, supported by Yehiel Tschlenow, Victor Jacobson, and Hans Gideon Heymann, presented the opposite viewpoint. It was decided to charge the preparatory committee with devising a scheme for a medical faculty, as well as other faculties. It was also agreed to try to persuade the baron to change the designation of the project from Research Institute *(Forschungs-Institut)* to Institute of Science *(Wissenschaftliches Institut).* Weizmann thus received, after the fact, the approval of the GAC for negotiations he had conducted all along with their authorization. Magnes, too, wrote in early June with some good news: Nathan Straus had agreed to

merge his health bureau in Jerusalem with the research institute. Moreover, a number of people at the Rockefeller Institute had expressed interest in the project.[179]

All was set for a meeting with the baron's representatives. At the
working committee meeting in Berlin on July 18 and 19, 1914, Weizmann
was charged with drafting a memorandum. The following points were
to serve as a framework for discussions with the baron's representatives:
The preparatory committee was to inaugurate the university with the establishment of scientific institutes in which the official language would
be Hebrew, though publications were also to appear in a European language; the House of Rothschild was to contribute to construction and
maintenance costs; the institutes were to be the property of the university once it received legal status; all matters connected with the institutes
were to be supervised by a committee composed of representatives of
the World Zionist Organization and representatives of Baron Edmond
de Rothschild.[180] The meeting of representatives of both sides was to take
place on August 12, 1914.[181] Nothing remained but the signing of papers. The rumblings of war were already audible when Chaim, Vera, and
Benjy Weizmann left England on July 30, passing through Paris the following day on their way to Switzerland. England's declaration of war,
which became effective August 4, came while they were vacationing in
Champex (Valais).[182] They were only able to return to England on August 28, 1914.

World War I dashed Weizmann's carefully constructed plans for a uni-
versity/research institute. Yet the foundation for the project had been
firmly established, and at the first opportune moment, with the war not
yet concluded, ground was broken on Mount Scopus in a moving ceremony celebrating the establishment of the Hebrew University. Perhaps
more important was the fact that by 1914 Weizmann had matured as a
scientist and a Zionist, struggling to find a balance between his two interests and, eventually, to harness chemistry in the service of Zion. To
find the synthesis between the two was not always easy, as he explained
to Julius Simon: ". . . it is inconceivable that I should give up things
here [in Manchester]. First, because I have many interesting problems in
the workshop through which I could well make a name for myself. Secondly, because for the sake of Zionism, too, and especially of my role in
the movement, I could not give up what I have achieved here. But serving two gods is unbelievably difficult . . . I do not want to use high-
sounding expressions, but I assure you, dear Julius, I am the veritable
tightrope dancer and am making desperate efforts to keep both going
and do them both well . . ."[183]

Weizmann could not possibly foresee in June 1914 how close he was
to realizing some of his most cherished aspirations. World War I set the
scene for his full emergence as a Zionist leader; the road to leadership
was facilitated—as Weizmann had predicted for many years—by his discoveries in chemistry.

XVII

Conclusion

Louis Lipsky's well-known remarks about Weizmann as he appeared to the former in 1913 provide a useful starting point for an assessment of Weizmann on the eve of World War I:

> When I first met Dr. Weizmann at the Vienna Congress in 1913, he seemed, on the surface, to be an easygoing young man, playing a modest part in its proceedings. He made the impression of indifference and fatigue. He was seen sauntering through the streets of old Vienna, chatting with companions, visiting the cafes, drinking tea. He was still the promising young man who had crossed swords with Theodor Herzl in the first Congresses. Only his mournful eyes belied the superficial effect of the Bohemian. He had settled in England, but was alien to the conventional life of British Jewry and was already estranged from the disputes of the continental Zionist world . . .
>
> He was chairman of a committee called upon to settle internal problems. I sat in that committee and observed him for days. His rulings were a study in temperament. He was impatient with equivocations by delegates trained as lawyers and Talmudists. But he was meticulous and sharp in procedure. He had a penchant for Yiddish jests and made generous contributions to off-the-record observations. He was a partisan of the Russian group, but did not seem to be very much involved . . . In the meetings of the Russians the older men dominated. Dr. Weizmann stood in the rear of the hall where the caucuses were held, his eyes half closed, listening, rarely speaking. He was a shrewd debater, good at repartee; but there was no drive to him in Vienna. He seemed to be listening and waiting . . .[1]

Lipsky's memoir clearly indicates that as late as 1913 Weizmann had not yet become a dominant figure in the Zionist movement. Although he had been elected a member of the Grosses Aktions-Comité (1905), was a vice president of the English Zionist Federation, was chairman of the important Standing Committee during three successive congresses (1909, 1911, and 1913), and was consulted by the Zionist executive as their *Vertrauensmann* in England, he had not yet entered the inner circle of leadership. He had not been involved in a sustained fashion in the changes that took place within the World Zionist Organization after Herzl's death. He did not have a popular following, nor did he head even a minor organization or faction within the World Zionist movement, which could be seen as his power base. Although those active in Zionist affairs knew and respected him as a man of sterling Zionist credentials, many other Eastern and Western Zionists had earned equal standing by virtue of their personal qualities and service. It is not surprising, therefore, that when World War I broke out Weizmann was not viewed immediately as a potential leader who could chart a successful course for Zionism through the turbulent times that lay ahead.

Weizmann's ascension to a preeminent position within the World Zionist Organization was apparently not the natural culmination of his own activities and services within the movement. Even within the shaky English Zionist Federation movement, others were seen as more appropriate representatives of the World Zionist Organization in its negotiations with Great Britain.[2] Some even viewed Weizmann's initiatives as a breach of Zionist discipline, as the actions of a usurper.[3] World War I upset many well-founded and established principles concerning rank, priority, and order in the Zionist movement. Circumstances coalesced to give Weizmann a position of leadership within a relatively brief period, and it is indisputable that he acquitted himself well in his new role.

Weizmann's development as a Zionist before 1914 can be seen roughly in terms of five phases which overlap somewhat. Each phase occurred in a different geographic location whose particular milieu and social circle left its mark on the forty-year-old Weizmann.

The dominant theme of the first eleven years in Motol was an intensive and exclusively Jewish upbringing. It was here that the young boy first heard of the beginnings of the Hibbat Zion and became aware of the need for the liberation of the Jewish nation.

In Pinsk, between 1885 and 1892, Weizmann's emotions and feelings became firmly anchored in the ideology of the Hibbat Zion. It was there that he acquired the regular habit of organizational activity.

As a student in the Charlottenburg Polytechnic in Berlin, between 1893 and 1897, Weizmann's ideological commitments and cultural identity were clearly defined under the impact of his Russian-Jewish peer group.

During the second part of his sojourn in Switzerland (1897–1904), as a *Privat-Dozent* in Geneva, Weizmann became a youth leader in his own right and began to develop both the skills of and the taste for a leadership role. Though for the most part he was still under instructions from his elders in the movement, he began to articulate and shape the views of his youth cohort.

It was only in Manchester, where he spent the ten years between 1904 and 1914, that Weizmann—detached from both the continental Zionists and Anglo-Jewry's Zionist leadership—began to sever his emotional and ideological dependence on the regional leaders in Russia. Guided only by Ahad Ha'Am—another lonely émigré—Weizmann began to develop his own, more independent Zionist weltanschauung. From his Manchester base Weizmann formulated his own position and entered the world of adult Zionist politics as a responsible and mature leader.[4]

The historiography of the past two decades favors giving Weizmann major credit for the attainment of the Balfour Declaration. Circumstances during the war permitted external forces to alter the hierarchical structure within the movement and thrust Weizmann into center stage of negotiations with Great Britain. These circumstances coalesced with his personal drive for power and leadership. What were the qualities of personality, experience, and ideology which prepared Weizmann for the task?

The most notable ingredient in Weizmann's makeup was his unqualified dedication to Zionism. Apart from Zionism and chemistry, Weizmann had few interests. Like Herzl, he believed that ideas could move people to action. Though he was more of a realist than Herzl, he also believed that just and important causes were bound to succeed, even in the face of great obstacles. Weizmann's single-minded determination insulated him from other processes which might interfere with his plans. This single-mindedness in the face of all obstacles also required courage and daring. It was no mean thing for a very junior academic to try to establish a university without any financial support from the World Zionist Organization. Only a man sure of the importance of his project could pursue it with such relentlessness and energy.

Weizmann has been described by Robert Weltsch, his friend and lifelong admirer, as "a demon, typically Russian, full of contradictions, something out of a novel by Dostoyevsky. His split personality contained a satanic impulse, like that of Ivan Karamazov."[5] Demon or not, when Weizmann was fired by an idea or cause he was absolutely relentless. He reveled in meaningful Zionist activity and did the work of an entire office staff—and his enthusiasm was contagious. The sheer physical capacity of a man who was often ailing and half the time suffered from "a case of nerves," as he put it, is astounding. Almost every year he undertook strenuous propaganda tours in Russia and the West. In those days it was de rigueur to hold debates that lasted three days, primarily because speeches that lasted less than an hour or two seemed superficial. Weizmann was often a major protagonist in such encounters with the Bund, Social Democrats, and the assimilationists. While campaigning for a cause, however few its supporters, he managed to convey the impression of speaking for a large and growing following. Often he spoke of an enterprise he had just begun—for example, the university vacation courses—as a fait accompli, aggrandizing his scheme and himself simultaneously. He understood the importance of publicity and public relations, and though the projects may have had little chance of success, he appreciated the importance of appearances and gave himself airs of leadership.

By temperament nervous, impulsive, and impatient,[6] he had the ability to wed his own goals to political and strategic possibilities and, if necessary, patiently take a backseat while others furthered his aims. He had the stamina to pursue a task or a project with tenacity over a long period of time—often exasperating his friends with a barrage of pleas and requests long after the project seemed to have deserved a decent burial. His colleagues often complied just to end the verbal and written onslaught. It is true that almost every one of his Zionist enterprises collapsed sooner or later, yet though he did not recognize it at the time, Weizmann himself had not totally failed. Projects such as the Democratic Faction and the student survey had gained him experience in organization and leadership. He had a chance to prove his skills as a political strategist and as an office manager. He made scores of contacts in both East and West. Moreover, he managed to involve young intellectuals in Zionist work, not only on the Continent but in England as well. His rise to leadership was not smooth and continuous. It proceeded in spurts. In its last phase he discovered that the foundations he had built in Geneva and Manchester among the younger generation bore fruit. His erstwhile collaborators, who had been on the margins of the movement or in opposition to its leadership at the turn of the century, had in the meantime risen to positions of power in the movement and supported Weizmann's policies.

Weizmann had the ability to immediately grasp original ideas and trends in the movement. He co-opted and soon was identified with them, often as if he had been their originator. He was sensitive to the slightest vibrations within the movement—and later also to general political trends—flexible in his political approach and quick to respond to new situations. He could analyze with force and clarity new social and political processes, set goals for meeting them, as well as outline the means for doing so. He did not build theoretical constructs, but always called for a defined and circumscribed action, providing priorities and organizational tools. In addition, Weizmann was able to recognize opportunities—for the movement as well as for himself. Once he did, he seized them with perfect timing. He was, as it were, finely attuned to the pulse of the Zionist movement.

It is interesting to observe how adaptable Weizmann was to his environment. A man who grew up in hostile Christian surroundings, with almost no personal contact with gentiles—except in his own work—was able, after 1904, to get along with British statesmen without undue complications. He was immediately well received by the British academic community, a process which, in turn, may have colored his perceptions of Christian-Jewish relations in England. While representing no one but himself, and hardly fluent in English, he gained access to some leading British politicians. Though he did not develop close ties with any of his Christian acquaintances until shortly before 1914, he soon grew accustomed to their company, language, mannerisms, and outlook on life. His professional standing placed him in the same class of gentile Britons which included England's ruling elite. He felt quite comfortable in the company of non-Jews, especially British gentiles.[7] His social and professional experience with this class undoubtedly prepared him for his negotiations after 1914. For many Weizmann was both the product and symbol of the encounter between East European Jewry and the West—in this case England. To this synthesis he contributed intellectual depth and brilliance, wit, and charm, while acquiring British civility and self-composure. It was in this congenial atmosphere that his Zionist and scientific ideas found their fullest expression.

In addition to the outward signs of acculturation, Weizmann possessed for both British gentiles and British Jews something that no native British Jew had: He personified the authentic Eastern Jew. He felt no ambivalence toward Jewish tradition, except for his resentment against extreme orthodoxy. Deeply influenced by the radical Russian revolutionaries, he was also a Jew free of any ghetto mentality or inferiority complex. He was a proud, unhyphenated, and uninhibited Jew[8] who, like Herzl, did not deny his Jewishness. On the contrary, he joked with gentiles about certain Jewish types without the slightest hint of apology, and was accepted by them without embarrassment. Though it became true in the formal sense only after 1911, when his friends controlled the World Zionist Organization, from the beginning Weizmann was viewed by both Jewish and gentile Englishmen as a representative of the world movement in Britain. Jews and gentiles saw him as the authoritative voice of East European Jewry. For his part, Weizmann continuously emphasized the difference between British Jews and himself and lived the life of a political émigré. This distance gave him the opportunity to express new ideas and drew into his orbit of influence those dissatisfied with the British Jewish and Zionist establishment.

Weizmann could speak to various constituencies in the movement with equally good credentials. His roots within and affinities for both Eastern and Western Jewry, his cultural work and firm belief in the importance of both practical and political tasks, and his long service to the movement prompted him to seek the widest possible consensus. Almost no other Zionist of his generation combined these qualities.

Added to this was his reputation as a first-rate scientist. Herzl had gained entry to the upper reaches of international diplomacy by virtue of his reputation as a journalist; Weizmann was eventually to gain entry by virtue of his scientific achievements. Both used their professions to advance the movement. Unlike Herzl, who first turned to the rich Jews and only later to the mases, Weizmann made the reverse journey, emerging, as it were, from among the masses and only much later hobnobbing with the well-to-do, powerful Jewish patricians. Like Herzl, he was by inclination an aristocrat. But coexisting with his contempt for the masses was an innate ability to move them through his folksy, intimate relations with the people.

Despite these small differences in orientation, both men were remarkably similar. Both preferred to conduct diplomacy single-handedly, sometimes without a proper mandate from the movement they led. The university project clearly demonstrates Weizmann's proclivity to work alone and establish contacts with notables and men who possessed the power to take immediate action. It also demonstrates that Weizmann understood intuitively what students of bureaucracy and social organizations have noted ever since, namely, that the person who controls the flow of information can often control an organization. Through his extensive correspondence, travels, and direct personal contacts, Weizmann placed himself in the center of activity and channeled major events in the direction that seemed most suitable to him. The founder of the Democratic Faction, who had often criticized Herzl for his undemocratic leadership, was later himself accused on the same count. The man who objected to Herzl's secret missions often informed his own colleagues of his negotiations after the fact. Both preferred to deal on a one-to-one basis with men of power, a trait that was evident in Weizmann even before his move to Manchester. Both spoke to statesmen not as timid intercessors *(shtadlanim)* but with authority and force. Like Herzl, Weizmann relied on his personal charm during negotiations with statesmen and felt equally justified in deviating from strict guidelines for these negotiations. Having criticized Herzl for making the Fourth Zionist Congress a showpiece in the English capital, Weizmann soon realized Britain's importance in the attainment of Zionist goals and acted on his convictions. Herzl had pointed the way but, paradoxically, it was left to Weizmann, the East-West Jew, to complete and complement in several significant areas the political actions of Herzl, the Western Jew. If Herzl laid some of the major ideological and organizational foundations of the movement, Weizmann's major contribution was to interpret, integrate, and synthesize these ideas in line with new developments within the World Zionist Organization. Eventually he converted these ideas into concrete action through skillful diplomacy.

Notes

I Origins

1. Shimon Yusuk, *Hurban Motoleh* (Jerusalem, 1957), pp. 3–5. The Swedish invasion actually began on July 29, 1655, with the conquest of Posen. See *The Cambridge History of Poland: to 1696*, ed. W. F. Reddaway et al. (Cambridge, 1950), pp. 519–25.
2. See Simon Dubnov, *History of the Jews*, vol. 4, trans. Moshe Spiegel (South Brunswick, N.J., 1971), pp. 29ff. See also Bernard D. Weinryb, "The Hebrew Chronicles on Bohdan Khmel'nyts'kyi and the Cossack-Polish War," *Harvard Ukrainian Studies* 1, no. 2 (June 1977): 153–77.
3. Yitzhak Nimzovitz, "Rabbi Ivan Smyoshkin the XIV," in *Hador*, September 25, 1955, p. 2.
4. See *Evreiskaia Entsiklopediia*, vol. 11, p. 344. This latter figure corresponds to the memoirs of the period, which list 200–250 Jewish families in Motol. See Chaim Weizmann, *Trial and Error* (New York, 1949), p. 3, and Shmuel Yarden, *Sipurah shel Motoleh* (Jerusalem, 1979), pp. 12–13.
5. Weizmann, *Trial and Error*, p. 3.
6. Oksana Irena Grabowica, "About Polesie," in Joseph Obreski, *The Changing Peasantry of Eastern Europe* (Cambridge, Mass., 1976), p. i.
7. Ibid., p. ii.
8. Ibid., p. iii.
9. Shmuel Yarden, *Sipurah shel Motoleh*, pp. 13–14.
10. See Zvulun Ravid, "Motoleh, ha-Ayarah shebah nolad Weizmann," *Hadoar*, no. 27, May 17, 1963, pp. 502–3. A popular saying in the district ran: "Fun Pinsk keyn Minsk, keyn Motoleh oif shabbes" ("When on the road, spend the Sabbath in Motol"). See "Pinsk noch'n ershten congress," *Haint*, May 9, 1937. Weizmann Archives (W.A.).
11. See Shaul Ginzburg, *Idishe Leiden in Tsarishen Russland* (New York, 1938). See also Simon Dubnov, *History of the Jews*, vol. 4.
12. On the origins of the Pale of Settlement, see Richard Pipes, "Catherine II and the Jews: The Origins of the Pale of Settlement," *Soviet Jewish Affairs* 5 (1975): 3–20, and J. D. Klier, "The Ambiguous Legal Status of Russian Jewry in the Reign of Catherine II," *Slavic Review* 35 (September 1976): 504–17.
13. On the determinants of the high growth rate of the Jewish population in the Pale, see Jacques Silber, "Some Demographic Characteristics of the Jewish Population in Russia at the End of the Nineteenth Century," *Jewish Social Studies* 42, nos. 3–4 (Summer–Fall 1980): 269–80.

14. Jacob Lestschinsky, "Ha-Reka ha-Kalkali shel Thum ha-Moshav la-Yehudim be-Russyah," *Heavar* 1 (1953): 31–44. See also Ezra Mendelsohn, *Class Struggle in the Pale* (Cambridge, 1970).

15. Jewish Colonization Association, *Recueil de Matériaux sur la Situation Economique des Israélites de Russie* (d'Après l'Enquête de la Jewish Colonization Association) (Paris, 1906), vol. 1, pp. 39, 41–43. See also Bernard W. Weinryb, *Neueste Wirtschaftsgeschichte der Juden in Russland und Polen* (Breslau, 1934), vol. 1, pp. 3ff.

16. Zeev Dov Rabinowitsch, *Ha-Hasidut ha-Litait me-Reshitah ve-ad Yamenu* (Jerusalem, 1961), p. 145. See also C. Chemerinski, *Ayarti Motoleh* (Tel Aviv, 1951), pp. 67ff. R. Shemaryah was not only the *rebbe* of Libeshei; he also officiated as *rav* in Libeshei and Kobrin. He had adherents in small towns like Yanovo, Telekhan, Homsk, and Motol. His sphere of influence stretched from Pinsk to Kobrin. According to hasidic tradition, he obtained the position of Rav in Kobrin in perpetuity for himself and his sons and was also empowered to appoint *dayanim* (Jewish judges) and *shohtim* (ritual slaughterers) as he saw fit. Consequently, the *dayanim* and *shohtim* of Kobrin were hasidim, even though most of the Jewish population were *mitnagdim* (opponents of hasidim). The appointment of the *Zaddik* of the Libeshei dynasty as Rav of all the neighboring small towns is the only instance of its kind in Lithuanian hasidism.

17. See Zeev Dov Rabinowitsch, *Ha-Hasidut ha-Litait me-Reshitah ve-ad Yamenu*, pp. 144ff.

18. They changed their names to Shapiro, Goldweitz, Rosensweig, Berman, and Weizmann. The two younger sons, Joseph and Chaim, retained the original, Fialkov.

19. "Em Weizmann," *Hegeh*, August 27, 1939. W.A.

20. In a letter to his wife, written in 1913, Weizmann provides us with a glimpse of relations between the Polish nobility and their Jewish subjects: "I remember *zeide* Michal, who had to kiss the hand of Polish noblemen and chant Jewish prayers for their pleasure, while great-grandfather [Moshe Yitzhak Chemerinski] was forced to climb a tree and imitate a cuckoo, on threat of being shot." Weizmann to Vera, January 22, 1913. *WL* 5, p. 355. (The letters of Chaim Weizmann, collected in twenty-three volumes, will henceforth be cited as *WL*, followed by volume and page number.) The story told by Weizmann may be true. It was not uncommon for the nobility—especially when under the influence of alcohol—to degrade their Jewish estate managers. See, e.g., Chone Shmeruk, "Ha-Hasidut ve-Iskei ha-Hakhirut," *Zion* 1970, pp. 182–92, esp. n. 23. At the same time, Weizmann's story closely resembles common folktales. See, e.g., Abraham Katz, "Ha-Paritz," *Yeda-Am* 2 (1954): 61ff.

21. See *Der Tog*, April 23, 1938, p. 5.

22. According to his own account, Weizmann was born on November 17, 1874. His Russian school-leaving certificate gives the date as November 12, 1873. This is also the date given in his *Abgangszeugnis* at the Polytechnic in Berlin and in his *curriculum vitae* printed in his doctoral dissertation at the University of Fribourg in 1899. See W.A. The catalogue of the University of Geneva of 1909 gives Weizmann's birth date as November 14, 1874. The discrepancies in the dates are most likely due to the differences in the Gregorian and Julian calendars, though 1873 can only be attributed to a clerical error. In all of Weizmann's documents from 1906 on, November 27, 1874, appears as the

date of his birth; this is also the date given in his English naturalization papers of 1910. See W.A. Weizmann himself adhered to this date. See Weizmann's letter to Military Authorities, August 31, 1916, *WL* 7, p. 290. Thus, the accepted birth date is November 27, 1874, or 18 Kislev, 5635.

23. *Der Tog*, April 23, 1938, p. 5.

24. Chaim was the third surviving child. After Miriam came Feivel in 1872, then Falk, who died in infancy.

25. Weizmann, *Trial and Error*, p. 6; Hayah Weizmann-Lichtenstein, *Be-Zel Koratenu* (Tel Aviv, 1948), p. 11.

26. According to the data of the Jewish Colonization Association of 1898–99, there were in that year, in the district of Grodno, 877 carters and 438 raftsmen. In the entire northwestern region of the Pale there were 5,916 carters and 1,975 raftsmen. W.A.

27. See Weizman, *Trial and Error*, pp. 7–10, and Hayah Weizmann-Lichtenstein, *Be-Zel Koratenu*, pp. 34–37. See also Chaim Chemerinski, *Ayarti Motoleh*, pp. 9–10.

28. There are a number of indications that the reins of Orthodoxy in the Weizmann household had been relaxed while Chaim was still young. See Hayah Weizmann-Lichtenstein, *Be-Zel Koratenu*, pp. 31, 67–68. See also Weizmann to Vera, August 31, 1902. *WL* 1, p. 390.

29. See Ezer Weizman, *Lekha Shamayim, Lekha Aretz* (Tel Aviv, 1975), p. 8.

30. Chaim Chemerinski, "Ayarti Motel," in *Reshumot*, vol. 2, ed. Alter Druyanov (Tel Aviv, 1926), p. 29.

31. See Abraham Joshua Heschel, "The Eastern European Era in Jewish History," in *Studies in Modern Jewish Social History*, ed. Joshua A. Fishman (New York, 1972), p. 9.

32. The *kahal* supervised every aspect of religious life. The rabbi was both the religious and secular leader, the synagogue the religious, cultural, educational and social center. There was no *shtetl* without at least one synagogue, a cemetery, a burial society, and a ritual pool for women. By the mid-nineteenth century, according to an official report, there were in Russia 604 synagogues, 2,340 prayer houses, 3,944 Jewish schools, and 954 rabbis. At the same time there were over 6,000 religious private schools in the Pale, ranging from *heder* to *Talmud Torah* and *Yeshivah*. See Isaac Alteras, "Jews under Tsarism and Communism," *Midstream*, 27, no. 5 (May 1981): 37.

33. Salo Baron, *The Russian Jew Under Tsars and Soviets*, 2nd ed., rev. (New York, 1976), pp. 27, 117–18. For a general study on *shtetl* culture, see Mark Zborowski and Elizabeth Herzog, *Life Is with People* (New York, 1952).

34. According to incomplete calculations of the ICA, there were in the Pale at the end of the nineteenth century 370,000 Jewish children in *hadarim*, as against 60,000 who studied in Russian and Jewish-Russian schools. Quoted in Yehuda Slutsky, *Ha-Itonut ha-Yehudit-Russit ba-meah ha-19* (Jerusalem, 1970), p. 13.

35. Weizmann, *Trial and Error*, p. 4.

36. Lichtenstein, *Be-Zel Koratenu*, p. 32; Rachel Leah Weizmann in *Der Tog*, April 25, 1938, p. 5.

37. Weizmann, *Trial and Error*, p. 5.

38. Lichtenstein, *Be-Zel Koratenu*, pp. 49–50.

39. Ibid., p. 52.

40. Rachel Leah Weizmann, *Der Tog*, April 25, 1938, p. 5.

41. Lichtenstein, *Be-Zel Koratenu*, p. 33.
42. During the *shmoneh esreh* (eighteen benedictions) he would often weep, and his teachers praised his religious zeal. See "Zikhronot al yalduto shel Chaim Weizmann," *Davar*, June 3, 1938, p. 8.
43. Lichtenstein, p. 2. Weizmann's mother related that Chaim was three when he moved to his grandparents'; see *Der Tog*, April 25, 1938, p. 5. Weizmann himself wrote that he was five or six when he moved there; see *Trial and Error*, p. 7, which conflicts with other evidence in his own memoirs and in his sister's memoirs.
44. See "Zikhronot . . . ," *Davar*, June 3, 1938, p. 8.
45. Rachel Leah Weizmann, *Der Tog*, April 25, 1938, p. 5. The Weizmanns were surrounded by uncles and aunts, mostly on Rachel Leah's side; she recalls five brothers and sisters in Motol. See *Der Tog*, April 28, 1938, p. 7.
46. Yakim, who called himself "the Weizmanns' goy," worked for the family from 1873 until 1912. See *Hegeh*. W.A.
47. Lichtenstein, *Be-Zel Koratenu*, p. 27.
48. Ibid., p. 29.
49. See Weizmann, *Trial and Error*, p. 12.
50. Lichtenstein, *Be-Zel Koratenu*, pp. 75–76.
51. Weizmann, *Trial and Error*, p. 13. See also Rachel Leah Weizmann in *Der Tog*, May 14, 1938, p. 6, concerning the ideological conflicts between Shmuel and Chaim Weizmann.
52. See Rachel Leah Weizmann in *Der Tog*, April 28, 1938, p. 7.
53. See Isaiah Berlin, *Personal Impressions* (New York, 1980), p. 52. Thirty years later Weizmann himself wrote that "the poor Jew of the darkest Russian ghetto, who has never seen an Englishman in his life, always turns to England hoping that salvation will come from this quarter." Weizmann to Alfred Zimmern, July 4, 1915. *WL* 7, p. 220.
54. Concerning the general influence of English culture and ideas on Russian intellectuals, see Ernest Joseph Simmons, *English Literature and Culture in Russia, 1553–1840* (Cambridge, Mass., 1935).
55. Weizmann to Shlomo Tsvi-Sokolovsky [Summer 1885], *WL* 1, pp. 35–37. Italics in original.
56. Chaim was apparently the first child from Motol to attend a high school in Pinsk. See Rachel Leah Weizmann in *Der Tog*, April 25, 1938, p. 5.

II Pinsk

1. Weizmann, *Trial and Error*, p. 10.
2. At the Weizmann house hung a painting, framed in black, depicting the assassination of Alexander II. See Lichtenstein, *Be-Zel Koratenu*, pp. 22–23.
3. Although at one point Chaim Lubzhinsky and his wife Miriam, Feivel (the oldest son), and Hayah (later Lichtenstein) contemplated immigration in 1892, they canceled their plans at the last minute. See Lichtenstein, *Be-Zel Koratenu*, pp. 58–60.
4. See Michael Aronson, "Geographical and Socioeconomic Factors in the 1881 Anti-Jewish Pogroms in Russia," *Russian Review* 39, no. 1 (January 1980): 18–31, and Leo Motzkin, *Die Judenpogrome in Russland* (Cologne, 1909).
5. See Shmarya Levin, *Forward from Exile* (Philadelphia, 1967), pp. 174–76, and Jacob Bernstein-Kohan, *Sefer Bernstein-Kohan* (Tel Aviv, 1946), pp. 67ff.
6. Baron, *The Russian Jew Under Tsars and Soviets*, p. 45.

7. For the attitude of the Russian officials toward the Jewish community on this and other issues, see Michael Aronson, "The Prospects for the Emancipation of Russian Jewry During the 1880s," *Slavonic and East European Review* 55, no. 3 (July 1977): 348–69; idem, "The Attitude of Russian Officials in the 1880s Toward Jewish Assimilation and Emigration," *Slavic Review* 34, no. 1 (March 1975): 1–18; see also Hans Rogger, "The Jewish Policy of Late Tsarism: A Reappraisal," *Wiener Library Bulletin* 25, nos. 1–2 (1971): 42–51, and Hans Rogger, "Russian Ministers and the Jewish Question, 1881–1917," *California Slavic Studies* 3 (1975): 15–76.

8. See the letter from a Jew in Vilna to the editor of *Nedelnaya Kronika Voskhroda* (February 1882) in Paul R. Mendes-Flohr and Jehuda Reinharz, eds., *The Jew in the Modern World: A Documentary History* (New York, 1980), pp. 328–29.

9. In January 1882 Count Nicholas Ignatiev, Minister of the Interior, allowed an interviewer to publish a statement in which he advised the Jews that the western borders were open to them if they wished to leave. Thus, the laws making it a criminal offense to leave Russia without a special permit would no longer be enforced. A short time later Ignatiev made a contradictory statement. In short, the Russian bureaucracy did not make it easy for Jews to emigrate.

10. In 1897 the Jewish population in Russia comprised 5,189,401 within a total population of 126,368,827. See Boris Goldberg, "Zur Statistik der juedischen Bevoelkerung in Russland laut der Volkszaehlung von 1897," *Juedische Statistik* (Berlin, 1903), pp. 259–65.

11. See Lloyd P. Gartner, "Immigration and the Formation of American Jewry, 1840–1925," in H. H. Ben-Sasson and S. Ettinger, eds., *Jewish Society Through the Ages* (New York, 1971), pp. 297–312.

12. Hans Rogger, "Tsarist Policy on Jewish Emigration," *Soviet Jewish Affairs* 3, no. 7 (1973): 29. See also W. W. Kaplun-Kogan, *Die Juedischen Wanderbewegungen in der Neuesten Zeit* (Bonn, 1919), pp. 19–25.

13. The yearly average of the Russian Jews going to the United States alone was 12,856 for 1881–86; it reached 28,509 in the next five-year period, rose to 44,829 from 1891 to 1895, and declined—perhaps due to the economic slump in America—to 31,278 from 1896 to 1900. The average yearly figures were 58,625 for 1901–5; 82,223 for 1906–10; and 75,144 for 1911–14.

14. For some of the refugees it was attractive to travel to Palestine because the price of a ticket was one eighth that of a ship ticket to America. See Shulamit Laskov, *Ha-Biluim* (Jerusalem, 1979), pp. 26–30.

15. For additional figures on immigration of Eastern European Jews, see Samuel Joseph, *Jewish Immigration to the United States, 1881–1910* (New York, 1914); Walter F. Willcox, ed., *International Migrations,* 2 vols. (New York, 1929, 1931); Mendes-Flohr and Reinharz, *The Jew in the Modern World,* pp. 529–30; and Salo Baron, *The Russian Jew,* pp. 69–74. See also Zosa Szajkowski, "How the Mass Migration to America Began," *Jewish Social Studies* 4, no. 4 (October 1942): 291–310, and Hans Weichmann, "Die Auswanderung aus Oesterreich und Russland ueber die Deutschen Haefen," Diss., Univ. of Heidelberg, 1913.

16. For an overview of anti-Semitism in these countries, see Jacob Katz, *From Prejudice to Destruction* (Cambridge, Mass., 1980).

17. For a comprehensive description and analysis of the Hovevi Zion, see David Vital, *The Origins of Zionism* (Oxford, 1975), pp. 135ff. See also Yitzhak Maor, *Ha-Tnuah ha-Zionit be-Russyah* (Jerusalem, 1973).

18. See Moshe Leib Lilienblum, *Kol Kitvei Moshe Leib Lilienblum* (Cracow, 1910), vol. 1, pp. 126ff. See also Zalman Epstein, *Moshe Leib Lilienblum, Shitato ve-Halakh Mahshavto* (1934–35).
19. Ben Halpern, "Ideology and Institutions of Israel," unpublished ms., chap. 1, p. 27.
20. These were the founders of *Am Olam* (Eternal People), the nationalist organization with the most strongly marked utopian socialist, populist character. Thus the *Am Olam* movement can be said to reflect the inverse image of the Bilu. See Abraham Menes, "The Am Oylom Movement," *YIVO Annual of Jewish Social Science* 4 (1949): 9–33. See also Eliyahu Tscherikower, *Geschichte fun der Idisher Arbeter-Bawegung in di Fereinikte Staaten* (New York, 1945), vol. 2, chap. 4, pp. 203–38, and Abraham Cahan, *Bleter fun mayn Lebn* (New York, 1926), vol. 2, pp. 20–24, who describes the arrival of an *Am Olam* group in Brody in 1882.
21. On the proto-Zionists, see Jacob Katz, "Le-Viur ha-Musag Mevasrei ha-Zionut," *Shivat Zion* (Jerusalem, 1950), vol. 1, pp. 91–105.
22. See Klausner, *Be-Hitorer Am*, pp. 440ff.
23. See Shmuel Ettinger, *Encyclopaedia Judaica*, 1st ed., s.v. "Hibbat Zion," and in greater detail in David Vital, *The Origins of Zionism*, pp. 154–60.
24. Laskov, *Ha-Biluim*, p. 38.
25. See their manifesto in Mendes-Flohr and Reinharz, *The Jew in the Modern World*, p. 421.
26. For detailed accounts on the Biluim, see Vital, *The Origins of Zionism*, pp. 74ff.; Laskov, *Ha-Biluim*, pp. 38ff.; idem, "The Biluim: Reality and Legend," *Zionism*, no. 3 (Spring 1981): 17–69.
27. He refers to Dr. Israel Yasinovsky, head of the Warsaw office of the Hovevei Zion, and to Dr. Leo Pinsker, both leading figures of the movement.
28. Weizmann, *Trial and Error*, p. 16.
29. The best accounts of Pinsk and its Jewish population are B. Hoffman, ed., *Toisent Johr Pinsk* (New York, 1941), and the much more comprehensive *Pinsk Historical Volume: History of the Jews of Pinsk, 1506–1941*, 2 vols., ed. Wolf Zeev Rabinowitsch (Tel Aviv and Haifa, 1973). Subsequent references are to the historical volume (1). In the nineteenth century the Jewish population of Pinsk-Karlin increased considerably. In 1897 the Jews of Pinsk constituted 74.2 percent and on the eve of World War I 72.4 percent of the total population.
30. *Pinsk*, p. 8. The overwhelming Jewish character of the city may have contributed to the fact that despite incitement against Jews, no pogroms were carried out in Pinsk. In 1883 mobs of peasants from the surrounding areas were forced to flee by the city's Jewish butchers, coachmen, and porters. During the years 1903–6, years of violence for Russian Jewry, no one dared start pogroms in Pinsk.
31. Ibid., p. 2.
32. Ibid., p. 4.
33. Ibid., p. 6.
34. Ibid., pp. 7–8. See also *Die Welt*, no. 11, 1898, pp. 3ff., and Jacob Lestchinsky, *Di Ekonomische Lage fun di Yidn in Poiln* (Berlin, 1931), pp. 100–111.
35. See Yaakov Yisraeli, *Beit Karlin-Stolin: Prakim be-Masekhet Hayehem shel Admorei ha-Shoshelet ve-Iyunim be-Mishnatam ha-Hasidit* (Tel Aviv, 1981) and Wolf Zeev Rabinowitsch, "Karlin Hasidism," *YIVO Annual of Jewish Social Science* 5 (1950): 123–51.

36. See Mordechai Nadav, "Kehilot Pinsk-Karlin beyn hasidut le-hitnagdut," *Zion*, 34, nos. 1–2 (1969): 98–108.
37. *Pinsk*, p. 10.
38. *Pinsk*, p. 47.
39. See Patrick L. Alston, *Education and the State in Tsarist Russia* (Stanford, Calif., 1969), pp. 130–39.
40. According to Weizmann, *Trial and Error*, p. 19, and Lichtenstein, *Be-Zel Koratenu*, p. 33, he was born in 1871. However, this is probably a mistake since Miriam, the oldest child, was born in 1871.
41. Lichtenstein, *Be-Zel Koratenu*, p. 33.
42. *Der Tog*, April 25, 1938, p. 5. According to his mother, Chaim was the first boy from Motol to attend the Pinsk *Real-Gymnasium*.
43. "Zikhronot al Yalduto shel Chaim Weizmann," *Davar*, June 3, 1938, p. 8.
44. *Der Tog*, April 25, 1938, p. 5.
45. Lichtenstein, *Be-Zel Koratenu*, p. 34.
46. Weizmann, *Trial and Error*, p. 20.
47. Ibid., p. 21.
48. See Lichtenstein, *Be-Zel Koratenu*, p. 52.
49. *Pinsk*, p. 94. See also Wolf Zeev Rabinowitsch, "Ha-Rothschildim shel Pinsk ve-Karlin," *Heavar* 17 (1970): 252–80.
50. *WL 1*, p. 40.
51. Ibid., p. 42.
52. Lichtenstein, *Be-Zel Koratenu*, p. 52.
53. Weizmann to Ovsey Lurie, November 23, 1890, *WL 1*, pp. 41–42.
54. See, e.g., *WL 1*, pp. 285ff., 351ff.
55. Weizmann to Ovsey Lurie, March 3, 1892. *WL 1*, pp. 45–46.
56. See Weizmann, *Trial and Error*, pp. 10, 11, 18, and 23.
57. *Pinsk*, p. 52.
58. See Alter Druyanov, *Ktavim le-Toldot Hibbat Zion* (Tel Aviv, 1930), vol. 3, p. 1330.
59. See Klausner, *Behitorer Am*, p. 454. However, he was not a member of the presidium of the Kattowitz Conference, as stated by Weizmann, *Trial and Error*, p. 24.
60. See Klausner, *Behitorer Am*, p. 379. See also Louis Lipsky, *A Gallery of Zionist Profiles* (New York, 1956), pp. 192–94, and Zvi Hirsch Masliansky, *Droshes fir Shabosim un Yomim Toyvim*, 2 vols. (New York, 1908).
61. *Pinsk*, p. 11.
62. Ibid., p. 52.
63. Ibid., p. 12.
64. The other two being Judah Leib Berger and Grigory Lurie.
65. Weizmann himself asserted that "I am in the Zionist movement since I was fifteen . . ." Weizmann to Charles P. Scott, December 9, 1914. *WL 7*, p. 77.
66. Weizmann, *Trial and Error*, p. 24.
67. In his memoirs Zvi Hirsch Masliansky relates that on one occasion, possibly in 1885, Chaim was appointed to lead some eight hundred students in the sale of Montefiore portraits, the proceeds to go to the Hibbat Zion movement. Chaim sold five times as many portraits as any other student. See "Me-Reshito shel Manhig." W.A.
68. Weizmann, *Trial and Error*, p. 27. When writing to the whole family, Weizmann used Yiddish.

69. *Pinsk*, p. 12.

70. Weizmann to Motzkin, January 23, 1896: ". . . about the model *heder* established in Pinsk; it is a great success and is creating an upheaval in all local educational affairs. . . ." *WL* 1, pp. 56–57.

71. See the interview with Aaron Eliasberg, who minimizes Weizmann's Zionist activities in Pinsk as well as Weizmann's involvement in the *hadarim metukanim*. W.A. Chaim *was* responsible for the first *Agudat Safah Berurah* in Motol, founded by the youngsters in the village, who were fascinated by his stories about Palestine and by Mapu's *Ahavat Zion* and *Ashmat Shomron*. See Lichtenstein, *Be-Zel Koratenu*, p. 45.

72. In Pinsk he met and worked with people like Isaac Naiditch, Judah Berger, and Georg Halpern, who rose to prominence in the movement and later worked with Weizmann.

73. The Weizmanns were always a close-knit family, and those among them who had attained a measure of economic security or independence always helped their younger brothers and sisters. In a letter to his father, Chaim advised him to sell his horse and fine cart in order to enable his younger brother, Moshe, to study at the Pinsk *Real-Gymnasium*. Ozer and Rachel followed his advice without hesitation. In 1892, as Chaim was leaving for Pfungstadt, Moshe arrived, aged thirteen, to commence his studies. See Rachel Leah Weizmann, *Der Tog*, April 25, 1938, p. 5, and Lichtenstein, *Be-Zel Koratenu*, pp. 69–70.

III   Berlin

1. See Louis Greenberg, *The Jews in Russia: The Struggle for Emancipation* (New Haven, 1965), pp. 85–86.

2. See Slutski, *Ha-Itonut ha-Yehudit-Russit*, p. 27.

3. Though he does not mention this in his autobiography, another reason for leaving on a raft rather than taking out a passport may have been connected to registration for military service.

4. Lichtenstein, *Be-Zel Koratenu*, pp. 53–54.

5. The non-Jewish population was 4,174 in 1871; there were 236 Jews. By 1900 the number of Jews began to decline due to immigration by the younger generation to the large cities. Paul Arnsberg, *Die Juedischen Gemeinden in Hessen* (Frankfurt am Main, 1971), vol. 2, p. 199.

6. Ibid., p. 200.

7. Leo Baeck has aptly described this situation as *"Milieufroemmigkeit."* See Monika Richarz, ed., *Juedisches Leben in Deutschland* (Stuttgart, 1979), vol. 2, p. 48.

8. The combined forces of the Agrarian League, the Conservatives, and other anti-Semitic groups proved very powerful. The success of the anti-Semites was spectacular. The anti-Semitic vote jumped from 47,000 in 1890 to 263,000 in 1893, raising the number of representatives of anti-Semitic parties from five to sixteen. See Jehuda Reinharz, *Fatherland or Promised Land? The Dilemma of the German Jew, 1893–1914* (Ann Arbor, Mich., 1975), esp. pp. 38–39.

9. See Weizmann, *Trial and Error*, p. 33.

10. Lichtenstein, *Be-Zel Koratenu*, pp. 54–55.

11. Ibid., pp. 67–68. Chaim's parents, however, continued to maintain an observant home. See Weizmann to Vera Khatzman, March 31, 1904. *WL* 3, p. 231: "It is a holy day [Passover] and therefore my family do not write." At

the same time, the parents were obviously tolerant in regard to their children's lack of observance of religious precepts.

12. Lichtenstein, *Be-Zel Koratenu*, p. 54.
13. See *Programm der Grossherzoglich Hessischen Technischen Hochschule zu Darmstadt fuer das Studienjahr 1892–1893* (Darmstadt, 1892). W.A.
14. He had to be tutored in mathematics by Nathan Katzenstein, a teacher in the boarding school. Interview with Mr. Ernst Katzenstein, November 1, 1981.
15. Weizmann, *Trial and Error*, p. 33.
16. Ibid., p. 165.
17. Even Pinsker's important nationalist tract *Auto-Emancipation* reveals his admiration for the West. Many of the East European intellectuals disdained the ghetto, i.e., the Pale of Settlement and its stifling physical and cultural atmosphere. See Leo Motzkin's testimony to this effect in Alex Bein, ed., *Sefer Motzkin* (Jerusalem, 1939), p. 267.
18. See Elias Hurwicz, "Shay Ish Hurwitz and the Berlin He-Athid: When Berlin was the Centre of Hebrew Literature," *Leo Baeck Institute Year Book XII* (London, 1967), pp. 85–102. See also Stanley Nash, "Tmunot mi-hug Shoharei ha-Ivrit be-Berlin (1900–1914)," *AJS Review* 3 (1978): 1–26. For a comprehensive treatment of the question of *Ostjuden* and the West, especially Germany, see Steven E. Aschheim, *Brothers and Strangers: The East European Jew in German and German Jewish Consciousness, 1800–1923* (Madison, Wisc., 1982).
19. Weizmann to Leo Motzkin, June 20, 1895, *WL* 1, p. 48.
20. The Hamburg-American Line, which carried about five thousand Russians annually in the 1870s, carried thirty thousand in 1886 and seventy-seven thousand in 1891. See Zosa Szajkowski, "The European Attitude to East European Jewish Immigration (1881–1893)," *Publications of the American-Jewish Historical Society* 41, no. 2 (December 1951): 127–60. See also H. Weichmann, *Die Auswanderung aus Oesterreich und Russland ueber die Deutschen Haefen* (Berlin, 1913), p. 5.
21. The German census figures for 1880 recorded 15,097 Russians passing through Germany; 46,971 for 1900; and 106,639 for 1905. By 1910 there were 137,697 Russians traveling or living in Germany—over half the total number of Russians in Western Europe. Among those coming to live temporarily or settle permanently in Germany were numerous Russian students. These were usually members of the lower middle class, many of them Jewish, who came to the technical high schools as well as universities to study medicine, chemistry, engineering, and law. The number of Russian students enrolled in German universities and high schools nearly tripled between 1900 and 1914. In the universities alone some 5,000 Russians registered during the summer and winter semesters of 1912–13, primarily in Berlin (1,174), Leipzig (758), Munich (552), Königsberg (435), Heidelberg (317), and Halle (283). See Robert C. Williams, *Culture in Exile: Russian Emigrés in Germany, 1881–1941* (Ithaca, N.Y., 1972), pp. 20, 25. See also Botho Brachmann, *Russische Sozialdemokraten in Berlin 1895–1914* (Berlin, 1962), pp. 1–30 and appendixes.
22. See Shalom Adler-Rudel, *Ostjuden in Deutschland 1880–1914* (Tübingen, 1959), pp. 21ff. By 1890 there were 11,390 *Ostjuden*—Jews from Russia, Austria-Hungary, Poland, and Rumania—in Prussia. In the entire German Reich there were 41,000 East European Jews in 1900 and more than 78,000 by 1910. Their percentage in the total German-Jewish population thus increased from 7 to 12.8 percent.
23. Ibid., p. 164.

24. See chap. 1 of Reinharz, *Fatherland or Promised Land?* In 1895 the Jewish population in Greater Berlin (including the suburbs of Charlottenburg, Schoenberg, Wilmersdorf and Neukoelln) was 94,391, which constituted 16.4 percent of the entire Jewish population in the German Reich. The suburb most favored by Jews was Charlottenburg, where 22,000 Jews lived in 1910. See Monika Richarz, ed., *Juedisches Leben in Deutschland*, pp. 22–23. See also Klara Eschelbacher, "Die Ostjuedische Einwanderungsbevoelkerung der Stadt Berlin," *Zeitschrift fuer Demographie und Statistik der Juden* 1–6 (January–June 1920): 2.

25. See Shalom Adler-Rudel, *Ostjuden in Deutschland*, p. 163, and Jack L. Wertheimer, "German Policy and Jewish Politics: The Absorption of East European Jews in Germany (1869–1914)," Diss., Columbia University, 1978, p. 596 (appendix).

26. See *Selbst-Emancipation*, no. 3 (February 2, 1891), p. 30. Alex Bein gives the date of founding as Autumn 1889. See Alex Bein, ed., *Sefer Motzkin*, p. 40. See also Jehuda Reinharz, "Ideology and Structure in German Zionism, 1882–1933," *Jewish Social Studies* 42, no. 2 (Spring 1980): 119 ff; idem, ed., *Dokumente zur Geschichte des deutschen Zionismus 1882–1933* (Tübingen, 1981), pp. 3–19.

27. See Central Zionist Archives (CZA), A125/12/1.

28. See CZA, A126/14/1. See also "Unsere Hoffnung" (in Yiddish), CZA, A126/14/1.

29. Other members of the Verein during different periods included Eliyahu Davidson, Lazare Kunin, David Makhlin, Isidore Eliashev, Joseph Lurie, Israel Motzkin, Selig Soskin, Judah Vilensky, Yehoshua Thon, Mordechai Ehrenpreis, David Farbstein, and Leo Estermann.

30. See N. M. Gelber, "Agudat ha-Studentim ha-Yehudim ha-Russim ha-Rishonah be-Berlin," *Heavar* 4 (1956): 48–50.

31. Weizmann, *Trial and Error*, p. 38.

32. Shmarya Levin, *Forward from Exile*, trans. and ed. Maurice Samuel (Philadelphia, 1967), p. 269. See also Marie Syrkin, *Avi-Nachman Syrkin* (Jerusalem, 1970), pp. 31ff.

33. Weizmann, *Trial and Error*, p. 38; Weizmann to Motzkin, September 10, 1895, WL 1, p. 51.

34. As late as 1910 even certain German Zionists made a distinction between themselves and all East European Jews, Zionists included. See the well-known essay on the subject by Franz Oppenheimer, "Stammesbewusstsein und Volksbewusstsein," *Die Welt*, no. 7 (February 18, 1910), pp. 139–43. See also Zosa Szajkowski, "The European Attitude to East European Jewish Immigration, 1881–1893," *Publications of the American-Jewish Historical Society* 41, no. 2 (December 1951): 138–41.

35. See Williams, *Culture in Exile*, pp. 7ff. See also "Zur Lage der russisch-juedischen Studenten in Deutschland," *Die Welt*, no. 15, April 11, 1902, p. 2.

36. For biographies, including fields of specialization, of Liebermann and his colleagues, see J. C. Poggendorff's *Biographisch-Literarisches Handwoerterbuch zur Geschichte der Exacten Wissenschaften*, vol. 4 (Leipzig, 1904).

37. Barnet Litvinoff, *Weizmann, Last of the Patriarchs* (New York, 1976), p. 21.

38. The Weizmann Archives contain an application for a patent: "Verfahren zur Herstellung von Farbstoffen durch Condensation von Anthrachinon und Anthrachinon-derivaten mit Resorcin." The application probably dates from 1897. The applicant is Christian Deichler; perhaps Weizmann, being a for-

eign student, was excluded from applying. In any case, the application for a patent was evidently not accepted. A rather accidental observation made by Weizmann in these practical studies proved to be of theoretical interest. He found that the reaction between phtholic anhydrides and phenols was catalyzed by boric acid, and that in the reaction vivid colors appeared. This was the beginning of the chemistry of borate complexes. See Ernst D. Bergmann, "The Example of Weizmann's Science," *The Jerusalem Post*, November 2, 1969, p. 3.

39. See CZA, A126/14.
40. Weizmann, *Trial and Error*, p. 37. It is not surprising that Berlin remained one of Weizmann's favorite cities, and he retained fond memories of his sojourn there. See Weizmann to Vera Khatzman, July 17, 1901. *WL* 1, p. 155.
41. See *Selbst-Emancipation*, no. 8 (November 16, 1891), pp. 5–6.
42. See Leo Motzkin, "Rede des cand. math. L. Motzkin, gehalten im russisch-jued. wiss. Verein in Berlin an dem IV Stiftungs- und Makkabaeerfeste desselben vor einem zum groesseren Theile aus deutschen Juden bestehenden Publicum," *Selbst-Emancipation*, no. 3 (February 1, 1892), pp. 31–32.
43. Levin, *Forward from Exile*, pp. 273–74. In the immediate period after the expulsion of the Jews from Moscow in 1891, members of the Verein also helped the destitute immigrants who poured into or through Berlin, often acting as the intermediaries between the new arrivals and the German-Jewish community. See Levin, pp. 278ff. See also N. M. Gelber, "Agudat ha-Studentim ha-Yehudim," pp. 50ff.
44. Gelber, "Agudat ha-Studentim ha-Yehudim," p. 53.
45. See Bein, *Sefer Motzkin*, p. 42.
46. At the beginning of 1893 his presence in Berlin appeared so dangerous to the Prussian officials that as an undesirable alien he was served with a police order to leave the capital. See Z. A. B. Zeman and W. B. Scharlau, *The Merchant of Revolution: The Life of Alexander Israel Helphand (Parvus)* (London, 1965), p. 25.
47. See Felix Weingartner, *Buffets and Rewards* (London, 1937).
48. Weizmann, *Trial and Error*, p. 40.
49. See Rachel Leah Weizmann in *Der Tog*, April 30, 1938, p. 5.
50. Esther, the fifteenth child, was born to the Weizmanns in 1894 but died in infancy.
51. See Lichtenstein, *Be-Zel Koratenu*, pp. 76–78.
52. *Der Tog*, April 30, 1938, p. 5.
53. See *Pinsk*, pp. 86ff.
54. Weizmann to Leo Motzkin, June 20, 1895, *WL* 1, pp. 48–49.
55. Weizmann to Leo Motzkin, September 10, 1895, *WL* 1, pp. 51–52. Italics in original.
56. Weizmann to Leo Motzkin, June 20, 1895, *WL* 1, p. 49.
57. Weizmann to Leo Motzkin, September 10, 1895, *WL* 1, p. 51.
58. Weizmann was probably influenced by similar ideas and suggestions for the education of the masses which were current in the Verein.
59. Weizmann to Leo Motzkin, September 10, 1895, *WL* 1, p. 52. The Pinsk group preceded in this aim the Verein, which in February 1896 formed a society for the distribution of Yiddish works among the masses, later known as Bildung: Verein zu Foerderung der Literatur in juedish-deutscher Mundart. See CZA, A126/17.
60. *Pinsk*, p. 52.

61. See Weizmann to Leo Motzkin, November 29, 1895, *WL* 1, p. 56.
62. The date of this incident is not clear. It may have taken place after 1895–96 on one of Chaim's visits to Pinsk. See Lichtenstein, *Be-Zel Koratenu*, pp. 87–88.
63. See Rachel Leah Weizmann, *Der Tog*, May 3, 1938, p. 5.
64. Lichtenstein, *Be-Zel Koratenu*, pp. 90–91.
65. Ibid., pp. 91–92. See also Rachel Leah Weizmann, *Der Tog*, May 3, 1938, p. 5.
66. Weizmann to Leo Motzkin, November 29, 1895, *WL* 1, p. 55.
67. Weizmann to Leo Motzkin, September 26–27, 1895, *WL* 1, p. 54.
68. Weizmann to Leo Motzkin, January 23, 1896, *WL* 1, p. 57.
69. Weizmann to Leo Motzkin, February 11, 1896, *WL* 1, p. 58.
70. Weizmann to Leo Motzkin, [March?] 19, 1896, *WL* 1, pp. 60–61.
71. See Leon Simon's biography *Ahad Ha'Am* (Philadelphia, 1960), pp. 10, 46–56, and Aryeh Simon and Joseph Heller, *Ahad Ha'Am, Ha-Ish, Poalo ve-Torato* (Jerusalem, 1955), pp. 11–37.
72. Ahad Ha'Am, "Shlilat ha-Galut," in Asher Ginsberg, *Kol Kitvei Ahad Ha'Am* (Tel Aviv, 1947), pp. 399–403. Subsequent references to this volume in the notes will be abbreviated as *KKAH*.
73. On the meaning of the term *merkaz ruhani*, see Leon Simon, "Ahad Ha'Am and the Future of the Diaspora," in *Between East and West: Essays Dedicated to the Memory of Bela Horovitz*, ed. Alexander Altmann (London, 1958), pp. 59–74.
74. "Dr. Pinsker u-Makhbarto," *KKAH*, pp. 43–48.
75. In his search Ahad Ha'Am was not always consistent, once declaring that the ideal of Judaism is absolute justice as revealed by prophecy, while elsewhere declaring that the essence of Judaism is absolute monotheism. See his essays "Moshe" and "Al Shtei ha-Seipim" in *KKAH*, pp. 342–47, 370–78.
76. The society was founded on the seventh of Adar, traditionally viewed as the date on which Moses died.
77. Letter from Judah Vilensky to Leo Motzkin, 1893. CZA, 126/20. See also the statutes of the Bnei Moshe in CZA, A25/32.
78. For a detailed account, see S. Tchernovitz, *Bnei Moshe u-Tekufatam* (Warsaw, 1914), pp. 61–62, 112–25. On the Bnei Moshe in general, see CZA, A35/22/11. See also Yosef Salmon, "Ha-Maavak al Daat ha-Kahal ha-Haredit be-Mizrah-Europa be-Yahas la-Tnuah ha-Leumit [1894–1896]," *Prakim be-Toldot ha-Hevrah ha-Yehudit be-Yemei ha-Beynaim uva-Et ha-Hadashah* (Jerusalem, 1980), pp. 330–68.
79. A branch of Bnei Moshe was organized in Pinsk under the name Zerubavel; see *Pinsk*, p. 52.
80. See Weizmann to Leo Motzkin, September 25, 1895, and January 23, 1896, *WL* 1, pp. 53–55, 57.
81. Israel Klausner, "Hibbat Zion be-Lita," in *Yahadut Lita* (Tel Aviv, 1959), vol. 1, pp. 502–3.
82. Simon, *Ahad Ha'Am*, pp. 130–33; see also Simon and Heller, *Ahad Ha'Am, Ha-Ish, Poalo ve-Torato*, pp. 40–44.
83. See Weizmann, *Trial and Error*, p. 34.
84. Weizmann to Leo and Israel Motzkin, September 20, 1896, *WL* 1, pp. 61–62.
85. See Yosef Salmon, "Ha-Imut beyn ha-Haredim la-Maskilim be-Tnuat Hibbat Zion bi-Shnot ha-80," *Zionism* [Tel Aviv] 5 (1978): 43–77.
86. See Maor, *Ha-Tnuah ha-Zionit be-Russyah*, pp. 81–103, and Klausner, *Mi-Kattowitz ad Basel*, vol. 1, pp. 387ff.
87. See Klausner, *Mi-Kattowitz ad Basel*, vol. 2, pp. 255–60.

88. See Maor, *Ha-Tnuah ha-Zionit*, pp. 111–14.
89. See the letters from Nathan Birnbaum to Menahem Ussishkin dated February 17, 1892, and March 18, 1892, in which Birnbaum berates Russian Zionists and the Hibbat Zion movement in general for having achieved so little. CZA, A9/141. See also "Aufruf" I and II, "An alle Freunde Zions!" signed by Nathan Birnbaum, Moritz Schnirer, Ruben Brainin, and Salomon Bauer, February 7, 1892. CZA, A9/141/4.
90. Weizmann, *Trial and Error*, p. 48. Weizmann claimed that he won a mandate from Pinsk. The procedures for attendance at the First Zionist Congress were, in fact, not clear-cut. Some delegates arrived at Herzl's personal invitation, while others were there as mere observers. See also Lichtenstein, *Be-Zel Koratenu*, p. 98.
91. Weizmann to Leo Motzkin, [July 1897], *WL* 1, p. 64. See also pp. 63 and 65.
92. Weizmann to Leo Motzkin, [July 31, 1897], *WL* 1, p. 65.
93. Weizmann, *Trial and Error*, pp. 48–49.
94. See *Ha-Kongress ha-Zioni ha-Rishon*, ed. Haim Orlan (Tel Aviv, 1978), p. 212.

IV Herzl

1. Weizmann to Leo Motzkin, January 23, 1896, *WL* 1, p. 57.
2. See *The Complete Diaries of Theodor Herzl*, ed. Raphael Patai and trans. Harry Zohn (New York, 1960), vol. 1, p. 300.
3. See Neville Mandel, "Ottoman Policy and Restrictions on Jewish Settlement in Palestine, 1881–1908," *Middle Eastern Studies* 10, no. 3 (1974): 312–32.
4. Quoted in Neville Mandel, *The Arabs and Zionism before World War I* (Berkeley, Calif., 1976), p. 19.
5. See Neville Mandel, "Ottoman Practice as Regards Jewish Settlement in Palestine, 1881–1908," *Middle Eastern Studies* 11, no. 1 (1975): 31–46.
6. *Ha-Enziklopedia ha-Ivrit*, vol. 6, col. 674, s.v. "Eretz Israel."
7. See Mordechai Eliav, *Eretz Israel ve-Yishuvah ba-Meah ha-19, 1777–1917* (Jerusalem, 1978), p. 498. See also Moshe Burstein, *Self-Government of the Jews in Palestine Since 1900* (Tel Aviv, 1934), p. 4, who states that sixty thousand Jews lived in Palestine in 1900.
8. Arthur Ruppin, in *The Jews of To-Day*, trans. Margery Bentwich (London, 1913), p. 284, estimates the number of Jews in Palestine for 1880 at thirty-five thousand, which is probably an overestimate.
9. See Israel Klausner, *Mi-Kattowitz ad Basel* (Jerusalem, 1965), vol. 2, pp. 31–44; *Hibbat Zion be-Rumanyah* (Jerusalem, 1958), p. 84.
10. One acre equals 4.5 dunams.
11. See David Gurevich and Aaron Gertz, *Ha-Hityashvut ha-Haklait ha-Ivrit be-Eretz Israel* (Jerusalem, 1938), p. 31, and Abraham Revusky, *Jews in Palestine* (London, 1938), pp. 10–12. See also Willy Bambus, *Die juedischen Ackerbaukolonien in Palaestina und ihre Geschichte* (Berlin, 1895); idem, *Palaestina in der Gegenwart* (Berlin, [1891]). See also *Protokoll des I. Zionistenkongresses in Basel vom 29. bis 31. August 1897* (Prag, 1911), pp. 192–207.
12. During the same period (1882–89) the total investment of all Hovevei Zion societies in Russia, Rumania, and Central and Western Europe was about eighty-seven thousand pounds. See Alex Bein, *Toldot ha-Hityashvut ha-Zionit*, 4th ed. (Ramat Gan, 1970), p. 10, n. 1. See also Israel Margalith, *Le Baron Edmond de Rothschild et la Colonisation Juive en Palestine, 1882–1889* (Paris, 1957), p. 142.
13. Quoted in Simon Schama, *Two Rothschilds and the Land of Israel* (New York,

1978), p. 82. For details on the period 1882–99, see the third and fourth chapters. Schama draws a clear distinction between the motivations and ideas of the baron as regards colonization in Palestine and that of his appointed administrators. For a critical view of the baron as well as his administration, see Laskov, *Ha-Biluim*, p. 342. See also Dan Giladi, "Pekidut ha-Baron Rothschild ve-ha-Moshavot be-Eretz Israel," *Divrei ha-Kongress ha-Olami ha-Shmini le-Madaei ha-Yahadut* (Jerusalem, 1982), pp. 145–51. Zionist historiography has usually dealt harshly with the Rothschild administration. Among the first to evaluate the baron himself in a more positive light was Weizmann. See *Trial and Error*, pp. 36 and 137.

14. See Ahad Ha'Am, "Emet me-Eretz Israel," 1891 and 1893, in *Kol Kitvei Ahad Ha'Am* (Jerusalem, 1947), pp. 23–24. See also Leo Motzkin's report to the Second Zionist Congress (1898) based on a nine-week sojourn in Palestine at Herzl's request, *Stenographisches Protokoll der Verhandlungen des II. Zionisten-Congresses gehalten zu Basel vom 28. bis 31. August 1898* (Vienna, 1898), pp. 99–127.

15. Halpern, "Ideology and Institutions of Israel," p. 40.

16. The Anglo-Palestine Company, the first Zionist institution in Palestine, began operating in Jaffa at the end of 1903, and the Palestine Office, which was responsible for Zionist affairs and reported to the headquarters in Germany, was established in Jaffa in early 1908 under the direction of Arthur Ruppin.

17. The standard biography of Herzl is still Alex Bein, *Theodore Herzl* (New York, 1962). For a critical assessment of Bein's work, see Jacques Kornberg, "Theodore Herzl: A Reevaluation," *Journal of Modern History* 52 (June 1980): 226–52. See also Amos Elon, *Herzl* (New York, 1975); Walter Laqueur, *A History of Zionism* (New York, 1972), chap. 3; David Vital, *The Origins of Zionism*, part 3. For a psychoanalytic interpretation of Herzl, see Peter Loewenberg, "Theodore Herzl: A Psychoanalytic Study in Charismatic Political Leadership," in Benjamin B. Wolman, ed., *The Psychoanalytic Interpretation of History* (New York, 1971), pp. 150–91. For a comparative analysis, see Carl E. Schorske, *Fin-de-Siècle Vienna: Politics and Culture* (New York, 1980), pp. 146ff. For a sociological analysis, see Jehuda and Shulamit Reinharz, "Leadership and Charisma: The Case of Theodor Herzl," in Jehuda Reinharz and Daniel Swetschinski, eds., *Mystics, Philosophers and Politicians: Essays in Jewish Intellectual History in Honor of Alexander Altmann* (Durham, N.C., 1981), pp. 275–313.

18. See, e.g., Max Bodenheimer, *So Wurde Israel* (Frankfurt am Main, 1958), p. 69; Elias Auerbach, *Pionier der Verwirklichung* (Stuttgart, 1969), p. 80; Yosef Eliash, *Zikhronot Zioni me-Russyah* (Tel Aviv, 1955), pp. 64–65; Menahem Ussishkin, "Ha-Tragiyut be-Haye Motzkin," in *Sefer Motzkin*, p. 16. See also Reinharz, "Leadership and Charisma." There were, of course, also those who at first adopted a critical, sometimes even hostile, stance toward Herzl. This was especially true of the inner circle of the Odessa Committee. See Klausner, *Mi-Kattowitz ad Basel*, vol. 2, pp. 341ff; idem, *Hibbat Zion be-Rumanyah* (Jerusalem, 1958), pp. 301ff; Menahem Ussishkin, "Pgishati ha-Rishonah im Herzl," *Sefer Ussishkin* (Jerusalem, 1944), pp. 352–54. On the other hand, the initial response from Galicia was more favorable. See N. M. Gelber, *Toldot ha-Tnuah ha-Zionit be-Galizia 1875–1918* (Jerusalem, 1958), pp. 282ff.

19. Herzl, *The Jewish State: An Attempt at a Modern Solution of the Jewish Question* (New York, 1946), pp. 75–76.

20. Ben Halpern, *The Idea of the Jewish State*, 2nd ed., rev. (Cambridge, Mass.,

1969), p. 141. Herzl did make some exceptions to his policy. In 1898 he issued a call to conquer the communities ("Eroberung der Gemeinden"), by which he meant that the Zionists should seize control of Jewish community institutions, but this plan was intended primarily as a tactical move to win the Jewish public over to the Zionist cause.

21. For an analysis of Herzl's charisma, including its sources and manifestations, see Reinharz, "Leadership and Charisma."
22. Quoted in Leon Simon, "Herzl and Ahad Ha'Am," *Herzl Year Book* (New York, 1960), vol. 3, p. 149. Italics in original.
23. See Halpern, "Ideology and Institutions of Israel," pp. 54–55.
24. See Israel Klausner, *Opposizyah le-Herzl* (Jerusalem, 1960), p. 11.
25. See Ben Halpern, "Herzl's Historic Gift: The Sense of Sovereignty," *Herzl Year Book* (New York, 1960), vol. 3, pp. 33–34.
26. The First Zionist Congress did not formally resolve upon the formation of a worldwide organization. However, the Third Zionist Congress of 1899 recognized in the *Organisations-Statut* which it adopted that such an organization had come into existence, comprising those Jews who signified their assent to the program of the Zionist congress and paid the shekel.
27. See Nathan Feinberg, "Mashmautah ha-Mishpatit shel Tokhnit Basel," in *Shivat Zion* (Jerusalem, 1950), vol. 1, pp. 131–37.
28. See Bein, ed., *Sefer Motzkin*, p. 48.
29. The idea of the Berlin congress failed because of its lukewarm reception by members of the Hibbat Zion, including Ahad Ha'Am.
30. See the letter of Ahad Ha'Am to M. Mandelstamm, July 22, 1898. CZA, A3/8.
31. See Lichtenstein, *Be-Zel Koratenu*, pp. 97–98.
32. Joseph Klausner claims that he met Weizmann in Montreux, Switzerland, immediately after the First Zionist Congress, where Chaim and fellow students were vacationing. Klausner's memory may have been inaccurate here; not having had sufficient funds to travel to Basel, it would seem unlikely that Weizmann would have had the money or the inclination to vacation. There are some other internal inconsistencies in the Klausner memoir. See Joseph Klausner, "Chaim Weizmann: Early Memories," in *Chaim Weizmann: A Tribute on His Seventieth Birthday*, ed. Paul Goodman (London, 1945), pp. 36–37.
33. The university attracted many Polish students and had a number of Polish faculty members, including Weizmann's mentor, Bistrzycki.
34. Little is known about Getzova and her relationship with Weizmann since their correspondence is in private hands and is unobtainable at this date. There is some information on Getzova in an article by Saul Stupnitzky, "Firer und Trauemer," published in *Frimorgn* [Riga], February 2, 1926. W.A.
35. See Johann Langhard, *Die anarchistische Bewegung in der Schweiz von ihren Anfaengen bis zur Gegenwart und die internationalen Fuehrer* (Berlin, 1903), pp. 186–327, and Jan M. Meijer, *Knowledge and Revolution: The Russian Colony in Zuerich (1870–1873)* (Assen, 1956), pp. 47–84.
36. For a description of the ideologies and debates of these and other revolutionaries, see J. P. Nettl, *Rosa Luxemburg* (London, 1966), vol. 1, pp. 63–112.
37. See Alfred Erich Senn, *The Russian Revolution in Switzerland, 1914–1917* (Madison, Wisc., 1971), pp. 3–4.
38. Ibid., p. 6. By 1907 the number of Russian citizens enrolled at the seven Swiss universities had grown to 2,343, representing 34.2 percent of the total en-

rollment. The 1,311 Russians studying medicine constituted 70 percent of the total enrollment in Switzerland's five medical schools. The 1,454 Russian women enrolled in 1907 made up the majority of female students at Swiss universities.

39. See A. Hermoni, *Be-Ikvot ha-Biluim* (Jerusalem, 1952), p. 101.
40. See Leonard Schapiro, "The Role of the Jews in the Russian Revolutionary Movement," *Slavonic and East European Review* 40, no. 94 (December 1961): 148–67; Elias Tcherikower, "Yidn revolutsionern in Russland in di 60er un 70er yorn," *Historishe Shriften Yivo* [Vilna] 3 (1939): 152–71; idem, "Nationalist and Revolutionary Ideologies among Russian Jewry," *The Early Jewish Labor Movement in the United States* (New York, 1961), pp. 27–50. See also Moshe Mishkinski, *Reshit Tnuat ha-Poalim ha-Yehudit be-Russyah* (Tel Aviv, 1981), esp. chaps. 8–9.
41. Algemeyner Yidisher Arbeter Bund in Lite Poyln un Russland.
42. See *Yidisher Arbeter*, no. 2 (1901): 97–102; repr. in Mendes-Flohr and Reinharz, *The Jew in the Modern World*, pp. 340–41. See also Jacob S. Hertz, "The Bund's Nationality Program and Its Critics in the Russian, Polish and Austrian Socialist Movements," *Studies in Modern Jewish Social History*, ed. Joshua A. Fishman (New York, 1972), pp. 30–94.
43. See Henry J. Tobias, *The Jewish Bund in Russia: From Its Origins to 1905* (Stanford, 1905), pp. 127–29. See also Koppel S. Pinson, "Arkady Kremer, Vladimir Medem and the Ideology of the Jewish Bund," *Jewish Social Studies*, July 1945, pp. 233–64.
44. Quoted in J. S. Hertz, "Der Bund un di andere Rikhtungen," *Die Geshikhte fun Bund*, ed. Gregor Aronson et al. (New York, 1960), vol. 1, p. 351.
45. Weizmann received a mandate from Pinsk for each successive congress.
46. This preliminary conference took place from August 19 to 22, 1898. See Yitzhak Gruenbaum, "Mi-Warsaw ad Helsingfors," and A. Rafaeli, "Veidot Artziot shel Zione Russyah," in *Katzir, Kovetz le-Korot ha-Tnuah ha-Zionit be-Russyah* (Tel Aviv, 1964), vol. 1, pp. 21–26 and 41–59 resp.
47. This was the first (illegal) convention of Russian Zionists. It was attended by some 160 representatives from 93 locales, most of whom also attended the Second Zionist Congress. Just prior to the latter congress there were 373 Zionist associations in Russia, representing approximately 41 percent of the 913 Zionist associations in the entire World Zionist Organization. See Maor, *Ha-Tnuah ha-Zionit be-Russyah*, pp. 151–52. See also Yitzhak Gruenbaum, "Mi-Warsaw ad Helsingfors," in *Katzir*, vol. 1, pp. 21–24.
48. *Stenographisches Protokoll* (II) (1898), pp. 99–127. See also the response to Motzkin during the debate that ensued at the congress: Willy Bambus, *Herr Motzkin und die Wahrheit ueber die Kolonisation Palaestinas* (Berlin, 1898). See also the following issues of *Die Welt*: October 14, 1898, pp. 2–5; November 4, 1898, p. 8; and November 18, 1898, p. 46. See also *Zion*, no. 8 (late August 1898): 14–16.
49. See *Stenographisches Protokoll* (II), pp. 137–51.
50. Weizmann, *Trial and Error*, p. 49.
51. *Stenographisches Protokoll* (II), p. 156. The resolution founding the bank was finally passed by acclamation. The Jewish Colonial Trust Limited was incorporated in London in March 1899. Its articles did contain provisions designed to secure control by the World Zionist Organization.
52. See Lichtenstein, *Be-Zel Koratenu*, pp. 99–101.
53. *Stenographisches Protokoll* (II), p. 242.

54. See Jacob Bernstein-Kohan, *Sefer Bernstein-Kohan*, ed. Miriam Bernstein-Kohan (Tel Aviv, 1946), pp. 213–21.

55. Weizmann to Leo Motzkin and Paula Rosenblum [September 24?], 1898, *WL* 1, pp. 66–67.

56. "I: Elektrolytische Reduktion von 1-Nitroanthrachinon; II: Ueber die Kondensation von Phenanthrenchinon und Nitroanthrachinon mit einigen Phenolen. Inaugural-Dissertation der mathematisch-naturwissenschaftlichen Fakultaet der Universitaet Freiburg in der Schweiz zur Erlangung der Doktorwuerde vorgelegt von Dr. Ch. Weizmann aus Pinsk. Bern 1899."

57. Carl Graebe had interests similar to Weizmann's. He had synthesized alizarin, proved it to be derived from anthracene, a coal tar substance, and had succeeded in synthesizing it from anthraquinone, a compound related to anthracene. He was professor at the University of Geneva from 1878 to 1906. See Berend Strahlmann, "Carl Graebe," *Neue Deutsche Biographie* (Berlin, 1963), vol. 6, pp. 705–6.

58. Abraham Lichtenstein became secretary, later president, of the Bern Academic Zionist Society. He married Chaim's sister Hayah in 1901.

59. See Weizmann, *Trial and Error*, pp. 50–51.

60. In *Trial and Error* Weizmann mistakenly called this first Zionist society Ha-Shahar, which was, in fact, the name of a Zionist society founded in Geneva in February 1902.

61. See Weizmann to Leo Motzkin, November 23, 1901, *WL* 1, pp. 209–10. See also A. Hermoni, *Be-Ikvot ha-Biluim*, pp. 90–92, and Isaiah Berlin, *Personal Impressions*, ed. Henry Hardy (New York, 1980), p. 49, note 1.

62. The official organ of the World Zionist Organization, *Die Welt*, reported one such speech at the end of January 1899. See *Die Welt*, no. 6, February 10, 1899, p. 13.

63. See Hirsch Abramowicz, "Historishe Debatn Weizmann-Tepper," *Pinsk*, vol. 2, pp. 469–71; idem, *Farschwundene Geshtaltn* (Buenos Aires, 1958), pp. 254–60. The latter is in the Yivo Archives. Abramowicz, who witnessed the debate, later wrote that Tepper was by far the best speaker, but this hardly mattered since each side, of course, claimed "victory." I am grateful to Dina Abramowicz for drawing my attention to her father's memoir.

64. See Yitzhak Berger, "Weizmann Tahat ha-Krashim," *Davar*, April 22, 1935, p. 2. See also Lichtenstein, *Be-Zel Koratenu*, pp. 86–87, and *Pinsk*, vol. 1, p. 53. An indication of the Bund's power in Pinsk is suggested by the fact that when Tepper was arrested soon after the debate with Weizmann, members of the Bund broke into the jail, which was located near the police station, and released him and others. Rachel Leah Weizmann, in *Der Tog*, May 14, 1938, p. 5, tells of searches for Bundists in the Weizmann house: "When the turn came for Chaim to be searched, he was not treated too politely. He stood there, pale and stiff, with a heavy heart, and it took him a long time until he recovered from the shock." Shmuel, Weizmann's brother, was a Bundist, and the two quarreled endlessly whenever Chaim came home, according to the same source.

65. See Weizmann to Leo Motzkin, February 3, 1901, *WL* 1, pp. 86–88, 91–92, 200–201. See also Saul Stupnitzky, "Firer and Trauemer," in *Frimorgn* [Riga], February 2, 1926. W.A.

66. At the time there were some 550 Jewish students in Bern, of which about 60 were Zionists. The majority belonged to the Bund and Social Democratic party. See *Hamelitz*, February 24, 1903, pp. 2–3.

67. Vladimir Medem, *Vladimir Medem, The Life and Soul of a Legendary Jewish Socialist*, trans. Samuel A. Portnoy (New York, 1979), p. 222. See also Koppel S. Pinson, "Arkady Kremer, Vladimir Medem and the Ideology of the Jewish 'Bund,' " *Jewish Social Studies* 7, no. 3 (July 1945): 233–64.

68. See *Hamelitz*, February 24, 1903, pp. 2–3, and March 9, 1903, p. 5.

69. In his memoirs Weizmann mentions that Buber was also invited. Buber was not in Switzerland at the time, though Weizmann tried to arrange a propaganda tour for him in January 1903. See Weizmann to Martin Buber, December 14, 1902, *WL* 2, pp. 93–94. See also Buber's reply to Weizmann, expressing doubt about his ability to come to Switzerland. Buber to Weizmann, January 23, 1903, in Martin Buber, *Briefwechsel aus sieben Jahrzehnten*. Vol. 1: 1897–1918, ed. Grete Schaeder (Heidelberg, 1972), pp. 185–86. An article in *Hamelitz*, February 24, 1903, corroborates Medem's account of the Zionist participants. See also Weizmann to Vera Khatzman, February 21, 1903, *WL* 2, pp. 260–61. Hermoni ascribes the locale of the debate to Lausanne. See A. Hermoni, *Be-Ikvot ha-Biluim*, p. 93. It is, of course, possible that Medem and Weizmann debated each other in that city as well.

70. Weizmann, *Trial and Error*, p. 51.

71. Weizmann described Aberson thus: "He had a brilliant mind . . . He was hated by the Russian Marxists because he understood their philosophy, had its terminology at his fingertips, met them on their own ground and invariably routed them in argument . . . The Bundists were terrified of him, and this man, who had so little to eat, was dubbed, with conscious irony, the *Bundistenfresser*, the gobbler-up of Bundists." Weizmann, *Trial and Error*, p. 65. For a brief description of Aberson, see A. Hermoni, *Be-Ikvot ha-Biluim*, p. 98.

72. This passage also does not agree with Weizmann's account, which claims that at the close of the meeting Plekhanov himself came up to him, furious at the success of the Zionists. Weizmann's response was: "But Monsieur Plekhanov, you are not the Czar!" This exchange may have taken place elsewhere—probably in Geneva, not Bern—in November 1901; it is the only record we have of a direct encounter between Weizmann and Plekhanov. See Weizmann to Leo Motzkin, November 23, 1901, *WL* 1, pp. 209–10. On the other hand, Medem may have exaggerated the power of the opposition and the limited resources of the Bund in order to aggrandize *his* victory.

73. The account in *Hamelitz*, February 24, 1903, pp. 2–3, is, on the contrary, full of praise for Weizmann's oratorical skills. See also *Davar*, December 23, 1932, p. 2.

74. Weizmann described Ansky, author of *The Dybbuk*, as a sort of universal uncle: "The Zionists liked him because of his tender Jewish understanding . . . The revolutionists found in him . . . a sympathetic soul. He had no very sharp political views, and was never really identified with any group." Weizmann, *Trial and Error*, p. 64.

75. Weizmann spoke on each of the three nights. Interestingly, he defended the "Mizrahi" from attacks by the Bundists but dissociated himself from Herzl's novel *Altneuland*, claiming that it did not represent a Zionist program. See *Hamelitz*, February 24, 1903, pp. 2–3.

76. Medem, *The Life and Soul of a Legendary Jewish Socialist*, pp. 261–62.

77. See CZA, Z1/295. See also the signature of Weizmann's letter to Max Bodenheimer on April 28, 1899, *WL* 1, p. 69. By the time Weizmann arrived in Geneva, there existed six Zionist societies in Switzerland; see *Stenogra-*

phisches Protokoll (II), p. 47, and *Die Welt*, no. 4, 1897, p. 11, and no. 30, 1898, p. 2. In 1897 the Union de Sionistes Suisses was founded and twelve Swiss Zionists attended the First Zionist Congress.

78. See Ben Halpern, "Weizmann ve-Doro," in *Ha-Ishiyut ve-Dorah* (Jerusalem, 1964), p. 163.

79. See Anthony R. Michaelis, "Appendix: The Scientific Papers and Patents of Dr. C. Weizmann" *Weizmann Centenary* (London, 1974), pp. 50–64.

80. A. Katchalsky, "Symbol of New Scientific Approach to Living," *The Jerusalem Post. Chaim Weizmann Memorial Supplement*, October 30, 1953, p. 5.

81. Vertrag zwischen der Aktionsgesellschaft unter der Firma "Farbenfabriken vorm. Friedr. Bayer & Co." in Elberfeld . . . und den Herren Dr. Chr. Deichler und Dr. Ch. Weizmann in Genf. . . ." The contract was signed on January 30, 1901. W.A.

82. Weizmann, *Trial and Error*, p. 56.

83. For more details see Lichtenstein, *Be-Zel Koratenu*, pp. 92–97. It is not quite clear from the Lichtenstein and Weizmann accounts whether the latter made a few thousand marks on his early discovery while still in the Polytechnic or later, when he was in Geneva, or whether this is the discovery he tried to sell in Russia in 1897 on the eve of the First Zionist Congress.

84. Weizmann to Vera Khatzman, July 5, 1902, *WL 1*, p. 285.

85. Weizmann to Vera Khatzman, July 30, 1902, *WL 1*, p. 332.

86. Vera Khatzman to Weizmann, August 6, 1902. W.A.

87. His first address in Geneva was rue de l'Ecole de Chimie.

88. Weizmann to Paula Rosenblum, August 5, 1899, *WL 1*, pp. 72–73.

89. Herzl stated, among other things: "I do not want to draw a picture of the homeland for you, for it will shortly begin in reality . . . I know what I am saying; I have never spoken so definitely before. Today I declare: I believe the time is not far off when the Jewish people will set itself in motion . . ." Quoted in Alex Bein, *Theodore Herzl*, pp. 281–82.

90. See Isaiah Friedman, *Germany, Turkey, and Zionism, 1897–1918* (Oxford, 1977), pp. 75–76, 88–89.

91. It took three years—until 1902—before the statutory minimum of 250,000 pounds, which permitted the Jewish Colonial Trust to commence operations, was paid up.

92. The composition of SAC (Engeres Aktions-Comité, or EAC) varied little between 1897 and 1904, the year Herzl died. In addition to Herzl, it was composed of Leopold Kahn, Oser Kokesch, Oskar Marmorek, and Moritz Tobias Schnierer.

93. See *Stenographisches Protokoll der Verhandlungen des III. Zionisten-Congresses gehalten zu Basel vom 15. bis 18. August 1899* (Vienna, 1899), pp. 67–71.

94. Ibid., pp. 70–71.

95. *Stenographisches Protokoll (III)*, pp. 63–65.

96. Ibid., p. 64.

97. "Herr Motzkin moechte, dass wir mathematisch und plannmaessig verschweigen, wenn irgend etwas Gutes in unserer Bewegung vorkommt . . . Er verspricht sich nur dann richtige Agitation . . . wenn man nicht ab und zu eine gute Mittheilung macht . . ." Ibid., p. 81. For Herzl's entire speech, see pp. 71–83.

98. Particularly Tschlenow, Weizmann, Nahum Sokolow, and Menahem Sheinkin. They, in turn, were opposed mostly by Rabbi Isaac Jacob Reines.

99. *Stenographisches Protokoll (III)*, pp. 198–206, 235.

100. Weizmann to Theodor Herzl [August 19], 1899, *WL* 1, p. 74.
101. Weizmann to Paula Rosenblum, August 5, 1899, *WL* 1, p. 72.
102. On the reception of Weizmann's speeches at Homel, see Yehuda Kahan-ovich, *Me-Homel ad Tel Aviv* (Tel Aviv, 1952), p. 29: "Dr. Weizmann held his lectures before mass gatherings in classic Yiddish . . . People came from all the neighboring towns. His inspiring speeches, full of content about Zion and the redemption, made a tremendous impact on his listeners, and the leaders of the Bund and S[ocial] D[emocrats], enemies of Zion, did not dare enter into a debate with him."
103. See letter from Isaac Dov Levine, October 19, 1964. W.A.
104. Weizmann, *Trial and Error*, p. 41.
105. Letter from Isaac Dov Levine, October 29, 1964. W.A.
106. Weizmann to Leo Motzkin, September 11, 1899, *WL* 1, pp. 75–76. For a more pessimistic evaluation of the Third Zionist Congress, see letter of Gaster to Mandelstamm, September 18, 1899. CZA, A3/8.
107. Weizmann to Leo Motzkin, June 9, 1900, *WL* 1, p. 79.
108. Ibid., p. 80.
109. Weizmann to Leo Motzkin, February 3, 1901, *WL* 1, p. 88. See also Weiz-mann to Leo Motzkin, November 23, 1901, *WL* 1, p. 208.
110. Weizmann to Leo Motzkin, February 3, 1901, *WL* 1, p. 81.
111. On the Fourth Zionist Congress in London and the reaction to it in the gen-eral press, see Benjamin Jaffe "Ha-Kongress ha-Zioni ha-Revii be-London ve-ha-Hedim ba-Itonut ha-Britit," *Haumah*, nos. 51–52 (1977): 394–405.
112. *Stenographisches Protokoll der Verhandlungen des IV. Zionisten-Congresses in London, 1900* (Vienna, 1900), p. 5.
113. The Fifth Zionist Congress of 1901 resolved upon the establishment of the fund within the near future. It was finally incorporated in 1907 under the name Juedischer Nationalfonds (Keren Kajemeth le-Jisroel) Limited.
114. Maor, *Ha-Tnuah ha-Zionit be-Russyah*, p. 178.
115. On Gaster's views on practical and cultural tasks at this stage, see Gaster to Mandelstamm, September 18, 1899. CZA, A3/8.
116. *Stenographisches Protokoll* (IV), pp. 222–23.
117. Ibid., p. 226.
118. Weizmann to Paula Motzkin, August [16?], 1900, *WL* 1, p. 83.
119. Weizmann, *Trial and Error*, pp. 56–57.
120. Herzl, *Complete Diaries*, vol. 3, p. 976. On at least one delegate, Shmarya Levin, the Fourth Zionist Congress had left an unforgettable impression. Perhaps this was due to the fact that it was the first congress he had at-tended. See Shmarya Levin, *Forward from Exile*, pp. 370–76.

V The Democratic Faction

1. See Vera Weizmann, *The Impossible Takes Longer* (New York, 1967), pp. 1, 12.
2. See Khatzman family tree in W.A.
3. Weizmann, *The Impossible Takes Longer*, p. 4.
4. *Evreiskaia Entsiklopedia* (St. Petersburg, 1913), vol. 7, p. 301.
5. Ibid., vol. 13, p. 678.
6. Weizmann, *The Impossible Takes Longer*, p. 5.
7. Ibid., p. 10.
8. Weizmann, *Trial and Error*, pp. 70–71.
9. Weizmann, *The Impossible Takes Longer*, p. 2.

10. Weizmann to Vera Khatzman [early 1901], *WL* 1, p. 84.
11. Ibid., pp. 84–85.
12. Weizmann, *The Impossible Takes Longer*, p. 13.
13. An added factor in the delay may have been due to the fact that Sophia's sister, who lived with her in Bern, was languishing due to a fatal illness.
14. Weizmann to Vera, [March 15?], 1901, *WL* 1, p. 97.
15. Weizmann to Vera, March 19, 1901, *WL* 1, p. 100.
16. Weizmann to Vera, July 17, 1901, *WL* 1, p. 155.
17. See Yaakov Cohen, "Krovim u-Rehokim," *Moznaim*, no. 2 (1960): 102.
18. Related to the author by Aryeh Motzkin, January 4, 1983. See also Helga Dudman, *Street People* (Jerusalem, 1982), pp. 138–39. The source for this episode comes from the Motzkin family. I could find no other corroborating evidence to substantiate it.
19. Related to the author by the daughter-in-law of Leo and Paula Motzkin. Interview with Naomi Motzkin, June 18, 1982.
20. Weizmann to Vera, September 8, 1901, *WL* 1, p. 179.
21. Weizmann to Vera, March 30, 1902, *WL* 1, p. 246.
22. Weizmann to Vera, April 1, 1902, *WL* 1, p. 248.
23. This is clear from Weizmann's joyful response: "And so on Sunday night I shall be with you, with you, with you, my darling . . ." Ibid., April 4, 1902, *WL* 1, p. 252.
24. See Weizmann, *The Impossible Takes Longer*, p. 15.
25. See, e.g., Jehuda Louis Weinberg, *Aus der Fruehzeit des Zionismus. Heinrich Loewe* (Jerusalem, 1946), pp. 97–112.
26. Halpern, "Ideology and Institutions of Israel," p. 58.
27. See Weizmann's summary of the reasons for opposition. Weizmann, *Trial and Error*, pp. 52–53.
28. See Herzl, *Complete Diaries*, vol. 2, p. 581.
29. Halpern, "Ideology and Institutions of Israel," p. 62.
30. See Herzl, *Complete Diaries*, vol. 2, p. 654.
31. See Yitzhak Gruenbaum, "Mi-Warsaw ad Helsingfors," in *Katzir, Kovetz le-Korot ha-Tnuah ha-Zionit be-Russyah*, vol. 1 (Tel Aviv, 1964), pp. 21–26.
32. See Halpern, *The Idea of the Jewish State*, pp. 28 ff.
33. See Yosef Salmon, "Ha-Imut beyn ha-Haredim la-Maskilim bi-Tnuat Hibbat Zion bi-Shnot ha-80." *Zionism* [Tel Aviv] 5 (1978): 43–55.
34. "Beschluss der Versammlung Zionistisch gesinnter Rabbiner zu Warschau." CZA, A147/23/11. Italics in original.
35. See Maor, *Ha-Tnuah ha-Zionit be-Russyah*, p. 154.
36. "Der Zionismus unternimmt nichts, was dem Religionsgesetze des Judenthums widerspricht." *Stenographisches Protokoll der Verhandlungen des II. Zionisten-Congresses gehalten zu Basel* (Vienna, 1898), p. 222.
37. *Stenographisches Protokoll der Verhandlungen des IV. Zionisten-Congresses in London* (Vienna, 1900), p. 226.
38. Klausner, *Opposizyah le-Herzl*, pp. 45–46.
39. Halpern, "Ideology and Institutions of Israel," p. 71.
40. See *Sefer Motzkin*, p. 48. One could perhaps go a step further and say that some of the ideas of the Democratic Faction can be traced back to the Bnei Moshe society, Ahad Ha'Am's training school for Zionists.
41. The term "Zionist Youth Conference" was employed from the beginning in order to make it clear the conference was not limited to students. The term "youth" was also ambiguous, since many of those involved were in their

twenties. Weizmann was then twenty-six and Motzkin thirty-four. On the other hand, Herzl was a mere forty-one at the time.

42. See CZA, A126/16.

43. See letter from Nemser to Motzkin, February 12, 1901. W.A. See also Courland to Kadimah, January 15, 1901. CZA, A126/14.

44. See, e.g., Menahem Ussishkin, "Dr. Chaim Weizmann," in *Sefer Ussishkin,* p. 365.

45. Weizmann to Leo Motzkin, February 3, 1901, *WL* 1, p. 87.

46. Weizmann to Leo Motzkin [February 22, 1901], *WL* 1, p. 89.

47. Weizmann to Motzkin [February 23?], 1901, *WL* 1, p. 90.

48. Weizmann to Motzkin, March 3, 1901, *WL* 1, pp. 90–91.

49. See Motzkin to Weizmann, March 15, 1901. W.A.

50. Weizmann to Motzkin, March 11, 1901, *WL* 1, p. 93.

51. "Circular of 15 March 1901." W.A.

52. *Hatzfirah,* no. 71, April 14, 1901, pp. 2–3; "Conferenz zionistischen Studenten in Muenchen," *Die Welt,* no. 16, April 19, 1901, pp. 7–8. See also CZA, A139/5.

53. Weizmann to Motzkin, March 30, 1901, *WL* 1, p. 103.

54. The report in *Hatzfirah* does indicate the presence of a delegate (Boris Gurevich) from Berlin who played a minor role in the proceedings. In a letter to Vera dated April 1, 1901, Weizmann speaks in the plural about "colleagues from Berlin."

55. Weizmann to Vera, March 19, 1901, *WL* 1, p. 99.

56. See letter of Catherine Dorfman in *Hapoel Hazair,* no. 10, December 15, 1933, p. 15; Kressel Collection, Oxford Centre for Postgraduate Hebrew Studies.

57. See *Hatzfirah,* no. 71, April 14, 1901. See also protocol on the preparatory conference, pp. i, ii and iii. W.A.

58. Until the Youth Conference was convened, it was assumed by Weizmann and others that a youth organization would be created.

59. This point in Weizmann's address is not altogether clear. He saw this task as an aid in the war against the Bundists, but in what way he did not specify.

60. For the proceedings of the conference, see CZA, A139/5. See also Klausner, *Opposizyah,* pp. 52–53.

61. Weizmann to Vera, April 2, 1901, *WL* 1, p. 108.

62. See CZA, A139/5. See also "Resolution of the Munich Conference of April 1–2, 1901" (in Hebrew). W.A. See also "Conferenz Zionistischer Studenten in Muenchen," *Die Welt,* no. 16, April 19, 1901, pp. 7–8.

63. See *Voskhod,* April 15, 1901. Reprinted in Chaim Weizmann, *Dvarim* (Tel Aviv, 1936), vol. 1, pp. 7–10.

64. *Voskhod,* May 3, 1901. English translation in W.A.

65. On conditions in Palestine at the time, see Yitzhak Gil-Har, "Ha-Gibush veha-Izuv ha-Irguni veha-Medini shel ha-Yishuv be-Reshit ha-Meah ha-20," *Hazionut* 6 (1981): 7–47.

66. Among other things, the baron informed the delegates that "I am the Yishuv" and that those who in future would show themselves incapable of earning their livelihood would be "impitoyablement éliminés." "Go and dirty your hands," he commanded, "send your wives and children to work," "occupez-vous de vos champs" instead of endlessly agitating against the administration. See Simon Schama, *Two Rothschilds and the Land of Israel* (New York, 1978), p. 139. For a report on the meeting, see Tschlenow's article

"Bericht der Delegation der Russischen Chowewe Zion ueber die Pariser Conferenz," in *Die Welt*, no. 21, May 23, 1901, pp. 2–3. For Herzl's reaction to the interview of the Russian Zionists with the baron, see Herzl, *Complete Diaries*, vol. 3, p. 1150.

67. See Ahad Ha'Am, "Shluhei Am Ani," *Kol Kitvei Ahad Ha'Am*, pp. 305–8.

68. Evidence for this can be gleaned from a letter from Ahad Ha'Am to Weizmann written on March 17, 1902, in which he refers to his earlier advice. See *Igrot Ahad Ha'Am*, ed. Aryeh Simon (Tel Aviv, 1957), vol. 3, pp. 135–36.

69. See Ahad Ha'Am to Weizmann, July 1, 1901, in *Igrot Ahad Ha'Am*, vol. 3, p. 61.

70. See Herzl, *Complete Diaries*, vol. 3, pp. 1110ff.

71. Dr. D. Pasmanik, "Der Congress der Zionistischen Studentenschaft," *Die Welt*, no. 26, June 28, 1901, pp. 5–6.

72. Pasmanik had at this point already been removed by Weizmann from the Organization Bureau; while writing in positive terms in *Die Welt* about the forthcoming Youth Conference, he was secretly warning Herzl about its implications. See Pasmanik to Herzl, July 25, 1901. CZA, HB112. See also Lazar Schoen, *Die Stimme der Wahrheit* (Würzburg, 1905), p. 357, and A. Hermoni, *Be-Ikvot ha-Biluim*, p. 99.

73. Herzl to Weizmann, July 2, 1901. W. A.

74. See Weizmann to Herzl, [July 5, 1901], *WL* 1, p. 148.

75. See Ahad Ha'Am to Weizmann, July 1, 1901, in *Igrot Ahad Ha'Am*, vol. 3, p. 61.

76. Weizmann to Catherine Dorfman, July 5, 1901, *WL* 1, p. 150.

77. Weizmann to Vera, July 6–7, 1901, *WL* 1, pp. 152–53. Italics in original.

78. Ibid.

79. Weizmann to Vera, July 19, 1901, *WL* 1, p. 156.

80. The letter was co-signed by Esther Shneerson, one of Weizmann's collaborators in the Oragnization Bureau.

81. Weizmann to Theodor Herzl, July 22, 1901, *WL* 1, pp. 157–58.

82. See letter of Herzl to Weizmann—"strictly confidential"—dated July 28, 1901. W.A.

83. In a confidential letter to Pasmanik dated July 28, 1901, Herzl revealed the reasons for his move: ". . . Nun hat mir Dr. Weizmann neulich geschrieben, dass diese Versammlung [the Youth Conference] keinen oeffentlichen Charakter haben werde. Ich kann selbstverstaendlich eine Verantwortung fuer diese ganze Sache nicht auf mich nehmen und muss es dem Ermessen und Gewissen der Herren ueberlassen, ob sie durch ihre Veranstaltung unsere schwer und muehsam errungenen Erfolge nicht gefaehrden werden . . ." CZA, HB112.

84. Halpern, "Ideology and Institutions of Israel," p. 72. Herzl, *Complete Diaries*, vol. 3, p. 1191.

85. See minutes of SAC, October 1, 1901. CZA, Z1/174.

86. See minutes of GAC, October 9–12, 1901. CZA, Z1/191. Herzl, too, spoke against the organizers of the Youth Conference.

87. According to Adolf Pollak, who was at the time on the staff of the Zionist office in Vienna, Buber was also present at the meeting. See Adolf Pollak, "Zionistische Chronologie," pp. 168–69. Copy in CZA, G/357. According to Pollak, Weizmann and Buber came to inform Herzl officially that concurrent with the Fifth Zionist Congress they planned to convene a Jungzionistisches Kongress. Herzl replied, "Warum wollt Ihr diese Tagung Kongress

nennen? Die Antizionisten werden sagen, aha, es gibt schon zwei Kongresse der Zioniten! Ich gebe Euch den Rat, dem Kinde einen anderen Namen zu geben und dann koennt Ihr uns, wenn Ihr wollt, die Koepfe herunterreissen!"

88. Herzl kept his promise. See *Die Welt*, no. 45, November 8, 1901, p. 16.

89. See Weizmann's letters to Ahad Ha'Am and Herzl dated October 31, 1901, *WL* 1, pp. 194–98. Evidently the meeting with Weizmann (and Buber) did not seem sufficiently important for Herzl to record. Weizmann is not mentioned at all in Herzl's diaries.

90. During the same period (1901) both Berthold Feiwel and Martin Buber, who were in sympathy with Weizmann's ideas, served as editors of *Die Welt*. Later, of course, they broke with Herzl and became Weizmann's closest collaborators.

91. See Weizmann to Vera, September 19, 1901, *WL* 1, p. 185.

92. Dorfman and Koenigsberg were his most steadfast assistants.

93. See Weizmann to Leo Motzkin, April 24, 1901, *WL* 1, pp. 114–15, and May 25, 1901, *WL* 1, pp. 116–18.

94. Weizmann to Leo Motzkin, June 26, 1901, *WL* 1, p. 138.

95. Weizmann to Leo Motzkin, November 30, 1901, *WL* 1, p. 212.

96. Motzkin's wife, Paula, apparently refused to have Weizmann in her house after his break with Getzova. Interview with Naomi Motzkin, June 18, 1982.

97. See Weizmann to Leo Motzkin, November 16, 1901, *WL* 1, p. 202, and March 21, 1902, *WL* 1, p. 239; Weizmann to Vera, July 18, 1902, *WL* 1, p. 309, and August [16], 1902, *WL* 1, p. 371. In 1925, when Weizmann was president of the World Zionist Organization and Sophia a lecturer in patholgy at the University of Bern, she did not hesitate to ask for her former fiancé's assistance in securing a position at the Hebrew University. See Weizmann to Sophia Getzova, January 31, 1925. *WL* 12, p. 301.

98. See Catherine Dorfman, "The Democratic Faction," *Hapoel Hazair*, no. 10, December 15, 1933, p. 15.

99. When the Organization Bureau included his name among the speakers at the Youth Conference, Motzkin threatened not to attend. See Weizmann to Leo Motzkin, December 9, 1901 (both telegram and letter), *WL* 1, pp. 212–14. Weizmann wrote, "I will do *anything, anything*—even at the expense of my pride—to see that not the slightest slur is cast on you . . . How can you suspect *me* of wanting to place you in an awkward position?" Ibid., p. 214. It is, of course, possible that Weizmann deliberately included Motzkin's name. There are similar complaints from Bernard Lazare. See his letter to Weizmann of June 24, 1901. W.A. There may have been an attempt to legitimize and give weight to the conference through the inclusion of important and well-known personalities. For the agenda of the Youth Conference, see *Die Welt*, no. 50, December 13, 1901, p. 8.

100. Weizmann to Leo Motzkin, November 7, 1901, *WL* 1, p. 198.

101. Weizmann to Leo Motzkin, May 25, 1901, *WL* 1, p. 116.

102. "Pour en revenir au fond même de la chose, je ne puis accepter de participer à aucun titre au Congrès des Jeunes Sionistes. Le Congrès accepte le programme de Bâle, et je ne l'accepte pas . . ." Bernard Lazare to Weizmann, June 24, 1901. W.A. On Lazare and his attitude toward Zionism, see Edmund Silberner, "Bernard Lazare ve-Hazionut," in *Shivat Zion* (Jerusalem, 1953), vols. 2–3, pp. 328–64.

103. Ahad Ha'Am to Weizmann, July 1, 1901, in *Igrot Ahad Ha'Am*, pp. 60–61.

104. See "Statuten des Vereins Hessiana." [June 8, 1901]. W.A. The first statute reads: "Der Verein 'Hessiana' ist ein wissenschaftlicher und befasst sich theoretisch mit der Frage der Begruendung eines juedischen Gemeinwesens auf kollektivistischer Grundlage in Palaestina und den unter England's Schutzherrschaft stehenden Nachbarlaendern." See CZA, A126. See also Marie Syrkin, "Socialist Zionism: A New Concept, 1898," *Jewish Frontier* 41 (October 1974): 9–13.

105. The lecture was printed in Berlin but published in London in order to avoid problems with the German police. See also Syrkin to Smaller Actions Committee, June 19 and 21, 1898. CZA, Z1/286 and Z1/287.

106. See *Kitvei Nachman Syrkin*, ed. Berl Katznelson (Tel Aviv, 1939), vol. 1, pp. 84ff. See also *Avi Nachman Syrkin*, pp. 55ff.

107. Weizmann to Leo Motzkin, June 23, 1901, *WL* 1, p. 133.

108. Weizmann to Vera, June 25, 1901, *WL* 1, p. 137.

109. It was not until the latter part of 1902 that Weizmann informed his parents. See, e.g., Weizmann to Vera, August 10, 1902, *WL* 1, p. 355.

110. Weizmann to Leo Motzkin, October 27, 1901, *WL* 1, p. 192.

111. Ibid., pp. 192–93.

112. See *WL*, n. 1 to letter 119–20, p. 173.

113. Weizmann, *Trial and Error*, pp. 76–77.

114. Weizmann to Vera, June 12, 1901, *WL* 1, p. 127.

115. Weizmann to Vera, June 25, 1901, *WL* 1, p. 136.

116. Ibid.

117. Weizmann to Vera, July 4–5, 1901, *WL* 1, p. 146.

118. See, e.g., Weizmann to Leo Motzkin, November 16, 1901, *WL* 1, p. 201.

119. Weizmann to Leo Motzkin, November 30, 1901, *WL* 1, pp. 211–12.

120. Weizmann to Catherine Dorfman, September 2, 1901, *WL* 1, p. 176.

121. Weizmann to Vera, July 4–5, 1901, *WL* 1, p. 146.

122. Weizmann to Leo Motzkin, June 9, 1900, *WL* 1, p. 80.

123. See Weizmann to Vera, June 21, 1901, *WL* 1, p. 131.

124. Weizmann to Vera, June 3, 1901, *WL* 1, p. 120. Italics in original.

125. Weizmann to Vera, June 8, 1901, *WL* 1, p. 122.

126. See Weizmann to Leo Motzkin, November 21, 1901, *WL* 1, p. 203.

127. Weizmann to Leo Motzkin, November 23, 1901, *WL* 1, pp. 205–8. As to the last point in Weizmann's program, a committee for the establishment of an aid fund for Russian-Jewish students regardless of their party affiliation was established in Berlin. The chairmen of the Geneva and Bern Zionist societies, Jacob Rabinovich and Jacob Salkind, severely criticized Weizmann for having taken an active part in setting up a Geneva aid fund, charging that this undermined efforts then being made to unify Zionist aid funds in Switzerland; they pressured him to withdraw. See Rabinovich and Salkind to Weizmann, November 6, 1901. W.A. Rabinovich, who was also a member of the board of the Geneva Agudat Israel, wrote a letter to the Smaller Actions Committee charging that Weizmann and others involved in the planning of the Youth Conference intended to launch an antireligious campaign. See Rabinovich to Smaller Actions Committee, November 4, 1901. CZA, Z1/326.

128. Weizmann to Leo Motzkin, November 23, 1901, *WL* 1, pp. 208–9.

129. See letter to *Voskhod*, no. 71, December 12, 1901. W.A. See also the article by P. Auerbach in *Hatzfirah*, no. 244, November 15, 1901, pp. 1–2. W.A.; and Ferdinand Kobler, "Zur Conferenz der Zionistischen Studentenschaft,"

Die Welt, no. 50, December 13, 1901, pp. 8–9, which echo Weizmann's ideas.

130. See Klausner, *Opposizyah*, p. 115, n. 1. There were also in attendance some one hundred guests as well as newspaper correspondents.

131. See Weizmann to Leo Motzkin, November 21, 1901, *WL* 1, p. 203.

132. See minutes in W.A. and CZA, A126/24/5/2.

133. Klausner, *Opposizyah*, pp. 118–120.

134. See Weizmann, *Trial and Error*, p. 65.

135. See agenda of the Youth Conference in *Die Welt*, no. 50, December 13, 1901, p. 8.

136. Weizmann speech of December 20, 1901, at the Youth Conference, W.A.

137. Weizmann apologized after the fact: ". . . should twenty or more such polemical skirmishes occur, my attitude to you—as to a human being and friend—will not waver. May all the saints protect me: in debate I always hit hard . . ." Weizmann to Motzkin, January 31, 1902, *WL* I, p. 221.

138. See Klausner, *Opposizyah*, p. 135.

139. For opposition to the Democratic Faction even before the Fifth Zionist Congress commenced its deliberations, see M. Glickson, "Zikhronot Rishonim," *Haaretz*, November 17, 1933. W.A.

140. Herzl, *Complete Diaries*, vol. 3, p. 1187.

141. See Herzl's diary entry for August 24, 1897. *Complete Diaries*, vol. 2, pp. 578–79.

142. *Stenographisches Protokoll der Verhandlungen des V. Zionisten-Congresses in Basel* (Vienna, 1901), pp. 114–15.

143. "Wir haben, seit wir Zionisten sind, Max Nordau Liebe und Verehrung entgegengebracht. Gerade deshalb aber muss ich hier Zeugnis ablegen, dass wir durch die Art, wie Nordau diese unsere Sache behandelt hat, in unserem tiefsten Empfinden, im Kerne unseres seelischen Zusammenhanges mit dem Zionismus verletzt wurden." *Stenographisches Protokoll* (V), p. 151. See also p. 152.

144. Ibid., pp. 126ff.; 312ff.

145. Ibid., pp. 70–71.

146. Ibid., pp. 389–92. The Jewish publishing house was to be granted a loan.

147. See Weizmann to Catherine Dorfman, [August 11?], 1901, *WL* 1, pp. 165–68. It is clear from this letter that other members involved in the preparation for the Youth Conference had also discussed this idea. According to Berthold Feiwel, however, the resolution concerning a Jewish university was presented by the cultural commission to the congress solely due to Weizmann's insistence. See Berthold Feiwel to Herzl, May 22, 1902. CZA, Z1/335.

148. *Stenographisches Protokoll* (V), pp. 392–93.

149. Ibid., p. 395.

150. Ibid., p. 402.

151. See M. Glickson, "Zikhronot Rishonim," *Haaretz*, January 17, 1933. W.A.

152. *Stenographisches Protokoll* (V), p. 417.

153. See Joseph Klausner, "Chaim Weizmann: Early Memories," in *Chaim Weizmann: A Tribute on His Seventieth Birthday*, ed. Paul Goodman (London, 1945), p. 40. What is more likely is that he fainted from sheer exhaustion.

154. Ibid., pp. 427ff.

155. See letters from Martin Buber to Paula Buber-Winkler dated December 26, 1901, and January 1, 1902, in Martin Buber, *Briefwechsel aus sieben Jahrzehnten*, vol. 1, p. 171.

156. *Stenographisches Protokoll* (V), p. 434. The speeches of members of the Dem-

ocratic Faction were praised in an editorial in *Die Welt*. See Oskar Marmorek, "Ein Epilog," *Die Welt*, no. 2, January 10, 1902, p. 2.
157. "Da ist Euerer Majestaet treueste Opposition." See Maor, *Ha-Tnuah ha-Zionit be-Russyah*, p. 194.

VI Public Ventures and Private Affairs

1. Herzl's telegram was dated December 25, 1901. See Herzl, *Complete Diaries*, vol. 3, p. 1189.
2. "J'ai soumis au pied du trône l'adresse d'hommage du Congrês, contenu dans votre télégramme et l'ordre de sa Majesté. Je m'empresse de vous en exprimer Sa haute satisfaction Impériale. Ibrahim [Chief of Protocol]." See *Stenographisches Protokoll der Verhandlungen des V. Zionisten-Congresses* (Vienna, 1901), p. 173.
3. See headnote to letter 155 in *WL* 1, p. 225. For Herzl's reaction, see *Complete Diaries*, vol. 3, p. 1192.
4. Weizmann to Herzl, February 3, 1902, *WL* 1, pp. 225–27. Copies of all the resolutions of the meetings are in CZA, Z1/94. See also "First Circular of the Democratic Faction," dated January 24, 1902. W.A.
5. Concerning the activities and membership of Hashahar, see CZA, A139/6.
6. See Weizmann, *Trial and Error*, pp. 64–66. See also the letter from Isaac Berger to Weizmann, February 3, 1902, W.A., asking about Aberson's brochure; letter from Weizmann to Menahem Ussishkin, December 28, 1902, *WL* 2, pp. 130–31. See also letter to Ussishkin dated January 13, 1903, *WL* 2, p. 192.
7. See CZA, Z1/295.
8. Weizmann to Ahad Ha'Am, February 5, 1902, *WL* 1, p. 228.
9. Weizmann to Herzl, February 2, 1901, *WL* 1, p. 225.
10. See Herzl, *Complete Diaries*, vol. 3, p. 1207.
11. Weizmann to Vera, February 17, 1902, *WL* 1, p. 232.
12. For a brief report to the GAC on Herzl's activities in Constantinople, see "Rundschreiben. Streng Vertraulich," signed by Kokesch and Herzl on behalf of SAC. CZA, Z1/225.
13. See *Hamelitz*, no. 25, January 30, 1902, p. 1, and no. 28, February 3, 1902, p. 3.
14. See letter from Ussishkin to I. L. Goldberg dated February 3, 1902. CZA, A9/132/1.
15. See Weizmann, *Trial and Error*, p. 59.
16. See *Die Welt*, no. 21, May 23, 1902, pp. 3–4.
17. See, e.g., the letter from Isaac Berger of Minsk to Weizmann, February 3, 1902. W.A. See also Nordau's attack in *L'Echo Sioniste*, January 15, 1902. W.A.
18. See Klausner, *Opposizyah*, pp. 149–53. See also Joseph Klausner's article, "Ha-Kongress ha-Zioni ha-Hamishi," *Hashiloah* 9 (January 1902): 63–83.
19. See Syrkin, *Kitvei Nachman Syrkin*, pp. 77–93. See also the introduction by Berl Katznelson, "Ha-Ehad ba-Maarakhah," pp. 97ff.
20. See Katznelson's introduction, pp. 102–3, 106.
21. See Weizmann to Motzkin, November 23, 1901, *WL* 1, p. 208.
22. See Katznelson's introduction, pp. 102–3.
23. See also Zangwill's speech at the Sixth Zionist Congress (1903), where he used more moderate language. Zangwill's address at this congress was reprinted as "Zionism and Charitable Institutions" in Israel Zangwill, *Speeches, Articles and Letters* (London, 1937), pp. 167–80.

24. See *Aus dem Protokoll der Kommission der Demokratisch-zionistischen Fraktion* (Berlin, 1902), p. 20. W.A.

25. Curiously, though, Weizmann's speech of December 20, 1901, at the Zionist Youth Conference was quite conciliatory toward ICA: "We cannot influence ICA by way of demonstrations and protests. What have we done in actual fact to get control of ICA? Nothing! . . . following Nordau's example, we are forever abusing ICA. If we had gone to them about the state of Jewry and the calamities that have befallen it, I do not know if they might not have met us half-way . . . We must not hold demonstrations but try to get ICA interested, to map out a field of activity for them. We have no right to abuse ICA while we ourselves have as yet accomplished nothing . . ." W.A.

26. See Jonathan Frankel, "Nachman Syrkin: The Populist and Prophetic Strands in Socialist Zionism," in *Zionism* 2 (Autumn 1980): 173–212. After he had delivered a scathing attack on the Second Zionist Congress (1898) and the Zionist movement, he had been forced to resign from the Bern Academic Society. When the report of the case was published in *Die Welt*, Syrkin replied that "as a socialist Zionist, I have nothing to do with the Zionism of the Second Congress in Basel." Weizmann had a hand in the resolutions of the Bern Academic Society against Syrkin. See *Die Welt*, no. 3, January 20, 1889, p. 11. See also *Stenographisches Protokoll der Verhandlungen des II. Zionisten-Congresses* (Vienna, 1898), pp. 163–64, concerning the debate between Herzl and Syrkin. See also *Die Welt*, no. 6, February 10, 1899, p. 8.

27. On the Hessiana, see CZA, A126.

28. In his diary Herzl recorded his negative reaction: "I rejected a proposal made by the Russian exaltados [extreme enthusiasts] Syrkin and Bukhmil: to put on mass demonstrations against the I.C.A. in the big cities . . ." *Complete Diaries*, vol. 3, p. 1192.

29. Toward the end of January other members of the Berlin Democratic Faction added their signatures to the document.

30. These are the names mentioned in the protest, but others associated with the faction who also participated in the discussion with Syrkin included Aberson, Abramovich, Gourland, Nemser, and Perelman.

31. The letter was signed by Lazare Kunin, David Glickman, A. Mandels, Victor Jacobson, Samuel Pevsner, Joseph Dubosarsky, and Leo Motzkin; later M. Berman, Berthold Feiwel, and Isidore Eliashev added their signatures. See "Confidential," January 9, 1902. W.A.

32. Weizmann to Motzkin, January 14, 1901, *WL* 1, p. 215.

33. Ibid., pp. 216–17.

34. Ibid., pp. 217–19.

35. See Motzkin to Weizmann, January 28, 1902. CZA, A126/24.

36. Weizmann to Motzkin, January 31, 1902, *WL* 1, pp. 221–24.

37. Both newsletters are in W.A.

38. See Weizmann to Motzkin, January 3, 1902, *WL* 1, p. 224.

39. See "Vertrag der Aktiengesellschaft . . . Bayer und Co. . . . und den Herren Dr. Chr. Deichler und Dr. Ch. Weizmann," p. 1. W.A.

40. Weizmann to Motzkin, March, 16, 1902, *WL* 1, p. 237.

41. Weizmann to Vera, March 28–29, 1902, *WL* 1, p. 245. Even before his letter reached her, Vera had written to Weizmann in care of Feiwel in Berlin: "I am outraged by the Ber[liners]. Heavens, what sort of people are they! One does not hear a single meaningful word from them . . ." Vera to Weizmann, March 27, 1902. W.A.

42.. Weizmann to Vera, April 1, 1902, *WL* 1, p. 247.

43. Weizmann to Vera, April 2, 1902, *WL* 1, p. 249.

44. See Weizmann to Esther Weinberg and Anna Ratnovskaya, April 4, 1902, *WL* 1, p. 251.

45. Weizmann was not a member of this committee, which consisted of Motzkin, Aberson, Bernstein-Kohan, Bukhmil, Feiwel, Klausner, and Sheinkin, with Leib Jaffe as an alternate.

46. Weizmann to Motzkin, March 2, 1902, *WL* 1, pp. 233–34.

47. Weizmann to Motzkin, April 25, 1902, *WL* 1, p. 258.

48. Those assembled at Heidelberg included Motzkin, Klausner, Aberson, Feiwel, and Jaffe.

49. See *Aus dem Protokoll der Kommission der Demokratisch-zionistischen Fraktion.* W.A.

50. Ibid., pp. 12–13.

51. Ibid., pp. 13–20.

52. Weizmann to Vera, July 5, 1902, *WL* 1, p. 286.

53. Ibid.

54. Weizmann to Motzkin, July 17, 1902, *WL* 1, pp. 307–8.

55. See "Tokhnit ha-Frakzia," *Hatzfirah,* no. 189, September 3, 1902, pp. 2–3, and successive issues up to and including no. 212, September 30, 1902, p. 3.

56. Weizmann to Motzkin, March 2, 1902, *WL* 1, p. 233.

57. See Weizmann to Vera, February 15, 16, and 17, 1902, *WL* 1, pp. 231–32. See also *Die Welt,* no. 11, March 14, 1902, pp. 10–11.

58. See the letter from Berger to Weizmann, February 3, 1902. W.A.

59. See Klausner, *Opposizyah,* pp. 163–68.

60. See "Juedischer Verlag, An die Mitglieder des V. Zionistencongresses zu Basel" [1901], Buber Archive, Ms. Var. 350/38.

61. *Stenographisches Protokoll* (V), pp. 390–91.

62. Ibid., p. 428.

63. See "Juedischer Verlag," January 1902. CZA, A102/135.

64. Its second publication was *Eine Juedische Hochschule,* also published in 1902.

65. See the report on the activities of the Juedischer Verlag in *Die Welt,* no. 44, October 31, 1902, p. 5, and no. 45, November 7, 1902, pp. 11–13.

66. See *Die Welt,* no. 44, October 31, 1902, pp. 3–6.

67. Other members of the committee were Nathan Birnbaum [Mathias Acher], David Farbstein, Alexander Hausmann, Abraham Kasteliansky, Abraham Korkis, Sigmund Kornfeld, Egon Lederer, Alfred Nossig, Felix Pinkus, and Davis Trietsch. See *Die Welt,* no. 14, April 4, 1902, pp. 8–9. See also CZA, Z1/335 and A102/10.

68. Ibid., p. 8.

69. See Alfred Nossig, ed., *Juedische Statistik* (Berlin, 1903).

70. See Weizmann to Herzl, May 21, 1902, *WL* 1, p. 265.

71. *Stenographisches Protokoll* (V), p. 248.

72. Weizmann to Ahad Ha'Am, February 5, 1902, *WL* 1, p. 229.

73. See Ahad Ha'Am's letter to Weizmann dated March 17, 1902, in *Igrot Ahad Ha'Am,* no. 5, p. 136.

74. With all other professions closed to Jews in Russia, the youth flocked to the departments of medicine and law in the schools of higher education. The Ministry of Education wanted to further reduce the number of vacancies open to Jews under the quota system. It ordered that, beginning with the academic year 1899–1900, the percentage of Jews eligible for admission should be calculated in relation not to the total student body but to that of each de-

partment. In 1901 the ministry ordered the reduction of the general quota on the ground that the number of Jewish students exceeded the legal limits. Louis Greenberg, *The Jews in Russia*, vol. 2, p. 49. There were similar restrictions against Rumanian Jews. See, e.g., "Die wichtigsten gegen die Juden gerichteten rumaenischen Gesetze," *Die Welt*, no. 40, October 2, 1902, p. 3.

75. Minutes of the Munich Conference. W.A.
76. *Stenographisches Protokoll* (V), pp. 392–93.
77. See Alfred Erich Senn, *The Russian Revolution in Switzerland*, p. 6.
78. Weizmann to Catherine Dorfman, August 11, 1901, *WL* 1, pp. 166–67.
79. Weizmann to Ahad Ha'Am, February 5, 1902, *WL* 1, pp. 229–30. See also Martin Buber's article on the subject of a Jewish university in *Die Welt*, no. 41, October 11, 1901, pp. 1–2, and no. 43, October 25, 1901, pp. 1–2.
80. See Feiwel's letter to Herzl dated May 22, 1902. CZA, Z1/335.
81. See "Enquêten und statistische Untersuchungen veranstaltet durch das Bureau: Juedische Hochschule." CZA, Z1/340.
82. See draft of letter to Herzl, probably sent on April 13, 1902. W.A.
83. See Herzl, *Complete Diaries*, vol. 4, p. 1276.
84. Ibid., p. 1279.
85. See Herzl to Feiwel, April 22, 1902, in CZA, HB266. It seems that Weizmann received the same letter. See also Feiwel to Weizmann, May 1, 1902. W.A.
86. Weizmann to Aaron Eliasberg, May 7, 1902, *WL* 1, p. 261. See also Feiwel's letter to Herzl dated May 22, 1902, in which he made it clear that it takes time to compose a thoughtful and well-balanced proposal for the university project. CZA, Z1/335.
87. See CZA, Z1/175.
88. Weizmann to Motzkin, May 21, 1902, *WL* 1, p. 266. Weizmann was responding to Herzl's charge that those dealing with the university project were not quite serious. Feiwel also remonstrated with Herzl: "Sie thuen Herrn Dr. Weizmann—und nebenbei mir—grosses Unrecht, wenn Sie uns, im Gegensatz zu Ihrer steten ernsten Behandlung des Hochschulprojectes mangelnden Ernst zum Vorwurf machen. Es ist Ihnen vielleicht nicht ganz unbekannt, dass speciell Dr. Weizmann neben den vielen Agenden, die er zu bewaeltigen hat, und trotz seiner geschwaechten Gesundheit das Hochschulproject auf das Energischste behandelt . . ." Feiwel to Herzl, May 22, 1902. CZA, Z1/335.
89. See "Preliminary Plan for a Jewish University." W.A.
90. See Weizmann to Herzl, June 12, 1902, *WL* 1, pp. 268–69.
91. See Feiwel to Herzl, May 22, 1902. CZA, Z1/335.
92. Weizmann to Motzkin, January 31, 1902, *WL* 1, p. 224.
93. Weizmann to Motzkin, June 2, 1902, *WL* 1, p. 265. We get an inkling of Weizmann's condition in June from a letter Vera wrote him during the summer, in which she recalls his condition before her departure: "Does your complexion look any different—has it changed from greenish-yellow, at least, to a normal pale?" Vera to Weizmann, August 2, 1902. W.A.
94. Weizmann to Vera, June 28, 1902, *WL* 1, p. 271.
95. The correspondence is particularly important since many of Vera's letters written to Weizmann when he was in England—after 1904—have been removed from the archives.
96. See interview with T. R. Fyvel (Berthold Feiwel's son). W.A.
97. Weizmann to Catherine Dorfman, June 30, 1902, *WL* 1, p. 273.
98. Weizmann to Vera, June 30, 1902, *WL* 1, p. 274.

99. Weizmann to Vera, July 29, 1902, *WL* 1, p. 330.
100. Weizmann to Vera, July 5, 1902, *WL* 1, p. 286.
101. Weizmann to Vera, July 10, 1902, *WL* 1, p. 293.
102. Weizmann to Vera, July 5, 1902, *WL* 1, p. 286.
103. Weizmann to Vera, July 26, 1902, *WL* 1, p. 325.
104. See Vera to Weizmann, July 14, 1902. W.A.
105. Vera to Weizmann, July 12, 1902, and Vera to Weizmann, July 14, 1902. W.A. Vera continued to control the Weizmanns' purse strings after their marriage. See the interview with Meyer Weisgal in *Musaf Yediot Aharonot,* November 1, 1974, p. 7.
106. Cf. Vera's note to Esther Shneerson: "Of course, I am bored here and even a bit depressed . . ." Note appended to letter to Weizmann, August 4, 1902. W.A. Cf. also her letter to Weizmann dated July 15, 1902: "As you see, my child, I spend my time very monotonously . . ." W.A.
107. Vera to Weizmann, August 24, 1902. W.A.
108. Vera to Weizmann, March 27, 1902. W.A.
109. Vera to Weizmann, June 27, 1902. W.A.
110. Weizmann to Vera, June [28?], 1902, *WL* 1, p. 272.
111. Vera to Weizmann, July 5, 1902. W.A.
112. Weizmann to Vera, June 30, 1902, *WL* 1, p. 274.
113. Weizmann to Vera, July 1, 1902, *WL* 1, p. 275–76.
114. Weizmann to Vera, July 3, 1902, *WL* 1, pp. 279–80.
115. Weizmann to Vera, July [8?], 1902, *WL* 1, p. 289.
116. Vera to Weizmann, July 14, 1902. W.A.
117. Vera to Weizmann, August 4, 1902. W.A.
118. Weizmann to Vera, July 21, 1902, *WL* 1, p. 311.
119. Weizmann to Vera, July 25, 1902, *WL* 1, p. 322.
120. Vera to Weizmann, July 29, 1902. W.A.
121. His health did improve over the summer. See Weizmann to Vera, July 29, 1902, *WL* 1, p. 329.
122. Vera to Weizmann, July 25, 1902. W.A.
123. Vera to Weizmann, July 26, 1902. W.A.
124. Vera to Weizmann, July 29, 1902. W.A.
125. See Weizmann to Vera, July 28, 1902, *WL* 1, p. 327.
126. Weizmann to Vera, July [8?], 1902, *WL* 1, p. 288.
127. Weizmann to Vera, July 10, 1902, *WL* 1, p. 293.
128. Weizmann to Vera, July 13, 1902, *WL* 1, p. 297.
129. Weizmann to Vera, July 31, 1902, *WL* 1, pp. 335–36.
130. Weizmann to Vera, July 26, 1902, *WL* 1, p. 323.
131. See her letter to Weizmann dated July 5, 1902. W.A.
132. Vera to Weizmann, August 7, 1902. W.A.
133. Weizmann to Vera, July 4, 1902, *WL* 1, p. 282.
134. Weizmann to Vera, July 11, 1902, *WL* 1, p. 294.
135. Weizmann to Vera, July 17, 1902, *WL* 1, p. 306.
136. Weizmann to Vera, [August] 3, 1902. *WL* 1, p. 341.
137. Weizmann to Vera, August 8–9, 1902, *WL* 1, p. 352.
138. Vera to Weizmann, August 2, 1902. W.A.
139. Vera to Weizmann, July 5, 1902. W.A.
140. Weizmann to Vera, July 11, 1902, *WL* 1, pp. 295–96.
141. Vera to Weizmann, August 23, 1902. W.A.
142. Weizmann to Vera, August 29, 1902, *WL* 1, p. 387.

143. Weizmann to Vera, July 3, 1902, *WL* 1, p. 280. See also Weizmann to Vera, July 17, 1902, *WL* 1, p. 307.
144. Weizmann to Vera, July 28, 1902, *WL* 1, p. 328.
145. Weizmann to Vera, August 2, 1902, *WL* 1, p. 340.
146. See Weizmann to Vera, August [7], 1902, *WL* 1, p. 348.
147. See Weizmann to Leo Motzkin, September 10, 1895, *WL* 1, p. 52.
148. See, e.g., his letter to Vera dated July 4–5, 1901, *WL* 1, p. 146.
149. Vera to Weizmann, March 27, 1902. W.A.
150. Vera to Weizmann, June 27, 1902. W.A.
151. See, e.g., Vera to Weizmann, July 15, 1902. W.A.
152. See Vera to Weizmann, July 25, 1902. W.A.
153. See Vera to Weizmann, July 26, 1902. W.A.
154. See Vera to Weizmann, July 15, 1902, and July 21, 1902. W.A.
155. See Vera to Weizmann, August 2, 1902. W.A.
156. See Vera to Weizmann, August 4, 1902. W.A.
157. See Vera to Weizmann, August 28, 1902, and August 30, 1902. W.A.
158. Vera to Weizmann, July 15, 1902. W.A.
159. Weizmann to Vera, July 24, 1902. W.A.
160. Weizmann to Vera, July 26, 1902, *WL* 1, p. 324.
161. Vera to Weizmann, July 31, 1902. W.A.
162. Weizmann to Vera, August 8–9, 1902, *WL* 1, p. 352. Yet the following sentence is the one in which he declares himself a savage!
163. Vera to Weizmann, July 15, 1902. W.A. She was, perhaps unconsciously, quoting a similar thought Weizmann had expressed to her a year earlier. See Weizmann to Vera, June 3, 1901, *WL* 1, p. 120.
164. Weizmann to Vera, July 4, 1902, *WL* 1, p. 281.
165. Weizmann to Vera, July 5, 1902, *WL* 1, p. 285.
166. Weizmann to Vera, July 30, 1902, *WL* 1, p. 332.
167. Bernstein-Kohan was given an annual expense allowance of 2,000 rubles, later increased to 6,000 rubles, after he had used his own financial resources to run the Kishinev Correspondence Center. His Zionist work caused him serious financial hardship. See Bernstein-Kohan, *Sefer Bernstein-Kohan* (Tel Aviv, 1946), pp. 92–137.
168. Vera to Weizmann, August 6, 1902. W.A. For a slightly different English translation, see Vera Weizmann, *The Impossible Takes Longer*, pp. 17–18.
169. Weizmann to Vera, August 12, 1902, *WL* 1, p. 364.
170. See, e.g., Weizmann to Vera, July 15–16, 1902, *WL* 1, p. 304.
171. Weizmann to Vera, July 31, 1902, *WL* 1, p. 334.
172. See interview with T. R. Fyvel [no date indicated]. W.A.
173. Ibid.
174. See Weizmann to Catherine Dorfman, July 17, 1902, *WL* 1, p. 305, where he states: "Shneerson arrived today."
175. Both Feiwel and Shneerson disliked Pinkus and tolerated his presence thanks to Weizmann. As soon as Weizmann left Leysin they moved to another vacation spot.
176. See Weizmann to Vera, July 24, 1902, *WL* 1, p. 319.
177. Weizmann to Vera, June [28?], 1902, *WL* 1, p. 272. Of course, Feiwel may not have known Sophia Getzova as did Motzkin, Bernstein-Kohan, and the other students from Eastern Europe. His easy relations with women may have also made him more empathetic to Weizmann and Vera's situation.

178. Weizmann to Vera [July 9, 1902], *WL* 1, p. 292. See also Weizmann to Vera, July 26, 1902, *WL* 1, p. 324.
179. See, e.g., Weizmann to Vera, July 15–16, 1902, *WL* 1, p. 303; July 28, 1902, *WL* 1, p. 329; August 8–9, 1902, *WL* 1, p. 351.
180. Weizmann to Vera, July 18, 1902, *WL* 1, p. 308.
181. Weizmann to Vera, July 4, 1902, *WL* 1, p. 281.
182. Weizmann to Vera, August 8–9, 1902, *WL* 1, p. 351.
183. Weizmann to Vera, August 8–9, 1902, *WL* 1, p. 352.
184. Weizmann to Vera, August 10, 1902, *WL* 1, p. 355.
185. "The matter of the University remains in my and Toldy's hands; *c'est convenu.*" Weizmann to Vera, July 5, 1902, *WL* 1, p. 286.
186. Weizmann to Herzl, June 25, 1902, *WL* 1, pp. 268–69.
187. Weizmann to Vera, July 15–16, 1902, *WL* 1, pp. 302–3.
188. Weizmann to Vera, July 28, 1902, *WL* 1, p. 327.
189. One of Buber's biographers claims that "Chaim Weizmann supplied the statistics . . . whereas Buber and Feiwel supplied the ideology." However, he cites no source to substantiate this claim. See Maurice Friedman, *Martin Buber's Life and Work: The Early Years, 1878–1923* (New York, 1981), p. 59. According to Buber's former secretary, Margot Cohn, Buber reluctantly lent his name to the pamphlet because he viewed its contents as misconstruing his own conception of the projected Jewish university. Buber had in mind something along the lines of a college of adult education. This information was related to Margot Cohn by Professor Gershom Scholem. I am grateful to Dr. Paul R. Mendes-Flohr for verifying this information for me (letter to the author dated December 3, 1982).
190. The manuscript, available in the Buber Archive, is in Feiwel's handwriting.
191. See Martin Buber, Berthold Feiwel, and Chaim Weizmann, *Eine Juedische Hochschule* (Berlin, 1902), pp. 3–31.
192. Ibid., pp. 31–36.
193. Weizmann to Vera, July 25, 1902, *WL* 1, p. 321.
194. Weizmann to Catherine Dorfman, July 31, 1902, *WL* 1, p. 334.
195. Ibid.
196. See their letter to Weizmann dated July 3, 1902. W.A.
197. See Weizmann to Theodor Herzl, July 16, 1902, *WL* 1, pp. 304–5, and Herzl to Weizmann, July 20, 1902. W.A.
198. Weizmann to Catherine Dorfman, July 14, 1902, *WL* 1, p. 299.
199. Weizmann to Vera, July 28, 1902, *WL* 1, p. 327.
200. Weizmann to Motzkin, July 28, 1902, *WL* 1, p. 329.
201. Weizmann to Catherine Dorfman, July 31, 1902, *WL* 1, p. 334.
202. Weizmann to Vera, August 14, 1902, *WL* 1, p. 369.
203. Weizmann to Vera, August 13, 1902, *WL* 1, p. 367.
204. Weizmann to Vera, August 12, 1902, *WL* 1, p. 363.
205. Vera to Weizmann, August 7, 1902. W.A.

VII Conflicts and Disappointments

1. Weizmann to Vera, August 20, 1902, *WL* 1, p. 375.
2. Weizmann to Vera, August 8–9, 1902, *WL* 1, p. 351.
3. Weizmann to Vera, August [16], 1902, *WL* 1, p. 371.
4. Weizmann to Vera, August 21, 1902, *WL* 1, p. 377.

5. Notably Hermann Senator, Louis Levin, Leopold Landau, and Raoul Pictet, who had tried—unsuccessfully—to help him in his Charlottenburg days to market his first discovery in dye-stuffs chemistry. See Weizmann to Vera, August 20, 1902, *WL* 1, p. 376.

6. See Weizmann to Vera, August 29, 1902, *WL* 1, p. 389. "Together with him we [Weizmann and Bernstein's daughter] cursed the assimilationists . . . he is on the road to Zionism." How far Bernstein was from Zionism in that period is evident from an article written by him during World War I, "Wie ich als Jude in der Diaspora aufwuchs," which was published in *Der Jude*. For an English translation, see Mendes-Flohr and Reinharz, eds., *The Jew in the Modern World*, pp. 227–30.

7. See Weizmann to Catherine Dorfman, August 27, 1902, *WL* 1, p. 384.

8. See Weizmann to Ovsey Lurie, September 4, 1890, *WL* 1, p. 39.

9. See Weizmann's letters to Motzkin in 1895 and 1896, e.g., the letters dated June 20, 1895, and September 10, 1895, *WL* 1, pp. 48–53.

10. See, e.g., Weizmann to Catherine Dorfman, August 4, 1901, *WL* 1, p. 162.

11. See Weizmann to Catherine Dorfman, August 27, 1902, *WL* 1, p. 384.

12. Weizmann to Vera, August 27, 1902, *WL* 1, p. 385.

13. See Weizmann to Vera, August 7, 1902, *WL* I, p. 165.

14. Ibid.

15. See "Dr. Chaim Weizmann's Family." W.A. See also Hayah Weizmann-Lichtenstein, *Be-Zel Koratenu*, pp. 119ff.

16. See Weizmann to Vera, August 25, 1902, *WL* 1, p. 379.

17. Weizmann to Vera, August 25, 1902, *WL* 1, p. 379.

18. See Yehuda Leib Fishman, "Toldot ha-Mizrahi ve-Hitpathuto," *Sefer ha-Mizrahi* (Jerusalem, 1946), p. 29.

19. Israel Klausner, "Be-Reshit Yisud ha-Mizrahi al Yedei ha-Rav J. Reines," *Sefer ha-Zionut ha-Datit*, ed. Yitzhak Raphael and S. Z. Shragai (Jerusalem, 1977), vol. 1, p. 344.

20. A notable exception was the historian Rabbi Zeev Yawetz, who advocated a positive cultural program with a religious Zionist orientation. His view was adopted within a few years.

21. *Die Welt*, no. 11, March 14, 1902, p. 2. The rationale for the Mizrahi was elaborated by Yawetz in "Kol Koreh." See *Hatzfirah*, no. 76, April 13, 1902, pp. 2–3.

22. See Fishman, "Toldot ha-Mizrahi," pp. 90ff.

23. See Yitzhak Malamud, "Sikur Veidat ha-Mizrahi ha-Rishonah be-Russyah," *Sefer ha-Zionut ha-Datit*, vol. 2, pp. 451–56.

24. It was also to be the last conference of Russian Zionists to take place in Russia before World War I. The third conference took place in Helsingfors, Finland (1906); the fourth in The Hague (1907); the fifth in Hamburg (1909); and the sixth in Basel (1911).

25. See Zvi Belkovsky, "Eikh husag ha-Rishayon le-Veidat Minsk?" *Hazioni Haklali*, no. 5, January 20, 1933. W.A. Permission was apparently given at the intercession of Manya Wilbushevitz (Shohat) and with the help of Sergei Zubatov, chief of the Moscow Okhrana from 1896 to 1902. See Moshe Mishkinski, "Ha-Sozialism ha-Mishtarti u-Megamot bi-Mediniyut ha-Shilton ha-Zari le-Gabei ha-Yehudim (1900–1903)," *Zion* 25, nos. 3–4 (1959): 243.

26. Concerning the estimate of delegates, see Israel Klausner's introduction to the book by Mordecai Nurock, *Veidat Zionei Russyah be-Minsk* (Jerusalem, 1963),

p. 32. See also the articles by David Zakai, Mordecai Nurock, Yaakov Berman, and Shmuel Eisenstadt in *Heavar* 9 (1962): 94–105.

27. Klausner, Introduction, p. 33. The remainder of the delegates were nonfactional. See also "Shishim Shanah le-Veidat Minsk," *Heavar* 9 (1962): 94–106.

28. Weizmann to Catherine Dorfman, August 27, 1902, *WL* 1, p. 384.

29. Weizmann to Vera, August 26, 1902, *WL* 1, p. 383. Vera's reply to Weizmann is interesting: "I can't understand why you reproach the office of the Minsk Conference when all questions concerning Zionism and the Zionists will be discussed and analyzed there . . . As to the fact that no one put himself down to report on the faction's question—whose fault is that? Generally, Chaimchik, I don't understand why you attack the conference beforehand . . . As to the rabbis and other orthodox groups, you should have gotten used to their snarling by now. You have not been at the conference yet, my baby, and you are already exasperated and outraged. I can imagine what will happen at the conference itself." Vera to Weizmann, August 30, 1902. W.A.

30. See Weizmann to Vera, August 31, 1902, *WL* 1, p. 391.

31. Ibid.

32. No minutes of the conference at Minsk have been preserved, but its proceedings were extensively reported in the Jewish press. See *Hamelitz*, nos. 209–51, September/November 1902; *Hatzfirah*, nos. 188–224, September/October 1902; *Die Welt*, no. 37, September 12, 1902, pp. 1–3, and no. 38, September 19, 1902, pp. 1–6. See also the extensive report by Nurock, cited above.

33. The central role accorded to Ahad Ha'Am at the Minsk Conference was a clear signal to Herzl and SAC that, on the whole, Russian Zionists valued Ahad Ha'Am's concepts and analysis of the Zionist situation, even if his ideas had not been welcomed in Vienna.

34. Nurock, *Veidat Zionei Russyah be-Minsk*, p. 65.

35. See A. Rafaeli, "Veidot Artziot shel Zionei Russyah," in *Katzir, Kovetz le-Korot ha-Tnuah ha-Zionit be-Russyah*, vol. 1, pp. 43ff.

36. For a summary of Ahad Ha'Am's speech in Minsk, see "Ueber die Kultur," *Ost und West*, no. 10, October 1902, pp. 655–60, and no. 11, November 1902, pp. 721–28. The October issue also contains Buber's thoughts on Ahad Ha'Am's speech. See Martin Buber, "Ein geistiges Centrum," *Ost und West*, no. 10, October 1902, pp. 663–72. See also Ahad Ha'Am, "Tehiyat ha-Ruah," *Hashiloah* 10, nos. 59–60 (November/December 1902): 385–99, 481–91.

37. See Nurock, *Veidat Zionei Russyah be-Minsk*, p. 68.

38. Ibid., p. 69.

39. Im Anfang war die Idee, nicht das Geld.

40. See *Hamelitz*, no. 242, November 5, 1902, pp. 1–2.

41. See "Resolutions" in Rafaeli, "Veidot Artziot shel Zionei Russyah," *Katzir*, vol. 1, p. 74. Those members of the Mizrahi who were "pure" political Zionists were unhappy with the compromise. On the controversy within the Mizrahi ranks, see Israel Klausner, "Be-Reshit Yisud ha-Mizrahi," *Sefer ha-Zionut ha-Datit*, vol. 1, pp. 353ff. There is no evidence that either of the two commissions set up in Minsk made any significant contribution to Zionist cultural activities.

42. See *Hatzfirah*, no. 24, October 22, 1902, p. 3.

43. On the condition of Rumanian Jewry at this time, see Elias Schwarzfeld, *Les*

Juifs en Roumanie depuis le Traité de Berlin (1878) jusqu'à ce jour (Paris, 1901); idem, "The Jews of Roumania from the Earliest Times to the Present Day" and "The Situation of the Jews in Roumania since the Treaty of Berlin (1878)" in *The American Jewish Year Book 5662* (Philadelphia, 1901), pp. 25–87; "Die wichtigsten gegen die Juden gerichteten rumaenischen Gesetze," *Die Welt*, no. 40, October 2, 1902, p. 3; and Bernard Lazare, *Les Juifs en Roumanie* (Paris, 1902). See also Zosa Szajkowski, "Jewish Emigration Policy in the Period of the Rumanian 'Exodus' 1899–1903," *Jewish Social Studies* 13, no. 1 (January 1951): 47–70.

44. For comparative figures, see Mark Wischnitzer, *To Dwell in Safety: The Story of Jewish Migration Since 1800* (Philadelpha, 1948), esp. pp. 98–140.

45. Ibid., p. 118. *The Jewish Encyclopedia*, 1905 edn., vol. 8, p. 585, estimates the number of permanent immigrants at one hundred thousand.

46. See V. D. Lipman, *Social History of the Jews in England 1850–1950* (London, 1954), pp. 134–35. The 1901 census showed that there were in the United Kingdom 94,425 Russians and Poles; nearly all of these can be regarded as Jews; in addition, some of the 10,130 Austrians in the United Kingdom were also Jews. They were highly concentrated in London. Ibid., p. 94. See also Georg Halpern, "Die juedische Einwanderer-Bevoelkerung Londons," in Alfred Nossig, ed., *Juedische Statistik* (Berlin, 1903), pp. 322–27.

47. Lipman, *Social History*, p. 138.

48. See the letter to Herzl from the Royal Commission dated May 29, 1902, and Herzl's reply in "Ha-Massa u-Matan beyn Herzl le-veyn Memshelet Britanyah ha-Gdolah be-Inyan El Arish," *Shivat Zion*, vol. 1, p. 184.

49. Herzl did go to Constantinople once more at the end of July at the invitation—in fact, insistence—of the sultan. Nothing of any substance came of his talks there with the grand vizier.

50. Herzl, *Complete Diaries*, vol. 4, p. 1283.

51. Ibid., pp. 1292–94. It seems that Uganda as a possible territory for settlement of Jews was mentioned for the first time during Herzl's meeting with Rothschild.

52. See *The Jewish Chronicle*, July 11, 1902, pp. 1–4.

53. See Herzl, *Complete Diaries*, vol. 4, p. 1295.

54. Ibid., pp. 1360–63.

55. Ibid., p. 1369.

56. Ibid., pp. 1370–71.

57. Weizmann to Vera, July 14, 1902, *WL* 1, p. 301.

58. Herzl, *Complete Diaries*, vol. 4, p. 1370.

59. Weizmann to Vera, September 16, 1902, *WL* 1, p. 401.

60. See Weizmann, *The Impossible Takes Longer*, p. 18.

61. Weizmann to Vera, October 15, 1902, *WL* 1, p. 405.

62. Ibid., pp. 404–5.

63. See *Die Welt*, no. 44, October 31, 1902, pp. 3–5, and no. 45, November 7, 1902, pp. 1–3.

64. He began his report by declaring: "This time I don't have a favorable report to give you." "Protokoll der Sitzung des Grossen A.C.," October 29, 1902. CZA, Z1/192.

65. Ibid.

66. See *Die Welt*, no. 45, November 7, 1902, p. 3.

67. See "Die Zionistische Jahresconferenz in Wien." CZA, Z1/168.

68. See Weizmann to Alexander Nemirovsky, November 6, 1902, *WL* 2, p. 4.

69. CZA, Z1/168.
70. See Weizmann to Samuel Shriro, November 5, 1902, *WL* 2, p. 3. Buber and Weizmann's names were left out, as was any mention of the Geneva bureau.
71. Weizmann to Israel Breslau, November 6, 1902, *WL* 2, p. 6.
72. Weizmann's plan for establishing a university in Europe before transferring it to Palestine is, in fact, not so dissimilar from Herzl's Uganda scheme.
73. Weizmann to Gregory Lurie, January 1, 1903, *WL* 2, pp. 144–45.
74. Weizmann to Isaac Rothstein, January 4, 1903, *WL* 2, pp. 157–58.
75. See Weizmann to Israel Breslav, November 6, 1902, *WL* 2, p. 6.
76. At the same time Weizmann agreed that Herzl would become the trustee for this money, which was deposited in a special account with the Jewish Colonial Trust. See Weizmann to Theodor Herzl, November 26, 1902, *WL* 2, pp. 32–33.
77. "You will recognize why I am so concerned with the financial independence of our Bureau . . . Both by aspiration and necessity we have to work in freedom. Woe to us if we have to turn to the treasury of some party, for then we shall be sold! Therefore we must leave nothing undone that may strengthen us!" Weizmann to Michael Kroll, January 8, 1903, *WL* 2, p. 176. See also Weizmann to Davis Trietsch, January 13, 1903, *WL* 2, p. 195.
78. His chemist friend Samuel Levinson was employed by the bureau as a secretary. When he emigrated to the United States in the spring of 1903, he was succeeded by Saul Stupnitzky. At the end of 1902 Moses Glikin, who had worked in Berlin for the Democratic Faction and the Jewish university project, was invited to work for the university and the Democratic Faction in Zurich on a salaried basis. See Feiwel to Glikin, November 26, 1902. CZA, A179/3. Motzkin had warned Glikin against working with Weizmann because of his own bad experiences with him; cited in Israel Klausner, *Opposizyah*, pp. 191–92. Glikin began his duties in January 1903. In the spring of 1903 he returned to Russia, where he worked for Yiddish and Russian-Jewish newspapers. Beginning in March 1903, Alfred Nossig became one of the bureau's permanent aides in Berlin, and in July 1903 Ben Zion Mossinson worked for the bureau in Bern.
79. See the letter from the bureau dated January 1903, which was appended to the questionnaire distributed to East European Jewish students. CZA, Z1/340.
80. Almost all of Weizmann's letters to his family have been lost.
81. There are, of course, allusions to his work in chemistry. See, e.g., Weizmann to Berthold Feiwel, January 22, 1903, *WL* 2, p. 216. On the whole, however, his last years in Geneva were not among his most productive in chemistry. See Weizmann's own account of these years in *Trial and Error*, pp. 74–92.
82. Martin Buber to Weizmann, December 12, 1902, in Martin Buber, *Briefwechsel aus sieben Jahrzehnten*. Vol. 1: 1897–1918, pp. 179–81. Buber proposed the establishment of four different kinds of bodies: a central committee, which would be set up in the spring of 1903 and would elect an executive committee; local committees in Vienna, Berlin, Munich, and elsewhere; local groups in Russia, which would raise funds for the bureau; and societies for members of the general public interested in supporting the project.
83. Weizmann to Martin Buber, December 14, 1902, *WL* 2, pp. 93–94.
84. See Buber to Weizmann, January 15, 1903. W.A. See also Buber to Weizmann, January 23, 1903, *Briefwechsel*, vol. 1, p. 185. Buber also invited Herzl to the meeting on the twenty-fifth. See Buber to Herzl, January 15, 1903,

Briefwechsel, vol. 1, p. 183. Since Adolf Schwarz, rector of the Israelitisch-theologische Lehranstalt in Vienna, and Leon Kellner refused to participate, Weizmann immediately suspected—incorrectly—that the Smaller Actions Committee had had a hand in their decision.

85. Weizmann to Buber, February 4, 1903, *WL* 2, p. 225. The inaugural meetings of the committee were first set for February 1, then February 8, until Buber finally gave up.

86. See Trietsch to Weizmann, February 5, 1903. W.A.

87. Consisting of professors Otto Warburg, Franz Oppenheimer, Wilhelm Meyerhoffer, Leopold Landau, and Alfred Nossig. See Weizmann to Vera, Sophia, Issay, and Theodosia Khatzman, March 17, 1903, *WL* 2, p. 272. See also the report of the Bureau Juedische Hochschule, May 1903, which also claims that a committee was set up in Mannheim. CZA, HVIII/915. See also Martin Buber's letter to the Smaller Actions Committee dated March 21, 1903, which lists the members of the Berlin committee as consisting only of professors Landau, Oppenheimer, and Warburg. CZA, Z1/343. There is no evidence that this small committee of distinguished academics was anything more than an ornament to the university project. It probably never met again once Weizmann had departed from Berlin.

88. See report of the Bureau Juedische Hochschule. Abteilung A. "Einzel-Enquête veranstaltet unter den auslaendischen (russischen, rumaenischen, usw.) juedischen Studierenden der westeuropaeischen Hochschulen." CZA, Z1/340.

89. See Berthold Feiwel, "Enquête unter den westeuropaeischen juedischen Studierenden," in Alfred Nossig, ed., *Juedische Statistik* (Berlin, 1903), p. 249.

90. Ibid., pp. 246–49.

91. Ibid., pp. 250–55. At the same time a survey was attempted by Michael Kroll and Abraham Idelson for Russian students. They distributed the materials in Moscow in February 1903 but received very few replies. See Weizmann to Abraham Idelson and Michael Kroll, February 6, 1903, *WL* 2, pp. 230–31.

92. Weizmann to Abraham Idelson and Michael Kroll, December 26, 1902, *WL* 2, p. 127. See also Weizmann to Gregory Lurie, January 1, 1902, *WL* 2, p. 146.

93. Weizmann to Joseph Pokrassa, February 4, 1903, *WL* 2, pp. 228–29.

94. Weizmann to Abraham Idelson and Michael Kroll, February 17, 1903, *WL* 2, p. 253.

95. Weizmann to Davis Trietsch, February 16, 1903, *WL* 2, pp. 245–46. See also Weizmann to Berthold Feiwel, February 16, 1903, *WL* 2, p. 249.

96. Weizmann to Berthold Feiwel, February 16, 1903, *WL* 2, p. 250.

97. See Buber to Weizmann, February 20, 1903. W.A.

98. Weizmann to Martin Buber, February 27, 1903, *WL* 2, p. 264.

99. See report of the Bureau Juedische Hochschule, May 1903. CZA, HVIII/915.

100. See CZA, A19/2 and S24/117. For Buber's conception of the periodical, see Maurice Friedman, *Martin Buber's Life and Work*, p. 60.

101. See the prospectus of *Der Jude* in Buber Archive, Ms. Var. 350.

102. See *Hamelitz*, no. 46, February 24, 1903, pp. 2–3.

103. See, e.g., Weizmann to Felix Pinkus, February 9, 1903, *WL* 2, p. 237; Weizmann to Abraham Idelson and Michael Kroll, February 17, 1903, *WL* 2, pp. 251–52. Motzkin's status had also declined in the eyes of those close to Weizmann. See, e.g., Michael Kroll to Weizmann, June 13, 1903. W.A.

104. Weizmann to Isaac Rothstein, November 6, 1902, *WL* 2, p. 9. See also Weiz-

mann to Berthold Feiwel, November 9, 1902, *WL* 2, p. 14: "I consider the University the only right and important thing just now."

105. Volme 2 of *WL* does not include all the letters, whose content was often repetitive or very similar; usually only one typical example is reproduced. Thus the volume includes only 423 letters. Of course, some letters were also lost (e.g., all of Weizmann's letters to his family in Pinsk).

106. See, e.g., Davis Trietsch to Weizmann, November 28, 1902, W.A., and Weizmann to Berthold Feiwel, December 1, 1902, *WL* 2, p. 46.

107. Weizmann to Berthold Feiwel, December 10, 1902, *WL* 2, p. 77. As to Weizmann's opinion of Buber, see *Trial and Error*, pp. 63–64.

108. Weizmann to Buber, December 10, 1902, *WL* 2, p. 78. For Buber's apologetic reply, see Maurice Friedman, *Martin Buber's Life and Work*, p. 58.

109. See Buber to Weizmann, December 12, 1902. W.A.

110. Weizmann to Buber, December 14, 1902, *WL* 2, pp. 93–94.

111. Weizmann to Moses Glikin, January 9, 1903, *WL* 2, p. 179.

112. See, e.g., Weizmann to Wolf (Zeev) Gluskin, December 29, 1902, *WL* 2, p. 124. See also Weizmann to Abraham Idelson and Michael Kroll, June 22, 1903, *WL* 2, pp. 395–400.

113. Weizmann to Michael Aleinikov, January 24, 1903, *WL* 2, p. 218.

114. See Weizmann to the Committee, Hashahar Circle, December 13, 1902, *WL* 2, pp. 89–90.

115. See, e.g., Weizmann to Jacob Bernstein-Kohan, December 27, 1902, *WL* 2, p. 128.

116. Weizmann to Berthold Feiwel, November 9, 1902, *WL* 2, pp. 13–14.

117. Weizmann to Isaac Rothstein, January 4, 1903, *WL* 2, p. 156, and Weizmann to the Democratic Faction, January 9, 1903, *WL* 2, pp. 180–181.

118. "Wohl aber stimmt dieses Verfahren zum Programm der 'Fraktion,' die sich thatsaechlich die Ausrottung der Religion zur Aufgabe gemacht hat." Josef Seliger, "Sonderbare Auswuechse," *Der Israelit*, no. 87, November 3, 1902, pp. 1823–24.

119. The passage most offensive to the Democratic Faction reads: "Man weiss, dass die christlich-russische Jugend durchseucht ist von nihilistischen Ansichten in politischer und religioeser Beziehung. Und diesen Nihilisten haben sich einige juedisch-russische Studenten assimiliert, sie haben den scharfen, unserer Rasse eigenem Kritizismus und die Goluseigentuemlichkeit der Disziplinlosigkeit mitgebracht und der Boden fuer die Fraktion war da . . . Gesaettigt mit nihilistischen Ideen, verbittert durch den Druck in geistiger und materieller Beziehung kommen sie aus ihrer russischen heimat nach Westeuropa . . ." Ibid., pp. 1824–25.

120. See CZA, Z1/340. Weizmann copied the declaration and sent it to *Die Welt*, which refused to publish it due to the declaration's insulting tone. The editor of the *Juedische Rundschau* refused to publish the letter on similar grounds, adding that he feared legal action by Schauer. See Heinrich Loewe to Moses Glikin, November 30, 1902. CZA, A179/3. Loewe stated, "I received the protest from Dr. Weizmann. Unfortunately I cannot publish it in its present form, because according to the law I would be liable to a heavy penalty . . ." A letter from the president of the Academic Zionist Society of Bern, D. Sch. Jochelman, correcting inaccuracies in the Schauer article was published by *Die Welt* in issue no. 49, December 5, 1902, pp. 7–8; a milder declaration by the faction was published in *Die Welt*, December 19, 1902, pp. 10–11.

121. See _Die Welt,_ no. 4, January 23, 1903, p. 4.
122. Weizmann to David Farbstein, January 7, 1903, _WL_ 2, p. 169.
123. See Theodor Herzl, _Altneuland_ (Leipzig, 1902).
124. Ahad Ha'Am's article was published in _Hashiloah_ 10, no. 60 (December 1902): 566–78. It was reprinted in _Kol Kitvei Ahad Ha'Am,_ from which the quote is cited on page 419. Even before it was published in _Hashiloah,_ a Russian translation appeared in _Voskhod._
125. _Kol Kitvei Ahad Ha'Am,_ p. 420.
126. Nordau saw the galleys of a German translation of the article which was to be published by _Ost und West,_ no. 4, April 1903, pp. 227–43.
127. See, e.g., Ahad Ha'Am, "Medinat ha-Yehudim ve-Zarat he-Yehudim" and "Yahid ve-Rabim," in _Kol Kitvei Ahad Ha'Am,_ pp. 295–98.
128. Max Nordau, "Achad Ha'am ueber Altneuland," _Die Welt,_ no. 11, March 13, 1903, pp. 1–5. See also Ahad Ha'Am's replies, "Ha-het ve-Onsho" and "Ha-Zionut ve-Tikun ha-Olam," in _Kol Kitvei Ahad Ha'Am,_ pp. 320–25.
129. See, e.g., his essay "Hikui ve-Hitbolelut" and "Avdut betokh Herut," in _Kol Kitvei Ahad Ha'Am,_ pp. 64–69, 86–89.
130. Weizmann to Vera, March 15, 1903, _WL_ 2, pp. 270–71. As a first symbolic act of support for Ahad Ha'Am, it was decided to inscribe his name in the Jewish National Fund's Golden Book. For a certain fee a person's name was entered in this book as a gesture of honor and respect. The fee was used for land reclamation. The suggestion for this gesture may have possibly originated with Weizmann, whose own name was inscribed in the Jewish National Fund's Golden Book in December 1902. See "Nachman Zeitlin aus Baku behufs Eintragung des Dr. Chm. Weizmann ins goldene Buch. Kr[onen] 253—" _Die Welt,_ no. 49, December 5, 1902, p. 9.
131. Even Nordau argued this point, albeit seven years later, when people like Franz Oppenheimer and others raised another controversy along these lines. See Max Nordau, "Ueber den Gegensatz zwischen Ost und West im Zionismus," _Die Welt,_ no. 11, March 18, 1919, pp. 1–2. See also the third chapter in Jehuda Reinharz, _Fatherland or Promised Land? The Dilemma of the German Jew, 1893–1914_ (Ann Arbor, Mich., 1975).
132. Shmarya Levin, "Ha-Binyan ve-Hastirah," _Bi-Yemei ha-Maavar_ (New York, 1919), pp. 207–12. Levin wrote his open letter before Nordau's article appeared in _Die Welt._ He later defended Ahad Ha'Am against Nordau.
133. Isaac Rothstein to Weizmann, [May 1903]. W.A.
134. Leo Wintz, "Die Juden von Gestern (Eine Erwiderung)," _Ost und West,_ no. 4, April 1903, pp. 217–26. See also Leo Wintz to Adolf Friedemann, August 15, 1903, in Michael Heymann, _The Uganda Controversy_ (Jerusalem, 1970), vol. 1, pp. 68–71.
135. See Berthold Feiwel to Siegmund Werner, March 19, 1903, in Heymann, _The Uganda Controversy,_ vol. 1, pp. 66–67.
136. See Steven E. Aschheim, _Brothers and Strangers_ (Madison, Wisc., 1982), p. 92.
137. See _Stenographisches Protokoll der Verhandlungen des V. Zionisten-Congresses_ (Vienna, 1901), pp. 39–41.
138. Ibid., pp. 54–55.
139. Weizmann to Theodor Herzl, May 6, 1903, _WL_ 2, p. 313.
140. A title that had been given to the illustrious medieval rabbi and scholar Gershom ben Judah. See Weizmann to Theodor Herzl, January 3, 1903, _WL_ 2, p. 151.

141. The affair began with a critique by Ahad Ha'Am of Herzl's *Altneuland*. Leo Wintz, editor of *Ost und West*, sent Herzl proofs of a German translation of this critique. Herzl forwarded it to Nordau, who attacked Ahad Ha'Am in an almost brutal *ad hominem* manner. Ahad Ha'Am was, according to Nordau, "a stunted, cringing victim of intolerance . . . who flattered himself by believing his works belonged to European literature." Nordau's attack was interpreted by most as that of a man of European culture who views with contempt the work of his ghettoized brethren. See Max Nordau, "Ahad Ha'Am ueber Altneuland," *Die Welt*, no. 11, March 13, 1903, pp. 1–5.

142. Weizmann to Kalman Marmor, July 25, 1903, *WL* 2, p. 439. Cf. also the undated letter from Isaac Rothstein to Weizmann [May 1903], W.A., who uses similar words: "Let us not forget that Ahad Ha'Am is our [ideological] opponent."

143. Buber stated clearly the Democratic Faction's debt to Ahad Ha'Am: "Ihre Ideen sind diejenigen denen unser Programm am naechsten steht, und wir koennen uns keinen so wie Sie als unseren Protagonisten denken . . ." Buber to Ahad Ha'Am, January 12, [1902]. Buber Archive, Ms. Varia 350. Those associated with the Juedischer Verlag were also closely tied to Ahad Ha'Am. Thus, Herzl viewed the Verlag, which disseminated Ahad Ha'Am's writings in German, as a center of opposition to his leadership. See Jehuda Reinharz, "Achad Haam und der deutsche Zionismus," *Bulletin des Leo Baeck Instituts* 61 (1982): 3–27.

144. Buber expressed this feeling in a letter to Markus Ehrenpreis: "Wir muessen nun in jeder Hinsicht mehr als je zu Achad-Haam halten, der vielleicht unsere staerkste Macht gegen diese ekelhafte Westlichkeit ist die sich bisher noch nirgend so abstossend wie in diesem Artikel Nordau geaeussert hat . . . Ich habe die Empfindung . . . dass zunaechst eine Aktion in Sachen Achad-Haam-Nordau unser aller Ehrenpflicht ist." Martin Buber to Markus Ehrenpreis, March 16, 1903. Ehrenpreis Archive, 40672/7.

145. Included among the signatories were Simon Bernfeld, Israel Friedlaender, Isadore Eliashev, Alfred Nossig, Davis Trietsch, and Saul Tchernichovsky.

146. See *Hazman*, no. 23, March 10, 1903, p. 10. See also *Hatzfirah*, no. 70, April 5, 1903, p. 3.

147. See Leo Wintz, "Die Juden von Gestern (Eine Erwiderung)," *Ost und West*, no. 4, April 1903, pp. 217–26. Concerning this article, see also Ephraim Lilien to Theodor Herzl, May 12, 1903. CZA, HVIII/511a.

148. Isaac Rothstein commented on this in his letter to Weizmann: "One can mistreat [someone else] in a vulgar manner, as Nordau did *with* sincerity; one can also do it gently, as did Ahad Ha'Am. The fact is, however, that mistreatment remains mistreatment." Rothstein to Weizmann [May 1903]. W.A.

149. Weizmann to Vera, March 15, 1903, *WL* 2, p. 271.

VIII   From Kishinev to Uganda

1. See report of the Bureau Juedische Hochschule, May 1903, signed by Buber, Feiwel, and Weizmann. CZA, HVIII/915.

2. Weizmann to Catherine Dorfman, March 18, 1903, *WL* 2, p. 276.

3. Weizmann to Vera, March 21, 1903, *WL* 2, pp. 276–77.

4. See report of the Bureau Juedische Hochschule, May 1903. CZA, HVIII/915.

5. Weizmann to Vera, March [25?], 1903, *WL* 2, p. 277.

6. Weizmann to Catherine Dorfman, May 4, 1903, *WL* 2, p. 297.
7. Ibid.
8. See report of the Bureau Juedische Hochschule, May 1903. CZA, HVIII/915.
9. Weizmann to Vera, March 29, 1903, *WL* 2, p. 280.
10. See report of the Bureau Juedische Hochschule, May 1903. CZA, HVIII/915.
11. Weizmann to Vera, March 29, 1903, *WL* 2, p. 280.
12. See Weizmann to Vera, March [25?], 1903, *WL* 2, p. 278, and March [31?], *WL* 2, p. 282.
13. See Weizmann to Vera, April 9, 1903, *WL* 2, p. 284. See also the letter from Michael Kroll to Weizmann dated May 3, 1903, in which he confirmed that it was best if Weizmann did not come to Moscow during the tsar's visit.
14. See report of the Bureau Juedische Hochschule, May 1903. CZA, HVIII/915.
15. Weizmann to Vera, April 9, 1903, *WL* 2, pp. 284–85.
16. For a description of the memorandum, see Aryeh (Raphaeli) Zenzipper, "Ha-Zionut be-Einei ha-Boleshet ha-Russit," *Shivat Zion* (Jerusalem, 1950), vol. 1, pp. 225–31.
17. Ibid.
18. Weizmann to Vera, April 14, 1903, *WL* 2, p. 287.
19. The Minsk Poalei Zion were not identical with the movement by the same name founded in 1906, whose aim was to combine acceptance of the Basel Program with that of Marxism.
20. See Yitzhak Berger, "Weizmann Tahat ha-Krashim," *Davar*, April 22, 1935, p. 2.
21. Weizmann to Catherine Dorfman, May 4, 1903, *WL* 2, p. 298.
22. See Zenzipper, "Ha-Zionut be-Einei ha-Boleshet ha-Russit," p. 231. The circular was not enforced, though it was not recalled either. Its psychological impact, however, was quite considerable.
23. Weizmann to Vera, April 23, 1903, *WL* 2, p. 290.
24. Cf. Weizmann to Vera, February 17, 1902, *WL* 1, p. 232: "My good girl, great things are happening in Zionism now. Our dear untiring leader is in Constantinople and yesterday I received a telegram from Buber in Vienna. 'Wide concessions expected.' Keep this secret, my little girl!"
25. Vera to Weizmann, April 19, 1903. W.A.
26. Today the capital of Moldavia (U.S.S.R.).
27. See Leo Motzkin, *Die Judenpogrome in Russland* (Cologne and Leipzig, 1910), vol. 2, p. 5.
28. There are many descriptions of the pogrom. Among the best known are Leo Motzkin, *Die Judenpogrome in Russland;* Michael Davitt, *Within the Pale: The True Story of Anti-Semitic Persecutions in Russia* (London, 1903); Henri Dagan, *Les Massacres de Kichinef et la Situation des Prolétaires Juifs en Russie* (Paris, 1903); [Berthold Feiwel], *Die Judenmassacres in Kischinew* (Berlin, 1903); and Bernstein-Kohan, *Sefer Bernstein-Kohan,* pp. 126–37.
29. See Cyrus Adler, ed., *The Voice of America on Kishineff* (Philadelphia, 1904), p. x.
30. See Dov Volchonsky, "Pogrom ha-Ptihah shel ha-Meah ha-20," *Heavar* 20 (1973): 176–94, and Eliyahu Feldman, "Plehve ve-Hapogrom be-Kishinov be-1903," *Heavar* 17 (1970): 137–50.
31. For an eyewitness account, see Mendes-Flohr and Reinharz, *The Jew in the Modern World,* pp. 329–30.
32. See Haim Nahman Bialik, "Gviyat Edut mi-Pi Nifgeei Praot Kishinev bi-Shnat

1903," *Heavar* 1, no. 1 (1953): 18–30. See also following volumes of *Heavar*. Bialik went in the company of the historian Simon Dubnov. See *Sefer Bernstein-Kohan*, p. 138.

33. See Haim Nahman Bialik, "In the City of Slaughter," trans. Abraham M. Klein, in *The Complete Works of Hayyim Nahman Bialik*, ed. Israel Efros (New York, 1948), vol. 1, pp. 129, 133–34; rpt. in Mendes-Flohr and Reinharz, *The Jew in the Modern World*, pp. 330–31. To avoid censorship Bialik originally entitled the poem "Masa Nemirov." See Ben-Zion Katz and Baruch Karu, "Hamishim Shanah la-Pogrom be-Kishinev," *Heavar* 2 (1954): 3–4. On the history of the poem, see Ben-Zion Katz, "Yahadut Russyah lifnei Hamishim Shanah," *Heavar* 1, no. 1 (1953): 5–17.

34. One of those seeking to avenge the blood of Kishinev's innocent victims was Peter Dashevsky, a friend of Moshe and Shmuel Weizmann, who had spent the Passover holiday of 1902 in their home in Pinsk. On June 17, 1903, he failed in his attempt to assassinate Pavel Krushevan, the editor of *Bessarabets*, for his role in inciting the mob against the Jews. Dashevsky was sentenced to five years in prison but was released in 1906.

35. See *Sefer Bernstein-Kohan*, p. 129.

36. Weizmann to Bernstein-Kohan, April 27, 1903, *WL* 2, pp. 291–92.

37. Weizmann to Vera, April 28, 1903, *WL* 2, p. 293.

38. Weizmann to Catherine Dorfman, May 4, 1903, *WL* 2, p. 300.

39. Weizmann, *Trial and Error*, pp. 79–81.

40. Weizmann to Dorothy de Rothschild, November 22, 1914, *WL* 7, pp. 52–53.

41. The pogrom in Homel took place five months later, two weeks after the close of the Sixth Zionist Congress (on September 11 and 14, 1903). On this occasion, too, Weizmann remained in Geneva. On the other hand, his brothers Moshe and Shmuel rushed to Homel in order to help in the self-defense effort by the city's Jews. See Hayah Lichtenstein, *Be-Zel Koratenu*, pp. 150–51.

42. See undated interview with T. R. Fyvel. W.A. Fyvel assumes that the memorandum was actually written by his father, Berthold Feiwel. See also Robert Weltsch, "Weizmann's Briefe aus dem Jahr 1903," *Mitteilungsblatt*, May 21, 1971, p. 2.

43. Weizmann to Theodor Herzl, May 6, 1903, *WL* 2, p. 307.

44. Ibid., pp. 308–9.

45. Ibid., p. 312.

46. Ibid., p. 313.

47. Ibid., p. 315.

48. See, e.g., the letter from Russian members of GAC dated April 24, 1903. CZA, Z1/501.

49. Weizmann to Theodor Herzl, May 6, 1903, *WL* 2, p. 317.

50. Ibid., p. 318.

51. Three months earlier he had declared that "our aims lie more in the achievement of a synthesis between *Ost und West* bringing the ghetto to Europe and Europe to the ghetto . . ." See Weizmann to Abraham Idelson and Michael Kroll, February 17, 1903, *WL* 2, p. 253. See also Weizmann's response to Alfred Klee at the Fifth Zionist Congress in *Stenographisches Protokoll der Verhandlungen des V. Zionisten-Congresses in Basel* (Vienna, 1901), pp. 53–55.

52. Weizmann to Theodor Herzl, May 6, 1903, *WL* 2, p. 321.

53. Theodor Herzl to Weizmann, May 14, 1903. Buber Archive, Ms. Var. 350/286.

54. See Weizmann to Theodor Herzl, June 27, 1903, *WL* 2, pp. 407–8.
55. See Weizmann to David Wolffsohn and Weizmann to Julius Moses, May 6, 1903, *WL* 2, pp. 323–25.
56. See Joseph Pokrassa to Weizmann, May 5, 1903, and May 21, 1903; Michael Kroll to Weizmann, May 31, 1903. W.A.
57. See Joseph Pokrassa to Weizmann, May 5, 1903, and Moshe Weizmann to Chaim Weizmann, May 4, 1903. W.A.
58. Samuel Shriro to Weizmann, May 24, 1903. W.A.
59. Ibid.
60. "Nach der Art und Weise, wie Sie gegen Dr. Nordau aufgetreten sind, kann ich, ohne ihn auf das Schwerste zu kraenken, an einer von Ihren geleiteten literarischen Unternehmung unmoeglich mitarbeiten." Theodor Herzl to Martin Buber, May 14, 1903. CZA, HB35.
61. See Buber to Herzl, May 18, 1903. CZA, HB35.
62. See Herzl to Buber, May 23, 1903. CZA, HB35.
63. See Herzl to Buber, May 28, 1903. CZA, HB35.
64. See Ephraim Lilien to Herzl, May 12, 1903. CZA, HVIII/511a.
65. Weizmann to Michael Kroll, May 9, 1903, *WL* 2, p. 333.
66. Weizmann to Vera, May 24, 1903, *WL* 2, p. 340.
67. Weizmann to Selig Weicman, May 31, 1903, *WL* 2, p. 348.
68. Weizmann to Moses Glikin, June 6, 1903, *WL* 2, p. 362.
69. Weizmann to Nahum Sokolow, June 7, 1903, *WL* 2, p. 366.
70. Weizmann to Vladimir Tyomkin, May 31, 1903, *WL* 2, p. 351.
71. See Weizmann to Martin Buber, June 1, 1903, *WL* 2, p. 353.
72. See Weizmann to Michael Kroll, June 3, 1903, *WL* 2, p. 359, and Weizmann to Martin Buber, June 9, 1903, *WL* 2, pp. 370–71.
73. Cf. Weizmann to Abraham Idelson and Michael Kroll, June 22, 1903, *WL* 2, p. 397: ". . . the Faction in Russia is without value outside the Congress and without justification as a *political party*. It must be converted into a league of freedom-loving Zionist elements . . ." See Martin Buber to Weizmann, June 12, 1903. W.A. Weizmann seems to be echoing an idea contained in a letter from Buber to himself.
74. "Wir brauchen auf Leben und Tod zwei tausend Rubel, sonst liegen wir brach auf der ganzen Linie." See "Circularbrief," Geneva, June 17, 1903. W.A. See also Martin Buber to Weizmann and Berthold Feiwel, June 12, 1903. W.A.
75. An exception to this was Joseph Pokrassa, who supported the tenor of Weizmann's letter to Herzl and took strong offense at Herzl's reply. See Pokrassa to Weizmann, June 28, 1903. W.A.
76. Abraham Idelson to Weizmann, June 15, 1903. W.A.
77. Joseph Pokrassa to Weizmann, June 3, 1903. W.A.
78. See Michael Kroll to Weizmann, June 30, 1903. W.A.
79. Martin Buber to Weizmann, June 12, 1903. W.A.
80. Victor Jacobson to Weizmann, June 18, 1903. W.A.
81. See Abraham Idelson to Weizmann, June 15, 1903. W.A.
82. Michael Kroll to Weizmann, May 31, 1903. W.A.
83. Weizmann to Michael Kroll, June 3, 1903, *WL* 2, p. 360, and Weizmann to Abraham Idelson and Michael Kroll, June 22, 1903, *WL* 2, p. 400.
84. See Abraham Idelson to Weizmann, June 30, 1903; Michael Kroll to Weizmann, June 30, 1903. W.A.
85. Michael Kroll to Weizmann, June 30, 1903. W.A.

86. Joseph Pokrassa to Weizmann, June 28, 1903. W.A. Weizmann himself had admitted to the elitist nature of his projects: "The irony of fate: that it should be the Democratic Faction which brings aristocratic undertakings into being—an *Elite-Organ, Hochschule, Kunstverlag,* etc." Weizmann to Abraham Idelson and Michael Kroll, February 17, 1903, *WL* 2, p. 253.

87. Weizmann to Davis Trietsch, July 7, 1903, *WL* 2, p. 422.

88. Weizmann to Joseph Pokrassa, July 7, 1903, *WL* 2, p. 426.

89. Weizmann to Kalman Marmor, July 25, 1903, *WL* 2, p. 436.

90. Weizmann to Selig Weicman, May 30, 1903, *WL* 2, p. 439.

91. Weizmann to Martin Buber, June 1, 1903, *WL* 2, pp. 353–54.

92. Weizmann to Martin Buber, June 9, 1902, *WL* 2, p. 370.

93. See Weizmann to Israel Breslav, November 6, 1902, *WL* 2, p. 6, and Weizmann to Gregory Lurie, January 1, 1903, *WL* 2, p. 145.

94. See Alfred Nossig to Weizmann and Berthold Feiwel, June 28, 1903. W.A.

95. See Martin Buber to Weizmann, February 9, 1903. W.A.

96. Michael Kroll to Weizmann, May 3, 1903. W.A. This was also the view of Kroll's colleague Abraham Idelson. See Abraham Idelson to Weizmann, June 15, 1903. W.A.

97. Michael Kroll to Weizmann, June 13, 1903. W.A.

98. On Ussishkin's suggestion to create the young guard Bnei Akiva, see Nurock, *Veidat Zionei Russyah be-Minsk,* p. 41. See also Weizmann to Menahem Ussishkin, January 13, 1903, *WL* 2, pp. 192–94.

99. See, e.g., Weizmann to Victor Jacobson, June 2, 1902, *WL* 2, pp. 355–57.

100. See Weizmann to Abraham Idelson and Michael Kroll, June 9, 1903, *WL* 2, p. 372. See also Weizmann's "Circularbrief" on June 17, 1903, W.A.

101. Weizmann to Saul Lurie, June 24, 1903, *WL* 2, p. 401. See also Weizmann to Alfred Nossig, June 30, 1903, *WL* 2, p. 411.

102. Weizmann to Ben-Zion Mossinson, July 4, 1903, *WL* 2, pp. 417–18.

103. See also Weizmann's telegram to Ussishkin, August [20?], 1903, *WL* 2, p. 450, and n. 1 to this telegram.

104. Joseph Pokrassa to Weizmann, June 28, 1903. W.A.

105. Herzl, *Complete Diaries,* vol. 4, pp. 1485–87. See also the letter from Lord Cromer to Lord Lansdowne dated May 14, 1903, and the letter from Boutros Ghali, the Egyptian Minister of Foreign Affairs, to Colonel Goldsmid dated May 11, 1903, in Raphael Patai, "Herzl's Sinai Project," *Herzl Year Book,* ed. Raphael Patai (New York, 1958), vol. 1, pp. 119–22. See also, in the same source, the report of the Sinai Technical Commission and Sir W. E. Garstin's "Note on the Irrigation of the Pelusiac Plan," pp. 128–39.

106. Though for a while Herzl tried to continue the negotiations for the El Arish valley, which did not need any of the waters of the Nile. See *Herzl Year Book,* vol. 1, pp. 122–27. For the exchange of letters on the subject, see also Alex Bein, "Ha-Massa u-Matan beyn Herzl le-veyn Memshelet Britanyah ha-Gdolah be-Inyan El Arish," *Shivat Zion* (Jerusalem, 1950), vol. 1, pp. 179–220.

107. Herzl, *Complete Diaries,* vol. 4, p. 1491.

108. See Chamberlain's own testimony regarding the impression Herzl had made on him as cited in Julian Amery, *The Life of Joseph Chamberlain* (London, 1951), vol. 4, pp. 268–69.

109. Herzl, *Complete Diaries,* vol. 4, pp. 1473–74.

110. Alex Bein, *Theodore Herzl,* p. 443.

111. See the letter from Leopold Greenberg to the Rt. Hon. Joseph Chamberlain M.P., H.M. Principal Secretary of State for the Colonies, dated July 13, 1903. CZA, HVIII/293.

112. Herzl, *Complete Diaries*, vol. 4, p. 1519. See also N. M. Gelber, "Bikuro shel Dr. Herzl be-Petersburg," *Heavar* 3 (1955): 12–19.

113. See Herzl, *Complete Diaries*, vol. 4, pp. 1522–24, and von Plehve's letter to Herzl dated August 12, 1903, in *Die Welt*, August 25, 1903, pp. 1–2.

114. See the letter from Sir Clement Hill to Leopold Greenberg dated August 14, 1903, in Heymann, *The Uganda Controversy*, vol. 2, pp. 124–25.

115. See the circular letter of June 12, 1903, signed by Herzl and Kokesch. CZA, Z1/212.

116. Weizmann to Vera, April 23, 1903, *WL* 2, p. 290.

117. Weizmann to Abraham Lichtenstein, July 2, 1903, *WL* 2, p. 415. See also Weizmann to Nahum Sokolow, July 31, 1903, *WL* 2, pp. 443–44.

118. Weizmann to Kalman Marmor, July 24, 1903, *WL* 2, p. 440.

IX The Uganda Controversy

1. See Weizmann, *Trial and Error*, p. 82.

2. Weizmann's memorandum dated May 6, 1903, is a case in point: It is a vote of no confidence in the leader of the movement even before Kishinev.

3. Representing 1,572 Zionist societies, an increase of 37 percent over the previous year. See Maor, *Ha-Tnuah ha-Zionit be-Russyah*, pp. 238–39.

4. The territory offered by the British to the Zionists has consistently and incorrectly been referred to in Zionist and British historiography as Uganda. The confusion stems from the fact that both the Uganda Protectorate, which was inland, and the East Africa Protectorate were under British rule in 1903. The offer to the Zionists involved a territory which was then part of the East Africa Protectorate and today corresponds to a portion of Kenya. The confusion of terminology is due to a number of factors: Uganda was much better known at the time, yet the famous Uganda railway, on which Chamberlain had traveled, lay exclusively within the East Africa Protectorate. As the offer was linked in people's mind to the Uganda railway, they thought immediately in terms of the inland protectorate. Another factor contributing to the confusion was the transfer, on April 1, 1902, of the Eastern Province of Uganda to the East Africa Protectorate. Two new provinces, Naivasha and Kisumu, were formed from the new additions, and some of the areas considered for Jewish settlement fell within the transferred land. See Robert G. Weisbord, *African Zion: The Attempt to Establish a Jewish Colony in the East Africa Protectorate, 1903–1905* (Philadelphia, 1968), pp. 9–11. As noted earlier, Herzl—and possibly Chamberlain—also mistakenly referred to the territory in question as Uganda. Julian Amery attributes the mistake to Herzl, who may have misunderstood what Chamberlain had been telling him about his trip. See Julian Amery, *The Life of Joseph Chamberlain*, p. 265. Work on the Uganda railway began in 1896 and was completed in March 1903. It was 582 miles long, connecting Lake Victoria Nyanza with the sea at Mombasa. See Robert C. Ensor, *England, 1870–1914* (Oxford, 1936), p. 381.

5. See *Protokoll der Sitzung des grossen A.C.*, Freitag, den 21. August 1903. CZA, Z1/193.

6. Ibid.

7. Ibid. Concerning Marmorek's position, see Max Bodenheimer, "Zikhronot

al Herzl u-Zmano," [1921]. W.A. See also Yehiel Tschlenow, *Pirkei Hayav u-Feulato, Zikhronot, Ktavim, Neumim, Mikhtavim* (Tel Aviv, 1937), pp 182–83. Tschlenow also points out that although this was not indicated in the official protocol, Victor Jacobson and Richard Gottheil had also immediately declared their opposition.

8. Herzl recorded the following in his diary for Agust 22: "The Sixth Congress. The old hurly-burly. My heart is acting up from fatigue. If I were doing it for thanks, I would be a big fool. Yesterday I gave my report to the 'Greater A.C.' I presented England and Russia. And it didn't occur to any of them for even a single moment that for these greatest of all accomplishments to date I deserved a word, or even a smile, of thanks. Instead, Messieurs Jacobson, [Gregory] Belkovsky and Tschlenow criticized me a number of times." Herzl, *Complete Diaries*, vol. 4, p. 1547.

9. See Tschlenow, *Pirkei Hayav*, pp. 183–87.

10. See *Stenographisches Protokoll der Verhandlungen des VI. Zionisten-Kongresses in Basel* (Vienna, 1903), pp. 3–11.

11. Shmarya Levin, *Forward from Exile* (Philadelphia, 1967), p. 380.

12. *Stenographisches Protokoll* (VI), p. 9.

13. In his memoirs Weizmann stated that "in the session of the Russian delegation, I made a violent speech against the Uganda project and swung to our side many of the hesitant . . ." See *Trial and Error*, p. 86. This account, as will be shown, is wholly fictitious, even if we allow that in hindsight Weizmann had merged in his memory his speeches to the Russian *Landsmanschaft* of both August 24 and 26. At the latter meeting he reversed himself on East Africa, but there is no proof that he swung votes, nor do contemporary accounts record that what he said was in the spirit of his memoirs.

14. See Michael Heymann, ed., *The Uganda Controversy* (Jerusalem, 1977), vol. 2, pp. 9–10.

15. See Max Nordau to Herzl, July 17, 1903. CZA, HVIII/6l5. Herzl wrote to Nordau after the attempt on the latter's life by an anti-African: "Sie, der Sie ueberhaupt gegen Ostafrika waren . . . werden als Ostafrikaner anrevolvert . . ." Theodor Herzl to Max Nordau, December 23, 1903. CZA, HVII/41.

16. See *Stenographisches Protokoll* (VI), pp. 62–72.

17. Ibid., p. 101. Weizmann also implied—incorrectly—that Herzl had decided of his own accord to drop the investigation and possible colonization of El Arish. Weizmann's main plea was to have the question examined thoroughly once again. Lastly, he pleaded for the cultural aspect of Zionism to take its rightful place beside the collection of funds, lest Zionism find itself bereft of a meaningful substance. See *Stenographisches Protokoll* (VI), pp. 101–3.

18. Heymann, *The Uganda Controversy*, vol. 2, pp. 10–11.

19. *Der Fraind*, no. 185, September 1, 1903, p. 4.

20. Ibid. See also the comments concerning Weizmann's behavior during the deliberations cited in Tschlenow, *Pirkei Hayav*, p. 190. Tschlenow alludes to Weizmann but does not mention him by name. On the other hand, Shmarya Levin, who spoke against Tschlenow's draft resolution, identifies Weizmann. See Levin, *Forward from Exile*, pp. 380–81.

21. *Stenographisches Protokoll* (VI), p. 166.

22. *Der Fraind*, no. 185, September 1, 1903, p. 4. Weizmann repeated his position at a meeting of 'Nay-Sayers' held two days after the congress ended, in which he claimed that as soon as he understood the implications of the East

Africa project—which was bound to deter Zionism from the course it chartered toward Zion—he became an opponent, though he was still in favor of emigration. See Chaim Weizmann, "Der Kampf um das Uganda-Projekt," in Chaim Weizmann, *Reden und Aufsaetze, 1901–1936*, ed. Gustav Krojanker (Tel Aviv, 1937), p. 17.

23. See Tschlenow, *Pirkei Hayav*, pp. 199–200.
24. Ibid., pp. 200–201.
25. See *Stenographisches Protokoll* (VI), pp. 224–227, and David Vital, *Zionism: The Formative Years* (Oxford, 1982), pp. 302, 479ff.
26. *Stenographisches Protokoll* (VI), pp. 224–25.
27. Ibid., p. 226. Weizmann's brother Shmuel and his brother-in-law Chaim Lubzhinsky were also present at the congress as observers. See Rachel Lea Weizmann, *Der Tog*, May 19, 1938, p. 7, and Hayah Weizmann-Lichtenstein, *Be-Zel Koratenu*, pp. 114–15. See also Weizmann, *Trial and Error*, pp. 85–86. The various accounts do not fully agree with one another except to indicate that the vote created a temporary rift among the various family members.
28. See the scathing attack of Ahad Ha'Am on the East European delegates to the congress in his article "Habokhim," *Hashiloah* 12, no. 28 (1903): 145–52.
29. Weizmann later tried to defend the ineffectiveness of the faction. See Chaim Weizmann, "Der Kampf um das Uganda-Projekt," p. 21. See also *Hamelitz*, no. 213, September 26, 1903, p. 1, which discusses the lackluster performance of the Democratic Faction and predicts its eventual demise since Weizmann had no time to devote to its organization.
30. On the Mizrahi's support for the East Africa proposal, see Ehud Luz, "Zion and Judenstaat: The Significance of the 'Uganda' Controversy," in *Essays in Modern Jewish History: A Tribute to Ben Halpern*, ed. Frances Malino and Phyllis Cohen Albert (Rutherford, N.J., 1982), pp. 217–39.
31. See Ahad Ha'Am's article "Ha-Bokhim" in *Kol Kitvei Ahad Ha'Am*, pp. 337–41, which berates the compromising stance of the *Nein-Sager*.
32. "Merkaz ha-Mizrahi be-Lida Meshiv le-Haver Shoel (be-Nose Uganda)," in *Sefer ha-Zionut ha-Datit*, vol. 2, pp. 479–80. See also Israel Klausner, "Be-Reshit Yisud ha-Mizrahi al yedei ha-Rav I. J. Reines," in *Sefer ha-Zionut ha-Datit*, vol. 1, pp. 361–71, and Ehud Luz, "Ha-Aktualiyut be-Vikuakh Uganda," *Kivunim*, no. 1 (November 1978): 54–59.
33. Anita Shapira, *Berl* (Tel Aviv, 1980), vol. 1, pp. 31–32.
34. See *Stenographisches Protokoll* (VI), p. 84. Syrkin declared unambiguously, "Dagegen begruesse ich es mit Freuden, dass eine neue Idee in die zionistischen Reihen geworfen wurde, das ist die Idee der Kolonisation Ostafrikas auf dem Boden einer juedischer Autonomie. Wenn Sie die Tragweite dieser neuen Idee ermessen werden, kann dieser Kongress ein Wendepunkt in der juedischen Geschichte werden . . ."
35. Tschlenow, *Pirkei Hayav*, p. 22.
36. Yasinovksy to Theodor Herzl, December 25, 1903. CZA, HVIII/397.
37. Motzkin, *Sefer Motzkin*, pp. 66–69. See also letter from Berthold Feiwel to Weizmann, September 26, 1903. W.A.
38. See Weizmann's account in *Trial and Error*, p. 87. See also Sokolow's views in *Hatzfirah*, no. 223, October 12, 1903, p. 1, and no. 227, October 19, 1903, p. 1.
39. See, e.g., the accounts of Yosef Chasanowitsch in *Die Welt*, no. 20, May 20, 1910, p. 469, and Josef Eliash, *Zikhronot Zioni mi-Russyah*, pp. 125ff.

40. The last instance prior to the Sixth Zionist Congress was in his memorandum to Herzl dated May 6, 1903.
41. For a critique of Herzl, culminating in his diplomatic steps surrounding the East Africa offer, see Jacques Kornberg, "Theodore Herzl: A Reevaluation," *Journal of Modern History* 52 (June 1980): 226–52.
42. Evidence for the direct link between the pogrom in Kishinev and Herzl's decision to explore the East Africa project can be gleaned from Herzl's opening address at the Sixth Zionist Congress. See *Stenographisches Protokoll* (VI), pp. 3–5.
43. Later Weizmann would call the scheme for University Vacation Courses his *Nachtasyl*.
44. See "Die Land Frage," *Der Fraind*, no. 199, September 4, 1903, p. 1. The Kishinev delegates voted against the East Africa project and walked out with the *Nein-Sager*.
45. See *Stenographisches Protokoll* (VI), p. 230. See also Hillel Zeitlin, "Hamashber," *Hazman* 1, no. 8 (August 1905): 278.
46. Weizmann, *Trial and Error*, p. 88.
47. See Tschlenow, *Pirkei Hayav*, pp. 284–85.
48. See *Stenographisches Protokoll* (VI), pp. 257–58. As to Herzl's whittling down of even this minor achievement by the *Nein-Sager*, see Heymann, *The Uganda Controversy*, vol. 2, pp. 21–22.
49. An important decision was the creation of the Commission for the Investigation of Palestine, with Professor Otto Warburg as its chairman and Professor Franz Oppenheimer and Dr. Selig Soskin as members; the commission had a budget of fifteen thousand francs. Its terms of reference included: the scientific and practical investigation of Palestine; the establishment of experimental stations; the establishment of an information bureau for agricultural and technical matters; the establishment of a medical examination station; and the publication of a periodical on the investigation of Palestine. See *Stenographisches Protokoll* (VI), 271–75. The commission did achieve tangible results. See CZA, Z1/170.
50. See *Stenographisches Protokoll* (VI), pp. 327–28.
51. Ibid., p. 340. Privately Herzl told his confidants that he might retire at the next congress. He noted in his diary, "The difficult great Sixth Congress is over. When, completely worn out, I had returned from the Congress building, after the final session, with my friends Zangwill, Nordau and Cowen, and we sat in Cowen's room around a bottle of mineral water, I said to them: 'I will now tell you the speech I am going to make at the Seventh Congress—that is, if I live to see it. By then I shall either have obtained Palestine or realized the complete futility of any further efforts . . .' " Herzl, *Complete Diaries*, vol. 4, p. 1547.
52. See Heymann, *The Uganda Controversy*, vol. 2, p. 26.
53. Weizmann, *Reden und Aufsaetze*, p. 17.
54. In a letter to Max Nordau dated July 13, 1903, Herzl revealed his motivations for pursuing the East Africa scheme: "Have you suddenly lost all faith in me? Do you consider me wholly thoughtless in such serious matters? When we failed at El Arish I simply had to return [to the Uganda offer]. An English colonialist will declare Uganda much better than El Arish; a Zionist will say it is much worse. This, then, is the purpose of leadership, to point the way . . . When I asked Jewry for money for the Sultan—by which we could

have made [Palestine] easily—I did not get any. *Eh bien, quoi?* We will just have to try another way, and this is it. We shall colonize [Uganda] on a national basis, with a flag, *s'il vous plaît,* and self-government. We make the formulas; we are not their prisoners. Where we will first break ground is only a question of opportunity, if only we are clear in our minds what kind of house we are building on the foundation. The settlement between Kilimanjaro and Kenya could be our first *political* colony. You already guess what I mean: a miniature England *in reverse.''* Quoted in Amos Elon, *Herzl* (New York, 1975), p. 376. Weizmann himself took an unsentimental view of the East Africa offer. In a speech given in Bern in December 1903 he described it as "a proposal which did not emanate from overfondness for the Jewish people, but rather from the attempt to solve the difficult Jewish problem which England faces in its own territory." See Weizmann, *Reden und Aufsaetze,* p. 18.

55. See Herzl, *Complete Diaries,* vol. 4, pp. 1550–54. A day earlier Greenberg informed Lansdowne, in Herzl's name, that the "Executive Committee [SAC] thankfully accepts your Lordship's offer in respect to the proposed Jewish settlement in British East Africa, and has now in preparation the arrangements for sending out a Commission for the purposes set forth in the letter referred to." See Greenberg to Lansdowne, September 4, 1903. See also Greenberg to Joseph Chamberlain, September 9, 1903. Both in CZA, HVIII/293.

56. See Herzl, *Complete Diaries,* pp. 1563–65. See also *Die Welt,* no. 1, January 1, 1904, pp. 4–5.

57. See Martin Buber to Paula Buber-Winkler, September 5, 1903, in *Briefwechsel aus sieben Jahrzehnten,* vol. 1, p. 208; Chaim Weizmann to Shmarya Levin (?), September 7, 1903, *WL* 3, pp. 6–7. See also the letter dated September 4, 1903, from G. Belkovsky, Victor Jacobson, E. W. Tschlenow, and Jacob Bernstein-Kohan to Theodor Herzl in Heymann, *The Uganda Controversy,* vol. 2, pp. 126–27. See also Martin Buber to Menahem Ussishkin, November 19, 1903. CZA, A24/117.

58. See *Die Welt,* no. 42, October 16, 1903, pp. 2–3. See also [Menahem Mendel Ussishkin], *Sefer Ussishkin* (Jerusalem, 1934), pp. 77–94. The Geulah Company was set up at the end of 1902 to purchase land in Palestine on behalf of private buyers.

59. See *Die Welt,* no. 44, October 30, 1903, p. 1, and *Hatzofeh,* no. 228, October 20, 1903, p. 982.

60. "Wie gross die diplomatischen Faehigkeiten des Herrn Ussishkin sind, weiss ich nicht. Aber dass er nicht einzukaufen versteht, das sehe ich . . . ,'' p. 1.

61. Ibid., p. 2. ". . . dann moege er nicht mit leeren Redensarten die Einigkeit im Zionismus stoeren, die mehr wert ist, als ein paar Grundstuecke in Palaestina." Ibid., pp. 2–3. Ussishkin replied to Herzl point by point on November 5, 1903. See *Hatzofeh,* no. 246, November 10, 1903, pp. 3–4.

62. For an analysis of the relationship between Herzl and the Russian Zionists, see Michael Heymann, "Herzl ve-Zionei Russyah—Mahloket ve-Haskamah," *Hazionut* 3 (1973): 56–99.

63. See *Vollmacht an die Herren Gr. Belkowsky, W. Temkin und S. Rosenbaum. Mitgliedern des von der russischen A.C.—Mitgliedern gewaehlten Delegation. Streng Vertraulich.* CZA/139/8/1. The deliberations of the Kharkov Conference became a matter of public knowledge by the end of December. See "Die Charkower Konferenz," *Die Welt,* no. 52, December 25, 1903, pp. 4–5.

64. See *Hatzfirah*, no. 289, December 30, 1903, p. 3.
65. See Leopold Greenberg's report in *Stenographisches Protokoll* (VI), p. 215.
66. See *Die Welt*, no. 5 (Separat-Ausgabe), August 28, 1903, p. 1.
67. There was also opposition in England itself. One of the most prominent opponents of the East Africa scheme was Sir Harry Hamilton Johnston, a scholar and African expert who had served from 1899 to 1901 as special commissioner in Uganda. At a speech in London on December 20, 1903, he stated that if he were a Jew he would reject the East Africa project for sentimental as well as practical reasons. See *The Jewish Chronicle*, December 25, 1903, pp. 12–13.
68. In January 1904 the Foreign Office finally offered the Zionists the Gwas Ngishu plateau, an area of about five thousand miles which lay northeast of the territory originally mentioned by Chamberlain, who had resigned from the government in mid-September 1903. See Weisbord, *African Zion*, pp. 81ff. See also Leopold Greenberg to Herzl, December 15, 1903. CZA, HVIII/293, and the letter from Lord Lansdowne to Sir Charles Eliot dated February 8, 1904. CZA, HVIII/294.
69. See Bein, *Theodore Herzl*, p. 485. See also Theodor Herzl to Max Nordau, December 23, 1903: "Ich wollte nur aus Ostafrika—Nilwasser herausschlagen, resp. in Elarish etwas kriegen." CZA, HBII/41.
70. See Herzl to Nordau, December 23, 1903. CZA, HBII/41: "Da kam die Nachricht Ihres Attentats. Ein politischer Entschluss musste sofort gefasst werden . . ."
71. *The Jewish Chronicle*, December 25, 1903, p. 8.
72. CZA, Z1/212.
73. Heymann, *The Uganda Controversy*, vol. 2, pp. 49–50.
74. Minutes of the SAC meeting of January 6, 1904. CZA, Z1/178.
75. Weizmann to Simon Rosenbaum, January 15, 1904, *WL 3*, pp. 190–92.
76. CZA, Z1/393.
77. See Bein, *Theodore Herzl*, pp. 491–92. See also Herzl, *Complete Diaries*, vol. 4, pp. 1568–1619.
78. "The Greater Actions Committee notes with satisfaction the continuous labors of the Smaller Actions Committee on behalf of Palestine. The GAC assumes that the SAC will undertake to dispatch the expedition to Africa in the spirit of the decisions of the Sixth Congress. However, since it will become necessary only at the Seventh Congress to decide on the substance of the question of colonization in East Africa, free discussion on this and other pending questions will continue in accordance with previous custom. Further, the GAC, after thorough discussion, has clarified and resolved the misunderstandings that have arisen in recent months due to the dispute which had raged too violently on all sides and had hampered the work of our movement.

"The East Africa scheme is open to free discussion. At the same time, however, each member of the Actions Committee pledges himself to avoid personal attacks not only in the official circulars, but also to exercise his influence to contain such attacks as well as any discussion which may have harmful consequences." See CZA, Z1/195–199. See also Jacob De Haas, *Theodor Herzl: A Biographical Study* (New York, 1927), vol. 2, pp. 230–31.
79. See Heymann, "Herzl ve-Zionei Russyah—Mahloket ve-Haskamah," pp. 70–71.
80. Weizmann to Nahum Sokolow, September 7, 1903, *WL 3*, pp. 7–8.

81. Sokolow abstained from voting on the scheme. See *Stenographisches Protokoll* (VI), p. 227.

82. See Weizmann to Abraham Idelson and Michael Kroll, September 6, 1903, *WL* 3, p. 2.

83. See Circular No. 1 of the Democratic Faction Bureau at Geneva. W.A.

84. See CZA, A24/117.

85. See letter of Berthold Feiwel to Weizmann, November 17, 1903. W.A.

86. Weizmann to Menahem Ussishkin, September 16, 1903, *WL* 3, pp. 10–12. Two days later Weizmann again declared his willingness to place himself at the service of the *Nein-Sager* among the regional leaders. "The points that may have divided us last year [viz. the Democratic Faction and the location of the university] have now largely, or entirely, lost their importance." Weizmann to Menahem Ussishkin, September 18, 1903, *WL* 3, pp. 16–17.

87. Ibid., p. 12.

88. Weizmann to Jacob Bernstein-Kohan, September 29, 1903, *WL* 3, pp. 30–31.

89. See *WL* 3, letter 29, n. 17, p. 33, and letter 61, n. 2, p. 68.

90. Weizmann to Martin Buber and Berthold Feiwel, September 25, 1903, *WL* 3, pp. 26–27.

91. See Martin Buber to Chaim Weizmann, October 2, 1903. W.A.

92. Weizmann to Vera, October 5, 1903, *WL* 3, p. 38.

93. Weizmann to Martin Buber, October 7, 1903, *WL* 3, pp. 40–41.

94. Weizmann to Menahem Ussishkin, October 20, 1903, *WL* 3, p. 62.

95. Martin Buber to Weizmann, October 10, 1903. W.A.

96. Weizmann to Martin Buber, October 13, 1903, *WL* 3, p. 50.

97. According to Weizmann, Ahad Ha'Am was to team-teach with Sokolow a course in modern Hebrew literature, though he had not yet received Ahad Ha'Am's consent.

98. Weizmann to Catherine Dorfman, October 16, 1903, *WL* 3, p. 58.

99. See Weizmann to Catherine Dorfman, October 16, 1903, *WL* 3, p. 58.

100. "The budget for the undertaking . . . comes to about 40,000 francs." Weizmann to Menahem Ussishkin, October 20, 1903, *WL* 3, p. 62. See also Weizmann to Moses Gaster, October 24, 1903, *WL* 3, p. 76.

101. Weizmann to Ben-Zion Mossinson, November 22, 1903, *WL* 3, p. 130.

102. Weizmann to Ben-Zion Mossinson, December 3, 1903, *WL* 3, p. 155.

103. Weizmann to Joseph Lurie, December 21, 1903, *WL* 3, p. 174.

104. The attack came mainly from Simon Bernfeld, who wrote, "You are not worthy of this activity; leave Jewish Studies to us who know a little of the Hebrew alphabet." See *WL* 3, letter 132, n. 1, p. 153.

105. Weizmann to Joseph Lurie, December 21, 1903, *WL* 3, p. 174.

106. Weizmann to Ben-Zion Mossinson, February 23, 1904, *WL* 3, p. 218.

107. Weizmann brought up the subject once more during the summer of 1904. He suggested to Narcisse Leven, president of the Alliance Israélite Universelle, that the agricultural school Mikveh Israel, near Jaffa, be converted into a university. The suggestion had first been made by Ussishkin during his trip to Palestine the previous summer. See Weizmann to Menahem Ussishkin, July 14, 1904, *WL* 3, p. 282 and n. 12.

108. See Martin Buber to Paula Buber-Winkler, September 5, 1903, in Buber, *Briefwechsel aus sieben Jahrzehnten*, vol. 1, p. 208.

109. See Weizmann to Abraham Idelson and Michael Kroll, September 6, 1903, *WL* 3, p. 2; Weizmann to Jacob Bernstein-Kohan, September 29, 1903, *WL*

3, p. 32. See also Weizmann to Menahem Ussishkin, October 26, 1903, *WL* 3, p. 80.

110. See Weizmann to Catherine Dorfman, October 16, 1903, *WL* 3, p. 59.

111. "Was ist mit dem Geld fuer den 'Juden'? Hast Du Nachricht von Jakobson? Von Ussishkin? Von den Anderen?" Martin Buber to Weizmann, October 10, 1903. W.A. See also Martin Buber to Weizmann, October 18, 1903. W.A.

112. Weizmann to Victor Jacobson, October 20, 1903, *WL* 3, p. 70.

113. Weizmann to Victor Jacobson, October 21, 1903, *WL* 3, p. 70.

114. See Weizmann to Menahem Ussishkin, February 2, 1904, *WL* 3, p. 205.

115. See Weizmann to Menahem Ussishkin, November 26, 1903, *WL* 3, p. 136, and Weizmann to Victor Jacobson, November 26, 1903, *WL* 3, p. 140.

116. Weizmann to Shmarya Levin, November 27, 1903, *WL* 3, p. 146.

117. The prospectus is undated and its date of publication can only be surmised on the basis of correspondence before and after it. See Weizmann to Martin Buber, November 27, 1903, *WL* 3, p. 144, and Weizmann to George Halpern, December 2, 1903, *WL* 3, p. 152. See also Moses Gaster to Martin Buber, November 19, 1903, in Buber, *Briefwechsel aus sieben Jahrzehnten,* vol. 1, p. 221.

118. The first prospectus announced publication for May 1903. See Buber Archive, Ms. Var. 350.

119. See Theodor Herzl to Martin Buber, May 14, 1903, in Buber, *Briefwechsel aus sieben Jahrzehnten,* vol. 1, p. 192.

120. See *Der Jude.* Herausgeber: Martin Buber und Chaim Weizmann. Buber Archive, Ms. Var. 350. See also *Der Jude* 1916/1917, p. 354.

121. Weizmann to Berthold Feiwel, February 16, 1903, *WL* 2, p. 250.

122. Weizmann to Martin Buber, February 27, 1903, *WL* 2, p. 264.

123. Weizmann to Catherine Dorfman, March 18, 1903, *WL* 2, p. 276.

124. Replying to Weizmann's letter on this issue, Buber wrote that he had no intention of crowding Feiwel out of the editorship. See Martin Buber to Weizmann, November 4, 1903. W.A. In his memoirs Weizmann described Martin Buber and Berthold Feiwel as "inseparable friends." See *Trial and Error,* p. 63. Yet there are indications that conflicts between them also arose in connection with the management of the Juedischer Verlag.

125. Weizmann to Berthold Feiwel, November 2, 1903, *WL* 3, p. 98.

126. See, e.g., the cable from Martin Buber to Weizmann dated June 14, 1903. W.A.

127. See Martin Buber to Weizmann, December 9, 1903. W.A.

128. Weizmann to Martin Buber, December 13, 1903, *WL* 3, pp. 162–63.

129. Martin Buber to Weizmann, December 27, 1903. W.A.

130. See Martin Buber to Weizmann, January 29, 1904. W.A.

131. See Weizmann to Victor Jacobson, February 4, 1904, *WL* 3, p. 215.

132. See Weizmann to the Russian Central Zionist Committee, June 21, 1904, *WL* 3, p. 264, in which Weizmann accounted for the income and expenditures of the Faction.

133. Weizmann to Nahum Sokolow, September 17, 1903, *WL* 3, p. 16.

134. Leopold Kessler and Joseph Cowen leaned toward Weizmann's interpretation of the role of the commission. Leopold Greenberg and Otto Warburg supported Herzl's more limited definition of the commission's terms of reference.

135. See Weizmann to Theodor Herzl, September 6, 1903, *WL* 3, p. 4.

136. Weizmann to William Evans-Gordon, September 7, 1903, WL 3, pp. 4–5.
137. See Evans-Gordon to Weizmann, September 13, 1903. W.A.
138. See Weizmann to Otto Warburg, September 7, 1903, WL 3, pp. 5–6, and September 16, 1903, WL 3, pp. 13–14.
139. Weizmann to Catherine Dorfman, October 1, 1903, WL 3, p. 34.
140. Weizmann to Vera, October 5, 1903, WL 3, p. 5. See also Weizmann to Vera, October 3, 1903, WL 3, p. 36.
141. Vera to Weizmann, October 7, 1903. W.A.
142. Martin Buber to Weizmann, October 10, 1903. W.A.
143. Weizmann to Martin Buber, October 7, 1903, WL 3, p. 40.
144. Weizmann to Menahem Ussishkin and Others, October 20, 1903, WL 3, p. 64. Weizmann had met representatives of the Alliance Israélite Universelle and the Jewish Colonization Association while he was in Paris in July 1903 and apparently found them to be sympathetic toward the Jewish university project, though they were more interested in setting up a secondary school. See Weizmann to Ben-Zion Mossinson, July 28, 1903, WL 2, p. 442. See also Berthold Feiwel to Martin Buber, July 17, 1903, in Buber, *Briefwechsel aus sieben Jahrzehnten*, vol. 1, p. 204.
145. Weizmann to Nahum Sokolow, September 7, 1903, WL 3, p. 8.
146. Weizmann to Vera, October 4, 1903, WL 3, p. 37.
147. Weizmann to Vera, October 5, 1903, WL 3, p. 39. Vera echoed his sentiments: "Oh, how these people disgust me! Chaimchik, do we need pogroms in order to awaken in these people a sense of their own dignity, pride, a consciousness of the fact that they are people and not pathetic slaves?" Vera to Weizmann, October 7, 1903. W.A.
148. Weizmann to Vera, October 8, 1903, WL 3, p. 44.
149. Weizmann to Vera, October 9, 1903, WL 3, pp. 45–46.
150. Ibid.
151. See, e.g., Moses Gaster, "Zionismus und Neu-Zionismus," *Ost und West*, no. 10 (October 1903): 669–79. Besides being an attack on Herzl and any scheme for settlement outside Palestine, the article also attacked Israel Zangwill, who wholeheartedly supported the East Africa scheme.
152. Weizmann to Vera, October 9, 1903, WL 3, p. 46.
153. Weizmann to Vera, October 12, 1903, WL 3, p. 47.
154. See, e.g., *Die Welt*, no. 37, September 11, 1903, pp. 1–8.
155. Weizmann to Moses Gaster, October 24, 1903, WL 3, p. 77.
156. Weizmann to Vera, October 12, 1903, WL 3, p. 47. Cowen, however, wavered on this point.
157. Weizmann to Vera, October 13, 1903, WL 3, p. 52. No wonder he found that he could manage to save his money. He lived in a good flat for which he paid two Swiss francs a day with breakfast. "Life here has proved far cheaper than I expected. Mainly because I am always invited out to dinner. I have dined at Gordon's, Gaster's (twice), Zangwill's, Kessler's, Bentwich's and so on and so on. I have been received everywhere in an exceptionally cordial manner." Weizmann to Vera, October 12, 1903, WL 3, p. 49.
158. Weizmann, *Trial and Error*, pp. 90–91.
159. It took Weizmann a year and a half in Manchester—and after the passage of the Aliens Act—to deal more cautiously with Evans-Gordon. Perhaps only then did he appreciate the full extent of Evans-Gordon's anti-Jewish campaign. When the latter was reelected by his East End constituency in Jan-

uary 1906, Weizmann remarked to Vera, "Unfortunately, Evans-Gordon has also been elected . . ." See Weizmann to Vera, January 18, 1906, *WL* 4, p. 224.

160. See Evans-Gordon to Weizmann, November 7, 1903, W.A., in which he relates his joy at the prospect of Weizmann settling in England.

161. Weizmann to Vera, October 15, 1903, *WL* 3, pp. 53–54.

162. Weizmann to Martin Buber, October 16, 1903, *WL* 3, p. 56. See also Weizmann to Catherine Dorfman, October 16, 1903, *WL* 3, p. 59.

163. Weizmann to Martin Buber, October 16, 1903, *WL* 3, p. 55.

164. "It is not without reason that I was striving to get here. This is the hub of the world, and, really, you sense the breathing of a giant, the city of cities." Weizmann to Vera, October 12, 1903, *WL* 3, p. 48.

165. Weizmann to Catherine Dorfman, September 17, 1903, *WL* 3, p. 15.

166. Ibid.

167. Weizmann to Vera, October 13, 1903, *WL* 3, p. 52.

168. Weizmann to Vera, October 15, 1903, *WL* 3, p. 54.

169. Weizmann to Catherine Dorfman, October 16, 1903, *WL* 3, p. 59.

170. Weizmann to Menahem Ussishkin and Others, October 20, 1903, *WL* 3, pp. 65–67.

171. See Weizmann to Martin Buber, October 16, 1903, *WL* 3, p. 56 and n. 9.

172. See Weizmann's detailed letter to Moses Gaster, in which he also summarized his trip. Weizmann to Moses Gaster, October 24, 1903, *WL* 3, pp. 75–80.

173. Weizmann to Menahem Ussishkin and Others, October 20, 1903, *WL* 3, p. 68; see also pp. 61–68. See as well Menahem Ussishkin to Weizmann, October 28, 1903, in *Heavar* 12 (1965): 59–60.

174. Weizmann to Menahem Ussishkin and Others, October 26, 1903, *WL* 3, pp. 81–82.

175. Ibid., pp. 82–85.

176. See Weizmann to Theodor Herzl, [August 19], 1899, *WL* 1, p. 74.

177. "I feel so wretched; something is stifling me, choking me, and I cannot get rid of a nightmare that torments me: I feel that something extraordinary is going to happen, that a prophet will appear in Israel, otherwise we are doomed. Everywhere . . . there prevails such a feeling of disappointment, such a terrible mood, that this will have to bring matters to a head." Weizmann to Vera, July 6–7, 1901, *WL* 1, p. 153.

178. Weizmann to Theodor Herzl, July 22, 1901, *WL* 1, p. 158.

179. Weizmann to Catherine Dorfman, September 2, 1901, *WL* 1, p. 176.

180. Weizmann to Vera, July 21, 1902, *WL* 1, p. 312.

181. Weizmann to Victor Jacobson, February 4, 1904, *WL* 3, p. 214.

182. Weizmann to Menahem Ussishkin, September 16, 1903, *WL* 3, p. 10.

183. Weizmann to Menahem Ussishkin and Others, October 20, 1903, *WL* 3, p. 63.

184. Weizmann to Jacob Bernstein-Kohan, September 19, 1903, *WL* 3, p. 32.

185. Weizmann to Victor Jacobson, October 20, 1903, *WL* 3, p. 70.

186. There were occasions when Weizmann seriously thought that a break with Herzl would be useful. One such occasion seems to have centered around the Kharkov delegation's mission to Herzl. See Weizmann to Jacob Bernstein-Kohan, December 16, 1903, *WL* 3, pp. 166–67.

187. See Weizmann to Vera, April 27, 1904, *WL* 3, p. 253. See also Weizmann to Moses Gaster, May 9, 1904, *WL* 3, p. 256.

188. Weizmann to Menahem Ussishkin and Others, October 26, 1903, *WL* 3, p. 83.

189. Menahem Ussishkin to Weizmann, November 6, 1903, in *Heavar* 12 (1965): 60–61.

190. Ibid., p. 60.

191. Weizmann to Martin Buber, November 6, 1903, *WL* 3, p. 108.

192. Weizmann to Ben-Zion Mossinson, November 4, 1903, *WL* 3, pp. 106–7, and Weizmann to Victor Jacobson, November 12, 1903, *WL* 3, p. 111.

193. See reports of the lecture and debate in issues of *Hatzofeh*, no. 253, November 18, 1903, p. 1086; no. 261, November 27, 1903, pp. 1118–19; no. 262, November 29, 1903, p. 1124; as well as December 19, 1903, to January 1, 1904.

194. See Weizmann, *Reden und Aufsaetze*, pp. 18–20. See Menahem Ussishkin to Weizmann, November 15, 1903, in *Heavar* 12 (1965): 61–62.

195. See Weizmann to Victor Jacobson, November 18, 1903, *WL* 3, p. 121, and telegram dated November 20, 1903, *WL* 3, p. 125.

196. Weizmann to Menahem Ussishkin, November 21, 1903, *WL* 3, p. 127.

197. Menahem Ussishkin to Weizmann, November 26, 1903, in *Heavar* 12 (1965): 62–63.

198. Weizmann to Victor Jacobson, November 26, 1903, *WL* 3, p. 140.

199. Weizmann to Ben-Zion Mossinson, December 3, 1903, *WL* 3, p. 155. See also Weizmann to Menahem Ussishkin, December 16, 1903, *WL* 3, p. 165.

200. Weizmann to Catherine Dorfman, November 16, 1903, *WL* 3, p. 117.

201. Weizmann to Regina Schimmer, November 26, 1903, *WL* 3, p. 143.

202. See Menahem Ussishkin and Bernstein-Kohan to Weizmann, December 6, 1903, in *Heavar* 12 (1965): 63–64. See also Weizmann to Martin Buber, December 13, 1903, *WL* 3, p. 163.

203. See Minutes of a Private Conference of Members of the Faction in Berlin, January 10–12, 1904. W.A.

204. Weizmann to Zionist Regional Leaders, January 8, 1904, *WL* 3, p. 187.

205. See Minutes of a Private Conference of Members of the Faction in Berlin, January 10–12, 1904. W.A. Weizmann's assessment of the meeting is contained in his letter to Georg Halpern dated February 2, 1904, *WL* 3, p. 207: ". . . in my view [it] has been pretty fruitless."

206. See Weizmann to Simon Rosenbaum, January 15, 1904, *WL* 3, p. 192.

207. Weizmann to Kalman Marmor, Uriah Moonitz, and Dov Aberson, January 17, 1904, *WL* 3, p. 195.

208. See Heymann, *The Uganda Controversy*, vol. 2, pp. 320–30.

209. Weizmann to Kalman Marmor, Uriah Moonitz, and Dov Aberson, January 17, 1904, *WL* 3, p. 195. See also Weizmann to Georg Halpern, February 2, 1904, *WL* 3, p. 208.

210. Weizmann to Kalman Marmor, Uriah Moonitz, and Dov Aberson, January 17, 1904, *WL* 3, p. 195.

211. See Weizmann to Ussishkin, January [25], 1904, *WL* 3, p. 199.

212. Menahem Ussishkin to Weizmann, January 29, 1904, in *Heavar* 12 (1965): 64–65.

213. So desirous was Weizmann of Ussishkin's friendship and so eager was he to be associated with him that in February 1904, in order to impress the *Haham*, he wrote Gaster that Ussishkin and he had met. In fact, Ussishkin had only written him a letter. See Weizmann to Moses Gaster, February 3, 1904, *WL* 3, p. 212.

214. Weizmann to Menahem Ussishkin, February 2, 1904, *WL* 3, pp. 201–5.
215. Weizmann to Abraham Idelson and Michael Kroll, February 3, 1904, *WL* 3, p. 213.
216. Weizmann to Catherine Dorfman, February 24, 1904, *WL* 3, p. 219.
217. See Weizmann to Vera, April 5, 1904, *WL* 3, p. 236. See also *Der Tog,* May 14, 1938, p. 5.
218. Weizmann to Vera, March 30, 1904, *WL* 3, p. 227.
219. Ibid.
220. Weizmann to Vera, March 31, 1904, *WL* 3, pp. 229–30.
221. Weizmann to Zvi Aberson and Rosa Grinblatt, April 3, 1904, *WL* 3, p. 233.
222. Ibid.
223. Weizmann to Vera, April 11, 1904, *WL* 3, p. 241.
224. Weizmann to Vera, April 14, 1904, *WL* 3, p. 244.
225. Weizmann to Vera, April 18, 1904, *WL* 3, p. 247.
226. Weizmann to Vera, April 22, 1904, *WL* 3, p. 247.
227. Weizmann to Vera, April 22, 1904, *WL* 3, p. 251.
228. Weizmann to Victor Jacobson, April 20, 1904, *WL* 3, p. 250.
229. Weizmann to Vera, April 22, 1904, *WL* 3, p. 251.
230. See Moses Gaster to Weizmann, October 29, 1903. W.A.
231. See Evans-Gordon to Weizmann, January 25, 1904. W.A.
232. Weizmann to Moses Gaster, January 18, 1904, *WL* 3, pp. 198–99.
233. See Moses Gaster to Weizmann, February 26, 1904. W.A.
234. Weizmann to Moses Gaster, March 22, 1904, *WL* 3, p. 224.
235. "Es ist eben der einzige Weg auf welchem Sie sich eine Zukunft in England verschaffen koennen." Moses Gaster to Weizmann, April 15, 1904. W.A.
236. Weizmann to Victor Jacobson, April 20, 1904, *WL* 3, p. 250.
237. See Moshe Rinott, *Hevrat ha-Ezra li-Yehudei Germanyah* (Jerusalem, 1971), pp. 109ff.
238. Weizmann to Menahem Ussishkin, May 17, 1904, *WL* 3, p. 259.
239. See Rinott, *Hevrat ha-Ezra,* p. 300, n. 14.
240. Weizmann to Menahem Ussishkin, June 21, 1904, *WL* 3, p. 262.
241. Weizmann to Moses Gaster, *WL* 3, p. 263.
242. See Ephraim Cohn-Reiss, *Mi-Zikhronot Ish Yerushalayim* (Jerusalem, 1967), p. 212. This reasoning is somewhat suspect since both Hildesheimer and Bambus were at odds with Herzl and would hardly have rejected someone solely for his opposition to Herzl. On the other hand, it may have told them something of Weizmann's character, particularly the fact that he did not always accept authority easily.
243. See Jehuda Reinharz, "The Esra Verein and Jewish Colonization in Palestine," *Leo Baeck Institute Year Book* 26 (1979): 261–82.
244. Weizmann, *Trial and Error,* p. 93.
245. Statements supporting his need to further his scientific career are contained in Weizmann to Vera, October 12, 1903, *WL* 2, p. 48; Weizmann to Victor Jacobson, April 20, 1903, *WL* 3, p. 250. See also Weizmann to Caroline Schuster, July 13, 1912, *WL* 5, pp. 313–14. Concerning Zionist opportunities in England, see Weizmann to Kalman Marmor, July 25, 1903, *WL* 2, p. 438; Weizmann to Vera, October 12, 1903, *WL* 3, p. 48; Weizmann to Catherine Dorfman, October 16, 1903, *WL* 3, p. 59; and Weizmann to Menahem Ussishkin and Others, October 20, 1903, *WL* 3, p. 68.
246. Weizmann to Victor Jacobson, March 15, 1904, *WL* 3, p. 233.
247. See Weizmann to Victor Jacobson, April 20, 1904, *WL* 3, p. 250.

248. Weizmann to Vera, October 12, 1903, *WL* 3, p. 48.
249. See Weizmann to Caroline Schuster, July 13, 1912, *WL* 5, pp. 313–14. In somewhat more general terms· Weizmann repeated this assertion in *Trial and Error*, p. 93. See also Barnet Litvinoff, *Weizmann: Last of the Patriarchs*, (New York, 1976), p. 49, who accepts Weizmann's assertion.
250. He moved to his birthplace, Frankfurt am Main. See *Neue Deutsche Biographie* S.V. "Carl Graebe," vol. 6, pp. 705–6.
251. See Weizmann to Vera, June 22, 1906, *WL* 4, pp. 301–2.
252. One need only mention their attitude toward him concerning the issue of the Kharkov Conference, Rosenbaum and Belkovsky's behavior after their meeting with Herzl, and the humiliation suffered by him at the time of the GAC meeting in April 1904.
253. Buber's pronouncement on the contemporary state of Zionism was especially harsh. He had been disaffected with the state of the movement since 1901, and by 1903–4 he had for all practical purposes ceased to be active in Zionist affairs. After Herzl's death he saw no hope for meaningful work in the near future: "With Herzl, the grand seigneur, it was *possible* to come to an understanding; it is *impossible* to deal with these pompous nonentities [*aufgeblasene Nullen*] . . ." See Buber to Markus Ehrenpreis, September 13, 1904. Ehrenpreis Archive, 40672/7. See also Jehuda Reinharz, "Achad Haam und der deutsche Zionismus,"*Bulletin des Leo Baeck Instituts* 61 (1982): 3–27.
254. Vera's attitude is well reflected in her letter to him dated August 6, 1902. With time her stand vis-à-vis dependence on the Zionist movement did not change. See Vera to Weizmann [August 29], 1904. Both letters are in W.A.
255. See Ahad Ha'Am to Yehoshua Eisenstadt, May 11, 1910, Asher Ginsberg [Ahad Ha'am], *Igrot Ahad Ha'Am*, vol. 4, p. 268.
256. See Weizmann to Caroline Schuster, July 13, 1912, *WL* 5, p. 314.
257. Two days prior to his departure he informed the Khatzman sisters that he planned to do Zionist work in England. See Weizmann to Vera, Sophia, Anna, and Rachel Khatzman, July 8, 1904, *WL* 3, p. 272.
258. See Weizmann to Vera, June 25, 1904, *WL* 3, p. 265.
259. See *Hansard's Parliamentary Debates*, 4th ser., vol. 134 (1904), cols. 561–69.
260. Ibid., col. 561.
261. See, e.g., Joseph Chamberlain's speech of November 11, 1905, in Julian Amery, *The Life of Joseph Chamberlain*, pp. 268–69.
262. The literature on the subject of British interest in Palestine and/or the restoration of the Jews is extensive. A good summary is contained in Barbara W. Tuchman's book *Bible and Sword: England and Palestine from the Bronze Age to Balfour* (New York, 1956). See also W. T. Gidney, *The History of the London Society for the Propagation of Christianity Among the Jews from 1809 to 1908* (London, 1908); Albert M. Hyamson, *British Projects for the Restoration of the Jews* (London, 1917), and *The British Consulate in Jerusalem in Relation to the Jews in Palestine, 1862–1914*, 2 vols. (London, 1939–41); Nahum Sokolow, *History of Zionism, 1600–1918* (New York, 1969); Laurence Oliphant, *Land of Gilead* (Edinburgh, 1881); Abdul Latif Tibawi, *British Interests in Palestine, 1800–1901* (London, 1961); Franz Kobler, *The Vision Was There: A History of the British Movement for the Restoration of the Jews to Palestine* (London, 1956); Brian Blakeley, *Colonial Office, 1868–1892* (Durham, N.C., 1972); Cedric J. Lowe, *The Reluctant Imperialists, 1878–1902*, 2 vols. (London, 1967); Joel H. Wiener, *Great Britain: Foreign Policy and the Span of Empire, 1689–1971* (New York, 1972); Kenneth Bourne, *Foreign Policy of Victorian England, 1830–1902*

(Oxford, 1970); Meir Vereté, "The Restoration of the Jews in English Prot-
estant Thought, 1790–1840," *Middle Eastern Studies* 8 (1972): 3–50; Michael
McKeon, "Sabbatai Sevi in England," *AJS Review* 2 (1977): 131–69; David S.
Katz, *Philo-Semitism and the Readmission of the Jews to England, 1603–1655*
(Oxford, 1982), esp. pp. 9–157.

263. See *Hatzofeh*, no. 453, July 15, 1904, p. 5.
264. Weizmann to Vera, July [6], 1904, *WL* 3, p. 270.
265. Weizmann to Vera, Sophia, Anna, and Rachel Khatzman, July 8, 1904, *WL*
3, p. 271.
266. See Max Nordau, *Erinnerungen* (Leipzig and Vienna, 1908), p. 234.
267. Weizmann to Vera, July 9, 1904, *WL* 3, p. 275.
268. Cf., e.g., Weizmann to Menahem Ussishkin, March 15, 1904, *WL* 3, p. 222:
"I should like to see you all the more because some personal plans will depend on our talk . . . However, I would not wish to take a definite decision before discussing it with you, with Kohan-Bernstein and Jacobson. . . ."
269. See Weizmann to Zvi Aberson, July 9, 1904, *WL* 3, pp. 273–74, and Weizmann to Menahem Ussishkin, July 14, 1904, *WL* 3, pp. 280–82.
270. See Richard Crossman, "The Torso of Greatness," *Encounter* 39, no. 5 (November 1972): 56.
271. Weizmann to Vera, July 8, 1904, *WL* 3, p. 271.
272. "What I would have liked is to talk, to recall the good old days; how good
they were, how young we were then, how everything has become stale since
then. Ah, old times . . ." See Weizmann to Catherine Dorfman, February
24, 1904, *WL* 3, p. 219.
273. See, e.g., *Hatzofeh*, no. 288, December 29, 1903, p. 2, and no. 290, December 31, 1903, p. 2.
274. Crossman, "The Torso of Greatness," p. 57.

X New Beginnings

1. Weizmann, *Trial and Error*, p. 93. See also Herzl's opening remarks at the
Fourth Zionist Congress in London: ". . . England ist eine der letzten Zu-
fluchtsorten, wo es noch keinen eingebuergerten Judenhass gibt . . ."
*Stenographisches Protokoll der Verhandlungen des IV. Zionisten-Congresses in
London, 1900* (Vienna, 1900), p. 3.
2. See Mark Wischnitzer, *To Dwell in Safety* (Philadelphia, 1948), pp. 118–20;
William Cunningham, *Alien Immigration to England, 1870–1914* (London, 1897);
Lloyd P. Gartner, "Notes on the Statistics of Jewish Immigration to England, 1870–1914," *Jewish Social Studies* 22, no. 2 (April 1960): 97–102; and
Walter F. Willcox, ed., *International Migrations*, 2 vols. (New York, vol. 1,
1929; vol. 2, 1931). See also Chaim Bermant, *Point of Arrival: A Study of London's East End* (London, 1975).
3. By 1881 there were approximately twenty thousand East European Jewish
immigrants in England, more than half of whom were in London. See A.
R. Rollin, "Russo-Jewish Immigrants in England before 1881," *Jewish Historical Society of England, Transactions*, sess. 1962–67, vol. 21 (1968): 211. See
also Georg Halperin, "Statistische Darstellung der russisch-Juedischen
Niederlassung in London," in *Die juedischen Arbeiter in London* (Berlin, 1903),
pp. 11–24.
4. See the second chapter in Bernard Gainer, *The Alien Invasion: The Origins of
the Aliens Act of 1905* (New York, 1972), pp. 17–35.

5. See Lloyd P. Gartner, *The Jewish Immigrant in England, 1870–1914* (London, 1960), pp. 57ff.
6. See, e.g., Alan Lee, "Aspects of the Working-Class Response to the Jews in Britain, 1880–1914," in *Hosts, Immigrants and Minorities,* ed. Kenneth Lunn (New York, 1980), pp. 107–33.
7. Gainer, *The Alien Invasion,* pp. 17–59.
8. Ibid.
9. *Stenographisches Protokoll* (IV), p. 4.
10. Gainer, *The Alien Invasion,* p. 168.
11. On White's views, see Arnold White, *The Modern Jew* (London, 1899), pp. 177–210.
12. Gainer, *The Alien Invasion,* pp. 83–84.
13. Gartner, *The Jewish Immigrant in England,* p. 45.
14. Gainer, *The Alien Invasion,* p. 175.
15. Gartner, *The Jewish Immigrant in England,* p. 48.
16. Gainer, *The Alien Invasion,* pp. 67–73. The membership of the League probably comprised only a few hundred, but its rallies were popular and awakened widespread sympathy. See Gisela Lebzelter, "Anti-Semitism—A Focal Point for the British Radical Right," in *Nationalist and Racialist Movements in Britain and Germany Before 1914,* ed. Paul Kennedy and Anthony Nicholl (London, 1981), p. 95. Lebzelter cites forty-five thousand members, which seems highly unlikely. Colin Holmes, *Anti-Semitism in British Society, 1876–1939* (New York, 1979), p. 91, cites twelve thousand.
17. See Evans-Gordon's views in his book *The Alien Immigrant* (London, 1903).
18. Gainer, *The Alien Invasion,* pp. 182ff. It was before this royal commission that Herzl had testified on July 4, 1902.
19. Quoted in Holmes, *Anti-Semitism in British Society, 1876–1939,* p. 27.
20. The following discussion is based on Gainer, *The Alien Invasion,* pp. 184–98, and accounts in *The Jewish Chronicle.*
21. See *The Jewish Chronicle* of June 24, 1904, pp. 7, 9–10; July 1, 1904, pp. 7, 14–17; July 8, 1904, pp. 28–31; July 15, 1904, pp. 7, 21–23.
22. See *The Jewish Chronicle,* July 28, 1905, p. 12.
23. See J. A. Garrard, *The English and Immigration* (London, 1971), and E. Rosenberg, *From Shylock to Svengali: Jewish Stereotypes in English Fiction* (Stanford, Calif., 1960).
24. His very entry into England signifies the difference between him and the Jewish masses who arrived in steerage: "I have just arrived on the soil of England. I managed perfectly well with the entry formalities, etc. A real gentleman . . . The crossing was beautiful . . ." Weizmann to Vera, July 10, 1904, *WL* 3, p. 276.
25. This is where he had boarded at a very reasonable rent in October 1903.
26. See, e.g, Moses Gaster, "Herzl . . . und dann!," *Ost und West,* nos. 8–9, August–September 1904, pp. 523–30.
27. They probably met and cooperated for the first time when both served on the Cultural Commission established by the Third Zionist Congress in 1899.
28. See Weizmann to Vera, July 11, 1904, *WL* 3, p. 277.
29. See Harry Sacher, "Dr. Gaster," in *Zionist Portraits and Other Essays* (London, 1959), pp. 72–75.
30. Due to his involvement in Zionist affairs, Gaster was also at odds with the Board of Elders of the Spanish-Portuguese Congregation (*Mahamad*), a fact

which did not deter him from pursuing these activities. See, e.g., *Die Welt*, no. 6, February 10, 1899, pp. 10–11.

31. See, e.g., *Hatzfirah*, no. 21, February 6, 1903, p. 1, on the condition of English Zionism; Paul Goodman, *Zionism in England, 1899–1949: A Jubilee Record* (London, 1949), pp. 15–16. See also Stuart A. Cohen, "The Tactics of Revolt: The English Zionist Federation and Anglo-Jewry, 1895–1904," *Journal of Jewish Studies* 29, no. 2 (Autumn 1978): 169–85.

32. See Elhannan Orren, *Hibbat Zion be-Britanyah, 1878–1898* (Tel Aviv, 1974), pp. 30–32.

33. Ibid., pp. 38–49.

34. Ibid., pp. 50–61.

35. Ibid., p. 63.

36. Goodman, *Zionism in England*, p. 11.

37. See *The Jewish Chronicle*, January 17, 1896, pp. 12–13.

38. Herzl recorded in his diary: "In the evening, my mass meeting in the East End . . . The Workingmen's clubhouse was full. People crowded into every corner . . . Great success . . . Great jubilation, hat-waving, hurrahs that followed me out into the street . . ." Herzl, *Complete Diaries*, vol. 1, pp. 418–19.

39. Ibid., pp. 419–20. One ought to mention here the trip to Palestine of twenty-one men and women under the nominal auspices of the Maccabean Club and headed by Herbert Bentwich. Those participating were not motivated by the Zionist idea. See Stuart Cohen, "The First Anglo-Jewish Pilgrimage to Palestine: 1897," *Zionism* 2, no. 1 (Spring 1981): 71–85. See also *The Jewish Chronicle*, April 9, 1897, p. 2, and Orren, *Hibbat Zion be-Britanyah*, pp. 134–136. The importance of this pilgrimage lies in the impact it had on the outlook of two of its participants, Herbert Bentwich and Israel Zangwill.

40. See Orren, *Hibbat Zion be-Britanyah*, pp. 146–56; *The Jewish Chronicle*, March 11, 1898, p. 17; Paul Goodman, *Zionism in England*, pp. 14–18.

41. Orren, *Hibbat Zion be-Britanyah*, pp. 153–59. See also *Die Welt*, no. 6, February 10, 1899, pp. 10–11. See also Benjamin Jaffe, "Ha-Pulmus ha-Yehudi be-Angliyah bitkufat Herzl (1895–1904)," *Kivunim* 8 (August 1980): 99–117.

42. Goodman, *Zionism in England*, pp. 17–18. See also the report by de Haas to the Fifth Zionist Congress in *Stenographisches Protokoll der Verhandlungen des V. Zionisten-Congresses* (Vienna, 1901), pp. 42–49.

43. See Cohen, "The Tactics of Revolt," p. 178.

44. For comparative purposes it may be interesting to note that in 1901 the EZF raised 7,212 shekel. See *Stenographisches Protokol* (V), p. 49. At the Eighth Zionist Congress, which took place in 1907, the EZF reported 8,307 shekel pledged for the previous year (of which only 4,067 had been paid) and 7,097 for the current year. See *Stenographisches Protokoll der Verhandlungen des VIII. Zionisten-Kongresses* (Cologne, 1907), pp. 46–47.

45. Stuart A. Cohen, *English Zionists and British Jews: The Communal Politics of Anglo-Jewry, 1895–1920* (Princeton, N.J., 1982), pp. 110–11.

46. See Vivian D. Lipman, "The Rise of Jewish Suburbia," *Jewish Historical Society of England, Transactions*, sess. 1962–67, vol. 21 (1968): 84–85. See Weizmann to Vera, July 12, 1904, and July 13, 1904, *WL* 3, pp. 278–79. In fact, Gaster was not elected to GAC in 1905, at the Seventh Zionist Congress.

48. See *The Jewish Chronicle*, July 15, 1904, p. 10.

49. Weizmann to Menahem Ussishkin, July 14, 1904, *WL* 3, p. 283.

50. Ibid., p. 284. All three moved to the United States when the funds for the newspaper did not materialize.
51. Weizmann to Menahem Ussishkin, July 17, 1904, *WL* 3, pp. 288–290.
52. Weizmann to Vera, July 18, 1904, *WL* 3, p. 293.
53. See Weizmann, *Trial and Error*, pp. 93–95.
54. Weizmann to Menahem Ussishkin, July 14, 1904, *WL* 3, p. 285.
55. Weizmann, *Trial and Error*, p. 89. Weizmann erroneously dated the meeting as having taken place in 1903 instead of July 1904.
56. Weizmann, *Trial and Error*, p. 89.
57. See the cover letter from Weizmann to Henry Algernon George, Earl Percy, July 26, 1904, *WL* 3, p. 304.
58. Weizmann was referring to the debate which took place in the House of Commons on June 20, 1904. See *Hansard's Parliamentary Debates*, 4th ser., vol. 134 (1904), cols. 561ff. See also the previous chapter. Percy had, of course, been less than straightforward in the debate and Weizmann took him at face value.
59. See P.R.O., F.0.2/848. See also Weizmann to Vera, August 1, 1904, *WL* 3, pp. 310–12, in which Weizmann summarizes the interview. Both versions are remarkably similar and his letter deviates only slightly from the official memorandum.
60. P.R.O., F.O.2/848.
61. Ibid.
62. Both replies are in W.A.
63. See Sir Clement Hill to Weizmann, August 4, 1904. W.A. In his reply Hill changed Weizmann's sentence somewhat. In his memoirs Weizmann ascribed this statement—in somewhat revised form—to Lord Percy. See Weizmann, *Trial and Error*, p. 89.
64. Weizmann's statement to Lord Percy that the East Africa Commission was on its way was not true but did not significantly alter the purpose or meaning of the discussion. Clement Hill wrote in his minutes that Weizmann advised him that the commission was already in Africa. See *The Manchester Guardian*, July 27, 1904, pp. 5–6, which denied these rumors. Weizmann's statements to Percy and Hill are all the more astonishing since he was a member of the East Africa Commission and should have known better.
65. P.R.O., F.O.2/848.
66. Ibid.
67. Percy to Weizmann, August 4, 1904. W.A.
68. Weizmann to Menahem Ussishkin, August 3, 1904, *WL* 3, pp. 314–15. "I must tell you, my child," he wrote to Vera, "that I am very suitable for the diplomatic corps. Though it's a pity I have neither an army nor a fleet to back me up." Weizmann to Vera, July 20, 1904, *WL* 3, p. 299.
69. Weizmann to Vera and Sophia Khatzman, August 5, 1904, *WL* 3, p. 320.
70. See Weizmann to Menahem Ussishkin, July 28, 1904, *WL* 3, p. 305.
71. Yehiel Tschlenow was furious when he heard of Weizmann's foray into "diplomacy" without any authorization from the movement.
72. Conscious of the similarity of their approach, he boasted, "I am convinced that I have achieved more than Herzl with all his diplomacy." Weizmann to Vera, July 31, 1904, *WL* 3, p. 309.
73. It is most likely that the interviews were conducted in French.
74. Weizmann to Menahem Ussishkin, July 28, 1904, *WL* 3, p. 305.

75. See Weizmann to Vera, July 22, 1904, *WL* 3, p. 301.

76. In his memoirs he wrote, "I picked Manchester as my place of exile," not indicating the difficult choice between London and Manchester. See Weizmann, *Trial and Error*, p. 95.

77. Weizmann to Vera, July 13, 1904, *WL* 3, p. 279.

78. See Benjamin Harrow, *Eminent Chemists of Our Time* (New York, 1920), pp. 41–58.

79. Weizmann to Menahem Ussishkin, July 14, 1904, *WL* 3, p. 285. This was also Vera's opinion: "I . . . would prefer it if you settle in London rather than in Manchester. Life there is more interesting, the Jewish community is bigger, and from the Zionist point of view London is a more important center. Remember, dearest, your dream to transfer the center of Zionist activities to London . . . So that if Ramsay offers you a laboratory in London, I would advise you to accept it and stay in London." Vera to Weizmann [July 24], 1904. W.A.

80. Weizmann to Vera, July 18, 1904, *WL* 3, p. 291.

81. Weizmann to Vera and Sophia Khatzman, July 19, 1904, *WL* 3, pp. 293–94.

82. Weizmann to Zvi Aberson and Saul Stupnitzky, July 20, 1904, *WL* 3, p. 296.

83. Weizmann to Vera, July 20, 1904, *WL* 3, p. 299.

84. Weizmann to Vera and Sophia Khatzman, July 19, 1904, *WL* 3, p. 294.

85. See Weizmann to Vera, July 22, 1904, *WL* 3, p. 301, and Weizmann to Vera and Sophia Khatzman, August 5, 1904, *WL* 3, p. 319.

86. Weizmann to Vera, July 20, 1904, *WL* 3, p. 299.

87. Weizmann to Menahem Ussishkin, July 14, 1904, *WL* 3, p. 285: "I shall do all I can to arrange to live in London and not Manchester."

88. Weizmann to Vera and Sophia Khatzman, July 19, 1904, ,*WL* 3, p. 294.

89. Weizmann referred to his new institutional setting alternately as Owens College, Victoria University, and Manchester University. The variable terminology is understandable, since the university was just then undergoing a major structural change. See G. N. Burkhardt, "The School of Chemistry in the University of Manchester (Faculty of Science)," *Journal of the Royal Institute of Chemistry* (September 1954): 448–60.

90. On July 15, 1903, a charter reconstituting the university under the name of Victoria University of Manchester was granted. See Edward Fiddes, "The Victoria University of Manchester," in *The Book of Manchester and Salford* (Manchester, 1929), pp. 63–64. See also W. H. Brindley, *The Soul of Manchester* (Manchester, 1929).

91. Edward Fiddes, *Chapters in the History of Owens College and of Manchester University, 1851–1914* (Manchester, 1937), p. 132. See also H. B. Charlton, *Portrait of a University, 1851–1951. To Commemorate the Centenary of Manchester University* (Manchester, 1951).

92. See Fiddes, *Chapters in the History of Owens College*, p. 137. Ten years later the number of students was 1,655.

93. F. Fairbrother, J. B. Birke, Wolfe Mays, and P. G. Morgan, "The History of Science in Manchester," in *Manchester and Its Region* (Manchester, 1962), pp. 187–91. See also various entries under Henry Roscoe and Carl Schorlemmer in the *Dictionary of Scientific Biography*, ed. Charles Coulston Gillespie (New York, 1974).

94. See Harrow, *Eminent Chemists of Our Time*, pp. 1–18. See also Ritchie Calder, "The Chemistry of Statesmanship," *Rehovot* 7, no. 4 (Winter 1974–75): 50.

95. See *Dictionary of Scientific Biography*, vol. 10, p. 517. For biographical information on Perkin, Jr., see *Owens College Union Magazine* for March 1896, housed in The Central Library, Manchester.

96. See Weizmann, *Trial and Error*, pp. 95–96.

97. Sir William Henry Perkin was still alive at the time and active in his own research in the magnetic rotatory polarization of certain organic compounds. One can only wonder whether he was aware that his son had engaged the services of Graebe's student.

98. Robert Robinson, later Sir Robert Robinson, FRS and Nobel Laureate in Chemistry (1947), was a student of Perkin, Jr., when Weizmann arrived in Manchester. He reports that Perkin was elated with Weizmann: "Robinson—I think we've got a good man." See Robert Robinson, "Chaim Weizmann at Manchester," *Rehovot* 5, no. 3 (Winter 1969–70): 30. Robinson ties this incident to the academic year 1905–6 instead of 1904–5.

99. See the *Bulletin of the Research Council of Israel (Weizmann Memorial Issue)* 3 nos. 1–2 (June–September 1953): 18ff.

100. The population of Manchester rose from 543,872 in 1901 to 714,333 in 1911. These are the two census dates. In the period mentioned the city also extended its boundaries. The figures are taken from the files of The Central Library in Manchester.

101. See Max Hesse, *On the Effective Use of Charitable Loans to the Poor Without Interest* (Manchester, 1901), p. 7. Hesse quotes *The Manchester Guardian*, which estimated the Jewish population of Manchester in 1880 at 10,000 and in 1901 at 24,300. In 1906 *The Jewish Chronicle* estimated the Manchester Jewish population to be 28,000 to 30,000. The Jewish population in all the provinces had increased from 33,000 in 1896 to 86,000 in 1905. See *The Jewish Chronicle*, June 15, 1906, p. 8.

102. See S. Rosenbaum, "The Manchester Jewish Community," in *The Jewish Chronicle*, June 22, 1906, p. 44.

103. Figures for foreigners (mostly Jews from Lancashire) in 1901 indicated the following countries of origin: Russia—10,500; Poland—2,235; Germany—4,314; Austria—1,483; all countries—28,603.

104. See *The Jewish Chronicle*, June 22, 1906, p. 44.

105. *The Jewish Chronicle*, June 15, 1906, p. 1.

106. See Bill Williams, *The Making of Manchester Jewry, 1740–1875* (Manchester, 1976), pp. 17ff.

107. See Gartner, *The Jewish Immigrant in England, 1870–1914*, pp. 90–92.

108. See Katharine Chorley, *Manchester Made Them* (London, 1950), p. 117. Behrens was the second Jew to hold the highest civic office. The first was Philip Goldschmidt (1885). Nathan Laski was elevated to the magisterial bench in 1906.

109. For details, see Bill Williams, *The Making of Manchester Jewry*, pp. 132ff. See also I. W. Slotki, *The History of the Manchester Shechita Board, 1892–1952* (Manchester, 1954).

110. The best-known and largest synagogues during Weizmann's sojourn in Manchester were the Great Synagogue, the Reform Synagogue, the Spanish and Portuguese Synagogue, the Central Synagogue, the South Manchester Synagogue, the North Manchester Synagogue, and the New Synagogue and Beth Hamidrash. There were, of course, also dozens of *minyanim* which met in private homes.

111. Already in 1804 the Manchester Hebrew Philanthropic Society had been es-

tablished, which had merged with the Jewish Board of Guardians by the time Weizmann arrived. This last organization, founded in 1867, functioned as the charity arm of Manchester Jewry for the relief of the Jewish poor. Manchester Jewry also supported the Home for the Aged and Needy and other charities. In June 1906 the Jewish Soup Kitchen was founded in Manchester.

112. The Jews' School was the successor to the Manchester Hebrew Association, founded in 1838. This was a day school which in 1905 had 672 boys as well as a special department for girls. The Talmud Torah School was founded in 1879 and had nearly 700 children who received Hebrew and religious instruction after school hours. See *The Jewish Chronicle*, June 15, 1906, pp. iii–iv.

113. Ibid., p. vi.

114. See the novel by Louis Golding, *Magnolia Street* (New York, 1932), which deals with life in Cheetham Hill.

115. See Williams, *The Making of Manchester Jewry*, pp. 176–78.

116. It was estimated that in 1906 2,500 Jewish children in Manchester were in "provided" schools and 2,300 in the Jews' School, out of a total Jewish population of some 30,000. See *The Jewish Chronicle*, June 22, 1906, p. 44.

117. See Weizmann, *Trial and Error*, p. 95.

118. See *Kelly's Directory of Manchester, 1905* (London, 1905), in The Central Library, Manchester.

119. See *Protokoll des I. Zionistenkongresses in Basel* (Prag, 1911), p. 220.

120. A sample of Massel's varied Zionist activities can be gleaned from John M. Shaftesley, "Nineteenth-Century Jewish Colonies in Cyprus," *Jewish Historical Society of England. Transactions*, sess. 1968–69, vol. 22, and *Miscellanies*, part 7, pp. 92ff.

121. See *Kelly's Directory of Manchester, 1905*, which lists Mrs. Rachel Levey's occupation as "householder."

122. Weizmann, *Trial and Error*, p. 100. See also Weizmann to Vera, August 11, 1904, *WL* 3, p. 325.

123. Weizmann to Vera, July 31, 1904, *WL* 3, p. 309.

124. Weizmann, *Trial and Error*, pp. 96–97.

125. Ibid., p. 96.

126. It may have been Schorlemmer's former laboratory. See Robert Robinson, "Chaim Weizmann at Manchester," *Rehovot* 5, no. 3 (Winter 1969–70): 30.

127. On this point, see the detailed description in a letter from G. Norman Burkhardt to Maurice Schofield, November 26, 1974. John Rylands Archives (University of Manchester), UA/18/16b. Burkhardt points out that, given the few available laboratories, Weizmann was "very lucky to get a private laboratory." All laboratories then in use were "half-basement laboratories in which quite senior research workers were." Burkhardt tends to think that Weizmann's first laboratory was in the Schunk Building, one of the oldest buildings on campus, in which many of the chemists had their laboratories.

128. See Weizmann to Vera, August 3, 1904, *WL* 3, p. 316.

129. See Weizmann to Vera and Sophia Khatzman, August 5, 1904, *WL* 3, pp. 318–19.

130. Weizmann began his work in the laboratory on Tuesday, August 2, 1904.

131. Weizmann to Moses Gaster, August 5, 1904, *WL* 3, p. 317.

132. Weizmann to Vera, August 11, 1904, *WL* 3, pp. 324–25. Until 1912, when they had a disagreement which soured their relationship, Perkin continued

to see to it that Weizmann would have excellent laboratory facilities. When
the Morley Laboratories were opened in 1909—apart from Perkin's rooms
on the upper floor—Weizmann got the best laboratory and his research students were in excellent half-basement laboratories below. See G. Norman
Burkhardt to Maurice Schofield, November 26, 1974. John Rylands Archives (University of Manchester), UA/18/16c.

133. Weizmann to Vera, August 1, 1904, *WL* 3, p. 310. The senior professor for
inorganic chemistry at Manchester was Harold B. Dixon. See *University
Catalogue for 1904–1905*, John Rylands Archives, UA/18/16h.

134. Weizmann to Vera, August 11, 1904, *WL* 3, pp. 324–25.

135. Weizmann to Vera, August 8, 1904, *WL* 3, p. 322.

136. Weizmann to Menahem Ussishkin, July 17, 1904, *WL* 3, p. 289.

137. Weizmann to Menahem Ussishkin, July 17, 1904, *WL* 3, p. 290. See also
Weizmann to Menahem Ussishkin, August 3, 1904, *WL* 3, p. 315.

138. Weizmann to Menahem Ussishkin, July 28, 1904, *WL* 3, p. 305.

139. Weizmann to Menahem Ussishkin, August 3, 1904, *WL* 3, p. 313.

140. See Moses Gaster to Weizmann, August 11, 1904. W.A.

141. See Moses Gaster to Weizmann, August 9, 1904. W.A.

142. The committee comprised the current members of SAC—Ozer Kokesch,
Leopold Kahn, Oscar Marmorek, Johann Kremenetsky—and five GAC
members, including Yehiel Tschlenow, Max Bodenheimer, Menahem Ussishkin, Alexander Marmorek, and Leopold Greenberg. The annual conference, which met from August 17 to 19, ratified this committee, to which it
co-opted Max Nordau, David Wolffsohn, Nissan Katzenelson, as well as Otto
Warburg. See *Die Welt*, No. 34, August 19, 1904, pp. 1–3. See also CZA,
Z1/170. In fact, the committee was really a Committee of Twelve, since
Nordau refused to join it.

143. See CZA, Z1/170 and Z1/203.

144. Weizmann to Vera, August 16, 1904, *WL* 3, p. 327.

145. Weizmann to Vera, August 18, 1904, *WL* 3, p. 328.

146. Weizmann to Moses Gaster, August 20, 1904, *WL* 3, p. 328.

147. See *Die Welt*, no. 34, August 19, 1904, p. 2.

148. Weizmann to Moses Gaster, August 20, 1904, *WL* 3, pp. 328–29.

149. CZA, Z1/203.

150. Weizmann to Vera, August 21, 1904, *WL* 3, p. 329. Vera was fully support-
ive: "I am happy that you left Geneva, with its absurd way of life; in England your life will possibly be tougher, but better; you will be free of all
the petty squabbles, be able to rest more, get back your strength. It is quite
superfluous for you to try to reassure me that it is not cowardice that prompts
you to think of retiring from working for the cause, as if such a thing could
ever have entered my head. I know you too well for that. You will rest,
dear child, and work with renewed strength for our beloved cause." Vera
to Weizmann, August [29], 1904. W.A.

151. Weizmann was greatly concerned over Moshe's marital problems. See
Weizmann to Vera, August 24, 1904, *WL* 3, p. 334. See also Vera's detailed
description of Moshe and Zina's marital problems in her letter to Weizmann dated August 12, 1904. W.A. Moshe Weizmann had married Zina,
daughter of Samuel Rivlin of Baku, in 1903. At this time she was working
toward a degree in dental surgery, while Moshe had been studying agriculture at the Kiev Polytechnic. Due to conditions in Baku and a reversal of

fortunes for his father-in-law, in 1905 he switched to chemistry in Geneva and later in Grenoble.

152. See Elias Auerbach, "Altneuland und seine Arbeit," *Juedische Rundschau*, no. 14, April 17, 1905, pp. 152–54.
153. Weizmann to Vera, August 24, 1904, *WL* 3, pp. 333–34.
154. Weizmann, *Trial and Error*, pp. 93ff.
155. Weizmann to Menahem Ussishkin, November 9, 1904, *WL* 3, p. 359.
156. Weizmann to Menahem Ussishkin, November 9, 1904, *WL* 3, p. 359.

XI   An Alien in Manchester

1. Weizmann to Vera, September 1, 1904, *WL* 3, pp. 334–35.
2. Weizmann to Vera, September 5, 1904, *WL* 3, pp. 337.
3. Weizmann, *Trial and Error*, p. 99. This discovery became important in the 1930s when research on synthetic carcinogenic substances began, prompted by the discovery that coal tar owes its carcinogenic action on the skin to the presence of a hydrocarbon, which is also an anthracene derivative and can be made synthetically.
4. Weizmann to Vera, September 20, 1904, *WL* 3, p. 344. On Weizmann's early research and publications, see Ernst D. Bergmann, "Obituary Notice—Chaim Weizmann," *Journal of the Chemical Society* (August 1953), part 3, p. 2841.
5. Samuel Shrowder Pickles and Charles Weizmann, "The Effect of Anhydrides on Organomagnesium Bromides," *Proceedings of the Chemical Society* 20 (1904): 201; idem, "Halogen Derivatives of Naphthacenequinone," *Proceedings of the Chemical Society* 20 (1904): 220. Weizmann's interest in the naphthacenequinones is usually attributed to the influence of his teacher Liebermann. Weizmann hoped to find in the substituted naphthacenequinones a clue to the synthesis of cochenillic acid. He was particularly impressed by the formation of dihydroxynaphthacenequinone from indandione, or from phthalic and succinic acids, by a series of processes. Soon he became more interested in the direct syntheses by condensation of various substituted phthalic acids and naphtols. See Robert Robinson, "Chaim Weizmann at Manchester," *Rehovot* 5, no. 3 (Winter 1969–70): 30–31.
6. Clearly, he must have used Charles in other forums since *The Jewish Chronicle* occasionally refers to him by this name. See, e.g., *The Jewish Chronicle*, February 24, 1905, p. 36.
7. See *Bulletin of the Research Council of Israel. Weizmann Memorial Issue* 3, nos. 1–2 (June–September 1953): 18–24, and Anthony R. Michaelis, *Chaim Weizmann* (London, 1974), appendix, pp. 50–64. Two papers co-published by Weizmann with William Henry Perkin, Jr., in 1907 are signed Carl Weizmann, but this must simply be due to an error.
8. See *Kelly's Directory of Manchester, 1908* (London, 1908), in The Central Library, Manchester. On the other hand, Weizmann seldom signed his letters Charles. One exception is his letter to military authorities dated August 31, 1916, *WL* 7, p. 290.
9. Weizmann to Vera, October 1, 1904, *WL* 3, p. 347.
10. See Weizmann to Moses Gaster, October 2, 1904, *WL* 3, p. 348.
11. Weizmann to Vera, October 1, 1904, *WL* 3, p. 347.
12. Weizmann to Menahem Ussishkin, November 9, 1904, *WL* 3, pp. 359–60. See also Weizmann to Vera, November 9, 1904, *WL* 3, p. 360.

13. E. N. Abrahart, "Weizmann and the Clayton Aniline Company Ltd.," Material given to the author in November 1982 by G. N. Burkhardt.

14. Weizmann to Martin Buber, January 12, 1905, WL 4, pp. 3–4. See also Weizmann's subsequent inaccurate descriptions of his position, e.g., Weizmann to Otto Warburg, January 21, 1907, WL 5, p. 12. To Judah Leon Magnes he wrote in 1912, when he was merely a senior lecturer, "I have achieved a professorship in biological and organic chemistry here . . ." Weizmann to Judah Leon Magnes, May 5, 1912, WL 5, p. 197.

15. The Manchester Directory for 1908 listed Weizmann's occupation as professor; this title was, no doubt, supplied by Weizmann. See *Kelly's Directory of Manchester, 1908.* The Central Library, Manchester.

16. See Weizmann to Vera, January 23, 1905, WL 4, p. 12; and March 3, 1905, WL 4, p. 47.

17. Weizmann to Vera, March 3, WL 4, p. 47.

18. Weizmann, *Trial and Error,* p. 101.

19. See Maurice Samuel, *Little Did I Know* (New York, 1963), p. 182. Samuel recorded his impressions of Weizmann's accent and manner of speech after Weizmann had already spent considerable time in Manchester. His very first lecture must have been all the more marked by linguistic peculiarities and was probably difficult to comprehend. See also W.G.W., "Dr. Weizmann in the Laboratory," *The Manchester Guardian,* October 1957.

20. Weizmann to Vera, January 23, 1905, WL 4, p. 12. See also Vera to Weizmann, January 25, 1905. W.A.

21. See, e.g., Weizmann to Vera, February 5, 1905, WL 4, p. 27; and February 24, 1905, WL 4, p. 41.

22. Weizmann to Vera, February 25, 1905, WL 4, p. 43.

23. Weizmann to Vera, December 1, 1904, WL 4, p. 374; and December 7, 1904, WL 4, p. 376.

24. See Weizmann to Vera, June 17, 1905, WL 4, p. 108; and July 2, 1905, WL 4, p. 118, where he claims that his annual stipend would be 120 pounds.

25. Robinson, "Chaim Weizmann at Manchester," p. 30.

26. W.G.W., "Dr. Weizmann in the Laboratory."

27. See Jan Quiller Orchardson and Charles Weizmann, "Some Derivatives of Naphthoylbenzoic Acid and of Naphthacenequinone," *Proceedings of the Chemical Society* 21 (1905): 307, and Charles Weizmann and Ernst Basil Falkner, "β-Naphthoylacetic Acid Ethyl Ester," *Proceedings of the Chemical Society* 21 (1905): 307.

28. Weizmann to Moses Gaster, October 2, 1904, WL 3, p. 348.

29. See, e.g., Weizmann to Vera, February 22, 1905, WL 4, p. 40; March 3, 1905, WL 4, p. 47; and April 13, 1905, WL 4, p. 76.

30. See, e.g., Weizmann to Vera, March 17, 1905, WL 4, p. 56.

31. Weizmann to Vera, February 13, 1905, WL 4, p. 33.

32. Weizmann to Vera, February 19, 1905, WL 4, p. 39.

33. See Weizmann to Vera, March 12, 1906, WL 4, p. 258; and March 13, 1906, WL 4, p. 259.

34. See Vera to Weizmann, April 1, 1905. W.A. Vera's own financial situation was quite desperate. See, e.g., Vera to Weizmann, September 17, 1905, and September 21, 1905. W.A. Yet she steadfastly refused to give up her own independence and accept money from Weizmann: "Chaimchik, it's so hard for me to be getting money from home, but it would be as hard, if not harder, to be helped financially by you. My dear friend, don't be offended by this. I

can't help this feeling. *C'est plus fort que moi.* I love you, I respect you, I think most highly of you, but I can't help feeling that the moment money enters our relationship something wrong will happen and it will lose its present pure character . . ." Vera to Weizmann, September 25, 1905. W.A.

35. Weizmann to Vera, January 18, 1905, *WL* 4, p. 9: "Mrs. Levey is sulking, of course, but I don't give a damn, as she was skinning us." Weizmann to Vera, February 7, 1905, *WL* 4, p. 30.
36. See Weizmann to Vera, May 20, 1905, *WL* 4, p. 94.
37. Weizmann rented his rooms from Mrs. Eleanor Gale, whose occupation was listed as "householder." Other occupants of the lodging houses in Parkfield Street in 1905 included: a butcher, a nurse, merchants, an optician, an engineer, a designer, a bookseller, commission agents, and an exporter. The street included one other Jew, who was a jeweler, and a few Muslims. See *Kelly's Directory of Manchester, 1905.* The Central Library, Manchester.
38. E.g., the chemist Henry Enfield Roscoe, the pathologist Sheridan Delepine, the physicist Arthur Schuster and the vice chancellor of the university, Sir Alfred Hopkinson. See Maurice Spiers, *Victoria Park Manchester: A Nineteenth-Century Suburb in Its Social and Administrative Context* (Manchester, 1976), pp. 52–53 and appendix.
39. See Weizmann to Vera, August 27, 1905, *WL* 4, pp. 127–28: ". . . am very pleased that I shall be living in cosier surroundings."
40. See Weizmann to Vera, August 29, 1905, *WL* 4, p. 131.
41. See Weizmann to Vera, October 7, 1905, *WL* 4, p. 177.
42. Weizmann to Vera, October 15, 1905, *WL* 4, p. 182.
43. See "Local History. Biographical Cuttings," the Central Library, Manchester. See also the biographical notes on Charles Dreyfus in W.A.
44. Weizmann to Moses Gaster, April 11, 1904, *WL* 3, p. 241.
45. Weizmann to Vera, November 25, 1904, *WL* 3, p. 371.
46. Weizmann to Menahem Ussishkin, December 12, 1904, *WL* 3, p. 378.
47. Weizmann was clearly pleased to be invited by the Dreyfus family, which belonged to Manchester's social and political elite. He became an almost weekly visitor in their homes. But familiarity also bred contempt. Eighteen months later he wrote to Vera, "I am filled with disgust whenever I meet the Dreyfuses . . . They're such snobs." See Weizmann to Vera, July 18, 1906, *WL* 4, p. 318. This did not deter him from continuing his social relationship with the family.
48. See Weizmann to Vera, January 27, 1905, *WL* 4, pp. 18–19. According to the official agreement, Weizmann was required "to perform research on behalf of the Company at the laboratories of Owens College and to attend at the works during vacational periods in excess of one month per annum." Several of Weizmann's research students subsequently joined the Clayton Aniline Company. Among these were W. H. Bentley and Rona Robinson. See E. N. Abrahart, "Weizmann and the Clayton Aniline Company Ltd." Material given to the author by G. N. Burkhardt in November 1982.
49. Weizmann to Vera, January 27, 1905, *WL* 4, pp. 18–19. Gaster advised Weizmann to consult a lawyer before signing the contract with Dreyfus. See Moses Gaster to Weizmann, December 13, 1904. W.A.
50. Weizmann to Vera, February 3, 1905, *WL* 4, p. 26.
51. Weizmann to Vera, January 31, 1905, *WL* 4, p. 24.
52. Weizmann to Vera, March 14, 1905, *WL* 4, p. 53.
53. Weizmann to Vera, May 20, 1905, *WL* 4, p. 94.

54. Weizmann to Vera, March 23, 1905, *WL* 4, p. 58.
55. Weizmann to Vera, March 25, 1905, *WL* 4, pp. 60–61.
56. Weizmann to Vera, March 27, 1905, *WL* 4, p. 62.
57. Weizmann to Vera, April 2, 1905, *WL* 4, p. 68.
58. Weizmann to Vera, April 20, 1905, *WL* 4, p. 80.
59. See *WL* 4, letter 65, p. 79, n. 1.
60. Weizmann to Vera, April 20, 1905, *WL* 4, p. 79.
61. In his memoirs Weizmann recorded that soon after his arrival in Manchester he and Joseph Massel attended a rather silly lecture at a meeting of the Manchester Zionist Association. When asked, at the end of the lecture, to move a vote of thanks, he severely attacked the speaker instead: "It took me months to live the incident down," he recalled. This was somewhat of an exaggeration. See Weizmann, *Trial and Error*, pp. 103–4.
62. Harry Sacher noted the following on this subject: "The Manchester Zionists were simple, hardworking folk, full of zeal, but not giants in the community. Weizmann's preeminence in any Zionist society was assured; here there was no competitor, and he acquired rapidly not only leadership but spiritual and intellectual authority as well." Harry Sacher, *Zionist Portraits and Other Essays* (London, 1959), p. 17.
63. See Simon Dubnov, *History of the Jews*, vol. 5 (London, 1973), pp. 725–29.
64. See *The Jewish Chronicle* for November 4, 1904, p. 9, and November 11, 1904, p. 11.
65. Weizmann to Vera, November [12?], 1904, *WL* 3, p. 361.
66. See *The Jewish World*, December 2, 1904.
67. Weizmann to Vera, November 27, 1904, *WL* 3, p. 371.
68. Weizmann continued to give speeches in Yiddish long after he had mastered English. In 1909 a correspondent of *Hazvi* in London noted: "Weizmann lectures in Yiddish, a language spoken by most English Jews. His Yiddish is rich with expressions, nuances and humor. He is a first rate public speaker and very much loved and appreciated by the masses." His Hebrew, on the other hand, was not as good. He understood Hebrew well but could not easily converse in the language. See *Hazvi*, July 15, 1909.
69. *The Jewish Chronicle*, September 11, 1885, p. 7. The records of Zionist activity in Manchester have not been preserved, and one must rely on published accounts in the local and national press. For a survey of Zionist activities in England from the turn of the century until 1917, see Josef Fraenkel, "Fun der Englisher Hibbat Zion Bavegung biz zu der Balfour—Deklarazie," *YIVO Bleter* 43 (1966): 72–147.
70. *The Jewish Chronicle*, September 11, 1885, p. 7.
71. Ibid., August 8, 1890, p. 13.
72. Ibid., December 19, 1890, p. 16, and April 10, 1891, p. 19.
73. Ibid., February 27, 1891, p. 19, and March 13, 1891, p. 11.
74. See, e.g., the creation of Agudat Achim in September 1892, and the Ben Zion Society in December 1892. *The Jewish Chronicle*, September 2, 1892, p. 13, and December 9, 1892, p. 19.
75. Ibid., March 29, 1895, p. 18.
76. One name that was associated with the Hovevei Zion in Manchester from its earliest years is that of Barrow I. Belisha. Possibly this is the same Belisha who had given the unfortunate lecture on "Stray Observations of a Wandering Jew," after which he was attacked by Weizmann. See Weizmann, *Trial and Error*, p. 104. Belisha became a supporter of Zangwill's Jewish Territo-

rial Organization (ITO) and therefore an obvious target for Weizmann.
77. See *The Jewish Chronicle,* August 14, 1896, p. 18.
78. Ibid., December 3, 1897, p. 32.
79. Ibid., December 3, 1897, p. 32.
80. Ibid., January 28, 1898, p. 28. One of the leaders of this group was Joseph
81. Ibid., January 21, 1898, p. 28.
82. Ibid., June 3, 1898, p. 28. A year after its founding there were reportedly eleven hundred Zionist members in Manchester. See *The Jewish Chronicle,* March 18, 1898, p. 29. By 1899 it was usually referred to in the English press as the Manchester Zionist Association.
83. *The Jewish Chronicle,* January 4, 1901, p. 23.
84. Ibid., October 18, 1901, p. 25.
85. Ibid., January 3, 1902, p. 34.
86. Ibid., May 16, 1902, p. 33, and May 23, 1902, p. 26.
87. Ibid., August 1, 1902, p. 21.
88. Ibid., March 20, 1903, p. 31.
89. Ibid., October 23, 1903, p. 27.
90. See, e.g., Weizmann to Vera, February 18, 1905, *WL* 4, p. 37, and February 22, 1905, *WL* 4, p. 40.
91. See, e.g., Weizmann to Vera, January 11, 1905, *WL* 4, p. 3.
92. The growth of the Manchester Zionist Association (MZA) had come to a halt. In March 1904 it had sold eight hundred *shkalim.* See *The Jewish Chronicle,* March 4, 1904, p. 35. A year later the revenue account and balance sheet showed a deficit of nineteen pounds, and the number of *shkalim* sold declined to six hundred. See *The Jewish Chronicle,* March 24, 1905, p. 26.
93. Weizmann to Menahem Ussishkin, December 12, 1904, *WL* 3, p. 378.
94. See, e.g., Weizmann to Vera, February [9], 1905. See also *The Jewish Chronicle,* February 24, 1905, p. 36, and March 24, 1905, p. 26.
95. Commenting on the affinity between Weizmann and the East European Jews in England, Vera wrote, ". . . I am so glad you entered the English Zionist world. There, of course, you will not have a young, responsive student body to influence and lead as you have in Geneva, but you'll have the masses, the people who need you so badly . . ." Vera to Weizmann, January 25, 1905. W.A.
96. See *The Jewish Chronicle,* January 20, 1905, p. 36.
97. Weizmann to Vera, January 23, 1905, *WL* 4, p. 12.
98. See *The Jewish Chronicle,* January 27, 1905, p. 29.
99. Weizmann to Vera, January 17, 1905, *WL* 4, p. 7.
100. See *The Jewish Chronicle,* January 27, 1905, pp. 29.
101. Weizmann to Vera, January 23, 1905, *WL* 4, pp. 12–13.
102. See *The Jewish Chronicle,* January 27, 1905, p. 29.
103. Dreyfus had initially been receptive to the East Africa project. See *The Jewish Chronicle,* September 11, 1903, pp. 10–13. At the Sixth Zionist Congress he abstained from voting on the East Africa project. He seems to have reversed himself sometime during 1904.
104. See Weizmann to Vera, February 13, 1905, *WL* 4, p. 33.
105. See Weizmann to Vera, January 28, 1905, *WL* 4, p. 19.
106. Weizmann to Menahem Ussishkin, January 29, 1905, *WL* 4, p. 211. See also Weizmann to Menahem Ussishkin, March 29, 1905, *WL* 4, p. 63. To Vera he wrote, "I intend to undermine Greenberg so as to promote Dreyfus . . .

He is a friend of Balfour and consequently holds stronger trumps than Greenberg. Moreover, in Zionist affairs Dreyfus will listen to me." Weizmann to Vera, January 30, 1905, *WL* 4, p. 21.

107. See, e.g., Weizmann to Vera, February 5, 1905, *WL* 4, p. 27; and February [9], 1905, *WL* 4, p. 30.

108. Weizmann to Vera, February 16, 1905, *WL* 4, p. 36.

109. See Weizmann to Vera, March 1, 1905, *WL* 4, p. 46; and March 29, 1905, *WL* 4, p. 65.

110. See, e.g., Weizmann to Menahem Ussishkin, March 29, 1905, *WL* 4, p. 63.

111. See Weizmann to Menahem Ussishkin, December 12, 1904, *WL* 3, p. 378, and n. 4 to this letter. In February 1905 he did speak in Manchester on "The Present Situation of the Zionist Movement." See *The Jewish Chronicle*, February 24, 1905, p. 36, which refers to him as Dr. Charles Weizmann. He also spoke in Manchester in March 1905 on "The Position of Zionism." See *The Jewish Chronicle*, March 24, 1905, p. 26.

112. Weizmann to Vera, February 27, 1905, *WL* 4, p. 44.

113. Weizmann to Vera, May 30, 1905, *WL* 4, p. 99.

114. Weizmann to Vera, May 12, 1905, *WL* 4, p. 89.

115. Cf. Weizmann to Menahem Ussishkin, March 29, 1905, *WL* 4, p. 64: ". . . the majority of Zionists [in England] read only Yiddish."

116. See Sacher, *Zionist Portraits and Other Essays*, p. 17.

117. Louis Kletz to David Wolffsohn, May 16, 1905. CZA, W58/II. Quoted by Camillo Dresner in his introduction to vol. 4 of the *Weizmann Letters*, p. xviii.

118. See Menahem Ussishkin, "Ha-Programah Shelanu," in *Sefer Ussishkin*, ed. R. Benyamin (Jerusalem, 1934), p. 125.

119. Ibid., pp. 113–16.

120. Ibid., p. 118. Ussishkin's article was later published as a pamphlet, translated into a number of languages, and widely distributed. His ideas were also echoed by Vladimir Jabotinsky and Ber Borochov. See Jonathan Frankel, *Prophecy and Politics: Socialism, Nationalism, and the Russian Jews, 1862–1917* (Cambridge, 1981), pp. 331–51.

121. See also the decisions and resolutions of the Zionei Zion in Warsaw, December 5, 1904, CZA, A115/28.

122. See *Hatzfirah*, no. 9, January 24, 1905, pp. 2–3. Though the center of activity of the Zionei Zion remained in Vilna, other Zionei Zion groups were also formed in the West in such cities as Berlin (see CZA, A24/81/1) and London (see *The Jewish Chronicle*, April 28, 1905, pp. 13–15).

123. Yitzhak Maor, *Ha-Tnuah Ha-Zionit be-Russyah* (Jerusalem, 1973), p. 297.

124. For a biography of Israel Zangwill, see Maurice Wohlgelehrnter, *Israel Zangwill* (New York, 1964).

125. See Israel Zangwill, "Der Zionismus und das Angebot England," *Die Welt*, no. 16, April 19, 1905, pp. 7–10; no. 17, April 28, 1905, pp. 3–5; no. 18, May 5, 1905, pp. 2–5; and no. 20, May 19, 1905, pp. 2–3.

126. Weizmann to Martin Buber, January 12, 1905, *WL* 4, p. 5.

127. See Weizmann to Vera, January 25, 1905, *WL* 4, pp. 15–16.

128. See *WL* 4, p. 17, n. 4.

129. See *The Jewish Chronicle*, April 28, 1905, pp. 13–15. See also J. K. Goldbloom, "Reminiscences of Zionism in Great Britain," in *The Rebirth of Israel*, ed. Israel Cohen (London, 1952), pp. 65–66.

130. Weizmann to Vera, April 25, 1905, *WL* 4, p. 81.

131. Ibid., p. 82.
132. Weizmann to Vera, February 10, 1905, *WL* 4, p. 32; Weizmann to Moses Gaster, March 12, 1905, *WL* 4, p. 50.
133. See Weizmann to Vera, April 2, 1905, *WL* 4, p. 68.
134. For the text of Zangwill's speech entitled "The East Africa Offer," see *Speeches, Articles and Letters of Israel Zangwill* (London, 1937), pp. 198–227.
135. Weizmann to Vera, April 10, 1905, *WL* 4, pp. 72–73.
136. See *The Manchester Guardian*, October 21, 1941, p. 6.
137. See *The Jewish Chronicle*, May 5, 1905, p. 33.
138. Weizmann to Moses Gaster, May 8, 1905, *WL* 4, p. 86.
139. See CZA, Z1/204.
140. Israel Cohen, *The Journal of a Jewish Traveller* (London, 1925), pp. 150–53.
141. For a detailed and fascinating description of the expedition, see Nahum Wilbush, *Ha-Masa le-Uganda* (Jerusalem, 1963), p. 44.
142. See Warburg to the Aktions-Comité, April 23, 1905. CZA, Z1/370.
143. See A. St. Hill Gibbons, Alfred Kaiser, and Nahum Wilbush, *Report on the Work of the Commission Sent Out by the Zionist Organization to Examine the Territory Offered by His Majesty's Government for the Purposes of a Jewish Settlement in British East Africa* (London, 1905), p. 15.
144. See "Sitzungen des Grossen Aktions-Comités, 22., 23., 24. Mai 1905." CZA, Z1/205.
145. Ibid.
146. See, e.g., the pamphlets in CZA, A115/28.
147. Weizmann to David Wolffsohn, May 29, 1905, *WL* 4, p. 97.
148. *The Jewish Chronicle*, June 9, 1905, p. 28. Present at the public meeting in the Manchester Hippodrome were Dreyfus and Weizmann, as well as Greenberg and Cowen. Alexander Marmorek had accompanied Wolffsohn to Manchester. Greenberg moved a resolution recommending that the congress not entertain the East Africa scheme. See also Weizmann to Vera, June 6, 1905, *WL* 4, p. 101.
149. See, e.g., Zangwill on this issue in *Die Welt*, no. 29, July 21, 1905, pp. 11–17.
150. See his speech in Liverpool against East Africa in *The Jewish Chronicle*, June 2, 1905, p. 30.
151. Ibid., June 16, 1905, p. 19.
152. Weizmann to Vera, June 13, 1905, *WL* 4, p. 103: "I have accomplished my Roosevelt-style mission. I feel very tired but am glad that everything came out well, although I am fed up to the teeth with Zionists. Nevertheless, I shall go to the Congress with the feeling that I did everything I could."
153. Weizmann to Menahem Ussishkin, June 27, 1905, *WL* 4, p. 114.
154. Ibid.
155. Weizmann to Vera, July 4, 1905, *WL* 4, p. 119.
156. Weizmann to Gaster, June 18, 1905, *WL* 4, p. 109.
157. Weizmann asked for fifty to sixty pounds, but Gaster could promise only ten pounds, later supplementing it with another fifteen pounds which he had borrowed on Weizmann's behalf from a friend. See Moses Gaster to Weizmann, June 23, 1905, and July 11, 1905. W.A.
158. Weizmann to Vera, July 21, 1905, *WL* 4, p. 124.
159. Cf. Weizmann to Vera, July 24, 1905, *WL* 4, p. 126, in which he describes the atmosphere even before the *Vorkonferenz* officially commenced: "Here it's hell: noise, commotion, din. A terrific amount of all kinds of riffraff."

160. *Stenographisches Protokoll der Verhandlungen des VII. Zionisten-Kongresses und des ausserordentlichen Kongresses in Basel* (Berlin, 1905), pp. 14–18.

161. Ibid., pp. 27–44.

162. "Weil eine autonome Kolonie ausserhalb Palaestinas bereits die Haelfte des Basler Programmes bedeutet. Es ist nicht Palaestina selbst, aber es ist eine oeffentlich-rechtlich gesicherte Heimstaette." *Stenographisches Protokoll* (VII), p. 74.

163. Ibid., p. 75.

164. Ibid., p. 12.

165. "Wir Zionisten zwingen niemanden, mit uns mitzugehen. Uganda steht Ihnen frei, gehen Sie hin!" Ibid., p. 115.

166. Ibid., p. 45.

167. Ibid., p. 132.

168. The English Zionist delegates were evenly split on the vote. Out of forty-six delegates from England—each representing two hundred shekel payers—to the Seventh Zionist Congress, twenty-three voted to reject the East Africa project. See J. K. Goldbloom, "Reminiscences of Zionism in Great Britain," in *The Rebirth of Israel: A Memorial Tribute to Paul Goodman*, ed. Israel Cohen (London, 1952), p. 66.

169. Ibid., pp. 133–34.

170. Ibid., p. 134.

171. Ibid., pp. 135–36.

172. See Israel Zangwill, "What Is Ito?" in *Speeches, Articles and Letters of Israel Zangwill*, pp. 231–33.

173. See Wohlgelernter, *Israel Zangwill*, pp. 158–74, and Richard Gottheil, *Zionism* (Philadelphia, 1914), pp. 140ff. Weizmann sharply attacked the territorialists during a meeting in Manchester held immediately after the Seventh Zionist Congress, in which he and Dreyfus reported on what had transpired at the congress; see *The Jewish Chronicle*, September 8, 1905, p. 25. For later controversies, see Max Mandelstamm to Alexander Marmorek [July 1910]. CZA A3/8.

174. *Stenographisches Protokoll* (VII), pp. 191–206.

175. Ibid., pp. 209ff.

176. Ibid., p. 297.

177. Ibid., p. 296.

178. Prior to the congress Weizmann calculated that the English members of GAC would be Greenberg, Gaster, and Dreyfus. See Weizmann to Menahem Ussishkin, June 27, 1905, *WL* 4, pp. 114–15.

179. Weizmann to Menahem Ussishkin, June 16, 1905, *WL* 4, p. 107.

180. Weizmann to Vera, June 17, 1905, *WL* 4, p. 108.

181. Weizmann to Vera, July 13, 1904, *WL* 3, p. 279.

182. Responding to Gaster's good wishes on the birth of his son, Benjamin, Weizmann expressed his feelings as an exile very clearly: "It will certainly be my greatest concern to make my son a good Jew . . . But it is not easy in this English *Galuth* to give a child a true Jewish education. Everything around is so terribly un-Jewish. One will therefore have to fight the whole environment. Even the 'Jews' here are Jews only in name. But I live in the hope that my son will grow up in Palestine." Weizmann to Moses Gaster, July 11, 1907, *WL* 5, p. 34.

183. Vera was well aware of this: "I must say, Chaimchik, that you have an un-

fortunate tendency to see everything in the darkest colors . . ." Vera to
Weizmann, June 6, 1905. W.A.

184. Weizmann to Vera, February 25, 1905, *WL* 4, p. 41.
185. Weizmann to Vera, February 19, 1905, *WL* 4, p. 38.
186. Weizmann to Vera, March 25, 1905, *WL* 4, p. 61.
187. Weizmann to Vera, September 8, 1905, *WL* 4, p. 142.
188. Weizmann to Vera, November 28, 1904, *WL* 3, p. 372.
189. See, e.g., Weizmann to Vera, April 5, 1905, *WL* 4, p. 70.
190. Weizmann to Vera, June 24, 1905, *WL* 4, p. 100.
191. Weizmann to Vera, July 8, 1906, *WL* 4, pp. 312–13.
192. Weizmann to Menahem Ussishkin, March 29, 1905, *WL* 4, p. 64.
193. Weizmann to Vera, April 14, 1905, *WL* 4, p. 77; and September 8, 1905, *WL* 4, pp. 141–42: "Whoever shows ability elevates himself to 'making money.' This is especially so among our Jews."
194. Weizmann to Vera, June 25, 1905, *WL* 4, p. 112.
195. Weizmann to Vera, September 9, 1905, *WL* 4, p. 143. A few years later Weizmann expressed himself in a similar vein. See *Hazvi,* July 15, 1909.
196. Weizmann to Vera, April 14, 1905, *WL* 4, p. 77.
197. Weizmann to Vera, March 19, 1905, *WL* 4, pp. 56–57.
198. See Weizmann to Vera, May 7, 1905, *WL* 4, p. 85, and May 8, 1905, *WL* 4, p. 86.
199. See the *Dictionary of National Biography,* ed. L. G. Wickham Legg (Oxford, 1949), pp. 3–5.
200. Weizmann to Vera, May 10, 1905, *WL* 4, p. 87.
201. Vera to Weizmann, July 6, 1904. W.A.
202. Vera to Weizmann, July 12, 1904. W.A. Vera's father died the following summer.
203. See, e.g., Weizmann to Vera, July 16, 1904, *WL* 3, pp. 287–88; and July 17, 1904, *WL* 3, pp. 290–91.
204. Vera to Weizmann, July 22, 1904. W.A.
205. See, e.g., Vera to Weizmann, July 24 and August 12, 1904, W.A.; Weizmann to Vera, September 1, 1904, *WL* 3, pp. 334–35.
206. Vera to Weizmann, July 22, 1904. W.A.
207. Vera to Weizmann, August 21, 1904. W.A.
208. Weizmann to Vera, September 8, 1904, *WL* 3, pp. 339–40. See also Weizmann to Vera, September 1, 1904, *WL* 3, pp. 335–36.
209. Vera to Weizmann, September 13, 1904. W.A. See also Weizmann's reply to Vera, September 20, 1904, *WL* 3, pp. 344–45.
210. Cf. Vera to Weizmann, September 6, 1904. W.A.: "Our financial circumstances are so bad . . ."; Vera to Weizmann, September 13, 1904. W.A.: "My nerves are absolutely shot to pieces, and I don't feel at all well . . ." See also Vera to Weizmann [September 16], 1904. W.A.
211. Vera to Weizmann, August 29, 1904. W.A. See also Weizmann's angry reply on September 8, 1904, *WL* 3, p. 339, and Vera to Weizmann, September 13, 1904. W.A.
212. See Vera to Weizmann, August 12, 1904. W.A. See also Vera Weizmann, *The Impossible Takes Longer* (New York, 1967), p. 24.
213. See, e.g., Vera to Weizmann, October 26, 1904; Vera to Weizmann, November 1, 1904. W.A. See also Weizmann to Vera, October 24, 1904, *WL* 3, p. 352.

214. See Weizmann to Vera, November 19, 1904, *WL* 3, p. 365; and January 11, 1905, *WL* 4, p. 3.
215. Vera to Weizmann, November 22, 1904. W.A.
216. See, e.g., Vera to Weizmann, February 17, 1905; Vera to Weizmann, February 23, 1905. W.A.
217. Weizmann to Vera, January 14, 1905, *WL* 4, p. 6. See also Vera to Weizmann, January 17, 1905, and January 19, 1905. W.A.
218. Weizmann to Vera, March 5, 1905, *WL* 4, pp. 47–48.
219. See Vera to Weizmann, February 1, 1905. W.A.
220. Vera was born on November 26, 1881.
221. See Weizmann to Vera, November 28, 1904, *WL* 3, p. 372; and November 29, 1905, *WL* 4, p. 209. See also Vera to Weizmann, November 26, 1904, and November 26, 1905. W.A. In 1904 he congratulated her too late, in 1905 much too early.
222. See, e.g., Vera to Weizmann, November 7, 1904; December 4, 1904; December 7, 1904; January 28, 1905; February 23, 1905. W.A.
223. Weizmann to Vera, June 26, 1904, *WL* 3, p. 266.
224. Weizmann to Vera, December 2, 1904, *WL* 3, p. 375.
225. Weizmann to Vera, February 24, 1905, *WL* 4, p. 41.
226. Vera to Weizmann, May 9, 1905. W.A.
227. Weizmann to Vera, May 15, 1905, *WL* 4, p. 90.
228. Weizmann to Vera, May 20, 1905, *WL* 4, p. 93.
229. Weizmann to Vera, June 20, 1905, *WL* 4, p. 110.
230. Weizmann to Vera, September 27, 1905, *WL* 4, p. 167.
231. See Weizmann to Vera, February 24, 1906, *WL* 4, p. 248: "It's our turn now, Verochka; we're a long way behind all our friends."

XII Wary Adjustment

1. See, e.g., Jeremiah Schneiderman, *Sergei Zubatov and Revolutionary Marxism: The Struggle for the Working Class in Tsarist Russia* (Ithaca, N.Y., 1976).
2. See Samuel H. Baron, *Plekhanov, the Father of Russian Marxism* (Stanford, Calif., 1963), p. 261.
3. See, e.g., David Lane, "The Russian Social Democratic Labour Party in St. Petersburg, Tver, and Ashkhabad, 1903–1905," *Soviet Studies* 15, no. 3 (January 1964): pp. 331–44.
4. See Father George Gapon, *The Story of My Life* (New York, 1906), pp. 174–215.
5. The Gaponovschina can be seen as having marked the beginning of the revolution of 1905. See Walter Sablinsky, *The Road to Bloody Sunday: Father Gapon and the St. Petersburg Massacre of 1905* (Princeton, N.J., 1976), pp. 272–91.
6. See Leon Trotsky, *1905,* trans. Anya Bostock (New York, 1971), pp. 83–117.
7. For the full text of the October Manifesto, see Sidney Harcave, *First Blood: The Russian Revolution of 1905* (New York, 1964), pp. 195–96.
8. See Nicholas V. Riasanovsky, *A History of Russia* (New York, 1963), pp. 452–53.
9. Weizmann to Vera, January 23, 1905, *WL* 4, p. 11.
10. See Weizmann to Vera, January 24, 1905, *WL* 4, p. 14.
11. Weizmann to Vera, June 8, 1905, *WL* 4, p. 102.
12. Vera to Weizmann, January 28, 1905. W.A.
13. Weizmann to Vera, January 28, 1905, *WL* 4, p. 19.

14. See Weizmann to Vera, January 30, 1905, *WL* 4, p. 22.

15. See Weizmann to Vera, February 5, 1905, *WL* 4, p. 27.

16. Weizmann to Vera, May 30, 1905, *WL* 4, p. 99.

17. Weizmann to Vera, March 6, 1905, *WL* 4, p. 49.

18. See "From Kishineff to Bialystok: A Table of Pogroms from 1903 to 1906," *The American Jewish Year Book 5667* (Philadelphia, 1906), p. 44.

19. See Leo Motzkin, *Die Judenpogrome in Russland*, vol. 2 (Cologne and Leipzig, 1910), pp. 44–58.

20. Shlomo Lambroza, "Jewish Self-Defense During the Russian Pogroms of 1903–1906," *Jewish Journal of Sociology* 23, no. 2 (December 1981); 123–34. See also *Hatzofeh*, September 21, 1903, p. 898.

21. See Simon Dubnov, *History of the Jews*, vol. 5 (New York, 1973), pp. 732–33.

22. Motzkin, *Die Judenpogrome in Russland*, vol. 2, pp. 60–79.

23. Weizmann to Vera, June 15, 1905, *WL* 4, p. 105.

24. See Motzkin, *Die Judenpogrome in Russland*, vol. 1, pp. 213ff. The total number of Jews murdered during 1905 was 1,002, while close to 2,000 were wounded.

25. Motzkin, *Die Judenpogrome in Russland*, vol. 2, pp. 109–34. See also *The Times*, November 6, 1905, p. 5. On the aftermath of the pogroms and the reaction within Russian Jewry, see *Hazman*, no. 12, January 15, 1906, pp. 3–4.

26. Weizmann to Vera, November 4, 1905, *WL* 4, pp. 192–93.

27. Weizmann to Vera, November 6, 1905, *WL* 4, p. 194.

28. See Weizmann to Vera, November 7, 1905, *WL*, 4, p. 194. A fortnight later he reiterated in a letter to Gaster: "It is painful; and a terrible irony, to be teaching chemistry to *goyim* now, and I laugh with derision at myself!" Weizmann to Moses Gaster, November 19, 1905, *WL* 4, p. 198.

29. See also Vera to Weizmann, September 13, 1905. W.A.

30. The pogrom in Rostov on November 1, 1905, did not affect the Khatzman family. See *The Times* of November 4, p. 5, and November 7, 1905, p. 5.

31. See Weizmann to Vera, February 16, 1906, *WL* 4, p. 244.

32. See Weizmann to Vera, March 23, 1906, *WL* 4, p. 262.

33. See Weizmann to Vera, February 14, 1906, *WL* 4, p. 243.

34. See Hayah Weizmann-Lichtenstein, *Be-Zel Koratenu*, p. 168.

35. Weizmann to Vera, September 10, 1905, *WL* 4, p. 148, and September 24, 1905, *WL* 4, p. 163.

36. Weizmann to Vera, September 20, 1905, *WL* 4, p. 160.

37. See Ronald Grigor Suny, *The Baku Commune, 1917–1918* (Princeton, 1972), pp. 35–37.

38. See James D. Henry, *Baku: An Eventful History* (London, [1906]), pp. 171ff.

39. Weizmann to Vera, September 8, 1905, *WL* 4, p. 142.

40. Weizmann to Vera, September 20, 1905, *WL* 4, pp. 159–60.

41. Weizmann to Vera, August 26, 1905, *WL* 4, pp. 126–27.

42. See Weizmann to Vera, January 25, 1906, *WL* 4, p. 229.

43. Weizmann to Vera, June 22, 1906, *WL* 4, p. 301.

44. See Moses Gaster to Weizmann, April 6, 1905. W.A. The Anglo-Jewish Association was founded in 1871 to protect Jewish rights in backward countries. The Board of Deputies of British Jews was *the* representative organization of British Jewry.

45. See Weizmann to Moses Gaster, April 8, 1905, *WL* 4, p. 71.

46. See Moses Gaster to Weizmann, April 10, 1905. W.A.

47. See, e.g., Weizmann to Vera, April 10, 1905, *WL* 4, p. 73.

48. See Weizmann to Menahem Ussishkin, June 16, 1905, *WL* 4, p. 106.
49. Weizmann's attitude on this subject did not change even in the 1940s. Writing his memoirs in the aftermath of the holocaust, and knowing full well that Britain had once again been less generous than it could have been in admitting Jewish refugees, Weizmann stated: "The Aliens Bill in England, and the movement which grew up around it, were natural phenomena only too familiar in our history. Whenever the quantity of Jews in any country reaches the saturation point, that country reacts against them. In the early years of this century Whitechapel and the great industrial centers of England were in that sense saturated. The fact that the actual number of Jews in England, and even their proportion to the total population, was smaller than in other countries was irrelevant; the determining factor in this matter is not the solubility of the Jews, but the solvent power of the country. England had reached the point when she could or would absorb so many Jews and no more. English Jews were prepared to be absorbed in larger numbers. The reaction against this cannot be looked upon as anti-Semitism in the ordinary or vulgar sense of that word; it is a universal social and economic concomitant of Jewish immigration and we cannot shake it off." Weizmann, *Trial and Error*, p. 90.
50. See *The Jewish Chronicle*, November 17, 1905, pp. 38–40.
51. Weizmann to Vera, November 13, 1905, *WL* 4, p. 196.
52. See Weizmann to Menahem Ussishkin, November 26, 1905, *WL* 4, p. 202.
53. Weizmann to Vera, November 26, 1905, *WL* 4, p. 203.
54. Weizmann to Menahem Ussishkin, November 26, 1905, *WL* 4, pp. 201–2.
55. Ibid., p. 202.
56. Ibid.
57. Weizmann to Vera, November 26, 1905, *WL* 4, p. 204.
58. See Sergei Witte, *The Memoirs of Count Witte*, trans. and ed. Abraham Yarmolinsky (Garden City, N.Y.: 1921), p. 293, who explicitly writes: "The loan to Russia was to be an international one . . . In 1905 I opened preliminary negotiations with Neutzlin, the head of the Banque de Paris et des Pays Bas . . . The other group of banks, known as the Jewish group, was headed by the Rothschild firm . . . Consequently, I instructed Rafalovich, our financial agent in Paris, to go to London and find out what was the attitude of the Rothschilds toward our loan. Rafalovich's reply was . . . that they would not be in a position to do so until the Russian Government had enacted legal measures tending to improve the conditions of the Jews in Russia." See, in addition, p. 299. See also C. C. Aronsfeld, "Jewish Bankers and the Tsar," *Jewish Social Studies* 35, no. 2 (April 1973): 87–104. Of interest in this context is also the attitude of Jewish bankers in the United States, which is discussed in Gary Dean Best, *To Free a People: American Jewish Leaders and the Jewish Problem in Eastern Europe, 1890–1914* (Westport, Conn., 1982).
59. See *The Jewish Chronicle*, December 15, 1905, p. 31.
60. See Moses Gaster to Weizmann, November 29, 1905. W.A.
61. Weizmann to Moses Gaster, December 6, 1905, *WL* 4, pp. 212–13.
62. See Moses Gaster to Weizmann, December 7, 1905. W.A.
63. Weizmann to Moses Gaster, December 6, 1905, *WL* 4, p. 212.
64. See Weizmann to Vera, November 26, 1905, *WL* 4, p. 203.
65. See *The Jewish Chronicle*, December 15, 1905, p. 32.
66. See Weizmann to Vera, November 30, 1905, *WL* 4, p. 210. In the same letter Weizmann summarized a debate he had in Manchester with the local orga-

nizers of the December meeting: "What can I tell you, Verochka? Seeing and talking with these people is worse than a pogrom, believe me. Why aren't they killed?"

67. Leopold Greenberg to David Wolffsohn, November 27, 1905. Quoted in Paul A. Alsberg, "Documents on the Brussels Conference of 1906," in *Michael*, vol. 2, edited by Shlomo Simonsohn and Jacob Toury (Tel Aviv, 1973), p. 144.

68. See *The Jewish Chronicle*, December 22, 1905, p. 28.

69. See Alsberg, "Documents on the Brussels Conference of 1906," pp. 150–52.

70. Max Nordau to David Wolffsohn, November 29, 1905. CZA, W96; see Yaakov J. Thon ed., *Sefer Warburg*, with an introduction by Yaakov Thon (Tel Aviv, 1948), p. 39.

71. See Israel Heilprin, "Nissayon shel Interventzia Politit le-Maan Yehudei Russyah aharei Peraot October," *Zion* 20, nos. 3–4 (1955): 103–74.

72. See *Die Welt*, no. 5, February 2, 1906, pp. 3–6.

73. See Leopold Greenberg to David Wolffsohn, February 4, 1906. CZA, W79I.

74. For a critique of the Brussels resolutions, see *Stenographisches Protokoll der Verhandlungen des VIII. Zionisten-Kongresses im Haag* (Cologne, 1907), p. 111.

75. See Weizmann to David Wolffsohn, December 19, 1905, WL 4, pp. 213–14.

76. See *The Jewish Chronicle*, December 15, 1905, p. 32, and December 22, 1905, p. 35.

77. Weizmann to Vera, January 12, 1906, WL 4, p. 220.

78. See Weizmann to Vera, January 19, 1906, WL 4, p. 225.

79. Weizmann to Judah Leon Magnes, February 13–17, 1906, WL 4, p. 241.

80. See Robert R. James, *The British Revolution*, vol. 1 (London, 1976), pp. 225–29.

81. See Harold M. Blumberg, *Weizmann: His Life and Times* (New York, 1975), p. 32; Harold Wilson, *The Chariot of Israel* (London, 1981), pp. 35–36; Blanche Dugdale, "Weizmann and Balfour," in *Chaim Weizmann*, ed. Meyer W. Weisgal (New York, 1944), pp. 129–34. See also Max Egremont, *Balfour: A Life of Arthur James Balfour* (London, 1980), pp. 204–5. In studying Weizmann's meetings with Balfour and Churchill, I have benefited from observations made by Richard H. S. Crossman as well as David Mitchell, "Spotlight on Balfour," *Middle East International* (1972)

82. Weizmann, *Trial and Error*, pp. 110–12. Weizmann's account in *Trial and Error* has received added credibility from William E. Rappard (a member of the Permanent Mandates Commission of the League of Nations), who in 1925 heard Balfour and Weizmann recollect their first meeting in Manchester. See William E. Rappard, "Great Humanitarian," *The Jerusalem Post: Chaim Weizmann Memorial Supplement*, October 30, 1953, p. 1. It should be kept in mind, however, that this conversation took place twenty years after the event, and that Rappard recorded it for the first time almost thirty years after hearing it, i.e., after *Trial and Error* had already been published. What makes his account suspect is the fact that it matches Weizmann's own wording and style.

83. Weizmann to Vera, January 9, 1906, WL 4, p. 219.

84. See Chaim Weizmann, *Dvarim*, vol. 1 (Tel Aviv, 1936), p. 134. In an introduction to Nahum Sokolow's *History of Zionism*, first published in 1919, Balfour mentions his conversation with Weizmann in January 1906 without reproducing its content. See Nahum Sokolow, *History of Zionism, 1600–1918* (New York, 1969), pp. xlix–1.

85. See Blanche Dugdale, *Arthur James Balfour*, vol. 1 (London, 1936), pp. 433–35.

86. Ibid., pp. 435–36, and Leonard Stein, *The Balfour Declaration* (New York, 1961), p. 152. Cf. Weizmann to Vera, March 23, 1906, *WL* 4, p. 262: "Balfour has written to Dreyfus that he would very much like to know me better."

87. See Blanche Dugdale, *Arthur James Balfour*, vol. 1, pp. 435ff. See also Kenneth Young, *Arthur James Balfour* (London, 1963), pp. 256–57, and Harry Sacher, *Zionist Portraits and Other Essays* (London, 1959), p. 18, where he writes: "If the international proclamation of the Jewish National Home bears in history the name of Balfour, that is due to Weizmann's evangelistic effort some twelve years before." Another theory has it that the wife of Laurence Oliphant, Rosamund Oliphant Templeton, was the first to interest Balfour in Zionism. See Aryeh Winshel, "Hashpaatah ha-Zionit shel Geveret Oliphant al Balfour," *Haumah*, no. 2 (April 1960): 226–28.

88. See Weizmann, *Trial and Error*, p. 109.

89. Dugdale, *Arthur James Balfour*, vol. 1, pp. 433–35; idem, "Weizmann and Balfour," p. 132. Concerning Balfour's intellectual interests, see L. S. Jacna, "Science and Social Order in the Thought of A. J. Balfour," *ISIS* 71, no. 256 (March 1980): 11–34.

90. Young, *Arthur James Balfour*, p. 255. See also Egremont, *Balfour*, p. 205. According to William E. Rappard, *it was Weizmann* who asked for the interview with Balfour, who was puzzled by this request. See *The Jerusalem Post: Chaim Weizmann Memorial Supplement*, October 30, 1953, p. 1.

91. See *The Jewish Chronicle*, September 8, 1905, p. 25.

92. See the letter from Joseph Cowen reprinted in English Zionist Federation, *General Election, 1900: Opinions of Parliamentary Candidates on Zionism* (London, 1900), pp. 1–2; my thanks to Professor Stuart A. Cohen for obtaining this pamphlet for me. See also *The Jewish Chronicle*, October 5, 1900, p. 9, and *The Jewish Chronicle*, January 12, 1906, p. 37. On the general question of the Jewish vote in England, see Geoffrey Alderman, *The Jewish Community in British Politics* (London, 1983). For the Zionist dimension, see pp. 86ff.

93. *The Jewish Chronicle*, January 12, 1906, p. 44.

94. Quoted in *Hansard's Parliamentary Debates*, 4th ser., July 10, 1905, Vol. 148, cols. 155–56.

95. Ibid., cols. 803–4.

96. See, e.g., Young, *Arthur James Balfour*, p. 257. Young quotes a letter from Balfour to Lady Elcho, dated August 17, 1899, in which he told her of a dinner party at the Sassoons', which he found difficult to stomach: "We were dragged . . . to a long, hot and pompous dinner . . . peopled with endless Sassoon girls . . . I believe the Hebrews were in an actual majority—and tho' I have no prejudices against the race (quite the contrary) I began to understand the point of view of those who object to alien immigration!" Ibid., p. 139.

97. See "Mr. Balfour and the Jewish Community," *The Jewish Chronicle*, July 14, 1905, pp. 6–7.

98. Letter of Winston Churchill to Nathan Laski, May [30], 1904. Quoted in Randolph Churchill, *Winston S. Churchill*, vol. 2 (companion vol.), Part 1, 1901–1907 (London, 1969), pp. 354–56.

99. Ibid., p. 357.

100. See *The Jewish Chronicle*, November 24, 1905, p. 15.

101. See *The Jewish Chronicle*, January 12, 1906, p. 44.

102. Ibid. See also Robert G. Weisbord, *African Zion* (Philadelphia, 1968), pp. 232–35.

103. See Weizmann to Nahum Sokolow, November 28, 1905, *WL* 4, p. 208.

104. See Oskar K. Rabinowicz, *Winston Churchill on Jewish Problems* (New York, 1956), p. 36.

105. Writing to Vera after the elections, Weizmann noted, "I have a feeling that the Liberal government will not be making any concessions either. They had promised a great deal before the elections. But after the elections promises, particularly those given to Jews, are reduced to zero." Weizmann to Vera, February 26, 1906, *WL* 4, p. 251.

106. See Weizmann to Menahem Ussishkin, November 26, 1905, *WL* 4, p. 201.

107. See Weizmann to Nahum Sokolow, November 28, 1905, *WL* 4, p. 208.

108. See Weizmann to David Wolffsohn, December 28, 1905, *WL* 4, p. 216.

109. See *WL* 4, p. 216, n. 8.

110. Weizmann to Vera, January 12, 1906, *WL* 4, p. 220.

111. Cf. the letter from Nathan Laski to Winston Churchill dated July 14, 1904: "Doubtless also, you would have learnt that Dr. Dreyfus—one of the principal supporters of Mr. Balfour—will support your candidature—and as he is a likely Lord Mayor—I know he refused the honor last year—he will prove a valuable ally . . ." Quoted in Randolph S. Churchill, *Winston S. Churchill,* vol. 2 (companion vol.), Part 1, 1901–1907, p. 357.

112. Geoffrey Alderman, *The Jewish Community in British Politics,* p. 96, states that "the suspicion must remain . . . that in January 1906 Weizmann allowed himself to be used for the propaganda purposes of the Conservative party." Alderman's statement is not based on any concrete evidence. Alderman also mistakenly claims that Weizmann did not meet Churchill during the election campaign. See p. 95.

113. This, in any case, is what he claimed twelve years later: "Conversations I held with Dr. Weizmann in January 1906 convinced me . . . that if a home was to be found for the Jewish people . . . it was vain to seek it anywhere but in Palestine." See Arthur James Balfour, "Introduction," *History of Zionism, 1600–1918,* by Nahum Sokolow (New York, 1969), pp. xlix–1.

114. See *The Jewish Chronicle,* January 19, 1906, p. 33.

115. See Dugdale, *Arthur James Balfour,* vol. 1, p. 436.

116. See Elie Halévy, "Epilogue," *A History of the English People,* trans. E. I. Watkin (London, 1934), vol. 2, pp. 8–12.

117. See Sydney H. Zebel, *Balfour: A Political Biography* (Cambridge, 1973), pp. 142–43. For a more detailed statistical breakdown of the results, see James, *The British Revolution,* vol. 1, pp. 229–30.

118. Dreyfus was also elected to the executive of the EZF. See *The Jewish Chronicle,* January 19, 1906, p. 29.

119. On the whole, the Glasgow Conference was uneventful. It is interesting and indicative of Weizmann's attitude toward Wolffsohn and the direction in which the World Zionist Organization was moving that at Glasgow he moved the following resolution, seconded by Joseph Cowen: "That this mass meeting of Glasgow Zionists and delegates from the Federated Zionist Association of the United Kingdom, gathered under the auspices of the English Zionist Federation, declares its fullest confidence in the Chief Executive Committee of the Zionist Organization, appointed at the last Congress, and its president, Mr. David Wolffsohn. It pledges itself loyally to abide by the decisions of the Zionist Congress and to work earnestly in accordance there-

with, under the direction of the Chief Executive Committee." *The Jewish Chronicle*, January 19, 1906, pp. 30–31. Though the resolution was a ritual that was repeated at each convention, it still indicates Weizmann's favorable attitude toward Wolffsohn at the time.

120. Weizmann to Vera, January 14, 1906, *WL* 4, p. 221.

121. See Lucien Wolf to Israel Zangwill, September 1, 1905. F. O. 2/948. See also *The Jewish Chronicle*, November 3, 1905, p. 25.

122. See David Vital, *Zionism: The Formative Years* (Oxford, 1982), p. 437.

123. See Stuart Cohen, *English Zionists and British Jews* (Princeton, N.J., 1982), p. 94.

124. See *The Jewish Chronicle*, September 15, 1905, p. 24.

125. *The Jewish Chronicle*, December 8, 1905, p. 34.

126. *The Jewish Chronicle*, July 13, 1906, p. 46.

127. See Oskar K. Rabinowicz, "Zionist-British Negotiations in 1906," in *Essays Presented to Chief Rabbi Israel Brodie*, ed. H. T. Zimmels, J. Rabinowitz, and I. Finestein (London, 1967), pp. 311–12. See also *The Jewish Chronicle*, September 1, 1905, p. 23.

128. Acknowledging Greenberg's letter on August 25, 1905, which informed him of the decisions of the Seventh Zionist Congress, Lucas then added: "With regard to the concluding part of your letter, I am to state that any endeavor to ameliorate the condition and raise the status of the Jewish People will always command the sympathy and goodwill of the British Government." Quoted in Josef Fraenkel, "Chaim Weizmann and Haham Moses Gaster," *Herzl Year Book* (New York, 1964–5), vol. 6, p. 209.

129. See Weizmann to Vera, September 7, 1905, *WL* 4, n. 3, p. 140.

130. See Weizmann to Vera, September 7, 1905, *WL* 4, p. 140.

131. Weizmann to Vera, October 30, 1905, *WL* 4, p. 189.

132. See Mordechai Eliav, *David Wolffsohn, ha-Ish u-Zmano* (Tel Aviv, 1977), pp. 68–69. See also *The Jewish Chronicle*, February 2, 1906, p. 8.

133. Weizmann to Vera, February 12, 1906, *WL* 4, p. 239.

134. See Weizmann to Vera, February 20, 1906, *WL* 4, p. 246.

135. Weizmann to Vera, March 5, 1906, *WL* 4, pp. 253–54.

136. Weizmann to Vera, March 9, 1906, *WL* 4, p. 257.

137. See Weizmann to Vera, April 29, 1906, *WL* 4, p. 274.

138. See *The Jewish Chronicle*, July 12, 1907, pp. 32–33.

139. See Weizmann to Vera, June 7, 1906, *WL* 4, pp. 296–97.

140. See *The Jewish Chronicle*, March 23, 1906, p. 13.

141. On the long-standing relationship between them, see Florian Sokolow, *Nahum Sokolow: Life and Legend* (London, 1975), pp. 90–91.

142. See Weizmann to Moses Gaster, June 25, 1906, *WL* 4, p. 305.

143. See Weizmann to Nahum Sokolow, June 12, 1906, *WL* 4, p. 299.

144. See Weizmann to Menahem Ussishkin, April 5, 1906, *WL* 4, p. 269; Weizmann to Vera, May 5, 1906, *WL* 4, p. 278.

145. The total number of members in the First Duma was 497. See Sidney S. Harcave, "The Jews and the First Russian National Election," *American Slavic and East European Review* 9 (1950): 33–41.

146. See M.H., "M. Vinaver ve-Hamahapekha ha-Russit," *Heavar* 15 (1968): 203–7.

147. See Sidney Harcave, "The Jewish Question in the First Russian Duma," *Jewish Social Studies* 6, no. 2 (April 1944): 162ff.

148. See Yitzhak Maor, "Yehudei Russyah bi-Yemei ha-'Dumot,' " *Heavar* 7 (1960): 49ff.

149. See "Report of the Duma Commission on the Bialystok Massacre," *American Jewish Year Book, 1906–7* (Philadelphia, 1906), pp. 70–89. See also *The Jewish Chronicle*, July 13, 1906, pp. 11–14.

150. See Harcave, "The Jewish Question in the First Russian Duma," p. 172.

151. After its dissolution, some two hundred Duma deputies—the Jewish deputies among them—met in the Finnish town of Viborg and signed a manifesto that denounced the government and called for passive resistance by the people. Subsequently the Viborg participants were sentenced to three months in jail and lost their right to stand for election to the Second Duma. Thus, the Jews—Zionists and non-Zionists—were deprived of their most effective leadership.

152. See, e.g., Greenberg's attack on Zangwill and the ITO in Liverpool on April 22, 1906, in *The Jewish Chronicle*, April 27, 1906, pp. 22–24, and Zangwill's counterattack on May 27, 1906, in *The Jewish Chronicle*, June 1, 1906, pp. 23–28, and June 8, 1906, pp. 21–22.

153. See *The Jewish Chronicle*, June 22, 1906, pp. 24–25.

154. Weizmann to Percy Baker, June 24, 1906, *WL* 4, p. 302.

155. Weizmann to Moses Gaster, June 25, 1906, *WL* 4, pp. 304–5.

156. Moses Gaster to Weizmann, June 25, 1906, and to Percy Baker, July 27, 1906. W.A. See also Moses Gaster to Max Shire, July 29, 1906. W.A. Percy Baker had actually resigned from the executive after Wolffsohn's visit to London in mid-July 1906, but his resignation was not accepted.

157. Weizmann to Moses Gaster, June 25, 1906, *WL* 4, p. 304.

158. Weizmann to Percy Baker, July 8, 1906, *WL* 4, pp. 311–12.

159. See CZA, Z2/226. Weizmann still believed in early July that Wolffsohn was "ignorant of the current situation." Weizmann to Ben-Zion Mossinson, July 8, 1906, *WL* 4, p. 314.

160. Writing to Max Mandelstamm a few months earlier, Wolffsohn stated: "Freund Zangwill, der ebenfalls zu den Ehrlichsten gehoert, und gewiss vom besten Willen beseelt ist, wird, wie ich zuversichtlich hoffe, bald den Weg zu uns wiederfinden . . . Fuerchten Sie nicht, dass sich der Zionismus jetzt zuviel mit sogennanter praktischer Arbeit in Palaestina, die uns zum alten Chowewe Zion Standpunkt fuehren koennte, abgeben wird. So lange ich bei der Leitung bin, wird die politische Richting immer die Oberhand behalten . . ." David Wolffsohn to Max Mandelstamm, October 5, 1905. CZA, A3/8.

161. See "Eine Konferenz in London," *Die Welt*, no. 29, July 20, 1906, p. 20, and no. 30, July 27, 1906, p. 5. See also Margery and Norman Bentwich, *Herbert Bentwich, the Pilgrim Father* (Jerusalem, 1940), p. 148.

162. Weizmann to David Wolffsohn, September 28, 1905, *WL* 4, p. 168. See also his resolution at the Glasgow Conference on pledging loyalty to Wolffsohn and SAC. *The Jewish Chronicle*, January 19, 1906, pp. 30–31.

163. Weizmann to Vera, February 14, 1906, *WL* 4, p. 244.

164. Weizmann to David Wolffsohn, July 24, 1906, *WL* 4, pp. 319–22.

165. See *The Jewish Chronicle*, July 27, 1906, pp. 18–20. See also David Wolffsohn to Weizmann, August 2, 1906. W.A.

166. Weizmann to Wolffsohn, August 5, 1906, *WL* 4, pp. 326–27.

167. See, e.g., Moses Gaster to Weizmann, June 25, 1906, and Moses Gaster to Percy Baker, July 27, 1906. W.A.

168. See Weizmann to David Wolffsohn, July 24, 1906, *WL* 4, p. 320.

169. See *The Jewish Chronicle*, July 2, 1906, p. 44.

170. See *The Jewish Chronicle*, March 2, 1906, p. 32.

171. "On the whole, I know very little about what goes on in the Zionist world." Weizmann to Vera, September 6, 1905, *WL* 4, p. 139.
172. "Altogether there is nobody here of our kind." Weizmann to Vera, September 7, 1905, *WL* 4, p. 140. See also Weizmann to Vera, September 9, 1905, *WL* 4, p. 143.
173. See Weizmann to Vera, October 8, 1905, and October 9, 1905, *WL* 4, pp. 177–79.
174. Weizmann to Vera, September 24, 1905, *WL* 4, p. 163.
175. Weizmann to Vera, September 9, 1905, *WL* 4, p. 143.
176. Weizmann to Vera, October 3, 1905, *WL* 4, p. 174.
177. Weizmann to Judah Leon Magnes, February 13–17, 1906, *WL* 4, p. 242.
178. See, e.g., Weizmann to Vera, March 24, 1906, *WL* 4, p. 263, and March 26, 1906, *WL* 4, pp. 265–66.
179. See *The Jewish Chronicle*, July 13, 1906, p. 46.
180. See Weizmann to Vera, October 31, 1905, *WL* 4, p. 190.
181. See Weizmann to Vera, February 12, 1906, *WL* 4, p. 239.
182. Weizmann to Vera, March 18, 1906, *WL* 4, p. 260.
183. See Weizmann to Vera, March 28, 1906, *WL* 4, p. 266.
184. Weizmann to Vera, May 2, 1906, *WL* 4, p. 276. The Clayton factory applied for a patent on February 28, 1906. See Weizmann to Moses Gaster, March 1, 1906, *WL* 4, p. 253; it would seem, though, that Weizmann found out about the German company—the "Badische-Anilin-und Soda-Fabrik"—only at the end of April or the beginning of May.
185. See Weizmann to Vera, January 17, 1906, *WL* 4, p. 223, and Weizmann to Vera, January 21, 1906, *WL* 4, p. 227.
186. See Weizmann to Vera, February 24, 1906, *WL* 4, p. 248.
187. See Weizmann to Vera, January 18, 1906, *WL* 4, p. 223.
188. Weizmann to Vera, January 20, 1906, *WL* 4, p. 226.
189. Weizmann to Vera, January 25, 1906, *WL* 4, pp. 227–28.
190. Weizmann to Vera, February 5, 1906, *WL* 4, p. 234.
191. Weizmann to Vera, February 7, 1906, *WL* 4, p. 235.
192. Weizmann to Judah Leon Magnes, February 13–17, 1906, *WL* 4, p. 240.
193. Weizmann to Vera, May 4, 1906, *WL* 4, pp. 276–77.
194. See Weizmann to Vera, May 21, 1906, *WL* 4, p. 286.
195. Weizmann to Nahum Sokolow, June 26, 1906, *WL* 4, p. 306. Weizmann's reaction to this tragedy was not as sympathetic as Vera had expected; he complained to her instead of the long delay in her replies. Weizmann to Vera, June 22, 1906, *WL* 4, p. 301.
196. See Weizmann to Judah Leon Magnes, June 1, 1906, *WL* 4, p. 294.
197. See Weizmann to Vera, June 17, 1906, *WL* 4, p. 300.
198. Weizmann to Vera, July 1, 1906, *WL* 4, p. 308.
199. Weizmann to Vera, July 3, 1906, *WL* 4, p. 310.
200. See Weizmann to Vera, July 18, 1906, *WL* 4, p. 318.
201. See Weizmann to Vera, May 19, 1906, *WL* 4, p. 284, and July 14, 1906, *WL* 4, p. 315.
202. See Weizmann to Vera, July 3, 1906, *WL* 4, p. 311. In February 1906 Weizmann and Vera had briefly contemplated marrying in Russia. See Weizmann to Judah Leon Magnes, February 13–17, 1906, *WL* 4, p. 242.
203. Weizmann to Vera, July 30, 1906, *WL* 4, p. 324, and August 1, 1906, *WL* 4, p. 325.
204. See Hayah Weizmann-Lichtenstein, *Be-Zel Koratenu*, p. 164.

205. See Weizmann, *Trial and Error*, p. 112, and Vera Weizmann, *The Impossible Takes Longer* (New York, 1967), p. 29.
206. See Weizmann, *Trial and Error*, p. 112. According to the protocol of GAC, its session on August 30, 1906, began at four thirty in the afternoon and ended at five thirty the morning of August 31.
207. Vera Weizmann, *The Impossible Takes Longer*, p. 29.

XIII The Theory and Practice of Synthetic Zionism

1. ". . . ein bemerkenswerter Fortschritt auf dem Wege der Einigung der juedischen Kraefte . . ."
2. See "Spezialbericht ueber die III. Zionistische Jahreskonferenz," *Die Welt*, no. 35, August 31, 1906, pp. 1–4.
3. Ibid., pp. 6–8.
4. See *Stenographisches Protokoll der Verhandlungen des VII. Zionisten-Congresses und des ausserordentlichen Congresses in Basel* (Berlin, 1905), pp. 209–20.
5. Ibid., p. 219.
6. He was supported by Leopold Greenberg, Arthur Hantke, Nissan Katzenelson, Simon Rosenbaum, and even Zalman David Levontin, director of the Anglo-Palestine Company in Jaffa, who had made the long trip in order to take part in the proceedings. See CZA, Z2/208.
7. See *Die Welt*, no. 35, August 31, 1906, p. 14.
8. Ibid., pp. 14–15, and CZA, Z2/208.
9. Cf. Marmorek's veiled threat: "Herr Weizmann hat eine politische Rede gehalten die eigentlich nicht hierher gehoerte . . . ich moechte feststellen, dass eine Antwort auf eine Frage, die Herr Weizmann vorgebracht hat, vom Engeren A.-C. gegeben werden muss. Und Sie koennen sich darauf verlassen, sie wird gegeben werden." *Die Welt*, no. 35, August 31, 1906, p. 15.
10. Reasons for Ussishkin and his colleagues' absence from Helsingfors are outlined by Yehuda Slutzky, "Menahem Ussishkin—Ha-Tkufah ha-Russit," *Heavar* 12 (1965): 3–28.
11. On the atmosphere and mood of the delegates at Helsingfors, see Hayah Weizmann-Lichtenstein, *Be-Zel Koratenu* (Tel Aviv, 1948), pp. 174–75.
12. See Yitzhak Gruenbaum, "Yovel Shenishkah (Hamishim Shanah le-Veidat Helsingfors)," *Heavar* 5 (1957): 12.
13. Ibid., pp. 14–17. See also A. Rafaeli, "Veidot Artziot shel Zionei Russyah," *Katzir, Kovetz le-Korot ha-Tnuah ha-Zionit be-Russyah* (Tel Aviv, 1964), vol. 1, pp. 86–102.
14. See Yehiel Tschlenow, "Hitpathut ha-Zionut ha-Medinit ve-Teudot ha-Shaa," in *Yehiel Tschlenow: Pirkei Hayav u-Feulato, Zikhronot, Ktavim, Neumim, Mikhtavim*, ed. Shmuel Eisenstadt (Tel Aviv, 1937), pp. 339–53.
15. See Rafaeli, "Veidot Artziot shel Zionei Russyah," p. 84. David Vital, in his *Zionism: The Formative Years* (Oxford, 1982), p. 469, credits Idelson with this formulation but does not cite the source. Another historian attributes the term to the journalist Abraham Coralnik in an editorial written for *Die Welt*. See Mordechai Eliav, *David Wolffsohn, Ha-Ish u-Zmano* (Tel Aviv, 1977), p. 96, and n. 50, p. 345. What is clear, though, is that the term "synthetic Zionism" surfaced either during the proceedings of the Helsingfors Conference or immediately afterward.
16. See Rafaeli, "Veidot Artziot shel Zionei Russyah," pp. 97–98.
17. See Weizmann to Moses Gaster, January 2, 1907, *WL* 5, p. 1.

18. See *WL* 5, p. 8, n. 33. The full text may be found in in CZA, Z2/411.
19. See *The Jewish Chronicle,* September 7, 1906, p. 29. In January 1907 Greenberg also took over as controlling editor and director for life of *The Jewish Chronicle.* See [Cecil Roth], *The Jewish Chronicle, 1841–1941* (London, 1949), pp. 124–40. See also CZA, Z2/271 and Z2/223.
20. Weizmann to Moses Gaster, September 30, 1906, *WL* 4, p. 331. That same day he also lobbied a member of the EZF executive to support his plan. See Weizmann to Harris Morgenstern, September 30, 1906, *WL* 4, p. 332.
21. Weizmann to David Wolffsohn, November 4, 1906, *WL* 4, p. 335.
22. Weizmann to Moses Gaster, December 6, 1906, *WL* 4, pp. 337–38.
23. See Weizmann to Moses Gaster, January 2, 1907, *WL* 5, p. 1.
24. See Weizmann to Martin Buber, October 13, 1903, *WL* 3, p. 50; Weizmann to Vera, August 24, 1904, *WL* 3, p. 332.
25. Weizmann to Vera, March 5, 1906, *WL* 4, p. 253, and March 6, 1906, *WL* 4, p. 255.
26. See Weizmann to Moses Gaster, January 15, 1907, *WL* 5, pp. 4–5. See also Percy Baker to Moses Gaster, January 20, 1907. W.A. Baker made the same suggestion, obviously after consultation with Weizmann.
27. See Moses Gaster to Weizmann, January 8, 1907. W.A. Gaster wrote to Percy Baker in the same vein: "I expect to receive *loyal* assistance, and unless my wishes are strictly adhered to, and every effort made to carry them into effect, I am convinced that no good work can be done for Zionism, and it is useless for me to allow myself to be brought into any direct relation with the EZF . . . You know my conditions, and it is only under these conditions, I again repeat, that I might see my way to cooperate in the future." Moses Gaster to Percy Baker, January 4, 1907. See also Moses Gaster to Percy Baker, January 7, 1907. W.A.
28. "Ich habe Anderes und Besseres zu thun."
29. Moses Gaster to Weizmann, January 17, 1907. W.A.
30. Weizmann to Moses Gaster, January 18, 1907, *WL* 5, pp. 8–9. Cf. Percy Baker to Moses Gaster, January 20, 1907. W.A.: Dr. Weitzman [*sic*] has shown me your letter to him of the seventeenth . . . This morning I received intimation that you have also been nominated as president and have instructed my clerk to write you again . . ." Though he owed his position in the EZF to Gaster, Baker showed more courage than Weizmann: "I still maintain, and I say it with all due respect to yourself . . . that you have made a big mistake in not accepting nomination as vice president . . . as it is, people say: Dr. G[aster] has not worked within the ranks for years and we are afraid of him . . ." See Percy Baker to Moses Gaster, January 29, 1907. W.A.
31. Moses Gaster to Weizmann, January 21, 1907. W.A.
32. See Moses Gaster to Weizmann, January 17, 1907, and Moses Gaster to Percy Baker, January 22, 1907. W.A. See also Percy Baker to Moses Gaster, January 29, 1907. W.A. Baker was unable to comply with this last demand.
33. See Moses Gaster to Weizmann, January 30, 1907. W.A.
34. See *Die Welt,* no. 6, February 8, 1907, p. 14, and *The Jewish Chronicle,* February 9, 1907, p. 23.
35. *The Jewish Chronicle,* February 8, 1907, p. 23.
36. *Die Welt,* no. 6, February 8, 1907, pp. 14–15.
37. Ibid., p. 15.
38. See *The Jewish Chronicle,* February 8, 1907, pp. 23–24.
39. *The Jewish Chronicle,* February 8, 1907, p. 26.

40. The term "Manchester School of Zionism" seems to have been employed for the first time by Harry Sacher. See Harry Sacher, "The Work of 'The Zionist Banner,' " *The Zionist Banner*, no. 1, April 1910, p. 2.
41. Harry Sacher, "The Manchester Period," in *Chaim Weizmann*, ed. Meyer W. Weisgal (New York, 1944), p. 190.
42. See *Die Welt*, no. 6, February 8, 1907, p. 15.
43. Greenberg was elected a member of the EZF executive. See *The Jewish Chronicle*, February 8, 1907, p. 24. Moreover, despite Gaster's objections, Greenberg was presented in Birmingham with a testimonial "as a lasting token of the esteem and regard felt for you not only as Hon. Secretary of the EZF . . . but also as a valuable testimony of the appreciation of your great and self-sacrificing services in the case of Zionism . . . [T]o mark our further gratitude we have decided . . . to have your name and your dear wife's name jointly inscribed in the Golden Book of the Jewish National Fund. . . ." Ibid., p. 25.
44. See Weizmann to Joseph Cowen, February 7, 1907, *WL* 5, pp. 14–15, and Weizmann to Moses Gaster, February 7, 1907, *WL* 5, pp. 16–17. See also Moses Gaster to Weizmann, February 11, 1907. W.A.
45. In the aftermath of the Birmingham Conference, after considerable prodding by Weizmann, Gaster did produce a "peace manifesto." See *The Jewish Chronicle*, March 1, 1907, p. 19.
46. Contemporary recognition of his active Zionist life in Manchester is contained in the following passage, which appeared in *The Jewish Chronicle*: "Dr. Weizmann, who has been in Manchester for the last three years, has gained the support and confidence of all parties, Zionist and non-Zionist, and although he is busily occupied at Manchester University as a lecturer in chemistry, he still finds time to devote a large amount of attention to the Jewish community. The quarterly report council [of the Manchester Zionist Association] spoke of the valuable services rendered by him to the Zionist movement, not only in Manchester but all over the country. In recognition of those services, it has been decided to enter the name of Dr. Weizmann and Miss Chatzman in the Golden Book of the J.N.F." The association also presented them with a mahogany bureau and a bookcase. See *The Jewish Chronicle*, November 30, 1906, p. 34. Weizmann's first entry in the Golden Book of the J.N.F. took place in 1902. See *Die Welt*, no. 47, December 5, 1902.
47. See Vera Weizmann, *The Impossible Takes Longer* (New York, 1967), p. 29, and Chaim Weizmann, *Trial and Error*, p. 112, where the account varies slightly from Vera's.
48. Vera Weizmann, *The Impossible Takes Longer*, pp. 30–32.
49. See Weizmann to Moses Gaster, December 6, 1906, *WL* 4, p. 338.
50. Weizmann, *Trial and Error*, p. 113. Hayah Weizmann-Lichtenstein notes in her memoirs that Weizmann's parents came for a visit to Manchester—probably at the end of June 1907. They were apparently so taken aback by their son's impecunious circumstances that upon their return to Pinsk they sent the young couple blankets, sheets, and tablecloths. See Hayah Weizmann-Lichtenstein, *Be-Zel Koratenu*, p. 195. See also Vera Weizmann, *The Impossible Takes Longer*, p. 35.
51. See Weizmann to Moses Gaster, March 17, 1907, *WL* 5, p. 22, and Vera Weizmann, *The Impossible Takes Longer*, p. 34.
52. Weizmann's neighbor at 55 Birchfields Road was an income tax assessor; his neighbor at number 59 was retired. Other neighbors had the following oc-

cupations: analytical chemist, minister, managers, jute merchant, and journalist. See *Kelly's Directory of Manchester, 1908* (London, 1908), in The Central Library, Manchester. Weizmann is listed in the directory as Professor Charles Weigman.

53. Weizmann to Moses Gaster, February 7, 1907, *WL* 5, p. 16.
54. See Weizmann to Moses Gaster, February 7, 1907, *WL* 5, pp. 16–17, and February 18, 1907, *WL* 5, p. 18.
55. See *The Jewish Chronicle*, March 1, 1907, p. 19.
56. Weizmann to Moses Gaster, February 18, 1907, *WL* 1, p. 19.
57. See L. Jaffe, *Sefer ha-Kongress* (Jerusalem, 1950), pp. 353–54.
58. *Die Welt*, no. 46, November 16, 1906, p. 14.
59. Weizmann to Moses Gaster, January 15, 1907, *WL* 5, p. 6.
60. Weizmann to Vera, March 31, 1907, *WL* 5, p. 23.
61. Weizmann to Vera, April 2, 1907, *WL* 5, p. 24.
62. Weizmann to Vera, April 8, 1907, *WL* 5, p. 26.
63. Weizmann to Vera, April 10, 1907, *WL* 5, pp. 26–27.
64. Weizmann to Johann Kremenetzky, April 19, 1907, *WL* 5, p. 28.
65. Ibid., p. 29.
66. See Weizmann to Moses Gaster, June 17, 1907, *WL* 5, p. 33. There is no evidence extant to support this, but it is quite possible that an additional reason for his willingness to postpone the circumcision was the imminent arrival of his parents at the end of June.
67. See Weizmann to Vera, January 22, 1913, *WL* 5, p. 356.
68. See, e.g., Weizmann to Moses Gaster, July 14, 1907, *WL* 5, p. 37.
69. Weizmann to Moses Gaster, July 11, 1907, *WL* 5, p. 34. In his memoirs Weizmann wrote, "I did it [i.e., correcting papers] at odd hours, day or night, very often with my new-born son, Benjy, in my lap. I held him there partly out of affection and partly to give my wife an occasional rest. Now and again he set up a great wailing, as infants will, and I can only hope that I was never driven to do any injustice to my unfortunate examinees." Weizmann, *Trial and Error*, p. 113. Weizmann continued to supplement his income by marking examinations until 1911. See *WL* 5, pp. 129–30, 135, 137, 138, 143, and 255.
70. Weizmann to Moses Gaster, July 14, 1907, *WL* 5, p. 37, and Weizmann to Johann Kremenetzky, July 22, 1907, *WL* 5, p. 39.
71. It seems that these negotiations were unsuccessful.
72. Weizmann to Moses Gaster, July 14, 1907, *WL* 5, p. 37.
73. Weizmann to Otto Warburg, January 21, 1907, *WL* 5, p. 12.
74. Weizmann to Moses Gaster, July 14, 1907, *WL* 5, p. 37.
75. See "At a Meeting of the Council [of the University of Manchester] held on October 23rd, 1907," which states "that Mr. C. H. Weizmann, Ph.D., be appointed Senior Lecturer in Chemistry for three years from the 29th September 1907 . . ." John Rylands Archives, RA/29/1, vol. 3, p. 85, and "Minutes of Council," RA/3/1 (1906–8), vol. 4, p. 234.
76. *The Jewish Chronicle*, March 29, 1907, p. 24.
77. Weizmann to Moses Gaster, July 11, 1907, *WL* 5, p. 35, and Gaster to Weizmann, July 12, 1907. W.A.
78. See *The Jewish Chronicle*, July 12, 1907, pp. 32–33, and *Die Welt*, no. 29, July 19, 1907, pp. 13–15.
79. See *Die Welt*, no. 31, August 2, 1907, pp. 9–18.

80. Weizmann to Vera, July 24, 1907, *WL* 5, p. 40.
81. See *Stenographisches Protokoll der Verhandlungen des VIII. Zionisten-Congresses im Haag* (Cologne, 1907), pp. 159–214. In 1908 the amendment was finally effected by means of an addition to the statutes which did not require court approval.
82. See *Die Welt*, no. 33, August 14, 1907, pp. 5, 8.
83. Ibid., pp. 5–9.
84. *Haolam*, no. 34, August 20, 1907, p. 421.
85. Ibid.
86. See *Die Welt*, no. 33, August 14, 1907, pp. 9–10.
87. *Stenographisches Protokoll* (VIII), p. 10.
88. Ibid., p. 45.
89. See, e.g., the statements by Alfred Nossig and Daniel Pasmanik. Of course, there were also those, like Adolf Friedemann and J. Niemirower, who defended Wolffsohn and SAC. See *Stenographisches Protokoll* (VIII), pp. 66–102.
90. Ibid., pp. 64–65, 108–9, 264–71. Sokolow proposed that Hebrew be declared the official language of the movement. Ibid., pp. 226–28. This was accepted by the congress, but, of course, it was not implemented until many years later.
91. Ibid., pp. 128–94.
92. Ibid., pp. 214–26.
93. Ibid., pp. 282–98.
94. See Weizmann to Vera, August 21, 1907, *WL* 5, p. 45.
95. *Stenographisches Protokoll* (VIII), pp. 298–305.
96. See, e.g., Adolf Boehm, *Die Zionistische Bewegung bis zum Ende des Weltkrieges*, 2nd ed., rev. (Tel Aviv, 1935), pp. 382–83.
97. Weizmann, *Trial and Error*, p. 122. Weizmann made this claim for the first time in a speech before the Eleventh Zionist Congress in September 1913. See *Stenographisches Protokoll der Verhandlungen des XI. Zionisten-Kongresses in Wien* (Berlin, 1914), p. 155.
98. See *Stenographisches Protokoll* (VIII), p. 298.
99. At one point, referring to Maromorek's lament that certain Zionists had left the movement, Weizmann turned to the latter and said, "Don't speak to us of tolerance, Dr. Marmorek, don't count those who had departed, because I could also produce a list: Where is Ahad Ha'Am?" Ibid., p. 302.
100. Adolf Boehm, who himself took an active part in the debate, wrote that "Weizmann's speech made an extraordinary impression . . . not only for its content but also because of the manner in which it was delivered . . . it was as if an otherworldly power had used the speaker as its instrument to speak in a prophetic voice . . ." Boehm, *Die Zionistische Bewegung*, p. 383.
101. See Menahem Ussishkin, *Unser Programm* (Vienna, 1905), pp. 5, 30.
102. Martin Buber, "Das Juedische Kulturproblem und der Zionismus," in Lazar Schoen, ed., *Die Stimme der Wahrheit* (Würzburg, 1905), pp. 209–10.
103. "Der VII. Zionisten-Kongress beschliesst, dass parallel mit der politisch-diplomatischen Taetigkeit, als reale Unterlage und zur Staerkung derselben, entsprechend dem Punkte 1 des Basler Programmes, die systematische Ausgestaltung unserer Positionen in Palsestina erfolgen muesse . . ." *Stenographisches Protokoll* (VII), p. 209.

104. See the speeches by Adolf Friedemann, Alfred Nossig, Daniel Pasmanik, J. Niemirower, and A. Salz in *Stenographisches Protokoll* (VII), pp. 67–70, 83, 91, 94, and 103.
105. The only one to use this term at the congress was J. Niemirower, a delegate from Jassy. See *Stenographisches Protokoll* (VII), p. 94.
106. See Evyatar Friesel, "Weizmann and 'Weizmannism,' " *Judaism* 26, no. 1 (Winter 1977): 75, who expresses a different view.
107. *Stenographisches Protokoll* (VII), pp. 326–28. See also *Die Welt*, no. 2, January 10, 1908, pp. 3–5.
108. The others were Gaster, Greenberg, Bentwich, Moser, and Montefiore. *Stenographisches Protokoll* (VIII), pp. 396–97.
109. Weizmann to Vera, August 21, 1907, *WL* 5, pp. 44–45.
110. See Weizmann to Johann Kremenetzky, July 22, 1907, *WL* 5, p. 39, and July 24, 1907, *WL* 5, pp. 40–41.
111. A British journal published an article a few years ago which flatly stated that Weizmann's first trip to Palestine took place in 1918. See D. E. Knox, "Weizmann's First Visit to Palestine," *The Wiener Library Bulletin* 28, nos. 33–34 (1975): 2–13.
112. See Alex Bein, *Toldot ha-Hityashvut ha-Zionit mi-Tkufat Herzl ve-ad Yamenu*, 4th ed. (Ramat Gan, 1970), pp. 28–29. See also Moshe Braslavsky, *Tnuat ha-Poalim ha-Eretz Israelit: Ziyunim u-Mekorot* (Ein Harod, 1942), p. 33.
113. See Abraham Yaari, *Igrot Eretz Israel* (Tel Aviv, 1943), pp. 492–502.
114. See Weizmann to Vera, August 22, 1907, *WL* 5, p. 47. It is quite possible that Weizmann met Manya Wilbushevitz at the Russian Zionist Conference in Minsk in 1902.
115. See Dimitry Pospielovsky, *Russian Police Trade Unionism: Experiment or Provocation?* (London, 1971), pp. 89–115, and Jeremiah Schneiderman, *Sergei Zubatov and Revolutionary Marxism* (Ithaca, N.Y., 1976), pp. 229–34.
116. See Walter Laqueur, *A History of Zionism* (New York, 1972), p. 288.
117. Weizmann to Vera, August 23, 1907, *WL* 5, pp. 47–48.
118. Weizmann to Vera, August 25, 1907, *WL* 5, p. 49.
119. Weizmann to Vera, August 29, 1907, *WL* 5, p. 50.
120. See Nachum Gross, "Kalkelat Eretz Israel be-Sof ha-Meah ha-19 ve-Reshit ha-20," in *Bankai le-Umah be-Hithadshutah* (Tel Aviv, 1977), p. 52.
121. Weizmann to Vera, September 2, 1907, *WL* 5, p. 51.
122. Weizmann to Vera, September 8, 1907, *WL* 5, p. 52.
123. Jaffa was then the second largest city in the country, with a Jewish population of six thousand, approximately 10 percent of the entire Jewish population in Palestine. In June 1907 Ahuzat Bayit, a society composed of sixty Jews, was founded with the aim of building a new suburb outside Jaffa. This became the cornerstone for the founding of Tel Aviv in 1909.
124. See A. Yodfat, *Prakim be-Toldot Jaffa* (Tel Aviv, 1972). See also Ruth Kark, "Aliyatah shel Jaffo be-Merkaz ha-Yishuv he-Hadash: Hebetim Hevratiyim ve-Tarbutiyim," in *Sefer ha-Aliyah ha-Rishonah*, ed. Mordechai Eliav (Jerusalem, 1981), pp. 297–318.
125. Weizmann to Vera, September 11, 1907, *WL* 5, pp. 53–54.
126. Weizmann to Vera, September 14, 1907, *WL* 5, pp. 54–55. Emphasis in original.
127. Weizmann to Vera, September 18, 1907, *WL* 5, p. 56.
128. Weizmann, *Trial and Error*, p. 131.

129. See Yaakov Yaari-Poleskin, *Yehoshua Hankin, Ha-Ish u-Mifalo* (Tel Aviv, 1933), pp. 69–72. See also Moshe Smilanski, *Yehoshua Hankin* (Jerusalem, 1946), pp. 25–27.

130. See Weizmann to Johann Kremenetzky, September 26, 1907, *WL* 5, pp. 58–59, and *WL* 5, December 4, 1907, pp. 68–69.

131. It is estimated that Rothschild invested 5.6 million pounds in Jewish settlements in Palestine, of which 1.6 million was invested between 1883 and 1889; during the same period (1882–89), the total investment of all Hovevei Zion societies in Russia, Rumania, and Central and Western Europe was about 87,000 pounds. See Israel Margalith, *Le Baron Edmond de Rothschild et la Colonisation Juive en Palestine, 1882–1889* (Paris, 1957), and Alex Bein, *Toldot Ha-Hityashvut ha-Zionit*, p. 10, n. 1.

132. Weizmann, *Trial and Error*, pp. 126–27.

133. Ibid., p. 129.

134. See *Stenographisches Protokoll* (VIII), p. 153. Ruppin went to Palestine in May 1907.

135. See "Bericht ueber die Sitzung des Grossen Aktions Komitees am 6. und 7. Januar 1908," *Die Welt*, no. 2, January 10, 1908, p. 2. See also Leah Doukhan-Landau, *Ha-Hevrot ha-Zioniyot lirkhishat Karkaot be-Eretz Israel, 1897–1914* (Jerusalem, 1979), pp. 98–171.

136. See Arthur Ruppin, *Pirkei Hayai*, 3 vols. (Tel Aviv, 1968); Arthur Ruppin, *Die landwirtschaftliche Kolonisation der Zionistischen Organisation in Palaestina* (Berlin, 1925), and Alex Bein, "Arthur Ruppin: The Man and His Work," *Leo Baeck Institute Year Book* 17 (1972): 117–71.

137. See his "Memorandum an das Aktionskomitee der Zionistischen Organisation (10. November 1907)," in *Dreissig Jahre Aufbau in Palaestina* (Berlin, 1937), pp. 9–18.

138. This was tried by Rothschild in 1889 in Yesod Ha-Maalah. See Shmuel Avizur, "Ha-Haklaut, ha-Melakhah ve-ha-Taasiyah," in *Sefer ha-Aliyah ha-Rishonah*, p. 241.

139. Weizmann to Johann Kremenetzky, September 26, 1907, *WL* 5, pp. 57–62. Emphasis in original.

140. See *WL* 5, p. 94, n. 2.

141. Due to the quarantine in Beirut and other unexpected expenses, Weizmann spent five hundred francs more than he had anticipated. The total cost for the Palestine trip came to ninety pounds. See Weizmann to Johann Kremenetzky, December 4, 1907, *WL* 5, pp. 68–69. The trip to Italy and southern France cost another ten pounds.

142. See *WL* 5, p. 220.

143. The Atid Company eventually failed, apparently due to management problems.

144. Kremenetzky already had some interests in Palestine before 1914, including citrus groves, a chemistry laboratory attached to the Palestine Office, and the Migdal farm.

145. See Weizmann, *Trial and Error*, p. 127.

146. See Weizmann to Vera, September 14, 1907, *WL* 5, p. 55.

147. Weizmann to Nahum Sokolow, November 19, 1907, *WL* 5, p. 67.

148. Ibid.

149. See *Die Welt*, no. 44, November 1, 1907, p. 16. See also *Hayehudi*, October 1907. W.A.

150. The annual income of the JNF for 1908 was 13,700 pounds.
151. See *The Jewish Chronicle*, October 25, 1907, pp. 29–30.
152. Weizmann to Nahum Sokolow, November 19, 1907, *WL* 5, p. 67.
153. Weizmann to Moses Gaster, October 27, 1907, *WL* 5, pp. 63–64.
154. See Moses Gaster to Weizmann, October 28, 1907. W.A.

XIV   The End of the Wolffsohn Era

1. See Weizmann to Moses Gaster, April 14, 1908, *WL* 5, p. 79.
2. Ibid.
3. See Weizmann to Ahad Ha'Am, July 26, 1908, *WL* 5, p. 82.
4. Weizmann to Ahad Ha'Am, August 25, 1908, *WL* 5, p. 85.
5. On November 13 Weizmann was due to address the Manchester Zionists Junior Branch. Since he was ill, P. Horowitz substituted for him.
6. Weizmann to Johann Kremenetzky, December 13, 1908, *WL* 5, p. 94.
7. His brother, Moshe, was then working for the same company.
8. See Weizmann to Vera, December 29, 1907, *WL* 5, p. 70.
9. See the summary of the proceedings in *Die Welt*, no. 2, January 10, 1908, pp. 3–11.
10. Ibid., p. 8. See also *Haolam*, vol. 2, no. 2, January 15, 1908, p. 26.
11. See P. A. Alsberg, "Mediniyut ha-Hanhalah ha-Zionit mi-Moto shel Herzl ve-ad Milhemet ha-Olam ha-Rishonah" (diss., The Hebrew University, 1957), pp. 22–31.
12. *Die Welt*, no. 2, January 10, 1908, p. 8.
13. See the letter from Leopold Greenberg in *The Jewish Chronicle*, June 19, 1908, p. 23.
14. See *The Jewish Chronicle*, February 7, 1908, p. 25.
15. See *Die Welt*, no. 6, February 7, 1908, p. 15, and no. 7, February 14, 1908, pp. 14–16.
16. Winston Churchill to Moses Gaster, January 30, 1908. W.A. Churchill had also mentioned the necessity to take care of the immediate needs "of those who suffer from day to day."
17. See Leon Simon, *Ahad Ha'Am* (Philadelphia, 1960), pp. 214ff.
18. See Weizmann to Ahad Ha'Am, January 26 and January 31, 1908, *WL* 5, p. 76.
19. Simon, *Ahad Ha'Am*, p. 216.
20. The following is indicative of Weizmann's attitude: "I shall be in London . . . We shall talk about everything then. I shall come to you as to a spiritual doctor, quite apart from the fact that I should like to see you generally." Weizmann to Ahad Ha'Am, March 7, 1909, *WL* 5, p. 105.
21. See, e.g., Weizmann to Ahad Ha'Am, July 21, 1911, *WL* 5, p. 257: "For heaven's sake forgive my bothering you again with financial requests . . . If you could lend me £25 . . . I should be extremely grateful to you . . ."
22. See Percy Baker to Weizmann, February 21, 1908. W.A. Baker suggested that Weizmann appoint a proxy to represent his views whenever he could not participate due to ill health.
23. See the telegram from Weizmann on August 11, 1908, announcing his inability to attend the annual conference. CZA, Z2/209.
24. Weizmann to Otto Warburg, December 5, 1908, *WL* 5, p. 93.
25. Other student Zionist societies preceded the one in Manchester (e.g., Oxford established one in December 1906, Cambridge in February 1908, and

Leeds sometime in 1908). See Weizmann's presidential address on January 29, 1909, on the history of Zionist societies, reprinted in *The Jewish Chronicle,* February 5, 1909, p. 30. The University of London established a Zionist society in March 1909. Weizmann delivered the keynote address, "What's Zionism?" See *Die Welt,* no. 13, March 26, 1909, p. 288.

26. The results of the election were: honorary president—Sir Francis Montefiore; president—Gaster; London vice president—Greenberg; provincial vice president—Moser; treasurer—Rubinstein; honorary secretary—Rosenberg; London members of the executive: Jacob Goldbloom, Israel Cohen, Percy Baker, Leon Simon, Herbert Bentwich, H. Ginzburg, Samuel Daiches. Provincial members of the executive: Weizmann, S. Cohen, Fuchs, Sacher, Raskin, Isaacs, Danziger, Lewis, and Jacobs. See CZA, Z2/311. Israel Cohen wrote a report describing the proceedings at Sheffield. See Leopold Greenberg to David Wolffsohn, February 8, 1909. CZA, Z2/311.

27. See *The Jewish Chronicle,* February 12, 1909, p. 29; March 19, 1909, p. 35; and *Die Welt,* no. 7, February 12, 1909, pp. 151–52. The others resigning included Bentwich, Rosenberg, Baker, Daiches, and Lewis.

28. See Leopold Greenberg to David Wolffsohn, February 8, 1909, and February 15, 1909. CZA, Z2/311.

29. See Leopold Greenberg to David Wolffsohn, February 8, 1909. CZA, Z2/311.

30. Ibid.

31. See David Wolffsohn to Samuel Goldreich, March 4, 1909. CZA, Z2/311.

32. See Weizmann to David Wolffsohn, February 9, 1909, WL 5, pp. 97–98.

33. Weizmann to David Wolffsohn, February 21, 1909, WL 5, pp. 100–1.

34. See Weizmann to David Wolffsohn, February 1, 1909, WL 5, p. 95.

35. See David Wolffsohn to Leopold Greenberg, February 18, 1909. CZA, Z2/311.

36. Samuel Goldreich to David Wolffsohn, March 2, 1909. CZA, Z2/311.

37. See David Wolffsohn to Samuel Goldreich, March 4, 1909. CZA, Z2/311. Gaster, too, wanted to found a new federation in the provinces. See Moses Gaster to Weizmann, February 3, 1909. W.A.

38. Greenberg's letter to Wolffsohn is quoted in full in a letter from David Wolffsohn to Weizmann dated March 28, 1909. CZA, Z2/322.

39. This was formally requested by the Manchester Zionist Association (MZA), which met on February 7, 1909. See Weizmann to David Wolffsohn, February 9, 1909, WL 5, p. 97.

40. See *The Jewish Chronicle,* April 2, 1909, pp. 25–27.

41. See *Die Welt,* no. 5, February 4, 1910, p. 100.

42. See Leopold Greenberg to David Wolffsohn, July 15, 1910. CZA, Z2/330. The decision to dissolve the EZF came after the OAM received some recognition by SAC in June 1910.

43. See Paul Goodman, *Zionism in England* (London, n.d.), pp. 27–28, and *The Jewish Chronicle,* March 1, 1912, p. 37. Kessler was named provisional EZF chairman and served until June 1, 1913, after which Joseph Cowen assumed the presidency. See *The Jewish Chronicle,* June 6, 1913, p. 29.

44. See Elhannan Orren, *Hibbat Zion be-Britanyah 1878–1898* (Tel Aviv, 1974), pp. 132–33.

45. See Margary and Norman Bentwich, *Herbert Bentwich, the Pilgrim Father* (Jerusalem, 1940), p. 151.

46. See Stuart Cohen, *English Zionists and British Jews* (Princeton, 1982), pp. 47ff.

47. This was achieved that same year by the Mizrahi and Poalei Zion.

48. See David Wolffsohn to Herbert Bentwich, September 23, 1909. CZA, Z2/358.

49. See I. Israel, Grand Secretary of the OAM to the Central Zionist Office in Cologne, December 12, 1909. CZA, Z2/252.

50. In a letter to Wolffsohn, Israel Cohen charged that though it sold three thousand shekels, the OAM only had thirteen hundred members; that it was a secret society more loyal to its own leaders than to the World Zionist Organization; that the EZF was fully capable of leading English Zionism; that the creation of a second, competing organization would only damage Zionist work in England, leading to chaos and confusion; and that the motivation for constituting the OAM as a *Sonderverband* was based on personal rivalry. See Israel Cohen to David Wolffsohn, December 22, 1909. CZA, Z2/252 and Z2/214.

51. See Moses Gaster to Weizmann, November 5, 1909, and November 6, 1909. W.A. Wolffsohn managed to stall on the recognition of the OAM as a *Sonderverband*, but in June 1910 the order again formally reiterated its demand (see OAM to GAC, June 1910. CZA, Z2/214), while the EZF continued its opposition to such recognition. See EZF to David Wolffsohn, June 17, 1910. CZA, Z2/214. See also OAM to David Wolffsohn, June 21, 1910, which denied some of the statements made by the EZF. CZA, Z2/214.

52. See *Die Welt*, no. 19, May 13, 1910, pp. 421–22, and no. 9, March 3, 1911, p. 197.

53. CZA, Z3/524. The official name was the Joint Zionist Council of the United Kingdom.

54. Cf. *The Zionist*, no. 1, June 1912, p. 2: "The 'Joint Zionist Council of the United Kingdom' is an accomplished fact." See also "Memorandum of the English Zionist Federation on the Joint Zionist Council," June 27, 1912. CZA, Z3/809.

55. Weizmann to Moses Gaster, March 2, 1910, *WL* 5, p. 198.

56. "Sie waren zwei Tage in London und haben mich *nicht aufgesucht* . . . Ich weiss auch sonst Ihre Bewegungen in London, die mir von anderer Seite gleich mitgeteilt wurden, und ich ziehe meine eigene Schluesse . . . Auf meinen langen Brief habe ich auch von Ihnen keine Antwort erhalten. Ich weiss woran ich bin. Ich will hoffen, dass Sie es auch wissen . . ." Moses Gaster to Weizmann, March 22, 1909. W.A. Emphasis in original. Cf. also Weizmann's explanation for meeting Leopold Greenberg and his assertion: "I did not betray you . . . Greenberg achieved nothing by the interview . . ." Weizmann to Moses Gaster, March 29, 1909, *WL* 5, pp. 113–14.

57. Leopold Kessler was also elected vice president. See *Die Welt*, no. 9, March 3, 1911, p. 197.

58. See *The Zionist Banner*, vol. 2, no. 12, February–March 1911, p. 180. The paper's editorial called the proceedings "The Peace Conference."

59. See *Die Welt*, no. 23, June 6, 1913, pp. 732–33.

60. See *The Jewish Chronicle*, February 20, 1914, p. 33.

61. This was the opinion of Sokolow. See Nahum Sokolow to Weizmann, January 4, 1911. W.A.

62. See Moses Gaster to Weizmann, December 14, 1909. W.A.

63. See David Vital, *Zionism: The Formative Years* (Oxford, 1982), p. 459.

64. See Bernard Lewis, *The Emergence of Modern Turkey* (London, 1961), pp. 203–5.

65. Ibid., pp. 209–14.

66. Ibid., pp. 206–7.

67. Alsberg, "Mediniyut ha-Hanhalah ha-Zionit," pp. 32–41.

68. See *The Jewish Chronicle*, January 29, 1909, p. 31.

69. See Max Nordau, *Erinnerungen* (Leipzig and Vienna, 1928), p. 238.

70. Alsberg, "Mediniyut ha-Hanhalah ha-Zionit," pp. 43–45.
71. See Mordechai Eliav, *David Wolffsohn* (Tel Aviv, 1977), pp. 146–47.
72. CZA, Z2/304.
73. See CZA, Z2/237. Weizmann chose not to attend the GAC meetings even though he was in Paris at the time; the occasion was his first visit to the Pasteur Institute.
74. The newspapers supported by the Zionists included: *Le Jeune Turc, L'Aurore, Il Judeo,* and the newly created weekly *Hamevaser.* For a detailed description of Jabotinsky's activities in Constantinople, see Joseph B. Schechtman, *Rebel and Statesman: The Vladimir Jabotinsky Story. The Early Years* (New York, 1956), pp. 154–58.
75. See *Die Welt,* no. 8, February 19, 1909, pp. 169–71.
76. See *Die Welt,* no. 48, November 26, 1909, pp. 1056–59. Implicit in their demands was their opposition to Wolffsohn's dictatorial behavior and his complete control of the purse strings of the movement.
77. *Haolam,* no. 39, November 10, 1909, p. 15.
78. Weizmann to Moses Gaster, November 14, 1909, *WL* 5, p. 162.
79. Weizmann to Moses Gaster, December 12, 1909, *WL* 5, p. 162. Arthur Lapworth and Robert Robinson, Weizmann's colleagues at Manchester, had been elected to the Royal Society in the spring, which no doubt spurred Weizmann to redouble his efforts.
80. Moses Gaster to Weizmann, December 14, 1909. W.A.
81. Ibid.
82. Cf. Weizmann to Moses Gaster, December 14[?], 1909, *WL* 5, p. 163: "I rely on you implicitly. If you tell me the decisions [arrived at by Gaster and his confidants], it will be all right."
83. Ibid.: "Whether the attack on Wolffsohn will succeed is questionable."
84. Ibid.
85. See *Stenographisches Protokoll der Verhandlungen des IX. Zionisten-Kongresses in Hamburg* (Cologne, 1910), pp. 5–8.
86. "True, our future lies in Turkey, but our present is, in the interim, still in Europe and America . . . the demands of the present should . . . make it imperative that for the time being we maintain our center outside Turkey." Ibid., pp. 20–21.
87. Ibid., pp. 21–23.
88. Ibid., pp. 23–25.
89. With Nordau as president.
90. Ibid., pp. 38–44.
91. Ibid., pp. 67–86.
92. Ibid., pp. 102–4.
93. Ibid., pp. 105–6.
94. Ibid., p. 265.
95. Ibid., pp. 195ff. See also *Die Welt,* no. 53, December 31, 1909, pp. 1235–41.
96. *Stenographisches Protokoll (IX),* p. 333.
97. Ibid., pp. 333–34. On the attitude of the German Zionists to this and other issues at the Ninth Zionist Congress, see Yehuda Eloni, "Beayot Ideologiyot, Irguniyot u-Mivniyot ba-Zionut ha-Germanit, me-Reshitah ad Milhemet ha-Olam ha-Rishonah" (diss., Tel Aviv University, 1981), pp. 217–31.
98. *Stenographisches Protokoll* (IX), pp. 335–36.
99. Ibid., p. 341.
100. Ibid., p. 343.

101. Ibid., pp. 343–44.
102. See Weizmann to Julius Simon, January 14, 1910, *WL* 5, p. 170.
103. He had been identified at the Ninth Zionist Congress as a member of the opposition and had no choice but to resign his official post in Cologne. See Simcha Kling, *Nahum Sokolow: Servant of His People* (New York, 1960), p. 87.
104. Weizmann to Nahum Sokolow, January 7, 1910, *WL* 5, pp. 166–67. Emphasis in original.
105. See Weizmann to Julius Berger, January 10, 1910, *WL* 5, p. 167.
106. See *The Jewish Chronicle,* January 28, 1910, p. 11. Weizmann spoke on January 23, 1910.
107. See *Die Welt,* no. 5, February 4, 1910, p. 101.
108. "Was die innere Politik anbelangt, so scheint mir, dass die Chancen der Opposition nicht sehr guenstig sind." CZA, L1/93. Warburg mistrusted such opponents as Davis Trietsch and Selig Soskin, whose motivations, he thought, were personal rather than ideologically grounded.
109. See Jacob Moser to David Wolffsohn. CZA, W65I. Moser wrote that he understood that on the last night of the congress Wolffsohn had taken part in the standing committee's deliberations concerning the composition of SAC and the JCT. He could not understand, then, Wolffsohn's subsequent conduct when the full congress reconvened. Moser also stated his support for a seven-man SAC located in Berlin and headed by Wolffsohn.
110. David Wolffsohn to Jacob Moser, February 2, 1910. CZA, W29I.
111. Weizmann to David Wolffsohn, February 12, 1910, *WL* 5, pp. 181–85. Emphasis in original. Wolffsohn did not reply. See Weizmann to Julius Berger, March 2, 1910, *WL* 5, p. 197.
112. Weizmann to Vera, March 20, 1910, *WL* 5, p. 200.
113. It was published by the Juedischer Verlag.
114. See Jacobus Kann, *Erez Israel, das jüdische Land* (Cologne, 1909), pp. 167ff.
115. See Schechtman, *Rebel and Statesman*, pp. 161–65.
116. See: Protocoll der Conferenz der Mitglieder des Grossen Actionscomités und Zentralcomités der Zionistischen Organisation in Russland, die am 13. und 14. Maerz [1910] in Petersburg stattgefunden hat. CZA, Z2/437.
117. For a brief summary of these events, see Eliav, *David Wolffsohn,* pp. 238–43.
118. Most of the signatories were Western Zionists.
119. *Die Welt,* no. 8, February 25, 1910, pp. 172–73. The editors of *Die Welt* had no choice but to print this manifesto, but not without voicing their own reservations, calling the signatories a new "faction" in the movement and explaining it away as the creation of those who failed to depose the Zionist leadership in Hamburg.
120. See *The Jewish World,* April 15, 1910, and *The Zionist Banner,* vol. 1, no. 2, May 1910, pp. 29–31.
121. See *Juedische Rundschau,* no. 13, April 1, 1910, pp. 145–47.
122. See *Die Welt,* no. 15, 1910, pp. 323–28.
123. *Die Welt,* nos. 16–17, April 22, 1910, p. 375.
124. See the letter from Nahum Sokolow to Weizmann dated April 8, 1910. W.A. Sokolow stated that he was writing at Weizmann's request to be informed of events in the movement and in preparation for Wolffsohn's visit. His *Suendenregister,* as he put it, against the leadership included: failure to comprehend Middle Eastern and Jewish national politics; belittling the work of Zionist representatives in Constantinople; and disregard for proposals

brought by Turkish Jewish delegates to the Ninth Zionist Congress. Sokolow also belittled the activities of the Cologne bureau and called *Die Welt*
an inconsequential paper. He mentioned the lack of resources placed at the
disposal of the PLDC and the general lack of support for work in Palestine.

125. The paper was printed by the firm belonging to Weizmann's first Manchester friend, Joseph Massel and Son. The EZF annual conference held on
February 1911, which saw the return of Weizmann as vice president, decided to support the paper, which appeared as *The Zionist* starting in April
1911 and was edited by Harry Sacher, Leon Simon, and Samuel Landman.
See Harry Sacher, "The Manchester Period," in *Chaim Weizmann*, ed. Meyer
Weisgal (New York, 1944), p. 190.

126. See *The Zionist Banner*, vol. 1, no. 1, April 1910, pp. 19 and 21.

127. Ibid., pp. 19–21. For a somewhat different version in German, see CZA,
W65 III. *The Zionist Banner* also supported Weizmann's point of view in an
editorial. See *The Zionist Banner*, vol. 1, no. 2, May 1910, pp. 23–26.

128. See *The Jewish Chronicle*, May 9, 1910, p. 12.

129. Wolffsohn stated: "Eight years ago five men, among them Dr. Weizmann,
wished to found a Jewish university. They collected twenty-five thousand
francs. Of those only forty pounds are today deposited with the JCT, and
these gentlemen have not founded the university. Dr. Weizmann wanted
to establish a new chemical industry. He needed the necessary funds. Those
funds were provided by a private source, and Dr. Weizmann went to Palestine. No one has since heard about his practical suggestions." See *Die Welt*,
no. 19, May 13, 1910, p. 422.

130. This was also Wolffsohn's interpretation. Weizmann attended a reception
in his honor after the speech and did not seem to take offense at what was
said. See the Protokoll of the annual conference of June 1910. CZA, Z2/212.

131. Weizmann to Wolffsohn, May 23, 1910, *WL* 5, p. 218.

132. Weizmann to Johann Kremenetzky, May 24, 1910, *WL* 5, pp. 219–20. Kremenetzky did not publicly refute Wolffsohn's charges. On the contrary, he
took Weizmann to task for having failed to provide full reports on his Palestinian trip. See Johann Kremenetzky to Weizmann, June 22, 1910. W.A.

133. See David Wolffsohn to Weizmann, May 29, 1910. CZA, W29.

134. See: Die Beschluesse der Konferenz der russischen Z.Z.K. mit den russischen Mitgliedern der A.C. stattgefunden am 22.–24. Mai a. St. Petersburg 1910. *Streng Vertraulich.* CZA, Z2/369. The resolution read: "Nach
Beurteilung der Frage ueber die Rede des Praesidenten in Manchester . . .
wird die Konferenz Gg. Dr. Weizmann ihre Hochachtung und Anerken-
nung seiner Verdienste in der Bewegung und insbesondere fuer die Ver-
breitung der Idee einer Juedischen Hochschule in Palaestina aus, und spricht
ihr Bedauern aus ueber dieses Verhalten des Praesidenten gegenueber einem unserer Besten." The conference also defended Jabotinsky and supported his stand against Kann's book.

135. See, e.g., Weizmann's letters to Ahad Ha'Am on May 15, 1910, and to
Menahem Ussishkin on May 22, 1910, *WL* 5, pp. 215–17.

136. Weizmann to David Wolffsohn, June 4, 1910, *WL* 5, pp. 221–22.

137. See *Die Welt*, no. 25, June 24, 1910, pp. 607–8.

138. Wolffsohn made a similar comment at the June annual conference. See CZA,
Z2/212.

139. See David Wolffsohn to Weizmann, June 17, 1910. CZA, W29. See also Johann Kremenetzky to Weizmann, June 22, 1910. W.A.

140. See: Bericht ueber die Sitzungen der Jahreskonferenz, den 27. Juni 1910. CZA, Z2/212. See also the "Resolution of Conciliation." CZA, Z2/219.

141. See Weizmann to Moses Gaster, November 10, 1910, WL 5, p. 239.

142. Weizmann only applied for naturalization in early November 1910. See the form letter from Edward Traup, Office of the Secretary of State, to Weizmann, November 5, 1910. Gaster Papers, U.C.L.

143 See Weizmann to Moses Gaster, November 6, 1910, WL 5, p. 238.

144. See Herbert Samuel to Moses Gaster, November 11, 1910. CZA, A203/28. Weizmann's naturalization certificate is dated December 17, 1910. W.A.

145. Weizmann to Ahad Ha'Am, February 26, 1910, WL 5, p. 196.

146. See Moshe Rinott, Hevrat ha-Ezrah li-Yehudei Germanyah be-Yezirah uve-Maavak (Jerusalem, 1971), p. 185.

147. See CZA, A20/53.

148. At the Eighth Zionist Congress Shmarya Levin had expressed strong interest in a Hochschule in Palestine. Thus he was most receptive to Nathan's suggestion.

149. For a brief history of these developments, see: Protokoll der Sitzung des Kuratoriums des "Juedischen Instituts fuer technische Erziehung in Palaestina" am 3. Oktober 1909. CZA, A20/53.

150. See: Satzung des "Juedischen Instituts fuer technische Erziehung in Palaestina," Berlin, 19. March 1909. CZA, A20/56. Members of the board, which also included the executive committee, were: Cyrus Adler, Dr. Gawronsky, R. Gotz, Eugen Landau, Julian Mack, Martin Philippson, Julius Rosenwald, Mortimer Schiff, Samuel Strauss, M. Sulzberger, Berthold Timendorfer, Moritz Warburg, J. Zetlin, David Wissotzky, Louis Marshall, and Solomon Schechter. Later Yehiel Tschlenow was also co-opted.

151. Weizmann to Ahad Ha'Am, February 26, 1909, WL 5, p. 102.

152. Weizmann to Ahad Ha'Am, March 7, 1909, WL 5, p. 105.

153. See, e.g., Ahad Ha'Am to Weizmann, October 19, 1909. Asher Ginsberg, Igrot Ahad Ha'Am (Berlin and Jerusalem, 1908–12), vol. 4, pp. 232–33.

154. See the report on Weizmann's public lecture concerning the Technicum, published in Hazvi [Jerusalem], July 15, 1909.

155. Weizmann to Ahad Ha'Am, May 21, 1911, WL 5, pp. 253–54.

156. See, e.g., Ahad Ha'Am to Weizmann, May 16, 1911. Ginsberg, Igrot Ahad Ha'Am, vol. 4, p. 380.

157. Weizmann marked exercise books from other universities as late as 1911. See Weizmann to Ahad Ha'Am, June 25, 1911, WL 5, p. 255.

158. See Weizmann to Vera, June 18, 1909, WL 5, pp. 135–36. Moses Gaster to Weizmann, June 28, 1909. W.A. At Weizmann's request Gaster had gathered information on the fringe benefits attached to a professorship in India.

159. He left for Kiev in the spring of 1909 after he lost his job in Manchester.

160. See Weizmann to Vera and Shmuel Weizmann, March 21, 1909, WL 5, pp. 107–8.

161. See Anna Weizmann, "My Brother 'Chaimke,' " The Jerusalem Post. Chaim Weizmann Memorial Supplement, October 30, 1953, p. 3. Anna Weizmann was appointed research student in chemistry at the University of Manchester on November 6, 1913. See John Rylands Archives, RA/3/5.

162. See Weizmann to Moses Gaster, August 1, 1910, WL 5, p. 230. From Freiburg Ozer went to yet another spa in Druskenniki, Lithuania.

163. See Hayah Weizmann-Lichtenstein, Be-Zel Koratenu (Tel Aviv, 1948), p. 197. Moshe and Shmuel Weizmann and their families also arrived for the seder.

164. Weizmann to Vera, April 10, 1911, *WL* 5, p. 247.
165. Weizmann to Vera, April 15, 1911, *WL* 5, p. 250.
166. See also Weizmann-Lichtenstein, *Be-Zel Koratenu*, p. 197.
167. Weizmann to Vera, April 15, 1911, *WL* 5, pp. 249–50.
168. Ibid., p. 250.
169. Louis Greenberg, *The Jews in Russia* (New Haven, Conn., 1965), pp. 84–88.
170. It was thought to be in connection with Passover, in this case.
171. For details, see Maurice Samuel, *Blood Accusation: The Strange History of the Beilis Case* (Philadelphia, 1966), and Mendel Beilis, *Die Geschichte fun Meine Leiden* (New York, 1925). See also the memoirs of Oscar Gruzenberg, the lawyer who defended Beilis: *Yesterday: Memoirs of a Russian-Jewish Lawyer*, ed. Don C. Rawson (Berkeley, Calif., 1981), pp. 104–24.
172. See Paul A. Alsberg, "Ha-Sheelah ha-Aravit bi-Mediniyut ha-Hanhalah ha-Zionit lifnei Milhemet ha-Olam ha-Rishonah," *Shivat Zion*, vol. 4, ed. Ben Zion Dinur and Israel Heilprin (Jerusalem, 1956), pp. 161–62. See also Yaakov Roi, "Yahasei Yehudim-Aravim be-Moshavot ha-Aliyah ha-Rishonah," in *Sefer ha-Aliyah ha-Rishonah*, ed. Mordechai Eliav (Jerusalem, 1981), pp. 245–68; idem, "The Zionist Attitude to the Arabs, 1908–1914," *Middle Eastern Studies*, no. 3 (April 1968): 198–242. See Neville J. Mandel, *The Arabs and Zionism before World War I* (Berkeley, Calif., 1976), p. 55. See also Haim Kalvariski-Margalit, "Ha-Yehasim beyn ha-Yehudim ve-Haaravim lifnei Milhemet ha-Olam ha-Rishonah," *Sheifotenu*, no. 2 (1931): 50–55. For the Yishuv's attitude toward the conflict with the Arabs in Palestine, see Yosef Gorni, "Shorasheha shel Todaat ha-Imut ha-Leumi ha-Yehudi-Aravi ve-Hishtakfutah ba-Itonut ha-Ivrit ba-Shanim 1900–1918," *Hazionut*, vol. 4, ed. Daniel Carpi (Tel Aviv, 1975), pp. 72–113.
173. Wolffsohn disclaimed any Zionist designs to found a Jewish state in Palestine. Shlomo Kaplansky dealt with Zionist-Arab relations.
174. See CZA, Z2/212. At the GAC meeting, which took place after the Tenth Zionist Congress, Nahum Sokolow expressed the concern of the Zionist movement in light of growing Arab nationalism and suggested the following practical steps to deal with it: ". . . Wir halten es fuer notwendig, in Palaestina eine gewisse Beeinflussung der arabischen oeffentlichen Meinung einzuleiten . . . Als zweiten Punkt . . . halten wir die Schaffung eines juristischen Beistandes . . . Das dritte Mittel . . . ist ein Anfang der Organisation des palaestinensischen Judentums . . . durch die Errichtung zweier Chachambaschi posten . . . in der Tuerkei und in Palaestina . . . Wir muessen auch dafuer sorgen, dass wir einen besseren Zusammenhang zwischen diesen Gemeinden und der arabischen Bevoelkerung schaffen. Wir werden ferner trachten Beruehrungspunkte zu schaffen, durch welche wir dem Ideenkreis der mohamedanischen Welt naeherkommen . . . es muss eine Fuehlungnahme mit dem denkenden Arabertum in Angriff genommen werden . . ." CZA, Z1/430. The subject of Arab attitudes to Zionist colonization in Palestine became a permanent concern of SAC, and various methods were devised to deal with this issue. See, e.g., the letter from SAC to members of GAC [February 20, 1913]. CZA, Z3/462.
175. See the protocols of the meetings in CZA, Z2/212. The gist of Marmorek's attack was quickly communicated to Weizmann, who expressed his satisfaction: "It is not noble, I know, to harbor feelings of vengeance, but I must say—I was not free of them when I read your letter . . . Marmorek in particular pleased me." See Weizmann to Julius Berger, July 9, 1910, *WL* 5, p.

227. See also Julius Berger to Hugo Schachtel [August 12], 1910. Schachtel wrote in the same spirit: "Marmorek should be made an honorary member of the opposition." CZA Z2/369.

176. See, e.g., *The Zionist Banner*, vol. 2, October 1911, p. 120.

177. This particular item had already aroused controversy at Hamburg as well as at the GAC meetings of June 1910. Thirteen members of GAC dissociated themselves from this particular proposal. See CZA, Z2/219.

178. See the resolutions of the Zionist Conference of 1910: "Resolution of Conciliation." CZA, Z2/219.

179. Weizmann to Julius Berger, July 9, 1910, WL 5, pp. 227–28.

180. See Julius Berger to Hugo Schachtel [August 12], 1910. CZA, Z2/369. See also Julius Simon to Menahem Ussishkin, November 8, 1910. CZA, A24/77.

181. See Emil Bernhard Cohn, *David Wolffsohn, Herzl's Successor* (New York, 1944), pp. 234–38; and Mordechai Eliav, *David Wolffsohn*, pp. 266–76.

182. See *Die Welt*, no. 1, August 1911, p. 792.

183. See Chaim Weizmann, *Dvarim*, vol. 1 (Tel Aviv, 1936–37), p. 50.

184. See *Stenographisches Protokoll der Verhandlungen des X. Zionisten-Kongresses in Basel* (Berlin, 1911), p. 14.

185. Prior to the congress Weizmann engaged in a public debate on this theme with a supporter of the Mizrahi. See *The Zionist*, no. 3, June 1911, p. 51.

186. Ibid., pp. 273–92.

187. Ibid., pp. 338–39.

188. Ibid., p. 340. The proposals of the standing committee were ready on the penultimate day of the congress. As late as that date Weizmann feared that Wolffsohn and his friends would surprise him with a last-minute "bomb," as he put it. See Weizmann to Vera, August 14, 1911, WL 5, p. 259.

189. Ibid., pp. 339–40.

190. Ibid., p. 341.

191. This was foreseen by the "practicals" after the GAC meetings in June 1910. See Julius Simon to Menahem Ussishkin, November 8, 1910. CZA, A24/77. See also Menahem Ussishkin to Weizmann, May 5, 1911. W.A.

192. Ibid., pp. 107–8.

193. Ibid., pp. 342–46.

194. Levin's election greatly pleased Ahad Ha'Am, too, who attended the Tenth Zionist Congress, his first since 1897.

195. The previous year Hantke was elected president of the Zionistische Vereinigung fuer Deutschland (ZVfD), replacing Max Bodenheimer. The central office of the ZVfD was then moved to Berlin. Thus, changes in German Zionism presaged those that would take place in the World Zionist Organization. For a detailed discussion, see chaps. 3 and 4 in Jehuda Reinharz, *Fatherland or Promised Land? The Dilemma of the German Jew, 1893–1914;* idem, ed., *Dokumente zur Geschichte des deutschen Zionismus 1882–1933* (Tübingen, 1981).

196. Weizmann joined the political committee established by SAC in November 1911.

XV Society, Science, and the Professorship

1. See, e.g., CZA, Z3/424. See also Nahum Sokolow to Weizmann, January 5, 1912. W.A.

2. See CZA, Z3/429–30 and Z1/430.

3. Weizmann to SAC, December 28, 1911, *WL* 5, p. 266. See also Weizmann's remarks at GAC meetings of November 1911, in which he advocated an information campaign in England. CZA, Z1/430.
4. Weizmann to SAC, December 28, 1911, *WL* 5, p. 266.
5. See "Nachmittagssitzung des GAC, den 6. November [1911]." CZA, Z1/430.
6. See Weizmann to SAC, January 14, 1912, *WL* 5, p. 269.
7. Weizmann to SAC, December 28, 1911, *WL* 5, p. 266. At this early stage Weizmann suggested that Nahum Sokolow come to England to negotiate with British statesmen. See Weizmann to SAC, November 9, 1912, *WL* 5, p. 320.
8. See Arthur Hantke to Weizmann, February 13, 1912. CZA, Z3/524. Weizmann was not always welcome as a Zionist propagandist. In some Zionist circles he apparently had the reputation of initiating sharp and unpleasant controversies. See, e.g., the letter from the Comité Central de la Fédération Zioniste Belge of December 2, 1912, in which the Belgian Zionists specifically asked the Central Zionist Office in Berlin to refrain from sending Weizmann on propaganda tours. CZA, Z3/772.
9. The tour was very successful. In Vienna and Prague his lectures on "Zionismus und Staatsbuergertum" were very well received. See *Die Welt*, no. 15, April 12, 1912, p. 451. Robert Weltsch, who led the Bar Kochba group in Prague at the time, also recalled Weizmann's visit some sixty-three years later. See *Haaretz*, January 22, 1975, p. 6.
10. Weizmann to Arthur Hantke, February 25, 1912, *WL* 5, p. 276. Emphasis in original.
11. The contract with Bayer was signed on January 30, 1901. See document in W.A.
12. See Anthony R. Michaelis, *Weizmann Centenary*, pp. 57–58; and *Bulletin of the Research Council of Israel* 3, nos. 1–2 (June–September 1953): 22.
13. The camphor patent was sold in 1907 to Leon Givaudan, who owned a plant producing perfumes and aromatics in Vernier, near Geneva. Weizmann owed his interest in camphor to William Perkin, who had encouraged him to investigate the field as soon as Weizmann arrived in Manchester in 1904. Arthur Lapworth, Perkin's brother-in-law, who came to the University of Manchester in 1909 and taught in the same department, was also interested in camphor and, in fact, was the one to point the way out of the labyrinth of camphor chemistry.
14. Seven hundred pounds per year, according to Weizmann. See Weizmann to Ahad Ha'Am, January 17, 1912, *WL* 5, p. 270. This is clearly an exaggerated figure for this period, probably intended to boost his salary at the Technicum should he get a job at that institution. Weizmann ceased working for the Clayton Aniline Company in 1910.
15. See senate committee minutes of April 23, 1912, John Rylands Archives, RA/3/4, vol. 5, p. 27. See also Weizmann to Ahad Ha'Am, April 28, 1912, *WL* 5, p. 291. It seems that in light of his new university obligations and salary, Weizmann invented for himself the title of "Independent Lecturer." In fact, he was still a senior lecturer, but his teaching duties were apparently reduced in the spring of 1912. His new salary and responsibilities became effective in October 1912. See the list of appointments of faculty members of the University of Manchester, John Rylands Archives, UA/18/16R.
16. The loans from Ahad Ha'Am continued throughout 1914, i.e., after Weizmann had been promoted to the position of reader, which carried with it the

considerable salary of six hundred pounds. At that point Vera was also earning a salary. Their combined annual income prior to World War I must have been close to one thousand pounds—then a considerable sum.

17. See Vera's extensive communications to Weizmann on these matters between 1902 and 1905, e.g., September 17, 21, 25, 1905. W. A. Concerning Weizmann's relationship with Vera and their attiude toward financial matters and English society, I owe a debt to the Rt. Hon. Richard H. S. Crossman.

18. See Vera Weizmann, *The Impossible Takes Longer*, p. 35. Vera maintains that she did learn how to cook. Nevertheless, Weizmann's constant references to the cook indicate that Vera's contributions in the kitchen were minimal.

19. See the interview with T. R. Fyvel (W.A.), who describes their lifestyle in London later on; one can assume that these inclinations and tastes were not cultivated overnight. See also Israel Sieff, *Memoirs* (London, 1970), p. 77, who writes of Vera: "She took with her a bourgeois background, gaiety and a taste for the good life."

20. Weizmann, *The Impossible Takes Longer*, p. 37.

21. Ibid., pp. 31, 35.

22. Israel Sieff recalls that during the 1913–14 period "I often gave lunch to [Chaim] and to Vera . . . not only for their company but because I thought it helped them out . . ." *Memoirs*, p. 79.

23. See Richard Lichtheim, *Rueckkehr: Lebenserrinerungen aus der Fruehzeit des deutschen Zionismus* (Stuttgart, 1970), pp. 17–26.

24. Weizmann to Vera, March 22, 1912, *WL* 5, p. 283.

25. Weizmann to Vera, March 29, 1912, *WL* 5, p. 287.

26. Weizmann to Vera, April 1, 1912, *WL* 5, p. 288.

27. The immigrants concentrated in and around the lower part of Cheetham Hill; as their economic condition improved, they moved up the hill. Weizmann always lived a few miles away from this area, in close proximity to or south of the university.

28. Israel M. Sieff, "The Manchester Period," in *Chaim Weizmann: A Biography by Several Hands*, ed. Meyer W. Weisgal and Joel Carmichael (New York, 1963), p. 90. When Weizmann spoke on Zionist affairs in the heart of the immigrant community, he frequently did so at the Jewish Working Men's Club. The club was established by well-to-do Jews *for* workers, to help "protect" them from socialist influences.

29. See Weizmann to Vera, May 30, 1912, *WL* 5, p. 309.

30. In her memoirs Vera recorded that while Weizmann visited Massel, "I would sit in silence, sniffing the smell of print, waiting for us to go home." *The Impossible Takes Longer*, p. 32.

31. Vera's ignorance of Judaism was such that she was often unaware of the date of the high holidays and needed to be reminded by Weizmann. See, e.g., Vera to Weizmann, September 17, 1905. W.A.

32. Sieff, *Memoirs*, p. 66.

33. Weizmann, *The Impossible Takes Longer*, p. 32.

34. See *The Owens College Union Magazine* for February 1897. The Central Library, Manchester.

35. See the *Dictionary of Scientific Biography* s.v. "Arthur Schuster," vol. 12, ed. Charles Coulston Gillespie (New York, 1975), p. 238. On both Schuster and Rutherford, see F. Fairbrother et al., "The History of Science in Manchester," in *Manchester and Its Region*, pp. 193–94.

36. See Weizmann, *The Impossible Takes Longer*, p. 33.
37. See Sieff, *Memoirs*, p. 66, for a description of Weizmann in 1913. See also Jacob Hodess, "Weizmann: Scientist and Statesman," in *The Jerusalem Post: Chaim Weizmann Memorial Supplement*, October 30, 1953, p. iii.
38. See the letter from Norah H. Nicholls dated April 9, 1969. W.A. In the spring of 1913 Caroline wrote to Weizmann: "My very dear friend and teacher, . . . I realized that there is no longer any question of the permanence of my interest in Zionism being dependent on whether your influence were removed or not. I can therefore now promise you that whatever may happen to you in future years, I shall not waver in my devotion to the Jewish nation and will do all the little in my power . . . to advance their cause. I am deeply grateful to you for bringing me to a true understanding of the matter and teaching me the only solution of the problem . . . I can never thank you enough or express how honored I feel by being admitted to the inner counsels of the Movement . . ." Caroline Schuster to Weizmann, March 18, 1913. W.A.
39. Weizmann, *Trial and Error*, pp. 116–17.
40. See the *Dictionary of Scientific Biography* s.v. "Arthur Schuster," vol. 12, p. 238.
41. Weizmann to Moses Gaster, January 15, 1907, *WL* 5, p. 6.
42. See Weizmann to Ahad Ha'Am, December 16, 1912, *WL* 5, p. 329.
43. The Manchester School for Mothers. See Weizmann, *The Impossible Takes Longer*, p. 40. See also Weizmann to Berthold Feiwel, May 16, 1913, *WL* 6, p. 73.
44. Weizmann, *Trial and Error*, p. 133.
45. See Albert Delaunay, *L'Institut Pasteur, des Origines à Aujourd'hui* (Paris, 1962), pp. 114ff. At the Pasteur Institute, Fernbach had become known in 1910 for his research, in which he—along with other scientists—anticipated Buchner's classic grinding of yeast cells with fine quartz or sand to yield cell contents for examination. See Maurice Schofield, "Weizmann's success as Manchester biochemist." W.A.
46. Weizmann, *Trial and Error*, p. 133.
47. This entire account is based on an article by Boris Guriel, "Lenin u-Weizmann," *Haaretz*, November 3, 1967, p. 3. There is no other evidence for this meeting, but the article is filled with sufficient detail to make it plausible. If indeed the meeting took place, it must have been between the end of March and mid-April 1910, when Weizmann came over to work at the Pasteur Institute. The two most detailed Western biographies of Lenin do not mention Weizmann. See Louis Fischer, *The Life of Lenin* (New York, 1964), and Adam B. Ulam, *Lenin and the Bolsheviks* (London, 1965).
48. Lenin stayed in Paris for three and a half years, beginning in December 1908. See Fischer, *The Life of Lenin*, p. 67.
49. On Lenin's attitude toward Jews, see Chimen Abramsky, "Emdat Lenin Klapei ha-Yehudim," in *Harzaot bi-Knasei ha-Iyun be-Historyah* (Jerusalem, 1963), pp. 363–74.
50. The book was originally published in 1909.
51. The book was published under Lenin's 1909–10 pseudonym of V. I. Ilian. According to Guriel, Weizmann donated the book to the Soviet legation in Tel Aviv in 1948.
52. At the time, the price of natural rubber in England had soared to twelve shillings per pound and was still rising. See Harold Davies, "A Review of the Development of the Butyl Alcohol-Acetone Fermentation and Early Work on Synthetic Rubber," *Papers Collected to Commemorate the 70th Anniversary of Dr. Chaim Weizmann*, p. 5. W.A.

53. Ernst D. Bergmann, "Bergmann on Weizmann," *Rehovot* 8, no. 1 (Spring 1976): 54.

54. Probably in January 1910.

55. There are two main sources from which I have drawn the information in this chapter dealing with Weizmann's research during 1910–12 and his connections with William Perkin, Auguste Fernbach, and Strange and Graham Ltd. The first is court proceedings dealing with a suit brought by Weizmann and Commercial Solvents Corporation—a U.S.-based company—against Strange and Graham and Synthetic Products Company Ltd. in 1926. The proceedings are contained in a report called "Reports of Patent, Design, and Trade Mark Cases," vol. 43, no. 7 (London, 1926), henceforth referred to as "Reports of Patent." The second source is the letters and memoranda which were presumably used as evidence during the court proceedings. These are collected in a container labeled "In the High Court of Justice, Chancery Division, Mr. Justice Romer. Commercial Solvents Corporation v. Synthetic Products Company Limited. Correspondence, Agreed Bundle No. 1 from 10th May 1909 to 31st May 1919 and Correspondence, Agreed Bundle No. 2 from June 12 [to 1925]. Plaintiff's Solicitors," henceforth referred to as "Court of Justice." The entire documentation is housed in W.A.

56. See "Court of Justice." Agreement signed by W. H. Perkin and Ch. Weizmann, February 8, 1910. A month later, on March 14, 1910, Perkin hired another research assistant, Harold Davies, who worked closely with Weizmann on all experiments. See Harold Davies, "A Review of . . . Early Work on Synthetic Rubber," p. 5.

57. Court of Justice, Strange to Fernbach, April 16, 1910.

58. See Court of Justice, Weizmann to Fernbach, August 8, 1910; Strange to Fernbach, September 22, 1910, and Fernbach to Strange, November 11, 1910.

59. Concerning Schoen's expertise and work, see Albert Delaunay, *L'Institut Pasteur*, p. 114.

60. Court of Justice, Weizmann to Fernbach, August 8, 1910: "The questions which we want to study at once are: 1st. Rice Albumin . . . 2ndly. Amyl and iso-butyl alcohols."

61. Court of Justice, Fernbach to Strange, February 10, 1911, and Weizmann to Strange, March 14, 1911; Reports of Patent, p. 211. Weizmann isolated this bacillus from garden soil taken from the "Vice Chancellor's garden," while Fernbach had isolated his bacillus from a water source in or near Paris. See Harold Davies, "A Review of . . . Early Work on Synthetic Rubber," p. 7.

62. Reports of Patent, p. 211.

63. See, e.g., Court of Justice, Fernbach to Strange, January 23, 1912.

64. As it turned out, he was wrong. An interesting and rather unexpected property of the minute, rodlike bacterium, subsequently given the systematic name Clostridium acetobutylicum Weizmann (nicknamed B-Y), was its ability to ferment starch directly, i.e., without prior treatment, since it contains maltase, which can split starch to "fermentable" sugars. See Ernst D. Bergmann, "The Example of Weizmann's Science," *The Jerusalem Post*, November 2, 1969, p. 3; see also Weizmann, *Trial and Error*, p. 134.

65. Weizmann to Ahad Ha'Am, December 2, 1911, *WL* 5, p. 264.

66. See Court of Justice, Strange to Perkin, February 24, 1912; Weizmann to Strange, February 27, 1912; Strange to Weizmann, February 28, 1912; and Weizmann to Strange, March 3, 1912.

67. See, e.g., Court of Justice, document by E. Moore Mumford, an assistant to Weizmann, dated April 30, 1912.

68. Court of Justice, Strange to Perkin, March 29, 1912. Kane also experimented with the isolation of other butyl-producing bacteria. On May 1, 1912, he isolated one from barley which he called "160." Reports of Patent, p. 186.

69. The power of producing acetone in the fermentation of carbohydrates was not peculiar to the bacillus BF. It is the property of all butylic ferments of starch.

70. Court of Justice, Strange to Perkin, March 29, 1912.

71. Ernst D. Bergmann, "Bergmann on Weizmann," *Rehovot* 8, no. 1 (Spring 1976): p. 54. See also Court of Justice, Strange to Fernbach, May 10, 1912: "I had a further interview with two of the Nobel Dynamite Trust people yesterday . . . and they admitted that the diminishing supply of acetone and the increasing demand for it by several countries for explosive manufacture is a matter of great concern to the British Government and particularly the Admiralty . . ."

72. See, e.g., Court of Justice, Strange to Weizmann, November 17, 1911.

73. Court of Justice, Strange to Weizmann, April 30, 1912. A more modest name was finally chosen for the company: Synthetic Products Company Ltd.

74. Reports of Patent, p. 214.

75. See Reports of Patent, p. 214: "The report states that it was 43 per cent of the dry substance of the potato, but this must have been a clerical error. No such yield has been observed with any bacterium discovered hitherto."

76. Court of Justice, Strange to Weizmann, April 30, 1912.

77. Early on in their collaborative research, when Strange published a prospectus that used Weizmann's and Perkin's names, the latter wrote to Strange— perhaps at Weizmann's insistence: "The prospectus has the appearance, at least, of being an attempt to raise money on our names and reputations and it was widely enough circulated to create a very unfavorable impression in scientific circles. We have every reason to object strongly to such a document being sent out without our knowledge or sanction." Court of Justice, Perkin to Strange, July 27, 1910. Clearly, Perkin's qualms about the use of his name had in the meantime been allayed by the prospect of making his fortune.

78. See Court of Justice, Strange to Weizmann, April 30, 1912, and Reports of Patent, p. 214. In a letter to Fernbach dated May 8, 1912, Strange wrote, "Perkin is to read a paper to the Society of Chemical Industry on June 17 setting out such portions of our position as we deem wise . . . We are anxious to get our statement ahead of the big German boom which is being engineered for September at the Congress of Applied Chemistry in Washington . . . I am writing up the paper for Perkin and I will send you an advance copy for your criticisms . . ." Court of Justice, p. 391.

79. Court of Justice, Fernbach to Strange, May 9, 1912, and Fernbach to Weizmann, May 9, 1912.

80. Court of Justice, Fernbach to Strange, June 11, 1912, and Reports of Patent, p. 232. Fernbach stated clearly: "Our large fermentation experiment on maize has been going on with very great speed for ten days when it stopped suddenly. The result is about the same as what you have yourself obtained at Rainham . . . the fermentation of maize is far from being so easy as the fermentation of potatoes."

81. Reports of Patent, p. 232. Fernbach wrote the following: "I have discovered

fermentation processes which by employing starchy substances, namely, cereal grains such as maize, as raw materials produce higher alcohols and acetone . . . In addition to working on the laboratory scale I have conducted the process successfully in large-size vessels and under certain conditions obtained over 42 per cent of the starch employed converted into mixed higher alcohols."

82. Cf. Court of Justice, Strange to Perkin, July 3, 1912: "We were only asking for the £450,000 on the off chance that the public might like to give it to us."
83. See, e.g., Court of Justice, Fernbach to Weizmann, May 9, 1912, and Moses Schoen to Weizmann, June 14, 1912.
84. Court of Justice, Fernbach to Weizmann, May 9, 1912.
85. Court of Justice, Weizmann to Fernbach, May 12, 1912, and May 13, 1912.
86. Court of Justice, Strange to Weizmann, April 30, 1912.
87. Weizmann to Vera, May 18, 1912, *WL* 5, p. 299.
88. Court of Justice, Weizmann to Strange, May 22, 1912.
89. See Court of Justice, Strange to Fernbach, July 19, 1912. In this letter Strange reviewed developments in Manchester after Weizmann returned from Paris in May.
90. Weizmann to Vera, May 21, 1912, *WL* 5, p. 302.
91. Court of Justice, Weizmann to Strange, May 22, 1912. Perkin seems to have been right in this case, though the evidence is somewhat ambiguous. In its meeting of April 1912 the senate of the university resolved "that Dr. Weizmann's stipend be raised to £450 per annum, it being understood that his position as to external work be the same as that of other members of the staff." Senate committee minutes of April 23, 1912. John Rylands Archives, RA/3/4, vol. 5, p. 27. The council of the university had monitored Weizmann's work outside the university all along. See, e.g., "At a Meeting of the Council Held on November 13th, 1907," John Rylands Archives, RA/29/1, vol. 3, p. 85, which regulated Weizmann's work for the Clayton Aniline Company.
92. Court of Justice, Strange and Graham to Weizmann, May 23, 1912.
93. Court of Justice, Perkin to Strange, May 30, 1912.
94. See Court of Justice, Strange to Weizmann, August 1, 1911. Weizmann to Strange, September 1, 1911. On September 6 Strange wrote to Matthews, "You will note that behind what I have stated is the feeling that if we are not careful Weizmann will endeavor to secure credit for himself which only belongs to him as a unit of the Research Organization. I am beginning to think that our association with Weizmann may have to come to an end unless he is prepared to accept the position as part of the machine . . ."
95. Court of Justice, Strange to Fernbach, June 3, 1912.
96. Court of Justice, Strange to Perkin, June 1, 1912.
97. See Weizmann to Vera, May 30, 1912, *WL* 5, p. 307.
98. Court of Justice, Fernbach to Strange, June 1, 1912.
99. Cf. Court of Justice, Strange to Fernbach, June 3, 1912: "My private opinion is that Perkin is not such a robber and blackguard as Weizmann makes out . . . I think an arrangement something on the lines you indicate can probably be put through . . ."
100. See Court of Justice, Weizmann to Perkin, June 5, 1912.
101. Court of Justice, Fernbach to Weizmann, n.d.
102. Court of Justice, Strange to Perkin, July 3, 1912. See also Fernbach to Strange, July 11, 1912.

103. Court of Justice, Strange to Fernbach, July 19, 1912.
104. Reports of Patent, p. 214, and Weizmann to Ahad Ha'Am, June 25, 1912. *WL* 5, pp. 311–12.
105. Court of Justice, Strange to Fernbach, July 19, 1912.
106. Ibid.
107. Court of Justice, Fernbach to Weizmann, August 16, 1912; Weizmann to Fernbach, August 22, 1912; Fernbach to Weizmann, August 24, 1912; Weizmann to Fernbach, October 28, 1912; Fernbach to Weizmann, October 29, 1912; Strange to Fernbach, November 13, 1912; Strange to Weizmann, December 9, 1912; and Fernbach to Weizmann, December 17, 1912.
108. See Court of Justice, Addleshaw Sons and Latham to Clapham, Fraser, Cook and Co. [Strange's solicitors], December 23, 1912, and January 7, 1913.
109. See Weizmann to Caroline Schuster, July 13, 1912, *WL* 5, pp. 313–14.
110. See Weizmann to Nahum Sokolow, August 2, 1912, *WL* 5, p. 315.
111. Weizmann to Ahad Ha'Am, September 26, 1912, *WL* 5, pp. 316–17. Weizmann sent Ahad Ha'Am a formal request, to be forwarded to the Hilfsverein, in which he declared his readiness to come to the Haifa Technicum in two years' time as professor of chemistry, at an annual salary of ten thousand marks, with sufficient facilities to conduct research and a guaranteed budget for five years. He himself undertook to raise one hundred thousand marks.
112. The professorship was offered to Perkin on November 23, 1912. Perkin accepted on December 10, 1912. See Oxford University Archives, "Minutes of meetings of electoral boards and other meetings chaired by the Vice Chancellor, 1898–1937," pp. 113 and 118. Perkin officially resigned from the University of Manchester on December 18, 1912. See Minutes of council, 1912–1914. John Rylands Archives, RA/3/1, p. 49.
113. For the widespread publicity connected with Perkin's work for Strange and Graham, see Henry Roscoe Record Notebook. John Rylands Archives (Deansgate).
114. Weizmann to Ahad Ha'Am, December 8, 1912, *WL* 5, p. 328.
115. Perkin's last patent with Weizmann was registered on October 4, 1912.
116. In tracing materials related to the appointment of Perkin's successor, searches were conducted in Manchester in the university archives, the records of the organic chemistry department, the records of the faculty of science, and the university registrar's office. The full files of the committee which dealt with the appointment to Perkin's chair are missing. Yet the record shows that in its first meeting the committee heard the views of Perkin and Dixon as to how to proceed in filling the vacancy. See "Committee on Arrangements in Consequence of Professor Perkin's Resignation," January 28, 1913. John Rylands Archives, RA/3/3. Council Committee's Book, February 1909–January 1916.
117. Court of Justice, Strange to Weizmann, December 9, 1912.
118. See "Arrangements," January 28, 1913. John Rylands Archives, RA/3/3.
119. See list of appointments of faculty members of the University of Manchester. John Rylands Archives, UA/18/16h. See also Senate committee minutes of April 23, 1912. John Rylands Archives, RA/3/4, 1912–13.
120. See minutes of February 14, 1913. John Rylands Archives, RA/3/4. Senate Committee Book. This decision was reaffirmed after the committee met on April 17, 1913, and read the letter received from Professor Theodore William Richards of Harvard University.

121. See minutes of March 11, 1913. John Rylands Archives, RA/3/4. Senate Committee Book.

122. Report of Committee on Arrangements consequent to Professor Perkin's Resignation. John Rylands Archives, RA/3/5. Senate committee minutes, vol. 4 (1912–14), p. 68.

123. Cf. Minutes of the Senate of The Victoria University of Manchester, May 1913. John Rylands Archives, RA/3/1 (25.9.1912–10.6.1914), ms. pp. 123–25: "That Dr. Charles Weizmann be appointed Reader in Bio-Chemistry at a stipend of £600 per annum, his duties being to give such instruction in Bio-Chemistry and the Chemistry of Colouring Matters as may be required . . . That the appointment be made in the first instance for three years, as from 29th September 1913 . . ." See also John Rylands Archives, RA/29/1.

124. When Dixon informed Weizmann of the committee's deliberation, he must have offered Weizmann the position of reader, though in January 1913 it had not yet been decided that Lapworth would get the chair. Thus, it seems that from the outset Weizmann was ruled out as the successor to the chair in organic chemistry.

125. See Weizmann to Ahad Ha'Am, December 27, 1912, WL 5, p. 332.

126. Weizmann to Vera, January 28, 1913, WL 5, p. 362. Emphasis in original.

127. See, e.g., Weizmann to Norah Schuster, May 12, 1913, WL 6, p. 64; Weizmann to Ahad Ha'Am, May 25, 1913, WL 6, p. 78; and Weizmann to Isaac Straus, May 25, 1913, WL 6, p. 82. Weizmann was so angered by the fact that he did not receive the professorship that he delayed signing his new contract as long as possible. He was the last of the entire faculty to do so— on November 13, 1913. See John Rylands Archives, RA/3/4.

128. Weizmann to Vera, January 28, 1913, WL 5, p. 362.

129. See, e.g., Weizmann to Vera, July 2, 1909, WL 5, pp. 140–41; January 23, 1913, WL 5, p. 357; and H. B. Speakman, "Dr. Weizmann's Contributions to Microbiology," in *Chaim Weizmann: Statesman, Scientist, Builder of the Jewish Commonwealth*, ed. Meyer Weisgal (New York, 1944), pp. 265–66.

130. In 1913 both had roughly the same status in the department. Weizmann had slight seniority since he had been appointed senior lecturer in 1907, while Lapworth was appointed in 1909. See Senate committee minutes of April 23, 1912. RA/3/4. 1912–13.

131. See the *Dictionary of Scientific Biography* s.v. "Arthur Lapworth," vol. 8, p. 32. There is, of course, no agreement as to who deserved the professorship. Lapworth's student George Norman Burkhardt has a different view on the merit of the case. According to Burkhardt, Weizmann's choice of topics for research was determined more "by commercial rather than scientific considerations. In 1913 he was only beginning to establish himself" in bio-chemistry. Lapworth, on the other hand, "had done notable work in the structural organic chemistry of camphor and related compounds. His general report was regarded as a classic. But it was his work on the formation and decomposition of cyanohydrins of ketones and on the bromination of acetone . . . that was recognized as one of the foundations of a new branch of chemistry (physical organic)." Yet even Burkhardt admits that much of Lapworth's work could not, by 1913, be thought of as being relevant to a chair of *organic* chemistry. Information provided by G. N. Burkhardt in November 1982. See also G. N. Burkhardt, "Prof. A. Lapworth, F.R.S.," *Nature* 147 (June 21, 1941): 769.

132. Weizmann was unable to become F.R.S. despite the fact that Arthur Schus-

ter was the secretary of the society from 1912 to 1919. It is most likely that Perkin withdrew his backing of Weizmann for an F.R.S.

133. See Weizmann to Vera, February 1, 1913, *WL* 5, p. 369, and Weizmann, *Trial and Error*, pp. 134–35.

134. Weizmann to Vera, February 11, 1913, *WL* 5, p. 381.

135. Weizmann to Vera, February 13, 1913, *WL* 5, p. 383.

136. See, e.g., Alfred Hopkinson to Norman Collie, February 18, 1913. John Rylands Archives, VCA, no. 5.

137. See minutes of council, September 25, 1912–June 10, 1914, John Rylands Archives, RA/3/1.

138. Richards was one of the most eminent chemists in the United States. In 1914 he was awarded the Nobel Prize in chemistry, the first chemist in the United States to be so honored. See the *Dictionary of Scientific Biography* s.v. "Theodore William Richards," vol. 11, pp. 416–17.

139. Alfred Hopkinson to T. W. Richards, February 18, 1913. Harvard University Archives, HUG/1743/1/6 (1912–1913), Box 1. Hopkinson wrote in a similar vein to the other chemists consulted by the committee. It should be pointed out that not all the potential candidates held the title of F.R.S. Crossley and Forster, who were F.R.S., had supported Weizmann's candidacy to the Royal Society.

140. Theodore William Richards to Alfred Hopkinson, March 7, 1913. Harvard University Archives, HUG/1743/1/6 (1912–1913), Box 1. On May 22, 1913, Hopkinson informed Richards of the decisions concerning Lapworth and Weizmann. See Harvard University Archives, HUG/1743/1/5 (1911–1913), Box 5; a copy of Hopkinson's reply is also contained in the vice-chancellor's letter book, John Rylands Archives, VCA, No. 5.

141. See Weizmann to Caroline Schuster, July 13, 1912, *WL* 5, pp. 313–14.

142. Weizmann to Caroline Schuster, December 7, 1912, *WL* 5, pp. 326–27.

143. Weizmann to Caroline Schuster, January 6, 1913, *WL* 5, pp. 336–37.

144. Weizmann to Vera, February 4, 1913, *WL* 5, p. 373.

145. In old age Norah Nicholls wrote, "I have no idea how these letters may strike other people, but I want to make it quite clear that there was no secret liaison between me and Chaim Weizmann. He was the soul of honor, as honor was understood in those days, and would never have dreamt of abusing my parents' hospitality in such a way . . . The nearest he ever got to a declaration was to say that if he had been free, he would have asked me to marry him, but callow though I was at the time, I didn't take that seriously, though naturally it embarrassed me." Letter from Norah N. Nicholls, April 9, 1969. W.A.

146. Weizmann to Norah Schuster, February 8, 1913, *WL* 5, pp. 377–79.

147. Weizmann to Vera, January 14, 1913, *WL* 5, p. 345. Interestingly, Vera published this letter in her memoirs—calling it "one of his most delightful letters"—but with some significant substantive changes, particularly the last three sentences quoted here. See Weizmann, *The Impossible Takes Longer*, pp. 38–39.

148. See, e.g., Weizmann to Vera, January 29, 1913, *WL* 5, p. 365, and February 1, 1913, *WL* 5, p. 370.

149. Weizmann to Vera, February 8, 1913, *WL* 5, p. 376. A few days later, in response to Vera's letter, he again declared that he loved and appreciated her more than anything else. "That love is clear and unshakable now and for ever." Weizmann to Vera, February 13, 1913, *WL* 5, p. 382.

150. Weizmann to Vera, January 15, 1913, *WL* 5, pp. 346–47.
151. Weizmann to Vera, February 20, 1913, *WL* 5, p. 390.
152. Weizmann to Vera, February 23, 1913, *WL* 5, p. 394.
153. Weizmann to Vera, February 24, 1913, *WL* 5, p. 395.
154. See, e.g., Weizmann to Norah Schuster, February 27, 1913, *WL* 5, pp. 397–402.
155. See the letter by Norah Nicholls dated April 9, 1969. W.A. Weizmann himself conceded in May 1914 that "all that part of my life and activities about which I would have liked to write [i.e., Zionism] must necessarily interest you very little." Weizmann to Norah Schuster, May 17, 1914, *WL* 6, p. 371.
156. See Weizmann to Norah Schuster, May 12, 1913, WL, 6, p. 64. Norah even kept a Jewish National Fund box—presumably sent to her by Weizmann—in her room in Cambridge.
157. Weizmann, *The Impossible Takes Longer*, p. 40.
158. Weizmann to Vera, March 6, 1913, *WL* 6, p. 7. See also the letter from Victor Jacobson to Weizmann dated February 27, 1913, and Arthur Hantke to Weizmann, February 27, 1913. W.A.
159. Weizmann to Norah Schuster, March 3, 1913, *WL* 6, p. 5.
160. Weizmann to Vera, March 6, 1913, *WL* 6, p. 7.
161. In the summer of 1902, after Weizmann declared his intention to give up chemistry and work for the university project, Vera wrote: "Is it possible that you are considering living off Jewish money? . . . I want only to advise you not to sever yourself from chemistry . . ." Vera to Weizmann, August 6, 1902. W.A.
162. See Weizmann to Berthold Feiwel, May 16, 1913, *WL* 6, p. 73.
163. Weizmann, *The Impossible Takes Longer*, p. 39. See also Weizmann, *Trial and Error*, p. 135.
164. Weizmann to Vera, February, 13, 1913, *WL* 5, p. 383.
165. Weizmann to Vera, January 29, 1913, *WL* 5, p. 366.
166. Weizmann to Vera, February 5, 1913, *WL* 5, p. 375.
167. He did try to rationalize the fact that he was appointed reader rather than professor because the subject of biochemistry was new and its beginnings in Manchester were small. See Weizmann to Charles P. Scott, December 9, 1914, *WL* 7, p. 77.
168. See, e.g., Weizmann to Herbert Bentwich, January 13, 1914, *WL* 6, p. 203: ". . . I don't think it is compatible with my position at the University to become a Director of the Company. Although it is not a money-concern in the real sense of the word, still the outsiders don't know the meaning of it, and I lay myself open to comments, which are not desirable . . ." Cf. also the letter from Weizmann's attorneys—Addleshaw Sons and Latham—to Strange's attorneys—Clapham, Fraser, Cook and Co.—dated January 7, 1913. "Our client cannot enter into the Agreements . . . unless they are modified so as to meet the requirements of the University . . ." Court of Justice.
169. Weizmann to Julius Simon, June 4, 1913, *WL* 6, pp. 84–85, and June 14, 1913, *WL* 6, pp. 95–96.
170. Cf. Weizmann to Ahad Ha'Am, May 25, 1913, *WL* 6, p. 78: "In the winter I have only one lecture a week; in the summer three and two days of practical work, and that's all. In many respects this position is better than a professorship. The difference in the salary is only £100, while I have almost no duties." See also Weizmann to Isaac Straus, May 25, 1913, *WL* 6, pp. 81–82.

XVI A Hebrew University in Jerusalem

1. Weizmann to Judah Leon Magnes, May 5, 1912, *WL* 5, pp. 295–97.
2. Judah Leon Magnes to Isaac Straus, January 8, 1913. W.A.
3. Weizmann to Vera, April 1, 1912, *WL* 5, p. 289.
4. The terms "Hebrew University" and "Jewish University" were used interchangeably by Weizmann and his friends in the 1912–14 period, whereas the term "Jewish University" (*Juedische Hochschule*) was most often employed between 1901 and 1904.
5. See, e.g., Richard Lichtheim to SAC, October 3, 1913. CZA, Z3/43. See also P. Alsberg, "Mediniyut ha-Hanhalah ha-Zionist . . . ," pp. 93–101.
6. Arthur Ruppin and Victor Jacobson visited the baron, who expressed interest in purchasing land, provided the Zionists would participate financially. See the report from Victor Jacobson to David Wolffsohn, July 10, 1913. CZA, W 143 II. There were even earlier reports about the baron's interest. See Arthur Hantke to Yehiel Tschlenow, April 7, 1913. CZA Z3/521: "[Henri] Frank [ICA] sagte ausdruecklich, dass der Baron Rothschild sich entweder direkt an der PLDC, oder zusammen mit irgend jemand an einer Landesgesellschaft unter einem neuen Namen mit einer Summe von mindestens einer Million Francs zu beteiligen gedenke . . ."
7. See *The Jewish Chronicle,* October 25, 1907, pp. 29–30.
8. Protokoll des GAC, November 6, 1911. CZA, Z3/430.
9. "I feel that I don't belong to Manchester at all. Everything here is 'temporary' and 'alien.' " Weizmann to Vera, March 13, 1913, *WL* 6, p. 13. See also Weizmann to Ernst Lesser, March 23, 1913, *WL* 6, p. 20.
10. "Of course the Zionist activities are an enormous comfort. It somehow lifts you above these little failures . . . It's not a mere autosuggestion, but I really find comfort in the thought that my true ambitions are not in the Victoria University but somewhere else and my real work is still before me." Weizmann to Norah Schuster, May 12, 1913, *WL* 6, pp. 64–65.
11. Unlike the discussions surrounding the site of a university which took place in 1901–4, no other option but Palestine was considered this time by GAC and Weizmann.
12. For the decisions of the GAC, see CZA, Z3/437.
13. Weizmann to Vera, March 8, 1913, *WL* 6, p. 8.
14. See Weizmann to Vera, March 10, 1913, *WL* 6, p. 10.
15. Weizmann, *Trial and Error,* pp. 140–41.
16. Ehrlich does not seem to have had a private practice. See Martha Marquardt, *Paul Ehrlich,* with an introd. by Sir Henry Dale (New York, 1951).
17. See Weizmann to Vera, March 10, 1913, *WL* 6, p. 11. See also Weizmann to SAC March 13, 1913, *WL* 6, p. 14. "No mortal has been able to talk to him for such a long time in the last few years, especially on a subject that was neither chemistry nor medicine."
18. See, e.g., Harry Sacher to Weizmann, March 3, 1913. W.A. Sacher outlined the tactics that ought to be taken to promote the university project.
19. Weizmann to Vera, March 13, 1913, *WL* 6, pp. 12–13.
20. Weizmann to Vera, March 16, 1913, *WL* 6, pp. 15–16.
21. See Arthur Hantke to Weizmann, April 7, 1913. W.A.
22. "It does one so good to feel again the living contact which prevails in the group, in the *Frakzije.*" Weizmann to Ernst Lesser, March 23, 1913, *WL* 6, p. 20.

23. See Berthold Feiwel to Weizmann, May 1, 1913 (W.A.), informing the latter of Buber's interest in joining the commission; see also Weizmann to Martin Buber, May 4, 1913, *WL* 6, p. 62, in which he extends such an invitation. Julius Becker, a journalist and Zionist activist, made a similar request and was also co-opted. See Weizmann to Julius Becker, May 25, 1913, *WL* 6, p. 79.
24. Weizmann to Ahad Ha'Am, April 4, 1913, *WL* 6, p. 32.
25. See Carl Alpert, *Technion: The Story of Israel's Institute of Technology* (New York, 1982), pp. 31–34. See also Shmarya Levin to Ahad Ha'Am, March 2, 1912, and March 26, 1912, in *Igrot Shmarya Levin* (Tel Aviv, 1966), pp. 158, 162. Paul Nathan offered the job to Alphonse Finkelstein, who began his duties in Haifa in October 1913.
26. ". . . if anything works out in Berlin [at the curatorium meetings] both Vera Isayevna and I will gladly move to Haifa at any time. I await news from you with impatience." Weizmann to Ahad Ha'Am, April 16, 1913, *WL* 6, p. 38.
27. Weizmann to Menahem Ussishkin, March 25, 1913, *WL* 6, pp. 22–23.
28. Weizmann to Judah Leon Magnes, April 19, 1913, *WL* 6, p. 41.
29. Judah Leon Magnes to Weizmann, May 25, 1913. W.A. Magnes reiterated his position three months later. See Magnes to Weizmann, August 14, 1913. W.A. This was also Sokolow's position. See Nahum Sokolow to Weizmann, August 14, 1913. W.A. Yehiel Tschlenow preferred a philosophical-historical faculty as a first step. See "Protokoll der Sitzung des GAC vom 15. und 16. Juni 1913." CZA, Z3/440. According to Victor Johnson, Baron Edmond de Rothschild was also interested—in the spring of 1913—in an archaeological institute. CZA, Z3/440.
30. Weizmann to SAC, June 12, 1913, *WL* 6, p. 93. See also Weizmann to Judah Leon Magnes, June 15, 1913, *WL* 6, p. 98, in which he agrees with him in principle but reiterates the importance of a medical school in view of the discrimination against Jewish students in Russia and the West.
31. See, e.g., Weizmann to Menahem Ussishkin, March 25, 1913, *WL* 6, p. 23, and Weizmann to Judah Magnes, June 15, *WL* 6, p. 98.
32. Weizmann to Menahem Ussishkin, March 25, 1913, *WL* 6, p. 23.
33. Ibid., p. 24. See also Weizmann to Julius Becker, May 25, 1913, *WL* 6, pp. 79–80, and Weizmann to Julius Becker, June 8, 1913, *WL* 6, pp. 88–90.
34. Weizmann to Menahem Ussishkin, March 25, 1913, *WL* 6, p. 23, and Weizmann to Judah Leon Magnes, April 19, 1913, *WL* 6, p. 41.
35. See, e.g., Weizmann to the Rector of St. Joseph University in Beirut, May 21, 1913, *WL* 6, pp. 73–74, and Weizmann to Isaac Lipavsky, May 21, 1913, *WL* 6, pp. 75–76.
36. See, e.g., the letter from Leo Motzkin to Weizmann, May 29, 1913 (CZA, Z3/1598), in which he outlined the division of labor among himself, Berthold Feiwel, Weizmann, and others.
37. Weizmann to Julius Becker, May 25, 1913, *WL* 6, p. 79.
38. Weizmann to Julius Simon, June 8, 1913 *WL* 6, p. 91. See also Weizmann to Isaac Straus, June 25, 1913, *WL* 6, p. 103.
39. Cf. the resolution of GAC of June 16, 1913: "Das GAC appelliert . . . an den verehrten Altmeister der Organization [Nordau] . . . am XI. Kongress wie frueher die Eroeffnungsrede zu halten, und den Vorsitz zu fuehren."
40. See *The Jewish Chronicle*, August 1, 1913, pp. 22–23.
41. Weizmann to Vera, March 13, 1913, *WL* 6, p. 13.

42. See *Stenographisches Protokoll der Verhandlungen des XI. Zionisten-Kongresses in Wien* (Berlin and Leipzig, 1914), p. 196.
43. See Ber Borochov, *Ktavim*, vol. 3 (Tel Aviv, 1954–55), pp. 776–77. See Weizmann's indirect reference to this opposition in his speech to the student group Hehaver in Heidelberg on June 4, 1914. W.A. See also *The Jewish Chronicle*, August 15, 1913, p. 25.
44. See Nahum Sokolow to Weizmann, August 14, 1913, and Judah Magnes to Weizmann, August 14, 1913. W.A.
45. Cf. Berthold Feiwel to SAC, May 13, 1913 (CZA, Z3/1598): "Ich wiederhole: So wenig als moeglich nach aussen keine Propaganda—auf dem Kongress (wenn ueberhaupt): Beschraenkung auf das rein Prinzipiellste . . ."
46. See Arthur Hantke to Weizmann, April 7, 1913. W.A.
47. Weizmann to Berthold Feiwel, May 4, 1913, *WL* 6, p. 61.
48. See "Protokoll der Sitzung des Grossen Actions-Comités vom 15. und 16. Juni 1913." CZA, Z3/440.
49. The strongest proponent of the university project on SAC, Shmarya Levin, was in Palestine at the time and could not fully exert his influence from there.
50. Weizmann to Judah Leon Magnes, June 15, 1913, *WL* 6, p. 98.
51. See Weizmann's speech to the student group Hehaver in Heidelberg on June 4, 1914. W.A.
51. See Weizmann to Julius Becker, July 6, 1913, *WL* 6, p. 110.
53. See "Beschluesse" in Protokoll der Sitzung des GAC vom 15. und. 16. Juni 1913. CZA, Z3/440. See also Leo Motzkin to Weizmann, May 29, 1913. CZA, Z3/1598.
54. Weizmann to SAC, July 20, 1913, *WL* 6, p. 116. See also Weizmann to Julius Simon, July 27, 1913, *WL* 6, pp. 121–22.
55. See Weizmann to Judah Leon Magnes, August 4, 1913, *WL* 6, p. 129. Magnes agreed to serve on such a committee. See also Judah Magnes to Weizmann, August 14, 1913. W.A.
56. See Arthur Hantke to Weizmann, July 23, 1913. W.A.
57. On Zionist conditions in England, compare the remark by Pineas Cohen, secretary of the Manchester Zionist Association, to SAC, October 29, 1912 (CZA, Z3/806): "Die EZF is augenscheinlich vollkommen tot, und die Unfaehigkeit und Untauglichkeit des Joint Council macht sich in so auffallender Weise bemerkbar, dass die Ortsgruppen nur noch von der Berliner Zentrale Raten und Hilfe erwarten koennen." See also the detailed report on the same subject from Nahum Sokolow to Otto Warburg, February 23, 1913. CZA, Z3/403.
58. Weizmann to Moses Gaster, March 25, 1913, *WL* 6, pp. 25–26.
59. Moses Gaster to Weizmann, March 28, 1913. W.A.
60. See, e.g., Moses Gaster to Weizmann, April 16, 1913. W.A.
61. Cf. the letter from Leon Simon to Weizmann on April 13, 1913 (WA): "I do not consider Gaster of such enormous value as to warrant the destruction of the results of much hard work and the revival of old squabbles."
62. See Weizmann to SAC, April 15, 1913, *WL* 6, p. 35.
63. See Leon Simon to Weizmann, April 13, 1913. W.A.
64. See Arthur Hantke to Weizmann, April 21, 1913, W.A.
65. See Arthur Hantke to Moses Gaster, May 5, 1913, and Moses Gaster to Arthur Hantke, May 8, 1913. CZA, Z3/547.
66. See Arthur Hantke to Weizmann, April 21, 1913. W.A.

67. See Arthur Hantke to Weizmann, May 5, 1913. W.A.

68. See Harry Sacher to Arthur Hantke, April 13, 1913 (W.A.), and Weizmann to SAC, April 27, 1913, *WL* 6, p. 50.

69. See Arthur Hantke to Weizmann, May 5, 1913. W.A. Adolf Friedemann, one of the earliest German Zionists and a member of GAC, also attended the EZF conference.

70. See *The Jewish Chronicle*, April 25, 1913, p. 28.

71. See *Die Welt*, no. 23, June 6, 1913, p. 732. See also Josef Fraenkel, "Fun der Englisher Hibbat Zion Bavegung biz zu der Balfour-Deklarazie," *YIVO Bletter* 43 (1966): 135.

72. Fraenkel, "Fun der Englisher Hibbat Zion Bavegung," p. 133. See also *The Jewish Chronicle*, June 6, 1913, pp. 29–32.

73. See *Die Welt*, no. 9, February 27, 1914, p. 225, and Weizmann to SAC, February 16, 1914, *WL* 6, p. 256.

74. See, e.g., Weizmann to SAC, June 20, 1913, *WL* 6, p. 101. Cf. also the letter from Leon Simon to Weizmann, June 7, 1913 (W.A.): "The idea is to get as influential an OAM delegation as possible, so as to throw into relief the rottenness of the EZF, and to show that there is a decent element in English Zionism."

75. See the statutes of the Gesellschaft Juedischer Aerzte und Naturwissenschaftler fuer sanitaere Interessen in Palaestina, August 1913. W.A. Weizmann became a member of its international committee in 1913.

76. See Harry Sacher to Weizmann, May 19, 1913. W.A.

77. Weizmann to Harry Sacher, May 14, 1913, *WL* 6, p. 69.

78. See Aaron Sandler to Weizmann, May 21, 1913. W.A.

79. Weizmann to SAC, June 12, 1913, *WL* 6, p. 93.

80. *Stenographisches Protokoll* (XI), pp. 7–15.

81. For Nordau's critique of the new SAC, see *Die Welt*, no. 14, April 3, 1914, pp. 339–40.

82. *Stenographisches Protokoll* (XI), pp. 16–34.

83. Ibid., pp. 154–59. In a speech delivered in Paris in October 1913, Weizmann returned to the theme of Arab-Zionist relations: "The political work is made more difficult because of the Arabs, who today constitute the population of Palestine. They fear that Jewish settlement in Palestine will oust them from the country and we must dispel these fears and explain to them that there is room in Palestine both for us and for them. We must explain to them that we want to work together with them, and that it will be to their advantage if a great Jewish community arises in Palestine. But this work . . . is very difficult. The overhasty among us want to see results immediately. But every man of political understanding will grasp the fact that we have to exercise great patience . . ." Weizmann, *Dvarim*, vol. 1, p. 53.

84. For a summary of Arab-Zionist relations prior to World War I, see Israel Kolatt, "Ha-Tnuah ha-Zionit ve-ha-Aravim," in *Ha-Zionut ve-ha-Sheelah ha-Aravit*, ed. Yitzhak Cohen (Jerusalem, 1979), pp. 9–16.

85. *Stenographisches Protokoll* (XI), pp. 193–216.

86. Weizmann to Vera, February 23, 1913. *WL* 5, pp. 394–95.

87. *Stenographisches Protokoll* (XI), pp. 294–300.

88. See Weizmann to Berthold Feiwel, August 7, 1913, *WL* 6, pp. 132–33. See also Judah Magnes to Weizmann, August 14, 1913 (W.A.), in which he approved Weizmann's resolution before the congress.

89. *Stenographisches Protokoll* (XI), pp. 300–308.

90. Ibid., pp. 344–45. The "Protokoll-Buch des Grossen A.C. 1907–1914," dated Tuesday, September 9, 1913, has a different formulation of the resolution: "Das A.C. beschliest die Einsetzung einer Kommission bestehend aus den Herren Berthold Feiwel, Leo Motzkin, Prof. Weizmann . . . welche die Aufgabe hat, das Material zum Studium dieser Frage [viz. the university in Jerusalem] zu sammeln und dem A.C. bericht zu erstatten." CZA, Z2/237.

91. Weizmann to Jacob Moser, October 15, 1913, *WL* 6, p. 148. Later Wolffsohn attached various conditions to his donation. See David Wollfsohn to Aktions-Komitee der zionistischen Organisation, April 22, 1914. W.A.

92. *Stenographisches Protokoll* (XI), p. 358.

93. Ibid., p. 359.

94. Weiss had just been promoted to the position of Chancellor of the University of Manchester. The information on residents of Brunswick Road is contained in *Kelly's Directory of Manchester, 1913* (London, 1913), in The Central Library, Manchester.

95. The most sophisticated synagogue, established in Manchester in 1913 by well-to-do Jews who left the Great Synagogue. Charles Dreyfus, for example, was a member of the South Manchester Synagogue.

96. Information on the house and the neighborhood is based on this author's visit to 30 Brunswick Road in February 1981 and interviews with longtime residents on the street.

97. For the most comprehensive discussion of the subject, see Moshe Rinott, *Hevrat ha-Ezra li-Yehudei Germanyah bi-Yezirah uve-Maavak* (Jerusalem, 1971); idem, "Histadrut ha-Morim, ha-Tnuah ha-Zionit ve-ha-Maavak al ha-Hegmonyah ba-Hinukh be-Eretz Israel (1903–1918)," *Hazionut* 4 (1975): 114–45. See also P. A. Alsberg, "Ha-Orientazia shel Mediniyut ha-Hanhalah ha-Zionit erev Milhemet ha-Olam ha-Rishonah 1911–1914," *Zion* 22, nos. 2–3 (1957): 165–70, as well as his dissertation, "Mediniyut ha-Hanhalah . . . ," pp. 106–12; Leon Simon, *Ahad Ha'Am* (Philadelphia, 1960), pp. 230ff., and Adolf Boehm, *Die Zionistische Bewegung* (Tel Aviv, 1935), vol. 1, pp. 470–76. Primary and archival material on the dispute include: *Igrot Ahad Ha'Am*, vol. 5; Paul Nathan, *Palaestina und palaestinensischer Zionismus* (Berlin, 1914); and the reply of the Zionistiches Actions Comité, *Im Kampf um die hebraeische Sprache* (Berlin, 1914). A summary of the debate from a Zionist point of view is contained in CZA, A20/56. See also *Juedische Rundschau*, no. 45, November 7, 1913, pp. 479–80, and no. 47, November 21, 1913, pp. 502–3.

98. See Arthur Hantke to members of AC, October 30, 1913. CZA, A20/54. Tschlenow had made an official inquiry concerning the language of instruction already on April 8, 1913.

99. CZA, A20/54.

100. See Alsberg, "Ha-Orientazia shel Mediniyut ha-Hanhalah ha-Zionit," p. 166.

101. CZA, Z3/356.

102. See "Beschluesse der Sitzung des Aktions-Komitees vom 23. and 24. November 1913." CZA, Z3/443 and Z3/237. See also *Die Welt*, no. 48, November 28, 1913, p. 1626.

103. See the letter from SAC of October 30, 1913. W.A. For a summary of the events leading up to the resignation of the Zionist members, see Shmarya Levin's statement of November 3, 1913. W.A.

104. See the letter from Samuel Pevsner and others to Shmarya Levin, dated

November 9, 1913. W.A. See also Jehuda Reinharz, *Dokumente zur Geschichte des deutschen Zionismus, 1882–1933*, pp. 117–21, 127–28.

105. See the secret memorandum from Yehiel Tschlenow and Arthur Hantke to members of GAC, dated December 5, 1913. W.A. See also *Die Welt*, no. 51, December 19, 1913, pp. 1719–26, and "Bisheriges Ergebnis der Schulwerksaktion," *Juedische Rundschau*, no. 18, May 1, 1914, p. 188.

106. The American members also recommended that the World Zionist Organization support the Technicum and that Ahad-Ha'Am, Levin, and Tschlenow resume their membership on the curatorium. See the letter from Judah Magnes to Shmarya Levin, dated January 19, 1914. CZA, A20/58. See also "Cablegrams exchanged between the Zionist Actions Comité and Dr. Magnes, February 2–19, 1914." CZA, Z3/1586. On February 15, 1914, the American members reiterated their compromise resolution and suggested that the three Zionist members who resigned submit the names of those who would replace them. See CZA, Z3/1586.

107. See CZA, Z3/356.

108. See "Protokoll der 47. Sitzung des EAC vom 23. Februar 1914." CZA, Z3/356. See also "Protokoll der Sitzung des GAC," February 27, 1914. CZA, Z3/446.

109. See Rinott, *Hevrat ha-Ezra*, pp. 223–25. See also "Protokoll der Kuratoriumsitzung vom 17. Juli, 1914." W.A.

110. For a full discussion of the subject, see the fifth chapter in Jehuda Reinharz, *Fatherland or Promised Land?* For the advertisements, see *Handels-Zeitung des Berliner Tageblattes*, no. 64, February 5, 1914, p. 23, and *Vossische Zeitung*, February 5, 1914, p. 14. See also "Zionistenhetze in Deutschland," *Die Welt*, no. 3, January 16, 1914, pp. 69–70.

111. A number of "political" Zionists were, for different reasons, also unhappy about the World Zionist Organization's handling of the dispute with the Hilfsverein. See, e.g., Max Bodenheimer's reservations as articulated at a meeting of GAC on November 23 and 24, 1913. CZA, Z3/443. Jacobus Kann was probably most vociferous in his disagreements with SAC over this issue. See Jacobus Kann to Aktions Komité der Zionistischen Organisation, December 9, 1913. W.A. See also his letters of January 11, 1914, and February 22, 1914. W.A. Even Harry Sacher and Leon Simon were not sanguine about these developments. See *The Zionist* for January 9, 1914. Shmarya Levin, on the other hand, did not believe that the language debate had an impact on the university project. See Shmarya Levin to Weizmann, February 10, 1914, in *Igrot Shmarya Levin*, pp. 286–87.

112. Though he was aware, of course, of the simmering conflict. See Shmarya Levin to Weizmann, August 7, 1913. W.A.

113. See *Stenographisches Protokoll* (XI), pp. 307–8.

114. As late as June 1913 even Ahad Ha'Am did not believe that it was possible to conduct instruction at the Technicum in Hebrew. See Ahad Ha'Am to Shmarya Levin, June 10, 1913, in *Igrot Ahad Ha'Am*, vol. 5, p. 63.

115. For an extensive correspondence between Weizmann and SAC concerning the language debate, see CZA, Z3/525. See also "Aus dem stenographischen Protokoll der Sitzung des GAC," February 27, 1914. CZA, Z3/446.

116. Weizmann to Ahad Ha'Am, November 2, 1913, *WL* 6, p. 160. Indeed, he only joined the curatorium in May 1914, after it became clear that Ahad Ha'Am's resignation was final. In this connection, see the report of a meeting between Weizmann and Paul Nathan on March 2, 1914. W.A. Initially Nathan denied Weizmann the right to replace Ahad Ha'Am.

117. Weizmann to Ahad Ha'Am, November 2, 1913, *WL* 6, p. 157.
118. Weizmann to Shmarya Levin, February 4, 1914, p. 242. Emphasis mine.
119. Weizmann to Judah Leon Magnes, December 3, 1913, *WL* 6, p. 175.
120. See *Die Welt*, no. 9, February 27, 1914, p. 224.
121. Weizmann to Julius Simon, December 30, 1913, *WL* 6, p. 190.
122. Weizmann to SAC, February 7–9, 1914, *WL* 6, p. 247.
123. See Judah Magnes to Weizmann, October 14, 1913. W.A.
124. See Charles Fox to Weizmann, October 16, 1913. W.A. In Manchester Joseph Cowen shared the platform with Weizmann on October 26, 1913, in praise of practical work in Palestine. See "Asefah Zionit be-Manchester," *Hatzfirah*, no. 236, November 13, 1913, p. 2.
125. See the letter from Leon Simon to Weizmann dated March 3, 1913 (W.A.), and those from Harry Sacher and Leon Simon, November 3, 1913. W.A.
126. See the statement by the committee, chaired by Siegmund B. Sonneborn, October 1913. W.A.
127. See the letter from Joseph Sapir to Weizmann dated October 17, 1913 (W.A.), and from Weizmann to Joseph Sapir dated November 9, 1913, *WL* 6, pp. 163–64. See also Menahem Ussishkin to Weizmann, February 25, 1914 (W.A.), in which he describes his activities on behalf of the university.
128. See the letter from Walter Moses to Weizmann, with the accompanying list of student groups and the declaration of support, dated March 20, 1914. W.A.
129. See, e.g., "Asefah Zionit be-Paris," *Hatzfirah*, October 22, 1913, pp. 6–7, and October 27, 1913, p. 3.
130. In his memoirs Sieff records that he met Weizmann in the summer of 1913. See Sieff, *Memoirs*, p. 66. Simon Marks and Israel Sieff are mentioned for the first time in *The Jewish Chronicle* of June 5, 1914, p. 20. At a fund-raising event for Zionist schools—addressed by Shmarya Levin and Weizmann—which took place at the Midland Hotel in Manchester, Sieff and Marks moved the vote of thanks.
131. "Il participera certainement à cette oeuvre colossale, mais un plus plus tard."
132. See Joseph Spanien to Weizmann, October, 30, 1913. W.A.
133. Weizmann to SAC, November 15, 1913, *WL* 6, pp. 165–67.
134. See the meetings of SAC of November 19, 1913. CZA, Z3/356.
135. See "Beschluesse der Sitzung des Aktions-Komitees vom 23. und 24. November 1913" (CZA, Z3/443), and *Die Welt*, no. 48, November 28, 1913, pp. 1625–26.
136. See Weizmann to Heinrich Loewe, November 30, 1913, *WL* 6, pp. 170–71. See also *Die Welt*, no. 48, November 28, 1913, p. 1626, and Heinrich Loewe, "Eine Vorbedingung der Universitaet," *Die Welt*, no. 14, April 3, 1914, pp. 328–29, and "Kurzer Bericht ueber die Vorarbeiten zu einer Bibliothek fuer die hebraeische Universitaet zu Jerusalem," July 31, 1914. W.A.
137. See Weizmann to Judah Leon Magnes, December 3, 1913, *WL* 6, p. 174. See also Magnes's reply of December 15, 1913. W.A.
138. Weizmann to Menahem Ussishkin, December 14, 1913, *WL* 6, p. 178.
139. Weizmann was quite taken by the baron. Decades later he described the latter as he first appeared to him: "When I first met Baron Edmond he was a man in his sixties, very much alert, still something of a dandy, but full of experience and *sagesse*. Everything about him was in exquisite taste, his clothes, his home—or rather his homes—his furniture and his paintings, and there still clung to him the aura of the *bon vivant*, which he had once

been. In manner he could be both gracious and brutal; and this was the reflex of his split personality. For on the one hand he was conscious of his power and arrogant in the possession of it; on the other he was rather frightened by it, and this gave him a touch of furtiveness. To his family he was, with his tremendous interest in the Jewish problem, an enigma and a wild man . . ." Weizmann, *Trial and Error*, p. 138.

140. Weizmann to Vera, January 3, 1914, *WL* 6, p. 193.

141. Weizmann to Judah Leon Magnes, January 12, 1914. *WL* 6, p. 199.

142. See the telegram from Nathan Straus to Weizmann dated January 3, 1914. W.A. As early as May 1913 Weizmann knew of Straus's intentions to donate land for such a purpose. See the letter from Judah Magnes to Weizmann dated May 25, 1913. W.A.

143. On these negotiations, see the letter from Victor Jacobson to Weizmann dated February 11, 1914. W.A.

144. See "Protokoll der Sitzung des Universitaets—Arbeitsausschusses, die am 6. und 7. Januar . . . stattgefunden hat." CZA, Z3/1598. For a truncated Hebrew version, see CZA, Z3/916. See also the Hebrew letter from Menahem Ussishkin to Arthur Ruppin, marked "strictly confidential," dated January 5, 1914, empowering Ruppin to buy the desired land on Mount Scopus.

145. Simon Schama, *Two Rothschilds and the Land of Israel* (New York, 1978), p. 185.

146. See Judah Magnes to Weizmann, February 4, 1914. W.A.

147. See Judah Magnes to Nathan Straus, February 4, 1914. W.A.

148. Nathan Straus to Judah Magnes, February 9, 1914. W.A.

149. Weizmann, *Trial and Error*, p. 138.

150. Cf., in this connection, Ahad Ha'Am to Weizmann, January 16, 1914, in *Igrot Ahad Ha'Am*, vol. 5, p. 148. "If the Baron finds out [about these leaks] you can be sure that he will refuse to continue negotiating with you . . ."

151. See *Die Welt*, no. 6, February 6, 1914, p. 146, and *Hatzfirah*, February 1, 1914, p. 3. See also the letter from Yehiel Tschlenow to members of GAC, marked "vertraulich!," dated March 16, 1914 (W.A.), demanding discretion in all matters connected with the research institute.

152. Weizmann to Judah Leon Magnes, December 3, 1913, *WL* 6, p. 176.

153. Weizmann to Harry Sacher, January 17, 1914, *WL* 6, p. 210.

154. Weizmann to Judah Leon Magnes, January 23, 1914, *WL* 6, p. 223.

155. Weizmann to SAC, April 26, 1914, *WL* 6, p. 337.

156. Cf. Judah Magnes to Weizmann, December 15, 1913 (W.A.): "Such a school would, I think, interest all classes of Jews . . . Its archaeological department would certainly secure funds from all classes of Jews . . . For me the chief importance and attraction of such a school, as of the university in general, would be that the humanities would be taught by Jews, primarily on the basis of Jewish documents and of Jewish life . . ."

157. Cf. Judah Magnes to Weizmann, February 4, 1914 (W.A.): "The plan of having an institute somewhat like the Rockefeller Institute is, I think, the proper way to proceed . . . I also very much like the idea of building proper quarters for a great library and of developing an academic faculty gradually and, at first, unofficially about the library. That seems to me a splendid way of avoiding the difficulties which an academic or philosophic faculty doubtless presents." Later that year Magnes modified his views somewhat and wanted clear assurances that the institute would indeed develop into a uni-

versity. See Leon Simon to Weizmann, May 4, 1914. W.A. Simon's letter describes a meeting he had with Magnes.

158. Ahad Ha'Am to Weizmann, April 27, 1914, in *Igrot Ahad Ha'Am*, vol. 5, pp. 172–73.

159. See "Beschluesse der Sitzung des GAC vom 27. und 28. Februar und 1. Maerz 1914." W.A.

160. See the letter from Yehiel Tschlenow and Victor Jacobson dated March 11, 1914. W.A.

161. Weizmann to Gaston Wormster, January 15, 1914, *WL* 6, p. 205.

162. See Victor Jacobson to Yehiel Tschlenow, April 2, 1914. CZA, Z3/407.

163. Weizmann to Vera, March 27, 1914, *WL* 6, p. 303.

164. Weizmann to Ahad Ha'Am, March 28, 1914, *WL* 6, p. 304.

165. Weizmann to Vera, April 1, 1914, *WL* 6, p. 307.

166. It seems that Weizmann also saw Rothschild on April 3, 1914, but it is possible that he just handed materials intended for the baron to Wormser.

167. Weizmann to Paul Ehrlich, April 9, 1914, *WL* 6, p. 318.

168. Weizmann to SAC, April 13, 1914, *WL* 6, pp. 320–21.

169. Ibid., pp. 321–22. For a short description of James Rothschild, see Schama, *Two Rothschilds and the Land of Israel*, pp. 188–89.

170. E.g., in Paris in April 1914. See excerpts from his speech there in Sieff Archives, Marks and Spencer, London. Copy in W.A.

171. The only one to lavish praise on Weizmann was Magnes: "Ich kann es nicht umhin wieder Ihnen zu ihrer grosszuegigen, verstaendnisvollen, praktischen Arbeit zu gratulieren. Sie sind mit Energie, mit Gewissen, mit Muth und mit Verstand *(sekhel)* vorgegangen . . ." Magnes to Weizmann, June 8, 1914. W.A

172. *WL* 6, p. 335, n. 3. Underlying these criticisms—to which Yehiel Tschlenow was a party—was a certain resentment at the manner in which Weizmann conducted his negotiations and a disappointment at the comparatively small sums of money the baron was willing to expend on the university.

173. Weizmann to SAC, April 26, 1914, *WL* 6, pp. 335–39. The letter to SAC was sent "unofficially" to Shmarya Levin, who, of course, showed it to all concerned.

174. Victor Jacobson, e.g., did *not* share Jabotinsky's views. See Jacobson to SAC, May 10, 1914. W.A. On the other hand, Ernst Lesser, Leon Simon, and Arthur Ruppin were among those who did not favor the research institute as conceived by the baron.

175. Weizmann to Shmarya Levin, April 26, 1914, *WL* 6, pp. 341–42.

176. Ruppin asked Weizmann for a power of attorney signed by the Turkish consul in Manchester. See Arthur Ruppin to Weizmann, April 7, 1914. W.A. See also Arthur Ruppin to SAC, May 18, 1914 (CZA, Z3/1611), and Menahem Ussishkin to SAC, April 26, 1914 (W.A.), discussing the financial terms on which the land on Mount Scopus was to be purchased.

177. See "Sitzung des Arbeits-Ausschusses fuer die Universitaet vom 6. and 10. Juni 1914." W.A.

178. See "Beschluesse der Sitzung des Actions-Comité vom 7. and 8. Juni 1914." CZA, Z3/449.

179. See Judah Magnes to Weizmann, June 8, 10, 1914. W.A. See also Simon Flexner to Weizmann, July 22, 1914. W.A. Flexner expressed his interest in the project but recommended a training institute not exclusively devoted to research.

180. See "Besprechung des in Berlin anwesenden Mitglieder des Arbeitsaus-schusses am 18. und 19. Juli 1914." CZA, Z3/1601 and W.A.
181. Originally it was scheduled for the tenth. See CZA, Z3/1661. An updated proposal was prepared for this meeting, in line with the discussions of the preparatory committee on July 18 and 19, 1914. See "Denkschrift ueber die Begruendung eines Juedischen Medizinisch naturwissenschaftlichen Insti-tuts in Jerusalem." CZA, Z3/1602. A copy was sent to James Rothschild.
182. Weizmann's summer plans also included work in Ehrlich's Frankfurt labo-ratory.
183. Weizmann to Julius Simon, June 12, 1914, WL 6, p. 379.

XVII Conclusion

1. Louis Lipsky, "Weizmann—Bond Between Two Worlds," in *Chaim Weiz-mann: Statesman, Scientist, Builder of the Jewish Commonwealth,* ed. Meyer W. Weisgal (New York, 1944), p. 167. Another version of this recollection can be found in Louis Lipsky, *A Gallery of Zionist Profiles* (New York, 1956), pp. 51–52, and in *The American Zionist,* December 15, 1952. See also Jacob Ho-dess, "Weizmann: Scientist and Statesman," *The Jerusalem Post: Chaim Weiz-mann Memorial Supplement,* October 30, 1953, p. iii. Hodess's description of Weizmann prior to 1914 closely matches that of Lipsky.
2. Leonard Stein, "Koho shel Chaim Weizmann," *Haaretz,* November 2, 1962, p. 9.
3. That Weizmann was not even considered for the leadership of the World Zionist Organization is evident from a lead article in *The Jewish Chronicle* of July 2, 1915, pp. 7–8. The article, marking the anniversary of Herzl's death, states: "To-day . . . we miss the inspiring leadership of a Herzl—of a man who can seize with imagination and vigour the Jewish interests at stake and present them to the world when the welter of the conflict has subsided. . . ." *The Jewish Chronicle* was, of course, not favorably disposed toward Weizmann, but this particular article reflects a point of view that was prob-ably shared even by Weizmann's friends.
4. See Ben-Zion Dinur, "Yihudo shel Chaim Weizmann," *Molad* 11, no. 64 (October 1953): 159.
5. See Robert Weltsch in *Haaretz,* October 5, 1979.
6. See Hodess, "Weizmann: Scientist and Statesman," p. iii.
7. In 1911, at a conference of the English Zionist Federation in Manchester, Weizmann said, "The English Gentiles are the best Gentiles in the world." See Israel M. Sieff, "The Manchester Period," in *Chaim Weizmann: A Biog-raphy by Several Hands,* ed. Meyer W. Weisgal and Joel Carmichael (New York, 1963), p. 92.
8. See Leonard Stein, *Weizmann and England* (London, 1964), p. 13.

Bibliography

Archives and Libraries

Ahad Ha'Am Archive, Jerusalem
Brandeis University Library
Louis D. Brandeis Papers, University of Louisville
Bodleian Library, Department of Western Manuscripts (Stein Papers)
British Library, London
British Museum
Buber Archive, Jerusalem
Central Library, Manchester
Central Zionist Archives [CZA], Jerusalem
Ehrenpreis Archive, Jerusalem
Guardian Archives, Manchester
Harvard University Archives
Harvard University—Widener Library
HUC-JIR—The Klau Library, New York
Israel State Archives, Jerusalem
Jewish National and University Library, Jerusalem
Kressel Collection, Oxford Centre for Postgraduate Hebrew Studies
David Lloyd George Papers, House of Lords Record Office
Manchester Polytechnic Archives, Manchester Studies Unit
Mocatta Library, University College, London
New York Public Library
Oxford University Archives
Public Record Office, London
John Rylands Library of the University of Manchester (Campus Building and
    Deansgate Building)
University of Manchester, Files of the Department of Chemistry and Registrar's
    Office
Weizmann Archives [W.A.], Rehovot
YIVO Archives

Newspapers and Selected Reference Works

Bulletin of the Research Council of Israel
Davar

Der Jude
Der Fraind
Der Tog
Dictionary of National Biography
Dictionary of Scientific Biography
Die Welt
L'Echo Sioniste
Encyclopaedia Judaica
Evreiskaia Entsiklopedia
Frimorgn
Haaretz
Hadoar
Ha-Enziklopedia ha-Ivrit
Haint
Ha-Karmel
Hamelitz
Handels-Zeitung des Berliner Tagesblattes
Hapoel Hazair
Ha-Shahar
Hashiloah
Hatzfirah
Haumah
Hazman
Hazvi
Heavar
Hegeh
Herzl Year Books
The Jerusalem Post
The Jewish Chronicle
Jewish Encyclopedia
Juedische Rundschau
Kovez Hashomer
The Maccabaean
The Manchester Guardian
Mitteilungsblatt: Wochenzeitung des Irgun Olej Merkas Europa
Ost und West
The Owens College Union Magazine
Selbst-Emancipation
Shivat Zion
The Times of London
Voskhod
Vossische Zeitung
Yiddisher Arbeiter
The Zionist
The Zionist Banner

Primary Sources

Ahad Ha'Am [Asher Ginsberg]. "Habokkim." *Hashiloah* 9, nos. 59–60 (November–December 1902): 145–52.

————. *Igrot Ahad Ha'Am.* Vol. 4: 1908–12; Vol. 5: 1913–17. Berlin and Jerusalem: Yavneh & Moriah Press, 1923–25.

————. "Shlilat ha-Galut." In *Kol Kitvei Ahad Ha'Am,* pp. 399–403. Tel Aviv: Hozaah Ivrit, 1947.

————. "Tehiyat ha-Ruah." *Hashiloah* 9, nos. 59–60 (November–December 1902): 385–99, 481–91.

Aaronsohn, Aaron. *Yoman Aaron Aaronsohn.* Edited by Yoram Efrati and translated by Uri Kesari. Tel Aviv: Karny, 1970.

Asquith, Herbert Henry. *Memories and Reflections, 1852–1927.* 2 vols. Boston: Little, Brown, 1928.

————. *Moments of Memory.* New York: Scribner, 1938.

Auerbach, Elias. *Pionier der Verwirklichung.* Stuttgart: Deutsche Verlags-Anstalt, 1969.

Aus dem Protokoll der Kommission der Demokratisch-zionistischen Fraktion. Berlin: [n.p.], 1902. [W.A.]

Bambus, Willy. *Herr Motzkin und die Wahrheit ueber die Kolonisation Palaestinas.* Berlin: A. Weichert, 1898.

————. *Die juedischen Ackerbaukolonien in Palaestina und ihre Geschichte.* Berlin: H. Schildberger, 1895.

————. *Palaestina in der Gegenwart.* Berlin: B. Epstein, [1891].

Bashan, Rafael. *Sihot Hulin shel Weizmann.* Jerusalem: Ha-Sifriyah Ha-Zionit, 1963.

Beilis, Mendel. *Die Geschichte fun meine Leiden.* New York: Mendel Beilis Publishing Co., 1925.

Belkovsky, Zvi. "Eikh Husag ha-Rishayon le-Veidat Minsk?" *Hazioni Haklali,* no. 5, January 20, 1933. W.A.

Ben Yehuda. "Open Letter to the Editor of *Ha-Shahar.*" *Ha-Shahar* 10 (1880): 242–45.

Bentwich, Norman. *My 77 Years: An Account of My Life and Times, 1883–1960.* Philadelphia: Jewish Publication Society of America, 1961.

Berger, Yitzhak. "Weizmann Tahat ha-Krashim." *Davar,* April 22, 1935, p. 2.

Bernstein-Kohan, Jacob. *Sefer Bernstein-Kohan.* Edited by Miriam Bernstein-Kohan. Tel Aviv: Hug Yozei Bessarabia, 1946.

Bertie, Francis. *The Diary of Lord Bertie of Thame.* London: Hodder and Stoughton, 1924. Vol. 1.

Bialik, Haim Nahman. "Gviyat Edut mi-Pi Nifgeei Praot Kishinev bi-Shnat 1903." *Heavar* 1, no. 1 (1953): 18–30.

————. "In the City of Slaughter." Translated by Abraham M. Klein. In *The Complete Works of Hayyim Nahman Bialik,* edited by Israel Efros, vol. 1, pp. 129, 133–34. New York: Histadruth Ivrith of America, 1948.

Bodenheimer, Max. *So Wurde Israel.* Frankfurt am Main: Europaeische Verlagsanstalt, 1958.

The Book of Manchester and Salford. Manchester, Eng.: George Falkner and Sons, 1929.

Borochov, Ber. *Ktavim.* Tel Aviv: Sifriyat Poalim and Ha-Kibbutz Ha-Meuchad, 1954–55. Vol. 3.

————. *Nationalism and the Class Struggle.* Edited and introduced by Abraham G. Duker. Westport, Conn.: Greenwood Press, 1972.

Brodetsky, Selig. *Memoirs: From Ghetto to Israel.* London: Weidenfeld and Nicolson, 1960.

Buber, Martin. *Briefwechsel aus sieben Jahrzehnten.* Vol. 1: 1897–1918. Edited by Grete Schaeder. Heidelberg: Verlag Lambert Schneider, 1972.

————, Berthold Feiwel, and Chaim Weizmann. *Eine juedische Hochschule*. Berlin: Juedischer Verlag, 1902.

Cahan, Abraham. *Bleter fun mayn Lebn*. New York: Forward Association, 1926. Vol. 2.

Chamberlain, Joseph. *A Political Memoir, 1880–1892*. Edited by C. H. D. Howard. London: Batchworth Press, 1953.

Chemerinsky, Chaim. "Ayarti Motele." *Reshumot*. 2nd ed., edited by Alter Druyanov, vol. 2, pp. 5–124. Tel Aviv: Dvir, 1927.

————. *Ayarti Motele*. Reprint ed. Tel Aviv: Dvir, 1951.

Cohen, Israel. *The Journal of a Jewish Traveller*. London: John Lane, The Bodley Head, 1925.

Cohen, Yaakov. "Krovim ve-Rehokim, Mi-Pirkei Zikhronotai." *Moznaim* 2 (1959): 93–104.

Cohn-Reiss, Ephraim. *Mi-Zikhronot Ish Yerushalayim*. Jerusalem: Sifriyat Ha-Yishuv, 1967.

Dorfman, Catherine. Letter to *Hapoel Hazair*, November 10, 1933. Kressel Collection, Oxford Centre for Postgraduate Hebrew Studies.

Druyanov, Alter. *Ktavim le-Toldot Hibbat Zion*. Tel Aviv: Ha-Vaad le-Yishuv Eretz Israel, 1930. Vol. 3.

Dugdale, Blanche. "Weizmann and Balfour." In *Chaim Weizmann: Statesman, Scientist, Builder of the Jewish Commonwealth*, edited by Meyer W. Weisgal, pp. 129–34. New York: Dial Press, 1944.

Efros, Israel, ed. *Complete Poetic Works of Hayyim Nahman Bialik*. New York: Histadruth Ivrith of America, 1948.

Eiges, Yehuda. *Yalkut A. D. Gordon*. Jerusalem: Ha-Histadrut Ha-Zionit, 1958.

Eliash, Josef. *Zikhronot Zioni mi-Russyah*. Tel Aviv: Ha-Sifriyah Ha-Zionit, 1955.

English Zionist Federation. *General Election, 1900: Opinions of Parliamentary Candidates on Zionism*. London: Philip Johns, 1900.

Evans-Gordon, Sir William Eden. *The Alien Immigrant*. London: W. Heinemann, 1903.

Frederic, Harold. *The New Exodus: Israel in Russia*. London: W. Heinemann, 1892.

Gapon, Father George. *The Story of My Life*. New York: Dutton, 1906.

Gibbons, A. St. Hill, Alfred Kaiser, and Nahum Wilbush. *Report on the Work of the Commission Sent Out by the Zionist Organization to Examine the Territory Offered by His Majesty's Government for the Purposes of a Jewish Settlement in British East Africa*. London: Wertheimer, Lea, 1905.

Glickson, M. "Zikhronot Rishonim." *Haaretz*, November 17, 1933, p. 5.

Goldbloom, Jacob K. "Reminiscences of Zionism in Great Britain." In *The Rebirth of Israel: A Memorial Tribute to Paul Goodman*, edited by Israel Cohen, pp. 61–76. London: Edward Goldston and Son, 1952.

Gordon, Judah Leib. "Hakiza Ami." *Ha-Karmel* 6, no. 1 (1866): 1.

Gruzenberg, Oscar. *Yesterday: Memoirs of a Russian-Jewish Lawyer*. Edited with an introduction by Don C. Rawson. Berkeley: University of California Press, 1981.

Hansard's Parliamentary Debates. 4th ser., vol. 134 (1904), cols. 561–79; vol. 148 (1905), cols. 155–56.

Hermoni, Aaron. *Be-Ikvot ha-Biluim*. Jerusalem: Rubin Mass, 1952.

Herzl, Theodor. *Bifnei Am ve-Olam. Neumim Umaamarim Zionim: 1895–1899, 1899–1904*. Jerusalem: Ha-Sifriyah Ha-Zionit, 1975. Vols. 1 and 2.

————. *The Complete Diaries of Theodor Herzl*. Edited by Raphael Patai and translated by Harry Zohn. New York: Herzl Press, 1960.

———. *Der Judenstaat: Versuch einer modernen Loesung der Judenfrage.* Leipzig and Vienna: M. Breitenstein's Verlags-Buchhandlung, 1896.

Hesse, Max. *On the Effective Use of Charitable Loans to the Poor Without Interest.* Manchester: Central Library of Manchester, 1901.

Jewish Colonization Association. *Recueil de Matériaux sur la Situation Economique des Israélites de Russie.* Paris: Jewish Colonization Association, 1906.

Jewish University Bureau. Juedische Hochschule. Abeilung A. "Einzel-Enquête veranstaltet unter den auslaendischen (russischen, rumaenischen, etc.) juedischen Studierenden der westeuropaeischen Hoschschulen." [CZA]

Kahanovich, Yehuda Leib. *Me-Homel ad Tel Aviv.* Tel Aviv: Ha-Vaad le-Hotzaat Maamarei Y. L. Kahanovich, 1952.

Kelly's Directory of Manchester, 1905. London: Kelly's Directories, Ltd., 1905.

Kelly's Directory of Manchester, 1908. London: Kelly's Directories, Ltd., 1908.

Klausner, Joseph. "Chaim Weizmann: Early Memories." In *Chaim Weizmann: A Tribute on his Seventieth Birthday,* edited by Paul Goodman, pp. 36–41. London: Victor Gollancz, 1954.

———. "Ha-Kongress ha-Zioni ha-Hamishi." *Hashiloah* 9 (January 1902): 63–83.

Levin, Shmarya. *Forward from Exile.* Translated and edited by Maurice Samuel. Philadelphia: Jewish Publication Society of America, 1967.

———. "Ha-Binyan ve-Hastirah." *Bi-Yemei ha-Maavar,* pp. 207–12. New York: Assaf, 1919.

———. *Igrot.* Tel Aviv: Dvir, 1966.

———. *Youth in Revolt.* New York: Harcourt, Brace and Company, 1930.

Levontin, Zalman David. *Le-Eretz Avotenu.* Tel Aviv: n.p., 1928.

Lichtheim, Richard. *Rueckkehr: Lebenserrinerungen aus der Fruehzeit des deutschen Zionismus.* Stuttgart: Deutsche Verlags-Anstalt, 1970.

Lilienblum, Moshe Leib. *Kol Kitvei Moshe Leib Lilienblum.* Cracow: Joseph Zeitlin, 1910. Vol. 1.

Lilienthal, Max. "Meine Reisen in Russland." *Juedisches Volksblatt* 3 (1856): no. 28, pp. 110–11; no. 29, pp. 114–15; no. 33, pp. 129–31.

Lipsky, Louis. *A Gallery of Zionist Profiles.* New York: Farrar, Straus and Cudahy, 1956.

———. *Memoirs in Profile.* Philadelphia: Jewish Publication Society of America, 1975.

Litvinoff, Barnet, ed. *The Letters and Papers of Chaim Weizmann.* Vol. 1, ser. B: 1898–1931. New Brunswick, N.J.: Transaction Books, Rutgers University; Jerusalem: Israel Universities Press, 1983.

Lloyd George, David. *War Memoirs of David Lloyd George, 1915–1916.* Boston: Little, Brown, 1933.

Loewe, Heinrich. "Eine Vorbedingung der Universitaet." *Die Welt,* no. 14, April 3, 1914, pp. 328–29.

———. "Rede, gehalten in der ersten Sitzung des Juedisch-nationalen Vereins 'Jung Israel' in Berlin am 31. Mai 1892." *Selbst-Emancipation* 14 (July 18, 1892): 142–44.

Marmorek, Oskar. "Ein Epilog." *Die Welt,* no. 2, January 10, 1902, p. 2.

Masliansky, Zvi Hirsch. *Droshes fir Shabosim un Yomim Toyvim.* 2 vols. New York: Hebrew Publishing Co., 1908.

Medem, Vladimir. *Vladimir Medem: The Life and Soul of a Legendary Jewish Socialist.* Translated from the Yiddish by Samuel A. Portnoy. New York: Ktav Publishing House, 1979.

Motzkin, Leo. *Die Judenpogrome in Russland.* 2 vols. Herausgegeben im Auftrage des Zionistischen Helfsfonds in London von Der Zur Erforschung der Pogrome Eingesetzten Kommission. Cologne and Leipzig: Juedischer Verlag, 1909–10.

———. "Rede des cand. math. L. Motzkin, gehalten im russisch-jued. wiss. Verein in Berlin an dem IV Stiftungs- und Makkabaeerfeste desselben vor einem zum groesseren Theile aus deutschen Juden bestehenden Publicum." *Selbst-Emancipation* (February 1, 1892): 31–32.

———. *Sefer Motzkin.* Edited by Alex Bein. Jerusalem: Ha-Hanhalah ha-Zionit ve-ha-Congress ha-Yehudi ha-Olami, 1939.

Nimzovitz, Yitzhak. "Rabbi Ivan Smyoshkin the XIV." *Hador* (September 25, 1955): 2.

Nordau, Max. *Erinnerungen.* Leipzig and Vienna: Renaissance-Verlag, 1928.

———. *Ktavim Zionim.* 4 vols. Jerusalem: Ha-Sifriyah ha-Zionit, 1954–62.

Nurok, Mordecai. *Veidat Zionei Russyah be-Minsk.* Introduction by Israel Klausner. Jerusalem: Ha-Sifriyah ha-Zionit, 1963.

Pickles, Samuel S., and Charles Weizmann. "The Effects of Anhydrides on Organomagnesium Bromides." *Proceedings of the Chemical Society* 20 (1904): 201.

———. "Halogen Derivatives of Naphthacenequinone." *Proceedings of the Chemical Society* 20 (1904): 220.

Program der Grossherzoglich Hessischen Technischen Hochschule zu Darmstadt fuer das Studienjahr 1892–1893. Darmstadt: Technischen Hochschule, 1892.

Rappard, William E. *A la Mémoire de Chaim Weizmann.* Neuchâtel: Editions de la Baconnière, 1953.

———. "Great Humanitarian." *The Jerusalem Post: Chaim Weizmann Memorial Supplement,* p. 1. October 30, 1953.

"Report of the Duma Commission on the Bialystok Massacre." *American Jewish Year Book 1906–7.* Philadelphia, Jewish Publication Society of America, 1906, pp. 70–89.

Reznick, Shlomo. "Zror Mikhtavim shel Chaim Weizmann ha-Zair." *Karmelit* 14–15 (1969): 411–22.

Robinson, Robert. "Chaim Weizmann at Manchester." *Rehovot* 5, no. 3 (Winter 1969–70): 30–31.

Ruppin, Arthur. *Memoirs, Diaries, Letters.* Edited by Alex Bein and translated by Karen Gershon. New York: Herzl Press, 1971.

———. *Arthur Ruppin, Pirke Hayai.* Edited by Alex Bein. 3 vols. Tel Aviv: Am Oved, 1968.

———. "Memorandum an das Aktionskomitee der Zionistischen Organisation, 10. November 1907." In *Dreissig Jahre Aufbau in Palaestina,* pp. 9–18. Berlin: Schocken Verlag, 1937.

Samuel, Maurice. *Level Sunlight.* New York: Knopf, 1953.

———. *Little Did I Know: Recollections and Reflections.* New York: Knopf, 1963.

Samuel, Viscount Herbert. *Memoirs.* London: Cresset Press, 1945.

Scott, Charles Prestwich. *The Political Diaries of C. P. Scott, 1911–1928.* Edited by Trevor Wilson. New York: Cornell University Press, 1970.

Sefer Toldot Ha-Haganah. Tel Aviv: Am Oved and Ha-Sifriyah ha-Zionit, 1954. Vol. 1.

Seliger, Josef. "Sonderbare Auswuechse." *Der Israelit,* no. 87 (3 November 1902): 1823–24.

Sieff, Israel. *Memoirs.* London: Weidenfeld and Nicolson, 1970.

Simon, Julius. *Certain Days.* Edited by Evyatar Friesel. Jerusalem: Israel Universities Press, 1971.

Simon, Leon, ed. *Selected Essays of Ahad Ha'Am.* New York: Atheneum, 1970.

Smolenskin, Perez. "Foreword." *Ha-Shahar,* vol. 1 (1868), pp. 5–7.

Stenographisches Protokoll der Verhandlungen des II. Zionisten-Kongresses gehalten zu Basel vom 28. bis 31. August 1898. Vienna: Zionist Organization, 1898.

Stenographisches Protokoll der Verhandlungen des III. Zionisten-Kongresses gehalten zu Basel vom 15. bis 18. August 1899. Vienna: "Erez Israel" [at] "Industrie," 1899.

Stenographisches Protokoll der Verhandlungen des IV. Zionisten-Kongresses in London, 1900. Vienna: "Erez Israel" [at] "Industrie," 1900.

Stenographisches Protokoll der Verhandlungen des V. Zionisten-Kongresses in Basel vom 26. 27. 28. 29. und 30. Dezember 1901. Vienna: "Erez Israel" [at] "Industrie," 1901.

Stenographisches Protokoll der Verhandlungen des VI. Zionisten-Kongresses in Basel vom 23. 24. 25. 26. 27. und 28. August 1903. Vienna: "Erez Israel" [at] "Industrie," 1903.

Stenographisches Protokoll der Verhandlungen des VII. Zionisten-Kongresses und des ausserordentlichen Kongresses in Basel vom 27. 28. 29. 31. Juli, 1. und 2. August 1905. Berlin: Juedischer Verlag, 1905.

Stenographisches Protokoll der Verhandlungen des VIII. Zionisten-Kongresses im Haag vom 14. bis inklusive 21. August 1907. Cologne: Juedischer Verlag, 1907.

Stenographisches Protokoll der Verhandlungen des IX. Zionisten-Kongresses in Hamburg vom 26. bis inklusive 30. Dezember 1909. Cologne: Juedischer Verlag, 1910.

Stenographisches Protokoll der Verhandlungen des X. Zionisten-Kongresses in Basel vom 9. bis inklusive 15. August 1911. Berlin: Juedischer Verlag, 1911.

Stenographisches Protokoll der Verhandlungen des XI. Zionisten-Kongresses in Wien vom 2. bis 9. September 1913. Berlin and Leipzig: Juedischer Verlag, 1914.

Syrkin, Nachman. *Kitvei Nachman Syrkin.* Edited by Berl Katznelson and Judah Kaufman. Tel Aviv: Dvir, 1939.

Turgenev, Ivan. "The Jew." In *The Collected Works of Ivan Turgenev,* pp. 409–21. New York: Greystone Press, n.d.

Ussishkin, Menahem Mendel. *Sefer Ussishkin,* ed. R. Benyamin. Jerusalem: Ha-Vaad le-Hotsaat ha-Sefer, 1934.

———. "Ha-Programah Shelanu." *Sefer Ussishkin,* ed. R. Benyamin, pp. 95–125. Jerusalem: Ezriel, 1934.

Weinberg, Jehuda Louis. *Aus der Fruehzeit des Zionismus. Heinrich Loewe.* Jerusalem: Rubin Mass, 1946.

Weizmann, Chaim. *Dvarim: Neumim, Maamarim, u-Mikhtavim.* 4 vols. Tel Aviv: Mizpeh, 1936–37.

———. "Elektrolytische Reduktion von 1-Nitroanthrachinon; Ueber die Kondensation von Phenanthrenchinon und Nitroanthrachinon mit einigen Phenolen." Inaugural-Dissertation der mathematisch-naturwissenschaftlichen Fakultaet der Universitaet Freiburg in der Schweiz zur Erlangung der Doktorwuerde vorgelegt von Dr. Ch. Weizmann aus Pinsk. Bern, 1899.

———. *Israel und sein Land. Reden und Ansprachen.* London: Keren Hayessod, 1924.

———. *The Letters and Papers of Chaim Weizmann.* Edited by Meyer W. Weisgal et al. English ed., vols. 1–3, ser. A. London: Oxford University Press and Yad Chaim Weizmann, 1968–1972; vols. 4–7, ser A. Jerusalem: Israel Universities Press, 1973–75.

———. *Reden und Aufsaetze, 1901–1936.* Edited by Gustav Krojanker. Tel Aviv: Hitachduth Olej Germania, 1937.

———. *Trial and Error.* New York: Schocken Books, 1949.

———, and Richard Gottheil. *What Is Zionism?* London: Zionist Organization, 1918.

Weizmann, Leah. "Em Weizmann." *Hegeh,* August 27, 1939, p. 7.

Weizmann, Vera. *The Impossible Takes Longer.* New York and Evanston: Harper & Row, 1967.

Weizmann-Lichtenstein, Hayah. *Be-Zel Koratenu.* Tel Aviv: Am Oved, 1948.

Wilbush, Nahum. *Ha-Masa le-Uganda.* Jerusalem: Ha-Sifriyah ha-Zionit, 1963.

Wilbushevitz-Shohat, Manya. "Ha-Shmirah ba-Aretz." *Kovez ha-Shomer,* pp. 51–56. Tel Aviv: Sefer and Archive of the Labor Movement, 1937.

Wilson, Trevor, ed. *The Political Diaries of C. P. Scott, 1911–1928.* Ithaca, N.Y.: Cornell University Press, 1970.

Yaari, Abraham. *Igrot Eretz Israel.* Tel Aviv: Massadah, 1943.

Zangwill, Israel. *Speeches, Articles and Letters of Israel Zangwill.* London: Soncino Press, 1937.

Zeitlin, Hillel. "Hamashber." *Hazman* 1, no. 8 (August 1905): 278.

Zeldin, Morris A. "Chaim Weizmann ve-Shmarya Levin (Perek me-Zikhronotai)." *Bizaron* 62 (1971): 255–57.

Zionisten-Congress in Basel (29. 30. und 31. August 1897). Officielles Protocoll. Vienna: Verein "Erez Israel," 1898.

Zionistiches Actions Comité. *Im Kampf um die Hebraeische Sprache.* Berlin: Zionistiches Actions Comité, 1914.

Secondary Sources

Abramowicz, Z. "Tnuat 'Poalei Zion' be-Russyah." *Kazir* I (1964): 105–21.

Abramsky, Chimen. "Emdat Lenin Klapei ha-Yehudim." In *Harzaot bi-Knasei ha-Iyun be-Historyah,* pp. 369–74. Jerusalem: Ha-Hevrah Ha-Historit Ha-Israelit, 1963.

———. "Weizmann: A New Type of Leadership in the Zionist Movement." *Jewish Historical Society of England, Transactions,* sess. 1973–75, vol. 25, and *Miscellanies,* part 10, pp. 137–49. London: Jewish Historical Society of England, 1977.

Adams, R. J. Q. *Arms and the Wizard: Lloyd George and the Ministry of Munitions.* College Station, Tex.: Texas A & M University Press, 1978.

Adler, Cyrus, ed. *The Voice of America on Kishineff.* Philadelphia: Jewish Publication Society of America, 1904.

Adler-Rudel, Shalom. *Ostjuden in Deutschland, 1880–1940.* Tübingen: J. C. B. Mohr, 1959.

Alderman, Geoffrey. *The Jewish Community in British Politics.* London: Oxford University Press, 1982.

Almog, Shmuel. *Zionut ve-Historyah.* Jerusalem: Magnes Press, 1982.

Alpert, Carl. *Technion: The Story of Israel's Institute of Technology.* New York: American Technion Society, 1982.

Alsberg, Paul A. "Documents on the Brussels Conference of 1906." *Michael.* Edited by Shlomo Simonsohn and Jacob Toury, vol. 2, pp. 145–177. Tel Aviv: The Diaspora Research Institute, 1973.

———. "Mediniyut ha-Hanhalah ha-Zionit mi-Moto shel Herzl ve-ad Milhemet ha-Olam ha-Rishonah." Diss., Hebrew University, 1957.

———. "Ha-Orientazia shel Mediniyut ha-Hanhalah ha-Zionit Erev Milhemet ha-Olam ha-Rishonah 1911–1914." *Zion* 22, nos. 2–3 (1957): 165–70.

———. "Ha-Sheelah ha-Aravit bi-Mediniyut ha-Hanhalah ha-Zionit lifnei Milhemet ha-Olam ha-Rishonah." Edited by Ben Zion Dinur and Israel Heilprin. *Shivat Zion* 4, pp. 161–209. Jerusalem: Ha-Sifriyah ha-Zionit, 1956.

Alston, Patrick L. *Education and the State in Tsarist Russia*. Stanford, Calif.: Stanford University Press, 1969.

Alteras, Isaac. "Jews Under Tsarism and Communism." *Midstream* 27, no. 5 (May 1981): 37–40.

Amery, Julian. *The Life of Joseph Chamberlain*. London: Macmillan, 1951. Vol. 4.

Arnsberg, Paul. *Die juedischen Gemeinden in Hessen*. 2 vols. Frankfurt am Main: Societas-Verlag, 1971.

Aronsfeld, C. C. "Jewish Bankers and the Tsar." *Jewish Social Studies* 35, no. 2 (April 1973): 87–104.

Aronson, I. Michael. "Geographical and Socio-economic Factors in the 1881 Anti-Jewish Pogroms in Russia." *Russian Review* 39, no. 1 (January 1980): 18–31.

———. "The Attitude of Russian Officials in the 1880s Toward Jewish Assimilation and Emigration." *Slavic Review* 34, no. 1 (March 1975): 1–18.

———. "The Prospects for the Emancipation of Russian Jewry during the 1880s." *Slavonic and East European Review* 55, no. 3 (July 1977): 348–69.

Aschheim, Steven. *Brothers and Strangers: The East European Jew in Germany and German Jewish Consciousness, 1800–1923*. Madison: University of Wisconsin Press, 1982.

Avizur, Shmuel. "Ha-Haklaut, ha-Melakhah ve-ha-Taasiyah." In *Sefer ha-Aliyah ha-Rishonah*, edited by Mordechai Eliav, pp. 297–318. Jerusalem: Yad Yitzhak Ben-Zvi, 1981.

Ayerst, David. *The Manchester Guardian: Biography of a Newspaper*. Ithaca, N.Y.: Cornell University Press, 1971.

Azoury, Negib. *Le Réveil de la Nation Arabe dans l'Asie Turque en Présence des Intérêts et des Rivalités des Puissances Etrangères, de la Curie Romaine et du Patriarcat Oecuménique*. Paris: Plon-Nourrit, 1905.

Baker, Rachel. *Chaim Weizmann: Builder of a Nation*. New York: Julian Messner, 1950.

Bar-Nir, Dov. "Gadlut Utaharut shel Manhigim." *Al Hamishmar*, August 20, 1976, p. 8.

Baron, Salo W. *The Russian Jew Under Tsars and Soviets*. 2nd ed., rev. and enl. New York: Macmillan, 1976.

Baron, Samuel H. *Plekhanov, the Father of Russian Marxism*. Stanford, Calif.: Stanford University Press, 1963.

Barzilay-Yegar, Devorah. "Crisis as Turning Point: Chaim Weizmann in World War I." *Studies in Zionism* 6 (Autumn 1982): 241–54.

Bein, Alex. "Arthur Ruppin: The Man and His Work." *Leo Baeck Institute Year Book* 17 (1972): 117–71.

———. "Ha-Massa u-Matan beyn Herzl le-veyn Memshelet Britanyah ha-Gdolah be-Inyan El Arish." *Shivat Zion*, vol. 1, pp. 179–220. Jerusalem: Ha-Sifriyah ha-Zionit, 1950.

———. *Theodore Herzl*. New York and Philadelphia: Jewish Publication Society of America, 1962.

————. *Toldot ha-Hityashvut ha-Zionit mi-Tkufat Herzl ve-ad Yamenu.* 4th ed. Ramat Gan: Massadah Press, 1970.

————. ed. *Sefer Motzkin.* Jerusalem: Ha-Hanhalah ha-Zionit, 1939.

Ben-Sasson, Haim Hillel, and Shmuel Ettinger, eds. *Jewish Society Through the Ages.* New York: Schocken, 1971.

Bentwich, Margery and Norman. *Herbert Bentwich, the Pilgrim Father.* Jerusalem: Hozaah Iwrith, 1940.

Bergmann, Ernst D. "Obituary Notice—Chaim Weizmann." *Journal of the Chemical Society,* part 3 (August 1953), p. 2841.

————. "Avodato ha-Madait shel Chaim Weizmann," *Mada* 17, no. 3 (1972): 168–75.

————. "Bergmann on Weizmann." *Rehovot* 8, no. 1 (Spring 1976): 52–61.

————. "The Example of Weizmann's Science." *The Jerusalem Post,* November 2, 1969, p. 3.

Berlin, G. L. "The Brandeis-Weizmann Dispute." *American Jewish Historical Quarterly* 60 (1970): 37–68.

Berlin, Isaiah. *Chaim Weizmann.* Herzl Institute Pamphlet No. 8. New York: Herzl Institute, 1958.

————. "Chaim Weizmann 'ke-Resh Galuta.' " *Bitfutzot ha-Golah* 16, nos. 71–72 (1974–75): 7–11.

————. *Four Essays on Liberty.* London: Oxford University Press, 1969.

————. *Personal Impressions.* Edited by Henry Hardy. New York: Viking, 1980.

————, and Kolatt, Israel. *Chaim Weizmann as Leader.* Jerusalem: Institute of Contemporary Jewry, The Hebrew University, 1970.

Bermant, Chaim. *Point of Arrival: A Study of London's East End.* London: Eyre Methuen, 1975.

Best, Gary Dean. *To Free a People: American Jewish Leaders and the Jewish Problem in Eastern Europe, 1890–1914.* Westport, Conn.: Greenwood Press, 1982.

Blakeley, Brian. *Colonial Office, 1868–1892.* Durham, N.C.: Duke University Press, 1972.

Blumberg, Harold M. *Weizmann: His Life and Times.* New York: St. Martin's Press, 1975.

Boehm, Adolf. *Die Zionistische Bewegung bis zum Ende des Weltkrieges.* 2nd ed., rev. Tel Aviv: Hozaah Ivrith, 1935.

Bourne, Kenneth. *Foreign Policy of Victorian England, 1830–1902.* Oxford: Clarendon Press, 1970.

Brachmann, Botho. *Russische Socialdemokraten in Berlin, 1895–1914.* Berlin: Akademie-Verlag, 1962.

Braslavsky, Moshe. *Tnuat ha-Poalim ha-Eretz Israelit: Ziyunim u-Mekorot.* Ein Harod: Ha-Kibbutz Ha-Meuhad, 1942.

Brindley, W. H. *The Soul of Manchester.* Manchester: Manchester University Press, 1929.

British Association for the Advancement of Science. *Manchester and Its Region.* Manchester: Manchester University Press, 1962.

Burkhardt, G. N. "Prof. A. Lapworth, F.R.S." *Nature* 147 (June 21, 1941): 769–70.

————. "The School of Chemistry in the University of Manchester (Faculty of Science)." *Journal of the Royal Institute of Chemistry* (September 1954): 448–60.

Burstein, Moshe. *Self-Government of the Jews in Palestine Since 1900.* Tel Aviv: privately printed, 1934.

Butler, David, and Jennie Freeman. *British Political Facts, 1900–1967.* 2nd ed. London: Macmillan, 1968.

Byrnes, Robert F. *Pobedonostsev: His Life and Thought.* Bloomington: Indiana University Press, 1968.

Calder, Ritchie. "The Chemistry of Statesmanship." *Rehovot* 7, no. 4 (Winter 1974–75): 49–52.

Caplan, Neil. "Britain, Zionism and the Arabs, 1917–1925." *Wiener Library Bulletin* 31, nos. 45–46 (1978): 4–17.

Charlton, H. B. *Portrait of a University, 1851–1951. To Commemorate the Centenary of Manchester University.* Manchester: Manchester University Press, 1951.

Chorley, Katharine. *Manchester Made Them.* London: Faber and Faber, 1950.

Churchill, Randolph. *Winston S. Churchill,* vol. 2. Companion vol., part 1, 1901–1907. Boston: Houghton Mifflin, 1969.

Cohen, Israel. *A Jewish Pilgrimage.* London: Vallentine, Mitchell, 1956.

———. *A Short History of Zionism.* London: Frederick Muller, 1951.

———, ed. *The Rebirth of Israel.* London: Edward Goldston and Son, 1952.

Cohen, Stuart A. "The Tactics of Revolt: The English Zionist Federation and Anglo-Jewry, 1895–1904." *Journal of Jewish Studies* 29, no. 2 (Autumn 1978): 169–85.

———. "The First Anglo-Jewish Pilgrimage to Palestine: 1897." *Zionism* 2, no. 1 (Spring 1981): 71–85.

———. *English Zionists and British Jews: The Communal Politics of Anglo-Jewry, 1895–1920.* Princeton: Princeton University Press, 1982.

Cohn, Emil Bernhard. *David Wolffsohn, Herzl's Successor.* New York: Zionist Organization of America, 1944.

Cook, Chris, and Brendan Keith. *British Historical Facts, 1820–1900.* London: Macmillan, 1975.

Crossman, Richard H. S. "The Torso of Greatness." *Encounter* 39, no. 5 (November 1972): 52–57.

Cunningham, William. *Alien Immigration to England, 1870–1914.* London: S. Sonnenschein, 1897.

Dagan, Henri. *Les Massacres de Kichinef et la Situation des Prolétaires Juifs en Russie.* Paris: Impression de Suresnes, 1903.

Davies, Harold. "'A Review of the Development of the Butyl Alcohol-Acetone Fermentation and Early Work on Synthetic Rubber." In *Papers Collected to Commemorate the 70th Anniversary of Dr. Chaim Weizmann.* Jerusalem: privately printed, 1944.

Davitt, Michael. *Within the Pale: The True Story of Anti-Semitic Persecutions in Russia.* London: Hurst and Blackett, 1903.

Dawidowicz, Lucy S., ed. *The Golden Tradition.* Boston: Beacon Press, 1967.

De Haas, Jacob. *Theodor Herzl: A Biographical Study.* New York: The Leonard Co., 1927.

Delaunay, Albert. *L'Institut Pasteur, des Origines à Aujourd'hui.* Paris: Editions France-Empire, 1962.

Dinur, Ben-Zion. "Yihudo shel Chaim Weizmann." *Molad* 11, no. 64 (October 1953): 159–63.

Dorfman, Catherine. "The Democratic Faction." *Hapoel Hazir,* no. 10, December 15, 1933, p. 15.

Doukhan-Landau, Leah, *Ha-Hevrot ha-Zioniyot Lirkhishat Karkaot be-Eretz Israel, 1897–1914.* Jerusalem: Yad Yitzhak Ben-Zvi, 1979.

Dubnov, Simon. *History of the Jews.* 4th rev. ed. 5 vols. Translated from the Russian and edited by Moshe Spiegel. South Brunswick, N.J.: Thomos Yoseloff, 1971 (vol. 4); 1973 (vol. 5).

―――. *History of the Jews in Russia and Poland.* 3 vols. Philadelphia: Jewish Publication Society of America, 1916–20.

Dudman, Helga. *Street People.* Jerusalem: The Jerusalem Post/Carta, 1982.

Dugdale, Blanche E. C. *Arthur James Balfour.* 2 vols. London: Hutchinson, 1936.

Egremont, Max. *Balfour: A Life of Arthur James Balfour.* London: Collins, 1980.

Elam, Yigal, *Mavo le-Historyah Zionit Aheret.* Tel Aviv: A. Lewin-Epstein, 1972.

Eliav, Mordechai. *David Wolffsohn: ha-Ish u-Zmano.* Tel Aviv: Tel-Aviv University and the Chaim Weizmann Institute for Zionist Research, 1977.

―――. *Eretz-Israel ve-Yishuvah ba-Meah ha-19, 1777–1917.* Jerusalem: Keter Press, 1978.

―――. "Meoraot Jaffa be-Purim 1908." *Hazionut* 3 (1973): 152–97.

Elon, Amos. *Herzl.* New York: Holt, Rinehart and Winston, 1975.

Eloni, Yehuda. "Beayot Ideologiyot, Irguniyot u-Mivniyot ba-Zionut ha-Germanit, me-Reshitah ad Milhemet ha-Olam ha-Rishonah." Diss., Tel Aviv University, 1981.

Ensor, Robert Charles. *England, 1870–1914.* Oxford: Clarendon Press, 1936.

Epstein, Zalman. *Moshe Leib Lilienblum, Shitato ve-halakh Mahshavto.* Tel Aviv: Dvir, 1934–35.

Errera, Leo. *The Russian Jews: Extermination or Emancipation?* London: Macmillan, 1894.

Eschelbacher, Klara. "Die Ostjuedische Einwanderungsbevoelkerung der Stadt Berlin." *Zeitschrift fuer Demographie und Statistik der Juden* 1–6 (January–June 1920): 2.

Esco Foundation for Palestine. *Palestine: A Study of Jewish, Arab, and British Policies.* New Haven: Yale University Press, 1947. Vol. 1.

Etkes, Emanuel. "Immanent Factors and External Influences in the Development of the Haskala Movement in Russia." Paper presented at the Leo Baeck Institute symposium on "The Impact of German-Jewish Modernization on World Jewry." Haifa, March 1983.

Ettinger, Shmuel. *Ha-Antishemiyut ba-Et ha-Hadashah.* Tel Aviv: Moreshet, 1978.

―――. "Hibbat Zion." *Encyclopaedia Judaica,* 1st ed.

―――. "The Jews in Russia at the Outbreak of the Revolution." In *The Jews in Soviet Russia Since 1917,* edited by Lionel Kochan, p. 17. New York and Toronto: Published for the Institute of Jewish Affairs and Oxford University Press, 1970.

Fairbrother, F., J. B. Birks, Wolfe Mays, and P. G. Morgan. "The History of Science in Manchester." In *Manchester and Its Region,* edited by C. F. Carter, pp. 187–91. Manchester: British Association for the Advancement of Science, 1962.

Feinberg, Nathan. "Mashmautah ha-Mishpatit shel Tokhnit Basel." *Shivat Zion,* vol. 1, Jerusalem: Ha-Sifriyah ha-Zionit, 1950, pp. 131–37.

―――. "Le Toldot ha-Munah 'Bayit Leumi Yehudi' (Al Hagdarato befi Chaim Weizmann bifnei Veidat ha-Shalom)." *Zion* 37 (1972): 111–16.

Feiwel, Berthold. "Enquête unter den westeuropaeischen juedischen Studierenden." In *Juedische Statistik,* edited by Alfred Nossig, pp. 245–55. Berlin: Juedischer Verlag, 1903.

―――. *Die Judenmassacres in Kischinew.* Berlin: Juedischer Verlag, 1903.

Feldman, Eliyahu. "Plehve ve-Hapogrom be-Kishinov be-1903." *Heavar* 17 (1970): 137–50.

Fiddes, Edward. *Chapters in the History of Owens College and of Manchester University, 1851–1914.* Manchester: Manchester University Press, 1937.

———. "The Victoria University of Manchester." In *The Book of Manchester and Salford,* pp. 63–64. Manchester: Manchester University Press, 1929.

Fischer, Louis. *The Life of Lenin.* New York: Harper and Row, 1964.

Fishman, Joshua A., ed. *Studies in Modern Jewish Socvial History.* New York: Ktav and YIVO, 1972.

Fishman, Yehuda Leib. "Toldot ha-Mizrahi ve-Hitpathuto." *Sefer ha-Mizrahi,* pp. 5–381. Jerusalem: Mosad ha-Rav Kook, 1946.

Florinsky, Michael. *Russia: A History and Interpretation.* New York: Macmillan, 1953.

Fraenkel, Josef. "Chaim Weizmann and Haham Moses Gaster." *Herzl Year Book,* vol. 6, pp. 183–237. New York: Herzl Press, 1964–65.

———. "Fun der Englisher Hibbat Zion Bavegung biz zu der Balfour-Deklarazie." *YIVO Bletter* 43 (1966): 72–147.

———. *Lucien Wolf and Theodor Herzl.* London: Jewish Historical Society of England, 1964.

Frangopulo, N. J., ed. *Rich Inheritance: A Guide to the History of Manchester.* Manchester: Manchester Education Committee, 1962.

Frankel, Jonathan. *Prophecy and Politics: Socialism, Nationalism, and the Russian Jews, 1862–1917.* Cambridge: Cambridge University Press, 1981.

Friedman, Isaiah. "Lord Palmerston and the Protection of the Jews in Palestine." *Jewish Social Studies* 30, no. 1 (January 1968): 23–41.

———. *Germany, Turkey, and Zionism, 1897–1918.* Oxford: Clarendon Press, 1977.

Friedman, Maurice. *Martin Buber's Life and Work: The Early Years, 1878–1923.* New York: Dutton, 1981.

Friesel, Evyatar. *Ha-Mediniyut ha-Zionit le-Ahar Hatzharat Balfour, 1917–1922.* Tel Aviv: Tel Aviv University and Ha-Kibbutz Ha-Meuhad, 1977.

———. "Weizmann and 'Weizmannism.' " *Judaism* 26, no. 1 (Winter 1977): 73–83.

"From Kishineff to Bialystok: A Table of Pogroms from 1903 to 1906." *American Jewish Year Book 5667,* pp. 34–89. Philadelphia: Jewish Publication Society of America, 1906.

Frumkin, Jacob, Gregor Aronson, and Alexis Goldenweiser, eds. *Russian Jewry, 1860–1917.* New York: Thomas Yoseloff, 1966.

Gainer, Bernard. *The Alien Invasion: The Origins of the Aliens Act of 1905.* London: Heinemann Educational Books, 1972.

Garrard, J. A. *The English and Immigration.* London: Oxford University Press, 1971.

Gartner, Lloyd P. "Immigration and the Formation of American Jewry, 1840–1925." In *Jewish Society Through the Ages,* edited by Haim Hillel Ben-Sasson and Shmuel Ettinger, pp. 297–312. New York: Schocken, 1971.

———. *The Jewish Immigrant in England, 1870–1914.* London: George Allen & Unwin, 1960.

———. "Notes on the Statistics of Jewish Immigration to England, 1870–1914." *Jewish Social Studies* 22, no. 2 (April 1960): 97–102.

Gaster, Moses. "Zionismus und Neu-Zionismus." *Ost und West,* no. 10, October 1903, pp. 669–79.

Gat, Ben-Zion. *Ha-Yishuv ha-Yehudi be-Eretz Israel, 1840–1881.* Jerusalem: Yad Yitzhak Ben-Zvi, 1964.

Gelber, Nathan Michael. "Agudat ha-Studentim ha-Yehudim ha-Russim ha-Rishonah be-Berlin." *Heavar* 4 (1956): 48–50.

————.*Toldot ha-Tnuah ha-Zionit be-Galizyah, 1875–1918.* 2 vols. Jerusalem: Ha-Sifriyah ha-Zionit, 1958.

Gidney, W. T. *The History of the London Society for the Propagation of Christianity Among the Jews from 1809 to 1908.* London: London Society for Promoting Christianity Amongst the Jews, 1908.

Giladi, Dan. "Pekidut ha-Baron Rothschild ve-ha-Moshavot be-Eretz Israel." *Divrei ha-Kongress ha-Olami ha-Shmini le-Madaei ha-Yahadut,* pp. 145–51. Jerusalem: World Union of Jewish Studies, 1982.

Gil-Har, Yitzhak. "Ha-Gibush veha-Izuv ha-Irguni veha-Medini shel ha-Yishuv be-Reshit ha-Meah ha-20." *Hazionut* 6 (1981): 7–47.

Ginsburg, Shaul. *Idishe Leiden in Tsarishen Russland.* New York: S. M. Ginsburg Testimonial Committee, 1938.

Glouberman, Emanuel. "Fedor Dostoevsky, Vladimir Soloviev, Vasilii Rozanov and Lev Shestov on Jewish and Old Testament Themes." Diss., University of Michigan, 1974.

Goldberg, Abraham. *Sefer Abraham Goldberg. Kovez Maamarav ve-Divrei Haarkha al Hayav u-Feulotav.* New York: Histadruth Ivrith of America, 1945.

Goldberg, Boris. "Zur Statistik der juedischen Bevoelkerung in Russland." In *Juedische Statistik,* edited by Alfred Nossig, pp. 259–86. Berlin: Juedischer Verlag, 1903.

Golding, Louis. *Magnolia Street.* New York: Farrar and Rinehart, 1932.

Goldstein, David I. *Dostoyevsky and the Jews.* Austin: University of Texas Press, 1981.

Goodman, Paul. *Zionism and the Jewish Diaspora.* London: English Zionist Federation, 1921.

————. *Zionism in England, 1899–1949: A Jubilee Record.* London: English Zionist Federation, 1949.

————, ed. *Chaim Weizmann: A Tribute on His Seventieth Birthday.* London: Victor Gollancz, 1945.

————. *The Jewish National Home.* London: J. M. Dent and Sons, 1943.

Goren, Arthur A., ed. *Dissenter in Zion. From the Writings of Judah L. Magnes.* Cambridge: Harvard University Press, 1982.

Gorni, Yosef. "Ha-Otzmah sheba-Hulshah: Dmuto shel Chaim Weizmann ke-Manhig ha-Tnuah ha-Zionit." *Skirah Hodshit,* no. 1 (January 1978): 25–33.

————."Ha-Shinuyim ba-Mivneh ha-Hevrati ve-Hapoliti shel ha-Aliyah ha-Shniyah ba-Shanim 1904–1940." *Hazionut* 1 (1970): 204–45.

————. "Ha-Yesod ha-Romanti ba-Ideologyah shel ha-Aliyah ha-Shniyah." *Asufot* 10 (1966): 55–74.

————. "Shorasheha shel Todaat ha-Imut ha-Leumi ha-Yehudi-Aravi ve-Hishtakfutah ba-Itonut ha-Ivrit ba-Shanim 1900–1918." *Hazionut,* vol. 4, ed. Daniel Carpi, pp. 72–113. Tel Aviv: Tel Aviv University, 1975.

————, and Gedalia Yogev, eds. *Medinai be-Itot Mashber. Darkho shel Chaim Weizmann ba-Tnuah Ha-Zionit 1900–1948.* Tel Aviv: Tel Aviv University, 1977.

Gottheil, Richard. *Zionism.* Philadelphia: Jewish Publication Society of America, 1914.

Grabowica, Oksana Irena. "About Polesie." In *The Changing Peasantry of Eastern Europe,* edited by Joseph Obreski, pp. vii–ix. Cambridge, Mass.: Schenkman, 1976.

Great Britain. Foreign Office. *Documents on British Foreign Policy.* Series 1, vol. 4. London: His Majesty's Stationery Office, 1952.

Greenberg, Louis. *The Jews in Russia: The Struggle for Emancipation*. New Haven: Yale University Press, 1965.

Gross, Nachum. "Kalkelat Eretz Israel be-Sof ha-Meah ha-19 ve-Reshit ha-20." In *Bankai le-Umah be-Hithadshutah*, pp. 24–63. Tel Aviv: Massada, 1977.

Gruenbaum, Yitzhak. "Mi-Warsaw ad Helsingfors." In *Katzir, Kovetz le-Korot ha-Tnuah ha-Zionit be-Russyah*, vol. 1, pp. 21–42. Tel Aviv: Massada and Ha-Vaad ha-Ziburi le-Toldot ha-Tnuah ha-Zionit be-Russyah, 1964.

———. "Yovel Sheniskah (Hamishim Shanah le-Veidat Helsingfors)." *Heavar* 5 (1957): 11–17.

Grunwald, Kurt. "Jewish Schools under Foreign Flags in Ottoman Palestine." In *Studies in Palestine during the Ottoman Period*, edited by Moshe Maoz, pp. 164–74. Jerusalem: Magnes Press, 1975.

Guinn, Paul. *British Strategy and Politics, 1914 to 1918*. Oxford: Clarendon Press, 1965.

Gurevich, David, and Aaron Gertz. *Ha-Hityashvut ha-Haklait ha-Ivrit be Eretz Israel*. Jerusalem: Department of Statistics of the Jewish Agency for Palestine, 1938.

Guriel, Boris. "Lenin u-Weizmann." *Haaretz*, November 3, 1967, p. 3.

Haim, Sylvia G., ed. *Arab Nationalism. An Anthology*. Berkeley: University of California Press, 1962.

Halévy, Elie. *A History of the English People*. Translated by E. I. Watkin. London: Ernest Benn Limited, 1929, 1934. Vols. 4, 5, and 6.

Halperin, Georg. *Die juedischen Arbeiter in London*. Berlin: J. G. Cotta, 1903.

———. "Die juedische Einwanderer-Bevoelkerung Londons." In *Juedische Statistik*, edited by Alfred Nossig, pp. 322–35. Berlin: Juedischer Verlag, 1903.

Halpern, Ben. "The Disciple, Chaim Weizmann." In *At the Crossroads: Essays on Ahad Ha-Am*, edited by Jacques Kornberg, pp. 156–69. Albany: State University of New York Press, 1983.

———. "The Drafting of the Balfour Declaration." *Herzl Year Book*, vol. 7, pp. 255–84. New York: Herzl Press, 1971.

———. "Herzl's Historic Gift: The Sense of Sovereignty." *Herzl Year Book*, vol. 3, pp. 27–35. New York: Herzl Press, 1960.

———. *The Idea of the Jewish State*. 2nd ed., rev. Cambridge: Harvard University Press, 1969.

———. "Weizmann ve-Doro." *Ha-Ishiyut ve-Dorah*, pp. 157–68. Jerusalem: Ha-Hevrah Ha-Historit Ha-Israelit, 1963.

Halpern, Israel. *Sefer ha-Gvurah*. Tel Aviv: Am Oved, 1950. Vol. 3.

Hammond, John Lawrence. *C. P. Scott of the Manchester Guardian*. New York: Harcourt Brace, 1934.

Harcave, Sidney S. *First Blood: The Russian Revolution of 1905*. New York: Macmillan, 1964.

———. "The Jewish Question in the First Russian Duma." *Jewish Social Studies* 6, no. 2 (April 1944): 155–76.

———. "The Jews and the First Russian National Election." *American Slavic and East European Review* 9 (1950): 33–41.

Harrow, Benjamin. *Eminent Chemists of Our Time*. New York: Van Nostrand, 1920.

Heilprin, Israel. "Nissayon shel Interventzia Politit le-Maan Yehudei Russyah aharei Peraot October." *Zion* 20, nos. 3–4 (1955): 103–74.

Henry, James D. *Baku: An Eventful History*. London: A. Constable, 1906.

Hertz, Jacob S. "The Bund's Nationality Program and Its Critics in the Russian,

Polish and Austrian Socialist Movements." In *Studies in Modern Jewish Social History*, edited by Joshua A. Fishman, pp. 80–94. New York: Ktav and YIVO, 1972.

———. "Der Bund un di andere Rikhtungen." In *Di Geshikhte fun Bund*, edited by Gregor Aronson, et al., vol. 1, pp. 281–358. New York: Farlag Unser Tsait, 1960.

Herzl, Theodor. *Altneuland*. Leipzig: H. Seeman Nachfolger, 1902.

Heschel, Abraham Joshua. "The Eastern European Era in Jewish History." In *Studies in Modern Jewish Social History*, edited by Joshua A. Fishman, pp. 3–23. New York: Ktav and YIVO, 1972. Reprinted from *YIVO Annual of Jewish Social Science*. New York, 1946, vol. 1, pp. 86–106.

Heymann, Michael. "Herzl ve-Zionei Russyah—Mahloket ve-Haskamah." *Hazionut* 3 (1973): 56–99.

———, ed. *The Uganda Controversy*. Vol. 1. Jerusalem: Israel Universities Press, 1970; Vol. 2. Jerusalem: Ha-Sifriyah ha-Zionit, 1977.

Hirshfield, Claire. "The British Left and the 'Jewish Conspiracy': A Case Study of Modern Anti-Semitism." *Jewish Social Studies* 43, no. 2 (Spring 1981): 95–112.

Hodess, Jacob. "Weizmann: Scientist and Statesman." In *The Jerusalem Post: Chaim Weizmann Memorial Supplement*, October 30, 1953, p. iii.

Hoffman, Benzion, ed. *Toyznt Yor Pinsk*. New York: Workmen's Circle, 1941.

Holmes, Colin. *Anti-Semitism in British Society, 1876–1939*. New York: Holmes and Meier, 1979.

Hook, Sidney. *The Hero in History: A Study in Limitation and Possibility*. New York: J. Day, 1943.

Hurwicz, Elias. "Shay Ish Hurwitz and the Berlin He-Athid: When Berlin Was the Centre of Hebrew Literature." *Leo Baeck Institute Year Book XII*, pp. 85–102. London: East and West Library, 1967.

Hyamson, Albert M. *The British Consulate in Jerusalem in Relation to the Jews in Palestine, 1862–1914*. 2 vols. London: Edward Goldstein for the Jewish Historical Society, 1939–41.

———. *Palestine: The Rebirth of an Ancient People*. New York: Knopf, 1917.

———. *British Projects for the Restoration of the Jews*. London: n.p., 1917.

Jacna, L. S. "Science and Social Order in the Thought of A. J. Balfour." *ISIS* 71, no. 256 (March 1980): 11–34.

Jaffe, Benjamin. "Ha-Kongress ha-Zioni ha-Revii be-London ve-ha-Hedim ba-Itonut ha-Britit." *Haumahnos* 51–52 (1977): 394–405.

———. "Ha-Pulmus ha-Yehudi be-Angliyah bitkufat Herzl (1895–1904)." *Kivunim* 8 (August 1980): 99–117.

Jaffe, Leib. *Sefer ha-Kongress*. Jerusalem: Ha-Histadrut ha-Zionit ve-ha-Direktoryon shel Keren Ha-Yessod, 1950.

James, Robert Rhodes. *The British Revolution: British Politics, 1880–1939*. London: Hamish Hamilton. Vol. 1, 1976; Vol. 2, 1977.

Jay, Richard. *Joseph Chamberlain, A Political Study*. London: Oxford University Press, 1981.

The Jerusalem Post: Chaim Weizmann Memorial Supplement. October 30, 1953.

Jewish Agency. *Chaim Weizmann*, 2nd ed., rev. New York: Jewish Agency, 1962.

Johnson, William Herman Eckart. *Russia's Educational Heritage*. Pittsburgh: Carnegie Press, 1950.

Joseph, Samuel. *Jewish Immigration to the United States, 1881–1910.* New York: Columbia University Press, 1914.

Judd, Denis. *Balfour and the British Empire: A Study in Imperial Evolution, 1874–1932.* New York: Macmillan, 1968.

Kalvariski-Margalit, Haim. "Ha-Yehasim beyn ha-Yehudim ve-Haaravim lifnei Milhemet ha-Olam ha-Rishonah." *Sheifotenu,* no. 2 (1913): 50–55.

Kann, Jacobus. *Erez Israel, das juedische Land.* Cologne: Juedischer Verlag, 1909.

Kaplun-Kogan, W. W. *Die juedischen Wanderbewegungen in der Neuesten Zeit.* Bonn: A. Marcus and E. Weder, 1919.

Kark, Ruth. "Aliyatah shel Jaffo be-Merkaz ha-Yishuv he-Hadash: Hebetim Hevratiyim ve-Tarbutiyim." In *Sefer ha-Aliyah ha-Rishonah,* edited by Mordechai Eliav, pp. 297–318. Jerusalem: Yitzhak Ben Zvi, 1981.

Katz, Abraham. "Ha-Paritz." *Yeda-Am* 2 (1954): 61–64.

Katz, Ben-Zion. "Yahadut Russyah lifnei Hamishim Shanah." *Heavar* 1, no. 1 (1953): 5–17.

Katz, David S. *Philo-Semitism and the Readmission of the Jews to England, 1603–1656.* Oxford: Clarendon Press, 1982.

Katz, Jacob. *From Prejudice to Destruction.* Cambridge: Harvard University Press, 1980.

———. "Le-viur ha-Musag Mevasrei ha-Zionut." *Shivat Zion,* vol. 1, pp. 91–105. Jerusalem: Ha-Sifriyah ha-Zionit, 1950.

Kedourie, Elie. *England and the Middle East. The Destruction of the Ottoman Empire, 1914–1921.* London: Bowes and Bowes, 1956.

———, and Sylvia Haim, eds. *Palestine and Israel in the 19th and 20th Centuries.* London: Frank Cass, 1982.

Kelly, Fred C. *One Thing Leads to Another.* Boston: Houghton Mifflin, 1936.

Klausner, Israel. *Be-Hitorer Am.* Jerusalem: Ha-Sifriyah ha-Zionit, 1962.

———. "Be-Reshit Yisud ha-Mizrahi al Yedei ha-Rav I. J. Reines." *Sefer ha-Zionut ha-Datit,* edited by Yitzhak Raphael and S. Z. Shragai, vol. 1, pp. 361–71. Jerusalem: Mossad ha-Rav Kook, 1977.

———. *Hibbat Zion be-Rumanyah.* Jerusalem: Ha-Sifriyah ha-Zionit, 1958.

———. "Hibbat Zion be-Lita." In *Yahadut Lita,* vol. 1, pp. 489–507. Tel Aviv: Am ha-Sefer, 1959.

———. *Mi-Kattowitz ad Basel.* 2 vols. Jerusalem: Ha-Sifriyah ha-Zionit, 1965.

———. *Opposizyah le-Herzl.* Jerusalem: Achiever, 1960.

Klausner, Joseph. *Manihe ha-Yesod shel Medinat Israel.* Jerusalem: Achiasaf, 1953.

Kleiner, Joseph. *Professor Dr. Chaim Weizmann. Hayav, Mipulotav, ve-Shitato ha-Zionit.* Krakow: Y. Meiler, n.d.

Kleinman, Moshe. *Chaim Weizmann.* Tel Aviv: Yavneh, 1945.

Klier, J. D. "The Ambiguous Legal Status of Russian Jewry in the Reign of Catherine II." *Slavic Review* 35 (September 1976): 504–17.

Kling, Simcha. *Nahum Sokolow: Servant of His People.* New York: Herzl Press, 1960.

Knaani, David. *Ha-Aliyah ha-Shniyah ha-Ovedet ve-Yahasah la-Dat ve-la-Masoret.* Tel Aviv: Sifriyat Poalim, 1976.

Knox, D. E. "Weizmann's First Visit to Palestine." *Wiener Library Bulletin* 28 (1975): 2–13.

Kobler, Franz. *The Vision Was There: A History of the British Movement for the Restoration of the Jews to Palestine.* London: Published for the World Jewish Congress, British Section, by Lincolns-Prager, 1956.

Kobler, Ferdinand. "Zur Conferenz der Zionistischen Studentenschaft." *Die Welt,*
no. 50, December 13, 1901, pp. 8–9.
Kohn, Hans. *Martin Buber: Sein Werk und seine Zeit.* Cologne: Joseph Melzer Ver-
lag, 1961.
Kolatt, Israel. "Ha-Tnuah ha-Zionit ve-ha-Aravim." In *Ha-Zionut ve-ha-Sheelah ha-
Aravit,* edited by Yitzhak Cohen, pp. 9–35. Jerusalem: Merkaz Zalman Sha-
zar, 1979.
––––––. "Ideologyah u-Metziut bi-Tnuat ha-Avodah be-Eretz Israel, 1905–1919."
Diss., Hebrew University, 1964.
––––––. "Mi-Kibush ha-Avodah le-Kidush ha-Avodah." *Baderekh* 1 (1967): 29–61.
––––––. "The Organization of the Jewish Population of Palestine and the Devel-
opment of Its Political Consciousness Before World War I." In *Studies in Pal-
estine during the Ottoman Period,* edited by Moshe Maoz, pp. 211–45. Jerusa-
lem: Magnes Press, 1975.
Kornberg, Jacques. "Theodore Herzl: A Reevaluation." *Journal of Modern History*
52 (June 1980): 226–52.
Lambroza, Shlomo. "Jewish Self-Defense During the Russian Pogroms of 1903–
1906." *Jewish Journal of Sociology* 23, no. 2 (December 1981): 123–34.
Lane, David. "The Russian Social Democratic Labour Party in St. Petersburg, Tver,
and Ashkabad, 1903–1905." *Soviet Studies* 15, no. 3 (January 1964): 331–44.
Langhard, Johann. *Die anarchistische Bewegung in der Schweiz von ihren anfaengen
bis zur Gegenwart und die internationalen Fuehrer.* Berlin: Verlag von O. Haer-
ing, 1903.
Laqueur, Walter. *A History of Zionism.* New York: Holt, Rinehart and Winston,
1972.
Laskov, Shulamit. *Ha-Biluim.* Jerusalem: Ha-Sifriyah ha-Zionit, 1979.
––––––. "The Biluim: Reality and Legend." *Zionism* 3 (Spring 1981): 17–69.
Lazare, Bernard. *Les Juifs en Roumanie.* Paris: Editions des Cahiers, 1902.
Lebzelter, Gisela. "Anit-Semitism—A Focal Point for the British Radical Right."
In *Nationalist and Racialist Movements in Britain and Germany Before 1914.* Lon-
don: Macmillan with St. Anthony's College, Oxford, 1981, pp. 88–105.
Lee, Alan. "Aspects of the Working-Class Response to the Jews in Britain, 1880–
1914." In *Hosts, Immigrants and Minorities,* edited by Kenneth Lunn, pp. 107–
33. New York: St. Martin's Press, 1980.
Lestschinsky, Jacob. *Di Ekonomishe Lage fun Yidn in Poyln.* Berlin: n.p., 1931.
––––––. "Ha-Reka ha-Kalkali shel Thum ha-Moshav la-Yehudim be-Russyah."
Heavar 1 (1953): 31–44.
Levin, Nora. *While Messiah Tarried: Jewish Socialist Movements, 1871–1917.* New
York: Schocken, 1977.
Levitats, Isaac. *The Jewish Community in Russia, 1772–1884.* Jerusalem: Posner,
1981.
Lewis, Bernard. *The Emergence of Modern Turkey.* London: Oxford University Press,
1961.
Lipman, Vivian D. "The Rise of Jewish Suburbia." *Jewish Historical Society of En-
gland, Transactions,* sess. 1962–67, vol. 21 (1968): 84–85.
––––––. *Social History of the Jews in England, 1850–1950.* London: Watts, 1954.
Lipsky, Louis. *Herzl, Weizmann and the Jewish State.* Rehovot: Yad Chaim Weiz-
mann, 1956.
Litvinoff, Barnet. *Weizmann: Last of the Patriarchs.* New York: Putnam, 1976.
––––––, ed. *The Essential Chaim Weizmann: The Man, the Statesman, the Scientist.*
New York: Holmes and Meier, 1982.

Loewe, Heinz-Dietrich. *Antisemitismus und reaktionaere Utopie: Russischer Konservatismus im Kampf gegen den Wandel von Staat und Gesellschaft, 1890–1917.* Hamburg: Hoffmann und Campe, 1978.

Loewenberg, Peter. "Theodor Herzl: A Psychoanalytic Study in Charismatic Political Leadership." In *The Psychoanalytic Interpretation of History,* edited by Benjamin B. Wolman, pp. 150–91. New York: Basic Books, 1971.

Lowe, Cedric James. *The Reluctant Imperialists, 1878–1902.* London: Routledge and Kegan Paul, 1967. Vols. 1 and 2.

Lunn, Kenneth, ed. *Hosts, Immigrants and Minorities: Historical Responses to Newcomers in British Society, 1870–1914.* New York: St. Martin's Press, 1980.

Luz, Ehud. "Ha-Aktualiyut be-Vikuakh Uganda." *Kivunim,* no. 1 (November 1978): 54–59.

———. "Zion and Judenstaat: The Significance of the 'Uganda' Controversy." In *Essays in Modern Jewish History: A Tribute to Ben Halpern,* edited by Frances Malino and Phyllis Cohen Albert, pp. 217–39. Rutherford N.J.: Fairleigh Dickinson University Press, 1982.

McKeon, Michael. "Sabbatai Sevi in England." *AJS Review* 2 (1977): 131–69.

Malamud, Yitzhak. "Sikur Veidat ha-Mizrahi ha-Rishonah be-Russyah." *Sefer ha-Zionut ha-Datit,* edited by Yitzhak Raphael and S. Z. Shragai, vol. 2, pp. 451–56. Jerusalem: Mossad ha-Rav Kook, 1977.

Mandel, Neville J. *The Arabs and Zionism before World War I.* Berkeley: University of California Press, 1976.

———. "Ottoman Policy and Restrictions on Jewish Settlement in Palestine, 1881–1908." *Middle Eastern Studies* 10, no. 3 (1974): 312–32.

———. "Ottoman Policy as Regards Jewish Settlement in Palestine, 1881–1908." *Middle Eastern Studies* 11, no. 1 (1975): 31–46.

Maor, Yitzhak. "Ha-Kruz ha-Antishemi shel 'Narodnaya Volhya.' " *Zion* 15 (1940): 150–55.

———. *Ha-Tnuah ha-Zionit be-Russyah.* Jerusalem: Ha-Sifriyah ha-Zionit, 1973.

———. "Yehudei Russyah bi-Yemei ha-'Dumot.' " *Heavar* 7 (1960): 49–90.

———. "Yehudei Russyah bi-Tkufat Plehve." *Heavar* 6 (1958): 38–59.

Margalith, Israel. *Le Baron Edmond de Rothschild et la Colonisation Juive en Palestine, 1882–1889.* Paris: Librairie M. Rivière, 1957.

Marquardt, Martha. *Paul Ehrlich,* with an introd. by Sir Henry Dale. New York: Henry Schuman, 1951.

Marriott, John Arthur Ransome. *The Eastern Question: An Historical Study in European Diplomacy.* 4th ed. Oxford: Clarendon Press, 1940.

Medzini, Moshe. *Dr. Chaim Weizmann, Skirah Biografit.* Jerusalem: Defus ha-Sefer, 1934.

———. *Ha-Mediniyut ha-Zionit me-Reshitah ve-ad Moto shel Herzl.* Jerusalem: Defus ha-Sefer, 1934.

Meijer, Jan M. *Knowledge and Revolution: The Russian Colony in Zuerich (1870–1873).* Assen: Royal Van Gorcum, 1956.

Melchett, Lord. "Chaim Weizmann." In *Twelve Jews,* edited by Hector Bolitho, pp. 271–88. London: Rich and Cowan, 1934.

Meltzer, Julian. *The Chaim Weizmann Memorial Lectures.* Rehovot: Zionist Federation of Great Britain and Ireland, 1973.

Mendelsohn, Ezra. *Class Struggle in the Pale.* Cambridge: Cambridge University Press, 1970.

Mendes-Flohr, Paul R., and Jehuda Reinharz, eds. *The Jew in the Modern World: A Documentary History.* New York: Oxford University Press, 1980.

Menes, Abraham. "The Am Oylom Movement." *YIVO Annual of Jewish Social Science* 4 (1949): 9–33.

Michaeli, Ben-Zion. *Sejera, Toldoteha ve-Isheha*. Tel-Aviv: Am Oved, 1973.

Michaelis, Anthony R. *Weizmann Centenary*. London: Anglo-Israel Association, 1974.

Mintz, Matityahu. "Ber Borochov." *Studies in Zionism* 5 (Spring 1982): 33–35.

———. *Ber Borochov: Ha-Maagal ha-Rishon 1900–1906*. Tel Aviv: Ha-Kibbutz ha-Meuhad, 1976.

Mishkinski, Moshe. "Ha-Sozialism ha-Mishtarti u-Megamot bi-Mediniyut ha-Shilton ha-Tsari le-Gabei ha-Yehudim (1900–1903)." *Zion* 25, nos. 3–4 (1959): 238–49.

———. *Reshit Tnuat ha-Poalim ha-Yehudit be-Russyah. Megamot Yesod*. Tel Aviv: Ha-Kibbutz ha-Meuhad, 1981.

Morgan, K. O. *The Age of Lloyd George*. London: George Allen and Unwin, 1971.

Nadav, Mordechai. "Kehilot Pinsk-Karlin beyn Hasidut le-Hitnagdut." *Zion* 34, nos. 1–2 (1969): 98–108.

Nash, Stanley. "Tmunot mi-Hug Shoharei ha-Ivrit be-Berlin (1900–1914)." *AJS Review* 3 (1978): 1–26.

Nathan, Paul. *Palaestina und palaestinensischer Zionismus*. Berlin: H. S. Hermann, 1914.

Nawratzki, Curt. *Die Juedische Kolonisation Palaestinas*. Munich: E. Reinhardt, 1914.

Nettl, J. P. *Rosa Luxemburg*. London: Oxford University Press, 1966.

Newton, (Lord) Thomas Wodehouse Legh. *Lord Lansdowne. A Biography*. London: Macmillan, 1929.

Nordau, Anna and Maxa. *Max Nordau: A Biography*. New York: Nordau Committee, 1943.

Nordau, Max. "Achad Ha'am ueber Altneuland." *Die Welt*, no. 11 (March 13, 1903): 1–4.

———. "Discours d'Introduction." *L'Echo Sioniste*, no. 1 (January 15, 1902): 21–30.

———. "Ueber den Gegensatz zwischen Ost und West im Zionismus." *Die Welt*, no. 11, March 18, 1910, pp. 231–32.

Nossig, Alfred, ed. *Juedische Statistik*. Berlin: Juedischer Verlag, 1903.

Oliphant, Laurence. *Land of Gilead*. Edinburgh: W. Blackwood and Sons, 1880.

Oppenheimer, Franz. "Stammesbewusstsein und Volksbewusstsein." *Die Welt*, no. 7, February 18, 1910, pp. 139–43.

Orlan, Haim, ed. *Ha-Kongress ha-Zioni ha-Rishon*. Tel Aviv: Ha-Histadrut ha-Zionit ha-Olamit, 1978.

Orren, Elhannan. *Hibbat Zion be-Britanyah, 1878–1898*. Tel Aviv: Ha-Kibbutz ha-Meuchad, 1974.

Pasmanik, Dr. D. "Der Congress der Zionistischen Studentenschaft." *Die Welt*, no. 24, June 28, 1901, pp. 5–6.

Patai, Raphael. "Herzl's Sinai Project." In *Herzl Year Book*, edited by Raphael Patai, pp. 119–22. New York: Herzl Press, 1958.

Patterson, David. *The Hebrew Novel in Czarist Russia*. Edinburgh: Edinburgh University Press, 1964.

Perlmutter, Amos. "Dov Ber Borochov: A Marxist-Zionist Ideologist." *Middle Eastern Studies* 5, no. 1 (January 1966): 32–43.

Pinkus, Lazar Felix. *Vor der Gruendung des Judenstaates*. Zurich: Art. Institut O. Fussli, 1918.

Pinson, Koppel S. "Arkady Kremer, Vladimir Medem and the Ideology of the Jewish 'Bund.' " *Jewish Social Studies* 7, no. 3 (July 1945): 233–64.

Pipes, Richard. "Catherine II and the Jews: The Origins of the Pale of Settlement." *Soviet Jewish Affairs* 5 (1975): 3–20.

Plekhanov, George. "The Role of the Individual in History." In *Essays in Historical Materialism*, part 2, pp. 5–62. New York: International Publishers, 1940.

Poggendorff, J. C. *Biographisch-Literarisches Handwoerterbuch zur Geschichte der Exacten Wissenschaften.* Leipzig: Professor Dr. A. J. von Oettingen, 1904. Vol. 4.

Pollak, Adolf L. *Hurban Motele.* Edited and translated by Shimon Yuzuk. Jerusalem: Vaad Yozei Motele, 1956.

Pospielovsky, Dimitry. *Russian Police Trade Unionism: Experiment or Provocation?* London: Weidenfeld and Nicolson, 1971.

Rabinowicz, Oskar K. *Fifty Years of Zionism.* London: Robert Anscombe, 1950.

————. *Winston Churchill on Jewish Problems.* New York: Thomas Yoseloff, 1956.

————. "Herzl and England." *Jewish Social Studies*, no. 1 (January 1951): 27–32.

————. "New Light on the East African Scheme." In *The Rebirth of Israel. A Memorial Tribute to Paul Goodman*, edited by Israel Cohen, pp. 77–97. London: Edward Goldston and Son, 1952.

————. "Zionist-British Negotiations in 1906." In *Essays Presented to Chief Rabbi Israel Brodie*, ed. H. T. Zimmels, J. Rabbinowitz, and I. Finestein, vol. 2, pp. 311–33. London: Soncino Press, 1967.

Rabinowitsch, Wolf Zeev. "Karlin Hasidism." *YIVO Annual of Jewish Social Science* 5 (1950): 123–51.

————. *Ha-Hasidut ha-Litait me-Reshitah ve-ad Yamenu.* Jerusalem: Mossad Bialik, 1961.

————. "Ha-Rothschildim shel Pinsk ve-Karlin." *Heavar* 17 (1970): 252–80.

————, ed. *Pinsk Historical Volume: History of the Jews of Pinsk 1506–1941.* 2 vols. (abridged from the Hebrew). Tel Aviv and Haifa: Association of the Jews of Pinsk-Karlin in Israel. Vol. 1, 1973; vol. 2, 1977.

Rabinowitz, Ezekiel. *Justice Louis D. Brandeis: The Zionist Chapter of His Life.* New York: Philosophical Library, 1968.

Rafaeli, A. "Veidot Artziot shel Zionei Russyah." In *Katzir, Kovetz le-Korot ha-Tnuah ha-Zionit be-Russyah*, vol. 1, pp. 43–102. Tel Aviv: Massada and Ha-Veadah ha-Ziburit le-Toldot ha-Tnuah ha-Zionit be-Russyah, 1964.

Raphael, Chaim. "Chaim Weizmann: The Letters." *Midstream* 20, no. 9 (November 1974): 2–15.

————. "Chaim Weizmann: Thoughts for a Centenary." In *Encyclopaedia Judaica Year Book, 1975/6.* Jerusalem: Keter, 1976.

Raphael, Yitzhak, and S. Z. Shragai, eds. *Sefer ha-Zionut ha-Datit.* 2 vols. Jerusalem: Mossad Ha-Rav Kook, 1977.

Ravid, Zvulum. "Motoleh, ha-Ayarah shebah nolad Weizmann." *Hadoar*, no. 27, May 17, 1963, pp. 502–3.

Redford, Arthur. *The History of Local Government in Manchester.* London: Longmans, Green, 1940.

Reifer, Manfred. *Chaim Weizmann. Der juedische Staatsmann.* Czernowitz: Juedischer Klub Masada, 1933.

Reinharz, Jehuda. "Achad Haam und der deutsche Zionismus." *Bulletin des Leo Baeck Instituts* 61 (1982): 3–27.

————. "Ahad Ha-Am, Martin Buber and German Zionism." In *At The Cross-roads: Essays on Ahad Ha-Am,* edited by Jacques Kornberg, pp. 142–55. Albany: State University of New York Press, 1983.

————. "Chaim Weizmann and the Elusive Manchester Professorship." *AJS Review,* vol. 9, no. 2 (Fall 1984).

————. "Chaim Weizmann: The Shaping of a Zionist Leader before the First World War." *Journal of Contemporary History* 18 (1983): 205–31.

————. *Dokumente zur Geschichte des deutschen Zionismus, 1882–1933.* Tübingen: J. C. B. Mohr, 1981.

————. "The Esra Verein and Jewish Colonization in Palestine." *Leo Baeck Institute Year Book* 26 (1979): 261–82.

————. *Fatherland or Promised Land? The Dilemma of the German Jew, 1893–1914.* Ann Arbor: University of Michigan Press, 1975.

————. "Ideology and Structure in German Zionism, 1882–1933." *Jewish Social Studies* 42, no. 2 (Spring 1980): 119–46.

————. "Laying the Foundation for a University in Jerusalem: Chaim Weizmann's Role, 1913–14." *Modern Judaism,* vol. 4, no. 1 (February 1984): 1–38.

————. "Science in the Service of Politics: The Case of Chaim Weizmann." *English Historical Review* (Spring 1985).

————. "Weizmann and the British General Elections of 1906." *Studies in Zionism* 5, no. 2 (Autumn 1984): 201–12.

————, and Shulamit Reinharz. "Leadership and Charisma: The Case of Theodor Herzl." In *Mystics, Philosophers and Politicians: Essays in Jewish Intellectual History in Honor of Alexander Altmann,* edited by Jehuda Reinharz and Daniel Swetschinski, pp. 275–313. Durham, N.C.: Duke University Press, 1982.

Revusky, Abraham. *Jews in Palestine.* London: Vanguard Press, 1938.

Riasanovsky, Nicholas V. *A History of Russia.* New York: Oxford University Press, 1963.

Richarz, Monika, ed. *Juedisches Leben in Deutschland: Selbstzeugnisse zur Sozialgeschichte im Kaiserreich.* Stuttgart: Deutsche Verlags-Anstalt, 1979. Vol. 2.

Ridley, Jasper. *Lord Palmerston.* New York: Dutton, 1971.

Rinott, Moshe. *Hevrat ha-Ezra li-Yehudei Germanyah bi-Yezirah uve-Maavak.* Jerusalem: Beit Ha-Sefer le-Hinukh shel ha-Universitah ha-Ivrit ve-shel Misrad ha-Hinukh veha-Tarbut, 1971.

————. "Histadrut ha-Morim, ha-Tnuah ha-Zionit ve-ha-Maavak al ha-Hegmonyah ba-Hinukh be-Erez Israel (1903–1918)." *Hazionut* 4 (1975): 114–45.

Robinson, Robert. "Chaim Weizmann at Manchester." *Rehovot* 5, no. 3 (Winter 1969–70): 30–31.

————. *The Structural Relations of Natural Products.* Oxford: Clarendon Press, 1955.

Robinson, Ronald, John Gallagher, and Alice Denny. *Africa and the Victorians: The Climax of Imperialism.* New York: St. Martin's Press, 1961.

Rogger, Hans. "The Jewish Policy of Late Tsarism: A Reappraisal." *Wiener Library Bulletin* 25, nos. 1–2 (1971): 42–51.

————. "Russian Ministers and the Jewish Question, 1881–1917." *California Slavic Studies* 8 (1975): 15–76.

————. "Tsarist Policy on Jewish Emigration." *Soviet Jewish Affairs* 3, no. 1 (1973): 26–36.

Roi, Yaakov. "Yahasei Yehudim-Aravim be-Moshavot ha-Aliyah ha-Rishonah." In *Sefer ha-Aliyah ha-Rishonah,* edited by Mordechai Eliav, pp. 245–68. Jerusalem: Yad Yitzhak Ben-Zvi; Ministry of Defense, 1981.

———. "The Zionist Attitude to the Arabs, 1908–1914." *Middle Eastern Studies* 3 (April 1968): 198–242.

Rollin, A. R. "Russo-Jewish Immigrants in England before 1881." *Jewish Historical Society of England, Transactions,* sess. 1962–67, vol. 21 (1968): 202–13.

Rose, Norman. *Lewis Namier and Zionism.* Oxford: Clarendon Press; New York: Oxford University Press, 1980.

Rosenbaum, S. "The Manchester Jewish Community." *The Jewish Chronicle,* June 22, 1906, p. 44.

Rosenberg, E. *From Shylock to Svengali: Jewish Stereotypes in English Fiction.* Stanford: Stanford University Press, 1960.

Rosenthal, Leon. *Toldot Hevrat Marbei Haskalah be-Israel be-Eretz Russyah.* St. Petersburg: H. Pines, 1885.

[Roth, Cecil]. *The Jewish Chronicle, 1841–1941: A Century of Newspaper History.* London: The Jewish Chronicle, 1949.

Ruppin, Arthur. *Der Aufbau des Landes Israel.* Berlin: Juedischer Verlag, 1919.

———. *Die landwirtschaftliche Kolonisation der Zionistischen Organisation in Palaestina.* Berlin: Verlag "Aufbau," 1925.

———. *The Jews of To-Day.* Translated by Margery Bentwich. London: G. Bell and Sons, 1913.

Sablinsky, Walter. *The Road to Bloody Sunday: Father Gapon and the St. Petersburg Massacre of 1905.* Princeton: Princeton University Press, 1976.

Sachar, Howard M. *A History of Israel.* New York: Knopf, 1976.

Sacher, Harry. *Zionist Portraits and Other Essays.* London: Anthony Blond, 1959.

Salmon, Yosef. "Ha-Imut beyn ha-Haredim la-Maskilim bi-Tnuat Hibbat Zion bi-Shnot ha-80." *Zionism* [Tel Aviv] 5 (1978): 43–77.

———. "Ha-Maavak al Daat ha-Kahal ha-Haredit be-Mizrah-Europa be-Yahas la-Tnuah ha-Leumit [1894–1896]." *Prakim be-Toldot ha-Hevrah ha-Yehudit bi-Yemei ha-Beynayim uva-Et ha-Hadashah,* pp. 330–68. Jerusalem: Magnes Press, 1980.

Samuel, Viscount Herbert. *Grooves of Change.* Indianapolis: Bobbs-Merrill, 1946.

Samuel, Maurice. *Blood Accusation: The Strange History of the Beilis Case.* Philadelphia: Jewish Publication Society of America, 1966.

Sanders, Ronald. *The High Walls of Jerusalem.* New York: Holt, Rinehart and Winston, 1983.

Schama, Simon. *Two Rothschilds and the Land of Israel.* New York: Knopf, 1978.

Schapiro, Leonard. "The Role of the Jews in the Russian Revolutionary Movement." *Slavonic and East European Review* 40, no. 94 (December 1961): 148–67

Schechtman, Joseph B. *Rebel and Statesman: The Vladimir Jabotinsky Story. The Early Years.* New York: Thomas Yoseloff, 1956.

Scheinhaus, Leon. *Ein deutscher Pionier (Dr. Lilienthal's Kulturversuch in Russland).* Berlin: M. Poppelauer, 1911.

Schneiderman, Jeremiah. *Sergei Zubatov and Revolutionary Marxism: The Struggle for the Working Class in Tsarist Russia.* Ithaca, N.Y.: Cornell University Press, 1976.

Schoen, Lazar, ed. *Die Stimme der Wahrheit: Jahrbuch fuer wissenschaftlichen Zionismus.* Würzburg: N. Philippi, 1905.

Schorske, Carl E. *Fin-de-Siècle Vienna: Politics and Culture.* New York: Knopf; dist. Random House, 1980.

Schwarz, Solomon M. *The Jews in the Soviet Union*. Syracuse: Syracuse University Press, 1951.

Schwarzfeld, Elias. *Les Juifs en Roumanie depuis le Traité de Berlin (1878) jusqu'à ce jour*. New York: Macmillan, 1901.

———. "The Jews of Roumania from the Earliest Times to the Present Day." *The American Jewish Year Book 5662*, pp. 25–62. Philadelphia: Jewish Publication Society of America, 1901.

———. "The Situation of the Jews in Roumania Since the Treaty of Berlin (1878)." In *The American Jewish Year Book 5662*, pp. 63–87. Philadelphia: Jewish Publication Society of America, 1901.

Schweid, Eliezer. "Mishnato shel Aharon David Gordon." In *Ideologyah u-Mediniyut Zionit*, edited by Ben-Zion Yehoshua and Aharon Kedar, pp. 50–59. Jerusalem: Merkaz Zalman Shazar, 1978.

Senn, Alfred Erich. *The Russian Revolution in Switzerland, 1914–1917*. Madison: University of Wisconsin Press, 1971.

Shaaltiel, Eli. "Zionism as the Art of the Possible: The Tragedy of Weizmann's Greatness." *Forum on the Jewish People, Zionism, and Israel*, nos. 30–31 (Spring and Summer 1978): 89–99.

Shaftesley, John M. "Nineteenth-Century Jewish Colonies in Cyprus." *Jewish Historical Society of England, Transactions*, sess. 1968–69, vol. 22, and *Miscellanies*, part 7, pp. 92–107. London: Jewish Historical Society of England, 1970.

Shapira, Anita. *Berl*. Tel Aviv: Am Oved, 1980. Vol. 1.

———. "The Origins of 'Jewish Labor' Ideology." *Studiees in Zionism* 5 (Spring 1982): 93–113.

Shapiro, Yonathan. "Ha-Mahloket beyn Chaim Weizmann le-beyn Louis Brandeis 1919–1921." *Hazionut* 3 (1973): 258–72.

Shatzmiller, Joseph;. "Bernard Lazare, Haim Weizmann et les 'Jeunes Sionistes.' " In *Mélanges André Neher*, edited by E. Amado Levy-Valensi et al., pp. 407–13. Paris: Maisonneuve, 1975.

Shazar, Zalman. *Mahzir Ha-Atarah*. Rehovot: Yad Chaim Weizmann, 1959.

———. *Or Ishim*. 2 vols. Jerusalem: Ha-Sifriyah ha-Zionit, 1964.

Shmeruk, Chone. "Ha-Hasidut ve-Iskei ha-Hakhirut." *Zion* 35 (1970): 182–92.

Silber, Jacques. "Some Demographic Characteristics of the Jewish Population in Russia at the End of the Nineteenth Century." *Jewish Social Studies* 42, nos. 3–4 (Summer–Fall 1980): 269–80.

Silberner, Edmund. "Bernard Lazare ve-Hazionut." In *Shivat Zion*, vols. 2–3, pp. 328–63. Jerusalem: Ha-Sifriyah ha-Zionit, 1953.

Simmons, Ernest Joseph. *English Literature and Culture in Russia, 1553–1840*. Cambridge: Harvard University Press, 1935.

Simon, Leon. *Ahad Ha'Am*. Philadelphia: Jewish Publication Society of America, 1960.

———. "Ahad Ha-Am and the Future of the Diaspora." In *Between East and West: Essays Dedicated to the Memory of Bela Horovitz*, edited by Alexander Altmann, pp. 59–74. London: East and West Library, 1958.

———. *Chaim Weizmann*. Jerusalem: Magnes Press, 1953.

———. "Herzl and Ahad Ha'Am." *Herzl Year Book*, vol. 3, pp. 145–51. New York: Herzl Press, 1960.

———, and Joseph Elias Heller, eds. *Ahad Ha'Am. Ha-Ish, Poalo ve-Torato*. Jerusalem: Magnes Press, 1955.

Simon, Skena D. *A Century of City Government: Manchester, 1838–1938.* London: George Allen & Unwin, 1938.

Slotki, I. W. *The History of the Manchester Shechita Board, 1892–1952.* Manchester: Manchester Shechita Board, 1954.

Slutsky, Yehuda. *Ha-Itonut ha-Yehudit-Russit ba-Meah ha-Tsha-Esreh.* Jerusalem: Mossad Bialik, 1970.

———. "Menahem Ussishkin—Ha-Tkufah ha-Russit." *Heavar* 12 (1965): 3–28.

———. "Zmihatah shel ha-Intelligentsia ha-Yehudit-Russit." *Zion* 25 (1960): 212–37.

Smilanski, Moshe. *Yehoshua Hankin.* Jerusalem: Jewish National Fund, 1946.

Sokolow, Florian. *Nahum Sokolow: Life and Legend.* London: Jewish Chronicle Publications, 1975.

Sokolow, Nahum. *History of Zionism, 1600–1918.* New York: Ktav, 1969.

———. *Sefer Sokolow.* Jerusalem: Ha-Histadrut ha-Zionit ha-Olamit and Mossad Bialik, 1942–43.

Speakman, H. B. "Dr. Weizmann's Contributions to Microbiology." In *Chaim Weizmann: Statesman, Scientist, Builder of the Jewish Commonwealth.* New York: Dial Press, 1944.

Spiegel, Shalom. *Hebrew Reborn.* Cleveland: World Publishing Company and the Jewish Publication Society of America, 1930.

Spiers, Maurice. *Victoria Park Manchester: A Nineteenth-Century Suburb in Its Social and Administrative Context.* Manchester: Cheetham Society, 1976.

Stanislawski, Michael. *Tsar Nicholas I and the Jews. The Transformation of Jewish Society in Russia 1825–1855.* Philadelphia: Jewish Publication Society of America, 1983.

Stein, Leonard. *The Balfour Declaration.* New York: Simon and Schuster, 1961.

———. "Koho shel Chaim Weizmann." *Haaretz,* November 2, 1962, p. 9.

———. *Weizmann and England.* London: W. H. Allen, 1964.

Strahlmann, Berend. "Carl Graebe," *Neue Deutsche Biographie,* vol. 6, pp. 705–6. Berlin: Dunker & Humbolt, 1963.

Stupnitzky, Saul. "Firer and Traeumer." *Frimorgn* [Riga], February 2, 1926.

Suny, Ronald Grigor. *The Baku Commune, 1917–1918: Class and Nationality in the Russian Revolution.* Princeton: Princeton University Press, 1972.

Syrkin, Marie. *Avi, Nahman Syrkin.* Jerusalem: Ha-Sifriyah ha-Zionit, 1970.

———. "Socialist Zionism: A New Concept, 1898." *Jewish Frontier* 41 (October 1974): 9–13.

Szajkowski, Zosa. "The European Attitude to East European Jewish Immigration, 1881–1893." *Publications of the American-Jewish Historical Society* 41, no. 2 (December 1951): 127–60.

———. "How the Mass Migration to America Began." *Jewish Social Studies* 4, no. 4 (October 1942): 291–310.

———. "Jewish Emigration Policy in the Period of the Rumanian 'Exodus' 1899–1903." *Jewish Social Studies* 13, no. 1 (January 1951): 47–70.

Tamir (Mirski), N., ed. *Pinsk: A Memorial Volume.* Tel Aviv: Association of the Jews of Pinsk-Karlin in Israel, 1966.

Taylor, A. J. P. *English History, 1914–1945.* New York: Oxford University Press, 1965.

Tcherikower, Elias. *Geshikhte fun der Yidisher Arbeter-Bavegung in di Fareynikte Shtatn.* New York: YIVO. Vol. 1 (1943); vol. 2 (1945).

————. "Yidn revolutsionern in Russland in di 60er un 70er yorn." *Historishe Shriften Yivo* [Vilna] 3 (1939): 152–71.

————, ed. *The Early Jewish Labor Movement in the United States.* Condensed, translated, and revised by Aaron Antonovsky. New York: YIVO, 1961.

Tchernowitz, Samuel. *"Bnei Moshe" u-Tekufatam.* Warsaw: Zefirah, 1914.

Teveth, Shabtai. *Kinat David: Hayye David Ben Gurion.* Jerusalem and Tel Aviv: Schocken, 1976. Vol. 1.

Thon, Yaakov Johanan. *Sefer Warburg. Korot Hayav, Divrei Haarkhah, Neumim u-Maamarim.* Tel Aviv: Massada, 1948.

Tibawi, Abdul Latif. *British Interests in Palestine, 1800–1901.* London: Oxford University Press, 1961.

Tobias, Henry J. *The Jewish Bund in Russia from Its Origins to 1905.* Stanford: Stanford University Press, 1972.

Toledano, Joseph. "Weizmann, l'Homme de la Synthese." *Israel Hebdo* 52 (November 19, 1976): 26.

Trotsky, Leon. *1905.* Translated by Anya Bostock. New York: Random House, 1971.

Tschlenow, Yehiel. *Pirke Hayav u-Feulato, Zikhronot, Ktavim, Neumim, Mikhtavim.* Edited by Shmuel Eisenstadt. Tel Aviv: privately printed, 1937.

Tuchman, Barbara W. *Bible and Sword: England and Palestine from the Bronze Age to Balfour.* New York: Minerva Press, 1956.

Ulam, Adam B. *Lenin and the Bolsheviks.* London: Secker & Warburg, 1965.

Ussishkin, Menahem. "Ha-Tragiyut be-Haye Motzkin." In *Sefer Motzkin,* edited by Alex Bein, pp. 15–19. Jerusalem: Ha-Hanhalah ha-Zionit ve-Hanhalat ha-Congress ha-Yehudi ha-Olami, 1919.

Vereté, Meir. "Madua Nosdah Konsulia Britit be-Eretz Israel." *Zion* 26, nos. 3–4 (1961): 225–31.

————. "The Restoration of the Jews in English Protestant Thought, 1790–1840." *Middle Eastern Studies* 8 (1972): 3–50.

Vital, David. *The Origins of Zionism.* Oxford: Clarendon Press, 1975.

————. *Zionism: The Formative Years.* Oxford: Clarendon Press, 1982.

Volchonsky, Dov. "Pogrom ha-Ptihah shel ha-Meah ha-20." *Heavar* 20 (1973): 176–94.

Webster, Sir Charles Kingsley. *The Founder of the National Home.* Rehovot: Yad Chaim Weizmann, 1955.

Weichmann, Hans. *Die Auswanderung aus Oesterreich und Russland über die Deutschen Haefen.* (Inaugural dissertation, University of Heidelberg) Berlin: Juristische Verlagsbuchhandlung, 1913.

Weingartner, Felix. *Buffets and Rewards.* London: Hutchinson, 1937.

Weinryb, Bernard D. *Neueste Wirtschaftsgeschichte der Juden in Russland und Polen.* Breslau: M. & H. Marcus, 1934. Vol. 1.

Weisbord, Robert G. *African Zion: The Attempt to Establish a Jewish Colony in the East Africa Protectorate, 1903–1905.* Philadelphia: Jewish Publication Society of America, 1968.

Weisgal, Meyer, ed. *Chaim Weizmann: Statesman, Scientist, Builder of the Jewish Commonwealth.* New York: Dial Press, 1944.

————, and Joel Carmichael, eds. *Chaim Weizmann: A Biography by Several Hands.* New York: Atheneum, 1963.

Weizman, Ezer. *Lekha Shamayim, Lekha Aretz.* Tel Aviv: Sifriyat Maariv, 1975.

Weizmann der Fuehrer. Anlaesslich seines Besuches in Wien im Januar 1925. Vienna: Zionistisches Landeskomitee fuer Oesterreich, 1925.

Weizmann, Leah. "Zikhronot al yalduto shel Chaim Weizmann." *Davar*, June 3, 1938, p. 8.

Weltsch, Robert. "Weizmanns Briefe aus dem Jahr 1903." *Mitteilungsblatt*, May 21, 1971, p. 2.

Wertheimer, Jack L. "German Policy and Jewish Politics: The Absorption of East European Jews in Germany, 1868–1914." Diss., Columbia University, 1978.

White, Arnold. *The Modern Jew*. London: W. Heinemann, 1899.

Wiener, Joel H. *Great Britain: Foreign Policy and the Span of Empire, 1689–1971*. New York: Chelsea House, 1972.

Wilensky, Mordecai. *Hasidim u-Mitnagdim, le-Toldot ha-Pulmus she-Beinehem, ba-Shanim, 1772–1815*. Jerusalem: Mossad Bialik, 1970.

Willcox, Walter F., ed. *International Migrations*. 2 vols. New York: National Bureau of Economic Research. Vol. 1, 1929; vol. 2, 1931.

Williams, Bill. *The Making of Manchester Jewry, 1740–1875*. Manchester: Manchester University Press, 1976.

Williams, Robert C. *Culture in Exile: Russian Emigres in Germany, 1881–1941*. Ithaca, N.Y.: Cornell University Press, 1972.

Wilson, Harold. *The Chariot of Israel: Britain, America and the State of Israel*. London: Weidenfeld and Nicolson and Michael Joseph, 1981.

Winshel, Aryeh. "Hasphaatah ha-Zionit shel Geveret Oliphant al Balfour." *Haumah*, no. 2 (April 1960): 226–28.

Wintz, Leo. "Die Juden von Gestern (Eine Erwiderung)." *Ost und West*, no. 4 (April 1903): 217–26.

Wischnitzer, Mark. *To Dwell in Safety: The Story of Jewish Migration Since 1800*. Philadelphia: Jewish Publication Society of America, 1948.

Witte, Sergei. *The Memoirs of Count Witte*. Translated and edited by Abraham Yarmolinsky. Garden City, N.Y.: Doubleday, Page, 1921.

Wohlgelernter, Maurice. *Israel Zangwill*. New York: Columbia University Press, 1964.

Wolf, Lucien. *Notes on the Diplomatic History of the Jewish Question*. London: Jewish Historical Society of England, 1919.

———, ed. *Menasseh ben Israel's Mission to Oliver Cromwell: Being a Reprint of the Pamphlets published by Menasseh ben Israel to promote the Re-admission of the Jews to England, 1649–1656*. London: Published for the Jewish Historical Society of England by Macmillan and Company, Limited, 1901.

Wolfsberg, Isaiah. *Chaim Weizmann*. Jerusalem: Ha-Sifriyah ha-Zionit, 1962.

Yaari-Poleskin, Yaakov. *Arthur James Balfour, Hayav ve-Hatzharato*. Tel Aviv: Holmim ve-Lohamim, 1930.

———. *Holmim ve-Lohamim*. Petach Tikvah: S. Z. Gissin, 1922.

———. *Yehoshua Hankin, Ha-Ish u-Mifalo*. Tel Aviv: Massadah, 1933.

Yanait-Ben Zvi-Rachael. *Manya Shohat*. Jerusalem: Yad Yitzhak Ben Zvi, 1976.

Yarden, Shmuel. *Sipurah shel Moteleh*. Jerusalem: Megamah le-Umanuyot ha-Dfus, 1979.

Yisraeli, Yaacov. *Beit Karlin-Stolin: Prakim be-Masekhet Hayehem shel Admorei ha-Shoshelet ve-Iyunim be-Mishnatam ha-Hasidit*. Tel Aviv: Hotsaat Keren Yaakov ve-Rahel, 1981.

Yodfat, A. *Prakim be-Toldot Jaffa*. Tel Aviv–Jaffa: Iryat Tel Aviv–Jaffa, 1972.

Young, Kenneth. *Arthur James Balfour*. London: G. Bell and Sons, 1963.

Yusuk, Shimon. *Hurban Motoleh*. Jerusalem: n.p., 1957.

Zborowski, Mark, and Elizabeth Herzog. *Life Is with People*. New York: International Universities Press, 1952.

Zebel, Sydney H. *Balfour: A Political Biography*. Cambridge: Cambridge University Press, 1973.

Zeman, Z. A. B., and W. B. Scharlau. *The Merchant of Revolution: The Life of Alexander Israel Helphand (Parvus), 1867–1924*. London: Oxford University Press, 1965.

Zenzipper, Aryeh (Raphaeli). "Ha-Zionut be-Einei ha-Boleshet ha-Russit." *Shivat Zion*, vol. 1, pp. 225–231. Jerusalem: Ha-Sifriyah ha-Zionit, 1950.

Zipperstein, Steve Jeffrey. "The Jewish Community of Odessa from 1794–1871: Social Characteristics and Cultural Development." Diss., University of California at Los Angeles, 1980.

Index

Abdul Hamid II (Ottoman sultan), 77, 78, 87, 92, 93, 102, 172, 318, 325
Aberson, Zvi, 41, 56, 58, 85, 92, 97, 104, 105, 139, 197, 207, 208, 218, 260
Ahad Ha'Am, 55, 60, 147, 313, 339
  and Chaim Weizmann, 39, 41–42, 73, 76–80, 83, 101, 139, 143, 162, 186, 194, 205, 206, 310, 319–20, 338, 348, 349, 354, 360, 361, 369–71, 378, 403
  and cultural Zionism, 71, 73, 78, 85, 124, 139
  East-West schism and, 141–44, 174
  evaluation of, 49
  goals of, 49, 50
  and Hibbat Zion, 39–40, 124
  and the Jewish university project, 101, 380, 381, 391, 392, 397
  and the Rothschilds, 47, 95
  and Theodor Herzl, 49, 50, 140, 143
  and the Youth Conference, 77, 81, 125
  and Zionism, 77, 90, 93, 169
Alexander, Samuel, 255–56, 349, 360, 361, 364, 390
Aliens Act, 214, 243, 266, 268, 272–77, 284
Aliyot
  First Aliyah, 46, 314
  Second Aliyah, 204, 311, 312, 315
Alliance Israélite Universelle, 31, 46, 99, 189, 269, 307
All-Russian Zionist Conference, 119, 123–25, 139, 146, 154, 163
Anglo-Jewish Association, 266, 267, 269
Anglo-Palestine Company (APC), 129, 170, 289, 312
Anti-Semitism
  Ahad Ha'Am on, 40
  causes of, 16–17
  Chaim Weizmann and, 264–65, 363–67
  cures for, 17–18

dealing with, 190
  in Rumania, 62, 212
  in Russia. See Pogroms; Russia
  in Western Europe, 16, 28, 205, 214, 274
Arabs, and Zionism, 342, 384, 385
Assimilation, 17, 36, 99, 135, 145–46, 404

Baker, Percy, 281, 282, 284, 295–96, 300, 320
Balfour, Arthur James, 244, 270–75, 276–78, 347
Balfour Declaration, 39, 50, 206, 251, 317, 404
Basel Program, 71, 81, 92, 98, 123, 167, 170, 174, 245, 246, 249, 250, 291, 319, 327
Belisha, Barrow, 247–48, 255, 275, 276
Belkovsky, Gregory, 177, 178, 184, 197, 198
Bentley, William, 287, 302
Bentwich, Herbert, 189, 216, 281, 284, 298, 300, 319, 321–24, 331, 333, 383
Bentwich, Norman, 299, 331, 334, 344, 349
Berlin
  appeal of, to East European Jews, 30, 31
  Chaim Weizmann's studies in, 30–36, 41–43, 50
Bernstein, Eduard, 121
Bernstein-Kohan, Jacob, 54, 63, 73, 76, 77, 80, 82, 83, 90, 130, 147, 181, 197, 250, 252, 267
  and the Democratic Faction, 94
  and the Jewish Statistical Bureau, 101
  and the Kishinev pogrom, 149–50
  and the Sixth Zionist Congress, 167, 170
  and the Youth Conference, 85
Bialik, Haim Nahman, 149, 389
Bilu, 18, 25, 46

557

Birmingham Conference, 299, 300, 320
Birnbaum, Nathan, 182
Bloch-Blumenfeld, Zvi, 10
Blumenfeld, Joseph, 351
Bnei Moshe, 24, 40, 41, 49, 93
Board of Deputies of British Jews, 266, 269, 275
Bodenheimer, Max, 167, 169, 306, 329
British Brothers' League, 125, 213, 274
Brussels Conference, 269, 270, 282, 289, 330
Buber, Martin, 88, 90, 134, 205, 310, 331, 334, 378
  and Chaim Weizmann, 93, 101, 131, 137, 143–45, 159, 160, 162, 175, 187, 191, 197, 203
  and the Juedischer Verlag, 100, 118, 129, 132, 135, 151, 181, 183–85
  and synthetic Zionism, 309
  and Theodor Herzl, 158
Bukhmil, Joshua Heshel, 50, 85, 95
Bund, the (General Jewish Workers' Union)
  and Chaim Weizmann, 55–56, 82, 100, 103, 135, 148, 152, 158, 196, 266, 281, 404
  and socialism, 51–52, 352
  and Zionism, 51–52, 55–56, 81, 132, 294

Campbell-Bannerman, Henry, 271, 275, 276
Chamberlain, Joseph, 127–28, 164–66, 177, 207
Charlottenburg Polytechnik, 30, 31, 33, 36, 50, 122, 403
Chemerinski, Gittl-Rivka, 5
Chemerinski, Yehiel-Michel, 7, 12, 21
Chemistry. *See* Weizmann, Chaim: as scientist
Churchill, Winston, 213, 272, 275–78, 319, 338
Commission for the Investigation of Palestine, 231, 251, 290
Committee for a Jewish University, 133, 145
Constantinople, 318, 325–27, 334, 373
Cowen, Joseph, 243, 252, 279, 281, 282, 289, 299, 319, 321, 323, 344, 383
  and Chaim Weizmann, 189, 217, 229, 283, 295, 296, 298, 300, 301, 304, 309, 324
  and Theodor Herzl, 215–16, 381
Cultural Zionism. *See* Zionism
Cyprus, 127, 279

Darmstadt, Chaim Weizmann's studies in, 27, 29–30
Deichler, Christian, 33, 58, 97, 105, 121, 347
Democratic Faction, 70, 87–89, 95, 119, 146, 154, 175, 183, 186, 195, 218, 246, 266, 280, 378
  and Ahad Ha'Am, 93, 139
  and Chaim Weizmann (founder). *See* Weizmann, Chaim
  criticism of, 93–94, 139, 180, 181
  and cultural Zionism, 88, 90, 124–25
  decline of, 125, 131, 138, 162, 171, 196–97
  end of, 198, 310
  and the Mizrahi, 123–25
  problems of, 94–96, 100, 123, 125, 147
  program of, 87, 95, 98–99, 119, 121, 309
  and Poalei Zion, 147–48
  role and obligations of, 86–87, 91
  significance of, 87
  and the World Zionist Organization, 86–87, 91, 92, 194
Diaspora, 9, 16, 45, 153, 192, 208, 373
  Zionist attitude toward and plans for, 48, 52, 245, 246, 291, 306, 310
Die Welt. See Welt, Die
Dixon, Harold Baily, 224, 239, 284, 338, 362, 363
Dorfman, Catherine, 80, 84, 119, 131, 145, 150, 184, 199
Dreyfus, Charles, 202, 241, 272, 273, 277, 322
  and Chaim Weizmann, 191, 237–39, 240, 242–44, 247, 249, 252, 280, 285, 300, 349, 390
Dugdale, Blanche, 272
Duma, 261–62, 265, 280–81, 305, 341

East Africa. *See* Uganda controversy
East Africa Commission, 186, 189, 229, 247, 248
East Africa Survey Expedition, 248, 249
Eastern Europe
  emigration of Jews from, 16, 46, 126, 211, 226
  Jews of, 3–4, 16, 49, 85, 122, 133, 153, 154, 174, 209, 211, 212, 230, 240, 241, 243, 250, 261, 289, 299, 406
  and roots of Chaim Weizmann, 26
East-West conflict of Zionism, 140–44, 154–55, 170, 174, 192–94, 208, 334, 405
  synthesis of Eastern and Western Zion-

ists, 142, 155, 171, 193, 208, 344, 405, 407
Education. *See also* Jewish university project
Chaim Weizmann on, 23, 26, 33
in Germany, 27, 30
in the Pale of Settlement, 9, 20, 27, 36, 102
in Palestine, 306–7, 379–81
in Pinsk, 20
and World Zionist Organization, 339, 392, 399, 401
Egypt, 128, 164, 165, 190
Ehrenpreis, Marcus, 41, 182, 306
Ehrlich, Paul, 377–78, 393–94, 396, 397, 399
El Arish, 127, 164–66, 168, 190, 207, 279
Eliashev, Isidore, 41, 85, 94
Eliot, Charles, 177, 186, 207
Engeres Aktions-Comité, 231, 252, 269
England. *See also* English Zionist Federation; English Zionists; Uganda controversy
anti-alien movement in, 126, 211–14
Chaim Weizmann and, 179, 186–91, 202, 204–10, 214, 217–29, 233–49, 252–56, 265–87, 310, 320, 346–74, 402, 404–7
Jewish immigration to, 16, 126, 205, 211, 212, 226
Jews of, 254–55, 266–70, 272, 277, 284, 403
role of, in Jewish history, 13, 14, 31, 206–7, 266, 281, 346–47, 381, 407
Zionism in, 273, 278
English Zionist Federation (EZF), 215–18, 229, 242–44, 247, 249, 268, 273, 278–84, 290, 294–302, 310, 317–24, 340, 346, 381–82, 393, 402
English Zionists, 208, 215, 217, 249, 278, 283, 284, 291, 297–99, 320, 322–24, 340, 344, 381, 382
Enlightenment *(Haskalah)*, 8, 16, 17, 20
Eretz Israel, 5, 18, 291
Evans-Gordon, William, 125–27, 213, 268
and Chaim Weizmann, 128, 186, 189–90, 191, 202, 214, 217, 266

Feiwel, Berthold, 98, 100, 101, 103, 115, 116–18, 132, 282, 331, 334
and Chaim Weizmann, 56, 97, 98, 102, 104, 115, 119, 131, 133–35, 137–39, 143–45, 151, 175, 181, 184–85, 191, 197, 246, 256, 269, 290, 310, 348, 376, 386

and Theodor Herzl, 90, 115, 158
Fernbach, Auguste, 351, 353–60, 364, 379
Figner, Vera, 51, 55
Fischer, Jean, 380, 384
Fribourg, University of, 50–51
Friedman, David, 24, 25

Gaster, Moses, 60, 63, 90, 217, 247–49, 252, 267, 268, 276, 284, 295, 296, 299, 317, 320, 322, 323, 344
ambitions of, 217, 221
and Chaim Weizmann, 182, 188, 191, 202, 203, 208, 214–16, 228–30, 237, 266, 280, 281, 283, 297, 302, 304, 324, 331, 338, 348, 381–83
and Theodor Herzl, 189, 194
Gegenwartsarbeit, 291, 294, 330
Gederah, 18, 25, 46
General Jewish Workers' Union. *See* Bund, the
Geneva, 51, 87, 205, 207–10, 403
Geneva, University of, 54, 205
Geneva Information Bureau, 95–97
Geneva Zionist Society, 57, 92
George, Lloyd, 272
Germany
anti-Semitism in, 16, 28, 205
appeal of, to Russian Jews, 30, 31
attitude of, toward East Europeans, 32–33
education in, 27, 30
Getzova, Sophia, 51, 52, 54–56, 66–69, 73, 81, 85, 86, 94, 116, 121, 146
Ginsberg, Asher. *See* Ahad Ha'Am
Gordon, Judah Leib, 10
Graebe, Carl, 33, 54, 205, 222, 224, 225, 238, 266, 377
Greater Actions Committee (Grosses Aktions-Comité [GAC]), 54, 59, 60, 79–80, 128–30, 160, 163, 166–68, 170, 172, 173, 175–78, 195, 198, 202, 217, 229–31, 248–50, 252, 269, 279, 298, 300, 302, 306, 310, 311, 318, 320, 323, 325, 326, 329, 334, 336, 342–44, 346, 376, 377, 380, 381, 390, 394, 397, 399, 400
Greenberg, Leopold, 126, 128, 165–66, 177, 189, 215–18, 221, 229–31, 243, 247–50, 252, 269, 277–84, 290, 295–97, 299–301, 304, 319, 321, 322, 335, 344, 402
Grinblatt, Rosa, 80, 260

Hadera, 42, 375
Haifa, 314, 339, 341

Halévy, Joseph, 181
Hamelitz, 17, 40, 42, 93
Hantke, Arthur, 329, 344–47, 374, 382,
    389
Hashahar, 92, 93, 138, 259
Hashiloah, 41, 49, 94, 140
Hasidism, 5, 20, 54, 116
Haskalah. *See* Enlightenment
Hatzfirah, 145, 178, 280, 396
Hebrew language, 10, 11, 21
  revival of, by Zionists, 25, 40, 99, 124,
    143, 241, 343, 384, 386, 389, 391–93,
    396, 399, 401
Hebrew studies, 24, 25, 99, 143
Hebrew University in Jerusalem. *See* Jew-
    ish university project
Heder, 5, 9, 10, 20
  metukan, 25, 37
Helsingfors Conference, 291, 293–94, 306,
    310, 330
Helsingfors Program, 297, 330
Herzl, Theodor, 24, 45, 158, 184, 188, 189,
    196–97, 204, 221, 250, 279, 302, 323,
    380
  Altneuland (novel), 134, 139–44, 157
  and Chaim Weizmann, 77–79, 83, 90–
    91, 93, 95, 118, 141, 143, 144, 151–57,
    166, 167, 169, 178, 186, 190, 193–95,
    205, 207, 208, 222, 387, 396, 407
  challenge to leadership of, 70, 73, 77,
    87, 167, 175–78, 193–94, 210
  charisma of, 48–49
  contribution of, 48, 50, 141, 407
  critics of, 59–61, 70, 73, 92, 407
  and cultural Zionism, 60, 64, 72, 88, 90
  death of, 178, 214, 217, 230, 245, 311,
    402
  and England, 59–60, 126–29, 211, 216
  goals of, 48, 50, 407
  influence of, 48–50, 141, 279, 406
  and the Jewish university project, 102–
    3, 118, 119
  Judenstaat, Der (The Jews' State), 45, 147,
    216, 241
  and the kaiser, 59
  as leader of the Zionist cause, 45, 47–
    50, 52, 54, 61, 99, 141, 174, 243, 293,
    327
  and Nathaniel Meyer Rothschild, 26–27
  and Orthodox Judaism, 64, 71–72, 90,
    153
  policies of, 48, 50, 70–71
  and a political homeland for the Jews,
    48, 50, 127, 148, 164–66, 231
  Sultan Abdul Hamid II and, 77, 78, 87,
    92, 93, 102, 103, 129, 172

and the Uganda controversy, 167–74,
    230
and the World Zionist Organization, 50,
    51, 70
and the Zionist congresses, 50, 62–63,
    72, 87, 88, 90–91
and the Zionist press, 132
Hibbat Zion, 14, 24, 42, 188, 245, 293. *See
    also* Weizmann, Chaim
  and agricultural settlements in Pales-
    tine, 46
  and Ahad Ha'Am, 39–40, 124
  beginning of, 16, 18
  and Bnei Moshe, 40
  and Herzl's leadership, 45, 61
  and the Kattowitz Conference, 13, 18,
    24
  and Ottoman policy, 45–46
  and the revival of Hebrew, 25
Hilfsverein der deutschen Juden, 203–5,
    245, 269, 307, 339, 391–93
Hill, Clement, 165–66, 217, 219–21, 229,
    272
Hirsch, Maurice de, 42
Hovevei Zion, 17, 18, 24, 42, 71, 77, 290
  in England, 215–16, 240–41

Idelson, Abraham, 160, 161, 291
Immigration by Jews
  to Canada, 16
  to England, 16, 126, 205, 211, 212
  to Germany, 31
  to Palestine, 16, 24. *See also* Palestine
  to the United States, 16, 31, 205
Inner Actions Committee (SAC), 59, 60,
    79, 80, 103, 119, 157, 170, 176–78,
    195, 198, 250, 279, 282, 289, 290, 295,
    302, 306, 311, 324, 326–29, 331, 334,
    342–47, 376–78, 380–85, 389, 391–95,
    397–99

Jabotinsky, Vladimir, 291, 326, 334, 399–
    400
Jacobson, Victor, 32, 94, 119, 160–61, 171,
    175, 183–84, 195, 196, 203, 204, 208,
    267, 281, 312, 325, 326, 344, 345, 382,
    389, 400
Jaffa, 40, 46, 129, 312–14, 391
Jerusalem, 25, 46, 272, 294, 313–14, 386,
    391, 395–97
Jewish Chronicle, The, 216, 240, 267, 274,
    281, 335
Jewish Colonial Trust (JCT), 53, 59, 147,
    170, 177, 192, 206, 251, 281, 295, 304–
    6, 318, 329, 342, 344, 346, 384, 385

Jewish Colonization Association (ICA), 47, 62, 77, 94–96, 99, 100, 148, 175, 187, 245, 269
Jewish Historical Commission, 149
Jewish National Fund, 63, 90, 99, 148, 170, 192, 290, 295, 302, 306, 339, 344
Jewish nationalism, 31–34, 71
  Bnei Moshe and, 40
  Chaim Weizmann and, 38, 153
Jewish Question, 83, 127, 250, 274. *See also* Anti-Semitism; Pogroms
Jewish Statistical Association, 101, 151
Jewish Statistical Bureau, 100–101, 102, 129
Jewish Territorial Organization (ITO), 251, 267–69, 273, 276, 278, 279, 281–83, 304
Jewish University Bureau, 131–33, 164
Jewish university project, 88–90, 99, 101, 117–19, 121, 125, 146, 157, 172, 181–83, 185, 236, 336, 374, 375, 381, 386–90, 393–99, 401, 404, 406
  language for, 391–93
  plans for, 379–80
  site for, 129–31, 162–64, 387
Jews. *See* Anti-Semitism; Assimilation; Eastern Europe; East-West conflict of Zionism; Germany; Motol; Pogroms; Russia; Zionism
Joint Zionist Council, 323, 382
Jude, Revue der Juedischen Moderne, Der, 135, 136, 145, 151, 154, 158, 175, 179, 180, 183–85
Juedische Statistik, 101
Juedischer Almanach, 100, 115
Juedischer Verlag, 90, 100, 101, 115, 118, 121, 129, 132, 134, 138, 145, 151, 154, 158, 185

Kann, Jacobus, 311, 324, 329, 331, 333–34
Karlin, 19, 20, 22, 24
Kattowitz Conference, 13, 18, 24
Kenya, 177
Kessler, Leopold, 189, 216, 321, 323, 381
Kharkov Conference, 176–78, 182, 196–97, 245
Khatzman, Issay, 65, 287
Khatzman, Rachel, 303, 351
Khatzman, Sophia, 301, 303
Khatzman, Theodosia, 65, 128–29
Khatzman, Vera, 65–66, 67–70, 92, 104–11, 121, 128, 131, 135, 136, 146, 148–49, 205, 237, 256–60, 265, 268, 284, 287, 318, 338, 356, 361, 367, 373, 390, 401

  letters of Chaim Weizmann to, 78–79, 81–83, 93, 97, 98, 120, 123, 141, 158, 187, 205, 234–36, 243, 253, 254, 263, 278, 280, 285, 312–16, 333, 352, 357, 363, 370–72, 374, 378, 385–86
  lifestyle after marriage, 348–51
  marriage of, 256, 287–88, 300–301, 303, 311
  medical studies of, 102, 351, 373
  and Zionism, 111–15, 259
Kiev, 4, 54, 175, 212, 240
Kornienko, 22
Kremenetzky, Johann, 302, 303, 311, 315, 318, 335
Kroll, Michael, 160, 161, 163

Landau, Leopold, 377, 393, 397, 399
Lansdowne, Henry Charles, Lord, 128, 165, 177, 221
Lapworth, Arthur, 361–63, 365–67
Laski, Nathan, 247–48, 255, 268, 275, 276
League for the Attainment of Complete Equal Rights for the Jewish People in Russia, 264, 281
Lenin, Vladimir Ilyich, 51, 55, 352, 353
Levey, Rachel, 227, 234, 237
Levin, Shmarya, 32, 50, 68, 94, 141, 168, 170, 173, 267, 306, 311, 339, 342, 344, 345, 384, 389, 391, 393, 400
Lichtenstein, Abraham, 55, 82, 123, 170, 318
Lichtheim, Richard, 334, 348
Liebermann, Carl Theodor, 33, 224, 225, 258
Lilien, Ephraim M., 90, 100, 121, 131–34
Lilienblum, Moshe Leib, 17, 18, 42
Lipsky, Louis, 402
Loewe, Heinrich, 329, 394–95
Lubzhinsky, Chaim, 12, 22, 35, 122, 145, 223, 287, 341
Lubzhinsky, Eva, 265, 341
Lubzhinsky, Fanya, 122, 287
Lurie, Grigory, 22, 36
Lurie, Joseph, 49, 50
Lurie, Ovsey, 22, 23
Lurie, Saul, 22, 25, 163

Magnes, Judah Leon, 266, 287, 375, 378–80, 386, 393–95, 397, 400
Manchester, 202, 215, 258–60, 270, 271, 273, 274, 295, 320–24, 333
  Chaim Weizmann in, 55, 58, 222–25, 228, 233–39, 249, 253, 254, 265, 277–

Manchester *(continued)*
  80, 284, 287, 291, 303, 305, 316, 376, 378, 390, 403
  Jews of, 211, 225–27, 273, 275, 276
Manchester, University of, 203, 222–25, 234, 255, 258, 338, 341, 347, 351, 376, 390
Manchester Chemical Society, 235, 239, 242
Manchester Conference, 319, 320
Manchester School of Zionism, 299, 300
Manchester Zionist Association (MZA), 237, 239, 240–44, 284, 297, 298, 300, 322, 325
Mandelstamm, Max, 171, 175, 246, 267, 278
Marks, Simon, 299, 391, 394
Marmorek, Alexander, 90, 167, 250, 252, 266, 290, 304, 307, 309, 326, 342, 343
Marxism, and Zionism, 55–56
Maskilim, 9, 16, 17, 61
Massel, Joseph, 227, 239, 241, 242, 349
Meyenberg, Alexander, 239, 284–85
Mizrahi, 123–25, 153, 170, 171, 193, 343
Mohilewer, Shmuel, 42, 71, 123
Montefiore, Francis, 177, 218, 243, 253, 279, 281, 283, 296, 299, 301, 321
Montefiore, Moses, 12, 13, 18, 47, 66
Moser, Jacob, 252, 301, 319, 321, 322, 331, 332, 337, 383
Motol, 3–5, 7–10, 13, 15, 18, 20, 22, 24, 28, 347, 403
Motolianski, Abraham Isaac, 10, 11, 20
Motzkin, Leo, 30, 32, 36, 38, 49, 101, 102, 119
  and Chaim Weizmann, 33, 35, 37, 39–41, 43, 45, 51, 54, 61, 62, 68, 73–74, 80–83, 86, 94–100, 103, 115, 121, 136, 163, 171, 180, 217, 311, 377, 378, 380, 386
  and Theodor Herzl, 60, 72–73
  and Zionism, 50, 52–53, 59, 63, 76, 82, 85–86, 93, 99, 125, 307, 381
Munich Conference, 73–75, 80

Nathan, Paul, 278, 338–39, 391
National home for Jews in Palestine. *See* Palestine
Nemser, Alexander, 73, 74, 76
Nordau, Max, 85, 88, 139, 140–44, 158, 169, 177, 181, 182, 186–87, 189, 207–98, 248, 250, 251, 267–69, 272, 304, 312, 325–27, 331, 334, 380, 384

October Manifesto, 261–62, 264
Odessa Committee (Society for the Sup-

port of Jewish Farmers and Artisans in Syria and Palestine), 24, 42, 49, 324, 326
Oliphant, Laurence, 24, 188 .
Order of Ancient Maccabeans (OAM), 323, 324, 326, 340, 343, 346, 381–83
Organization Bureau, 75, 78, 80, 83
Orthodox Judaism, 28, 37, 40, 63–64. *See also* Weizmann, Chaim
  and Zionism, 71–72, 81, 90
Ottoman Empire
  revolution in, 325
  and Zionism, 42, 45, 46, 77, 78, 87, 126, 127, 129, 172, 298, 304, 318–19, 327, 331, 333–34, 340, 342, 376, 379, 381, 384, 395–97
Owens College, 223–224, 350

Pale of Settlement, 3, 5, 10, 13, 34–36, 43, 65, 66, 123, 128, 146. *See also* Pogroms
  conditions in the, 5, 9, 15, 26, 51, 122, 151, 200–201
  education in the, 9, 20, 27, 36, 102
  Judaism in the, 9
  Zionist conditions in, 43
Palestine, 167, 245, 318
  Ahad Ha'Am on, 39–40, 47, 49
  Bilu and, 18
  Chaim Weizmann's first visit to, 311–17
  Chaim Weizmann's interest in settling in, 203–5, 330, 331, 334, 343, 381
  education in, 306–7, 379–81
  Herzl's policy regarding, 48, 77, 78, 127, 231
  importance of, to Zionism, 87, 208, 384
  Jewish colonization of, 16, 17, 24, 46, 215, 241, 245, 289, 329, 345, 397
  as the Jewish homeland, 27, 169, 172, 174–76, 179, 180, 191, 196, 231, 249–51, 266, 273, 277, 281, 282, 297–98, 381
  Leo Motzkin's report on, 52–53, 59
  Ottoman Empire and Zionism in, 42, 45–46, 126, 127, 325, 333–34
  preparations needed by Zionists for, 46, 99, 289, 290, 294, 297–98, 306, 311, 334
  as site for the Jewish university, 130, 131, 162–64, 182, 183, 187, 279, 307, 376, 387
Palestine Land Development Company (PLDC), 315, 320, 336
Palestine Office, 310–11, 315
Pasmanik, Daniel, 76, 77, 80, 291, 327
Pasteur Institute, 351, 352, 355, 395

Percy, Earl, Lord, 190, 217, 219–21, 229, 272
Perkin, William Henry, Jr., 203, 222–28, 233–35, 238, 242, 249, 284, 338, 349, 352–65, 367, 371, 374, 375
Pevsner, Samuel, 197, 313–15
Pfungstadt, 27, 31, 37
  education in, 27–29, 33
  Chaim Weizmann as teacher in, 27–30
Pinkus, Felix, 97, 98, 116, 119
Pinsk, 3–5, 8, 19–20, 24, 29, 122, 256. *See also* Pinsk *Real-Gymnasium*
  Chaim Weizmann in, 10, 12–14, 18, 21–24, 26, 30, 36, 37, 39, 43, 45, 50, 54, 200, 341, 403
  and Hibbat Zion, 18
  Jews of, 18–20
  Weizmann family's move to, 35
  and Zionism, 43, 52
Pinsk, *Real-Gymnasium*, 13, 15, 20–22
  Chaim Weizmann at the, 20, 21, 27, 41
  Moshe Weizmann at the, 35
Pinsker, Leo, 17, 18, 42
Plehve, Vyacheslav von, 123, 148, 149, 165, 167, 174, 190
Plekhanov, G. V., 51, 55
Poalei Zion (Zionist Workers), 55, 147, 380
Pogroms, 15–16, 24, 135, 157, 215, 239–40, 262–66, 269, 270, 274, 276, 279
  at Bialystok, 281
  at Homel, 187, 311
  at Kishinev, 149–51, 157, 165, 167, 172, 175, 200, 212, 216, 264, 276, 284, 311
  at Odessa, 264
Pokrassa, Joseph, 160, 164, 196
Polesie, 3–4
Political Zionism. *See* Zionism: political
Poretchye, 7
Practical Zionism. *See* Zionism: practical

Rabinovich, Solomon, 90, 265
Ramsay, William, 202, 222–23, 355
Rehovot, 40, 42, 313, 314
Reines, Isaac Jacob, 90, 123–25
Richards, Theodore William, 362, 365–66
Rossenbaum, Simon, 147, 152, 177, 178, 197, 198, 202, 265, 291, 306
Rosenblum, Paula, 51, 54, 59
Rothschild, Edmond James de
  criticism of, 53
  and the Jewish university project, 376, 381, 383–84, 394–99, 401
  and Zionism, 46–47, 49, 77, 314, 315
Rothschild, James de, 46, 398, 399
Rothschild, Nathaniel Meyer, 126–29, 187, 226, 267

Rothschild family, 12
Rothstein, Isaac, 141–42
Royal Commission on Alien Immigration, 213, 216–17
Ruppin, Arthur, 311, 314–15, 380, 385, 400
Russia, 3, 5, 43. *See also* Pogroms
  anti-Semitism in, 212, 341–43, 387
  Chaim Weizmann's attitude toward, 27, 42
  culture of, 22, 25–26
  Jewish emigration from, 16, 46
  Jews in, 15–16, 30, 31, 165, 250, 262–63, 266, 269, 270, 281, 294, 341–43
  political unrest in, 261–66
Russian Zionists, 59–61, 82, 84, 87, 93, 94, 98, 123, 138, 155, 160, 162, 163, 169–72, 178, 179, 195, 196, 205, 249, 252, 291, 300, 305, 310, 325–27, 330, 331, 336, 343, 379, 403
Russischer juedischer wissenschaftlicher Verein—Kadimah, 35, 40, 41, 73, 93
  Chaim Weizmann and the, 33, 38, 39, 51, 121
  characteristics of the, 32–34
  purpose of, 31–32, 34, 50
Rutherford, Ernest, 352, 360, 361, 364

Sacher, Harry, 294, 297, 299, 300, 303, 319, 322, 324, 331, 334, 346, 349, 373, 381–83, 390, 394
Samuel, Herbert, 338
Schapira, Zvi Hermann, 18, 63, 89, 379
Schauer, Rudolf, 138, 139
Schiff, Jacob H., 339, 391, 393
Schuster, Arthur, 350–51, 360–64, 367, 373, 390
Schuster, Caroline, 205, 350–51, 368–70, 371–73
Schuster, Norah, 367, 369–70, 371–73, 390
Shneerson, Esther, 80, 115–17, 119, 256, 260
Shriro, Samuel, 119, 129, 157–58, 183, 206, 236
Sieff, Israel, 299, 394
Simon, James, 278, 339, 391
Simon, Julius, 348, 374, 376, 378, 394, 401
Simon, Leon, 299, 319, 321, 324, 331, 334, 349, 381, 382, 394
Sinai, 127, 164, 166, 207, 279
Smolenskin, Perez, 10, 17
Socialism, 16, 34, 226, 404
  and Zionism, 51–52, 62, 82, 132, 147, 152–53, 170, 251, 311
Sokolovsky, Shlomo Tsvi, 11, 13, 18

Sokolow, Nahum, 60, 63, 90, 124, 145, 150, 151, 159, 170, 178–79, 181, 186, 208, 280, 306, 316, 326, 329–31, 335, 344, 349, 380, 384, 389, 396, 397
Sprachenkampf, 391–93
Strange, Edward Halford, 352–61
Straus, Nathan, 375, 393, 395–97, 400–401
Switzerland, 43, 50, 98, 151, 403
   as refuge and place of study for East Europeans, 51
   Zionist activities in, 136, 139
Synthetic Zionism. *See* Zionism
Syrkin, Nachman, 32, 55, 72, 81–82, 94, 95, 171, 250, 251, 306

Technicum, 338–40, 345, 375, 377–79, 391, 392, 395
Technische Hochschule in Darmstadt, 29–30
Tschlenow, Yehiel, 184, 191, 231, 291, 294, 310, 311, 324–26, 329, 342, 384, 390
   and Chaim Weizmann, 230, 267, 306
   and David Wolffsohn, 344
   and the Jewish university project, 391, 399, 400
   and Max Nordau, 334
   and Theodor Herzl, 60
   and the Uganda controversy, 167, 169, 171–74, 195
   and Zionei Zion, 250
Turkey. *See* Ottoman Empire
Tyomkin, Vladimir, 146, 175, 177, 291, 306

Uganda controversy, 125, 165–210, 216, 217, 219–20, 229–31, 243, 245–51, 271–73, 275, 279, 305, 311, 319, 383
Ussishkin, Menahem, 53, 66, 77, 147, 164, 167, 172, 176, 181, 184, 215, 245, 248, 268, 290, 309, 311, 312, 326
   and Chaim Weizmann, 194–98, 202, 203, 205, 208, 209, 217–19, 221, 223, 229–30, 234, 242, 244, 252, 267, 276, 280, 291, 294, 320, 330, 337, 379, 380, 392, 395
   as extremist, 173, 175
   and the Jewish university project, 130, 162–63, 386, 394
   as leader of the Russian Zionists, 87, 93, 94, 157, 231, 325
   and practical Zionism, 324, 384
   and synthetic Zionism, 245
   and Theodor Herzl, 180

Verein, the. *See* Russischer juedischer wissenschaftlicher Verein—Kadimah

Warburg, Otto, 162, 186, 203, 231, 248, 250–52, 269, 290, 304, 306, 311, 314, 320, 326, 328, 329, 331, 344, 345, 382, 384, 385, 389
Warsaw Conference, 123, 124
Weitzmann, Selig, 170
Weizmann, Anna, 123, 236, 341
Weizmann, Benjamin (Benjy), 303, 311, 318, 340, 348, 351, 361, 401
Weizmann, Bracha, 21, 22
Weizmann, Chaim, 5, 279. *See also* Ahad Ha'Am; England; Khatzman, Vera; Motzkin, Leo; Zionist congress
   ambitions of, 179–81, 186, 210, 252, 321–22, 404
   ancestors of, 5
   and anti-Semitism, 149–51, 157, 214, 265
   and Arthur James Balfour, 271–75
   on assimilation, 36, 145–46, 404
   bar mitzvah of, 21
   birth of, 7
   character of, 22, 42, 54, 78–80, 150, 209, 221–22, 336, 404–5
   and chemistry vs. Zionism, 55, 58, 114, 232, 233, 401, 404
   cultural interests of, 122–23
   and cultural Zionism, 60, 63–64, 88, 90, 124–25, 169
   and David Wolffsohn, 282–83, 328, 331–37, 343, 344
   as debater, 53–56
   and the Democratic Faction, 73, 86, 90, 91, 94, 96–99, 124, 125, 136, 138, 142, 151, 153–54, 159–62, 179, 405, 407
   as diplomat, 190–93, 219–21, 407
   disappointments of, 136–37, 363, 374
   early influences on, 9–13, 20–26
   East-West conflict and, 141, 142–43, 154–55, 192–93, 208, 331, 334, 405
   East-West synthesis and, 142, 155, 171, 174, 193, 208, 334, 344, 405, 407
   on education, 23, 26, 33
   education of, 10–11, 15, 20–26, 27, 29–30, 31–36, 41, 50–51, 54
   and elitist approach to Zionism, 83, 101
   on English Jews, 266–70
   family of, 7–8, 12–13
   and gentiles, 24, 26, 349–51, 363, 405
   and German Jews, 29, 36

goals of, 26, 344
health of, 103–5, 121, 136, 196, 199, 244,
  301–2, 318
and the Hibbat Zion movement, 13–14,
  18, 24–26, 403
influence of the Verein on, 33, 34
and the Jewish Colonization Association, 94–95
and Jewish nationalism, 38, 42, 153
and Jewish university project, 88–89,
  99, 101–3, 117–19, 125, 129–33, 136,
  138, 146, 147, 154, 157, 163, 164, 172,
  181–83, 185, 335, 374, 375, 379–81,
  387–90, 392–401, 404, 406
Judaism of, 13–14, 210, 406
lifestyle of, after marriage, 48–51
lure of Palestine for, 373–74
as a man of action, 83–84, 135, 136, 209
marriage of, 256, 287–88, 300–301, 303
and Marxism vs. Zionism, 55, 62
military service and, 37–38
as orator, 309
and Order of Ancient Maccabeans
  (OAM), 326, 340
and Orthodox Judaism, 28, 37, 63–64,
  406
personality of, 23, 66, 78–79, 209
and plans of for publications, 134–35
as politician, 209
and professorship at the University of
  Manchester, 361–67
reasons for success of, 404–7
roots of, 24
sacrifices of, for Zionism, 84, 136, 205,
  210, 244, 340, 404
and the Schauer affair, 138–39
and the Schuster affair, 367–74
as scientist, 22, 26, 33, 51, 97, 112, 118,
  121, 204, 206, 209, 227–29, 232, 284–
  85, 287, 304, 326, 338, 351–60, 374,
  401, 406
setbacks for, 82, 83, 198–99, 230, 279–
  80, 363, 374, 400
and settling in Palestine, 203, 345
and synthetic Zionism, 290, 307–10,
  317, 330, 384
as teacher, 27, 54, 228, 234–36, 284
and the Technicum, 339–40, 375, 376,
  378, 379
and Theodor Herzl, 50, 54, 77–79, 83,
  90–93, 95, 118, 141, 143, 144, 151–57,
  166, 167, 169, 178–79, 186, 190, 193–
  97, 205, 207, 222, 386, 387, 404
and the Uganda controversy, 168–74,
  179, 186–90, 195, 208

a visit to Palestine by, 311–17
and Western culture, 30, 36–37, 67, 142
and Winston Churchill, 276–78
and the Youth Conference, 73–77, 79–
  83, 85–87, 92–94, 125, 168
and Zionism, 25, 26, 37, 43–53, 112,
  204, 209–10, 223, 316–17
as Zionist leader, 57–59, 80, 135, 136,
  209–10, 323–24, 345, 401, 403, 405
and Zionist unity, 323–24, 330, 334
Weizmann, Chilik, 12, 123
Weizmann, Feivel, 20–22, 35, 37, 122, 287,
  288
Weizmann, Fruma, 123, 265
Weizmann, Gita, 123, 265
Weizmann, Hayah, 7, 10, 82, 123
Weizmann, Masha, 123, 236
Weizmann, Minna, 123
Weizmann, Miriam, 10, 12, 35, 122, 145,
  287, 341
Weizmann, Moshe, 35, 122, 124, 170, 199,
  231, 265, 266
Weizmann, Ozer, 5, 7, 11, 13, 22, 35, 37,
  38, 41, 44, 120, 123, 170, 199, 287, 288
  accomplishments of, 8–9
  death of, 341
  on education, 20–21, 23
  on religion, 29, 37
Weizmann, Rachel Leah, 7, 12, 13, 20, 35,
  123, 199, 288
Weizmann, Shmuel, 122–24, 152, 199,
  236, 265, 341
Weizmannism, 330
Welt, Die, 99, 129, 140, 158, 175, 178, 246,
  282, 302, 332, 334–36, 396
Weltsch, Robert, 404
White, Arnold, 125, 212
Wintz, Leo, 134, 142, 144
Wissotsky, David, 339
Wissotsky, Kalman (Wolf), 339
Wissotsky Fund, 339
Witte, Sergei, 165, 261
Wolffsohn, David, 53, 157, 244, 248, 250,
  252, 269, 277, 279, 282, 289, 295, 304,
  306, 311, 314, 318–19, 321–27, 329,
  330, 334, 342, 343, 380, 384, 385, 389.
  See also Weizmann, Chaim
  death of, 390
World Zionist Organization, 44, 47, 48,
  71, 72, 76, 77, 80, 129, 163, 167, 179,
  185, 208, 245, 251, 252, 269, 277, 279,
  300, 321, 323, 330, 331, 336, 338, 343
  and Ahad Ha'Am, 77
  and Chaim Weizmann, 402–4, 406, 407
  and cultural Zionism, 123

World Zionist Organization (*continued*)
democratic nature of, 210
and education, 339, 392, 399, 401
and England, 128, 171, 216, 217
and the Mizrahi, 123
and the Ottoman Empire, 324–25, 327
and the program of the Democratic Faction, 98
reform of the, 88, 90
in Russia, 147
and Theodor Herzl (founder), 50, 51, 61, 70, 73, 77–79, 188
and the Uganda controversy, 171, 177, 229, 246, 249, 250, 251
unity and disunity in, 87
and the Youth Conference, 85
Wormser, Gaston, 394, 397–99

Yasinovsky, Isidore, 167, 171, 278
Yellin, David, 60, 400
Yeshivot, 20, 21
Yishuv, 312, 313, 326, 339, 384, 391, 392
Young Turks, 325, 331
Youth Conference
and Ahad Ha'Am, 77, 81, 125
Chaim Weizmann and, 73–77, 75–87, 93–95, 125, 168
purposes of, 75, 85
and Theodor Herzl, 78–80

Zangwill, Israel, 90, 95, 168, 182, 188–89, 212, 215–17, 246, 247, 249–51, 279, 281, 282, 304
as threat to Zionism, 278
Zion, 17, 25, 55, 169, 401
Zionei Zion, 170, 173, 245–47, 249, 250
Zionism, 16, 31, 37, 38, 42, 116, 180, 226. *See also* East-West conflict of Zionism; Herzl, Theodor; Jewish university project; Uganda controversy; Weizmann, Chaim; World Zionist Organization; Zionist congress
and Ahad Ha'Am, 39–40, 71
attack on, in Russia, 146–47
attraction of, to Chaim Weizmann, 25, 26, 37, 50
conservative faction of, 139, 153
cultural, 60, 70–72, 88, 90, 99, 123, 124, 139, 151, 169, 210, 245, 309, 330, 343
democratic principles of, 79, 98
and England, 346–47

financial contributions to, 42
and Germany, 30
Jewish intelligentsia and, 133
and Marxism, 55–56
militancy of, 49
opposition to, 138–39
and Orthodox Judaism, 40, 63–64, 71–72, 81, 124
and the Ottoman Empire, 45–46. *See also* Ottoman Empire
Palestinian-centered, 174, 249, 310
political, 57–59, 123, 138, 139, 169, 217, 243, 245, 290, 291, 297
practical, 59, 71, 217, 290, 291, 294, 297, 298, 300, 304, 306, 307, 310, 311, 315, 317, 324, 326, 330, 331, 334, 383, 384
press of, 132
principal goals of, 79, 81, 87, 249
proposed reform of movement by Chaim Weizmann, 195
publicity for, 42–43
roots of, 16–18
and socialism, 51–52, 57, 62, 81, 152, 251, 311
socialist, 55, 99
in Switzerland, 55–58, 136
synthetic, 142, 155, 171, 174, 193, 208, 245, 290, 293, 307–10, 317, 330, 331, 334, 384, 407
and a territorial solution, 164–66, 281, 299
and the Verein, 33
Zionist Congress
First, 24, 43, 44, 46, 50, 52, 63, 70, 71, 89, 216, 241
Second, 52, 53, 59, 60, 70–72
Third, 58–61, 304
Fourth, 60, 62–64, 72, 87, 95, 305, 407
Fifth, 69, 74, 87–91, 93, 100–102, 118, 129, 237
Sixth, 90, 151, 159, 165–75, 178, 179, 183, 194, 195, 237, 330
Seventh, 230, 245–46, 248, 250, 252, 266, 269, 272, 273, 278, 279, 284, 289–90, 304, 309–10
Eighth, 297, 304–11, 317, 319, 330
Ninth, 323, 324, 326–31, 334, 337, 338, 340, 342, 344
Tenth, 324, 330, 331, 334, 340, 342–45
Eleventh, 377, 390, 379–81, 384–90, 394, 399
Twelfth, 390